Eric Blackburn was born in Hull in 1928, and after an elementary education, left school at 13 to become a farmer's boy. His childhood interest in steam locomotives, however, had a stronger pull than muck, toil, and poverty, and with a little prompting on his part, the Fates determined he should become an engine driver. Not satisfied with that, these fickle mistresses saw him heading off to East Africa in 1955, for more steam-related adventures. In 1965, Eric married Shirley, the love of his life, with whom he lives in a little village at the foot of the Yorkshire Wolds.

To my wife, Shirley, my constant friend and companion.

With love.

Eric Blackburn

GOODBYE MR KRUPPS

Memoirs of an Engine Driver – from the Hull & Barnsley to East African Railways

AUSTIN MACAULEY PUBLISHERS
LONDON * CAMBRIDGE * NEW YORK * SHARJAH

Copyright © Eric Blackburn 2024

The right of Eric Blackburn to be identified as author of this work has been asserted by the author in accordance with sections 77 and 78 of the Copyright, Designs and Patents Act 1988.

All rights reserved. No part of this publication may be reproduced, stored in a retrieval system, or transmitted in any form or by any means, electronic, mechanical, photocopying, recording, or otherwise, without the prior permission of the publishers.

Any person who commits any unauthorised act in relation to this publication may be liable to criminal prosecution and civil claims for damages.

The story, experiences, and words are the author's alone.

A CIP catalogue record for this title is available from the British Library.

ISBN 9781035843121 (Paperback)
ISBN 9781035843138 (Hardback)
ISBN 9781035843145 (ePub e-book)

www.austinmacauley.com

First Published 2024
Austin Macauley Publishers Ltd®
1 Canada Square
Canary Wharf
London
E14 5AA

I would like to thank Tony Ives for his time, diligence and perseverance in transcribing and sub-editing the original manuscript—a Herculean effort, not least because he was one of the few people able to decipher my somewhat inimitable style of handwriting! Thank you, Tony!

Also, a special thanks to my son, James, for his time and effort in preparing the manuscript for publication. Without his help and dedication, this book would never have been published.

Table of Contents

Prologue	12
Chapter 1: Growing Pains	16
Chapter 2: The Call of Steam	26
Chapter 3: A Farmer's Life for Me!	65
Chapter 4: A Leg Up to Railway Work	90
Chapter 5: Terror in a Blacked-Out Chapel	106
Chapter 6: A Medal for Running and Jumping	115
Chapter 7: Move to the Locomotive Department	124
Chapter 8: A (Rogues) Gallery of Drivers	143
Chapter 9: Promotion to Fireman	166
Chapter 10: The Art of Administering Cough Drops	182
Chapter 11: Pounding the Main Line	193
Chapter 12: A Failed Experiment	218
Chapter 13: National Service	228
Chapter 14: Eighth Railway Training Regiment, Longmoor	248
Chapter 15: Back to Civvy Street and Becoming a Passed Fireman	261
Chapter 16: An Encounter with Some Crossing Gates	276
Chapter 17: Stuck for Steam (Or, Not a Grand Day Out)	289
Chapter 18: Africa Ho!	310
Chapter 19: Feeling My Way	328

Chapter 20: A New Class of Engine	366
Chapter 21: A Non-Fictional Encounter with a Lion	408
Chapter 22: Funny Business at the Shed	427
Chapter 23: Locomotive Inspector, Tabora	443
Chapter 24: Rescuing 3013	461
Chapter 25: Keeping Mwanza Going	474
Chapter 26: Upheaval and Mutiny	480
Chapter 27: Life at Dar es Salaam	498
Chapter 28: Goodbye, Mr Krupp	523
Epilogue	540

East African Railways 30 Class, that Rolls Royce of locomotives, and the pinnacle of the author's driving career. Here number 3012 can be seen hauling a goods train at Tabora in 1956, with the author (in hat) on the footplate. (By kind permission of Alon Siton / Historical Railway Images).

Prologue

It had proved a long, hot and busy day for the driver of Hull Paragon Station's pilot locomotive. Now, it was late evening and he was nearing the end of his shift and enjoying a brief respite from his labours. It being Sunday, and the culmination of a glorious mid-summer weekend, the citizens of Hull, wearied with work, dirt, and living in a city still devastated by war and plagued by years of harsh unrelenting rationing, had flocked to take advantage of the weather and the many cheap Seaside Specials running that day.

These trains had all returned, been shunted and marshalled, ready for Monday morning's rush hour, with only one train remaining for the pilot to shunt—a Troop Train Special, returning from Hellifield on the Leeds-Carlisle section of the old Midland Railway main line. With a feather-light train of only four coaches and headed by a London North-Eastern Railway (LNER) D49 poppet-valve Hunt, plus an enthusiastic and fired-up crew, it was now racing flat out for home.

The pilot engine driver was alerted to the train's approach by the hiss and crash of nearby electro-pneumatic points slamming home, followed in succession by a whole series, as the signalmen set the route for the incoming train. "Come on, mate," the pilot driver shouted to his fireman, and stepping back on his engine, he automatically glanced at its gauges. All was in order, with steam pressure well up, and three-quarters of a glass of water. Satisfied, he shifted his gaze, staring down the long station yard for this last train of the day coming in.

He picked it out on the far side of the yard and followed its progress as it snaked across the maze of lines that made up Paragon Station's running lines from D-line to C-line, from C-line to B-line, and finally, to A-line, the line that would direct the special into the vacant number two platform. He watched as the lowering sun picked out the burnished tyres and flanges of the leading pair of front bogie wheels, as they gently moved across under the engine, following the path laid out for them. The engine looked well, he thought, as it drifted in quietly, with only the flanges complaining a little on the curves, and the snifter valve behind the chimney flacking gently. With approval he noted that the fireman, a lanky but amiable-looking young feller, had his side under control, with the chimney clear of smoke. Mark well that young fireman, dear reader, for we shall hear more of him, and his exploits, in the forthcoming pages!

As the engine passed, the pilot driver observed with interest the evidence of high speed running: the weather glasses grimed with exhaust smoke and splattered with oil, the blackened faces of the crew, and, most telling of all, the marks on the main frame scored by the coupled wheels, as the engine had oscillated violently above its boxes, indicating a rough ride. But he could hear the nearside injector singing healthily, and it was obvious to him that the crew had everything well in hand.

On the train engine, the driver 'ran down to the bottom', stopping just short of the dead end, to wait for his train to be drawn by the pilot engine, thus releasing him to return to the shed. As the train stopped the driver made a full application of his vacuum brake, simultaneously shutting his vacuum ejector off by closing its small ejector steam valve. The engine, when released, would now be worked back to the shed under the control of its steam brake. At the same time, his young fireman, satisfied that he had both his fire and boiler where he wanted them, shut off his injector, then eased the blower until it just prevented firebox fumes from escaping back into the cab.

Assured that all was in order, he stepped out onto the platform and rearranged his headlamps for light engine running back to the shed. Passing the cab he asked his mate to 'nip 'em up', which the driver obliged by screwing his engine into reverse gear, and with a whiff of steam, compressed the buffers between engine and train, relieving the tension on the screw coupling and allowing the fireman to 'lowse' off.

After uncoupling, the fireman walked back to the cab, wiping his hands on a ball of cotton waste. Climbing on board, he glanced at the steam and water gauges. With three-quarters of a glass of water showing and nearly full steam pressure, he swung open the firehole door, the better to examine the condition of his fire. It was well run down—there would be no complaints from the stabling fireman about too much fire, or even too little. Content with what he had found, he closed the firehole door and, with the engine standing silent under the station canopy, he made himself comfortable to wait for the train to be 'drawn', releasing them for the shed. He wiped his face with a clean white cotton 'sweat rag' and gently cleaned the corners of his eyes of gritty microscopic smokebox ash.

It was time for the young fireman to relax, to ease the strains and tensions of what had proved to be the fastest run he had ever made, or, indeed, was ever to make on a steam locomotive, during which time he had observed a strange effect at the locomotive's 'front end', when the cylinders appeared to be devouring steam at a faster rate than the boiler, at full working pressure, could supply them; a locomotive which had run so fast that its flashing pistons began to drain steam faster than the regulator valve and superheater could deliver—in effect, a locomotive running itself breathless. It now seems presumptuous of me to hazard a guess as to what speed that Hunt class locomotive achieved that glorious summer's evening between Selby and Hull, but it was surely more than one hundred miles per hour, and perhaps as much as one hundred and fifteen. The year was 1953, and I was that young fireman.

Now, however, it's time I stayed my over-enthusiastic pen, for I'm getting ahead of myself, and the full story of this high-speed run, realised by a driver with the appellation 'Sir Henry', must be reserved for a forthcoming chapter, rather than being laid bare here in the prologue. For the reader should know that this book is not simply about railways and railwaymen, but that it also chronicles a journey, as well as a love affair.

It is a journey charting a course from boyhood to adulthood, as well as a journey in the more conventional travel sense of the word, from a small village in East Yorkshire, to the vast untamed wilds of East Africa. It is also a chronological journey, from the rural idyll, poverty, and unrelenting graft of 1940s England, through to the exotic sights, sounds and smells of tropical Africa in the 1960s. As part of this journey the traveller will bear witness to a changing world, a Britain transitioning from war to peace, and from empire to Commonwealth, and an African territory passing from the steadying hand of colonialism to the vibrant birth of a new country.

Most of all, though, it is a story of one man's love affair—a love affair with railways, with steam engines, and with living the life of a footplateman. From the awestruck wonder of a little boy watching steam trains on the Hull and Barnsley Railway (H&BR), to the assured self-confidence of a locomotive inspector on East African Railways. A life of adventure and hardships, and of triumphs and disasters, but a life that I loved—or as Robert Louis Stevenson more ably worded it: "There's the life for a man like me, there's the life forever"; to which I add a sincere and heartfelt "Amen!" And with it, I hope that you, intrepid reader and fellow traveller, will find something of interest in this autobiography and its tales of the steam age and more.

Chapter 1
Growing Pains

Through all the changing scenes of life,
in trouble and in joy

Hymn, Nahum Tate (1652-1715).

To begin at the beginning, I was born in Hull (or to give it its full name, Kingston upon Hull) on 3 July 1928, shortly before my parents moved to Cottingham, a village to the west of that city. A child of what, in those days, were classed as parents of old age, my father, Joseph Thomas Blackburn, by calculation, being then in his late fifties, and my mother, Ethel, at 43, considered well past child-bearing age. By all accounts, I was born looking more like a skinned rabbit than a human being. Always poorly, I hovered somewhere between life and death for many months. Afraid that the latter was imminent at any time, my parents quickly had me baptised. Yet, despite the dire prognosis and the headshaking, I somehow clung on to life, during a time which must have been a nightmare for my parents, as they fought to keep the spark of life alight in me.

At that time, with the effects of the Great Depression biting ever more deeply, my parents must have found themselves under severe financial pressure. My father had lost his employment when the firm he worked for, the celebrated Hull firm of organ builders, Forster and Andrews, had gone out of business, and, at his age, with mass unemployment rife, it was impossible for him to find work. With two existing sons, one aged ten and the other five years old, my arrival, even had I been in the best of health, must surely have spread dismay throughout an already hard-pressed household. Certainly, as far as my mother was concerned, I was very much the unwanted child, something I was frequently reminded of when "I wish I'd never set eyes on you" was flung at my head. In sickness or in health, in times of failure, or times of success, I can never remember a kind word, a kiss or a hug, to help me on my way. Nothing but cold bitter indifference to the emotional needs of a small child, punctuated by bursts of opprobrium and anger. Apologies if the next few paragraphs seem somewhat Dickensian, but that's how things were.

From an early age I learned my mother's word, once given, was law—absolute, unconditional, set in stone law. To defy her in any way was more than I dare. Even to mildly question her orders would immediately bring a flash of anger, often with the retort: "You won't get the better of me, My Lord. I'll hang for you first." If something displeased her she often reacted with a blow, landed without warning or explanation, although I always knew the reason. When she grew fretful with me, but busy with something else, she would warn me with "You're asking for it, My Lord, and I'll make sure you get it."

The epithet 'My Lord' always served as a warning, and it was used often. Whilst I never heard either of my parents swear in any shape of form, mother had a whole range of expressive words to fling at my head without pause or hesitation. "Guttersnipe", "good-for-nothing", "not worth the salt you were born with", "devious", "underhand", "ne'er-do-well", "ragamuffin" was some I remember, and usually delivered with a flurry of blows. Plainly, as a little boy, I had no wish to master or upset her or anyone else; all I wanted was to play quietly, in safety, and be comforted when sick or hurt.

A telling illustration of my mother's unfeeling attitude to me was her liberal use of iodine, that fiery yet potent antiseptic of the day—a remedy so painful and powerful that it was normally applied to a wound delicately and with care and consideration. I was by nature an adventurous little boy, always interested in the things around me, wanting to explore and investigate the trees, fields and hedgerows where I played. This resulted in me often arriving home suffering cuts, abrasions, burns and sometime more serious wounds. Then, not for me the kind word and gentle wiping away of tears. In short order, I would be told that I was a fool and would never learn (and there was a lot of truth in that!), and that it was my own fault. This was followed by what I feared most: "Get the iodine bottle and stop snivelling." Then despite my tears and pleadings, the burning corrosive liquid would be poured into the open wound. After continuous doses of iodine had been roughly applied, or after another of the frequent and sound thrashings, I often fell asleep sobbing and feeling lost, my last thoughts being "I hope I never wake up, that will make her sad." This had a very beneficial effect, cheering me up immensely, banishing my woes and proving no end of a tonic.

Of course, over time I learned to conceal any injury, whatever the pain, treating them as best I could by myself, but as a result leaving many bright scars on my body as testimony.

At mealtimes I always occupied a position at the head of the table. Don't rush, however, into thinking that this was a place of honour. Far from it! Until age and height made it no longer practical, I had to stand, where I was conveniently positioned within easy reach of my mother's large and powerful hand. Whether this arrangement was a discipline, a way to teach me my place, or a means of instructing me in the finer points of table manners, I have never been able to decide. At the time this was simply 'the norm' in our household, and it's only afterwards that I came to perceive the strangeness of this arrangement. I had two older brothers, Joe (10 years my senior) and Bernard (five years my senior), and paradoxically, I never remember either of them having to stand at the table, but then, as I was often reminded, they, unlike me, were no trouble.

My walk to school or the village shops was about two miles, a total there and back, twice a day, of about eight miles. To save her both time and her legs, mother sometimes gave me strict instructions, on leaving school, to bring home some small article of grocery, such as a pound of sugar or a packet of tea. Occasionally, it was a large block of salt, wrapped in thick blue cartridge paper to protect it from the damp, and to keep it dry, kept at home in a warm cupboard alongside the kitchen range. As and when salt was required a slice was cut off, using a carving knife, then using a rolling pin it was crushed to a powder on a baking board.

Often excited at being free from the restrictions school imposed, and among my friends who might, when the weather permitted, be playing marbles along the gutters of the empty main street, or in season, the equally exciting whips and tops, or whatever took our fancy, I sometimes forgot the groceries. "Where is it then?" mother would demand when I returned home empty-handed. My reply would receive short shrift. "Get back down there," she would order, "before the shops shut." Rain, hail, snow or blow, healthy or sick, made no difference. I would turn and retrace my steps, adding a further four miles to the eight already walked. On my return, and observing my weariness, mother would remark, "You haven't the sense you were born with, have you? Your head will never save your legs!"

At home birthdays were never celebrated, in any shape or form, for any of us, passing unnoticed as part of the daily round, without acknowledgement or comment by any member of the family. Consequently, I am unaware of any of my family's birthdays. In the cemetery at Cottingham my parents' gravestone stands engraved with names and dates of deaths, but lacking the important dates of birth, indicating that my brothers who erected it, were as ignorant of their birthdays as I am. Likewise, toys, as my brothers before me, I did without. This never upset me, it being a case of, if you don't expect anything, then you won't be disappointed. Besides, I was blessed with much more: the wide-open country to play in. Woods with trees to climb, and above all, somewhere to go off and explore and discover all sorts of new and exciting things. Christmas, it has to be said, though, was celebrated, with my parents going to some trouble to decorate the house and make it a festive and jolly affair, albeit without presents.

None of this rather Spartan way of life was due to narrow doctrinal beliefs, but rather mirrored the hard times my parents had fallen on. To illustrate this the family did without toothpaste, relying on a finger dipped in salt, a treatment which proved its worth in years to come. For all our washing, bathing and laundry needs we used cheaper, but probably just as effective blocks of 'plain washing soap'—either *Fairy Green* or *Sunlight Yellow,* which brings to mind the rough and ready way, as a child, my mother used to wash me. Dressed only in some kind of tiny pants, or even stripped to the buff (my mind is a bit vague at this point) I recall that mother would pick me up and carry me into the cold unheated scullery, and dump me down unceremoniously on a large dresser which lived there. A dresser about which I you will hear more, shortly. What I most vividly remember, as I kicked my little legs impatiently in helpless frustration, was the cold, dripping wet cloth trailing back and forth across my bare chest, and my mother grumbling at me to keep still.

When I was a little older, maybe five, and became more adventurous I thought it well worth a try climbing the aforementioned dresser, and having successfully scaled its main part I continued ascending by means of the plate rack, which formed part of the back, as a sort of ladder. All went well until I was about half way up when, inevitably, the whole thing, plates, pots and jugs, came away from the wall, throwing me down on the stone floor, as the broken plate rack and its shattering crockery fell on top of me. I should have been killed, but miraculously I escaped unhurt, and in a panic ran off, hiding under one of the bridges which spanned the roadside stream in front of the house—a hiding place from which I was quickly and summarily extracted (although, mercifully, I can no longer recall the punishment I received). As I write this I shudder with dismay when I recall the valuable antique pottery I unwittingly destroyed that day.

For all my mother's harsh puritanical nature (and I have damned her enough in these pages) or perhaps because of it, she, without thought for herself, fought to provide for her family. In her housekeeping, three things were paramount: the best of food to maintain and nourish us; a good fire to warm and cheer us; and stout leather boots on our feet to keep us dry. All else, including her wants, were of secondary importance. In her we had a plain but praiseworthy cook, and as such, able to transform any offal or other cheap meats, be it humble rabbit, pigs trotters, ox tails, neck of lamb or sheep's brains, into the most savoury and delicious meals. It is said that the English have a different pudding for each day of the year. If my mother failed to attain these lofty heights, she was, nevertheless, able to produce a seemingly endless supply of different puddings, along with home-baked bread, scones, waffles, pastry pies and tarts. She also had the advantage of a large garden, which father faithfully 'tented' with care and devotion. A garden whose bounty of fruit and vegetables mother exploited to the full.

I have fewer memories of my father than I do of my mother, as he wasn't always around, having had various odd jobs when I was a child, and at one time being employed as a night-watchman. I remember him as a kindly man, though, and when he was at home he was the person I always used to run to when I was in trouble.

To wander off the pathway somewhat, Monday, whatever the weather, was sacrosanct as washday. Monday, with its memories of *Reckitt's Blue* additive staining the washing water (but, miraculously, not the washing) deep blue, and its large posters displayed in prominent positions around Cottingham, usually house gable ends, for which a rent was paid, and showing, blowing in the breeze, a line of brilliant white washing, under clear azure blue sky, with a pretty and obviously delighted young housewife pointing to her handiwork and announcing "Out of the blue comes the whitest of wash." On washing day, and equally fixed, the main meal consisted of cold meat, sliced from the Sunday joint, boiled potatoes, and steamed along with them, a vegetable. For a pudding, one of mother's diverse puddings, placed in the oven early on and left to simmer away gently until required. A feast fit for a king, but one, which in view of the busy day, could pretty much be left to look after itself.

Saturday, on the other hand, was given over to cooking for the coming week until, to help financially in the dark days of the Depression, my parents took on the job of caretakers of Cottingham's Congregational Church where, as a family, we worshipped every Sunday. Thereafter, Friday became the operative day for baking. This commenced first thing after breakfast, when mother prepared bread dough in two large china wash-hand basins, covering them with cloths before placing them in the warm hearth to rise. It was important to get bread making out of the way, leaving the oven for other baking, which went on near enough to bedtime, usually ending with 'hot cakes' for supper—bread cakes drawn straight out of the oven, cut open and thickly buttered.

It might be of interest to record our meals throughout a typical day, at least until the 1939-1945 war broke out, when, along with everyone else, our days of plenty ended. Breakfast always consisted of bacon and eggs, with field mushrooms in season, bread and butter, or if the bread was becoming a bit dry, fried to a crisp in the frying pan's bacon fat. In winter this meal was fortified by the addition of a bowl of porridge. The stamina provided, gave me the strength and purpose to plod onwards, on my way to and from school, however deep the snow or vile the weather. Lunch, or dinner, as it was generally known in those less sophisticated times, was the heartiest meal of the day. Always with meat of one sort or another, and vegetables fresh and crisp from the garden. But it was mother's puddings which proved the *tour de force* of dinnertime. A speciality in winter months were milk, or as the purists would have it, baked puddings. Puddings loaded with a knob of butter and rich with creamy milk. And if a list seems tedious, nevertheless, it is worth a mention, for the family benefitted and enjoyed plain rice pudding, ground rice, sago, semolina, lemon pudding, bread pudding, barley pudding, and a favourite of mine, tapioca pudding. And when the cupboard was bare, macaroni was pressed into service as a substitute, making, I might add, a jolly fine milk-based pudding. Mother always made sure milk puddings went into the oven early on, to bake slowly over the full length of the morning.

During spring and early summer and continuing until such time as the fruits in the garden had ripened, we enjoyed a variety of boiled or steamed puddings—puddings cooked in a pudding basin immersed in boiling water, and when ready, served with a thick custard or cornflour sauce. Although mother had a whole range of flavours up her sleeve, chocolate and ginger were among the favourites.

Come fruit-picking time, starting when rhubarb became fit, either as pies or served as a cold dish with custard, and not ending until the last of the cooking apples signalled the end of summer's bounty, came suet puddings. Unable to preserve fruit, other than by making jam, mother concentrated on steamed suet puddings. These were cooked in a pudding basin lined with a suet mixture and loaded with fruit from the garden—bramble, gooseberry, raspberry, etc. Sometimes, with my palate a little jaded by the continuation of such rich fare, I would be unable to finish a meal, and then my mother would round on me: "Don't you dare turn your nose up at good food, My Lord" and with a nod in the direction of the cemetery, "Just you wait until I'm in there, then you'll find out!" In the years to come, this proved all too prescient. A change and relief, in terms of diet, came in the shape of date, fig and currant suet puddings, all served with mother's speciality—a thick sauce or custard, brought to a pitch of creamy perfection by adding a small pinch of salt and stirring vigorously whilst boiling.

Tea time, when due to mother's prudence, we ate our fill, usually of cold meat which, if mother's purse ran to it, might be boiled ham. If not, one of the cheaper meats processed at the butchers, and brought home on leaving school: haslet, polony, black pudding and chitterlings. Sometimes in the winter months, tripe and onions cooked in milk, and served up piping hot to help cold hands and frozen feet. If money was really tight, a not infrequent occurrence at that time, it was either bland tasteless brawn, saved by homemade chutney or piccalilli or mother's homemade jam and bread, and none the worse for that, and a feast in itself. Nor must we forget old fashioned standbys: poached eggs on toast, boiled eggs with bread and butter, and hard boiled eggs. Apart from hot cakes on baking day, I went to bed following a bowl of bread and milk which, after being baked slowly, more resembled a bread pudding. This leaves me convinced to this day that milk puddings, together with other puddings, always layered with a thick dollop of custard were, especially where I was concerned, mother's way of building up strength into a body open to every infection going. What a present-day nutritionist, beset by thoughts of modern ills, might make of a diet rich in sugar and fats, not to mention salt, I shudder to think, fearing it might bring on an attack on their central nervous system, leading to a fit of delirium tremors, if not something worse. However, as I re-read this paragraph at the age of 95, I think to myself that it can't have done me too much harm!

By the way, as a sure and certain cure for my frequent chest infections, mother had a sovereign remedy, and one so effective that I offer it to any budding entrepreneur wishing to make, in short order, his or her fortune:

- One part ipecacuanha-wine
- One part syrup of squills
- One part paregoric

Mother would send me off to school carrying a medicine bottle, with instructions to call at the chemists on the way home. About one-third of the bottle was filled with this mixture and was then diluted by filling the remainder with water. This proved pleasant to the tongue[1], in stark contrast to the family doctor's bitter and eye-watering medication. Not that this homespun concoction prevented me contracting the dreaded tuberculosis, resulting in me being off school for at least six months.

Compensating for her Victorian nature, mother had another side. Often the house was filled with laughter, music and song. She was blessed with a fine, rich, velvety contralto voice; smooth, deep, always on pitch. A voice she used to good effect when things were going right. Father, a trained musician, loved to accompany her either on the piano, which lived in the 'front room', a room only used on Sundays, or on his American reed organ, which lived with us in the kitchen. At times, when the day's work was over, the house hushed and quiet, and the family gathered together, dad frequently moved to his beloved organ. "Come on, mother, let's have a song," he might suggest.

Then dad, often playing without music, for music was expensive and hard to come by, gathered us around for a singsong. Over time, aided by school and chapel, I learned a huge range of songs and hymns. Dad was first and foremost an organist, having been made, I understand, a Fellow of the Royal College of Organists, and religious music was one of his loves. On one occasion my brother Bernard, who had been learning to play, gave a family recital, and when he'd finished asked father what he thought of his playing. "Very good—very good indeed," he replied. "You're coming along nicely. Mind you, when you can do

---

[1] Ipecacuanha being a species of plant native to parts of South America, and squill being a type of plant found in Mediterranean regions—both of which seem harmless enough; however, I now understand that paregoric is tincture of opium—so there's little wonder I considered it pleasant!

this," he said, swapping places with Bernie at the instrument, "you'll know you're really on your way." and with this he swapped his hands left to right, and played the hymn cross-handed, perfectly, to my brother's astonishment, and to mine.

Father once asked me whether I'd like him to teach me the violin, an offer which almost brought on a heart attack. Seeing the suggestion had fallen on barren ground, he never asked again—something I have deeply regretted all my life. We were never short of a variety of different hymn books to sing from, and it was listening to mother and father singing in close harmony that I first started to appreciate and then love the haunting poetry of hymns, and the beauty and depth and delightful harmonies that hymn tunes offered.

Despite father being unemployed and, unfortunately due to his age, unwanted, he led a full and busy life until his health broke down completely. As a member of the large and well-attended Congregational Church in Cottingham, he took on the duties of caretaker, which meant most of the family spending much of each Saturday cleaning and preparing the church and Sunday school for Sunday worship, though I suspect that much of the remuneration was returned via the church collecting plate. Much of his time was spent cultivating our large well-stocked garden, but as an organ builder and highly skilled wood worker, he was often in demand for odd jobs. One of my childhood memories is of him going to some job or other, carrying his 'bass' of tools. He made, at home, an attractive chest of drawers for someone, and for someone else, a glazed mahogany bookcase. On such jobs it was a delight to watch him chopping out fine dovetail joints with practiced ease. At one time a harmonium arrived to have parts made and a complete overhaul, including polishing the case. He also spent time making new stable doors for a farm just along the road, and also a wheelbarrow, with its planked bottom in three sections. And thereby hangs a tale! Dad was a joker, and taking me along with him, he delivered the wheelbarrow minus its central plank, which I was carrying concealed in sacking. "So, what do you think of that then?" dad enthused to the farmer, putting on a show.

"Why, it's only got half a bottom!" the customer protested.

Dad carefully explained, "Well now, that's to let the water out when it rains."

"When it rains?" snorted the farmer with some exasperation. "If you think I'm paying for half a barrow, you've another thing coming. And that's all there is tiv it. You can keep ya barrow!"

"Oh well, if that's the way you feel about it, I'd better make it right," and taking the missing section, dad gently tapped it into place.

If dad worked long and hard, mother's life would now be classed as one of never-ending drudgery. If it was drudgery, it was drudgery in a most noble of causes: service to her family, and as such, gladly given. Her only break throughout the year, Sunday evening service and the annual, one day, Sunday school outing to the seaside town and fishing port of Bridlington. Mother's warning to me on this occasion: "Don't you dare show me up or you'll be for it when we get home," whilst solemnly noted, did nothing to quell the excitement of riding on a steam train. On that special day, in those more simple times, the farm workers in the fields, aware of a special train, and the excited children it carried, would straighten up from their toil and wave, delighting in the carefreeness of its happy occupants. Nor, on returning to Cottingham Station after a day of wonders, tired yet excited by all I had seen and done, was I at all mindful of the long walk home.

Such was my early life in Cottingham. A time of exploration of the great outdoors, sparsity, wholesome if humble meals, milky puddings, and mother, ruling the roost with a rod of iron.

Chapter 2
The Call of Steam

Aged five or six years old, in the calm silence of a bitterly cold winter's night, a night when Jackie Frost's hoary hand had gripped the land, weaving intricate patterns on the inside of my bedroom windows, something woke me. I lay listening snuggled deep against the cold within my soft, warm, feather mattress, wondering what, in the middle of the night, had disturbed my dreams. My bedroom window faced west and, on mother's instructions, was always left open: "The fresh air will do you good," I was told. Through the open window came a new and unfamiliar sound. Faint and far away it fell softly on my ears, a progression of precise drum-like beats. As I lay trying to make something of this strange mysterious sound, the steady purposeful rasp, now beginning to interest me, was interrupted by a thunder, rolling down the slope of the Yorkshire Wolds. However, unlike thunder, rumbling and then fading away, this stopped abruptly as if cut off sharply by an unseen hand, to be replaced by a lighter, slower beat. Now, fully awake, I listened with bated breath, as the sound slowly but surely picked up and quickened pace.

 Then without warning, another distant rumble and roar arched through the freezing midnight air, again cut off quickly and effectively. And with these confusing sounds came the realisation, this was some form of human activity. Childlike, this was my first intimation, that unlike myself and those I knew and loved, not everyone was sleeping in a warm, safe and comfortable bed, and somewhere in the cold and dark, for reasons I was unable to fathom, some sort of mighty struggle involving human beings and powerful machines was in progress. With this recognition came a pang of disquiet. Anxious, my body stiffened, willing whoever was involved to continue onwards. As I strained to pick up the distant sounds, they began to recover, growing more confident and sure. Feeling the worst of the distant battle was over, I relaxed, until without warning, the straining locomotive, for that is what it was, again 'lost its feet' roaring mightily in protest at the heavy train dragging its drawbar. Again the crew fought to get a grip on the ice-bound rails. Cautiously, with skill and patience, they controlled the engine, coaxing the train further along the grade, until entering Skidby cutting (about three miles from my house), the sounds of struggle faded out of earshot. In the future, and only on rare occasions, when the countryside lay frost-bound, with the moon riding high in a cloudless sky, and all was still and silent, I recognised, far to the west, the faint sound of a locomotive fighting against the grade of Little Weighton Bank.

My first real encounter with the wonders of the railway would come sometime later when, with my brother Bernard, we went exploring. Together we ambled westwards along an empty road, its grassy verges thick with meadowsweet, which together with clumps of wild honeysuckle in the hedges, dispersed a sweet and delicate fragrance all around. Stopping frequently, we examined anything which might interest us, before turning left at the foot of Castle Hill to explore an abandoned chalk pit, and a little beyond, a dilapidated brick-built folly or observation tower. Called Thompson's Tower, it still stands to this day, the only reminder of the long demolished so-called Cottingham Castle, a former country house, now the site of the massive Castle Hill Hospital. At the time, the observation tower, which from its commanding position overlooked a wide expanse of rolling countryside, still retained floors and stairs, but was in too dangerous a condition to climb.

Anyway, back to our walk. As my elder brother and I ambled along the heavily scented and sunlit road, we traversed the crossroads at the bottom of Castle Hill, and shortly passed an active chalk pit on our left, whose brick-built kilns produced powdered lime and quicklime. It was worked by two stalwarts who deserve a mention in these pages. They used to pass my home together just after 6 am each weekday morning, striding out purposefully, and in step. In winter their iron-shod boots, ringing on the hard road surface, often woke me to another day of life's rich tapestry. In summer, roused by the calls of a multitude of different birds, I was often sitting on the grass verge at the front of our house when they passed, bronzed and weather-beaten by working at the pit face in all weathers. Summer and winter they wore the same thick heavy cord trousers, and, in the manner of the day, gathered just below the knee by leather straps. Depending on the weather, both strode by with sleeves rolled up, wearing waistcoats, and sporting a bright red neckerchief to enhance their rather sombre garb. Underarm, each carried a square wickerwork lunch box. Striding out, in step, were they former First World War soldiers, I have often wondered? Intent on the work ahead, they passed the little boy, sitting on the grass verge alone, without speaking. Yet they remain clear in my mind as if it were only yesterday.

By now, having wandered far beyond anywhere I had ventured before, we passed Near Stions farmstead, which later played a pivotal role in my life, before reaching the tiny hamlet of Eppleworth. Shaded by venerable trees, it lay somnolent and quiet in the heat of the day. Passing through its rustic charms, my brother suddenly exclaimed, "Look, there's Five Arches!" High soaring, the Hull and Barnsley Railway's (H&BR's) Eppleworth viaduct spanned the Raywell Valley on five huge brick arches. Eagerly, we dashed the further half mile, anxious to view it at close quarters. From the deserted road, having arrived breathless and excited, I gazed upwards in awe and wonder at the massive arches with the bricks expertly laid askew.

Whilst examining the viaduct's broad-shouldered pillars, we heard the sound of an approaching train, its locomotive working hard against the grade. "Quick!" ordered my brother. "Let's get underneath and listen to it going overhead."

Five Arches viaduct, sadly demolished in 1977

Standing under the central arch, I felt an overwhelming sense of excitement as the train passed above to a cacophony of sounds. The deep dull thud of the engine's exhaust reverberating over the surrounding countryside, mingled with strange mechanical sounds, followed by the measured thump and crunch as the train of waggons passed over slightly yielding rail joints. As an added delight, something only a working locomotive can diffuse, a never-to-be-forgotten whiff of hot oil and exhaust steam. In that heady moment a lifetime's love of steam locomotives was surely conceived!

From then on, mostly on school summer holidays but excluding Saturday's when I helped clean and polish the Chapel and Sunday school (and certainly not on a Sunday when I attended morning service, Sunday school in the afternoon and evening service); but at every other opportunity, fortified by some of mother's baking, I sped on willing feet to meet my first love, FIVE ARCHES! There, on one such expedition, an evil and malign thought began to sully my brow. I had frequently heard a faint indistinct crunch as the end arches took the first shock of a moving train. Gazing upwards, I studied the viaduct and its approach embankments carefully as an idea began to form. What, I wondered, would be the sensation if I climbed the embankment to where it buttressed the viaduct, and wedged myself in the tiny space, hard up against the brick work of the leading arch? Cunning and devious (perhaps my mother was right after all!), I studied the landscape for any sign of watching eyes. Nothing moved to disturb the peace or observe the movements I was about to undertake.

Stiffening my resolve, I climbed to where the sweep of the viaduct's initial arch bisected the slope of the embankment, then, looking round for a final check, I wriggled my way in as tightly as I could and, lying full length, waited for the first train to pass close above me. As I lay wedged between the brick arch and the embankment, doubts and fears began to vex me. Clear before my eyes I began to have visions of the arch crumbling and breaking as the train passed over, whilst a form of claustrophobia tormented me. I steadied myself with the thought that this bridge had carried millions of tons of coal over the years, remaining as firm and solid as ever, and a few more tons were unlikely to affect it.

As I lay tense, ears attuned to the slightest sound, I became aware of an approaching train. Fear quickly turned to terror at its rumbling approach, and it was all I could do not to leap to my feet and race down the embankment, out of the way of this terrible iron monster. Common sense, however, told me the viaduct was safe. I lay stiff with fear as the train passed from the solid embankment to the slender airy arches of the viaduct, rumbling and clacking loudly through the thin brick 'skin' I was pressed against. I descended shaking and trembling after the train had moved on. Nearly frightened out of my wits by the experience, it was nevertheless a thrill I could not resist, and time and time again, one that I had to experience. That is until I found even more excitement when I ventured along a cart road alongside the railway embankment, which running up the slope of the valley led to an out-of-the-way Wold farm.

Cautiously, afraid I might be challenged and have to beat a hasty retreat, I crept along to where the embankment gave way to a cutting. There, upon the few yards of level ground between the two, I discovered an isolated and seldom if ever used, gated accommodation crossing, which from then became a little heaven. There, with long-distance views of the railway in both directions, with only the hum of the honey bees and the sound of the crickets in the grass as company, I spent many happy hours at the gate, thrilled by the procession of trains, when sharp-eyed and jovial engine crews would spot the little boy standing wide-eyed, and give me a warm-hearted wave, and sometimes, to set my pulse racing further, give me a 'pop' on the whistle.

The majority of the trains burnishing the H&BR metals were, and always had been, coal trains. Those working towards Hull and its docks, conveying fresh wrought coal, truly black diamonds to everyone connected, miners, railwaymen in general and dockers. In the interwar years, many of the coal waggons were privately owned and painted in their colliery owner's colours, and proudly embellished with the name of their pits. Names which still resonate: Denaby Main, Thurcroft, New Oaks, Frickley, Brodsworth, Yorkshire Main and, incongruously, believe it or not, Nostell Priory. Each set my imagination soaring. One in particular always caught my attention, giving me cause for thought, the splendidly named Prince of Wales Colliery.

The Down trains came rumbling out of the yawning gap of far-away Little Weighton cutting, passing at a steady 15 mph, the locomotives' brake blocks juddering red hot under the strain of controlling the train. The waggons, mainly grease lubricated and loaded to the limit, thumped over each rail joint, and sometimes, adding to my excitement, under the weight of its load, running a hot journal, its box on fire, and streaming a trail of acrid smoke to mark its passage.

In the other direction came waggon loads of pit props and other colliery stores and equipment bound for the mines of West Yorkshire. The locomotive was usually a GC Robinson 'O4' 2-8-0, but occasionally a splendid Raven three-cylinder NE 'T3' 0-8-0. The engines, working hard against the grade, brought on a surge of excitement within me. From my vantage point, I would follow the progress, and from its chimney, the efforts of its firemen. Far down the line, with the train little more than a speck in the distance, the exhaust was normally clear. Then from the chimney, as I watched with growing exhilaration, would come a sudden spurt of smoke, clearing almost immediately to a thin haze as the fireman bent to his task. This would be his last firing over this section, as he arranged his fire, with it being run down at the top of the grade and in a fit condition for the long descent through Drewton tunnel and beyond. As the Up trains approached Eppleworth Viaduct, the effort the engines were putting in became obvious, from the pall of smoke being produced, to the roar of exhaust reverberating over the surrounding countryside, all adding spice to my day. And a further thrill, every so often, a dashing passenger train thundered past, including several Sentinel rail cars. Painted cream and green, they carried the names of former stagecoaches once active in the East Riding of Yorkshire: Hero, Tally-Ho and Robin Hood. These passed in a whirl of gears and the whine of the Sentinel patent chain drive and, it seemed, always accompanied by clouds of black smoke as the fireman strove to maintain pressure in the railcars diminutive high-pressure boiler.

With no one ever to disturb me, it wasn't long before I decided to climb the crossing gate, ignoring the cast iron notice, warning me of the penalties of trespassing on railway property. I savoured the thrill of not only defying the railway authorities, by doing a bit of exploring, but on a hot summers day, the heady smell of creosoted sleepers, liberally stained over many years by superfluous engine oil thrown from the engines motions, plus gobs of axle box grease, whose composition interested me. Emboldened by the solitude of my lookout position, and the fact that I never saw anyone apart from the engine crews, I went a step further, and began placing small stones on the railhead and watching them disappear in a puff of dust as they were crushed under the leading wheels of passing locomotives. From there I graduated to placing old nails on the rails to be flattened. One time I toyed with the idea of placing a farthing (one-quarter of an old penny) on the line, and by doubling its size and thereafter passing it off on some unsuspecting shopkeeper as a halfpenny. But having an unfortunate, and unlikely to be improving, deficit of that or any other coin, I was forced to abandon this 'get rich scheme' once and for all. It's as well that the railway authorities never learned of these reprehensible activities, for if they had they would surely prejudice my later career.

Meanwhile at home in an outbuilding a few rusty nuts and bolts were kept company by some ball bearings. Seeing them, and of an inquiring mind, a germ of an idea began to form. What would the effect be I wondered, if instead of a nail, something I was beginning to lose interest in, I placed a ball bearing on the rail. Would it, I reflected, shatter, flinging many dangerous fragments far and wide, or would, and this was equally if not more of a possibility, fly with the speed of a bullet when the engine wheel connected? Time, I decided, to try an experiment. At the first opportunity I was off, as fast as my eager legs would carry me.

Arriving at my secret den, breathless and impatient, I looked around and about for signs of human activity, the dappled fields lay empty and quiet, likewise the line of railway, shimmering in the morning heat. Satisfied no one was about to observe my mischief, I climbed the crossing gate and with a further glance around to reassure myself, I walked a short distance down the line. For, I reasoned, if the ball bearing was to fly when the engine wheel connected, I wanted to be behind rather than in front. Glancing around again, I placed the ball bearing in the centre of the near side rail, where I could observe the effect, securing it with a blob of axle box grease, tiny enough I hoped, to escape the notice of hawk-eyed engine crews.

Retreating, I took up my position behind the safety of one of the crossing's stout gate posts, and with growing excitement, awaited developments. Before long, far away, deep in Little Weighton cutting, I saw an approaching coal train. Its driver, his face blackened by his day's toil, twigged me, and in passing gave me a cheerful wave. Crouched behind the gatepost, and a little afraid of what might happen, I listened and watched intently. The engine rolled on undisturbed over where I had fixed the ball bearing. Disappointed by the lack of effect, I waited until the train had travelled down the line and out of sight, convinced my ball bearing had dislodged and disappeared. However, when I went to investigate, I discovered something which took my breath away; something which truly astonished me.

I found the ball bearing had neither been dislodged, shattered, nor impelled forward, but against all expectations and imaginings, driven deep, whole and undamaged into the surface of the rail. Astonished it was unscathed, I ran my fingers over the rail, finding the ball bearing hammered in flush. Then something equally strange and exciting caught my eye. About every four feet, at regular intervals, a ring had been imprinted on the rail, a clear indication the ball bearing had produced an indentation and a raised ring on the locomotive's left leading pony tyre. Delighted by what I considered a splendid outcome, I continued with this wicked and criminal practice until my supply of ball bearings sadly ran out. Why plate laying staff never discovered what, in effect, could be counted as criminal damage, remains a mystery. Or perhaps they did, but by returning to school after the summer holidays, I was saved from the clutches of the law. For, as events turned out, it was a long time before I renewed my love affair with railways.

I have mentioned, if only briefly, Near Stions, the farmstead I passed on my forays to 'Five Arches'. It was farmed by a family with the splendidly appropriate name of Summerland. The family were well known to us, having been near neighbours until they moved there a few years before. Sometime in February or early March of the following year we received the sad news that Arthur Summerland senior had died in a farming accident. My memory of the morning of his funeral is still distinct and clear. The sky dawned wild and tempestuous, with squalls of driving sleet, which continued as mother, father, my two brothers and I lined up on the grass verge outside, to pay our respects. Standing buffeted about by wind and sleet, we had a long view down the road, as we watched the slowly approaching cortege. Arthur Summerland's coffin was conveyed on one of his farm carts, drawn by his favourite horse, Prince, a handsome gentle skewbald led by his son, also Arthur. The coffin, to protect it from the jars and shocks transmitted from the unsprung iron-shod wheels, was laid on a folded horse blanket. Plodding behind stoical and silent, heads bent against the sleet, came a little group of mourners, led by Mrs Summerland. For them, the road swept by sleet must have been hard as it was long, that cold blustery morning. As the cortege passed, mother curtsied to the coffin, which, although she attended the Congregational church long and faithfully, I found that gesture a bit of the Catholic. Dad on his part removed his cap and bowed. I especially remember his white hair blowing in the wind. We three lads stood gazing dumbly, unaware that in a few short years, both our parents would follow the same bitter and melancholy path.

Shortly after the funeral, mother told me to go to Near Stions and help in any way I could. Young Arthur had the responsibility of the farm resting on his teenage shoulders, and was in dire need of help, and so, whenever I had some free time, I went to help in any way I could. There I learned to milk, to suckle young calves, to 'fother up', to mow and to hoe, and in a small way, become a farmer's boy. In the summer months, when the grass was lush, I often 'tented' (tended to) Arthur's small herd of cows along the roadside verges. With the roads more or less devoid of traffic, apart from the occasional ploughman riding his two heavy horses sideways on to work, it was an easy way for a boy to spend the day.

Events however soon took on an ugly and far more serious turn when, one Saturday afternoon, I became involved in a near fatal and traumatic accident which, in a flash, transformed a peaceful country setting into one of horror and confusion. It was caused in the first place by a cow unexpectedly and illegally calving outside the farm, in a distant pasture field. Engaged in some task or other behind the farm buildings, I was made aware of the situation when Arthur, in some state of concern, came dashing towards me. "Quick," he called, "bring a wheelbarrow, a cow's calved in the bottom field"; a field, incidentally, and in view of what developed later, that was fortunately in plain sight of the first cottage of the tiny hamlet of Eppleworth.

At the time, Jersey Longhorns, on account of the superior quality of the milk they produced, were the preferred breed of milking cow, and this cow was of that kind. Jersey Longhorns, as the name implies, where noted for their long, gracefully curving horns, and this cow was no exception. Nevertheless, she stood placid and undisturbed as we lifted the helpless calf into the wheelbarrow. That accomplished, with Arthur and the wheelbarrow in the lead, I followed with the mother, who plodded along behind the calf, her huge swollen udders swinging painfully from side to side, with her giving soft comforting moos to the calf, as the little procession set off down the road for the safety and shelter of the farm.

That afternoon the warm and kindly weather had brought out a young family on bicycles. The wife riding in front, followed by her husband, who had a small boy riding on a seat attached to the crossbar. As they approached, Arthur concentrating on his wheelbarrow and its precious load, and myself walking behind, attending the cow, both failed to notice a real and evident danger, something obvious to any countryman. Running loose alongside the man was a family dog. The man together with his child and dog where on the point of passing Arthur, when the dog became aware of the calf. By then it was too late. The dog's keen nose had already picked up an interesting scent, the smell of a new-born calf. The dog's nose lifted, and it wheeled sharply towards the wheelbarrow. In an instant the peaceful bucolic scene was transformed into one of fear and panic.

Despite having just given birth, the cow reacted with surprising speed and agility. Snorting and bellowing she lunged at the dog, and with a mighty sweeping swing, tried to impale it. The dog, however, leaping aside, easily evaded the points of the cow's needle-sharp horns; the man and the boy, though, were not so fortunate. The upward sweep of those long curving horns caught the man between the legs, severing an artery, and lifting him off his seat and over the handlebars, causing the bicycle with the child strapped on, to swing away before crashing on the verge, trapping the child underneath.

Pandemonium erupted, with screaming from the child and its mother adding to the nightmare, as Arthur and I tried to control the maddened and lunging cow, before it inflicted further injury on someone else, including Arthur and myself. As we fought to calm the cow, the man struggled to his feet begging us to help his son who was trapped beneath his father's bike by the straps that were to help keep him safe and secure but were now suffocating him. It was then with horror, I saw a fountain of blood gushing from the bottom of his trouser legs, swamping his foot, and spreading over the road. Appalled and faint from the sight, I knew instinctively the man was quickly bleeding to death.

Then an event occurred which undoubtedly saved his life. Running from the nearest cottage came Mrs Gowthorpe, clutching a bedsheet, followed by her husband. From her cottage she must have observed what happened, in itself a miracle, and then reacted with amazing speed. Sometimes I wonder if she had trained as a nurse, for when she arrived her actions were entirely professional. Taking charge of the injured man, who had now collapsed, she tore his trousers off, at the same time shouting for me to run as fast as I could to the landmark Skidby Mill, which possessed the only telephone for miles around, to ask them to ring for a doctor and ambulance.

Even as a child I was never a good runner, being always short of breath as I wheezed my way along, and Skidby Mill was over a mile and half away by road and to add to my difficulties located on the summit of Skidby Hill. Instead of taking the way round by road, aware that time was of the essence, I chose a shorter path, one diagonally across the fields in a straight line, forgetting in my panic, that Near Stions' boundary hedge, without gates to pass through, barred my route. Desperate, I forced my way through the hedge, tearing my clothes, and being stabbed a dozen times by the vicious blackthorn bushes, before arriving at the mill bloodied and exhausted, my boots seemingly filled with lead, and in a state of near collapse, to gasp out my message to the astonished mill owner, who concerned at my condition called his wife, who helping me recover, made me a cup of tea.

And what of the little boy trapped beneath the bike? It was the quick intervention of old Mr Gowthorpe which saved his life, and it was old Mr Gowthorpe, who after releasing him, held him gently in his arms and comforted him. The upshot of this double tragedy, which marred a peaceful Saturday afternoon, was that thanks to Mrs Gowthorpe's prompt and expert attention, the man survived. Though how she was able to staunch that massive flow of blood escapes me.

One incident I was involved in used to be part and parcel of farm life. One day young Arthur came bustling out of the house with an old hessian bag in his hand. Pointing out one of several cats, kept to keep down rats and mice, he ordered, "Fetch 'od a that black moggy. Grab it by the scruff of its neck, then it won't scratch, and drop it in this sack," which I naively and obediently did. "It's been killing me chicks, and I'm going to settle its hash once and for all!" he announced. As Arthur tied the neck of the sack with a length of Massey Harris binder twine, the cat, suddenly sensing its time was nigh, responded by hurling itself against the inside of the sack and howling most piteously. Arthur, however, unmoved by its lamentations, picked up his ancient Akrill twelve bore hammer gun, stepped back a few paces, raised it, and with one shot despatched the unfortunate creature to the next world. Such were the times back then, and at least it was over quickly for the unfortunate cat.

During that period of my life, with no time available between school and helping out at Near Stions, the call of the H&BR Main Line began to fade and lose its appeal. This was around 1938 and, increasingly, wars and rumours of wars began to dominate at home, but with both my brothers now in full-time employment, the financial situation had begun to improve, with little luxuries appearing, and thanks to this and Mr Gibbs and his dentifrice, I now cleaned my teeth using his excellent product, rather than with salt.

At Sunday lunch 1939 my father suffered a massive heart attack, made all the more dreadful by him choking on his food. Childishly impotent I watched in mounting horror and despair, as with rolling eyes he collapsed in his chair, dragging his plate of food to the floor. My eldest brother, by sticking his fingers down his throat, managed to clear his airways. Mumbling incoherently, and in great pain and distress, dad was helped to bed. As far as I am aware a doctor was never called to assist, mother ministering to his needs. It marked the start of the steady decline of a much-loved father, who for the rest of his life, as his heart slowly failed, remained an invalid.

With war now certain, my eldest brother, aged 21 volunteered for the army, and as a dental technician, was drafted into the Royal Army Medical Corps (RAMC), where on the outbreak of war, his regiment moved to France as part of the British Expeditionary Force (BEF). As France collapsed, his regiment was forced to join the 'race for Dunkirk', marching day and night to keep ahead of the triumphant German panzer groups, now roving the countryside mopping up any remnants of the BEF they could find. Even in this desperate situation, the British 'Tommy' could often make a joke of things, as the following anecdote vividly illustrates.

My older brother, Joe (an affable and kindly big brother), rarely spoke of his experiences during the war, but years later he unbent a little, and one day told me an amusing incident during that harrowing retreat. As they marched on, discarding by the roadside equipment, and anything else which might hinder their progress, one man, a private, fell out footsore and exhausted, as the rest, abandoning him to his fate, continued their headlong flight. Eventually they were forced to rest, taking cover in a wood, from where the sentries and lookouts had a clear view of the road. After resting for several hours they prepared to move off, when a cry of alarm was sounded. "Stand to, someone's approaching." The regiment now formed up and, helpless, prepared to surrender, when instead of the expected enemy, to their surprise, clip clopping down the road, bestride a large white farm horse, came their abandoned comrade. Barefoot, boots with his socks stuffed inside tied around his neck, and most incongruous of all, much like a commanding officer riding on parade with a drawn sword, holding a stick vertically in his right hand.

Urging his horse forward with a mixture of French verbs and English adjectives, he approached the astonished sergeant major, saluting him with an exaggerated flourish of his stick. "Bring the men to attention," he ordered. "I wish to inspect them."

On the beaches of Dunkirk, whilst others were evacuated as fast as possible, the RAMC were ordered to stand fast, set up first aid posts, and attend to the wounded and dying. My brother, among the last to be rescued, escaped under the cover of darkness in a small boat, as the enemy occupied the beaches. This delay, and in the confusion that followed, resulted in him being posted missing. With the horrors and conditions of the First World War fresh in their minds, this grim news deeply affected my parents, and did much to hasten the death of my father, already a sick man.

Arriving home eventually, my brother appeared exhausted and hungry, his uniform torn and, from his time in the sea, water stained, with his little cachet of personal letters and photographs no longer legible. Despite all the privations and humiliations he had suffered on that epic retreat, he wasn't averse to being referred to as a member of what was whimsically known in the British Army as the 'Dunkirk Harriers'. After a brief leave he was kitted out and quickly posted to the Eighth Army in the Middle East where, if he hadn't done enough running about, he was chased around the desert by Rommel's Africa Corps for the next few years. Of this period, all I can remember him reflecting on was General Montgomery's promise, that under his command, each man would receive a bottle of beer per man, per day – an announcement received with stunned incredulity and perhaps disbelief (although whether this promise was kept he never did say).

But all this was hidden in the future, and when war was declared on 3 September 1939, the news was met at first by a deep despair, for mother in particular had first-hand experience of war and its shattering effects. At this juncture, I vividly remember her remarking in agony "Has the world gone mad, it's only 20 years since the last war!" Both her brothers had served throughout the war with the East Yorkshire Regiment, and in view the casualties suffered, only survived by a miracle, although not without cost. One brother, Ernest, was badly gassed then taken prisoner, leaving him with damaged lungs and poor health for the remainder of his life. Billy, the other brother, was badly wounded by a nearby shell burst, which disfigured his face, driving stones and bits of uniform and equipment into his body, making his recovery a long and harrowing experience.

To me, a small boy, Uncle Billy was always a bit peculiar in his ways, although a lot of fun, having become rather too fond of the bottle, something of an anathema to mother. After recovering from his wounds, and unmarried, he went to sea, where perhaps on the deep rolling oceans, far from the horrors he had seen and endured, he was able to find some kind of calm and peace. Every so often he would return from sea, and out of affection, for he dearly loved his sister, he would visit mother, who would spy him navigating an unsteady and erratic approach. This rolling swaying motion could be put down not only to wobbly sea legs, but to the amount of Hull Brewery Pale Ale he had consumed on his slow and uncertain passage through Cottingham. "Here's your Uncle Billy," mother would exclaim. "Just look at him, can't pass a pub door for the life of him."

If Uncle Billy expected an affectionate welcome he was in for a disappointment, receiving only a blast of indignation. Smiling sweetly despite the odium, he would sing, with an oblique hint of reproach and a little emphasis on the hymn 'Tell Me The Old Old Story'. Despite all this, mother always made sure he went away well fed. He would tell me of the strange far-away places he had visited, Vladivostok, Murmansk, Kobe in Japan, and many others, which despite his beery breath, excited my imagination.

Infrequently, for before the 1939/45 war she lived far away in London, mother's sister, Lilian, would visit us. And from conversation overheard as I played in the house, I learned of the suffering everyone endured during that first conflict: of the times their two brothers came home on infrequent leave from the front, uniforms thick with Flanders mud and infected with lice; of how they had to strip naked in the back yard, and wash down before entering the house; and how their uniforms and underclothing was dropped in a copper of boiling water as they changed into clean civilian clothes.

Uncle Ernie told me that, when walking through the streets of Hull in his civilian clothes, he was accosted by a woman who angrily demanded to know, as a fit young man, why he wasn't at the front. "I shall be returning there the day after tomorrow, Madam," he assured her. And so the brothers would return with uniforms lovingly cleaned, mended and pressed. Living in the Old Town part of Hull, which on several occasions had been bombed in Zeppelin raids, they spoke about their experiences, and although they were careful what they said when I was around, 'little ears' are sharp, and I heard more than was intended, with stories of dead or dying friends and neighbours being recovered from bombed houses, and the like. Adding to these lasting impressions was the appalling news of loved ones killed or injured in the earlier war, a scale which was expected to rise considerably in the coming conflict.

The first day of war affected me deeply. Not from any war-like activity, for isolated at home, the day passed quietly, if subdued, but rather from an extraordinarily vivid and spectacular moment. Towards evening, spreading from the west, with a deep azure blue sky as background, came a series of menacing, swiftly moving, dense back clouds. Illuminated from behind by a sun burnishing the edges with gold, and shot through as a contrast with shafts of bright flashing sunlight. As the sun continued its slow decline, it turned the underside of each bank of cloud a fierce and disturbing blood red, which spread dramatically across the sky, and in places, becoming coloured with different shades of lilac and mauve. I gazed upwards with a sense of awe and wonder, spellbound by its changing glory. When the sun tipped the horizon a change began. As an eerie glow spread the birds fell silent, as if afraid. Bathing everything, my home, and the familiar trees and fields around me, in an unearthly and ghastly rose pink, before fading slowly to a darkening uniform grey, the whole spectacle from start to finish lasting about three-quarters of an hour. As darkness fell, I went into the house to overhear my parents, obviously affected, discussing the strange and disturbing meteorological event. Was it, I wondered, a portent of the blood-bath about to engulf the whole world?

From the earliest days of the war, Cottingham was used by the military as a holding area for large concentrations of soldiers. First British, then Dunkirk survivors, followed by Canadian, French Algerian and African-American. They were billeted in various church and chapel halls, dotted about the village, and in several large houses and villas, previously used as Halls of Residence by Hull University, and now, with other work for the undergraduates, standing empty.

The first to arrive were the Lancashire Fusiliers. At that early stage of the war, probably all regular soldiers who, I remember, still favoured marching in columns of four. It was they who set up a firing range in the now abandoned lime pit near Eppleworth. Rigging up an ingenious system of wires and pulleys, whereby small wooden models of German aircraft were made to sweep back and forth across the width of the pit and worked from behind the cover of the brick-built lime kilns, the Lancashire Fusiliers, with massive expenditure of small arms ammunition, would try in vain to shoot them down. This failure never dampened their ardour. Returning, they passed along the road, marching at ease with rifles slung, singing heartily such World War I favourite as 'Pack up Your Troubles in Your Old Kit Bag' and 'It's a Long Way to Tipperary'.

When tending cows in the vicinity of the pit, and the Fusiliers were no longer about, I would spend a fruitful hour or so digging bullets out of the chalk face, to show my friends, at school, and make swaps. After a few weeks the Fusiliers vanished as quickly and silently as they had arrived. Later, rumour had it, they had been sent to Norway to stem the German invasion there and had been decimated in that futile and costly campaign.

In stark contrast to the smart and confident Fusiliers, our next visitors were some of the sorry remnants of the BEF. Passing on my way to and from school, my main impression was, lacking all forms of equipment, how disorganised and aimless they were. A cookhouse of sorts was set up on West Green, a grassed area, which quickly became a sea of mud. Out in the open, without shelter, the cooks had only Dixies suspended over open wood fires to provide a minimum of tea, porridge and a watery stew to the lines of men patiently waiting, whatever the weather, ankle-deep in mud. Later the cooks improvised primitive field ovens, using oil drums embedded in the clay and mud which surrounded them. Things improved when two large army marquees arrived, giving a modicum of shelter for the soldiers to sit in whilst eating. A little later, Soyer stoves arrived and were established outside various billets, and whilst the cooks had to work outdoors in all weathers, the men could now sit in the warmth and comfort of these billets.

The threat of invasion hung heavily on everyone, and to counter it the Local Defence Volunteers (LDV), a forerunner of the Home Guard, was formed. In these early days they armed themselves with any weapon they could lay their hands on, no matter how feeble and ineffective: old hammer shotguns (all thoughts of licences being quickly forgotten), muzzle-loading guns (again, how quickly, when the need arose, all thoughts of gunpowder licences was dropped), and even spears were pressed into service. Wooden rifles were issued, not I hasten to add to impress the enemy (they wouldn't!) but to practise rifle drill.

Barricades were hastily erected, on the main approach roads to the village, using anything lying at hand. One, just along the road from the family home, was typical of others, using parts of rotten and broken farm carts, a couple of junk washing tubs filled with earth; likewise a pair of old rusty milk churns. Even as a child none of this filled me with confidence, especially when I observed the open fields either side, affording easy passage for enemy tanks. Without wishing in any way to disparage the courage of the LDV volunteers, men determined to sell their lives as dearly as possible, in defence of their homes and enemy, I cannot help thinking, having pitied their weakness, that many Germans would have died, not from shotgun pellet, muzzle-loading ball, or a spear thrust, but from incredulous laughter. At that time, from spring 1940, such was the very real fear of invasion that I had in my mind's eye a clear vision of columns of heavily armed German soldiers marching past my home in their alien uniforms, singing and cheering, much as the Lancashire Fusiliers had done, but this time with different songs.

Almost nightly, adding to our fear and foreboding, the wail of the air raid siren prevented sleep. Many nights no air activity was detected, making everyone wonder why the alarm sounded so frequently. It wasn't until long after the war we learned that, under the cover of darkness, the Luftwaffe, up to no good, was busy laying mines in the shipping lanes along the East Yorkshire coast, and at low tide, in the mouth of the Humber, to carry them upriver on the rising tide, where before sufficient mine clearing vessels became available, they claimed many ships.

Our next visitors were the men of the Green Howards; men as yet untouched by war, well equipped, and as keen as mustard. Unlike the pitiful Dunkirk survivors, who had wandered around in small groups, these men marched about purposefully and disciplined, as they went about their duties. One of the first acts they undertook was commandeering the university-owned, but now uninhabited, former Cottingham Grange, and criss-crossing its extensive parklands with series of trenches, strong points and redoubts. Re-enacting the battles of World War I all over again, and with alarming efficiency and little regard for the Chancellor of The Exchequer's pocket, they proceeded to demolish these fortifications with trench mortar bombs and hand grenades. Week after week, Cottingham was rocked by explosions as the Green Howards set to with a will.

In school, we children, tired, our sleep interrupted by the nightly air raid alarms, and heads drooping, would be jerked into full consciousness, when a particularly violent explosion set the classroom windows rattling. But after school, when the Green Howard's had finished for the day, I would venture to look around Cottingham Grange, it being only a short distance from home, and there amid the wreckage, and the exciting smell of recent explosions, marvel at the scale of destruction and pick up shards and fragments of both hand grenades and trench mortar bombs, hand grenade levers and the solid filling caps. Trench mortar bomb fins seemed to escape major damage, laying about in profusion, a few to be gathered up and taken to school. Here I did a good trade amongst friends, bartering them for other exciting treasures.

At this early stage of the war, Hull lay open, at the mercy of the Luftwaffe, it's only defence a bank of barrage balloons to the west of the city, flying serenely above us, always head to wind and hardly noticed, except as accurate wind indicators. But they were memorable targets, as proved one afternoon, when a number fell to the attack of a single Luftwaffe fighter pilot. Pleased by our welcome release from the rigours of the school day, chattering and laughing amongst ourselves, a small group of us had gathered outside the school gates, when our attention was diverted by the sound of a hard driven aircraft diving steeply. My eyes searched the sky as it developed into the scream of a fighter plane diving at full throttle, and I picked it out, hurtling down at an acute angle towards one of the tethered balloons. Then unexpectedly, for no air raid warning had sounded, a burst of machine gun fire ripped from the plane, shocking our little group into silence. We watched awestruck, as the balloon under attack suddenly deflated, folding in on itself before bursting into flames and falling to Earth, leaving a trail of black smoke in the sky to mark its passing. For the next few minutes, our little group, excited and thrilled by the skill and daring of the German pilot, felt like the Ranks of Tuscany, an urge to cheer him on, watching in admiration, as after each 'kill', he roared skyward nearly vertical, his engine howling in effort, before rolling his aircraft over at the apex of his climb in a tight turn, then diving, all guns blazing, at his next target, and probably hoping at the same time, to tickle up some of the ground crew. Unopposed, he methodically and with supreme skill, went the rounds, before departing for home in an easterly direction at high speed, ammunition presumably exhausted.

As children we had grown a little wise in the ways of the war, and as the implications of this attack sank in, we realised it might be the opening move to an all-out air raid on Hull that night. Fortunately, it failed, for whatever reason, to materialise—a simple change of plan perhaps? But which begs the question, if one fighter aircraft was able to wreak such havoc, why not send a flight over as the prelude for launching full scale raids? With this one highly effective sweep, it became clear the vaunted balloon barrage had proven entirely ineffective and was there to lull the citizens of Hull into a false sense of security, and for the enemy, something not worth risking lives and aircraft on.

Rather, I like to think, some Luftwaffe pilot, perhaps a little bored, decided to pop over from occupied Holland or Denmark and have a bit of fun at our expense. Whatever the explanation, I have no doubt he flew home more than satisfied with his afternoon's work, and later that evening, in the comfort of his mess and among his comrades, he felt he had well and truly earned his bottle of Schnapps. Whilst it was all in the past, this attack raises a further question, which might also be asked of two similar but much more mystifying occasions, when again, solitary enemy aircraft, in the latter instances low-flying bombers, had, in broad daylight, been able to penetrate so far in land without warning.

Standing amongst friends in the school playground during the morning break in the summer of 1940, I heard, rising above the commotion of the children playing and letting off steam, the deep pulsating roar of an approaching, low-flying aircraft. In the absence of any air raid warning I assumed, naturally enough, this must be some kind of new, and therefore exciting, British bomber. Still hidden from view by the school buildings, I waited for it to pass over. Quickly the roar of its engines increased, filling the playground with resonance, and glancing upwards I was in time to observe the aircraft emerge from behind the school's roof. A large, all black, twin-engined aircraft, flying northwards as if following the railway line, at no more than 3,000 feet, and about half a mile to the east. And whilst its stubby blunt nose was almost obscured by its massive engines, its shape and form showed clear and distinct against the deep blue of a cloudless sky. It seemed in no hurry, as admiringly, I followed its stately progress with interest.

Then as I watched, to my astonishment, a black ball appeared as if from nowhere, hanging motionless in the sky, above yet in close proximity to the aircraft. Confused, I stared more keenly, unable to understand what it was and where it came from. Then two things occurred simultaneously. As the aircraft flew steadily on, without deviation in height, course or speed, a cluster of mysterious objects appeared in front of the aircraft. At the same time came a thudding concussion, the hollow whanging drum of an air burst, which jolted the playground and frightened the other children into silence, sending them scurrying for cover. More interested than concerned, I followed the course of the aircraft, as it continued its unhurried low-level flight, until the teachers, now fully alive to the situation, rushed out and quickly ushered us into the greater safety of the school buildings. The next day we heard the aircraft, a Junkers 88 had crashed somewhere in the Plain of Holderness.

This incursion, deep into British airspace, that bright summer's morning, seems on the face of it, to defy all logic, raising so many questions it becomes difficult to know where to begin. In strict sequence might be the most sensible starting point to examine the details as I knew them. In sending over, without the protection of a fighter escort, a lone, lightly armed, slow and vulnerable aircraft, makes one question the motives of the German command. Nor does it take into account the alarm of the unfortunate crew, who must have felt they were they being sacrificed on the altar of some obscure suicide mission. What was the purpose? We knew from the direction it arrived over Cottingham that it had closely skirted the line of Hull's western barrage balloons. Was it probing and examining the extent of Hull's then feeble defences? If so, surely this was work for one of the Luftwaffe's fast and agile photo reconnaissance aircraft, which in the hands of a specially trained pilot, could make his runs with impunity. In any case, what use was this largely futile and empty information to an enemy sending bombers and fighters to Hull on an almost nightly basis, and on their return, closely debriefing the crews, especially over the defences?

If indeed it was a reconnaissance mission, why did the crew, their work complete, fail to leg it home by the shortest route, due east, where the comparative safety of the wide open North Sea beckoned? The mystery deepens: why did they continue flying at such a low altitude, when height would have added much to their safety, and inexplicably, why continue flying north, towards Beverley, and the large Leconfield airbase just beyond, where a squadron of Polish fighter pilots resided, all thirsting for revenge and marked as such on all Luftwaffe maps by a vivid red line as somewhere to be avoided at all costs?

Then there is the mystery of the aircraft continuing its straight, level and unhurried flight, even when coming under anti-aircraft fire. Perhaps that first ranging shot, which even some distance away shook the school, had, by bursting near the aircraft, wrought such havoc amongst the crew that they had, if only temporarily, become incapable of controlling the aircraft. We shall never know. What we do know is, the aircraft turned in an easterly direction shortly afterwards, before nose-diving into a field and killing all the crew.

Bearing in mind no air raid warning had sounded, there remains a final twist to this extraordinary series of events. It concerns the action, or apparent lack of action, on the part of the extensive radar system, set up all along the East Coast specifically to warn of any approach from the seaward side by aircraft. An important part of this system were many Royal Observer Corps posts located in strategic positions—cliff tops, tall buildings, etc., and in the main, manned by aviation experts who, by means of tracking instruments, telescopes and field glasses, observed and recorded the height and direction of all passing aircraft, friend or foe. Perhaps the benign weather and the total lack of air activity that day lulled the defenders into a false sense of security. Years later, when I was one the many hapless National Service conscripts, I learned from a German Prisoner of War another possible reason, although I pass it on only in jest: speaking in perfect if slightly accented English, he remarked: "We always knew where you were at 10 am to 3 pm." Astonished, I asked him to explain. "Yes, for you English, the war had to stop between 10 o'clock in the morning and 3 o'clock in the afternoon."

"Had to stop?" I enquired, wondering what part of my military training came into this.

"Yes," he continued, "whilst you stopped and made the cup of tea!" Maybe this solitary bomber, like the fighter aircraft before, the one which came in shooting down balloons, had sneaked in, as the British attended to their daily ritual of making tea.

The following summer, at home helping my mother in the rear garden one afternoon, I watched a similar episode which, for the solitary low-flying German bomber and its crew, had an equally foregone and grisly conclusion. Like the first, the presence and actions of the aircraft were unexplained by any logic or reason. Daylight hours normally signalled a time free from strife and other warlike alarms, and this day was no different. No air raid warning, bringing up its spasm of fear, had sounded. The countryside, basking in the sun, lay peaceful and quiet. The only reminder we faced a ruthless and implacable enemy, the line of silvery balloons, like guardian angels above us, each glinting in the sun as it tugged and heaved on its mooring cable.

Then far to the west, without warning, its precise location hidden from us by the bulk of the house, came the faint but unmistakeable roar of concentrated machine gun fire. Startled by this unexpected and unwelcome interruption into our peaceful activities, we paused, listened and wondered. Then again, this time much nearer, ripping the heavens apart, with a cacophony of sound, came a long and sustained burst. Now thoroughly alarmed, we raced to the front of the house, to gain a better view, arriving in time to witness, first-hand, the horrifying destruction of a German bomber and its entire crew.

Sweeping low across our front from west to east, not 500 yards distance, and between ourselves and the landmark Skidby Mill, came a single German bomber. What made us draw our breath in sharply, was the sight of three Spitfires hanging on its tail, harrying it without pity or mercy, as they raked it from end to end in a drumroll of machine gun fire, in what appeared to be a slow, very deliberate and cold blooded execution. Were they Polish airmen from RAF Leconfield, I wonder?

Notwithstanding the punishment being inflicted, the bomber gave no appearance of returning fire, giving an indication that the crew had to a large extent already been killed or injured. Still pursued by the avenging Spitfires, the bomber flew straight and level, its mighty Mercedes Benz engines roaring lustily. Watching the death of the bomber in horrified silence, my mother, no friend of the Germans, was moved to whisper a prayer. "God help them, they are some mothers' sons." We followed the aircraft's course as it disappeared behind the trees shading the cemetery, then by the indistinct bursts of gunfire, and the fading sound of its engines. It crashed a few miles further on, its engines still on full power as it ploughed into the ground. There were, of course, no survivors.

Once again there was the unaccountable behaviour of a lonely German bomber overflying the East Riding in daylight, this time from west to east. Where on earth had it come from and what were its intentions that day? I really don't know. Below were only a scattering of agricultural villages and isolated farms, and not much of interest. And what of the crew, and their failure to respond when attacked?

In response to the increasing scale and frequency of bombing attacks, Hull's defences slowly strengthened. Unlike in the past, now German pathfinder aircraft droned and circled overhead, as they searched for their chosen targets, dropping clusters of magnesium parachute flares, which drifted slowly down, illuminating the helpless city below in one ghastly white glare. And having discovered their target, they continued by dropping, and adding to our fears, vivid red target indicators for the following bombers to aim at. Now, barrages of anti-aircraft gunfire were flung over the outlying villages to the west of the city, in an effort to deter or disrupt the attacks.

Hull docks became an early target, causing widespread destruction, and setting fire to acres of sawn, stacked timber, which from the 'observation post' of the family home, stained the night sky over Hull a fearful crimson red, visible, it was reported, from as far away as Denmark. The timber which survived was quickly dispersed into open country, much of it being stacked in the fields surrounding my home. For the horses engaged in this task, it meant a long hard pull from the far side of the city, and I well remember the exhausted state of these pathetic creatures, struggling through Cottingham with heavy loads.

Among a series of severe wartime winters, 1940/41 stands out as particularly long and harsh. Apart from my father's slow and painful decline, it is chiefly remembered for week upon week of intense cold, leaving the local streams and becks frozen solid for most of the time. And adding to people's misery, lowering black clouds blotted out all sunlight, leaving everyone slipping and floundering on ice-bound pavements and roads, whilst cursing the everlasting cold and darkness.

As silent witness to that cruel winter, the emaciated bodies of innumerable birds, of all kinds, littered the snow in all directions. But mainly these were wild pigeons who, having arrived in vast flocks, decimated private gardens, allotments and market gardens in the quest for survival. However, their numbers seemed to recover quickly, and to such an extent, the government introduced Friday evening pigeon shooting, with a plentiful issue of free cartridges to help things along. More tragic, then, was the effect on that gentle and graceful bird, the lapwing, so called because of its actions in flight (also known as peewit, which describes its shrill call, or more simply called the green plover), whose large flocks, lazily flapping across the heavens, had been such a delightful feature of my childhood. That winter they disappeared and have never returned. Now, even the sight of a solitary bird is, I find, a rare treat.

Father was now very ill, suffering progressive heart failure, which had developed into dropsy, effecting both lungs and both legs. Mother nursed him with care and devotion, binding his swollen and weeping legs with wide strips, cut from her precious and irreplaceable store of bed linen. When the bombardment from the enemy, and our own guns, was at its most intense, the three of us, father, mother and I would gather in the entrance hall, a place deemed best able to withstand a bomb, and there huddled together for natural warmth and comfort, we'd watch the electric light shade start swinging back and forth, and then around in ever increasing circles, as the house shook to the repeated concussions from Hull and the surrounding areas. Mother would wrap her arms around us both and whisper, "Please God, if we have to go, let us all go together." Sitting in the cold, on a hard chair, in great pain and discomfort, my dying father stoically endured those long and terrifying hours without complaint.

Returning in the dark one evening, having attended a woodworking class at chapel, I was caught in the open by an early air raid and the ensuing anti-aircraft barrage. Fortunately, I was in the vicinity of an empty barn on the edge of a wood, and with shell splinters thudding into the ground around me and through the trees, cutting off the smaller branches and twigs, I ran in fear of my life towards the barn. Shaken, I crouched down in a corner, listening to the rain of shell splinters striking the pantiles, which every so often jumped up several inches under the impact of shell bursts. Crouching in the darkness, with the pantiles lifting above me, I began, if only in a small way, to understand the appalling effect on aircrews, our own included, when being hammered, in largely unprotected aircraft, by these shell bursts.

But with morning would come relief from the fires and alarms of the night before, and on my way to school came the excitement of picking up shards of razor-sharp steel, littered about the streets, the residue from overnight gunfire. The most prized discovery of all was finding brass shell heads, each finely inscribed with settings for height and range. I have one today that I picked up in the garden at home. Now it serves me well as a paper weight, yet as I handle it, it gives me pause for thought. Unlike others, this one is different, being deeply grooved and scarred. Most telling, the foremost part of its head is missing, destroying what I take to be its detonating mechanism. And examining it, there is evidence that any explosion which followed was small and incomplete. Had it, I sometimes wonder, been fired with such accuracy, that during flight, it had struck an enemy aircraft, been damaged, and failed to fully explode? And if so, what of the aircraft's crew? Did they return with a nasty hole in their plane, and shrugging their shoulders, count themselves lucky, or did they return carrying dead and wounded?

Meanwhile, as part of the city of Hull's defences, a searchlight and crew took up position in a ploughed field opposite home. At first, the searchlight, its crew, with generators and other equipment, were left, exposed to all weathers on the bare ploughed field, and had to make do with tents, bare cooking facilities and open latrines. A tent for those exposed to the freezing winter of 1940/41 calls for stamina and fortitude. For defence, a Lewis machinegun was mounted, its single barrel pointing defiantly to the skies. Now and again the gunner, inviting retribution in the shape of a big fat bomb, would let fly in the general direction of an enemy bomber as it flew overhead. Unharmed, unconcerned, probably unaware, the enemy passed on, to where the target indicators lit the night sky, calling attention to more desirable objectives in the centre of Hull.

Wooden accommodation was eventually erected for the searchlight crew, together with proper latrines and a cookhouse. At the same time a large circular pit was excavated by the Royal Engineers, with revetted walls to house the searchlight. As a further delight, Auxiliary Territorial Service (ATS) girls arrived to man direction indicators, to act as cooks and to drive trucks, all swelling the encampment, and adding an air of importance to its activities. This continued until the middle of 1944 when, with air raids falling away dramatically, the site was abandoned, the huts broken up and burnt on site. The protecting pits were filled in, the brick cook house chimney demolished and the field returned to the plough.

However, there is a sequel. The site was located a little way outside Cottingham and obscured by hedges, was little known and soon forgotten. The field was next to the municipal cemetery, and as demand for space continued without fail, it became necessary to incorporate the field into this indispensable requirement. What, I wonder, must be the astonishment of the present generation of gravediggers when, going about their melancholic task, they find in places the ground strangely soft, or in digging graves in what they suppose is virgin ground, they find, well down, a collection of spent .303 cartridges?

Prior to the war the Royal Engineers had already chosen a site for what they euphemistically called 'bomb cemeteries'—a safe place to store unexploded bombs, which in this case were two abandoned chalk pits, nestling in a fold of hills and largely hidden from view by trees straddling the 'old' Beverley to Cottingham road, to the north-west of Cottingham. Being only two miles from home, both were familiar to me, having spent many happy hours playing both in and around them. The frequent passage through the streets of Cottingham by these resolute bomb disposal men, with their deadly cargo, were first heralded by two motor bike riders, riding abreast, and as a warning to everyone, flying red pennants attached to the rear of each motor bike. These were followed by the bomb-carrying vehicle, easily recognised by its pillar-box red bonnet and front mudguards. Each bomb securely locked down and, like the soldiers riding with it, thickly coated in clay from which, at the risk of a catastrophic explosion, it had been laboriously excavated.

To a small boy, interestingly they carried no lifting gear to unload the bombs with, and I presumed that having manoeuvred the truck into position, they simply rolled the bombs down a wooden ramp or, even more a matter of concern, unceremoniously tipped them over the side, before positioning them in neat rows along the bottom of the pits.

Disposing of unexploded bombs wasn't always the straightforward affair the engineers hoped for. One team escaped death by seconds when, perhaps alerted by an ominous ticking beginning to emerge from the depths of the bomb they carried, or by some 'sixth sense' they, in haste, abandoned the truck and bomb in the entrance of the pit, where, as they legged it, it exploded, scattering the remains of the truck far and wide over the surrounding countryside. Its engine and front suspension was found hundreds of yards away, thus adding insult to injury, as it were, by obliging the team to walk many miles back to base on the far side of Hull.

I'm not sure what size bomb it was, but the explosion left a peculiar and interesting crater in the solid chalk of the entrance. It created, as if excavated and formed by hand, a perfect circle, about 10 feet in diameter, about five feet deep with sheer walls and a flat level bottom. The effect on the trees forming a canopy above was less pleasing, leaving them like bare poles, stripped of all leaves and branches.

One of my great thrills as a boy was riding a homemade bogie (local parlance for what is nowadays generally referred to as a 'go-kart') down the vertiginous Castle Hill, which in those days was located well outside Cottingham and surrounded by fields. This hill's steepness (it has since been levelled) was exemplified by the fact that some early cars could only conquer it by going up in reverse. Astride my bogie, built from old pram wheels and leftover bits of planking, with rope 'reins' for steering, it was extraordinary the speed that I could attain on it, the exhilaration of the wind in my hair and the roadside vegetation speeding by in a blur. It's just as well that, in those days, seeing a car was a very rare occurrence, and my friends and I had the road to ourselves as we went hurtling over the crossroads at the bottom. As will become apparent when you read more of this narrative, speed has always held a fascination for me, and whether experiencing such rapid velocity at a young age is the reason for this enduring passion, resulting in, as I grew up, the need to travel even faster to experience the same thrill, I do not know.

Towards the end of the war, and quite by accident, I made a remarkable discovery in the vicinity of Castle Hill. I had gone exploring by myself, my primary aim to examine Cottingham Castle's abandoned observation tower, and of course, anything else of interest. With curiosity satisfied, and whilst making my way back by skirting the top of the abandoned chalk pit at the foot of the hill, I tripped over a ring bolt, set flush with the ground and hidden in the grass. Why, I wondered, should a ring bolt be hidden in a belt of fine hardwood trees, and in such an out of the way place? Intrigued, my curiosity aroused, I tugged and heaved in an attempt to pull it out, when to my astonishment I lifted a hinged steel tray, roughly four inches deep by two feet square, filled level with earth, and growing the same type of grass which covered the ground around. Now fully open this revealed a wood-lined shaft, with an attached ladder descending about 20 feet. Being alone, I peered down the shaft with some uncertainty, unaware of its purpose, and of what lay at the bottom.

Plucking up courage, I descended cautiously, finding the vertical shaft led to a wood-lined tunnel, which in turn led to a substantial chamber about 12 feet square, with ample head room and lined throughout with well-cut and finished timbering. Opposite to where I had entered, a low tunnel, at floor level, threw a faint light. Looking around I found evidence of past occupation but nothing of note. Convinced that the place was no longer in use, I crawled through the low tunnel, finding myself on the floor of the chalk pit among a heap of huge cut down tree trunks and a tangle of equally large tree roots, concealing the tunnel entrance. Even to me, then an unworldly school boy, this clearly was some kind of secret military base, and one skilfully constructed by proficient military engineers.

History now reveals it was probably constructed for what was known as Home Guard Special Units. Covert groups of hand-picked dedicated men prepared to fight to the last, a secret kept hidden even from close companions in the same platoon. But I'm afraid that both its location, and the men who occupied it, would have been short-lived had the Nazis invaded. The chalk pit lay on the boundary of the former Castle Hill Isolation Hospital and sanatorium, then a much smaller affair than now, and being located in open country, ripe for requisition by a German occupying force. It only needed a German, interested in the tower like me, to trip as I did, for the base to be discovered. The pit itself, isolated and hidden from prying eyes by its belt of trees, was ideal if the Germans wished to carry out the execution, by firing squad, of undesirables, something they were wont to do in occupied countries during the war years. It only wanted one inquisitive German to poke about a little and the escape route would have been discovered in a jiffy.

Early in 1941, three massive air raids on Hull were mounted, with many deaths and massive destruction. At times, I walked to the higher ground to the north, and from that vantage point watched in dismay as acrid black smoke drifted over the stricken city, at the same time, hearing the thud of distant explosions as the engineers demolished unsafe buildings and cleared blocked streets. In fear of their lives, refugees began leaving the city, seeking safety in the open country, pushing hand carts, wheelbarrows, prams, anything which might help to carry precious possessions. To accommodate large numbers of bombed-out homeless people, the village school, a rather grand affair, with separate schools for boys, girls and infants, was closed for several weeks, which we children, totally ignoring the victim's plight, welcomed with open arms.

On 4 April 1941, aged 13, after a night free of enemy air activity, I rose as usual at 6.30 am. The house was cold, and I crouched in front of a tiny fire, trying to extract a little warmth from its feeble glow. Whilst I knew mother was somewhere about, the house was silent and still. Suddenly she appeared from the direction of father's bedroom. Tall and imperious, she stood in the doorway, swayed a little, then leant against the door jamb. I looked at her, surprised by a sign of weakness never seen before. She straightened up, and without warning delivered the most terrible bombshell I had experienced in my life up until then. A blow which rocked me back and nearly broke me. She announced, "Your father has just died." For some unexplained reason, I looked at the old family clock hanging on the wall, a clock which hangs in my current hallway to this day, and which showed 10 minutes to seven.

I knew father was ill, but in my childish ignorance never dreamt he was dying. He wasn't that old, of course he'd get better! Shocked by this appalling announcement, if that wasn't enough mother continued: "Go into your father's bedroom and get your brother's bicycle." This was a top of the range Sunbeam, which for safe keeping had been placed behind a wash-hand stand, for when, and if, he returned from the war. "Go into Cottingham," she ordered, "and tell the doctor and the Wright Brothers [the village undertakers] your father has died."

Fear now struck home adding to my sense of desolation and despair. Fear of seeing my much-loved father on his deathbed. Yet for all my dread of the unknown, I dare not defy my mother. Sick to my stomach, my world suddenly black, I crept shaking into his bedroom. I had to pass close to his bed and in the half-light of a spring morning I found my father laid on his back, the ghastly blue-grey pallor of death disfiguring his face. His eyes were closed, but what upset me more, his jaw had dropped and his mouth, filled with black blood, gaped open. His poor legs, wrapped in strips of precious and irreplaceable bed linen, the only dressings mother had to soak up the dropsy fluid leaking from his grossly swollen legs, which lay on other folded sheets. What sort of night mother had comforting him in his last hours can only be imagined. Whimpering with fear and shock, I struggled to move the heavy wash-hand stand, illogically afraid noise might disturb him. Finally, having freed my brother's bicycle, I turned to face another shock. Dad's eyes, now blank silvery discs, stared straight into mine in the spreading light of morning, no longer the familiar blue, having now taken on a blank, white and lifeless stare, a stare as white as the head resting on the pillow. Crushed, gasping for breath and completely undone by now, I kept the bicycle between myself and dad's body as I fled the room and the house.

Too upset and frightened to return home that early morning, I hung about the school entrance, waiting for it to open, bringing, I hoped, some sense of normality to my shattered world. During the dinner break, still afraid to return home, I wandered about the village, lost, and was deeply upset when I met the two Wright brothers, making their way out of the village, carrying between them a long flat board. With night falling, and the school with its warm classrooms and companionship closed (although school could never be called a bed of roses—more on this later), and with hunger gnawing at my belly, not having eaten since the day before, and feeling the cold, I was forced to make my way home.

Mother, only a shadow of her normal self, had prepared a meal for me. Acutely aware of father's body nearby, and hungry though I was, the meal lost its ability to please, and I could only pick at it. Mother, usually ever ready to lash out, either with tongue or hand, if I dared leave food on my plate, but now past caring, chose to ignore my failure. I went to bed mourning father, my mind full of childish fears and fancies, until exhaustion and sorrow finally closed my eyes.

In the week before his funeral, the presence of my father hung heavy in the house. This was in no way lessened by the arrival of his coffin on Wednesday morning. Handmade by the Wright Brothers in their workshop, it was trundled through the streets, and along the road on a handcart, its form and shape scarcely concealed under a canvas sheet. Mother and I then had to endure the thumps and bangs of the undertakers going about their work. Leaving little to the imagination, they first asked my mother if she had any unwanted rags or clothing, and secondly by informing her, father's body was deteriorating and the coffin had to be sealed. In a final act of love, mother picked daffodils out of the garden that father had carefully tended, and placed them around his coffin, with the result that, whilst admiring daffodils for their beauty, elegance and promise of spring, I still cannot stand their smell.

A week after his death, for his funeral, Arthur Summerland, in a much-appreciated act of kindness, harnessed up Prince, the same steady and faithful horse which had drawn his father a few years before, and attached to the same cart that was to carry dad the short distance to the cemetery. The small cemetery chapel was packed for the short service, and whilst my older brother, awaiting his call-up, attended, my eldest brother, serving with the Eighth Army in the Middle East, was of course unable.

Apart from his grieving family and friends, and in view of all that was happening around the world, dad's death was of little consequence. But I have added it to emphasise the change of attitudes, where death has become sanitised, and to a large extent hidden from view.

Whilst not on the scale of the Blitz, heavy air raids continued on Hull, and sometime in mid-April, two bombs fell on open grassland to the south-west of Cottingham, stripping a nearby farmhouse of its pantile roof, blowing in doors and windows and killing several grazing cattle, but fortunately causing no further casualties. I mention this for the two enormous craters the bombs left behind. The following day word spread quickly around the school, and as it was not far out of my way, I decided, on leaving school, to go and investigate.

With a friend I approached the site by crossing a grass field. One first indication of what lay ahead was two separate and enormous circles of huge clay boulders. Familiar with the large craters left by the dreaded parachute land mines, these craters, perhaps 30 feet deep by 40 feet or more across, took my breath away. Together, my friend and I climbed and scrambled up to the crater's edge, between the raised mass of mammoth clods, and peering into the depths, cautiously descended, where to our surprise, we began to discover something to gladden the heart of any schoolboy. Trophies, in the shape of inch-thick, heavy, jagged and razor-sharp pieces of bomb casing. Examining each one carefully, I found them deeply stressed and riven on the explosion side. Here indeed was something worthy of display at school the next day.

At school the following day, with several of my prize items safely hidden in the compartment under my desk lid, the classroom door was flung open, and in strode the headmaster, one Robert Beckett Brooks, otherwise known as 'Fatman'—a man long in name, short in stature, and corpulent in form, hence his nickname. By nature he was a sadist and a bully, and as such, hated and feared by pupils and teachers alike. His presence was an abomination, with records of his brutality legion. In a history of the school, the chronicler was more than charitable when he described him merely as a 'strict disciplinarian'. The following may read like *Tom Brown's School Days*, but it is all perfectly true.

This was a man who prowled the boys' school, carrying as his constant companion a two-foot six-inch length of thick heavy and iron-hard Malacca cane. I can confirm how effective it was by its frequent encounters with me. This he employed as an implement of brutality and torture when, for his own apparent amusement and enjoyment, he thrashed some poor unfortunate, but not before an extended period of what I can only describe as a twisted form of foreplay, during which, using his stick, he poked and prodded his victim into position. Not content, next came a tapping of the trembling outstretched hand. Tap it upwards a little, no tap it down, that's not quite right, so let's start all over again, *I must get that hand perfectly in position!* This psychological torture traumatised the helpless victim before any blow was struck, and who then had to suffer, on both hands, three, and often more, vicious cuts across the middle joints of his fingers causing the fingers to inflame and swell alarmingly, but leave no incriminating evidence such as raised welts. It was a condition we learned could be eased a little by holding the cold cast iron legs of one's desk. To pull the hand away in a futile attempt to escape was to invite more serious punishment, something no one ever risked. Facing him, as I quite often did, for either my face didn't fit, or he discerned a look of contempt and rebellion in my eyes, I used to say to myself: *You can hit me as hard as you like, but you'll never make me cry*. Though I must confess, I was near to it at times.

If you think my account impossible, and Beckett Brooks' brutality grossly exaggerated, may I give you a further example, one recounted by my brother Bernard, many years later, about when the school was on the point of breaking up for the Christmas holidays. After the children had finally put their school books away and cleared their desk lids, Brooks burst in, stick in hand, and as was his custom, thwacking it excitedly against his leg, whilst threatening his cowering pupils. "Stand up there," he ordered two boys, hacking his leg even more vigorously.

In the class at that time, unusually, three boys had the same initials, 'BB': Brian Beal, Brian Bramly and my brother Bernard Blackburn. For some reason, a lapse of memory perhaps, Brooks failed to call out my brother, who thereafter, expecting to be called out next had, in fear and trembling, a ringside seat of the proceedings. Brooks, or Fatman, as I chiefly remember him, had spent a little time examining the worn lids of the ancient desks used by generations of boys, who in moments of boredom had scratched their initials, and on two of these had discovered the damning characters 'BB', probably inscribed years before.

With the two innocents standing uneasily before him, Fatman, in view of the 'Season of Goodwill', indulged in a little jollity: "We break up for the Christmas holidays," he observed, addressing Beal and Bramly. "And I'm going to give each of you a Christmas present. It's a present you'll remember for the rest of your lives, and it's for causing damage to school property." Unlike Doctor Samuel Johnston's headmaster, who perhaps genuinely believed thrashing his pupils saved them from the hangman, Brooks had no such excuse, when he set about giving each boy four hard vicious cuts on either hand. A more wanton, malicious and evil man it is hard to imagine.

But one way or another, some pupils had their revenge, as did two, big for their age, strong farm lads, who in their final hour at school, having taken in waggon ropes, tied Fatman securely in his headmaster's office chair, gagging him to muffle his squeals of dismay, then shutting the door, left him to stew, until the school caretaker found him much later, bedraggled and semi-conscious.

Someone bravely, or recklessly, once pencilled a ditty on the whitewashed walls of the boy's lavatories, which drew a discerning picture of Fatman, who on discovering it, and in keeping with his dastardly character, made every boy write out the first line, on paper, for him to examine, in an attempt to uncover the culprit. The stanza, replete with schoolboy humour, I still remember, as follows:

"Mr Brooks is a very good man,
Who goes to church on Sunday,
He prays to God to give him strength,
To thrash his lads on Monday!"

Indeed, whether he attended church is another matter. He certainly didn't attend chapel.

Occasionally, a perturbed and vengeful mother, screaming blue murder, would appear at the school gates the day after her son had received a thrashing, in which case Fatman would order the nearest child: "Boy, fetch a policeman!" Today, it's Fatman who would have been arrested, but in those days it was the mother who risked incarceration for threatening behaviour towards a public figure. The school, under its strict regime, did, however, function smoothly; a regime where not only the headmaster, but the teachers in general, were quick to use the stick to maintain its character. And many raised by that system might agree with its sentiments, for we were rebellious, and given half a chance, a defiant lot to deal with. Yet school was not all doom and gloom. In compensation we sometimes found ways of 'tweaking the teacher's ear'.

One teacher, nicknamed 'Brass', had been knocked about in World War I, leaving him hard of hearing, and after being gassed, with chest problems. Finding life a little difficult, he opted for a more peaceful existence, and as a consequence he was more than happy to let us go our own way, providing we behaved ourselves. Towards this end, he permanently posted a boy at the classroom door, watching through the upper glazed part, for any signs of Fatman on the prowl. At the cry of "He's coming!" we quickly grabbed our books, and if he came in, gave the appearance of being totally engrossed in our work. The morning's first lesson, an hour-long arithmetical period, formerly a pain in the neck, was easily disposed of by Brass, who wrote each sum on the blackboard, and from his answer book, not only the working out, where applicable, but the answers as well. What could be easier than that, even if we learned little under his guidance?

But on two memorable occasions we had a bit of fun at his expense. Happily blessed with a fine elegant 'copperplate' hand, Brass was extremely particular when writing up the class register, something he completed morning and afternoon, and which thereafter lay open on his desk for the rest of the day. One morning, a friend arrived at school, hiding a large, realistic-looking false ink blot made of painted tin, with the sole intention of placing in the centre of someone's exercise book. With a mind always full of evil intentions, and without thinking of the inevitable consequences, I immediately recognised the potential for greater amusement, diversion and a bit of fun, and suggested it might be more entertaining if, during the dinner break when the classroom was empty, we placed the blot in the centre of Brass' precious register, and at the afternoon roll call, await developments.

Sitting in our place after the break, with growing impatience and many nudges, winks and sniggers, we waited for the first moves in the drama. Brass entered, sat down, and looking round at his class in preparation, drew the register forward, using his left hand, and with the other picking up his pen and dipping it into his inkwell. The stage was now set, and deliciously aware, we knew the 'balloon was about to go up'. Brass looking round the class, called the first name. "Here, Sir," came the reply. The class hushed and still, waited expectantly; Brass' pen rose, and his eyes swept the register to be met by, horrors of horrors, the sight of an enormous pool of blue-black ink defacing its page. He gave a sharp intake of breath. "Whatever's happened?" he wailed. At that, we knew we had scored a hit. But in providing even more entertainment for us little devils, the course had far to run.

Brass now added to our delight by taking a square of blotting paper, and using a corner, tried vainly to soak up the ink. This went on, to our intense amusement, for some time, as he tested one corner after another without success. He followed this by wetting the corners of the paper with his lips, and trying again, further swelling our feelings of glee at his discomfort. Becoming more agitated and desperate, Brass took his handkerchief, and tried a corner, dangling it ineffectively in, or should I say on, the offending blot. However, at this point, his suspicion began to form, and taking his pen, Brass tentatively poked the blot, and so discovered its true identity.

With the plot uncovered Brass reacted with fury. "Who's responsible for this?" he thundered. "By heavens, I'll have the skin off his back!" I now realised that what I had conceived as a bit of an amusing prank had got out of hand, and if found out, I was in serious trouble. "Stand up, the boy who did this," he demanded. Afraid of his wrath, and with others involved, I remained seated. Again he asked, and again I stayed silent. He then struck me a crucial verbal blow: "I see," he told the class, "we have a coward amongst us, someone afraid to stand up." I squirmed as the taunt struck home, but mental funk triumphed again. "Very well," Brass went on. "I'm going to stick everyone in the class, then I'll know I've got whoever did it!"

That afternoon fortune favoured me, when Brass commenced his retributory punishment on the far side of the class, and with a combination of about 35 boys, and lungs scarred by chlorine gas, he was soon running out of steam, with his blows becoming progressively weaker until, by the time he had reached me, they had become quite ineffective. At the same time, the threat of revenge attacks, as hinted by Brass, was decidedly low. I was generally popular with the other boys, who having thoroughly enjoyed the show, and putting themselves in my place, thought the 'sticking' a price worth paying and were ready to forgive my lack of moral fibre.

The next event involved Brass again, who despite all, we liked and admired, not least for his war service and the suffering he had endured. At a time when discipline was rigidly enforced, this was as unexpected and entertaining as anything that we could imagine. In about 1936 or 37, a group of Dutch growers settled in and around Cottingham, the children a familiar sight clumping along in wooden clogs. One family, the Rosenbruicks, had a boy called Tony in our class, who carried a sneering and unpleasant attitude towards the English, which he must have got from his parents, and which helps to explain his actions, together, perhaps, with discovering one of the idiosyncrasies of the English language. Something which, with dullness of mind, had always failed to register with us.

The classroom faced south, the afternoon was hot, and to allow a cooling breeze to sweep in, the upper portions of the large windows had been opened. Tony Rosenbruick, sitting in the full glare of the sun, stood up and raised his arm. "Yes boy?" Brass enquired.

Then to a shocked and horrified class Rosenbruick, looking Brass squarely in the eye, announced, "You're daft, Sir!"

Brass reared up, but because of his deafness, was unsure he had heard correctly. "You what?" he shouted. "What did you say?"

Rosenbruick, all sweetness and light, replied with a little more resonance, "There's a draft, Sir!" – something which amused us immensely, and which we thought was very clever. Satisfied with the explanation, Brass told him to close the top windows, which tickled us even more, making it even more difficult to hide our glee, especially when Rosenbruick, standing up, gravely closed the windows one by one.

The following afternoon, Rosenbruick rose to his feet and raised his hand. This time a certain hardness could be detected in Brass. "Yes Rosenbruick?"

Rosenbruick stood and solemnly declared "You're daft, Sir!"

Perhaps Brass had mulled over Rosenbruick's words. Perhaps the look of uninhibited glee on our faces had given the game away, and convinced Brass his ears had not, in the first place, deceived him. "Daft, am I? I'll show you whether I'm daft or not," snarled Brass, reaching for his stick. "I'll make you dance you clever little bugger." In short bursts, Brass could wield a stick with the best of them, and for the next minute or two, Rosenbruick received a stinging lesson in corporal punishment—a punishment we all agreed, in view of his unpleasant attitude towards us, he justly deserved.

On the subject of 'jolly japes', one day I had the idea of employing a humble piece of school stationary as a device of entertainment. At the start of school each of us had been issued with an ordinary wooden ruler, but this was an object to be cherished and lovingly cared for. Woe betides anyone who lost or damaged their ruler! To effect this witticism, I carefully, over many days and weeks, bent my ruler, making the wood gradually more pliable over time, until eventually I could bend the ends right round so that they touched each other. Now it was just a case of seeking a gullible victim to become the butt of my joke: "Hey, Bogey, look what our rulers can do"—bend! "Ooh, I never knew that, let me try with mine!"—Snap! "…Boy! What have you done to your ruler! Bend over…!" Setting fire to inkwells was another much-loved form of entertainment, but a seriously perilous one if a teacher caught you!

I've mentioned that we were an unruly bunch of boys, and another of our favourite pastimes was fighting each other. In fact we were forever scrapping. Not the "Are we fightin' or are we dancin'?" kind of slap and tickle affairs, but proper fist fights, although what we fought about I can no longer remember. Perhaps it wasn't important. In my case it didn't matter who my opponents were, or how many of them there were, with my back against the wall I'd take on all comers. On one occasion I had, for some reason, upset Bogey Botham (possibly it was the ruler incident, possibly something else), and he being the treacherous underhanded so-and-so that he was, he lay in wait for me within some laurel bushes by the school, ready to ambush me on my way home. As I was passing, he suddenly jumped out on me and: Whump! Yes, my reactions were faster than his, leaving him, I'm sorry to say, with a broken and blood-streaming nose. Poor old Bogey!

But all this has been a digression from a particular moment when Fatman burst into the classroom, surprisingly without his stick. The reason for this unusual (i.e. stick-free) behaviour quickly became apparent when he was followed into the classroom by two army officers. As Fatman harangued and threatened in his usual manner, one of the officers curtly put a stop to his rant: "You've done nothing wrong, children," he assured us, "but we are very anxious to obtain parts or pieces of the two large bombs which fell the night before last."

Charmed by his pleasant manner, and recognising the army was more than a little interested in our prized possessions, those of us who had parts withdrew them from the secret places in our desks, handing them over with the feeling we were helping the war effort. The thickness of the bomb casing, and the depth of the craters, may have indicated a new type of armour-piercing and deep penetration bomb. What devastation they would have caused had they fallen on a built up area is difficult to imagine.

Speaking of German bombs brings me to another of my wartime adventures. During and after the Blitz attacks on Hull, the activity of the bomb disposal teams increased considerably, finding them passing frequently through Cottingham with their always large bombs. The smaller bombs, if there were any, were presumably taken to some other isolated part of Holderness, perhaps somewhere on the remote Humber foreshore, far from human habitation, where they could be exploded harmlessly. Not that this explains why they brought the larger (and still live) ones through inhabited areas!

All this activity inspired me to go and examine the 'bomb cemeteries'. So at the first opportunity I set off and walked the mile or two to the site, at the same time, fully aware that curiosity had killed the cat, and this venture might kill me. The two pits, on either side of the main road lay largely hidden in the lower part of a steep field, having in times past been excavated into the rising ground, for the chalk they contained. Not knowing what to expect, and wishing first to make a survey, I approached carefully, not by the road and the normal way in, but cautiously, by means of the surrounding fields. With ears straining for any warning sounds, and a furiously beating heart, I crept the last few yards on hands and knees to the rim of the first pit and, parting the undergrowth, gazed down. First, in the bottom a movement caught my eye: a pair of frisky rabbits assured me no humans were present, and without interference I could make a survey. What caught my attention more however, bringing with it a sharp intake of breath was, in the bright sunlight flooding the pit, row upon row of unexploded bombs, all tidily arranged, and enough to blow Cottingham to Kingdom Come. Momentarily frightened by the scale, I wriggled back a few yards to escape and draw breath, until, with reason prevailing, I crept back. With keen eyes I looked around. With no sign of human activity, and having reasoned myself the bombs must be stable, I stood up boldly, and made my way around the perimeter of the pit, and into its entrance.

Before me lay row after row of the Luftwaffe's finest. Each missing its guiding fins, and each with its filling cap removed, to expose the sometimes white, sometimes yellow, hard crystalline high explosive. On seeing this, my first instinct was to leave quickly, having seen enough and whilst still in one piece. Yet curiosity overcame my concerns, as I reasoned, if the bomb disposal engineers were confident of their safety, as they knocked the bombs about whilst unloading and arranging them, what had I to fear? I looked around; under the hot sun the pit lay quiet and deserted, the bombs large and menacing. The more recent arrivals I noticed, still coated with clay, those retrieved first, now swept clean by the weather.

I ran my hand around the cones of one or two of the cleaner bombs, feeling under my fingers the lathe marks where they had been trued up. Now more interested than concerned, I went on to examine the manufacturer's details stamped on the cones, and ever inquisitive, had a close look at some of the bombs' explosive contents. Looking round, I made a further chilling discovery. Behind some of the bombs lay small heaps of explosive, something I dare not investigate, and each with clear evidence the bombs had been hacked into. Stunned by the discovery, I asked what madman, at the risk of his life, would hammer and chisel rock hard explosive out of a bomb? Not, I was sure, any of the local farmworkers, who if they ever visited this place, had more sense, than risk their lives this way. Then were boys responsible, perhaps, although highly unlikely? From experience I knew other children never visited the concealed, out of the way, and largely forgotten pit. Yet wrack my brains as I might, I could see no other explanation.

With my reconnoitre complete, and my curiosity satisfied, I returned home contented. Years later, in a sudden flash of understanding, I realised those little heaps of explosive must have been the work of the bomb squad taking samples for examination and analysis. However, this no longer spoilt the end of my bomb cemetery adventures. Whilst at home, some twelve months later, I became aware of thick clouds of dense black oily smoke drifting across the horizon, from somewhere in the vicinity of the pits, and with it continuing for several days, arousing my curiosity. Over time, I had learned that a type of incendiary oil bomb was being dropped on Hull, and assuming this must be the engineers burning them off, decided to investigate.

Like some huge volcanic eruption, massive clouds of smoke rose slowly and heavily as I approached. At the same time, from the same source, a deep sustained roar began drumming my ears. Pressing on, I followed my previous route over the fields, approaching cautiously, on my belly for the last few yards, I inched forward and timorously looked over the edge to find myself looking down on a Dante's Inferno. Roaring below me, was not, as I expected, oil bombs burning away harmlessly, but laid alongside the others of its kind, two of Herman Göring's biggest and best, white hot, blasting out a stream of intense white flames, with a roar enough waken the dead.

There was nothing like looking down on a close-by white hot bomb to spur me into action, and fearing an imminent and massive explosion, with the next day's headlines: 'No Trace Found of Missing Schoolboy' I leapt to my feet and ran. But not before I had registered, in one quick flash, several other bombs, burnt out and rusting. It was months before I returned, long after the last of the smoke had drifted away. Looking around I found a number of burnt out bombs, but the majority still lay in rows, intact.

But my last hair-raising visit to the bomb cemetery no longer signalled the end of my acquaintance with bomb disposal, and its teams of brave and resolute men. Sometime after my panic-stricken retreat, whilst working at Arthur Summerland's, in a field bordering the road, I noticed the arrival of two bomb disposal trucks, and the unusual behaviour of the soldiers who had arrived with them. Initially they opened a gate in the field opposite, and to the desecration of farmer Johnny Cockrill's valuable and hard-won crop of ripe corn, drove into the field and disappeared behind its hedge. Sensing something was afoot, I leant on my hoe, watching events. After a few minutes the truck reappeared, parking up further along the road, where the soldiers, having left their vehicles, stood about smoking. The mystery deepened, something 'fishy' was going on it seemed. Then from behind the hedge, to the detriment of a further patch of Johnny's corn, two almost simultaneous explosions occurred. It wasn't so much the thud of detonation which has stuck in my mind, though they rattled my teeth, but the impressive sound from the two symmetrical and identical columns of earth thrown high into the sky.

A little later, across the wheat fields of the largest and most prosperous farms to the west of Cottingham, as the ripe corn waited on the attentions of the harvesters, Luftwaffe bombers dropped swathes of incendiary bombs, hoping it was said, to set the cornfields alight, and deprive the county of the wheat crops it so desperately needed. If this was indeed the intention, it failed completely, but left many live bombs laid about, again bringing in the bomb disposal men, for what were probably very welcome but always long, walks in the country, as they scoured the fields and hedgerows for those small elusive but deadly bombs.

Chapter 3
A Farmer's Life for Me!

Later that same day, alone in one of the top fields, with only myself for company, I was cleaning either turnips or wurzels, I cannot now remember which, but both required a sharp eye and a steady hand, to avoid chopping out the young tender plants, together with weeds, or what we called 'rubbish'. The row I was working on lay alongside a boundary hedge between ourselves and the next farm. In the empty landscape, my back to the hedge, I worked away, until I was startled by a voice behind me. "Now, me lad," I straightened up. Over the low hedge stood the neighbouring farmer. "Dost tha want a job?"

Did I want a job? You bet I did. Thirteen years of age, I was tired of school, of Fatman, of not learning anything, and of the time wasted. Also, I was aware my mother had difficulty making ends meet, and would be glad of every penny. Besides, whilst Arthur had never paid me, I enjoyed being a farmer's boy. Thus, to a large extent led astray, and soothed by the easy-going nature of things at Near Stions, I jumped at the chance.

"Canst thoo milk?" enquired the farmer in the same local twang.

"Yis Sir," I replied.

"Canst thoo get up in the morning?"

Again, I replied, "Yis."

"Right, we start milking at five-thirty. I'll pay you seven shillings and three pence a week [about 41 pence in today's money], and we'll see how you get on." This was Saturday afternoon, and I was told to start on the following Monday morning. That evening, I went home fully expecting an outburst from mother and an order to get back to school. To my astonishment, she quickly accepted my decision, merely asking what time I had to start, and saying she would get my breakfast ready.

Monday morning arrived. The night had proved quiet, with no air activity to disturb my sleep, and I left home in the clear light of a bright summer's morning. I had a good half hour's walk ahead as I strode out a bit before 5 am, eager to be on with my new-found work, my heavy iron-shod boots ringing on the hard surface of the otherwise empty road, and my nostrils filled with the heady perfume of wayside meadowsweet. All was silent as I strode over the crossroads, where in the past the bodies of malcontents may or may not have creaked and swung in the gentle breezes, which, similarly, now caressed my face. I strode on, past Near Stions and its abundance of memories, through the tiny tree-shrouded hamlet of Eppleworth, and with scarcely a glance at Eppleworth Viaduct looming ahead, I turned into the farm, marching boldly passed the medieval brick barn, with its narrow slits for windows, and its stout oak doors. On past the equally ancient stable block, where I could hear the horses stamping on the cobbled floor as they stirred themselves.

From this huddle of age-old buildings, I easily picked out the cow house and its attached dairy, a more recent addition to the farm, built between the wars, I guessed, and which held 14 milking cows. In the doorway, awaiting my arrival, stood the farm foreman. A short wiry man, about 40 years of age, his face brown and weather-beaten, he was dressed 'country style' in a pair of cord breeches (always referred to by my later shooting companion as 'choke-bored' trousers), stout hobnailed boots, knee-length, hard-wearing cotton leggings, and topped by a thick, warmly-lined jacket which, as the day wore on and the sun's rays increased, was usually divested, saying "It's gettin' yat, an I mun teck off a peeling", which then revealed a thick-sleeved waistcoat, which in due course, became another 'peeling'—thus exposing a thick collarless flannel shirt. To relieve this sombre attire, he wore around his neck a bright red neckerchief, and of course, the customary flat cap.

His pleasure was to chew tobacco, and shifting the plug of it in his mouth, he was able to impel an accurate and lethal squirt of juice at any impudent wasp or fly that had strayed too near or which had generally offended him. What he made of a lanky, bare-headed, 13-year-old boy advancing towards him in schoolboy short trousers, an innocent fool about to face the rigours of farm life, I shudder to think. Why didn't he throw up his hands in despair, I shall never know. "Thoo'll be the new lad?" he questioned.

Adopting the dialect I had grown up with, I answered "Yis."

"Thoo knows how ti milk, is it?"

"Yis," I replied.

"Then mek sure tha milks 'em out dry, an' remember this, I'm the foreman round here, on wot I sez goes, thoo understand?"

We both started milking from opposite sides of the cow house. It was pleasant enough work to start the day with, especially in winter, when, often arriving cold and wet, I welcomed the comfort of the cow house, which was kept warm by the animals, a place where I was able to thaw out my frozen fingers on their warm forgiving bodies. Each full pail of milk had to be decanted into a milk cooler, located in the attached dairy, from where it drained cold into 10 gallon milk churns. In those first few early days, I found lifting a full pail of milk above my head, to pour into the cooler, without spillage, a heavy and trying task.

By now, 7.30 am, with milking complete, the foreman checked my work. Satisfied I had milked my cows dry, we turned them out into the steeply inclined grass fields to graze until the evening's milking. "Now then, get in that barn there, an' muck the cow house out, an I want it clean!" he ordered. And turning abruptly, he entered the farmhouse to breakfast. It was then that I had my first encounter with what has remained firmly fixed in my mind as 'The Monster'…

Cautiously, I entered the barn, and there it loomed before me, a huge brown body sitting on two gnarled stumpy legs, its two long arms outstretched menacingly towards me—a brooding, reeking thing of massive proportions which instantly filled me with trepidation and dismay: for 'The Monster' was in fact an enormous wheelbarrow. Its stout commodious body had been further extended by the addition of wooden planks nailed on, and all thoroughly soaked in the cow-house effluence it was designed to carry. Its massive iron wheel, cast by some long-gone Victorian iron master, with the clear intention of it performing its duties for a further 200 years or more, was fitting tribute to his skill.

This wheelbarrow, top heavy and unstable even when empty, required the arms, back and sinews of a Samson to lift and control. I staggered about as I manoeuvred it into the cow house, and loaded with what I thought I could manage. It seemed a pitying small amount, but I had to barrow each load a good 100 yards, past the old weather-beaten barn, and on to the end of the stack yard, where a large muck heap awaited my attention.

As I finally completed my task, the foreman reappeared refreshed and rested, carrying that multipurpose tool, a swan-necked hoe. "Get thi sen up them top fields," he ordered. "Thoo'll find a field of sugar beet, it's gotten a bit mucky, so start cleaning it."

For the next six weeks I spent each day hoeing, coming down only for the evening's milking. With hands unused to such unrelenting punishment, it left them blistered and bloody, until they were hardened. After a few days working in splendid isolation, I was surprised by a visit from the foreman, who came into the field on horseback. Like all countrymen, he didn't believe in walking if he could ride, and having thrown a bridle over one of the farm horse's heads, had ridden up, bare-backed and sideways on, as was the custom with such a heavy horse. He swayed easily with its movements, the bones of his backside comfortably and safely hooked over the horse's spine. Without speaking he rode slowly up and down the rows I had cleaned, bending down and examining the quality of my work, and searching for evidence of any back-sliding on my part. Then without a word, he pulled his horse round, and with a "Girup", rode back to the farm.

On that, my first day of employment, I left the field and made my way down for evening's milking, which I completed by about six o'clock. If I thought that signalled the end of the day, I had another 'think' coming. After milking ended I was led into another section of the dairy. Unknown to me, the farm had an extensive milk round, a 'nice little earner' by all accounts, and worked by an attractive Land Army girl, whose sole duty was delivering milk. To that end she was provided with a smart and handsome milk float, nicely painted and decorated, and for added show, set off by a long leather whip held vertically at her right front. The float was drawn by an equally fine-looking and high-spirited bay cob which, when out on its rounds delivering milk, made an attractive sight with its polished harness and gleaming brasses.

The float, kept under cover when not in use, was brought out and the cob harnessed to it by the foreman. He then loaded the crates of bottled milk and pails of milk with tight hinged lids, each with its own set of measures (for in those days, many customers preferred milk delivered that way). Likewise on its return, mid-afternoon, the foreman made it his business to stay behind and unload the float, piling the used and often dirty contents on the dairy floor which, I now discovered was, for the want of a better description, the farm's bottling plant. By present-day standards, primitive in the extreme, and housed in a concrete-floored extension, about 15 feet by 15. In the far left corner a large square galvanised cold water tank was mounted, fed by a cold water tap; under wartime conditions, cold water, brushes and elbow grease being the only means of cleaning equipment. What's that, sterilisation? Come on, don't make me laugh!

To the right of the tank, a long zinc draining tray occupied the remainder of the wall, and above, a wooden shelf held a variety of hand brushes: stiff ones for scrubbing clean the returned milk pails and measures, churns or anything else of that nature; and specially-shaped hand rotated brushes, so shaped to simultaneously clean the inside of a milk bottle and its inside neck, and outside rim.

A heavy wooden bench used to bottle milk stood to the right of the drainer, above a wooden cupboard containing a supply of waxed cardboard, milk bottle tops, and several blocks of *Monkey Brand*, a mild benign abrasive, used for cleaning and polishing metal dairy objects. The foreman then carefully explained the procedures I had to follow, with the warning that everything had to be perfectly clean, and if not, he would make my life a misery. He left with a final warning: "Make sure you switch off the light when you finish, an' make sure yat's shut [the door's shut] beyont you, me dayn't want any stinking moggies gettin' in, an' helpin' themselves ti milk." Then, leaving me to it, he went into the farmhouse, closing the door with a thud, which spoke clearly that as far as he was concerned, his day's work had ended.

I finished my work about 9.30 pm in the evening, and with the sun sinking fast behind me, trudged home slack-footed and weary, along a road empty of fellow creatures. Yet, despite a long day of constant work, in no way did I feel downhearted. Indeed rather the opposite, being pleased with the way things had gone, and as for the foreman's short and crabby attitude, well, it seemed no different to what I what I was used to both at school and home, and for that matter from grown-ups in general. As I made my way home, along a road heavy with the scent of honeysuckle and meadowsweet, I had as further encouragement the happy thought my wages would help lighten the load that my mother carried.

When I entered the house, mother, ever ready to condemn, gave me a sharp look, one which begged the question, where have you been until now? I had no need to explain, my worn condition provided the answer. Yet as always she had a fine hearty meal prepared for me, frequently making me wonder if, during those hard and hungry times, she went without, sacrificing much of her rations for my well-being. With time to reflect on subsequent events, I am convinced she did.

My first day as a farmer's boy set the pattern for my six-day working week. My daily round commenced at 5.30 am, at first milking, followed by mucking out the cow house and stables, which included my daily wrestle with both the foreman and The Monster. Then, under his instructions, going out into the fields on such jobs as he ordered; returning for the evening's milking, followed by milk bottling and dairy cleaning. And whilst the hours were such, and it was hard work, I didn't mind.

Here, I'm reminded of those former hardy sons of the soil, who in old age, regaled my boyhood years with stories of their farming days. One I knew worked for over 60 years on the same farm, without even one day off, before retiring aged 75—perhaps something of a record, but not all that unusual in those days. Another old boy, explaining his first day as a live-in 12-year-old, chuckled as he recounted being told by the farm foreman: "Thoo needn't get up much afore fower, as thou'll ony be burnin' candle (You don't need to get up much before 4 am, as you'll only be using up candles)."

Another in conversation told me that at harvest and muck spreading time, "Why, when thoo'd finish work, thoo climbed inter bed at yar side, an straight out at t'other, and it nivver had time to git warm."

After my stint of hoeing, haymaking arrived, when most of my time was spent with a hayfork, turning hay for it to dry and mature in the wind and sun. When fit and ready, using a horse-drawn rake, I formed it into large rows, the better to load and transport down to the farm's stack yard. After the field had been cleared, the stacks built and made rainproof and watertight, I was sent to scruffle a half field of 'coo tonips' (swedes) our all-important crop of main winter feed, and where I learned to 'scruffle'.

"Tek owd Violet," I was instructed. "Thoo'll find scruffler chucked in hedge bottom, just through yat hole (field entrance)." I had never scruffled before, although all my life I had observed, with little interest I might add, men scruffling. It always seemed a straightforward, easy sort of job, with nothing much to it. First, line up the horse and scruffler on the headland, between the rows, and the horse, knowing what it was about, would do the rest. I expected the most arduous part would be lifting, at full stretch, the heavy cumbersome horse collar over the head of a reluctant, playful and excitable horse, as it shied away. With collar and blinkers fitted, and its bit between its teeth, I took off, my two trace chains wrapped round the horse collar 'yaws'.

I rode as befitted a farmer's boy, bare-backed and sideways on, up to the more level fields on the 'tops' where the scruffler rested, and where, after much huffing and puffing, I pulled it free, and facing the field, onto the headland. It took only a minute to lay out the traces and hang Violet on. Then taking hold of the scruffler's handles, with a "Gir up, Violet", I confidently set off, Violet plodding dutifully and with precision, between the rows.

All went well for the first few yards, then things quickly began to go awry. To my consternation, the scruffler began to drift away to one side. No matter how I strained, heaved and fought with all my strength to bring it back into line, in dismay I watched as the scruffler cut through the precious crop. I stopped Violet, who must have wished she was back in her stable, and repositioned the scruffler and set off again, with the same melancholy results. Reaching the far headland, I turned the rig and looked with consternation at the havoc I had caused. Much less confident, but hoping that things might improve, I set off again.

From beginning to end, it proved a nightmare. By the time I reached the end of the row, I had not only caused more damage, but fighting the heavy scruffler every inch of the way, I was becoming exhausted. Knowing I couldn't go on, and desperate for a solution, I turned on the headland, straightened the scruffler up, and began to study how to steer this malevolent machine. I took particular interest in its single wheel, a fixed wheel at the front which I felt must hold the answer to its steering. I crouched alongside and fiddled with it. It had 'play' enough, but no means of steering as far as I could see. Afraid to inflict further damage, not knowing which way to turn, in desperation I took hold of the wretched wheel and shook it violently, hoping this might offer enlightenment of some kind. When enlightenment came, it came from an unexpected quarter, in an unexpected way.

I nearly jumped out of my skin as a voice behind me bellowed, "Wat's tha' doin' on tha's backside? Get up, thoo idle bugger. Don't thoo ever sit down in a field agin."

I leapt to my feet, frightened, but protesting my innocence. Yet in a flash, and with an overwhelming sense of relief, I recognised that whilst I was in deep trouble, here was a kind of deliverance, "I can't steer it," I whimpered.

"Can't steer it? Can't steer it?" howled the foreman. Then the implications of what I was asserting struck home. If I couldn't scruffle, he would have to! Immediately, his attitude and tone changed. "Can't steer it?" He cooed, "Why, it's 'iver so easy when tha' knows hoo. Jist thoo walk alongside of me, an' I'll show thee how it's done."

Taking Violet's guide strings, the foreman and I set off, both studiously ignoring the violent damage I had inflicted. He showed how, by closely watching the head of the scruffler, and that wheel, for any slight deviation from the straight, a slight pressure on the scruffler's opposing handle brought it back easily into line. Reaching the end of the row, the foreman turned Violet and lined her and the scruffler up. "Now," he told me, "get a hold a them handles, an' let's see how tha frames." He walked beside me, monitoring my progress, offering advice, and keeping me right.

By the end of the row, he was satisfied I'd got the hang of it. He watched me turn on the headland, before departing with a warning: "Keep tha mind on't job. Thoo's done enuff damage already." No more was said regarding the two rows of turnips I had more or less destroyed. It paid the foreman to keep quiet, the responsibility being his of course. As for myself, I was more than happy nothing more was said, and the farmer never found out.

One lovely summer's morning, after mucking out, and after the foreman had breakfasted and rested a little, he came out to me. "Chuck a bridle over Star's head," he ordered, "an tek him over to Billy Buggs", who was the nearest blacksmith, with a shop in the village of Skidby, near the church and alongside the green, and sheltered by an old tree. "Tek Star an' get 'im shod all round," he ordered, "an' whilst thoo's there, bring back a couple of Billy's swan-necked hoes."

This surprised me, as it was the sort of cushy job the foreman usually reserved for himself. A fine morning, a leisurely ride out, a chat with Billy as he shod the horse, and perhaps a stroll to the nearby shop for a plug of chewing tobacco, was just up his street. And by the time he arrived back, the morning would have passed, and pie-time would be beckoning.

Star, so named from a distinctive star-shaped white flash he carried on his forehead, was a large powerful horse, used for the heaviest work, but quiet and even-tempered. To mount, I had to walk him to the nearest five-barred gate, climb up it, and then, making a leap of faith, jump on his back. Riding Star bare backed, we set off along a sun drenched road, ablaze in the morning sunlight. I revelled in the power of the horse beneath me and the sweetness and beauty of the countryside around. Meanwhile, Star, giving little snorts and snuffles, seemed to be enjoying the outing as much as I was.

I knew Billy Bugg from way back, and this morning, riding out, I was looking forward to meeting an old acquaintance. Before the war I had been great friends with a boy whose family had subsequently moved to Skidby, where at every opportunity I walked over to visit him. Billy Bugg's smithy forge was a favourite port of call, especially when the weather was cold. Sheltered within its walls we used to take advantage of his fire by using his bellows, with its long handle, fancifully beautified at its tapering end by the addition of a large imposing cow horn.

Apart from Bill's abilities to make sparks fly and form things, as a former company sergeant major in the First World War, he had a wealth of stories, thrilling us with tales of derring-do. Although, as a blacksmith, I suspect Billy's war was fought far from the front line. Maintaining cavalry units perhaps, or in one of the many railway workshops and locomotive sheds operated by the Railway Operating Division in northern France. It was Billy who, one day as my friend and I sheltered from an icy blast, unthinkingly placed an iron rivet on his anvil, striking it hard with a heavy forging hammer.

Picking up the rivet in his horny calloused hand he unthinkingly pressed it, hot from the blow, into my friend's soft tender paw saying, "Here's a shillin', lad, gan and git thasen a bag of sweets fra shop." As the hot rivet seared his hand, my friend let out a howl of pain. Instantly mortified and contrite, poor Billy, for he was really a kindly man, raked about in his trouser pocket for a mollifying coin, dragging out a tiny silver thruppenny 'dodger'. My friend, amazed and delighted by this munificence, shut off his tears with the speed of light, and before you could say 'Jack Clapperson', was loping off to the shop to begin a thorough exploitation of his new-found wealth.

Having just escaped the fiasco of scruffling, it wasn't long before I came another cropper, once again verifying the age-old dictum: a little knowledge is a dangerous thing. As the year progressed, I began leading turnips from the high tops down to the farm, where the foreman, covering them with straw and earth, formed piles, for the winter months. Each morning after my work around the farm, I walked up to the field, where I spent the rest of the morning 'top and tailing' cow turnips or wurzels, before leading them in the afternoon, with Violet drawing one of the most useful and indispensable of farm vehicles, the humble muck cart. To the casual eye, like most farm equipment, it looked crude and primitive. Yet it was the end result of much careful thought and ingenuity. The body so finely balanced that fully loaded it bore down little on the horse. Its rear door allowed it to be tipped, and its contents discharged easily and quickly. Whilst its large diameter, iron-shod wheels, ungainly and out of proportion it seemed, were designed to smooth its passage over rough or broken ground and were particularly effective in reducing the risk of the cart being 'gripped' in a slop hole or other calamity. At the body end of the fixed shafts, was positioned a platform, from which, if he so wished, either standing or sitting, the driver could control the horse, although many, under normal circumstances, preferred walking alongside the horse's head.

My first afternoon leading, I prepared Violet, after the usual tussle with her collar. This was followed by fitting her gear, then harnessing her to the muck cart. I walked beside her up the steep side of the valley. I was young and lithe, and apart from my little 'Tansad' folding pram, every step of my life had been taken on my own two feet, consequently, I found the climb no effort. Arriving at my workplace, together we moved slowly along the rows of prepared fodder, of the type known as 'coo tonnips', forking them into the cart using a long-handled pitchfork, another of those simple but highly efficient, multipurpose farm tools. I forked them in two at a time, using both tines, until I had a load, and it was time to return. On Near Stions' more gentle slopes, I had grown accustomed to working with a horse and muck cart, so walking at Violet's head, unconcernedly I set off. At first the cart track remained fairly level, until we reached the crest of Raywell Valley. Here, for some inexplicable reason, Violet halted. "Go on," I urged, clicking my tongue. Dutifully, Violet moved off. Part of a draft horse's harness was a thick strong leather band, a 'britchburn', which passed around the rear quarters, well down. It was attached to the cart shafts on either side, by a short length of chain and, for the comfort of the horse as it worked, this was always left loose and slack. It was something I had never given any thought to, and this was about to be my undoing.

Once over the brow, the track began to steepen. Walking alongside the horse, blissfully unaware, I began to feel the heavy cart pushing Violet, who stiffened her back legs, and surefootedly dug her hind hoofs in. The angle of descent increased, and as it did so, all hell broke loose, and in an instant I discovered the purpose of the britchburn. As the cart began to impel her, Violet's hind legs shot forward, she then threw her weight rearwards, in effect sitting in the britchburn; except, hanging loose, and by riding up over her rump it no longer operated. Freed, she sat down on her backside, her hind legs stuck forward at a grotesque and painful angle, as the cart shafts crashed down on either side of her. Supported only by her front legs, and with the full weight of the loaded cart now bearing down on her back, Violet looked a pitiful sight indeed. Even as I looked on in shock, and fully alive to what was occurring, her straining front legs began to give, as she fought to keep her chest off the ground, and certain suffocation. I could have flipped the rear door of the cart open, and decanted much, if not all of the load, then helped Violet to her feet, but panic overcame reason, and I raced towards the farm, shouting "Violet's down!"

Immediately the foreman appeared, and together we raced to where Violet, sweat-stained, eyes rolling and trembling, fought against the weight of the cart. In a flash, the foreman was fighting to unbuckle her restraining and tightened harness. With a desperate heave, he slipped the main buckle, instantly freeing the distressed animal. Snorting with fear and shock, she was helped to her feet. Was that a look of reproach Violet gave me? Trembling, she was led away to recover in the safety and quiet of her familiar stable. As for me, I stood head bowed, as I endured the wrath of the foreman who, in unsurprisingly verbose and colourful language, swore by all the gods, who may or may not in times past have circled the globe, to knock some sense into my uncommonly thick and unresponsive head. My failures were caused less by an exaggerated sense of my own abilities, but more by a lack of wit and intelligence. I was on the whole, you might say, a bit thick. My promise to try harder, lasted for only a few more weeks, when I became unfortunately responsible for a similar and equally serious event involving a horse.

In this case, for once, I was around the farm when the Land Army girl returned, stepping down daintily from her float, before disappearing into the farmhouse with her leather cash bag, and list of customers, to render her accounts. This afternoon, the foreman called me over. "Unload the float and back it under cover," I was ordered. "Then lowse the pony out, then bring her round, and water and stable her." I was now well-practised in detaching draft animals from a variety of farm implements, and this present job seemed simple and matter of fact, and as such held no terrors. As I backed the float under cover, I congratulated myself in how easy it had proved, and how responsive the pony had been to my demands, I began to release the pony from between the float shafts.

Here I ought to shy away from my account and explain the sequence of events leading up to this next failure, with results no less dire, for the pony. When being loosed out, the heavy draft animals I was familiar with had been taught to remain motionless between the shafts as they were freed, the shafts then being lowered to the ground. With a muck cart with fixed shafts, heavy and difficult to lower, and more difficult, if not impossible for the person in charge to raise, a pole, under the left shaft could be lowered, retaining the cart and its shafts in a horizontal position until such time as the cart was required again. With the horse standing patiently within the shafts, its harness finally released, and its guide strings neatly coiled and hung over one of the collar 'yams', then, acting on a gentle "Go on" or click of the tongue and only then, would the horse trot off by itself, its harness jingling, back to its stable, and the removal of its harness.

With the float safely under cover, I turned to the pony, unhooking both its collar and britchburn chains from the hooks on the float's two shafts, then following my normal practice, I released the pony's bellyband. As I did so, things went horribly wrong. Unbeknown to me, this was a signal for the pony to walk out of the shafts, shafts which I should, at this stage, have been holding up until the pony was clear and I could lower them to the ground. At this point I was caught unawares. The shafts fixed, and with the weight of the float on them crashed down. I have already remarked on the pony being highly strung and sensitive. This trait was aggravated by the foreman, who had some funny ways, surreptitiously, but in my presence, feeding the pony excess oats. For, quoth he, chuckling: "That'll mek it frisky, an' give 'er [the Land Army girl] summit to think about."

The pony, startled out of its wits by the crash behind, sprang forward in fear. When lowsing out, I was accustomed to leaving the guide strings until last, but in this case these were heavy leather reins, which extended back to the float, and hung over an ornamental iron rest fixed to the front of it. Things now went from bad to worse, as the pony, in its panic, leapt forward, its bit pulling fiercely at its mouth, and the reins, flying off the float, landing with a resounding 'thwack!' across the horse's rump, sending it, now maddened, screaming and rearing at full stretch through the stack yard, in a cloud of dust and flying stones, with me running behind, vainly pleading with it to stop.

If this wasn't enough, compounding its fear and confusion, the heavy reins became entangled in the pony's hind legs. Still kicking at the tormenting reins tearing at its mouth, it tore out of the farm entrance, and turned westwards along the road, before passing under the H&BR's Five Arches Viaduct, and on to the tiny insignificant hamlet of Raywell. There some stalwart and hardy son of the soil, risking life and limb, brought the crazed, sweat-lathered creature to a halt, and using all his guile quietened it down, before the foreman, pedalling furiously on his bike, arrived, to take charge. Here let me draw a veil over his reactions, leaving what happened to my reader's imagination, except to say "fool" and "blockhead" formed much of his verbal tirade.

Following this, a major part of my day was spent 'lookin' (a dialect term for hoeing) 'rubbish', mainly thistles, in cornfields or elsewhere. Among farmworkers of the time it was considered weary boring work, giving rise to the expression 'I'm lookin for night', which in plain English meant, 'I've had enough of this, I'll be glad when we're finished for the day'. To derive any kind of satisfaction from walking up and down alone, in an otherwise empty cornfield, required a very dull mind indeed. Perhaps that's why it appealed to me!

After my 'lookin' stint, I was sent to hoe sugar beet. Because of wartime shortages, this was a crop farmers had by law to cultivate, and the farm had about three acres, growing in a block with other root crops. The same routine which served when previously 'lookin', now applied to the sugar beet. Each morning, after farm duties, I went lifting and trimming the sugar beet using, as a point of interest, a curved brass-handled French bayonet, which according to its engraved inscription, had been manufactured by the St Etienne Government Armoury in about 1870. How a Franco-Prussian war bayonet had arrived on a small East Riding farm is, to this day, quite beyond me. During each afternoon, taking the usual muck cart, I spent time leading the trimmed sugar beet down to the farm, to await transportation to the nearest sugar beet factory, from where we received our processed beet back for use as a kind of stock feed, although now, in its dry and desiccated form, it proved of little nutritional value.

At that time we still suffered occasional air raids, now sporadic, and on a much reduced scale. After the devastation wreaked in Hull, the Luftwaffe seemed to have 'dusted its hands' on a job well done, whilst continuing small 'nuisance' raids designed to keep the city on the *qui vive*. Or perhaps, with its involvement in Russia, it had bigger 'fish to fry'. One afternoon, during this period, I was loading sugar beet and watched from the fields a grim drama being played out, when a visibly badly damaged twin-engine Wellington bomber, perhaps jumped on somewhere over the North Sea by a roving Messerschmitt fighter, came limping home. Flying low, very low, escorted by a Hurricane flying alongside, it headed north, its passage marked by a thin haze streaming behind, which thickened as I followed its progress, leaving me wondering if it managed to land safely.

A few days later, still busy amongst the sugar beet, I became involved in a highly charged drama of my own; a drama which for some time left me a quivering bag of nerves. Loading beet, I became aware of the sound of a low flying, fast approaching aircraft. Always interested in such things, I stopped forking, and searched the heavens for the elusive aircraft, hoping to identify its type and make. With a roar it swept over the brow of a hill, about 400 yards distance, and flying obliquely across my front, from north to south, with its two large and prominent engines, it was obviously a bomber, yet of a design unknown to me. As I studied it, its large glazed and bulbous nose, deep cockpit areas, and overly slim fuselage reminded me of some enormous and (if there was such a thing) venomous dragonfly. My interest now fully aroused; I followed its flight as it banked gently to the west and began to climb. Then catching my breath, I stiffened as a spasm of fear swept over me. Interested only in the aircraft's unusual shape, I had failed to notice its insignia, which showed clearly, this was in fact a German aircraft. Prominent in an otherwise empty landscape, our little group might prove a tempting, though difficult, deflection shot, for some enterprising German gunner wishing to practise his skill. Feeling exposed, I held my breath, as the plane flew on, slowly gaining height, and not relaxing until it was out of gunshot range, I followed its course as it passed over the H&BR main line, in the vicinity of Five Arches, and then whilst still slowly gaining height, watched it swing round in a wide arc. Had the crew spotted the viaduct, and now were gaining height in preparation for bombing it I wondered? After all, it would be rather counter-productive, if at a low height, they blew themselves up with their own bombs. The bomber adopted a shallow dive. Was I about to say goodbye to a well-loved structure? If so, this would prove a feather in the caps of its crew, for much of the South Yorkshire coal passed over Eppleworth Viaduct, and until it was repaired, its loss would be felt by much of the country. Then with growing dismay I realised it was aligned, not on the viaduct, but on a certain light-coloured muck cart closely associated with old Violet and me, who were stranded in the middle of a bare, open field, with neither place to hide, nor time to flee, where even dropping to the ground would offer no protection. Violet, used to the roar of low-flying aircraft, stood unmoved within the shafts, quietly standing with one hind hoof tilted, resting on the toe of its horseshoe. Standing helpless, with my back to the cart wheel, I felt much as a condemned man might feel when facing a firing squad. I gazed up into the huge glazed nose of the bomber, expecting my last sight would be the flash and twinkle of its forward machine guns. Automatically, with eyes half closed, I braced myself for the seemingly inevitable. Still it came on, 500 yards, 400, 300… any moment now it would be over. Two hundred yards, and suddenly the aircraft lifted, and howled close overhead. So close that even steady old Violet took exception, by shaking her head, backing a little and trampling about with her hoofs in a show of indignation. Little did she know how close she had come to being, like me, a bloody lifeless heap in the middle of a field. And who could say what momentary charitable thought had caused the gunner to stay his hand on the machine gun trigger?

A few days later, in the same field, I was alerted by the same roar. But this time without hesitation, I fled, leaving poor Violet to her fate, and making for the cover of a nearby hedge. Peering fearfully through its greenery, I watched the very same aircraft thunder past. But instead of the feared Luftwaffe symbols I was expecting, I was astonished to discover it now sported the familiar and more friendly roundels of the RAF. I can only assume this German aircraft had been captured somewhere, and I was undergoing tests by the RAF. Criticism might be levelled at the crew for diving a marked enemy aircraft on an exposed farm worker and his horse, a creature usually expected under such circumstances to bolt away in terror. On the other hand, the crew, flying in excess of 200 mph, may have caught only a flash of something below, and with the probability none were from a country background, may casually, without thinking, and on the spur of the moment as part of the evaluation of the aircraft performance, decided to mount the feigned attack—which left me deeply shaken from what I considered a miraculous escape.

Throughout the summer months I continued the daily tasks and common round until, with autumn upon us, the foreman began to take a closer interest in the condition of the corn crops, and whilst keeping his weather eye open, walked round frequently and often to test for fullness and condition. For upon his experience and word, depended the harvest, the culmination of a year's work, and the bedrock upon which the farm's future depended. In those days, unlike today's wholly mechanical operation, harvest, even at the best of times, proved a Herculean task, and as such, adding much toil and trouble to the already overburdened shoulders of farm workers. But first, preparations had to be made. From the shelter where it had slept since the last harvest, the self-binder was dragged out, to be checked over, fettled up and carefully oiled. Its two opposing cutting slides withdrawn, and on each, the succession of large triangular cutting teeth sharpened by first using a file, then honing each to a razor edge with a whetstone. With its working parts lubricated and draw-gear checked over, the weather set fair and the corn declared 'fit', the harvest operation could begin. Unlike other fields, where the headlands were left unploughed to facilitate the turning of horses and equipment, cornfields were ploughed out and sown to their limits. This meant that before a self-binder could enter, each field had to be 'opened out' by hand, using the shoulder developing instrument, a 'lay' (scythe), so called for the way that each sweep of its blade 'laid' whatever it was cutting into neat swathes.

With the foreman's broad shoulders on the lay, cutting out a passage, a 'breed' some 12 or 14 feet wide around the circuit of the field, the farmer, whom I seldom saw, arrived as a much-needed reinforcement, to help out. The foreman and I both followed, gathering up the cut corn and forming it by hand, into sheaves. With the field thus 'opened out' and ready, the farmer, it being his privilege, took over the management of the self-binder. Lacking the benefits of modern herbicides, and despite all the time and effort put into 'lookin' many dried thistles remained to torment bare hands and arms as, following the binder, we gathered up the bound sheaves, two, sometimes four, if pressed, at a time, under our arms, before forming them into 'stooks'.

Harvest time, 1941, favoured us with a spell of fine dry weather, but before we could start bringing in the harvest, a long period of wind and driving rain arrived to thwart our efforts. During this time I spent most days lifting and resetting sodden stooks, blown over by the wind. Although the days had shortened, eventually as they had to, sunshine and drying winds did their work, and we were able to lead the fruits of our labours home to the safety and security of the stack yard. Transporting sheaves on a four wheeled flat rully, required careful loading, to a set pattern, if it was to withstand the heave and roll of sloping fields, and the shock and jar of rough, potholed cart tracks. This was a skill I had learned well during my time at Near Stions, and because of this it was something I enjoyed doing. And so by mutual consent I was appointed chief loader, the fact I was young and lithe, and more able to scramble about on a swaying load, may also have influenced their decision.

As the rully moved slowly between the rows of stooks, the farmer on one side, using a pitchfork, forked sheaves of corn up to me, whilst on the other side the foreman did the same. To run smoothly, loading required a degree of cooperation between the forkers and the loader, this being governed by the rate the loader was able to correctly position and interlock the odd-shaped and slippery sheaves. To assist in this, those forking turned each sheaf in the direction it was being laid, singly and in time with the loader. I stress singly and in time with the loader, because hidden from the farmer by the load, the foreman was up to another of his tricks. Winking and grinning, he vented his spleen by forking up sheaves to me two at a time, throwing them haphazardly, with no care or scruple as to how or where they fell, leaving me scrambling about on the swaying load, as I fought to keep on top of things.

As each load arrived in the stack yard and drew alongside the growing stack, our roles changed somewhat. The farmer now taking on the business of 'stacking', the foreman on the rully 'teeming' and me left with the unenviable task of standing precariously on the edge of the stack, directly above the needle-sharp tines of the foreman's pitchfork, forking his sheaves crosswise over the stack, to the farmer. And woe betide me if I didn't make sure each fell the right way up, the right way round, and conveniently to hand. This gave the foreman a further chance to carry on with his wanton ways. Leering up at me with many a wink, he continued throwing up sheaves, two at a time, and often deliberately at me, leaving me struggling waist-deep in an ever-growing pile. Fighting to clear the backlog with a foreshortened pitchfork the result was, perhaps inevitably, that I stabbed myself, inflicting a nasty wound in my left leg. The pitchfork tine had entered my leg on the inside, just below the knee in a downward direction, missed the joint by a fraction, and exited behind the knee. In the heat of the moment I thought this was but a scratch, although at the time I was mildly surprised at the effort suddenly required to withdraw the fork.

I was fortunate in one respect, in that it happened towards the end of the final load of the day, although I still had the milk bottling to face. Working alone, late into the night, my knee began to ache and stiffen until, having finished my work, I hardly knew how to hobble the few miles home, where, after washing away a trickle of dried blood I'd discovered behind my knee, proof could be seen that the tine had penetrated my knee from front to rear. I fell into bed exhausted and in pain. Sleep brought relief, and in the morning, whilst the throbbing ache in my knee was much eased, I limped my way to work, stiff-legged on that side for some time. It says something, though I know not what, that although still wearing my school boy short trousers, now very raggy, patched and worn, and despite the often dirty conditions I worked in, the wound healed quickly and cleanly without infection.

With the stacks erected and topped out with straw as protection against the elements until the arrival of the threshing machine and its accompanying steam traction engine, work continued without let up. No sooner had the harvest been safely stacked, than it was 'muck plugging' time, the intermediate stage between harvest and ploughing-out the bare and empty cornfields. For the next fortnight, between milking, the foreman and I spent our days muck spreading, each using only a muck fork. This meant two weeks of hard solid graft, loading and spreading the many tons of tangled, often part-rotten manure, now piled up in heaps. Among generations of farm workers it had been said, often with a wistful sigh, "If only they could fit a seat to a muck fork." And blow me, it wasn't much longer before someone did—and called it a tractor!

This 'rural idyll' was broken when two lorry loads of basic slag arrived to be spread as a fertiliser and land conditioner. Apparently it was blast furnace slag ground to a fine powder, and probably full of heavy metals and as toxic as could be! Again, I had the dubious company of the foreman to lend a hand. Spreading it dry, it blew and swirled around us, covering our clothes in a grey powder, and filling our lungs at the same time. A spell of wet weather interrupted our labours and when we resumed, each shovelful, now as heavy as lead, clung like glue to our shovels. Even the foreman began to despair of ever spreading it, but spread it we did, even though each time it left me reeling with exhaustion. Yet, despite the long hours and harsh working conditions, I was generally content, happily accepting my lot and pleased to take home a weekly wage. At the same time, I was well aware that I was ill-equipped for any other kind of work, and accepting that fact I was content to remain a farm labourer for the rest of my working life.

With the vacant fields well mucked, the farm turned its attention to ploughing and preparing the bare empty cornfields for 'back-end' sowing. To plough the farm's rolling undulating contours required a special skill beyond me, and as the foreman ploughed out each field, it fell to me to follow on and harrow the soil, afterwards rolling it to a fine tilth. Was harrowing, as the word suggests, an explanation for the exhausting work it entailed, or was it synonymous with the term? Whatever, this was really man's work and, for a boy of 14, was utterly draining. Ache, pain, toil, exhaustion, one could go on until the cows came home, describing its effects. Sufficient to say it was 'hardwired' in the DNA of toughened farm workers to the extent that, when worn out by toil, they often remarked about "I's about been 'arrowed", or if completely done in, the more abrupt and certain, "I is 'arrowed."

Harrows in those days were formed by three overlapping, cast steel sections of an open diamond pattern covering, when set out for work, an area about seven feet square. At the junction of each diamond point, a large blacksmith-forged and tempered tine was bolted in. Forward facing, with a curved profile, it was designed to not only break up and level the surface of a ploughed field, but importantly, drag out any growing 'rubbish', and in those days, especially that bane of farmers' lives, the tough deep-rooted 'wicks', perhaps more widely known as couch grass. It was this initial phase of the operation which proved so back-breaking. Frequently, as each section of the harrow became clogged with weeds, stones and soil, and whilst maintaining a good steady walking pace, the section, heavy with its own weight, and against the pull of the horses, had to be lifted out of the ground and shaken vigorously, to clear it of its accumulated debris. This I found beyond my strength, leaving me with no other options than to stop each time and clear the harrows by hand. A slow time-consuming operation, and one not likely to find favour with the foreman, ploughing in an adjoining field. Disapproving he may have been, but I wonder, was he distantly grinning at my discomfort?

It brings to mind the times we went cutting hay from one or other of the haystacks. After hitching a spare horse to a suitable cart and leading it around to the stack, I would meet the waiting foreman, twirling a pitchfork, where he would greet me with "Come on lad, we haven't got all day" or something similar. To cut into the compressed hay required a hay knife, the foreman always granting me the privilege of using what I found to be a distinctively cumbersome tool. Made of heavy cast steel, its large triangular blade was sharpened on either side, using a whetstone. As I struggled to drive it down into the solid hay, I often felt the foreman, who sharpened it for me, could have put a keener edge on it, if he so wished.

Gently tearing apart the cut hay with his fork, he would urge, "Put tha' back into it lad, a bit hev work'll do tha good." About this time I purchased a second-hand bicycle. I say second-hand for lack of any of its former history. Delving into my scanty store of coin, I approached the old man selling it and, for perhaps half a crown in old Imperial currency, or about 12½ pence, I acquired it. What I actually paid has been lost in the mists of time, I may even have paid five bob, or 25 pence, though such a sum, nearly a full week's wages, and stretching my resources to the limit, would have brought a sharp intake of breath, and much sucking of teeth, as parting with such a princely sum filled my breast with doubts and fears.

Being of such unusual construction and doubtful heritage, this machine deserves both a mention and a more detailed examination. It was a massive 'sit up and beg' sort of bicycle, weighing 'a ton', and as such had become too heavy and cumbersome for its elderly owner to either mount or control. To propel it forward required the efforts of an eight-coupled goods engine and one at the peak of its performance. The main frame of this oddity, for never having seen its like before or since, was formed, not of single tubes, but of four small diameter steel tubes, firmly clamped together at intervals, the wheel struts, formed likewise of two similar clamped steel tubes. The handlebars seemed to stretch to infinity in graceful curves, whilst the mudguards, of a solid square section, were pressed from thick, heavy-duty steel. The leather saddle, softly sprung, was another distinctive feature of this peculiar machine, being of such generous proportions one could easily saddle a horse with it. Search as I might, I found no indication of where it was manufactured, or by whom. Was it a military bicycle from World War I, French perhaps? Or being roughly painted in a suspicious grey-green colour, was it perhaps a trophy captured from the Germans? The indications being, it had either been fashioned by a village blacksmith with a spare tin of greyish paint, or because of its massive construction, an early form of German armoured vehicle, built to withstand the rigours of war! Yet it did save some boot leather, and returning weary on a night it saved my legs. Mounted on the front was something I prized, a magnificent aluminium-bodied, carbide gas headlamp. It was well sprung to counter the uneven roads, and containing within its body, a bottom chamber holding carbide, and above it a reservoir of water, with a finely adjustable drip feed, to drip water at a controlled rate onto the carbide to produce acetylene gas. It threw a blindingly white glare far ahead, picking out nocturnal creatures, rabbits, sometimes a fox and occasionally a night owl. In its pristine condition, it would be worth a fortune in today's market. Whatever happened to it I wonder?

In late 1942, an early, and what was to prove again, another severe winter, was already making its unwelcome presence felt, as each morning, after completing my work round and about the farm, armed with a sharpened hedge slasher over my shoulder, I made my way up to the cold windswept top fields to cut kale. Kale, a winter crop, had an evil reputation: its leaves large and pendulous, held copious amounts of rain or snow, and with each slash at the thick stalk, flung a spray of wet around, drenching the cutter and ensuring the stigma of being bad to deal with. Nor in the afternoons, when forking the wet and dripping kale onto a cart, did things improve much. I, like all farm workers at this time, was woefully lacking any form of what is now described as 'protective clothing'. Instead, I wrapped old sacking around my lower limbs, secured with lengths of Massey Harris binder twine, and around my waist, as further protection against the wet and cold, any old mouse 'chavelled' corn sack I could lay my hands on. If the weather was particularly severe, it was usual to cover one's head and shoulders with another corn sack, after pushing in a corner to cover the head and ensure it held in place.

With the icy winds of winter scouring the desolate countryside and lacking both money and sufficient clothing coupons for anything better, I was still wearing my short school trousers, now very raggy and hardly decent. Furthermore, with bare knees, chapped and sore from the frigid blast of 'Old Man Winter', I was beginning to suffer from cold and wet. True, having worn short trousers all my life, I was accustomed to often harsh conditions, but these never extended to remaining exposed for hours in an open field. Despite the eldest of my brothers now serving in the Middle East and busy running backwards and forwards across the desert sands at Field Marshall Rommel's behest, and as such unlikely to return home soon, if ever, mother, taking pity on me, reluctantly (for my brother's possessions were sacrosanct), gave me a pair of his grey flannel trousers, an act of inestimable value at this time.

To the west of the H&BR main line, that section where it burst from the shelter of the deep Willerby Cutting and its adjoining chalk quarries, and on the exposed embankment leading to Eppleworth Viaduct, lay the farm's most distant field, given over that year to growing cow turnips and kale for winter feed. Having exhausted the nearer fields, I was put to work leading our daily wants of fodder from this far-flung field, which was aligned along the southern slope of the east-running Raywell Valley, and following its inclination, had been ploughed and sown in the same direction right up to and hard against the railway's boundary fence. In the meantime the weather, although bright and cold, turned even colder, with keen frosts persisting throughout the day. This bright and sunny period proved ideal for the job in hand, and whilst I was forced to kick each swede out of the ground before I could top and tail them with that good old French bayonet, the water held in the kale leaves, as I cut the kale down, flew away as frozen shards. That week, on the Friday night, the weather changed and a wet cold miserable thaw set in, bringing with it not only snow and sleet, but an unkind, north-east wind, which cut through clothing to the bone. Life became difficult for the horse and me, as we wallowed in what overnight had become a sea of mud. Nor could the thaw have arrived at a more inauspicious time, Saturday being the day I had to double up for Sunday with my supply of fodder.

Sharp after a snatched dinner break, I set off with Violet and a flat waggon to lead back the swedes and kale I had cut that morning. Two loads were required, and both Violet and I had our work cut out if we were to lead them home before the darkness, and milking overtook us. Donning my foul-weather gear of sacks and sacking, which always smelt strongly of rats and mice, especially when wet, I threw a couple of corn sacks over Violet's back, to keep her as warm and dry as possible, before fitting her harness.

Arriving in the field in the teeth of this weather, I worked back and forth along the rows, encouraging Violet as the load became heavier and the cart wheels sank further. Finally with a good load on, I pointed Violet down the valley slope towards the field's entrance where the hard road beckoned. Under its load the cart's ironclad wheels ploughed deep furrows in the thawing ground making hard work for the old lady. We had almost reached the field gate, when disaster struck. Immediately within the entrance, covered by a thick layer of ice, and concealed by a coating of mud waiting to catch an unaware innocent like me, a deep 'slop hole' had developed. During the week I had driven over it, without noticing and in safety. Now under its load, the cart crashed through the thinning ice, and stuck.

With both of us thrashing about in mud and water, I tried time and time again to coax Violet into pulling us free, however, time and time again she failed. With much still to do, and time pressing, I was becoming deeply anxious; also, by now Violet was showing signs of distress. Increasingly, it looked as I would have to admit defeat, lowse Violet out, abandon the cart and its load, and return empty-handed to the farm, for help. I shuddered at the thought of facing the irate foreman. Just then, however, I heard a voice behind me, "'Ello, what we got 'ere then?"

It was a youngish man I didn't recognise, unshaven and dressed in a long shabby coat, and wearing a cocked hat. Thinking back, and bearing in mind the desolate location, he may have been a poacher. Nevertheless, any port in a storm, I quickly appraised him of my situation which, in any case, was plain enough to see. "Ah, that's easily dealt with," he replied, picking up a plank of wood that was lying in the nearby hedge bottom. Then, positioning himself behind the horse: *Thwack*! Poor Violet reacted violently, and with a scream and a snort, lunged hard against her collar.

Under the sudden strain, her 'yams' broke away from her collar. "Ah well, she's free now!" the man casually observed, and before I quite knew what had happened, he'd nonchalantly strolled off, obviously making himself scarce. Unbelieving, and in despair, I stared, my hopes blighted. Not only was I up to my neck in mud, I was now adrift in a 'sea of troubles'. Without yams, my draw gear was gone, leaving me helpless. Once again the spectre of returning without a load, and the consequent vehemence of the Foreman, rose to haunt me. Then in a flash of recollection and inspiration, I remembered a length of old trace chain, also discarded in the nearby hedge bottom. With a bit of luck and some ingenuity, this could prove my saviour.

Before retrieving it, I spent a little time calming the distressed and trembling horse. From behind her blinkers, her eyes showed their whites. After her rough handling, which she seemed to attribute to me, I don't think she liked me anymore, and when I tried to stroke her neck to calm her, she turned her head away. Forlornly, picking up the chain, I was relieved to find it about six feet in length, so more than enough, after repositioning the yams, to bind them together. With a few kind words and some gentle coaxing, we set off, after carefully avoiding the treacherous slop hole. Entering the farm, I was met by a livid foreman, demanding to know where I'd been? "Stuck fast, stuck fast in a grip, wi' busted yams," I replied.

"Is that so?" he snarled, "Get this load teemed whilst I fetch another collar. An get back for t'other load."

Without calling his attention to my own condition, exhausted and caked in mud, I warned him, "I think I need a new horse, Violet's about done in."

The foreman looked her over carefully. "Get this load teemed, sharp, an' I'll fetch Star." Lowsing Violet out, he had her away to the peace and quiet of her own warm stable. Returning with Star, a big powerful horse, he harnessed him to the cart, before helping me with the remainder of the load. I swung Star and the cart round to return and resume where I had left off. "Get tha sen away quick, an' this time, don't get stuck," was his parting shot.

In the field, I worked my way along the rows, until nearing the railway boundary, I became aware of a goods train on the embankment above me, slowly drawing up to a signal. Usually immersed in my work, I seldom noticed passing trains, trains which had once formed such a large and exciting part of my life, enthralling and delighting me, but which now I had left behind. However, intrigued by the unusual circumstances of a train being stopped here, something outside my experience, it aroused both my curiosity and my interest. I gazed up at the engine on the embankment, high above me. The cab was sheeted against the weather, and through the drift of sleet and snow I could see one of the blue-clad crew, sitting relaxed, warm and comfortable. Unbidden, and not without reason, I felt a twinge of envy as I found myself comparing my current working conditions with those of the men, warm and dry, on the footplate. In a flash of sudden and vivid recollection, I remembered the always-cheery engine crews of yesteryear, who never failed to give me a wave as I sat on the five-barred gate, not half a mile from where I now toiled. And as a contrast I spontaneously dwelt a little on the foreman's sour and unbending attitude. And as I did, I experienced a kind of 'Road to Damascus' moment. Sweeping over me came the sure and certain conviction, a simple, "I can do that job"; nevertheless, at the present I had work to do. After about an hour I was alerted by the engine whistle, and as he prepared for the climb ahead, the clang of the fireman's shovel. Then in a cloud of hissing steam and barking exhaust, the engine got to grips with its heavy train, leaving me with a final view of that intimate moment, and a host of memories, the passing guards van, its cast iron chimney belching flames and sparks, as the guard made himself snug and warm for the journey ahead, and leaving behind, to mark its departure, a windswept trail of smoke.

Delayed by my earlier difficulties, darkness was upon me by the time I had finished loading. Now I was faced with the daunting prospects of negotiating a mile of open road in the darkness without warning lights, a darkness intensified by frequent squalls of snow and sleet. I pondered on my best course of action. Common sense told me to leave the cart and its load of Sunday fodder, and walk Star home along the safety of the grass verge. But leaving my load was out of the question. The foreman would never let me hear the last of it, and I feared the lash of his tongue more than anything. However, looming ever larger in my mind was the danger, without any form of warning lights, of collision with some other road user, on top of which, after a day of hard manual labour in atrocious conditions, I was without putting too fine a point on it, let's say 'arrowed. In all this I consoled myself with the knowledge that, along this road, traffic especially after dark, was to all intents, null and void. But there remained a nagging anxiety, however remote, that some army vehicle might be encountered with results which can only be imagined.

Feeling I was risking my life, not to mention that of my faithful horse, or even some poor unfortunate who might be despatched to eternity if impaled by a broken cart shaft crashing through his windscreen, I could see no option other than crossing my fingers, hoping for the best, and blindly making a dash for it. Bracing myself, I set off by leading Star on a long open driving string that, I hoped, just hoped, in the event of meeting an oncoming vehicle, would give me sufficient distance to prevent a collision. It was a mightily relieved farmer's boy who, thankfully, despite the mountain of work still awaiting him before finishing for the night, turned his horse and cart into the safety of the farmyard.

And what unusual circumstances had compelled the halting of the train close to Eppleworth Viaduct on that bleak and bitter Saturday afternoon so long ago? Years later I was to learn that, under conditions of extreme frost followed by sudden thaw, rock falls often occurred in the lofty near-vertical chalk walls of Little Weighton cutting, compelling the Little Weighton ganger to stop all traffic, and with his men, to clear the obstruction, before safe and normal running could be resumed.

Chapter 4
A Leg Up to Railway Work

Sunday, my day of rest, dawned bright but cold. The vision of the engineman had haunted me since I espied him lolling at ease on a warm and sheltered footplate, and now the more I dwelt upon it, the more convinced I became that his life was a better one than mine, and given the chance, I could make a go of it. Unsettled by these thoughts, my mind progressively shifted to those distant halcyon, sun-filled, dreamy days when eager steps led me to the H&BR Main Line and all its wonders. I recalled with delight the succession of jolly footplate men who, with a world opening before them, or so I imagined, never failed to offer a good humoured and cheerful wave, as they passed on their way to curious and exciting destinations. Having convinced myself these men enjoyed a better way of life, I cast around for ways of joining them. Unfortunately I had a problem with this: I lacked any means of contact with the railway world, a world which seemed to me, closed, distant, even secretive, with its notices of imminent prosecution for trespass upon its property, or other vague misdemeanours. Nor did I know anyone with railway connections who might help or offer advice. Seemingly unable to penetrate this blank wall, I began to despair, viewing my longings as an exercise in futility—nothing more than a fanciful delusion. I had been harbouring a will-o'-the-wisp, and as such it was something best forgotten.

However, whilst coming to terms with my disappointments, suddenly out of the blue, a wild and improbable idea flashed through my mind. How it arrived, where it came from, remains a mystery. Put simply, it was to contact someone I had never met, and I was never likely to meet, who lived in an area where casual visitors were not only unwelcome, but actively discouraged, and who lived, well, I didn't quite know where. None other, let it be said, than the Cottingham stationmaster—someone who must be a man of authority and responsibility; an imposing figure, and as such, more than likely to send me on my way with a flea in my ear for having the cheek to disturb him.

Nevertheless, having made up my mind, and steeling myself for the encounter, I spent the remainder of the morning cleaning and blacking my scuffed and work-worn boots, until I obtained upon them a faint but discernible sheen. In the afternoon, after making myself as presentable as my circumstances allowed, I mounted Old Peculiar, and with beating heart and many doubts and fears, rode off, to beard the lion in its den. After identifying the stationmaster's house (not so difficult—it was attached to the station), what followed has forever stayed in my memory. Strange as it may be, one of my strongest impressions of that momentous day was the pristine condition of the stationmaster's front door. Facing due west, and approached by a short path, and resplendent in North-Eastern Railway (NER) apple green, the sun reflecting like glass off its highly-varnished panels.

I raised the heavy, emblematic NER door knocker with trembling hands, knocked and waited. Nothing stirred, I knocked again, again no reply. Convinced the Fates were against me, I turned away, half glad that my attempt had failed, and as I did so, the door behind me opened, and a voice demanded, "Yes, what is it you want?"

I turned to face a slight, silver haired, sharp featured man, dressed for Sunday in grey flannel trousers, and grey open-necked pullover. I explained that I was looking for work. He shook his head and replied, "No, I've nothing for you." Defeated, I thanked him for his time, and with hope gone, walked dismally away. In that brief encounter, perhaps a tinge of pity at my appearance touched him. Maybe he saw something in me which appealed, for as I walked away he called, "Just a minute, young man. Give me your name and address, and if anything comes up, I'll get in touch with you." After thanking him again, I left. Deep down it was more or less what I expected, the classic 'brush-off', the stationmaster's way of being shot of a troublesome young man. A young man who, for a few hours, had dreamt an impossible dream.

Now fully reconciled to the life of a farm labourer, I was dumbfounded when only few days later I received an official-looking letter from the Railway District Offices, Hull. In effect, it informed me that a vacancy existed for the post of Lad Porter, at Cottingham Station. And if I wished to be considered for this position, to report, giving date and time, to the stationmaster at Cottingham, who would issue me with a third class return ticket to York. Once there, I was to report to the head office of the London and North-Eastern Railway in Rougier Street where, depending on the results of a medical and eyesight examination, consideration might be given to my employment. Bewildered by this sudden and abrupt change of fortune, I could scarcely believe what I was reading. Over the following years I have often had cause to reflect on the stationmaster's unexpected volte-face; a sudden change of heart which reset my life forever, leaving me to speculate on the 'why and wherefore' of his actions.

Was it kindness on his part? If so how did he justify a sudden and urgent need for increased staff? Or was it something more mundane? As the war developed in intensity, was there a genuine need for more staff? This I shall never know, but over time, having received nothing from him but kindness and consideration, I like to think it was the former. And in so doing, I take this opportunity to salute the memory of Charles Beckett, stationmaster, Cottingham, for the life-changing opportunities he bestowed on me.

At the farm I made my excuses for wanting a day off, and at the appointed time, brimming with excitement, and not a little apprehension, I reported to Cottingham Station. Up until then my only experience of train travel had been the two or three, pre-war Sunday school day trips to Bridlington, when, with face happily glued to the carriage window, I found delight in the passing and varied landscape, where men working in fields straightened up and waved, happy and delighted by knowing this was a very special train, one crowded with happy, cheerful and excited children. I rose at my normal time, old habits die hard, and in any case I had much to do before I presented myself at Cottingham Station, and to be ready for whatever lay ahead. I prepared myself with care, by again cleaning my boots of accumulated mud and manure, then applying thick layers of *Cherry Blossom* boot polish, before buffing them (as best I could) to some semblance of a polish. For this special occasion mother had loaned me my eldest brother's raglan overcoat. A poor, open weave sort of coat, through which the wind blew ferociously and without hindrance, but because it concealed many defects in my attire, something I was very grateful for.

What thrills the journey provided, speeding through a barren and frozen countryside, before alighting beneath the mighty curved roof at York. But even before I found the station exit, I was distracted by a massive roar, as standing on the northern curves of the station, an express locomotive struggled to start an enormous fully loaded train. Outside in the station forecourt, lost in the centre of a teeming city, I was confused on how to find the railway headquarters. A friendly porter, attending to passengers' luggage, pointed out my destination, thankfully only a short distance away. As befitting its builders, the mighty NER, it dominated everything around, high, solid, ornate and imposing.

The medical consisted of a thorough physical examination, followed by a series of rigorous eyesight tests, including colour identification, by means of a lantern, through which slides of various shades of red, green and yellow were exposed for me to identify. It all seemed to go well, and later, back at York Station, waiting for my train home, I had an unexpected thrill. From the northern end of the station I heard the rousing beat of an approaching train, and the wailing chords of its chime whistle. I gazed in wonder as the train, under light steam, passed on a through road at about 30 mph. Magnificent in power and beauty, and unlike anything I had seen gracing the humble metals of the H&BR, one of Nigel Gresley's splendid Streamlined Pacifics. Transported, I followed its progress, until leaving the station, I could hear the driver opening it out for the next section. At that moment, how I envied them, both driver and fireman, on the magic footplate of a London North-Eastern Railway (LNER) express locomotive, as, setting about the task ahead, and working the engine hard, they lifted the heavy train and its full complement of passengers cleanly away from York, on the next leg of an already long and arduous turn of duty. A journey which, no doubt, demanded a formidable feat of engine management from both men, and made all the more Herculean by wartime conditions.

With hopes raised, having glimpsed another world, waiting to be either accepted for railway service, or rejected, proved an anxious time. If it proved to be the latter, it left me with no other option but to continue with a life I now found increasingly unpleasant. Returning home from work each night, I searched anxiously for the letter which would seal my fate. When it arrived I tore it open, prepared for the worst. Almost in disbelief, I read that I had been accepted. At that moment, overjoyed, I can hardly describe the surge of happiness and relief which swept over me. The next morning, light of foot, I hurried to inform the foreman I was leaving. Grunting and spitting tobacco juice, he fished around for more information. "Wheers tha gyin then? The railway!" he scoffed. "Nay good that. There's too many gaffers bossing tha about." Yes, but none like you, I thought, and hoped!

On my last Saturday evening, before he shut the farmhouse door on me for the last time, the foreman paid my final week's wages: two half crowns, two one shilling pieces and three pennies, equalling seven shillings and threepence.

Roughly 38p translated into today's currency, which has lost its value enormously since then. Even by 1942 standards it was little for the work I put in every day[2]. Yet for my mother's sake, I had been happy to graft, and graft hard. In any case what else would I have done with my time?

In my account of farming life in the early 1940s, I may have been a little harsh on the foreman. Life for him was also hard. Like all farms, this one operated all year round, seven days a week, with stock having to be fed and watered, cows milked, and cowsheds and stables mucked out. And whilst I counted myself lucky for having been granted each Sunday off, the foreman continued working throughout the year without holidays, including having to turn out if and when a cow calved during the night.

Monday morning, when it came, found me excited beyond measure, if also a little daunted at facing the unknown. Yet I was ready and willing for the Great Adventure. Overnight a heavy fall of snow had blanketed the village and surrounding countryside. To make myself more presentable, and provide a little extra protection against a biting wind, my brother's overcoat was pressed into service. I chose to walk the nearly three miles to the station; not because I had little faith in Old Peculiar's ability to forge a path through the deep snow—its robust and unusual construction had been, I felt, developed for a more demanding and melancholy toil—the mud of Flanders battlefields. My decision to walk was for other reasons. Firstly, I didn't know if bikes were allowed to desecrate the hallowed compass of the station and its grounds. I was a very unworldly young man. Secondly, something I cringed at, I felt the station staff would find my strange machine, with its enormous saddle and archaic headlamp, a source of amusement.

Approaching the station I was caught up in a tide of fellow creatures hurrying to catch the train of choice. Unused to such a crush, and unsure of what to do or where to go, I joined a queue at the booking office window, where, conscious of the many curious eyes boring into the back of my head, and the inquisitive ears listening to my halting conversation, I explained to the booking clerk who I was, and why I was there. At his call the early shift senior porter appeared, and taking me under his wing, escorted me through the ticket gate and along the busy platform to that 'Holy of Holies', the porters' room. Entering, I was met by a welcome blast of heat, provided by a cast iron stove, which roared mightily up

---

[2] 38p in 1941 would be the same as earning £15.18 for a week's work in 2023.

the chimney. Not even a warm cow house on a freezing morning could match this for luxury. Inside, to greet me, two other lad porters, looking smart and confident in their uniforms, lounged at ease, waiting to attend the next train. It all seemed pleasantly relaxed and easy, and I warmed even more to the thought of becoming a railroad man.

The strident ring of a signal bell warned of an approaching train. "Stay with us, and we'll keep you right," my new-found friends assured me. Leaving the warmth and comfort of the porters' room I followed them on to a crowded, windswept, and snow-covered open platform, where one of the lad porters took up position at the ticket gate, ready to collect tickets from detraining passengers, whilst the other, together with the head porter, stood awaiting the incoming train. Among those crowding the busy platform, groups of service personnel, including Wrens, WAAFs and ATS girls, all in obvious good spirits, laughed and joked among themselves, their breath clear and distinct in the cold morning air. Used to a solitary existence in empty fields, and now jostled about by the crowd, and not sure what was expected of me, I drew my thin coat tightly around myself, feeling ill at ease, and out of place with my surroundings.

The train's arrival in the half-light signalled a change of mood. Its massive noisy locomotive stopping near to where I was standing, revived memories of childhood days alongside the H&BR line, and the almost forgotten, but thrilling aroma it gave off, a mixture of hot oil and firebox fumes. As I sensed the heat from its boiler, and heard the sustained roar from its chimney, I found its presence alongside strongly comforting and reassuring. Passing the engine cab, I found the blue-clad crew looking back along the platform, confident, relaxed, at ease with the heavy responsibilities resting on each of their shoulders.

On this, the first train I had attended, I was shown how to look out for carriage doors only partially locked, and warned of the dangers of passengers attempting to board a moving train, and it was here I was able to pick up my first rudimentary hand signals. By mid-morning, with the rush of passengers and trains much reduced, and the two lad porters going about other duties, the senior porter, perhaps to see how I framed, set me cleaning the platforms of snow and ice. After my long hours on the farm, and having to wrestle each morning with a heavy recalcitrant wheelbarrow and its load of fetid manure, this in comparison seemed easy work, and it was with utter surprise when I was informed it was now 12 o'clock and my lunch hour (a whole hour!). Amazed how quickly the morning had passed, I raced home on foot, and having noticed plenty of space at the station for bikes, throwing caution to the winds, I mounted Old Peculiar, and in triumph rode back to work. In the darkness of late afternoon I was handed a form, with illustrations and instructions for taking measurements for my railway uniform, with nod at the condition of my current apparel and the advice that the sooner I filled in and returned the form, the sooner I would receive my coveted uniform. Whilst, to my surprise, being informed it was now 5 pm and I had put my hours in (what short days the railway worked!) and after being reminded to start work at the highly agreeable time of 8 am the following morning, I was now free to go home.

Delighted with my work, and the friendly reception I had received at all levels, with my love of the railway restored to full vigour, and helped by what appeared to be a bright and agreeable future, I left clean, dry and tidy, after firing up my acetylene headlamp. It was with a profound feeling of satisfaction and hope for the future that I set off for home on that momentous day, these feelings engendered not least by the unaccustomed benefits which a warm friendly porters' room provided.

At this point a description of the porters' room, the hub of all the platform staff activities, might be of interest. Built by the York & North Midland Railway (YNMR) in 1845, as part of Cottingham Station, to a design by the YNMR resident architect (George Townsend Andrews), it was warm and snug, just off the platform between a storeroom and luggage room. Oblong in shape, it was dominated at the far end by a feature of Andrews' architecture, a handsome canted bay window, which overlooked the station's crowning glory: an extensive railway-owned nursery, tended by a railway gardener, who sent plants and cut flowers (by rail, of course) to grace and beautify the rooms and dining tables of both the York & Hull railway hotels. In spring and summertime its grounds became a blaze of myriad colours and scents. Its flower beds, greenhouses and cold frames set off by well-kept paths, lined with attractive neatly trimmed box hedging. As for the gardener, I shall come to him shortly.

The porters' room on one side, furnished with a plain but substantial pine table and form (bench) seating. Opposite, a stove blazed away mightily, consuming as it did so, huge quantities of coal. No wartime rationing here! And if the supply did begin to fail, well under the cover of darkness, hidden from prying and ill-disposed eyes, for what we were doing was misuse of railway assets, and penalties for that were severe, we would, without the driver's knowledge, approach the fireman of a Push and Pull train, alone on the footplate, who would happily fill our wheelbarrow with best quality Yorkshire Main or Maltby coal.

The gardener meanwhile, was a strange unapproachable man, who stepped down from a Hull train each morning, and without speaking, went about his solitary business. Each lunchtime it was his habit to eat his packed lunch silently in the porters' room. By his profound lack of contact with those around, he remained a remote and enigmatic figure. Was he, I wonder, a survivor of World War I, someone so shocked and traumatised that, locked in his own world, he was unable to converse with those around him? It is possible, for I clearly remember others like him, and he was of their age. Another such 'old boy', sometimes seen walking Cottingham's main street, obviously a veteran of the trenches and irrevocably scarred by his experiences, would suddenly and without warning stop, drop the little dog that had hitherto been clutched in the crook of his arm (it seemed remarkably unfazed by this), and shout to his imaginary comrades, "Steady men! Steady!" Perhaps the outburst had been caused by a car backfiring, or the whistle of a train, triggering a deep-rooted memory, meaning he was suddenly transported back to the trenches, being pounded by artillery—who can know?

Attending trains, I learned the art of securing carriage doors. Being something of a backwater, our passenger trains were, in the main, formed of pre-grouping stock, mostly of NER vintage, but often including Great Central (GC) and H&BR coaches. Each company, interestingly, had its own style of door lock. The NER favoured a double locking device, which, if the door failed to lock up fully, left it safe but slightly ajar—an indication to the platform staff the door required a good hard push, and something often done on the hop as the train moved off. GC coaches boasted large brass door handles, which in the company's heyday must have looked magnificent, highly polished, and gleaming bright against the varnished paintwork of the company's splendid coaches. But now neglected in that respect, and tarnished by smoke and grime, they looked cumbersome and ugly. To secure a GC door, each handle had to be turned by hand, something most passengers declined to do. And once inside, in bad weather, who could blame them? It meant having the window in the door lowered, letting in a blast of cold air, then leaning out to physically turn the handle. In those circumstances it's little wonder they left them to the porters, who were skilled at catching and turning handles on the move. As befitted the refined and gentle nature of Hull folk, and those further afield in the far-flung outposts of the South Yorkshire coalfields, the H&B door locks were of a more delicate and agreeable design. Self-locking, the dainty brass handles fitted the hand comfortably, and as the door shut, locked automatically. Conveniently positioned to assist passengers, each company had its own, often elaborate design of cast brass mounting handle, to further enhance and beautify its coaching stock.

Within a day or two of commencing what proved to be a happy and rewarding railway career, I was taking a turn on the ticket gate, where my request for tickets—"Tickets please"—often drew some rather sharpish looks from detraining passengers, who were at first reluctant to hand over their precious tickets to someone shabbily dressed in civilian clothes. However, my very presence at the gate gave me the necessary authority, and I was soon clipping first-class returns, and others, with the *sangfroid* of a veteran.

Leaving work on Saturday evening, I signed for my first week's pay. Unlike the farm, where my pay was doled out coin by coin into my outstretched hand, I now received it, all proper, you might say, in a sealed pay packet. In the absence of written terms of employment, a normal thing in those days, I was in the dark over my rates of pay, although having said that, I had learned my working week consisted of what I thought a very pleasant and easy 48 hours, divided into six, eight-hour shifts.

Pleased with all aspects of my work, proud as a peacock, and eager to hand my pay packet over to my mother, I pedalled off furiously, my acetylene headlamp blazing a brilliant white path to guide me. At home, to my surprise and delight, I discovered that not only had my working hours halved, but my pay had almost doubled, and now stood at the princely sum of 13 shillings and six pence—about 82½ pence. After sharing the bounty with mother, I had, for the first time, money to jingle in my pocket. However, there was a downside to my new-found wealth: in keeping with the majority, I took up smoking, a habit, or for me a pleasure, I pursued relentlessly and without fail for the next 30 years.

During the next days, in company with the other porters, I settled into the many and varied tasks a busy station demanded. Among them the all-important work of cleaning and trimming the station's two distinct sets of oil burning signal and road crossing lamps. Sitting atop the nearside platform, at the far end, in the Hull direction, stood a low brick building, about 15 feet square. The early, and long out of use, station signal cabin, in my day used as a very handy 'lamp room' and as such equipped on its three facing sides with benches and a variety of jugs and funnels, together with *Brasso* and cotton waste. On one side, the out of use but trimmed and ready set of lamps were lined up for inspection, whilst on the rear blank wall, a large tank contained the special long-burning paraffin, used in signal lamps and gate lamps, with two smaller tanks holding either rape or colza oils, for use in other lamps.

Fully aware of the importance of clear bright signals to engine crews, each lad porter took immense pride in cleaning and trimming each lamp, taking special care over cleaning the wicks of carbon crust built up over its two-week burning period, before finally polishing each brass burner to a state of dazzling brilliance. As part of his duties, the stationmaster frequently examined the lamp room and its contents, paying particular attention to the condition of the refurbished lamps without, I am pleased to say, ever finding fault.

Every two weeks the middle shift lad porter exchanged lamps throughout the station's signalling system, regardless of the weather conditions, fog being the most dangerous, although climbing signal ladders in a gale, whilst lugging heavy and awkwardly shaped signal lamps both up or down, ran it a close second. With 12 semaphore signals, plus Thwaite Street and Northgate crossings' eight gate lamps, and four ('dollies') ground signals, shunt signals, subsidiary signals, take your pick, a total of 24 heavy lamps had to be carried back and forth to the lamp room. Adding to this weight, the lad porter carried with him a stout leather satchel containing materials for cleaning the 'bull's eye' magnifying glass, and coloured aspects of each signal. In view of the high speeds attained in this section, especially between Beverley and Hull, the distant and outer home signals, as protection for the road crossings, were located far beyond the station limits, making heavy work, and frequent trips back and forth for the lad porter involved.

One late afternoon, three of four weeks after starting on my railway career, at that time of day, where between frequent stopping trains, I was able to enjoy the warmth, camaraderie and other benefits that a benevolent and cosy porters' room bestowed, I was handed two large brown paper parcels tied with string. Despite my lack of experience in these matters I didn't need telling these were my longed-for uniform and great coat. Leaving work scarcely able to contain my excitement, I balanced the two parcels on my handlebars, and pedalled home, anxious to examine and try on my uniform. The first held my uniform, comprising a pair of thick heavy, black serge trousers, a black serge waistcoat, with four pockets and long, close-woven cotton sleeves, and a heavy black serge jacket, each cut and machined from quality cloth. The second contained my railway overcoat and cap. Despite wartime shortages and restrictions it was in keeping with the rest of the uniform, top quality cloth, thick and wonderfully warm, its blue-grey herring bone lining thicker in itself than my brother's raglan coat. Trying on the uniform, mother expressed her delight at the quality and cut, and thanks to all her careful measurements, its superb fit. As the 'icing on the cake', I tried on the final bit of kit, my standard issue railway cap. Delighted, I felt I was now a full, complete and accepted member of the mighty LNER company, and when standing at the ticket gate, no longer would passengers view me with open suspicion, or guards and engine crews hesitate to accept my "Right Away."

It was still January, with a good deal of harsh weather about when I first wore my uniform to work. My lasting impressions of that proud day, are firstly, how warm my uniform felt, and how easily it tamed the biting wind. And secondly, resplendent, my uniform filling me with a new-found confidence, I was able to swagger and strut my stuff a little, as I moved among the patiently waiting passengers gathering on the platforms. With my uniform came the news I expected. I was told to commence shift working the following Monday. By now I was familiar with shift times and patterns of work. The 'First', or early shift opened the station at 5.30 am. This was done, not as one might expect by the senior porter, but by one of the 15-year-old lad porters, who unlocked the station office, waiting rooms and porters' room. (Nowadays I expect someone, lying in wait, would knock him on the head and steal the previous night's takings, before escaping in the blackout!). And in cold weather they prepared and lit fires in the office and porters' room, ready, for the senior porter arriving at about 6 am, and the first train a few minutes later, a local Push and Pull from Hull to Beverley, propelled by a stout North-Eastern 'G5' 0-4-4, which always departed as if the devil was after it, with a roaring exhaust and a shower of flying sparks. This shift, including an hour's meal break, ended at 3:30pm.

The middle shift came on duty at 10 am, and with an hour's meal break, left at 7 pm. This shift became a favourite, as over time I began to appreciate the pleasures of both a lie in and the fact I still had several hours of leisure at the end of my shift. 'Back', or late shift staff commenced duty at 2.30 pm, until 11.30 pm when, after the departure of the last train, the station was closed down and locked up. During dark evenings this shift often became a rich source of incidents, as passengers and visitors alike battled the effects of the blackout, and in some cases, a little too much to drink, which were sometimes minor, sometimes serious, and on occasion, hilarious.

Cottingham was blessed in many ways, by several large and profitable market gardeners, who in season, moved their produce by rail. Several times a week in summer, every barrow and truck was loaded with boxes of fresh vegetables, fruit and cut flowers. When these were fully loaded, the remainder were piled high on the platform. For these an empty bogie van was marshalled at the front of the requisite passenger train, whereupon arrival, the platform suddenly became a scene of frenzied activity, as the whole station staff turned out in an effort to cut delay to a minimum, including both male and female clerks. For despite war raging across Europe, on the LNER trains had to run on time.

One such market gardener was Alex West, a now forgotten head of a bitter war against the infamous Soviet-style 'Tomato Board' whose ranks of bureaucrats meddled into every aspect of commercial tomato growing, and made life a misery for the growers. Alex West resisted its nonsense, and for his pains was pursued relentlessly through the Courts. At the taxpayers' expense of course, and Alex West's ample but not unlimited pocket. Eventually common sense prevailed, and the board, with several others of the same ilk, were wound up, earning Alex West the accolade 'Tomato West' a handle he carried proudly for the remainder of his life.

Weather permitting, platforms were swept using a large platform brush, and offices and waiting rooms cleaned on a daily basis. Once a month the station's windows were cleaned, when in the absence of anything else, a mixture of bath brick and paraffin was applied, before polishing off with cotton waste. Surprisingly, despite the wartime shortage of paper, we frequently received posters to hang on the station poster boards. These occasionally extolled the virtue of travelling by train on the LNER, but most of it was of a government propagandist nature, by reminding viewers that 'Careless talk costs lives' or 'Walls have ears', and in view of the sometimes neighbouring posters reminding the general public to travel by the LNER, were ones asking 'Is your journey really necessary?' promoting one or two acidic comments from those who, sometimes reluctantly, were returning to active service.

Whilst on the whole I was a hard-working and conscientious employee of the LNER, I did occasionally revert to my more irreverent ways. On one such occasion a new lad porter joined us, and it was my job to help train him up. Not long after he'd started we were standing on the platform, and looking down at the tracks I said, "See these rails?", pointing out the gleaming metals of the main line, rendered shiny by the passing of numerous trains. "It's our job to keep them polished; we get thruppence a mile, but we've got to find our own *Brasso*. Tomorrow morning, come with a tin, and I'll set you to work polishing them."

Anyway, the next morning, he arrived punctually, complete with his tin of *Brasso* and some rags, whereupon I sent him off to the infrequently-used coal stage[3], with its rusty and pitted rails, with instructions to start polishing them. Off he set, and after about an hour, the stationmaster appeared and caught him polishing the rails (or at least trying to polish them), whereupon he was sent away with a flea in his ear and no doubt told to do something a little bit more productive. Incidentally, nothing was said to me, so perhaps old Beckett, who had a bit of soft spot for me, just smiled to himself and let it pass.

A melancholy, if infrequent station visitor, was an occasional coffined body, always carried in a locked van coupled to the rear of its assigned passenger train. After the train guard had unlocked the van, we, the lad porters, would place the coffin on a flat four-wheeled luggage trolley and, on its iron wheels, trundle it along the platform to the ladies' first class waiting room where, with the chairs moved aside, we placed the coffin on the large square table occupying the centre of the room. And there, with the window shutters closed, and the door locked, it was left to wait the attentions of the Wright Brothers (Cottingham joiners and undertakers). If the body arrived on the rear of a Hull-bound train, it suffered an even more bumpy ride, as the trolley, on its small diameter iron wheels, jarred and rattled its way along the full length of the far side platform. Then, with the coffin bouncing alarmingly, it made its rather perilous navigation over the accommodation crossing with its uneven surfaces and two running lines, at the end of both platforms.

In the early 1940s, with tractors almost unknown, most farms depended entirely on horses. These together with several livery stables around and about, gave the railway a steady trade not only in horses, but also in other livestock, and it was not unusual at that time to see cattle and sheep being driven through the streets. To offer a smooth swift and efficient transit, horse boxes were invariably attached to passenger trains. Although within the station limits, and under the watchful eye of the Cottingham North signalman, and under the protection of his signals, attaching or detaching horse boxes, in either direction, involved the

---

[3] An elevated brick-built structure that supplied locomotives with coal.

somewhat dodgy practise of leaving the train and its complement of passengers standing exposed during this operation on the main running lines. As the Harrow disaster on 8 October 1952, and many others have graphically demonstrated, trains sometimes overran signals, with disastrous results. A primary consideration during these shunting operations was the prevention of unnecessary delay to the passenger train, and more importantly, the avoidance of dangerous confusion. Both required a bit of nifty footwork, sound knowledge of the Rule Book, hand signalling and shunting operations. Much the same as the responsible and essential undertaking of opening the station was left to the ability of the early morning lad porter to get out of bed, so likewise the potentially hazardous activity, especially in fog or falling snow, was left to whichever lad porter was available at the time. Where you may well ask, was the senior porter, with his lifetime of experience on Cottingham Station, at these times? The answer is from 12 noon until 3 pm, he manned the signal post, Thwaites Gates, during which time the station was effectively in the hands of lad porters. What the current 'Elf & Safety' would have to say about these goings on I shudder to think. Yet this system operated perfectly well, for many years. Probably, as far as I know, since the station first opened for business in the early 1840s.

Another routine task for the busy mid-shift lad porter entailed working in the goods yard, sheeting waggons securely. Nothing was guaranteed to raise the ire of the traffic department more than reports of a goods train dashing through stations with wildly flapping tarpaulins. Even worse was one trailing along the platform, to the fear and consternation of waiting passengers! Part of the same operation was to fold surplus tarpaulins and return them to the station for logging by the Goods Clerk, before onward transmission to a central depot.

Before leaving the goods yard and its doings, albeit on a temporary basis, I have a curious story to relate. Throughout the war, Cottingham provided a home to many soldiers of different nationalities: British, Canadian, Free French, French Algerian and latterly, Americans, plus a sprinkling of others. To supply their manifold needs a small camp was erected on the outskirts of the village, manned by a detachment of Royal Army Service Corps personnel, under the command of a sergeant. They worked in the goods yard unloading and distributing waggons of service stores to the various military establishments dotted about; nothing out of the ordinary with that, one might say, after all, soldiers have to be fed and shod. What was so strange, even bizarre and certainly archaic about this business, was the manner in which it operated. It used nothing but horses and carts, and must, by then, have been the only unit in Britain without motorised transport. The little camp stabled six horses and three dark green, four-wheeled narrow, drop-sided, general service carts of World War I vintage. In those days, Cottingham was well used to horse drawn vehicles of every description, and towering above them all were the splendid waggons, each with three matched Shire horses in line ahead, which trundled through the main street delivering thrashed corn to Cottingham Station from the large outlying farms to the west of the village. Their 'wags' (waggoners) made each trip a field day, with brushed up, bob tailed and plumed horses. There was gleaming leather harnesses and polished brass martingales swinging below each horse collar. However, for all this pomp and glory, none could touch the magnificence of those six army horses and three carts, whose daily turnout could have graced London's Horse Guards Parade. Yet if their appearance was enough to draw admiring glances, even more so was the sergeant leading his little caravan, by riding the outside horse of the leading waggon on their errands around the village. Aged about 45 years, tall, ramrod straight, with a swarthy complexion and fine features, he had probably fought in the First World War. In appearance he possessed all the characteristics of a regular soldier and may have served all his life in the army. One might say, all in all, a fine figure of a military man! However, it was more than his physique and bearing which drew attention; mysteriously, for it was a mystery, he dressed not as other soldiers in battledress and gaiters, but in a long-out-of-date World War I cavalryman's uniform. From his peaked 'cheese cutter' cap held in place by a polished leather chinstrap, his burnished cap badge blazed like the sun. Instead of a battle dress blouse, he wore an old-fashioned military jacket, with highly polished buttons down the front, and on his epaulettes, polished brass Corps insignia. Diagonally, across his chest, hung a leather bandolier, polished often and lovingly to a deep mahogany hue. Buckled around his waist one of the early, wide webbing belts, long out of favour. A pair of cavalrymen 'choke-bored' trousers and, bless my soul, something I thought out of favour and discarded since the early days of World War I, when they were found hard to fasten on when chased by the enemy: a pair of puttees, of all things, though they did go with the uniform! From the heels of his bulled-up boots, a pair of plain but burnished steel spurs showed to good effect. Therefore, in every respect, the very essence of a military man and sergeant!

An everyday job was trawling the goods yard for discarded waggon tarpaulins and after folding these, returning those not wanted back to the station for onward transmission to the stores department. Allied to this was the frequent sheeting by the lad porters of open waggons conveying perishable goods, a function requiring care and attention. At the same time, the waggon ties, ties being lengths of tarred cord, used for fastening the waggon sheets securely, were carefully examined, and those frayed or worn replaced from stock carried by the station. Much depended on this simple task, as the following, potentially serious, near-accident clearly shows.

Imagine a fine summer's afternoon. I was standing on the Hull-side platform, with a small group of passengers, waiting for an approaching Hull bound goods train to pass. It was a long train, and with the engine crew having the end of their shift in sight, going at a fair lick, the engine working hard. Watching in some admiration, my approval was shattered when I noticed a waggon's tarpaulin adrift, halfway along the train, and as such, blowing and twisting violently in the wind on its passage. This posed a serious risk to the unsuspecting passengers, but in the short time left I was able to shout a warning and move them out of danger, as the heavy sheet, lashing and thrashing about, raced along the platform, sweeping all before it. Like so many minor incidents, it went unreported.

An important day job was positioning loaded coal waggons over the station's domestic coal drops. After examining the waggon labels to make sure which consignee coal merchant it was intended for, the lad porters moved each waggon over its correct coal cell using a specially designed, long handled pinch bar, inch by inch under one wheel. Once in position it was only a few minutes work to go round knocking out the pins which secured the waggon's bottom doors, discharging its contents in to the cells below.

Chapter 5
Terror in a Blacked-Out Chapel

As far as work was concerned, the 'back shift', from 2.30 pm until the station closed at 11.30 pm, was for the greater part the most easily worked. After the evening rush abated, and the stationmaster and clerical staff had left, the two duty porters, one a senior porter, and one the lad porter, vacated the porters' room and moved into the station office, where the senior porter continued issuing tickets and suchlike. During the summer months, where Double Summer Time made for long light evenings, the lad porter would busy himself around the station with the many little jobs requiring his attention. But in winter, with the blackout, things were different. Then, after shuttering the office windows and taking no heed of coal rationing, the 'back shift' porters, between trains, basked in the luxury of a large open fire. Outside, however, in the inky darkness, where the blackout ruled supreme, things happened. And whilst the ladies of the night arrived from Hull by train, seeking rich pickings from the many servicemen stationed in Cottingham, not all the nocturnal fun and games were of that nature.

Accidents and incidents, some trivial, others more serious, were a feature of the 'back shift', caused mainly by the blackout, and sometimes aided by a little too much drink (on the part of passengers, not staff, I hastened to add!). Unlike today's climate of blame and claim, these went unreported. If the unfortunate victim could walk, aided or unaided, they were left to their own devices. However, in retrospect, sometimes these incidents had an amusing side. One in particular, despite its relative seriousness, still brings a wry smile to my face from the way it developed into a kind of Keystone Cops or Charlie Chaplin comedy.

On a night where dense fog was proving a further hindrance to hard-pressed engine crews, a train from Hull, its brakes squealing in protest, overshot the station. In these circumstances, being nimble of foot, the lad porter would run down the train, warning the passengers to remain seated. Unfortunately in this instance, confusion and disorder reigned supreme, with error compounding error. To make matters worse, the engine began to blow off, drowning out my shouts as I ran down the train. With my hand lamp casting a feeble glow, I ran down the slope at the end of the platform to discover I was too late for one unfortunate passenger. Finding the train stopped, and my shouts unheard, he opened the compartment door and boldly stepped out, into thin air, falling flat on his face and sending his false teeth flying. With the open carriage door behind him, I found him rising unsteadily to his feet, shocked, hurt and disorientated. "Bloody 'ell," he muttered, staggering about. "What's happened?"

If this wasn't enough, things now went from bad to worse, for, just as the man straightened up, the driver, being equally confused, made the cardinal sin of setting back without permission, with the inevitable result, the swinging carriage door struck the unfortunate man from behind, throwing him to the ground from which, only moments before, he had risen shakily to his feet, and leaving him now in even greater confusion, convinced he had been set upon in the dark by a gang of evil-minded footpads intent on inflicting further injury. After dusting him down, as it were, we saw him leave the station a little unsteady on his feet, but under his own steam.

The office main door opened directly onto the platform. Seated comfortably one evening around the fire, we were disturbed by a persistent knocking on the door. The senior porter went to investigate, to find a woman complaining that a soldier had snatched her handbag containing her money and house keys, before running over the station footbridge, and throwing the ransacked handbag onto the tracks below. Could we, she pleaded, please retrieve her bag and keys? I was ordered to go and find them, so taking my hand lamp, I dropped down between the platforms, walking along until my lamp picked up the discarded handbag, its keys and a scattering of other objects, and in anticipation of a good trade, several packets of 'French letters' (which at that time I knew little about). But on the back shift, one grew up quickly!

At times the back shift provided more than its fair share of unwelcome frights and alarms. At ease, seated comfortably one dark and gloomy night, we were startled by a woman in high heels running the length of the deserted platform, before hammering frantically on the office door, the sound of her hard-to come-by high heels alerting us to this being something out of the ordinary. In a refined and educated voice, she sobbed, "There's a man laid on the line."

The senior porter, having survived the horrors of World War I, appeared unmoved by this tearful announcement. "Whereabouts is he?" he cheerfully enquired.

"Near the stationmaster's house," the woman whimpered.

Turning to me, he ordered, "Get your lamp, we'll go and see." What for me had, until then, been a quiet evening turned quickly into a nightmare. Dropping into the 'four foot' visions of a ghastly mangled body struck me with the force of thunderbolt. In the dark, frightened by what I had to face, I hung back, as the senior porter, his hand lamp flashing around, strode on purposefully between the tracks. "Here he is," he announced. Petrified and shaking, not wanting to be any part of it, I kept my distance as the body was examined and rolled over. "He's dead all right," I was solemnly informed. "Dead drunk, I reckon. Let's get him up on to the platform before the next train hits him." Between us we manoeuvred the man onto the platform and into the nearest waiting room, where we left him, sozzled but safe, in the tender care of the lady in high heels.

If this scene hadn't frightened me enough for one week, the following night I was given a similar fright. Cottingham North's signalman, the doughty Steve Barley, ever careful of his signals, rang in to say one of his signals was showing an indifferent light, and required attention. Whilst an infrequent call, this was the duty lad porter's responsibility, so taking my hand lamp I set off along a familiar path which led from the station to the goods yard, at one point skirting the goods warehouse and main lines. At the further end of the warehouse, an unguarded public pathway crossed the tracks. With the view at this point restricted by the warehouse, the crossing over the years had gained notoriety for being the scene of several fatal accidents, none more heartrending, in my mind, than the death there in 1935 of Mrs Moorsby, the retired head of Cottingham Infants School, and as such a popular and well-liked figure around the village who, unfortunately, being a little hard of hearing, had stepped from the shadow of the warehouse into the path of a speeding train. Remembering her well, this accident remained stuck in my memory.

This night, though clear, was also dark, and under wartime conditions, as silent as the grave, and as I approached the crossing a solitary bomber droned overhead. This distracted my attention from the path between the rows of waggons occupying the warehouse line and the main running lines. Immediately beyond the crossing, still gazing heavenwards, and wondering what had been the bomber's mission and how the crew had fared, I tripped over an object laid near to the main line. Something silent, something soft and yielding. Once again the spectre of a mangled body flashed through my mind. Recovering my balance, feeling all alone in a dark world, with the hair rising on the back of my neck and all of a dither, frightened by what I was about to discover, I shone my hand lamp towards the body. In its dim uncertain light I made out an unidentifiable form. Bracing myself for an unpleasant duty, I moved closer, discovering, not the body I feared, but a rolled up tarpaulin. Oh, such relief!

In the summer of 1943 the station was ordered to stand by for the arrival, later in the day, of two Troop Train Specials. Terminating at Cottingham, these out-of-the-ordinary workings rather set the cat among the pigeons, each requiring extra effort on our part as we detrained the occupants, and then had to carry out some rather, for us, complicated shunting movements, as we ran the engines around and rejigged the trains on the opposite lines, prior to their return 'empty stock'[4], to Hull.

We had grown accustomed to groups of foreign service personnel travelling by train. Polish airmen from the nearby Leconfield air force base, Canadian airmen from the large bomber base at Pocklington, and Free French airmen travelling to Elvington, via York, plus a mixture of other soldiers, sailors and airmen, and on occasion German officers, now prisoners of war, and travelling first class under armed guard. As I walked along the train checking doors and door handles, one such officer struck me in particular. Lounging at ease on the deep cushions, in the opulent grandeur of a North-Eastern clerestory[5] first class coach, our eyes met as he smoked, with evident enjoyment, the largest cigar I have ever seen. However, the two troop specials brought a different cargo that bright sunny afternoon, something totally outside our experience: black Americans. Brought up before multiculturalism became the plaything of the chattering classes, and there in the flesh, we could only stare in astonishment as this host of African-Americans, a seemingly unknown species, descended on Cottingham. Of a different culture, they spoke in unfamiliar terms. "Is this the railroad depot?" they wanted to know. Often when they spoke to us they prefaced it with "You's Limeys", which at first we misinterpreted as "You Slimies", something which, on ones your first acquaintance, we thought a bit uncalled for!

---

[4] As the name suggests, train movements carried out without passengers or freight, usually between a station and a siding or depot.

[5] Carriages where a portion of the roof is elevated, with windows in the sides for light and/or openings for ventilation.

Sometimes they would ask which "track" the Beverley train was on, all of which we found confusing. Employed on Hull docks as dock workers, they went off each morning in convoys of large American army lorries, returning in the evening to ogle and wolf whistle the local girls, sometimes to good effect.

Undamaged, Beverley unlike Hull, which had its centre destroyed and deserted, became the GI's centre of attraction, with ample stocks of Camel and Marlborough cigarettes, plus unobtainable nylon stockings and lipstick, and money to burn, they were very definitely overpaid, oversexed, and over here! And here one wonders how or why soldiers came by an abundance of such exotica as stockings and lipstick, as they, by night, descended on Cottingham Station, requesting a "round trip" to Beverley. Then in the darkness, confused by the blackout, and at times by inclement weather, in the unfamiliar surroundings of a platformed station, the fun and games would begin. On returning, and fuelled from a good night out in Beverley, like others before them, they sometimes mistook a silent but still moving train for one at rest, and stepping gaily out, paid the sure and painful penalty (including gashed and bruised faces, broken noses, etc.). Unaccustomed to raised platforms, they frequent climbed out of the train on the wrong side, and were left tripping, floundering and lost between the platforms, at the mercy of any train which might be approaching from the opposite direction.

With surprising regularity a similar but potentially more dangerous type of incident occurred, one with a touch of whimsy about it, yet carrying all the hallmarks of a multiple tragedy. I still wonder no one was killed or seriously injured in the mayhem which inevitably followed, included the two back-shift porters on duty at these times and whose lives were put at considerable risk as they fought to save the situation. In fair weather or foul, the lure of Beverley drew the Americans, who arrived at the station eager to sample all the delights the town offered. Coincidentally, at this particular time, two trains arrived at Cottingham almost simultaneously. The first to arrive was a train from Beverley to Hull, which occupied the far side platform, an arrangement which spelt danger. Impatient to catch the Hull to Beverly train, and seeing only indistinctly the faint lights of a train standing in the station, Americans would grab their tickets and, determined not to miss the Beverley train, would make a run for it. Then with flailing arms and legs, as if trying to become airborne, they would run off the edge of the platform, to crash down on the unforgiving iron rails below, an action that rather spoilt the unfortunate person's night out! How none of them landed under the wheels of the Hull bound train remains one of life's mysteries.

This posed a problem for the two staff on duty. The Hull to Beverley train was due at any moment, and on its tracks lay an injured man. Yet without hesitation, and at considerable risk to themselves, station staff, helped by the injured man's comrades, lifted him on to the platform out of harm's way, where thereafter his friends looked after him. At times it could be a close thing, and once I had to leave the crowd milling about on the tracks and run towards an approaching train, waving a red hand signal. Fortunately for everyone concerned, the driver feeling his way into the station was proceeding with caution, and was easily able to stop at my hand signal. Like all such minor incidents, these went unreported.

But back to railway routine. At 9.30 am each workday an express from Scarborough, and classed by us as the most important businessmen's train of the day, and running flat out, flashed through the station. To negotiate the trying humped-backed climb over the Wolds, between Scarborough and Bridlington, in style, its motive power was provided by either a Gresley three-cylinder 'K3', or an equally powerful, three-cylinder NE Class 'S' 4-6-0. In late 1943 however, an impressive, and to me unknown, type of locomotive began handling the train: engine 2165[6], one of Sir Vincent Raven's elegant and beautifully proportioned, three-cylinder NE Atlantics, which so delighted me I made a point of observing it closely whenever it was heading the train. An approach, heralded at first by a faint indistinct roar, which quickly developed into a full-throated, three-cylinder beat, drumming the air, as leaning into the curve through the station, its exhaust blasting from its shapely Wilson Worsdell form of chimney, they left behind an abiding memory, the acrid, but not unpleasant smell of perfectly combusted, hard Yorkshire steam coal.

Whilst at the same time I was deeply grateful for my position, the magic spell of footplate work began to dominate my thoughts. Daily I watched breathless as trains ripped through the station on time, in all conditions of weather, from high summer to deepest winter, with its fogs, snow and rain. This yearning became

---

[6] A word on locomotive notation, for the uninitiated: in the locomotive numbering system, the first two digits of a 4-digit number signify the class (the type) of locomotive, e.g. "21 Class", and the second two signify the sequential number of the locomotive in that class. Hence, locomotive 2164 is referred to as "Twenty-One Sixty-Four" (rather than "Two-One-Six-Four" or "Two-thousand and sixty-four", etc.).

further developed when, returning from 'lamping' one morning, I met by chance the daily pick-up, standing after shunting the yard at Cottingham North Inner Home signal, waiting for it to clear. I still had a further half mile to walk and the lamps were proving heavy, so seizing my chance I asked the driver if I could have a lift to the station. He agreed to my request: "Put your lamps on the running plate," he responded, "and jump up."

I climbed into the engine cab, one of Wilson Worsdell's hardy little NE Class 'C' 0-6-0 tender engines, which was a 'Tommy Owt' sort of engine—one which would go anywhere, and within reason, do anything. To my wondering eyes it presented a magical ordered world of cleanly swept footboards and footstools, and a bewildering array of steam valves, handles and, to mystify me further, strangely formed brass shapes spread around.

Hissing fiercely, we moved off to the accompaniment of hollow 'woofs' from deep within the firebox, which at first swirled the loose ash off the slumbering fire, then quickly whipped it up into a white heat. At first what surprised me most was the hard unyielding ride the engine gave as it rode over points, turnouts and rail joints. With signals giving us a clear run, the driver indulged in a bit of whimsy at my expense. "Ah well," he announced, "we've got the Right Away, so I can't stop now, I'll have to take you through to Hull." Seeing the look of consternation flooding my face, for how was I not only going to explain my long absence from work, but how on earth was I going to carry my heavy signal lamps all the way back from Hull, he relented: "Don't worry, lad, I'll drop you off." Thereafter, whenever I got the chance, be it by fair means or devious, I begged a lift back to the station, and each time further cementing my desire for a life on the footplate.

In the meantime, I added to my growing list of blood-curdling incidents, in this instance one only remotely connected to railway work, and only by virtue of my leaving work after the back shift. As mentioned, before the start of the war, with my father out of work, my parents had taken on the caretaker-ship of the Congregational church, and after my father's death my mother, single-handedly, bravely carried on what was to all intents and purposes a Herculean task. For her this meant the whole of each Saturday was spent in cleaning and preparing the church and its extensive schoolrooms for Sunday worship. This, when the weather demanded, required the cleaning out and lighting of a large, coke burning, central heating boiler, housed in its own boiler house, attached to the rear of the church premises, and accessed through the church itself. Lacking a pump it relied entirely on convectional currents slowly heating the system throughout and as such had to be lit early and maintained throughout the Saturday and Sunday. Accordingly, depending on which shift I was working, I helped whenever I could, and when returning home off the back shift on a Saturday night, always fired up the boiler, to save mother a long and potentially dangerous walk through the blackout late at night.

One Friday afternoon in late October of early 1943 or 1944, as I was preparing for my turn of duty on the back shift, I was told to stoke the church boiler after I left work. This rather surprised me, as during the war years the boiler had never been lit on a Friday, and I could only assume that some rather grand wedding was taking place on the Saturday. But like the cavalrymen of old, standing steady before they charged Balaclava, mine was not to reason why! Leaving work at 11.30pm, I drew up in front of the chapel. Apart from the cold wind soughing and sighing around the ancient building, all was quiet. In those law-abiding days, when despite soldiers from all parts of the world coming and going at all times, the church doors could safely remain unlocked, it nevertheless came as a surprise when I found them standing wide open. Unable to account for this I still strode boldly inside. The church is large, a monument to its independent strictures, and I was familiar with every inch. Despite the profound darkness I confidently picked up the line of central box pews, merely as a guide to the end, where on reaching it I turned right to cross over in front of the communion table, before turning left and passing alongside the organ case and into the vestry. From there a short passage led to the boiler house, a much later addition to the church.

Arriving at the end of the pews I turned, and as I stepped out something dreadful occurred. Concealed by the darkness I strode full tilt into a coffin, a coffin which juddered and rocked perilously on its wooden coffin stools. Shocked, in darkness so intense it could be literally felt, I listened to the coffin stools moving, afraid the coffin might crash to the floor with consequences too dreadful to contemplate. Not knowing how precariously the coffin was balanced, and almost fainting with shock and fear, I had to get around it somehow. Unable to mark its position, and afraid it might fall, I gently felt my way around its base, or was it the base? As a fresh fear filled me I wasn't sure, it might be the top edge and illogically I began to fear the coffin might be open and I would find myself stroking the face of its reclining occupant. Finding the coffin lid securely in place, and by now nothing but a bag of twitching nerves, I crept past and fled into the boiler house.

If I thought by closing the doors of the boiler house I had found a place of refuge I had another think coming. With only a faint glow from the boiler as illumination, my imagination began to run riot, and I began to sense strange unworldly creatures gathering in the passage outside. With each scrape and clang of my shovel my fears increased as I strained to hear a movement from outside, but all was as quiet as the coffin in the church. My fears increased though, until in sheer terror I began to hallucinate, plainly seeing dark shadows beyond the boiler, weird leering figures gazing hungrily at me. By now, frightened out of my wits, I finished stoking the boiler. Now nothing in the world could or would induce me to open the boiler house doors on to who knew what, and then pass through the church with its wobbly unstable coffin which, for all I knew, may now have fallen off its stools. Trapped in the boiler house to which I had fled as a sanctuary, but which had now become a prison, and desperate to escape the ghouls which surrounded me, I remembered the hatch through which coke was delivered. Its door was bolted from the outside, but if I could break it open it offered a means of escape. Taking a heavy fire-iron I attacked the door in a blind panic and succeeded in forcing it open. Scrambling up the heaped coke, I squeezed through the opening. Never had the cool night air felt so clean and sweet when I tumbled out of that malignant stoke-hole. Still haunted and pursued by demons, I ran past the church in a paroxysm of terror, grabbing my bike on the way, and pedalling at high speed away from my fears along a dark deserted but never more-friendly street. For some time, although I never challenged her over it, I held a grudge against my mother for not warning me of the coffin blocking my way. Later, after a more calm and sober assessment, I came to realise that she must have been unaware herself that a coffin had been left in the church overnight.

Chapter 6
A Medal for Running and Jumping

At this time, whilst gazing longingly at the blue-clad confident men manning the locomotives which swept through or into the station, my thoughts increasingly turned to a career among them, yet I hesitated in asking the stationmaster for a transfer. Hanging around my shoulders was the thought of approaching the silver haired and benevolent Mr Beckett and asking him for a transfer. After his many acts of kindness, it seemed like throwing them back in his face. Yet eventually the impulse became too strong, and plucking up courage I asked for a transfer. In the event my fears proved unfounded. With his customary courtesy and good humour, and after asking me a few questions, and seeing my heart was set on a transfer to the Locomotive Department, he not only gave me his blessing, but agreed to make out the application form and forward it on to the appropriate authorities.

But in the meantime two events occurred on the back shift, which emphasised the raw courage and grim determination of aircrews on both sides of the conflict. By late 1943, with the Luftwaffe under extreme pressure defending its homeland, and from its obligations to the savage fighting in Russia, air raids of Hull had almost become a thing of the past. However, one clear night when on duty on the back shift, the air raid sounded, its melancholy wail reverberating over Cottingham. Hull had lost its ineffective barrage balloons, most having been shot down, and was now heavily defended by batteries of anti-aircraft guns. This night the guns remained silent, however. Perhaps the alert was for an odd enemy aircraft slipping in to lay mines in the faraway mouth of the Humber, and as such, no concern of ours. Comfortably seated in front of a roaring open fire in the porters' room, we remained undisturbed. Suddenly, however, our peaceful rest was shattered by heavy anti-aircraft fire over Hull, and now intermingled by some particularly heavy air bursts. Things seemed to be warming up, and intrigued I stepped outside to see what was going on. It was from there I was able to watch the thrilling spectacle of a solitary enemy aircraft overflying Hull. Coned in the rays of a dozen searchlights, it was taking violent evasive action against concentrated anti-aircraft fire, and against a new and much more powerful weapon. As I watched the twinkling air burst seeking the illuminated aircraft, there came to my astonished eyes, formations of rockets streaking up into the skies manned, it was said, by members of the now defunct Home Guard. The rockets, exploding simultaneously, surely spelt certain destruction to any aircraft in their vicinity. I don't know what the aircraft's business was that night, certainly no bombs were dropped, but as it left (somehow unscathed) the orbit of the city's defences, something remarkable and unexpected occurred: taking a wide sweep, the pilot, with consummate skill and courage, turned and braved another pass over Hull before disappearing in an easterly direction.

About this time, perhaps my next turn of back shift working, I witnessed another act of what I have always thought as supreme courage, this time by *the many*, not *the few*. I'd left work after the last train had departed, and mounted my bike in the teeth of a nor'westerly gale. Overhead, a stream of British bombers were already flying in a southerly direction. From past scanning of similar conditions, I knew the aircraft would be flying sideways on in a peculiar crab like way, as they were forced to counter the effects of the gale, and the weight of bombs they carried. I had scarcely left the station premises when the gale suddenly developed into a violent and dramatic thunderstorm of uncommon ferocity, with spectacular sheet lightening, remarkable in its continuity, ripping across the sky from horizon to horizon, whilst at the same time dumping a deluge of lashing rain, which quickly overwhelmed the gutters and drains of Cottingham, flooding the streets in a torrent of rushing water.

Forced to take shelter in a shop doorway (despite my heavy railway overcoat) I had, by virtue of the lightening, an unparalleled view of the low-flying bombers as, with engines at full throttle, they struggled onwards, fighting to gain height and headway. Who were these young men, boys really, who flew through this war of the elements with such steadfast resolution? Free French Squadrons from RAF Elvington, near York, perhaps. Did they ever have to bomb their own towns and cities, I wonder? Canadians from RAF Pocklington, Polish aircrews from RAF Leconfield near Beverley, Australians and New Zealanders from RAF Holme-on-Spalding Moor, and the British, South Africans and many colonial airmen from RAF Lissett near Bridlington, who suffered especially grievous losses throughout the war, and whose sacrifices are remembered by an inscribed monument there and an annual Remembrance Service? It required a special kind of high courage to fly so resolutely though a storm of such intensity, with a full bomb load. Something I have never forgotten, nor ever will.

For passengers preparing to alight trains, the blackout posed a very real threat. This never more so when drivers, often further harassed by bad weather and other problems, and unsure of their whereabouts, a position made worse by the fact at that time the majority of LNER locomotives were driven from the right, or blind side, forcing drivers to grope and feel their way cautiously the last few yards along an obscure and often ill-defined platform. For those preparing to depart the train, this was the moment of greatest danger. The heavy, solidly-built wooden carriages of the period effectively deadened the sound and feel of any slow movement. Cocooned in dimly lit compartments unable to distinguish the outside world, unwary passengers lulled into believing the train had stopped, sometimes stepped out. In the vicious tumble which inevitably followed, it was nothing short of a miracle no one was seriously injured. In keeping with the times, such accidents were regarded as part and parcel of life, and as such went unreported.

Not so an accident I was deeply involved with which occurred on the night of 27 September 1944, as it was far too serious to be ignored. As the war made its slow progression and staff retired, the railways experienced an acute shortage of manpower. To fill the gap they began recruiting female employees, including lady passenger guards. About the same time Cottingham gained a lady porter, a Mrs May. That night, on duty with Mrs May, we both were attending the last train of the day, the 11.02 pm Beverley to Hull, and whilst Mrs May checked the train doors and handles, I was standing at the ticket gate taking tickets by the light of the hand lamp crooked in my arm. The night was dark and overcast but dry, with most of the detraining passengers, African American servicemen, who unseen and silent because of their rubber-soled shoes, loomed out of the surrounding darkness into the glow of my lamp. The train guard was a Mrs Mathers, a now familiar figure on the local trains, and the train locomotive a powerful Gresley 'J39' 0-6-0 tender engine, and as such, capable of making light work of its five-coach load.

Mrs May completed her check of the train, and I heard her "Right Away!" to the guard, followed by the guard's warning whistle. This signalled that the curtain was about to rise on an unexpected and serious accident. In the meantime, towards the rear of the train, hidden in the darkness, far beyond the range of our feeble hand lamp, another drama was being played out. A solitary African American soldier had stepped out of the still-moving train, had been flung to the ground and now lay unconscious and unseen upon the platform. Standing at the ticket gate, I scarcely heard the driver's whistled acknowledgement, or the bark of his engine's exhaust as he moved off, although I was aware, this being the last train of the day, that the engine crew would be looking for a quick end to their shift and a speedy departure for home, and as such would give little thought of sparing the engine.

Suddenly, from nowhere, along the dark impenetrable length of the station platform, bursting without warning on the normally calm and peaceful scene came, a blood curdling, long drawn out scream, horrifying in its intensity. Locked in my own tiny circle of light, shocked, confused and unable to make out the cause of the dreadful screams, I automatically lunged towards the accelerating but nearly invisible train, when in the light from my hand lamp, and to my horror, I saw the shrieking form of Mrs Mathers being dragged by the train along the platform, her legs flailing wildly in an vain effort to gain purchase and lever herself back into the guard's van. It later transpired that, in blackout she'd tripped over the unseen and unconscious American, and consequently missed her footing. For a brief space of time everything became a blur, as blind instinct swept over me. However, I remember clearly my hand lamp and the tickets I'd collected flying through the air as, knowing I only had the remaining length of the platform to have any chance of saving Mrs Mathers' life, I dropped everything and raced after the rapidly departing train. Once again I emphasise what a poor runner I had always been, quickly becoming winded, yet in this instance I was granted the strength and fleetness of foot to catch up with the departing train, dragging the now unconscious Mrs Mathers like an old sack. At that moment I remember with particular clarity the open door of the guards' compartment lit by the faint blue light from within, and a sense I must be near the end of the platform. Here I must have made a great leap, for the next thing I remember is teetering on the very edge of the guards van entrance and frantically scrabbling with hands and feet in a desperate bid to remain upright and not fall backwards to join Mrs Mathers. Having gained my footing I tried desperately to free Mrs Mathers and lift her to safety, but caught up somehow, I found it impossible. This left me with only one option. Feeling profoundly guilty at leaving her dangling precariously, and in imminent danger of falling away or being swept off by some line-side fixture, and deeply aware of her legs hanging perilously close to the spinning bogie wheels below, I made a grab for the only option left to me, the guard's brake application handle, and in my blind panic threw my full weight on it, as if my weight alone would accelerate its action. As the train shuddered to a halt I dashed over to Mrs Mathers where, to my intense relief I found her still hanging. Again I tried, and again failed to free her. Whilst struggling, the fireman arrived, enquiring as to why the train's brakes had been applied? Between us we freed the limp body, lifted it into the guardsvan, and laid it on the floor.

Aware that rules forbade the train to proceed without a guard, and anxious about Mrs Mathers, I volunteered to act as guard, but without a hand lamp as a means of communication I arranged with the fireman that on my releasing the brake, this would confirm the train was ready to proceed. Whilst discussing these arrangements, Mrs May, the lady porter arrived, after bravely making her way along the dark and perilous lineside tracks. Anxious to provide medical assistance for Mrs Mathers as quickly as possible, I asked Mrs May to return to the station and ring Paragon terminus requesting an ambulance be there to meet us. With the brakes released and the train again underway, there was little I could do, so seated in the guard's seat, I stared glumly at Mrs Mathers' inert body laid out before me. In the blue lights of the blacked-out van, her face had taken on a ghostly hue, reminding me all too strongly of my dead father, leaving me wondering if she too was dead. To emphasise my fears, her head appeared to lay at an unnatural angle to her body. Looking down at her torn and ripped uniform I shifted uneasily in my seat, feeling I should be doing something to help her. I thought about feeling for a heartbeat, but recoiled in horror at the thought she may come round to find me groping around in her tunic. Instead I placed my cap under her head as it bumped and jolted on the wooden floor and offering what aid I could, I took off my jacket, and to keep her warm laid it over her body.

At Paragon two policemen stood awaiting our arrival, and whilst one entered the guards van the other questioned me taking copious notes. As the questioning continued, two ambulance men, carrying a stretcher, came hurrying along the platform and into the van, coming out shortly after with Mrs Mathers wrapped in blankets, and with, I was very relieved to note, her face uncovered. Then, quickly, I found myself alone in the cavernous depths of Paragon Station, from where it seemed all but I had fled. With this came the realisation that, abandoned and left to my own devices, I had a long tramp of about 8 miles before I reached the comfort and solace of my bed. At the same time, I little expected that a further trial awaited me before I reached home.

Feeling at least somewhat content with what I hoped I'd achieved, namely the saving of a life, I set off in good heart through Hull's devastated streets, eating up the miles, until in the early hours I reached Cottingham, and there turning into Hallgate, the main street, I ran into more trouble. Without warning an electric torch shone directly into my face completely blinding me, and hidden behind its powerful glare I heard the harsh irascible, and familiar voice of Police Constable Gray, demanding to know what I was up to at that time of night? This was, of course, a time when policemen patrolled the streets at night. PC Gray's unfriendly attitude requires an explanation: a few years before, at school, during an altercation, I had punched his son, the apple of his eye, on the nose, causing an effusion of blood, and leaving it somewhat out of line. PC Gray had collared me by the scruff of the neck, and in no uncertain terms vowed like for like punishment when the chance came along. At that moment, alone together in the pitch-black deserted street, unable to see, and held like a rabbit caught in a spotlight, it seemed a golden opportunity for him to exact revenge for the desecration of his son's snout. I steeled myself for a vicious blow coming unseen out of the darkness from either fist or truncheon. Neither landed, and after listening to my stuttered explanation, he remarked he had been informed of a serious accident occurring at the railway station, and with that switched off his wretched torch and resumed his 'beat' and left me to complete my long walk home.

The following afternoon I resumed duty to find two grave official-looking gentlemen in bowler hats, carefully examining the far side platform. After a while they called me over, wanting to know what happened, my precise position at the ticket gate and whereabouts I first saw the screaming helpless Mrs Mathers. They noted the paraffin stain on the platform where I had dropped my hand lamp as I raced to her aid, and from these positions they took measurements, carefully plotting the distance, clearly marked by Mrs Mathers' trailing feet along the platform's edging flags, where she had lost consciousness. And from there they measured the short distance, 20 yards or so, to where the platform sloped down to the accommodation crossing, level with the rails, at which point I would have lost her for good. As the train of events became clear, they questioned me, gently enough, on how I had been able, from my position at the ticket gate, to outrun and catch a rapidly departing train. To which in all honesty I had no recollection.

Several times they asked how, obscured by the blackout, had I been able to leap over and clear Mrs Mathers trailing body, and land in the doorway of the accelerating train. I replied that my only recollection of that event was seeing, bright and clear, the departing train's tail lamp, then faintly illuminated by the blue light from within the guard's open doorway, and that next I was in the doorway, frantically trying to claw myself upright before I fell backwards. Later they said I had achieved the impossible and I was very brave. They were wrong, I was very frightened, only blind instinct driving me on. They said I deserved a medal, and in the splendour of the former NER headquarter's panelled boardroom at York, they gave me one, standing by myself before the LNER board of directors as the citation was read out by Sir Ronald Matthews, Chairman of the LNER. I thus became the proud recipient of a silver medal, bestowed upon me for Courage and Resource[7].

LNER medal awarded to the author for Courage and Resource.

Overawed by the surroundings and the applauding grandees seated around the magnificent oval mahogany boardroom table, I must have cut a sorry and inarticulate figure as, shabbily dressed and tongue-tied, I was scarcely able to offer a feeble and indistinct thank you. As for poor Mrs Mathers, after recovering from her bodily injuries, I heard that, sadly, she had been committed to a mental hospital.

If my encounter with the Grim Reaper on the night of 27 September 1944 had been too close for comfort, I had an even closer escape, when one afternoon, with my attention diverted elsewhere, I walked stupidly and blindly into the path of a speeding express. Each day, about mid-afternoon, at a time when trains were

---

[7] This medal bears the LNER coat-of-arms on its face, with a scroll on the reverse naming the recipient and recording the date, superimposed on a laurel wreath. The medal recognises acts of courage and resource connected with the railway, equivalent to those acts that are recognised by the George Cross, the George Medal or the British Empire Medal.

few and far between, a Down express, now five miles out from Hull, on level track and running full tilt, ripped through the station. For the lad porters busy elsewhere, it usually passed through unnoticed, and thirty minutes after it had cleared, during the same quiet period, a stopping train rolled in from Scarborough via Bridlington, usually with only a few passengers alighting. However it often carried ten-stone boxes of wet fish for Cottingham suppliers, together with crates of homing pigeons for release (yes, even during the war!), the precise release time being recorded from the station clock (a clock carefully adjusted each morning by the stationmaster at 9 am from a central signal), and for the benefit of the pigeon owners, written on the basket's label. All this took time, and in the normal course of events the train had long left. But with nothing to unload, it was normal for the porter-in-charge to watch it leave the station safely.

Usually when passing from one platform to another, the platform staff, taking a short cut, dropped into the 'pit' between the two platforms, an action performed frequently each and every day. Unfortunately, on this occasion things began to stack up against me. For once the train arrived with nothing to unload, the first of a series of events occurring which marked my near demise. At that time I was busy at the front of the station, and being eager to complete my tasks, I omitted to stand and watch the train leaving the station; instead, I dropped down into the 'pit' immediately the last vehicle passed, and stepping from behind the train, hurried across the tracks. Things act in a mysterious way: something to my right now diverted my attention, and halfway across the opposite side 'four foot', and too late to turn back and save myself, I saw from my left, running late and under full steam, and right on top of me, thundered the Down express. If another time I vaulted for Mrs Mathers' life, I now, with a prodigious leap, jumped to save my own, and somehow landed safely on the platform, as the engine's buffer beam missed me by a hair's breadth, and the fireman, shocked at my sudden appearance from nowhere, right on the edge of his buffer beam, had only time to howl "Madman!" at me as he swept past. Unlike the Mrs Mathers accident which left me frightened and shaking, this incident, over and done with in a flash, left no time for fear. Unmoved by this close encounter with the Down express, I gave the fireman a genial thumbs up from the safety of the platform as, looking back in a state of shock, he waved his fist at me.

Shortly after my narrow escape, whilst working in the goods yard one afternoon I felt a distinct jolt underfoot, my first impression being that I had experienced some kind of minor earthquake. This was followed, almost immediately by a heavy rolling clap of thunder from the north-west. Astonished, for the day had remained bright and sunny throughout, I instinctively glanced that way, and in the distance, over the red pantiles of Cottingham's roofs, I saw an immense cloud of dark grey smoke rolling majestically heavenwards, and knew at once that the 'bomb cemetery', with its rows of ordnance, had exploded. I guessed that this was the work of the Royal Engineers, who, embarrassed by the bombs' continued presence, decided to get rid of them once and for all.

This excited my curiosity no end, and I determined to find out what effect this massive explosion had on the pit and surrounding countryside, and at the first opportunity, mounting Old Peculiar, I rode up to be met by a scene of utter destruction. Gone was the pit with its vertical sides, where as a child I had played for many happy hours. In its place lay a huge crater. Of the many mature trees surrounding it, few remained. Those nearest the explosion to have survived (somewhat), just shattered dismembered trunks; those further away, still standing, but shorn of all but their stoutest branches. If it was the work of the Royal Engineers, they were probably now more embarrassed by the resulting devastation than they had been by the bombs' continued presence. On that spot today stands a permanent travellers' encampment, and whilst passing on the new road which now bypasses the site, I sometimes wonder in passing if hidden somewhere beneath, biding its time, lies a big fat unexploded bomb…

Chapter 7
Move to the Locomotive Department

A few days after my transfer application had been submitted, I was ordered to attend the Railway HQ at York, Room 23, for further medical and eyesight examinations. In this matter, the Locomotive Department obviously had no trust in the Traffic Department's ability to carry out a thorough examination, even though I went through exactly the same procedures as before. Everything went perfectly, and confident I had passed with ease, I returned to my duties. A few days later the stationmaster called me into his office. He looked at me keenly, hesitated for a moment then, with a blow like a thunderbolt, he informed me I had failed my eyesight examination. This was a mighty blow indeed, which with all my hopes and dreams shattered, left me bereft and hopeless, and something I found hard to believe. "Do you think you passed?" enquired the stationmaster.
"Yes," I replied, "I'm certain." Despairing, I swore to forget life on the footplate, and instead be thankful for what was, after all, a very pleasant if mundane job.

Before I left for work that day, the stationmaster sent for me again: "Are you certain you passed the eyesight test?"

"Yes," I replied again, "as certain of that as I am of anything."

He looked me over carefully. "If I were you," he went on, "I would arrange an eyesight test with a private optician, both for colour and vision. If you pass, bring me the results." As soon as I was able, I purchased a Return Privilege Ticket to Hull, and found an optician. With things being different in those days, and short of trade in any case, he agreed to comprehensively test my eyesight there and then, and was able to confirm I had perfect eyesight, and to establish the fact, he filled in a form setting out the details of the tests I had undergone. I never spent a better five shillings (£0.25) in all my life, and armed with my independent proof, I gave the evidence to the stationmaster.

Next came an anxious wait, then, a couple of weeks later, I received confirmation that I had been accepted as a cleaner into that *Holy of Holies,* the Locomotive Department, at the same time giving me a starting date of the following Monday and a time of 8 am at Springhead Locomotive Shed, Hull. What strings the stationmaster was able to pull, and what lengths he had to go to in order to alter the railway's mind set, I have no idea, but he must have striven magnificently on my behalf. And for that I owe Charles Beckett, stationmaster, amiable gentleman and friend, a further deep and everlasting debt of gratitude.

Because of wartime restrictions, Sunday passenger services had been suspended for the duration in our neck of the woods, although goods trains still ran, mainly hauling train loads of bombs and suchlike, for the bomber air bases en route. Free of work each Sunday, I took the opportunity to go exploring, hoping to discover the whereabouts of the mysterious Springhead which, from discreet questioning, I knew lay to the west of Hull, in what had once been open country, but which had in the years before the war been extensively developed. It was now a labyrinth of roads, streets, houses and shops, extending in the north towards Cottingham and to the west as far as Willerby, and as such a part of Hull quite unknown to me. After many twists and turns and frustrating dead ends, yet guided by distant sounds of railway activity, I arrived at a sleeper wall, and following a sleeper path along its length, I arrived at a rough, rather decrepit, planked door, its ancient paint faded and peeling. For something as grand as a locomotive shed, at the same time unaware of the locomotive and carriage works on the same site, I thought it a poor thing. Yet, ramshackle and neglected, it was plainly an entrance into Springhead. Later I discovered the main entrance, broad and straight at the end of the works. Satisfied I had found my way, I marked the way in, yet I was surprised to find how near to Cottingham Springhead really was, and yet had remained unknown to me. I returned home and prepared for my big day, and its inevitable leap into the unknown.

Something I had failed to bargain for was rising on the Monday morning to a dense impenetrable and clinging fog. But with plenty of time in hand, I chose to walk the few miles to work, for I reasoned again, that my new workmates might find my faithful bike a source of amusement, and by connection, myself as well! Unfortunately, confused by the fog and early morning darkness, I quickly lost my way in the maze of unfamiliar roads and streets leading to Springhead. However, guided by the sound of engine whistles, I eventually found myself up against the sleeper wall. Instinct told me to turn right, and by now feeling I was running out of time, I groped my way along, searching for the elusive door, until to my dismay, the wall ended and I found myself in open country, with the sound of whistles far behind. Beginning to panic, for who wants to be late for work, especially on their first day, I retraced my steps. Along the way I overtook a solitary figure trudging along, buried deep in a railway overcoat, his shoulders hunched against the cold, and obviously making his way to the shed. On my asking for directions, he must have detected a note of anxiety in my voice, for he reassured me with, "Just come with me, I'm booking on at eight and we're in good time." Within a few yards, we had found the door, and on opening it I passed into a new and exciting world.

To my right, at the end of a spur line, and barely visible, stood a large turntable. In the past a single gas lamp on a tall pole had served to throw a little light over it, but was now extinguished for the remainder of the war. The cinder 'trod' soon gave way to a deepened walkway, and here, each accessed by its own set of rails, loomed a row of imposing gable ends, signalling a series of 'shops'. Reaching the end we turned left, where the shed, devoid of any lighting because of the blackout, rose massively in the fog and darkness. My friend escorted me inside. A straight through shed with eight roads, in its H&BR heyday it boasted an allocation of 120 engines, and as such was a large shed by any standards. Inside, stretching away in the darkness, all was quiet, peaceful even, giving it an air of some great lofty cathedral; a cathedral, perhaps, to the power and majesty of steam.

Entering the shed alongside number one engine road, I followed my new-found friend into the booking-on hall. Embedded flush within the shed's massive northern wall, it included the running office. This hall was provided with a long, deep and sloping desk, upon which those drivers booking off filled in the repair book relevant to the engine they worked, along with any reports they may have had to submit. In the hall, the driver and firemens' daily rosters were on prominent display, together with drivers' notices, warning drivers of speed restrictions, failure of water supply, signals out of order, or anything which might affect the safe and expeditious running of trains.

Situated behind, as an integral part of the booking-on hall, was the nerve centre of the shed: the running office. It was administered jointly by the running foreman, the roster clerk and the booking clerk. Like all the running staff, each a former footplate man, who through failing eyesight or other disability, had been required to leave the footplate. Next along, each flush with the shed wall came the shed stores, and finally the cleaner foreman's sanctum sanctorum.

My guide booked on at the hatch dividing the booking-on hall from the running office, before introducing me to the booking clerk. "Ah, a new man," he observed. "What's your name?" He shuffled through some papers, perhaps a summary of my service history. "I see you were on Cottingham Station," he remarked, before writing my name and the date in a ledger, and then handing me a copper disk stamped with a number. "Look after it," he warned, "it's your pay cheque, hand it in for your pay. And as you book off tonight, pick up measuring forms for your footplate uniform."

This comprised of two sets of blue cotton overalls and two blue cotton jackets, a black serge jacket, a heavy overcoat and a railway cap. As a result, I was soon to be the proud owner of two thick heavy railway overcoats, two black jackets and two railway caps! At a time of severe clothes rationing, this abundance left me, if not jumping for joy, at best mightily pleased with the way things were going.

From there I was directed to the cleaner foreman's snuggery, and here I have a confession to make. You, dear reader, will find few names in this narrative. From my earliest days, I have, generally speaking, been unable to remember with any certainty, the names of my acquaintances and friends, despite remembering the smallest details of many other things. It's a failing which often embarrasses me, and one I deeply regret, but there it is. Today, to tease and puzzle me, I have trawled up from some deep recess of my mind, the name Harry Levitt, which may be right, but equally may be wrong. I found him a man of about 60 years of age, wise beyond measure in the ways of engine sheds, and sitting at ease before a roaring fire. No coal rationing here I again mused, and why should there be, for Springhead consumed huge quantities each day. Like the majority of the running staff he favoured a quasi-uniform of bib and brace overalls, civilian jacket and flat cap. Of medium height and tubby build he proved to always be kind, thoughtful and scrupulously fair. I remember him, if not his name, with affection. But having said that, as a former engine driver, I remember him as someone who could 'crack the whip' when necessary.

In keeping with his character and wealth of experience, he showed no surprise at someone before him wearing the uniform of a railway porter. Instead he explained my duties, informing me I would work a three-shift rota, commencing with the 8am to 4pm shift I was already on, followed by a 4pm to

12 midnight shift, and the third, with the rather unusual times of 12.01 am until 8.01 am. The one minute adjustment, I was later told, a time-honoured agreement with the former H&B Railway to prevent the cleaners, on the first shift of the week, claiming a day's Sunday pay.

After my induction to the precepts, customs and rules of the noble and well-founded order of engine drivers and firemen, I followed my overseer to meet the day cleaner gang, who were already working on the south-facing side of the shed, on number eight line, the 'repair road' with its large windows running its length. Here the fitters, in well-lit conditions, worked on light repairs, and here the day shift cleaners were busy cleaning the valve gears of a 'dead', 2-8-0, Robinson 'O4' prior to repair work; a type of engine I was familiar with, after watching them thumping up Little Weighton grade years before.

Each cleaner had been provided with a deep, three-compartment tray, holding about three gallons of paraffin, used for cleaning off lighter and less obstinate gunge, scrapers for scraping off more obstinate dirt, and armfuls of clean cotton waste, for wiping down and finishing off. Perhaps alone during those times of desperate shortages, Springhead had a seemingly endless supply of precious paraffin and clean cotton waste. In its day the H&BR held an enviable reputation for its gleaming locomotives. It was a tradition that, despite the wartime shortages, had still to some extent persisted. We washed down with copious amounts of paraffin, sending the youngest cleaners 'underneath' to clean the shaft and scramble about cleaning the valve gear. To them also were left the wheels and rods. More senior cleaners worked on boilers, cab sides and tenders, polishing them up with an endless supply of clean cotton waste.

Cleaning locomotives, as I soon discovered, was not only a filthy job, but, until I learned to curb my youthful enthusiasm a little, one fraught with unexpected hazards. Split pins, taper pins, nuts of all shapes and sizes played havoc with dirty paraffin-soaked hands. Why none of us contracted dermatitis, skin rot or other foul diseases remains a mystery. Locomotives were often, but not always 'dead' when we cleaned them. We were young and full of fun and mischief. If, when cleaning a dead engine, we could lure an unsuspecting cleaner into the firebox, on some pretext, we closed the firehole door on them and left them locked in to stew. Or if opportunity arose, we placed a lighted torch lamp in the ash pan, the more smoky and foul the better. "When he comes out, he'll look like a smoked kipper!" was the agreed verdict. But circumspection ruled, for the cleaner foreman might appear without warning to inspect the quality of our work, and although a kindly man, we felt the less he knew about 'kippering', the better.

At a time when even passenger engines ran about in a state of filth and neglect, Springhead's unglamorous goods engines not only continued to sparkle, but with keen fitters to maintain them, and the erecting shop to fall back on, it follows they were kept in good working order. Each shift was allowed a 20 minute food break, sometime between the third and fifth hour. This was taken in the drivers' lobby. a concrete-floored, steel-framed, corrugated iron-clad structure, painted a dull sombre black, and facing due south, for which there was a very good reason, it being that the 'Dust Hole'[8] men could observe, over the locomotive yard and the main line, the arrival of the trains they relieved.

Like most drivers' lobbies it was sparsely furnished with long wooden tables and forms, in this case on three sides. In the centre stood a massive round stove which, burning night and day, was something, as part of their charge, the cleaners were expected to maintain. The top of the stove, and fitting it snugly, was what could be easily taken for the middle section of some long-discarded boiler, and probably was. This held hot water, which could be drawn off by means of a brass tap, although, as I found out, footplate men, at least in our part of the world, preferred their tea made at home, and carried in a screw-topped lemonade or beer bottle, which on the footplate rested gently stewing among the oil bottles on the tray above the firehole door. The top of the boiler held a variety of such tea bottles, again each gently stewing and belonging to those drivers and firemen whose duties centred around the lobby, mainly Dust Hole men. As the tea stewed, becoming thicker and less palatable, the owners would draw off hot water, and after swilling it around the bottle, swig it down with evident satisfaction and relish!

Full of strangers, I found entering the lobby for the first time a rather daunting experience. Here were the footplate men I had grown to admire: main line drivers, toughened by life on the footplate, together with their hardy firemen. And with them, at ease between jobs, men about whose abilities I lacked all knowledge: the Dust Hole men. Drivers and firemen whose hard, dirty and often dangerous work, stabling and preparing the engine for its next duty and receiving the crews of Down trains, on the main line, opposite the lobby, where, after a

---

[8] So named for their dirty and arduous work of cleaning the fires of clinker, the smoke boxes of ash, and raking out ash pans before stabling the engine and preparing it for its next turn of duty.

few words between them regarding the condition of the engine, particularly the fire, these Dust Hole men then worked the train forward, up onto the high-level section of the main line. From there they reversed the train under gravity into one of the sidings forming part of the extensive exchange sidings, to the south of Springhead, before returning to the shed 'light engine' (i.e. just the engine, with no carriages or waggons).

After the amalgamation of the H&BR with the NER, and later the formation of the LNER, all the Springhead passenger train working had been transferred to Botanic Gardens loco shed, leaving the H&B shed as a purely goods depot. In my day the famous H&BR 0-8-0 Class 'A' goods engines, nicknamed 'Tiny's' on account of their large size, had long gone, to be replaced by Robinson's 2-8-0, LNER Class 'O4'. Used extensively by the army during World War I, and known to us as 'Puggies', some still retained cast military insignia on the cab sides. By now beginning to age, they were in the process of being modernised by Edward Thompson who, as quickly as wartime conditions allowed, provided them with a modern front end layout, outside Walschaerts valve gear, a new modern boiler with the pressure raised from 175 to 225 pounds per square inch (psi), and a firebox with rocker grates. And at the front end, a self-cleaning smokebox, and at the other end the benefit of a typical and commodious, double-windowed LNER cab, with the unheard of luxury of padded bucket seats. In keeping with the traditions of the NER where he learned his trade, whatever might be said of Edward Thompson as a mechanical engineer, the comfort and well-being of engine crews was always paramount, especially anything to relieve the burden of fire, smokebox, and ash pan cleaning. And it is for these and his other innovations, he should be chiefly remembered.

After being relieved by the Dust Hole man, the main line crew, faces smudged and blackened by smoke, would swing down and make their way across the front of the shed to the lobby. Each fireman possessed his own shovel, slacker pipe and hand brush, which he deposited in the stores, to await his next turn of duty. Meanwhile the driver would make his way to the lobby to fill in his timesheet, and have a few words with old friends. Sometimes, if the spirit moved them, and if they had a receptive audience of cleaners, they would feed them, egged on by others in the lobby, the most outrageous tales of derring-do that febrile minds could devise. We cleaners believing, in the main, every word, would listen in awed silence, mouths agape, as the cold hand of fear touched our spines. To us they all seemed like gods, and some of their tales are worth repeating.

One cold spring day, with a gale rattling the lobby windows, and those inside the lobby glad of the warmth it provided, one of the main line drivers came in, after being relieved by the Dust Hole men. A big man, gnarled and weather beaten, it must have been a cold trip in the draughty cab of an 'O4', for he was wearing his thick heavy railway coat, with its collar turned up. Standing with his back to the stove, occasionally bending forward, he announced to all and sundry "I'm just warming the [w]hole of my body", a double entendre which remained with me over the years. Diving into the deep and generous pockets of his overcoat, he withdrew his tea bottle containing the last dregs of stewed tea. Unscrewing the top, he drained the bottle before glancing round. At one table sat a small group of cleaners; at another, chatting together, two spare drivers. One called out, "Had a rough trip, Bill?", which was the opportunity Bill had been waiting for.

"Aye!" he replied. "It's been a bit cowd an' windy," and then he slipped the two drivers a wink. "But not as bad as I had a few years back."

With the cleaners hanging on every word, the driver launched into a tale enough to make anyone's blood run cold. "It wor yar night with a great wind blowin'," he went on, "an I left wit a train hev coal empties, an' does tha know wat?"

"No Bill," chorused the two drivers, "tell us, tell us all!"

"Well, the wind got in them empties, an blew me all the way up the bank and inter Drewton tunnel, an' do you know, I never had to open the regulator, not once." He glanced at the cleaners listening with bated breath and warmed to his task. "An' to cut a long story short, when I got blown into Drewton, with the wind behind me shoving, we went faster an' faster. (And here, for those unfamiliar with the speed of an unbraked goods trains, this would be, under favourable conditions and at full stretch, about 28 to 30 mph, and with only engine brakes to rely on, a speed which required a long distance, and all the skills a driver possessed, to bring the train safely to a halt).

"Me an' the fireman screwed the hand brake on as hard as we could, but that didn't do any good, so I put the steam brake on full. But with the wind blowin' us, that didn't do any good either. Comin' out of Drewton, we must have been doin' ninety!"

"Oh calamity, calamity," cried the drivers in consternation, the cleaners, imaginations running riot, and the cold hand of fear gripping them at the horror of the driver and fireman on the footplate, hurtling through the night, desperately trying to bring a runaway train under control.

"However," continued Billy, "I still had another trick up mi sleeve. I wound the owd engin' inter back gear, then opened her out full. She didn't like that very much, an' yucked and yarked about, but that began to slow her down."

"Oh merciful heavens!" cried the drivers, stamping their feet in relief at a disaster averted. "Tell us what happened next?"

"Why, I looked over the side an' got a shock."

"A shock, Billy? A shock, whatever next?" cried the drivers in unfeigned consternation.

"Why, when I looked over the side, them coupled wheels was spinning round all red hot, wi' sparks flying off 'em like great big Catherine wheels. An' me brake blocks, white hot, was worm away to nowt. I had a right job ti stop when I got to yon end wi' all the brake blocks gone!"

"What a horrible experience!" wailed the drivers.

"Yes, it warr," confirmed Billy, "but that's not all. Cos we had to come home wi' a loaded coal train, an' engine wi' no brakes."

Intrigued, one of the drivers asked, innocently enough: "How did you get home, Billy, with no brakes?"

For a moment, Billy, never having thought things through to that extent, was at a loss for an answer, but his quick and fertile mind came to his rescue. "Why," quoth he, "Me an' me fireman raked about the colliery yard an' fun a great big iron bar. An' when we comes tiv a downhill bit, he slipped off an shoved it through the spokes and under the frames. That locked the wheels up tight, an' that way we got home safe."

"Yes," agreed the drivers sympathetically, "you can have some mighty rough trips on the 'raging main'."

Other tales from the 'raging main' continue to rekindle old memories of mine, bringing with them a fond smile. One, with its vivid (and of course exaggerated) description of tender first running, sent our youthful imaginations soaring to new heights. 'The Cream', as we knew him—and more about him later—drew our attention by declaring he had just had a rum sort of trip. "Why's that?" he was asked.

"Well, I went on ti Cudworth shed ti turn, ready for comin' home, an' some h'armeture had run inter the turntable an' bust it. So we had to come home tender first. Comin' downhill," he solemnly declared, "through South Kirby tunnel, we was goin' that fast, the coal was blowing back out hev the tender. So mi fireman opened the firehole big door, an' believe it or not, the coal went straight into the firebox. An' that way we got home without having to fire anymore. An' when we got back, all we had left in the tender was some big knobs of coal." And to bring his story to a fitting conclusion, he added, "Cos them knobs was as big as cart-'oss heads!"

One morning in the early hours, during that period when the cleaners were in the lobby dining off their meagre rations, an ancient hoary-headed driver came in after being relieved on the main line. In response to a question, he answered by saying he had been in a hurry to get home. "'Cos," he cackled knowingly, "me missus is waitin' for me in a nice warm bed."

"In that case," warned the fireman, "be careful, or you'll bain her."

Ignoring this crude implication, he went on, "Cos I wanted to get home as quick as I could, I had to ease down to ninety round that curve through Drax station." Everyone among the gathered engine men, now listened intently, wondering how far the story was going to extend, and trying to imagine a trundling 'O4', with fully loaded coal train racing through the night at a speed in excess of 90 mph. Even as inexperienced cleaners, we found that a bit hard to swallow, but it was a thrilling story, and we listened with keen interest.

The driver's elderly, but seemingly eager and willing wife, apparently now forgotten, he continued, "When I was through Drax, me tender was clatterin' and banging about that much, mi handbrake column came all lowse, an' the handbrake was wavin' about all over the place." As everyone sat up straight, and prepared for the grand finale, he paused in his narrative. "When we went through the station," he continued, "what with the tender rollin' about, an' the handbrake all lowse, why it hit every lamp post along the platform, an' snapped 'em all off, clean as a whistle. I'll bet the station boss won't half be narked when he gets up and finds them all smashed. I reckon he won't sleep for a week thinking about them!" Then to add a ring of credibility to his story, he went on, "I suppose I ought to make out a report for the owd man, or he'll be narked as well!"

Whilst moving through three shifts, I discovered, because of the blackout, that all cleaning work ceased, as darkness overtook the shed and its staff, and as a result the cleaners were put on other work. At times a pilot engine came on shed with a small train of waggons and vans containing shed stores, which the cleaners unloaded. Frequently a 10 ton waggon of sand had to be shovelled into the large brick-built sand dryer for Springhead engines, as working heavy trains up steep inclines out of low lying collieries meant they often returned with sand boxes empty. Now and then a waggon containing brake blocks arrived, for again, Springhead was heavy on brake blocks. Barrels of lubricating oil came in separate waggons which, when unloaded, we rolled some distance into what was known as the oil store. A large detached building, what its original purpose was, I've no idea, for it was far too grand to have been built to store, within its lofty and spacious interior, a few barrels of oil. From there, when required, we rolled barrels of oil around to the shed and into the stores, before hoisting them aloft by means of chain tackle and grabs, then decanting the contents into large ornately decorated and lined out oil tanks.

Supervised by the shed storeman, checking everything against a manifest, we unloaded smaller items, including brass and phosphor bronze bar, white metal and other valuable components for the erecting shop and repair line. In fact anything a busy shed required, including stationery for general office work. Being enthusiastic, I helped the Dust Hole men whenever I got the chance, and this included the thrill of chugging around the yard to the coal stage, to coal, water and turn our engine, our wheels grinding and groaning on the tight curves which, when emphasised by total darkness, added to the thrill of the experience. From here we returned to the front of the shed where, over the ash pits, the dirty mundane task of cleaning the fire, smokebox and ash pan commenced, and where, like generations before me and under the critical eyes of firemen, I learned to safely handle heavy red-hot clinker shovels, and other equally hot and dangerous fire irons, with the skill and dexterity required. With six sand boxes to each 'O4', four along the running plate for forward running, and two inside the cab below the seats for tender first running, and each box containing about eight buckets of sand, carrying them from the 'sand hole' and filling the sand boxes could be an arduous task, and in this respect, Dust Hole firemen were always glad of a little help, reminding me of the old maxim: "A little help is worth a lot of pity."

For the cleaners, the night shift proved just as busy, often completing outstanding work from the earlier shift. One night shift duty was 'knocking up' those drivers and firemen residing within one mile of the shed. Usually they were up and about when the knock came. but it was a service much appreciated, for however deep the night, the Locomotive Department didn't like its engine men sleeping in, and this was a guarantee against that happening. Knocking up one morning is remembered not only for the cold, but chiefly for a robin I found sheltering in a driver's porch. Huddled in the apex above the door, seemingly unafraid, it watched my every move, its tiny jet-black eyes glistening in the light from my hand lamp. A bonus well worth the effort.

Each morning, about 6am, the night shift cleaners split into groups to clean and prepare the shed's offices and other accommodation. As one group cleaned the driver's lobby and brought in a sufficiency of coal to maintain its massive stove (coal gleaned, of course, from the nearest engine), another group cleaned the foreman's snug and prepared and lit a fire, in preparation for him coming on duty at 8am. In the meantime, the reminder went to clean and prepare the shedmaster, Mr G. J. Gregory's, office; more about that gentleman later. This entailed a trek the length of the eight-bay loco shed, frequently in the dark, then a further trek to where, standing in splendid isolation, yet conveniently overlooking the shed and locomotive works, stood the shedmaster's office.

Dating from the railway's earliest days, and in stark contrast to the rest of Springhead which had been built to the highest standards, using top quality red engineering brick, the shedmaster's office was of a more humble construction, being double fronted and constructed entirely of wood, although in keeping with railway practice, built to last. However, its unpretentious exterior concealed a glorious past, for this was none other than the office of Matthew Stirling, the long-serving and only locomotive superintendent, or as that position is nowadays more widely and better known, the chief mechanical engineer, of the H&BR. Son of the illustrious Great Northern locomotive superintendent and mechanical engineer, Patrick Stirling, nephew of James Stirling, notable locomotive superintendent of the Glasgow and South-Western railway, and later occupying the position on the South-Eastern Railway, he came from a family of renowned Victorian locomotive engineers.

But H&BR tradition had it, that the office was erected in the first place for William Kirtley, at the time the Locomotive Superintendent of the London Chatham & Dover Railway, who had been engaged for a period, in an *ad hoc* advisory capacity, and as such was responsible for the design and implementation of the H&BR's first stud of locomotives, comprising the following three classes: ten 2-4-0 express tender engines, twenty 0-6-0 goods tender engines, and twelve '0-6-0' side tank, shunting engines. In total, 42 locomotives, to launch the fledgling railway on its way.

Off to the right of the entrance hall, although largely unused since the amalgamation with the hated NER on 31 March 1922, was the drawing office for Stirling's design and drawing staff. And on the left, still oozing character, and to me a place of wonder and enchantment, the former office of Matthew Stirling, now occupied by the shedmaster. It was a handsome, well-proportioned room, with a hardwood floor. To spread its comforting warmth all around, a large brick-built and tiled fireplace, with polished oak surround, and ornate brass fender and an array of fire irons, dominated its western side. Suspended on the rear wall by means of a backing board, was a full size model of a Stephenson link motion valve gear, upon which Stirling was able to work out the dimensions and proportions of valve gears, and also the intricacies of valve events for any type of locomotive under design.

But what drew my attention most of all were the large framed plate photographs adorning every wall—detailed photographs of every type of H&BR locomotive, including Kirtley's original prototypes. Although at that early stage in my career, I had little understanding of what was expected of these locomotives, nor their ability to carry that out. Nevertheless, I examined each plate with care and attention, and a sense of wonder. As a result, office cleaning was neglected until I had had my fill. I do hope they have survived, and are in safe keeping somewhere.

In the centre of the room stood Stirling's impressive desk, a desk which almost proved my undoing. One morning, long before the shedmaster's arrival, whilst basking in the warmth of a splendid fire, I cheekily occupied the great man's chair, and with my feet on the desk, laying back, I contentedly puffed on a fag, for in those days everyone smoked, especially if they could find some cigarettes hidden 'below the counter'[9]. Some, like *Passing Cloud,* were horrible, enough to make even a factory chimney cough, but we persevered. Anyway, there I was, imagining I was G. J. Gregory, master of all I surveyed, when suddenly, without warning, and to my horror, the man himself walked in. "Get yer bloody feet off my desk, you insolent little bugger!" he howled. "I've a good mind to sack you here and now!" Shaken to the core, and fearing the loss of my

---

[9] Although there was no rationing of cigarettes during the war, cigarettes were very hard to come by, and shopkeepers no longer put them on display, reserving them for their favourite customers by hiding them below the counter.

job, my hopes and dreams, I fled, before he put his threat into action. Later, I like to think he might well have chuckled to himself thinking "That frightened the little sod." He retired to Cottingham, where I remember him as a tall distinguished-looking gentleman who I sometimes met as I cycled to and from work. Recognising me as a footplate aficionado, he would glance my way, perhaps recognising me for the beardless youth he had booted out of his office long ago.

If things were a bit slack on one of the night shifts, my delight was being invited by Dust Hole firemen to accompany them when they relieved main line crews. This wasn't complete altruism on their part, for although cleaners learned basic firing techniques this way, they were expected to help the fireman stable the engine. What a thrill though, scrambling from the lobby to the main line in pitch darkness, with only a faint glow from the standing engine as a guide. Once aboard, the two drivers, after consulting watches, would agree the relieving time, an essential requirement when they filled in their time sheets. At the same time, the main line fireman would have a quick word with the relieving fireman, mainly regarding the condition of the fire, or anything else of importance, before making his way to the shed stores to park his shovel, slacker pipe and hand brush.

With the engine cab bathed in a gentle glow from a rundown fire, slumbering after a long 'shut off' down Little Weighton Bank, it offered to a young cleaner like me a confusion of sights, sounds and smells. Seen only dimly, the boiler pressure gauge, its needle standing where it might be more brightly illuminated by its gauge lamp, the boiler water levels gently bobbing up and down in the two gauge glasses, and sometimes, in unison with steam hissing under pressure, an injector might be singing strongly and merrily. For the relieving fireman this was the time for important decisions. By opening the firebox big door he was able to examine the dull red fire from back to front in detail. If he had been left with a fire too thick for straightforward uncomplicated cleaning, he had to devise a way of getting rid of the bulk, before arriving on shed. If on the other hand it was thin, perhaps with holes burnt in it, through which cold air could be drawn (setting in train dangerous opposing strains throughout the firebox and tubes, and also under such conditions, a fire unable to sustain the climb from the level and the subsequent sometimes lengthy disposal of its train), then he had a different and more urgent problem to deal with if he was to avoid bringing the engine on-shed with smoky unburnt coal, and one requiring a great deal of skill. For the bane of a Dust Hole fireman's life was 'paddling out' a mass of choking, burning coal.

But, by carefully choosing small coal of the right size for the conditions, and by firing little but often with coal that burnt away quickly, the fireman could keep control over his fire, bringing the locomotive in over the ash pits clean and smoke-free.

Meanwhile, after a warning whistle from the driver, things became even more exciting. On opening the regulator, strange unidentifiable squeaks, whistles and sighs from the front end, and clicks and bangs from the engine gathering up its strength, followed by the first deep exhaust, disturbing the fire, and sending a blizzard of fine, loose, white ash swirling round the firebox. And as the engine lifted its load, whipping the fire into a white hot glare, be the night ever so dark and stormy, this was bliss indeed!

But to return for a moment to the day shift, and more specifically to the winter months, when a cold and often bitter wind gusted the length of the shed, making conditions ripe for knocking more 'bark' off the cleaners' numbed unfeeling hands. To eliminate these conditions, stout wooden doors, covering each engine road had been provided; in practice, however, they had proved too heavy and cumbersome to be opened and closed each time an engine had to be moved, thus remaining open for the wind to blow through freely. Occasionally, however, a welcome escape happened, when some of us were sent into the erecting shop to clean engine parts. Once inside, I found the erecting shop a place of wonder and delight. Out of the nagging wind, the shop was warm and comfortable, as heat from its electric motors maintained an even temperature. Beneath its broad and lofty roof, its powerful overhead crane could be found lifting and moving locomotives to delight the heart of any steam enthusiast: perhaps a memorable H&BR locomotive, one out of the three classes of that company remaining, and still doing good work after a lifetime of increasing toil, or maybe an ailing Robinson 'O4', or any of the many different classes stabled at Hull's four different sheds.

Under the supervision of the erecting shop foreman we went to work on frames, wheels and rods, and if precision work was required, we prepared journals, axle boxes, big and little end brasses, and side rod bushes, or cleaned any other component that required a close precise finish by one of the machinists. Cleaning dismantled bottom parts gave me a deeper and more thorough understanding of the part played by the axle box, wedges and stayplates, and how they were adjusted to take up the wear and tear, than I could have learned in day to day shed cleaning. Crouched on the erecting shop's wooden block floor, my first assignment was cleaning the four bogie axle boxes from a former NER Class 'W', 4-6-2, now LNER Class 'A7', passenger tank engine, known from its NER designation as a 'Willie'. Being below, and in close proximity to the smokebox and its abrasive contents, I found the four axle boxes coated with a thick destructive mixture of smokebox ash and lubricating oil, to the extent it seemed impossible for them to move freely and vertically in the axle box guides, as they were intended. Sometimes engines came into the shop for valve and piston work, giving me an opportunity to try and solve one of the great mysteries to me of engine locomotion for, puzzle as I may, I was at a loss to understand how a locomotive was able to start from rest whatever the position of its rods and cranks. Enlightenment came, when one day, the erecting shop foreman discovered me peering into the innards of an open, defrocked, and empty steam chest belonging to a slide valve engine, as I tried to make sense of what little there was to see. Observing my interest, and in answer to a question, he began to explain in simple terms, for I was a simple lad, for whom the complexity of valve gear layout and the more esoteric features of steam distribution went far beyond my ability to understand. But for a start the foreman explained the purpose of the steam chest which, in common with the majority of British inside cylinder locomotives, was positioned between the two cylinders, and as such, formed an integral part of both, and which, without much comprehension, I had just been peering into. After pointing out the four steam ports connecting the steam chest with the cylinders, he took one of the engine's two bronze slide valves from a nearby bench, and began to instruct me in elementary steam distribution, by first showing how a slide valve was formed in the shape of a box, a box with an open face, and protruding bars at each end, whose purpose was to admit steam into the cylinders, and act as a bridge, spanning the steam ports to which they applied, whilst the open underside provided the passage to the blast pipe, for exhaust steam.

Taking a chalk from the top pocket of his waistcoat, the foreman drew a diagram, showing how, when the engine stood at rest with the reverser locked in mid-gear, the two valves covered the four ports, effectively shutting them off to steam. So far this had proved a lesson I was able to understand. Then, getting down to the meat of the matter (and without delving into the complexities of lap and lead and its effects on steam distribution), by taking the right cylinder as an example he demonstrated the following: when the reverser was moved from mid-gear, to say, full-forward gear, and (for ease of explanation) the piston in the cylinder had reached the limit of its forward stroke, at that point the front bar end of one valve was opening the front port to steam, prior to pushing the piston to the rear of the cylinder; and at the same time maintaining the rear port closed to admission, yet to clear the cylinder of steam, leaving it open to exhaust via the underside of the slide valve.

Conversely the left cylinder's piston would now be on the half-stroke, with the left back port having been fully opened to the steam, and now on the point of closing, leaving the front port closed to admission, and fully open to exhaust. Put simply, it still left me with a knitted brow, for I had failed to understand that a slide valve did just what its name implied: sliding backwards and forwards, opening and closing the steam ports in strict sequence. Yet I was beginning to understand the steam cycle of what, at best, could only be described as a primitive form of engine. But the big question remained! All along I have been distracted by the more obvious and exciting features of a steam locomotive—the large, and in some cases, very large driving wheels, and the whirling tinkling side rods, with their ungainly alternating motion, which when viewed head on, seemed to bear no relation to the steady uniform progress of the locomotive itself. Led astray by a locomotive's driving wheels, what still troubled me was its ability to start from any point around those wheels, although if I had thought about it more deeply, and with greater understanding, I would have recognised the foreman had already answered my question.

Showing admirable patience for a busy man, we went underneath, where nestling on the driving shaft, between the two connecting rod big-ends, and forming part of the valve gear, lay the eccentrics in fixed positions on the shaft. Eccentrics I had cleaned often enough, without ever understanding the part they played in the action of the valves. Without making a meal of it, the foreman explained how the greatly reduced throw of the eccentrics, around the shaft, mimicked the outer rotation of a locomotive's driving wheels, and working through the medium of the valve gear, and as the name implies, sliding the valves back and forth, opening and closing the steam ports in strict order, with the beauty being that, no matter where an engine's wheels stopped, two ports, one on either cylinder, and at opposing ends, remained open to a greater or lesser extent. And by what struck me at that time as very clever design, the engineers were able to make sure that however minute the opening of a port was to steam, the other port on the opposite cylinder opened to a greater degree, thereby ensuring that even under load, the engine was provided with enough power to move. Clever fellows!

By the winter of 1943/44 enemy air activity had in effect ended. No longer each night, either at home or at work, bringing with it the fear of air attack and sudden death. Instead of the night sky being filled with the sound of enemy bombers, it was now British bombers, heading south on their deadly missions. Then, after the last had passed overhead, a heart-warming but unreported drama became visible. North and south, as far as the eye could see, in a precise line, every searchlight shone its beam vertically, leaving them upright as welcoming beacons until the last of the sorely tried and often traumatised crews had returned home to safety and rest.

It was during this winter that a returning bomber, badly damaged by enemy gunfire, lost a propeller which, during the early hours, fell with considerable force narrowly missing the coal stage, to the fear of the coal stage 'black gang', who heard it scything unseen through the air towards them. Working around the shed late one morning I became distracted by the beat of an unfamiliar exhaust, which unlike the deep exhausts of Springhead's stock of goods engines, sounded syncopated, sharp and clean. With interest aroused I followed the engine's exhaust as, hidden by other locomotives and general yard clutter, the stranger made its way round to the ash pits, after coal and watering. As it swung into view, head on, I experienced a wild paroxysm of disbelief as, picked out in bold relief on its front buffer beam, I recognised its number and class: none other than my old friend from my lad porter days, when I had admired it so much as it raced through Cottingham 'belly to ground' on the final leg of its journey: 2165, one of Sir Vincent Litchfield Raven's magnificent Atlantics.

This was an opportunity not to be missed, and abandoning what I was doing, I climbed up into the cab, anxious not only to help the fireman stable and prepare the engine for its next turn of duty, but also to savour the experience of being on its footplate. After completing the dirty work, i.e. cleaning the fire, smokebox and ash pan, the fireman asked me to fill the engine's sight feed lubricator. Oh dear me, as I was about to discover, a little knowledge can be a dangerous thing! Feeling important, worldly and in charge of things, I closed, or thought I had, the lubricator's steam valve. Now I was about to experience one of the vagaries of a Detroit hydrostatic lubricator. Bracketed conveniently on the boiler's back plate, above head height on the fireman's side, it overhung the fireman's footstool. Unscrewing the lubricator's filling plug, I placed it on the fireman's box seat. As

I did, I heard from deep inside, a distinctive 'glug'; a glug which should have meant everything to me, but which in my ignorance, meant nothing. Taking a bottle of superheated cylinder oil, 'black oil', in our northern engine men's parlance, and ignoring further glugs, I filled the lubricator, and bending down, was about to replace the filling plug when, above me I heard a more pronounced and audible glug, followed by a searing pain as the lubricator deposited a large dollop of scalding, steam-heated cylinder oil down the back of my neck, adding a further scar to the many already dotted around my body. As they say, experience is the best teacher, and the worst experiences teach the best lessons— I certainly wouldn't be doing that again!

Chapter 8
A (Rogues) Gallery of Drivers

During that winter my career prospects began to further improve, after the cleaner foreman passed me out for firing duties. My first ever firing turn was a day job on one of the two pilots shunting at Springhead's extensive exchange sidings on a 24 hour roster, making up trains for transfer to Hull docks on the other side of the city. This was memorable on several counts, not least because this was the first time I had been trusted with the important task of firing a steam locomotive, and who among that privileged band could fail to remember such an occasion. Remembered also, with gratitude, is the amicable old driver, working out the remainder of his days on a shunting engine and who, by patiently telling me when to fire, kept me right. Though I say fire, in truth it was, on my part, more clumsily poking coal through the firebox door, than firing in the accepted sense. I also remember the weather conditions for, although it remained dry, a harsh cutting wind caught the engine, an H&BR 0-6-2 tank engine, sideways on, viciously blasting through the cab, making me thank God it didn't bring with it snow and rain. We endured these conditions until we rigged up a sheet on the windward side of the cab, held fast and tight with the aid of a couple of old fishplates suspended below it. At once, it transformed the cab into a warm cosy haven.

In the following weeks I began firing turns on a more regular basis. This was mainly dashing up and down the extensive sidings attached to Springhead, making up trains for onward transmission to the Hull docks, but rostered occasionally on the 'Shed Pilot', which included the thrilling experience of charging 'full tilt' up the steep incline and on to the coal stage whilst propelling loaded waggons of coal. During this period I occasionally went by means of a tiny Austin van to either Dairycoates or Botanic Gardens, to help out there in the

Dust Hole. I didn't much care for Dairycoates, with its huge series of meandering sheds to get lost in, especially in the dark and during the blackout.

Nor did I like being close to the Humber foreshore and the fish docks, where a large and odorous fish manure factory spread a thick and cloying stench of rotting fish over and around the shed. Despite my reservations, I once spent an interesting night shunting the nearby Neptune Street sidings with a massive ponderous, clanking, three-cylinder NER Class 'X' 4-8-0 tank engine, which for me, seemed to have an inordinately long firebox. Of the two sheds, I much preferred the smaller Botanic Gardens—even the name seemed to endow it with an air of romance, never mind its stud of high-stepping, long-legged passenger engines.

But back to Springhead. Before long I was booked for my first main line trip, and mighty proud I was too. Not, I hasten to add, a proper main line outing, up Little Weighton Bank, on to whatever lay beyond, but the mundane daily pick-up between Springhead and Hull docks, which, by poking its smokebox into all kinds of hitherto unknown sidings and yards, opened up a whole new world to my wondering eyes. Worth reporting, but little known, there was a daily practice which fell to the dock pick-up[10] crew: each morning, before departing Springhead sidings, they took on-board several five gallon cans of fresh water, for delivery to signalmen along the way who, isolated on the high-level section, lacked the luxury of a piped water supply. Hardly had we hauled our train out of the yard and up onto the high level, than we stopped at our first cabin, Springbank South, where in exchange for a full can, we were handed an empty one.

Ideal for this kind of work we pottered along with one of the gallant but quickly diminishing band of H&BR 'G3' 0-6-0 tank engines, dodging into a coal yard here and a goods depot there, and each a source of wonder to a country boy. This part of Hull, far from the better-known shopping and commercial centre, which the Luftwaffe had effectively rearranged a couple of years beforehand, was a district I was totally unaware of. Now rumbling along the high-level embankment above the city, what met my astonished eyes was a land of factories, industry and all manner of manufacturing activities. Close alongside the railway, and dominating the area stood Sculcoates power station, with its cluster of tall chimneys, and what for me was a first, its odd-shaped cooling towers, whilst

---

[10] A train going along the H&BR high level embankments around Hull, picking up and dropping off waggons.

opposite, in the middle distance, Rank's massive flour mill stood defiantly among the bombed ruins surrounding it.

As we approached, the next feature to draw a gasp of astonishment, the splendid bow girder swing bridge crossing the River Hull, which we rattled across in style, before shunting the last two yards on our route, Burleigh Street goods and Drypool goods, before entering the massive former H&BR Alexandra Dock. This was a dock so large it required its own locomotive depot, and a stock of 24 shunting engines to attend its many wharves' coal hoists, and miles of dock railway.

After taking water, and hanging on to a newly formed train of coal empties, we struck out for home, only to be turned off at Cannon Street Junction to travel the Cannon Street branch leading to Cannon Street station, about which I had heard so much from former H&BR men, it being the principal passenger station on the system, but which proved a disappointment. Long unused as a passenger station, it had an air of neglect about it as we dropped off a few empty waggons into a loading bay. But what the station lacked in grandeur was more than made up, as our gallant engine, whilst steaming freely, was thrashed up the grade and over a series of bridges and arches straddling the Hull and Hornsea branch line, and its near neighbour, the deep and sluggish Holderness Drain, to the extent that, under the intense heat from the engine's open 'flapper' (air deflector plate), both footstools began to smoulder, before bursting into flame. This was a moment of high drama, and as the engine flung a plume of smoke and steam skywards, I responded to the threat by dousing the spreading flames with water from the engine's bucket. Finally, gaining the main line once more, at Cannon Street Junction, I had my first experience of a triangle turning an engine. We entered Cannon Street branch 'bunker first', and by the time we took up the main line again, I found we were running 'engine first', an event which at the time rather spooked me, until I worked out the reason for this change of direction.

Shortly after this trip I was rostered to work my first through train, a chance coming my way which I was eager to take on. But this was not, it turned out, a train pulled by a Robinson 'O4', bravely clawing its way over the rolling Yorkshire Wolds by way of Little Weighton Bank and over Eppleworth Viaduct, past my secret hideaway and lookout which had granted me so many pleasures, and past the fields I had toiled in as a farmer's boy. No, this was rather more lowly work, conveying loaded 'trip' trains between Springhead and Alexandra Dock, over the six-mile high-level section, returning each time with a train of empties. After the thrash up from the sidings and on to the embankment, the track, apart from small variations, remained level throughout. And thereafter, whilst running at a steady 20 mph, and watching the exhaust thumping out of the engine chimney unremittingly, I was always surprised by how little coal the engine was expending for the tonnage it was happily drawing along. Just a few half-shovelfuls around the front of the box and a little in the back corner seemed sufficient.

What follows could well be dubbed '*A Winter's Tale*'. Shortly after this initial 'trip', I was booked on the same job again. However this time, instead of one of Springhead's dwindling band of H&BR tank engines, which gave protection whichever way they were running, the engine allocated proved to be a former NER Class 'C' 0-6-0 tender engine. And whilst its deep American-style cab provided excellent protection for the crew in most circumstances, returning tender first each trip from Alexandra Dock was something else. Now, whatever the weather was prepared to throw at us, was funnelled into the cab, where it drenched everything, forcing us into our greatcoats, and spitting and dancing off the boiler back plate and its fittings. It made one wonder how early engine crews, on the open footplates of the day, and lacking protection of any kind, could endure extremes of weather for hours on end. Perhaps there was more than a hint of truth in one horny-handed driver's quip: "When I was a young fireman," he announced, "it war wooden brake blocks an' men hev steel. Now look at 'em, it's steel brake blocks an men hev wood, an' that's all there is tiv it!"

My driver for the day, a short man, smoked a foul-smelling pipe, which he drew on with evident satisfaction. He wore a flat cap, which on account of it being favoured by main line men, was generally known as a 'mainliner' and in true H&BR style was pulled down low over his eyes. To my curious gaze, he seemed very old, very old indeed. And that may well have been true, for it was said, rightly or wrongly, but particularly at Springhead (which often seemed to make up its own rules) that because of wartime expediency, any driver of retirement age could, if he so wished, stay on. And this driver may well have been one of that small but resolute band.

Observing my beardless youth and underdeveloped physique, the gulf of age hung heavily between us. I found him a dour uncommunicative yet not unpleasant man, who let me get on with my work without interference, only asking when we first met, with a nod to the engine "Can you manage one hev these?" to which I eagerly replied "Yes!" Arriving back at Springhead sidings, after our fourth or fifth 'trip', our day's work done, and night closing in, the yard foreman gave us the tip for the shed.

Still coated up, all that remained was to leave the yard, run down the main line, still tender first, and stop alongside Locomotive Junction signal cabin, behind the dolly and points which, when activated, would allow us to cross over and enter Springhead locomotive yard. Standing in the cab, buffeted by wind and rain driving in, everything around us dank and wet, we both stood in our overcoats, our backs to the boiler for shelter and warmth, the driver impassively smoking his pipe as we waited for the dolly to clear.

Instead, the cabin window above us slid open. "Control wants you to run another trip," the signalman informed us. Without altering his position, the driver took the pipe from his mouth. "Shed," he replied, and replaced his pipe. The signalman closed his window and returned to his telephone, before opening the window once again. "Control wants another trip," he informed us. Patiently, the driver withdrew his pipe, and this time with a little edge to his voice, replied, "Shed."

As we stood mute against the boiler, expecting the message to have gone home and the dolly to turn, the cabin window slid open again. "Control says…" the signalman got no further. "Shed!" squealed the driver, his voice beginning to rise. Seeing the way things were going, and becoming afraid the driver's growing annoyance might be turned on me, I squeezed myself into a corner of the cab. Once again, the signalman tried to pass on Control's message. This proved the last straw.

As I cowered in the corner, the driver snatched the pipe from his mouth, and flinging his arms wide open in despair, sent a stream of tobacco juice and spittle swirling around the cab. "Control can go to bloody 'ell," he howled, "it's Shed!" With the rain sweeping the cab, we resumed our positions, each standing on his footstool near the boiler, the driver, his head bowed, and as silent as ever, quietly puffed his pipe, seemingly lost in his own little world, until he heard the points click over, followed by the dolly clunking into place. Sliding his side window open, the driver squinted into the rain swept darkness, and with a little grunt of approval, reached for the regulator.

With my time at Springhead ever increasing, so came a growing acquaintance with those staff whose idiosyncratic behaviour, quirky deeds, and in some cases, quirky misdeeds, deserve a mention. If they are to be identified in order of seniority, I suppose I ought to start with the shedmaster, George

Gregory. As a boy he followed his father, and Matthew Stirling, from the GNR to work the H&BR's incipient Locomotive Department, thereafter spending the remainder of his working life at Springhead. Retaining an immense pride in all things H&BR, he demanded a high standard from everyone, something made obvious by his well-maintained and well-cleaned engines, and equally clean, tidy and well-maintained locomotive shed. I can offer no other explanation for the quantities of cleaning materials we lavished on locomotives, even at that late stage of the war, but with admirable foresight he must have stockpiled large quantities of paraffin and other cleaning products against the coming war and its inevitable shortages.

At the time, 1944, a song became popular which went something like this:

Who's that looking through the window,
Who's that looking through the door,
Why it's old man sunshine, old man sunshine,
He's been here before.

On his daily rounds, George Gregory frequently stopped and looked first through the driver's lobby window, then the door, to see if the cleaners were gainfully employed and not lounging about. The cleaners, with youthful irreverence, quickly adapting the last two lines of the above ditty to:

Why it's old man Gregory, old man Gregory,
He's been here before.

Now I'd like to cast a light on some of the more colourful footplate staff. Step out from the shadows of the past that group of hardy individuals, whose funny little ways impressed me to the extent that they remain as clear and distinct as they did all those years ago.

Step forward then, the first of that illustrious brotherhood—Driver 'X'. His real name is unknown to me, for I only knew him as 'The Cream', or just 'Cream' for short. In 1944 he was reaching the end of his working life, but remained a tall, well-built and imposing figure, emphasised by a splendid shock of white hair, upon which, being a former H&BR man, he perched his peaked, soft topped engineman's cap, four square, and tilted slightly forward, with his fresh pinkish complexion set off by a magnificent white and bushy walrus moustache. He dressed in that manner favoured by a majority of footplate men when, for ease of movement, his blue cotton jacket was fastened by a single button, high up, against his collar, a tradition going back to the beginning of steam locomotion, as early photographs show.

Well turned out, and beautifully brushed up, he was particular about his appearance, one of the few drivers who could climb off his engine, after a long day, unmarked by his labours. What then of the nickname he carried with such distinction? Apparently, so the story went, he had entered into an altercation with a signalman, somewhere in the further reaches of the H&BR, an altercation which had become rather heated, and which he was in danger of losing, until he played his trump card: "Now Mr Bobby (signalman), I don't want to hear anymore; you must remember this, you is only a signalman, whilst I'm an ingin driver, and as you know, we is the cream." With these immortal words, Cream closed the argument, and from that moment Driver X earned his small niche in the annals of footplate lore, and a 'handle' he carried to his grave.

Next from that band of deep-rooted stalwarts—driver Alfred Drewton Marshall. Mark well his middle name. His father was employed by the H&BR as signalman at the lonely Drewton West signal box deep in Drewton Dale. In an idyllic and sheltered position alongside the clear Weedley Springs which, as a fountain, burst pure and silvery from just beyond the railway boundary fence, before passing beneath the railway as a stream on a bed of gleaming chalk, its banks in the spring a riot of golden primroses. And for company, a few sheep grazing the rolling hillsides, and of course, not forgetting the passing trains at that time. Drewton West signal box's sole purpose was to 'work forward' through Drewton tunnel, the heavy coal trains, pounding against the grade, along the sinuously winding Drewton Dale, before making the final assault on the Wolds through Drewton itself.

It was said of Alfred Drewton Marshall, or simply 'Drewton', as he was familiarly known, that his father, so taken with his employment by the H&BR and the beauty of his place of work, named his eldest child in honour of them both. That may well be the explanation for his unusual middle name. There might also be another reason. My future father-in-law, also a signalman, coincidentally spent a period of time in the same box, having rented a single room in the nearest village, South Cave. Occasionally his wife, weather permitting, and when the tiny accommodation palled and became tedious, would walk over the silent hills, and make her way by a narrow path through belts of trees to join her husband. It was a path long-used, and Drewton Marshall's mother would undoubtedly have used the same path to see her husband. One day, perhaps, (after work, of course) when the sun was still warm, the grass fresh and green, and dotted thickly with flowers of the field, and the air thick with scent from that lonely queen of the meadows, meadowsweet, maybe in those quiet and peaceful surroundings with only the songbirds for company, Alfred Drewton Marshall was conceived? Perhaps it's also no coincidence that the woman who was to become the love of my life, and whose father was also a signalman at Drewton West, was born at South Cave, and baptised in the village church there.

Step up to the mark now, driver Marley Burns, an eccentric, short, middle aged man built like a barrel, and as strong as a plough horse, whose feats of strength were the stuff of legend. One such was his ability to lift prodigious weights, never better exemplified when, as a young fireman, in company with others of his ilk, he came across a pair of waggon wheels outside the machine shop, waiting to be profiled. "Bet you can't lift a pair of those wheels," suggested one of his friends. At first Marley found it difficult getting a grip on the broad axle, but transferring it into the crook of his arms, and straightening up, lifted both wheels and axle well clear of the rails they rested on.

Not content, Marley, using his immense strength, slowly swung the wheels, before dropping them clear of the rails, remarking with a chuckle, "That'll mek 'em scratch their heads when they find them derailed!"

As a young man, with Hull fair in town, and a pint or two of Moors' & Robson's under his belt, and ready for anything, he was won't to frequent the fair's boxing booths, where for all his strength, he was no match for the fleet footed ex-pros who, by taking on all-comers for a three minute round, earned their crust of bread. As Marley stood flat footed, and as rooted as when firing an engine, the former pugs danced around him, evading his wild swings, then gently (relatively speaking) sitting him down on the canvas as the bell rang.

Unfortunately, he had a habit of grabbing any cleaner or young fireman in a bear hug, and almost squeezing the life out of them, sometimes having to be warned by other drivers, "That's enough, Marley, let him go."

I once witnessed a moment of high drama between Marley and a fireman: seeing Marley approaching I dodged out of his way by hiding on an engine, so Marley instead went for the fireman, who having just drawn his shovel was on his way to his engine. Hidden from view, I heard the fireman warn Marley, "Come near me, Marley, and I'll hit you with this bloody shovel."

Marley, not liking the steel in the fireman's voice or the look on his face, decided he had an appointment elsewhere. I never fired to him, but it was said, once on the footplate, he was a good considerate mate.

Yet Marley's eccentricities extended further. The most obvious, his unusual mode of dress to work, for he spurned wearing blues, which may have been a throwback to the early days on the H&BR, when its engine crews had to be content with only a cap and overcoat for uniform. Instead he wore ordinary civilian trousers and jacket. But what set him apart, and bizarre as it may seem, from his top pocket a coloured hankie dangled at all times, whilst of all things, he invariably turned up for work wearing a stiff white dicky front and dicky bow tie. It would be many long years before I witnessed another driver, dressed in similar fashion, mount his engine and drive off.

Next we have Rabbit Jack, a tall, spare, lanky sort of man. Born and bred in the country, and still a countryman at heart, he lived in the nearby village of Anlaby, a mile or so up the line from Springhead, and a village bisected by a H&BR main line embankment, where it gained height to assault the Wolds, and an embankment along which Rabbit Jack walked, to and from work. But this stretch of railway, being largely in open country, his instincts drove him to lay rabbit snares along the way. Stuffing the proceeds from this activity into his overcoat pockets, he was welcomed at Springhead with open arms by all.

Also drifting out of the mists of time, driver Tommy Whitehead, whose snow white head of hair vindicated his surname. A gentle, softly spoken man who, after oiling his engine, loved nothing better than to find someone to talk to. Looking for a sympathetic and friendly ear, heavy oil feeder held in both hands, he effected a special look of pleading, as if half afraid he was about to be spurned. But there was the rub: those in the 'know' were prepared for what was to come, the ignorant, less so. As Tommy became more engrossed in the conversation, so the spout of his feeder slowly began to droop, decanting a trickle of thick engine oil. The more fortunate might only find their footwear swamped; those less so received the oil down the front of their blues, and some of those more affected might later find one of their jacket pockets oozing oil. Those acquainted with this problem kept a wary eye on Tommy's feeder, warning him, "Get that spout up a bit, Tommy, whilst we're talking."

For those readers unacquainted with locomotive fire irons and their use, let me explain the purpose of two of them. The first, known as a 'straight dart' was formed from a long stout iron rod, one end being shaped into a round handle, and the other, the working end, forged into the shape of a large blunted arrow head. It was used for knocking up clinker along the length of the firebox, when cleaning a fire. With it came its companion, a bent dart. Made by bending a straight dart at right angles, and used for dislodging clinker from those hard-to-get-at back corners, and equally difficult areas below the firehole door, from where the fireman was able to push the dislodged and broken clinker forward for disposal. On tender engines, the fire irons were carried on the tender, and restrained from falling off by suitable brackets. However in the event of a collision, these in no way prevented the fire irons being hurled into the cab, often with fatal consequences for the crew. On the other hand, a side tank engine carried its fire irons much more safely, on the fireman's side tank top. Unfortunately lacking experience with any form of saddle tank engine, I am at a loss to know where, or how, or indeed if they did carry fire irons at all.

Step into the frame now our final worthy from that band of long-gone but gallant enginemen. A driver formally as tall and slim as the proverbial garden rake, or if you prefer, as tall and slim as a straight dart. In stoic silence he endured the pain of a bad back, made worse by the constant jarring and long hours on the footplate, fighting the 'raging main', leaving him round shouldered, bent over, and with a spine twisted like a corkscrew, giving his workmates no other option than to nickname him, Bent Dart.

Historically the administration of a locomotive shed was in the capable hands of former footplate men, who, because of failing eyesight, physical injuries, or other disabilities, had been forced to relinquish the footplate grade, filling instead the positions of running foreman, cleaner foreman, storekeeper, roster clerk, timekeeper, etc. Most sheds, and Springhead was no exception, carried one or two odd jobs men, who in local farming circles were descriptively known as 'Tommy Owt'. Men able to turn their hands to most things, but who mainly kept the shed and ash pits clean and tidy, gathering up fire irons discarded as burnt or worn out, for attention by the blacksmith, and dealing with anything about the shed and its surroundings which might offend the critical eye of George Gregory, the shedmaster.

One of that ilk, yet not of that ilk, was the pitiful figure of Wobbly Walt, who aided by a stout staff, was sometimes seen making his slow, painful and erratic way around the yard. His progress was marked by the jerky and disjointed movements of his legs which, failing to keep time with his body and each other, caused him to sway and veer about in a wildly irregular manner, a condition not helped by him becoming morbidly obese. To the footplate staff, whose thoughts and ideas were largely influenced by the engines they were closely linked to, it was evident that both knee joints were worn and loose and needed re-bushing. But worse, because of the jerky uncertain movements of his feet and legs, it was generally agreed his valve events were way out of sync, and needed resetting. But, when known, the truth regarding his distressing condition was much more harrowing. Imagine Wobbly Walt not as a broken man, but rather as a fine strapping senior fireman, full of life and vigour, who on the night in question had booked on to work the 11pm Night Mail, on its nightly, hell for leather dash, along the H&B main line. It was a foul night for anyone on the footplate, but especially for H&B crews, who only had Matthew Stirling's apology of a cab for protection.

For Wobbly and his veteran mate, the night had got off to a bad start. Instead of their regular engine, one of the new Class 'J' 4-4-0, they had been landed with an older and smaller Class 'H1' 2-4-0, whose cabs were even more Spartan. Not content with that, congestion inside the shed had forced them to prepare the engine outside, in the dark, where both were exposed to a night of freezing winds and blinding snow showers. After drawing the engine's stores, which included ample cotton waste, and a thick white cotton sweat rag apiece, Wobbly checked out his engine. Finding all in order, he turned his attention to the sight feed lubricator, filling it with thick black cylinder oil before opening its steam valve. One last task remained, taking his 'black oil' bottle he left the cab to fill the two ball lubricators affixed to the two cylinder covers, and which in the case of the 'H1' Class, were discreetly hidden beneath a hinged covering plate, located below the smokebox door. A door whose locking bar and bolt he would check at the same time, as part of the routine.

Meanwhile the driver, his work completed, had moved into the shelter of the shed for a few moments respite, before moving off and running light engine to Cannon Street station for his train. By the light from his flaming paraffin torch he checked his pocket watch, and with a little time to spare, filled his pipe and lit up. Suddenly his reverie was shattered by a long drawn out scream from the direction of his engine. Stumbling over, he was met by a scene of horror. His fireman had slipped on the snow-covered plating in front of the smokebox. Unable to help himself, he had sat down hard on an engine lamp bracket, and now lay bloody and impaled, his paralysed legs hanging helpless over the edge of the front buffer beam. By the time others arrived, alerted by his screams, he had lapsed into merciful unconsciousness. When lifted off the bracket, so extensive were his injuries, it was immediately obvious, only urgent medical attention could save his life.

To that end, Wobbly's inert body, covered by several overcoats to keep him as warm as possible, was placed on the footboards of the engine he was about to have manned, which was about to follow the same path made every night, when it ran tender first, light engine, to pick up its train stabled at Cannon Street station. In the meantime, alerted by Cannon Street, at that time only a short distance from Hull's premier hospital, the elegant Georgian, Hull Royal Infirmary (later wantonly demolished in the brutal mid-20th-century era), its horse drawn ambulance, with every minute counting, was being whipped through the streets. On arrival at Cannon Street, Wobbly, still unconscious, was quickly driven to the hospital, where surgeons battled heroically to save his life.

When Wobbly eventually returned, a broken man unfit for footplate work, the H&BR taking him under its sheltering wings, found a place for him in a corner of the stores, where warm and dry and sheltered from winter's icy blast, which had treated him so cruelly, he spent the remainder of his working life polishing and trimming locomotive headlamps gauge lamps, and making wool trimmings. Trimmings, made in a variety of ways, to lubricate locomotive moving parts. On my transfer to the Locomotive Department, I enrolled in Springhead's Mutual Improvement class, which met each Sunday morning in a room provided, and discussed engine management and the Rule Book. The highlight came one Sunday, when a trip to Doncaster plant was arranged. There a young engineer spent most of his Sunday showing us around the silent and deserted workshops, explaining in an entertaining and humorous manner the purpose and workings of each. The pièce de résistance was the large and lofty erecting shop, with many engines under repair, or in the course of erection. At the head of these, on its wheels, with its boiler plated over, stood the plant's magnum opus, Edward Thompson's rebuilding of number 4470, the 4-6-2 Pacific, Great Northern. The engineer's enthusiasm for the project has remained with me all my life, particularly when explaining the draughting arrangements in the smokebox, which he was at pains to point out, at ten feet long was the longest formed by Doncaster.

By mid-March 1944, with the end of war and its miseries in sight, and my career blossoming, I was blissfully unaware that my not uncomfortable world was about to end. Returning home from an early Saturday firing turn I was horrified to find my mother in a state of collapse, her face broken and bloody, both arms a series of bruises, and her right hand sliced to the bone. Shocked by her injuries I cleaned them and dressed her wound. When asked what had happened, she told me she had fallen while changing curtains and in an effort to save herself, had gashed her hand. It seemed a strange explanation for multiple injuries, but at the time, one that I accepted. As I became more worldly wise, I began to recognise her injuries were consistent with a violent and sustained attack. At that time a regiment of Algerian soldiers were stationed in Cottingham, many of them in the chapel's school rooms. It seems to add up: to them, a woman out at 5 am in the morning, as she went to stoke the chapel boiler, could mean but one thing: an approach; a sharp rebuttal; unfulfilled passions: violent retribution!

Tough and physically strong, mother soon recovered from her injuries until, a few weeks later, arriving home from work, I was dismayed to find her in bed. For a woman who enjoyed perfect health, and to which staying in bed an anathema, I knew something was seriously wrong, and despite her protestations I contacted the doctor. His examination, when he eventually came, was brief, and ended with him advising that she had a feverish cold and ought to stay in bed for a day or two. Despite his calming prognosis, and unable to get out of bed, her condition quickly became worse. More thoroughly alarmed I again contacted the doctor. This time his examination was more careful and ended by him saying a few days in hospital would do her good. Within an hour an ambulance arrived, and mother, looking drawn and frail, was stretchered into it and driven away.

Monday evening gave me an opportunity to visit her, when to my astonishment and relief I found her, not as I expected, laid prostrate in bed very ill, but sat up cheerful and in good heart. As I entered the ward she saw me, and for the only time in my life I can remember, she greeted me with a smile of welcome, something I have treasured ever since. I left the hospital buoyed up by the change in her, content she was in good hands, and confident she would soon be home. I intended calling the following night, but was thwarted when called to a firing turn. Leaving work, after missing visiting hour, I stopped at the first phone box and phoned through to the hospital, where after some difficulty, I got through to the ward. After some to-ing and fro-ing the ward sister came on the phone to tell me briefly "Mrs Blackburn died this morning"[11]. Expecting nothing

---

[11] Cause: septicemia.

but good news and her imminent discharge, this hammer blow almost felled me. Distraught, in a state of shock, I returned to a dark and now alien house, a house empty and devoid of life. Wracked by grief and alone, the silence of the night bore down heavily, and I began to experience an overwhelming sense of loneliness and isolation, so deep and profound I began to believe there was nobody on Earth but myself. The mental trauma continued late into the night, when eventually, the sound of a British heavy bomber passing overhead, from north to south, broke the spell. In the face of a dark uncertain future, the sound lifted my spirits, and went a long way to reassuring me I was not totally alone in the world.

With my two brothers away in some distant part of the world and unavailable, I found myself, aged sixteen, isolated, alone, and with the weight of responsibility resting on my shoulders. And adding to my concerns, I was keenly aware I was under-age and classed as an orphan, and if this came to the attention of the authorities I would be sent to an orphanage. The thought of this filled me with dread. For to the best part of my knowledge, the nearest orphanage was many miles away, and that fact, together with the restrictions placed on inmates must certainly spell the end of my railway career. In the meantime it was essential I got in touch with my place of work, and explain the situation I was in, and if possible, come to some arrangement with them. Booking on the next morning, I poured out my troubles to an understanding cleaner foreman, who without hesitation granted me a week's leave of absence, to see to my mother's affairs and organise her funeral.

As I started to overcome the waves of distress which numbed me, the harsh realisation came that I had to do something about my mother and make arrangements for the funeral. Adding to this burden was the grim fact that, apart from a few coppers carried in my pocket, I was without money, whilst a forlorn glance into my mother's purse, left in the house, merely confirmed what I expected, that it was equally empty. Such an insuperable problem left me disorientated, and I was unable to see any way forward. In this state of distress I spent the rest of the day, until, with evening coming on, I saw with a tremendous burst of relief, too difficult to describe, my friend and guardian angel, Auntie Pop, my mother's sister, who lived in London, and who on her rare visits always made a fuss of me, steaming at full speed to my rescue!

She swept into the house with a "Now young man," a gentle emphasis on the 'man' part, "I'm staying to look after things, and I want your help." Exhausted and broken in spirit I willingly laid all my burdens at her feet. Thereafter things became a blur until later.

After mother's funeral Auntie Pop put her arm around my shoulder. "I've got to go back to London," she informed me. "You know you can't stay here by yourself, and so I've arranged for you to go to live with Uncle Ernie in Hull." Uncle Ernie, my mother's brother, his lungs scarred in World War I, was left with a chronic cough, and lived with his family in a small terraced house in a narrow back street. The house, hemmed in on all sides by other terraced houses (unlike my family house which stood alone and open), was shut off from the sun, leaving it permanently in the shade.

Yet the house and its location held some surprises for a country lad accustomed to the myriad sounds of the country. This back street, empty of vehicles, and to a large extent pedestrians, without trees or shrubs to sway and rustle in the breeze, and by extension, bird song to catch the ear, seemed, for the centre of a large city, oddly quiet and peaceful. No longer did I wake to the cacophony of the 'dawn chorus', the gentle lowing of cattle in a nearby field, nor even to the loud and sometimes persistent crowing of unruly cockerels; but rather, I woke every day to an eerie and unaccustomed silence.

Despite being treated with the utmost kindness and consideration, I realised I was proving to be a burden on an already overcrowded family, which consisted of two girls, about my age, and two younger boys, who together with mother and father, were crammed into two small bedrooms, whilst I, because of the odd hours I worked, which in itself must have been a cause of disruption, slept in a small box room. Eventually I found lodgings with an elderly widow in a tiny 'two-up, two-down' terraced house in another part of town. But in the meantime, and this must be something for the psychologists, I found it very difficult to come to terms with the loss of my mother, despite her lifetime's rejection of me, and I felt compelled, with every fibre in my body, to visit her grave (which was that of my father too, although this compulsion was always focused on my mother) whenever possible, sometimes even in the dark, when once, tripping and stumbling over the heaving turf, I almost walked into another open grave.

Even my visits to the cemetery had moments of sheer horror as, when shortly after the funeral, and feeling in desperate need to be at the grave, I arrived to discover the soil on the grave not yet settled, but sunk below the level of the surrounding ground, with the outline of the grave standing in sharp relief. At this late stage of the war, with everything in short supply, coffins were being made of thin plywood or even cardboard. It was obvious to me that mother's coffin had all too quickly collapsed. Deeply distressed by what I had found, and its implications, it was some time before I found the courage to again visit her grave.

But life had to go on, and being booked on more and more firing turns, I found my work, and the friends I had made there, a source of comfort and hope. With springtime came a lifting of the spirits, and my first main line firing turn, bringing with it all my pent-up excitement. Not only was I about to renew, however fleetingly, my appointment with Eppleworth Viaduct and the secret lookout position which had proved such a delight in the past, but the fields where I had laboured in the mud and snow, and which, in the end, had set me on my present course which, as it was about to now unfold before me, meant I was to discover those mysteries of the railway which had previously teased and tantalised me. And this, with the added spice of the firing turns there and back in daylight hours, giving me the opportunity to study the railway and its works.

At the stores I had been handed, just for the trip, a good shovel, a slacker pipe and hand brush, to sweep up any bits of coal which might fly about, as I reduced large knobs coal to a more manageable size. For drivers, and rightly so, were particular about footplates being kept clean and dust free. Feeling proud and very important, and for the benefit of anyone watching, I carried my gear over to the engine, with what I hoped was the air of a seasoned main line fireman. At that time, Springhead's stud of main line locomotives consisted entirely of J. G. Robinson's tough, versatile and free-steaming 2-8-0 tender engines, LNER Class 'O4'. And on this day, mine still carried its Railway Operating Division flaming bomb and chevrons, denoting its service with the Royal Engineers in France during the First World War.

My driver, as expected, was an elderly man, who greeted me warmly, perhaps one of those who in the past had never failed to give me a wave and cheerful smile when passing Eppleworth years before. He would have been tipped off regarding my lack of main line experience, but didn't show it. The engine had been prepared and made ready, and as the driver went round the engine's oil boxes and oil cups, 'putting in trimmings', I weighed up my side of things. A quick peek at the fire showed it clean and spread around the box, the brick arch solid and in good order, and the tube plate free of bird nesting. Things there looked good, but not so when I had a squint at the contents of the tender. By that stage of the war, things on the Home Front were desperate, and this applied to coal as well. To eke out the supply to locomotives, it was increasingly being mixed with large square briquettes, whose composition remained a secret, and whose dark chocolate brown colour did nothing to inspire confidence in its ability to produce steam, for they burnt as dead as the proverbial door knocker, and for a firemen they offered only two alternatives. First, boot them over the side when they arrived on the shovelling plate. This was the preferred option, as the briquettes lining the trackside from end to end testified; although it is certain, in those times of severe want, Permanent Way men and line side farmers viewed this bounty as a gift from heaven, and which helped to fill coal houses for years to come. The alternative, by using the quartering hammer, was break them up into fist size lumps, and by keeping them away from the front of the firebox at all costs, feed them sparingly into the back corners, where they helped to fill a space. Unfortunately this option added to the fireman's workload, without in any way producing, in the way of steam, an adequate return for his labours.

Once I'd made up the fire, and with a full boiler, and up to the mark in steam, we moved off the shed and down the engine line, which was overlooked and controlled from the nearby Locomotive Junction cabin. At Springhead, exit was requested by a simple three pops on the whistle, a signal usually found unnecessary as the line was always under observation, except when darkness, fog or falling snow obstructed the signalman's view. On our approach, with both main lines clear of traffic, the signalman pulled off the engine line signal, allowing us to leave the yard, and cross over to the Up main line, and once over, reverse the few yards into Springhead's extensive Up departure sidings, and on to our train, where the guard already waiting, exchanged information, load, etc., with the driver.

Anxiously awaiting the guard's "Right away!" and excited by what lay ahead, but concerned over my ability to cope, for long experience at Eppleworth, watching engines thumping up the grade, left me in no doubt what the first few miles of 'collar work'[12] meant, I fretted and fidgeted, until the driver reassured me, "Don't worry, lad, I'll keep you right." With only an engine-length of level track before hitting the main line and Little Weighton Bank, a cold engine, and the marked retarding effect of a sharp turnout on a long heavy train, I knew the first half mile would show me what I was in for.

To my heartfelt relief, I found I was blessed with a free steaming engine. And as a boost to my confidence, I was now experienced enough, to keep the boiler

---

[12] A farming expression, relating to horses undertaking heavy work, requiring much pulling on their collars.

up to the mark and, under the driver's instructions, especially where changes in gradients occurred, I was able to relish the whole experience.

My senses, it seemed, had become dulled by living in a dirty bombed out city, where heaps of rubble from the destruction remained untouched, and where the rank smell of burnt and wrecked buildings hung over the city, offending both eyes and nose. Never, I felt, had the rolling Yorkshire Wolds looked so clean and beautiful, or the richly scented air so sweet. That day's lasting impressions burnt deep in my memory. Standing firing on a hot roaring locomotive, as the footplate jarred under my feet, and the exhaust roared over the countryside was, I felt, the high point of my long-held and cherished desires. As I passed high above the field where, years before, I had stood alongside faithful old Violet, as she sheltered me from the worst of the wind and sleet, and where I had vowed to become a footplateman, I raised my cap in salute to her memory. The field had been sown with beans and, now in full flower, that heady and most fragrant of plants scented the air in clouds. On through Skidby cutting with its graceful brick overbridges, and the approach to Big Hill, or as more generally known, Little Weighton cutting, whose sheer 85 foot cliffs, carved out of hard Wold chalk, never failed to make an impression on me, and which years before, and impossibly far distant, had fired my imagination and desire to see more.

With an early warning from the driver to ease on the firing, we breasted the summit at the sleepy hamlet of Little Weighton, before plunging into the dank and gloomy interior of Drewton tunnel which, with a length of 1 mile and 354 yards, was the longest on the H&BR, and marked the beginning of a seven-mile descent into the Vale of York. My memory of first passing through Drewton is of the driver shutting off, then utter steam-filled blackness engulfing us, the jar and thud of rail joints, and the groaning from the screwed-down tender hand brake reverberating from the walls of the tunnel. Bursting out into the brilliant sunshine, and carefully negotiating the falling gradients through the winding Newtondale, with its short Weedley and Sugar Loaf tunnels, gave me the opportunity to wonder at the scale of engineering required to conquer this quiet corner of the Wolds, before the driver opened out, as he bustled his train over the 20 or so miles of Vale of York flatlands.

The rich farmland, spread out broad and far, only altered when the wide and fast flowing River Ouse, the historic boundary between the East and West Ridings, and the site of what was without doubt the glory of the line, the massive River Ouse swing bridge, came into view. Hammering through its 250 feet centre span of open lattice work with its ornate cabin perched high atop its central span, some 650 tons in all, resting on a huge masonry pivot. This must be the bridge I had heard spoken of when a schoolboy, and which had first sparked my interest, filling my wondering childhood with visions, dreams and desires. In subsequent trips, gazing down at the turbulent waters eddying, boiling and buffeting the noble central column rising from the river, I allowed my mind to wander a little, making me wonder, as I still do, how it had been erected in the first place, and how it was able to withstand, stable and unmoved, the weight it had to carry, especially those times when two trains crossed together.

We drew up at Carlton Towers to replenish our tender tank in preparation for the stiff work ahead, tackling the rising grades which characterised the hilly South Yorkshire coal fields where we met a series of junctions leading to branch lines up to individual collieries, and which often, it seemed to me, were miles from anywhere. Each was guarded by a lonely signal box whose occupant, standing at an open window, waved us on our way. Hereabouts I received something of a shock when, for the first time since leaving Springhead, I noticed the square face of an H&BR mile post, which boldly announced 'Alexandra Dock—42 miles'. In this day and age 42 miles may seem of little consequence, but to me, whose world had been governed by the distance my legs could carry me, 42 miles and still travelling onwards, was difficult to comprehend, and I began to wonder how all this was going to end. But the engine was streaming freely, my injector working perfectly, and as common sense overruled my nervousness, and reassured, I settled down to enjoy the remainder of the trip.

In due course we arrived at Cudworth, our destination, and home of the Monckton Main Colliery, where after the driver had picked his way through a confusing tangle of conflicting lines and junctions, once belonging to both the former Midland Railway and Great Central Railway, we parked our train in Monckton Main Colliery sidings, from where we ran light to Cudworth shed, an eight-road through shed in the style of Springhead. Here we turned, took water, and carried out engine duties, mine being to clean the fire for the return journey. Returning light to Monckton Main Colliery, we picked up our train of 45 coal waggons, plus brake van, about 700 tons on the drawer bar, from where the driver, after receiving the guard's "Right Away!" slowly and carefully took up the slack in the train's loose couplings, until a flourish from the guards van assured him he hadn't inadvertently broken any couplings, and the train was complete and underway. So, feeling confident and in good heart, I looked forward to whatever the return trip might bring.

By now I had come to recognise I was blessed with a driver who, by taking advantage of every down grade, and letting the train gather momentum and roll, was prepared to ease the burden of firing a little. After once again drinking in the wonders of the River Ouse swing bridge, and shortly after passing Wallingfen station, and just beyond its stout girder bridge over the Market Weighton canal, we met, rising at first imperceptibly out of the flat flood plain, the long embankment, the start of an eight-mile slog up to and through that obstacle to all east-bound trains, Drewton tunnel. Feeling the rising embankment, the engine's beat took on a more serious and strident note, as the driver opened out and lengthened his cutoff. With the engine at full throttle, extreme care had to be practised when firing as the heavy exhaust drew smaller coal off the shovel and without deft wrist work, deposited it in a growing heap under the brick arch, to the detriment of the engine's ability to produce steam at the rate required. At the same time, on the approach to South Cave station, I was acutely aware it was time to prepare my fire for the haul through the long tunnel. Ideally my fire would be burnt through, leaving the chimney clear of smoke, and so arranged it would not only take us through the tunnel without further firing, but carry us down the bank to Springhead. And as an added twist to the exercise, to avoid the enmity of the Dust Hole men, it would allow me hand over a fire not so run down that it had to be fired during the disposal of the train, or perhaps worse, leave them a thick unmanageable fire, most of which had to be 'paddled out' using a variety of the engine's fire irons when arriving on shed.

Winding our way through the sinuous and magnificent Drewton Dale, a relic, I am told, of the Ice Age and subsequent melt water, I had prepared a thick but well burnt through and level fire, and now committed, all I could do was sit back and hope the traces of smoke at the chimney top would clear before we entered Drewton. Rounding the last curve before the entrance we found it blocked by thick clouds of sulphurous smoke rolling out slowly from the tunnel entrance and filling the cutting. In the moments before diving into this murk, the driver drew his head into the shelter of the cab. In that cold, damp and slippery tunnel, the passage through was fraught with many perils, not least the danger of slipping to a standstill. 100 yards outside the tunnel entrance we had passed through a set of trailing catch points, positioned to prevent the rear portion of a divided and runaway train from entering the rear section, but also effectively preventing a driver from setting back out of the tunnel, and trying again after slipping to a standstill.

With the driver's hand on the regulator, ready to steady the engine if instinct warned him it was about to slip, we passed, in the blink of an eye, from bright sunlight into a profound darkness devoid of all light. At the same time, the driver, lowering his head, protected his eyes from the maelstrom of white-hot fire which came ricocheting from the tunnel roof in all directions, many particles bouncing and fizzing around the cab, which on entering the tunnel had been engulfed in steam and smoke from the tunnel's reeking smoke-bound interior. At the same time he shouted across for me to open the engine's front sanders and continue working them through the tunnel. Now confined, the train's hard riding on the unyielding rock floor reverberated through the cab, setting anything which could move rattling and vibrating. With his eyes protected by the peak of his cap, the driver, every sense alert, stared blindly through his weather glass into 'nothing'. Whilst a thundering exhaust beat around our ears, increasing every sense of being at the centre of some kind of Dante's Inferno, I watched with curiosity and interest, the tunnel's reek being drawn back into the white-hot glare of the open flapper plate, where I suppose it provided some kind of recycling. Halfway through, with plenty of water in the boiler, I knocked off my injector, allowing me leeway to fill up afterwards and keep the engine quiet on the drift down to Springhead.

Then, through the weather glass, as indistinct and vague as the first morning, I spied a faint lightening, which rapidly grew stronger and more distinct, until, trailing streamers of steam from the engine and every waggon, we burst out into sunlight and clean pure air. Little Weighton signal box, half way between the tunnel and Little Weighton station, marked with exactitude the descent of Little Weighton Bank when, after shutting off, and with the train beginning to exert its weight, the driver ordered me to screw the hand brake hard on. Now relaxed and content, the driver basking in the late afternoon sun, lit up his pipe, and under the control of both hand brake and steam brake, we trundled down to our final destination, Springhead and its relieving Dust Hole crew, at a steady 15 mph.

Not every passage through Drewton went as smoothly. A few months later, shortly after the end of the war in Europe, Springhead began to receive ex-army, eight-coupled WD engines. Generally known among the staff as "Them army ingins", they were in good mechanical condition, still retaining the army's flat, earth-coloured finish, as well the insignia of former army units. Unlike the locomotives we were familiar with, but in keeping with the 'LMS practise', these engines carried the injector clack valves immediately behind the chimney, perhaps the most advantageous position from an economical working position as well as an engineering point of view, but in the rough and tumble of everyday working, anything but helpful.

On a Down train, hauled by a WD working forward through the tunnel, disaster struck when about a train length inside, and without warning, the fireman's injector clack valve stuck open, discharging the contents of the boiler at a furious and alarming rate. There was no other option than to keep going, but with the imperative of either freeing the recalcitrant valve or, failing that, shutting it down using the clack nut on the clack box. The driver, no longer a young man, handed the engine over to his fireman, and equipped with the appropriate inch and three eighth spanner, and against everything the engine and the tunnel could throw at him, heroically felt his way along the running plate, and by some supreme effort, in unimaginable conditions, managed to haul himself behind the bellowing chimney and its hurricane of cinders, and by tapping the clack box, succeeded in seating the valve. He then managed to return to the safety and shelter of the cab but, suffering from exhaustion, burnt hands and smoke inhalation, he ended up making an extended visit to Hull Royal Infirmary.

My route to and from work carried me on a well-worn 'trod' past the former H&BR two-road paint shop, long disused, and with its large double doors apparently firmly locked. When passing, I scarcely gave it a thought, except to regret such a fine building was no longer in use, until leaving work one afternoon I spied one of the small wicket doors, set in the main doors, slightly open. Intrigued by its silent interior, and my spirit of adventure fully roused, I decided to explore. After making sure I was unobserved, I slipped inside, to find the last thing I ever expected meeting my astonished eyes. Packed closely together around the walls were numerous grey-painted four-inch naval guns, whilst the centre of the wood block floor was piled high with hundreds of obsolete rifles. These were mainly single shot, single barrelled, Martini-Henry cavalry carbines, but also many hundreds of the American 'cowboy rifle', the low-powered and inaccurate Winchester .44 underlever repeating rifle. On examination these appeared to be in 'as new' unfired condition throughout. I had, in all innocence, stumbled on a huge arsenal of weapons, with enough rifles (though of dubious worth) to equip several regiments, or the IRA perhaps, for the next 100 years.

But in all this, what has remained a lasting mystery is this curious fact that, whilst the former H&BR men spoke fondly and at length about 'The Works' and all its doings, waxing lyrical over the care lavished in the paint shop on preparing, painting, varnishing and finishing locomotives and carriages to the highest possible standards, and although the weapons must have been stockpiled in full view of the Springhead staff and required the active involvement of many of them, not a hint, not a whisper escaped, regarding the new use the paint shop was being put to.

Chapter 9
Promotion to Fireman

Come Friday afternoon, whilst waiting in the booking-on hall to draw my weekly 'screw', having already scanned the next day's duty roster in vain, I turned to the drivers' notice board, which I found hard going, being of little or no interest, for it spoke of matters and places somewhere in the outer reaches of the system and as such far outside my knowledge. The notice board consisted mainly of a list of warnings: speed restrictions caused by pit subsidence on some unknown branch line, perhaps; or warnings of a defective signal somewhere; or maybe a restricted water supply at an essential water column. Somewhat disinterested in this obscure information, I nevertheless ploughed on, when at the bottom, against all odds, I read a notice that changed my life forever. Looking back I see it not only as a miracle, but also a matter of 'what ifs'. What if, tired of reading a boring list of unfamiliar place names, I had turned my attention elsewhere? What if someone had interrupted my reading? What if I had been called to draw my pay before reaching the bottom of the list? However, none of these things happened, and hence I read the notice that galvanised me, sending my pulse racing: a notice stating that a vacancy existed at Botanic Gardens for a fireman!

The surge of excitement and hope quickly faded when I realised that among Hull's four sheds, others more senior to me might like a stab at a 'plum' job. Unaware of how to apply, or even if the position was open to me, I turned to the cleaner foreman for advice. I had found him a kindly man who seemed to favour me a little. He it was who arranged for me to have time off for my mother's funeral, and who knew my circumstances. Yes, I could apply he informed me. Then he asked me, "Do want the job?" Did I want the job? You bet I did. My eagerness must have been obvious when I asked if he thought I had a chance. He looked me over thoughtfully. "Yes, you might well," he replied, and to my astonishment, and perplexity, gave me a wink.

By now it was late 1945, and I was 17 years of age. The long drawn out war had finally ended, and we were busy with coal pouring down the main line for export through Hull docks. This meant plenty of footplate work, and in the excitement I barely gave a thought to my application for promotion, which in any case I thought had little if any chance of success. Booking off after a hard day of Dust Hole work, the timekeeper handed me a typed memo. His voice held a note of congratulation. "Is this what you're looking for, Blackie?" Scarcely able to believe my good fortune, it confirmed my promotion to fireman, and instructed me to report to Botanic Gardens at 4:50 am the following Monday, for my rostered turn of duty. Over the following years, looking back, I've often puzzled over my unexpected promotion, and can only conclude there was more to the cleaner foreman's wink than I first realised.

Having accepted an honourable and responsible calling, my days as one of a gang of carefree, and at times, mischievous, cleaners had ended. Here I bowed in the direction of 'The Cream' and those other hardy footplate men I knew, including my guard and mentor, the cleaner foreman. It was a calling I coveted and felt passionate about. Now it was time to put away childish things, time to grow up, and time to act the man, and embrace the discipline and responsibilities that life on the footplate demanded. But first I had some sorting out to do. As my excitement subsided, my first clear thought, in view of the many early shift patterns at Botanic Gardens, was to purchase a loud and sonorous alarm clock. Locomotive sheds I had learned, took a very dim view of footplate men arriving late for work, and very strict discipline was observed regarding this.

With many different shifts, in particular the early ones, arrangements had to be made regarding packing up sandwiches. So short had food become that, to prevent me helping myself, my landlady had kept what little there was under lock and key, and understandably so, given the healthy appetite of a 17-year-old[13]. On the early shifts, breakfast was left out overnight for me to prepare the next morning, consisted, in those lean times, of a small bowl of barely-sweetened porridge, and a cup of weak tea sweetened with ersatz sugar, i.e. a saccharine tablet. The only filling available for packing up sandwiches, which we relied on

---

[13] Rationing continued for a number of years after the war, and in some instances it became even stricter, with bread, that most staple of foodstuffs, being rationed from July 1946 to July 1948.

to get us through the day, was either the rubbery 'bungy'[14] national cheese, or a thin watery jam, the contents of which provided a great deal of head shaking and debate. Its main characteristic was that it quickly soaked into the course grey bread of the day, reducing it to a soggy unpleasant mess. Nevertheless, with bellies often knotted with hunger, it was devoured quickly, although with little enthusiasm. One morning, my landlady primly informed me, "I've got a treat for you this evening for your tea: a bit of rabbit."

Now, I very much like rabbit, and so thanked her and enthusiastically replied that I was very much looking forward to it. That evening, as I sat expectantly down at table, I was greatly disillusioned to find placed before me the cooked head of a rabbit, its grey sightless eye sockets looking up at me forlornly. You can take it from me, there's really not much meat on (or even in) a rabbit's head. "Mmm, lovely," I declared as I delicately chewed on a miniscule sliver from its cheek.

Despite my impatience to take up my new position, the old doubts and fears came back to nag and vex me. I was keenly aware of my lack of experience and how I still lacked the skills of a truly experienced fireman; and reflecting on the amount of steam a speeding passenger locomotive consumed, I wondered if my unpolished firing could possibly satisfy its demands.

However, the following Monday, bursting with excitement and expectation, I arrived at Botanic Gardens to find the booking-on hall filled with men arriving on duty. Some scanning the notices, others examining their engine's individual repair book for anything they needed to check or keep an eye on. They were all strangers to me, yet amongst themselves they joked and passed the time of day in easy familiarity. Among the bustle of men I was an outsider, and ignored, leaving me feeling small and insignificant, and unsure of my place. I approached the booking-on clerk's window, wondering which 'Link' I was about to land in. As probably the youngest fireman on the shed, certainly in terms of seniority, I expected to start at the bottom, and wondered if it was to be the lowly Shunt Link, shunting Paragon Station, together with various yards and sidings; or the even more humble Dust Hole Link, where I would spend my days, on shed, stabling and preparing engines.

Before going further, a description of Hull's Botanic Gardens Locomotive Depot and its various 'Links' is required. 'Botanic' provided the motive power

---

[14] The filling consisting of hard and rubbery 'nationalised' cheese. This cheese was known as 'bungy' for reasons we need not go into here.

for Hull's passenger services. Classed a round shed, though in fact built square, it contained within its cavernous interior two 50-foot turntables and outside one 60-foot turntable, together with the usual offices, stores and machine shops. Towering above it all, and replacing the original coal stage, was a modern mechanical coaling plant. Botanic's allocation of locomotives is now lost in the mists of time, but number one Main Line Link consisted mainly of 'B1' 4-6-0 locomotives, brand new from the works. The first to arrive was 1010, and as if to recapture the LNER glory days, was resplendent in high-gloss apple green lined out with black and white bands. Another Botanic 'B1', which during my time in Spare Link I frequently fired, was the now famous 1306[15]. Number two main line locomotive stock was mainly the 4-4-0 Shires and Hunts with a sprinkling of other types such as 'K3's' and 'B16's' thrown in as and when required. During the war, and for some time after, the shed was graced by a solitary Great Northern (GN) Atlantic, and 2165, a North-Eastern Railway Atlantic. After the war Thompson 2-6-4 'L1' tank engines began to arrive, quickly earning themselves an unenviable reputation[16], but not, I hasten to add for lack of comfort, which was second to none. On fast trains with an 'L1' leading, the first two coaches had to be locked against passengers as the result of an unpleasant fore and aft movement which the 'L1's' generated. Eventually a separate L1 Link was formed.

Spare Link was, as its name implied (and to employ a farming term), a 'Tommy Owt' sort of Link, although in practice it covered mainly number one and number two Main Line Links. Continuing in descending order: Push and Pull Link consisted entirely of the delightful 'G5' (NER Class 'O') 0-4-4 side tanks of late Victorian vintage, adapted for Push and Pull working by means of a vacuum operated intermediate regulator, which in the Push mode was ignored, the fireman operating the regulator. The cabs, however, were comfortable and

---

[15] Since designated '61306', it's one of only two Thompson B1's to have survived, helping haul trains such as the 'Winter Cumbrian Mountain Express' that ran from London Euston to Carlisle in 2019, and used for operating a service from Waterloo to Windsor in Summer 2019, it being the first regular steam-operated service from that London terminus for 52 years.

[16] On paper, at least, the class should have been very free steaming and powerful engines but, in practice, they were not suited to the suburban passenger work to which they were assigned, which wore out axleboxes, crosshead slides and crank bearings in a remarkably short time.

well arranged with excellent foul weather protection. The 'G5' had a remarkable turn of speed for its comparatively small 5-foot 1-inch coupled wheels. Their only fault was the single slide bars with slipper block crossheads. The slide bars picked up dust and dirt especially when running bunker first, this wore the slipper blocks' white metal linings, which in turn affected the piston rod glands, as a result a 'G5' was usually marked moving off enveloped in a cloud of steam.

Tanky Link was composed of Great Northern (GN) 'C12' 4-4-2 tank engines. Dainty, long-legged and light-footed, and designed in the late Victorian era for commuter trains, rather than shunting, it required 12 turns on a stiff screw to put it into reverse, rather than the use of a lever, which was the much more preferred option for shunting purposes. Despite their ladylike appearance, or perhaps because of it, the 'C12's' required gentling, or they would erupt in a fury of spinning coupled wheels and roaring exhaust, and often, to emphasise their displeasure, would pick up their water and froth mightily at their chimney tops and at both valve and piston glands. Often in these circumstances the Ivatt regulator would stick open, much to the consternation of the driver as he fought to close it against water pressure. Not, then, a lady to be trifled with. The 'C12's' of Tanky Link were strengthened, if necessary, by a variety of NER 'A8', 'A7' and Great Central (GC) 'A5's' covering much of the branch line work. Shunt Link men shunted Paragon Station and Sculcoates goods. And finally, the Dust Hole Link the abode of drivers and firemen setting out on the respective careers.

Thrown together in Botanic's pot of locomotives were the odd NER 'D20' 4-4-0 and for a time a couple of H.A. Ivatt's GN '1321' Class (LNER 'D2') 4-4-0 tender engines with 6 feet 7 inch coupled wheels, heartily disliked, especially in winter, for their minimal cabs and lack of seats. Sometimes a former NER Class 'S' 4-6-0, both in original and rebuilt form, appeared, as did an occasional Gresley 'J39' 0-6-0. To strengthen Tanky Link you might find one of Wilson Worsdell's little Class 'P' 0-6-0 tender engines, equally at home on goods or passenger trains, although with only 4 foot 7 inch coupled wheels, working a branch line express into Hull did rather try them.

An interesting commentary on old habits refusing to die might be aired here. At the time about which I'm writing, most if not all of the Botanic enginemen had either served on the former NER, or had fired to former NER men who continued to use NER locomotive classifications, and by continued use passed them on to those of us who had never known the glories of the NER. Both for former NER men, and for us younger men, an NER Atlantic remained not a Class

'6' or '7' but either a 'V' or 'Z'. Similarly an LNER classified 'B16' was still spoken of as an Class 'S', and an LNER 'D20' 4-4-0 endured forever as a Class 'R'. Two types of 4-4-2, the LNER 'A8' and 'A7' tank engines, remained as Class 'D' and 'W' respectively. Wilson Worsdell's small but powerful 0-6-0 tender engines of 1896 vintage, LNER 'J21's' were never anything other than Class 'P', and Wilson Worsdell's small but remarkably agile 0-4-4 tank engines of 1894 remained fixed as Class 'O', which I understand was the last class of NER locomotives to meet the cutter's torch.

Before I leave my survey of Botanic motive power in the early 1950s I must mention a handful of London, Midland and Scotland Railway (LMS) Class '3' 2-6-2 tank engines which, after nationalisation, arrived from nowhere. Unimpressive in all respects, they were engines that visiting LMS crews, by their nods, winks and pointing, seemed glad to be shot of. If they thought they had rid of them on the cheap they were sadly mistaken: in no time Botanic men had the measure of them, condemning them thoroughly with abuse and bad language as little better than useless. So they departed to that never-never land as quickly as they had arrived.

So, getting back to where we left off, namely my 4.50 am arrival that first morning at Botanic, it was with much excitement and perhaps not a little apprehension that I approached the office window and explained who I was. The timekeeper ran his finger down his list. "Ah, here you are, you're in Tanky Link. Ingin 4514. It's on this end table, and you're mating Freddy Durdon."

Thrown completely off balance by my unexpected elevation, I didn't quite grasp what I was told, and in surprise stuttered, "Tanky Link?"

The timekeeper looked at me a bit sharply. "Yes, Tanky Link, and your injin's 4514."

Elated by the thought I had fallen into Tanky Link, with my own engine, and out on the road every day with new horizons to explore, I could hardly contain myself, even if I had much to learn. I hurried into the shed anxious to find my engine and be on with things. There I found her in her 'stall', work stained, war weary and run down, her attractive pre-war lined-out and shaded numbers and lettering almost obscured by years of grime and neglect. On the front buffer beam I was still able to make out the number 4514, her class 'C12' and her home shed, Botanic Gardens. This information, carefully and expertly sign written pre-war, with full shading, not only helped engine crews identify individual locomotives, but when, like the rest of the engine, kept sparkling clean, provided the public with a point of interest.

Introduced by H. A. Ivatt for the Great Northern, and built at Doncaster to an Atlantic wheel arrangement, they were, by any standards, very handsome locomotives. Despite her condition, she looked magnificent, her beautiful proportions set off to perfection by a tall and splendid chimney which towered above her smokebox. This chimney, a masterpiece of Victorian design, was cast in three sections, with a slim elegant waist forming the central part, giving the impression it was effective enough when in action to draw the boiler tubes out of the tube plates. It appeared a throwback to the illustrious Patrick Stirling's famous 'Single Spinners' and perhaps Doncaster had found one in some forgotten corner of the plant and, rather than destroy it, clapped it on to 4514. Unfortunately the performance of Great Northern (GN) Tanky's never matched their good looks, as I was about to find out.

Climbing into the roomy cab, I discovered a layout rather different from the H&BR and GC locomotives I was used to. Missing were the driver's and fireman's footstools, leaving a flat level floor. Unusually, the boiler back plate and its fittings, including the GN pull-out regulator, lay flush with the cab front. And because the former GN Railway frowned on its drivers and firemen sitting about looking untidy, there was a marked lack of seats. For its braking, this class of engine relied entirely on a vacuum brake, which sometimes proved awkward if, when low in steam, the engine had to be turned out of its 'stall'. Then, on the table, with negligible braking power, it became, first here, then there, a frustrating juggling act, as the crew tried to anchor the engine on the table balancing point.

With little or no thought for a cab layout, here a NER engineman might remark, "Cab, what cab!" And with little or no thought for the driver, a distinction of the GN Locomotive Department, the vacuum brake ejector body had its application handle on the right side, which was really a pattern for left drive engines. But on right drive GN Tanky's, the same type of combined ejector and brake handle was mounted, unhelpfully, close to the cab side in a difficult and inaccessible position; a position which prevented the driver using what on a right-hand drive locomotive, would be his left hand, leading me to the conclusion that, to control a Tanky engine whilst keeping a proper lookout, a driver required the neck of a giraffe and the body of a circus contortionist! I mused whether or not it might be more convenient and less stressful if he stood on his head, and applied the brake using the toe of his boot. In these circumstances, spare a thought for any driver shunting all day, often in adverse weather conditions, or in the dark, with one of those perverse and intractable engines. But on this, my first day, it all lay unknown, and shrouded in the future.

On the footplate, in the dim light thrown by a slumbering fire, I checked the steam and water gauges. Satisfied on that score, I made my way over to draw the engine's daily allocation of stores. Unless someone had filched something, the engine's equipment, fire irons, lamps etc., normally remained complete, leaving me only to replenish the engine's two oil 'bottles' (actually tin containers), the larger one with the day's allocation of engine oil, and the smaller with cylinder oil, or as we knew it, 'black oil', so called for its thick treacly consistency and its deep black hue. Even at that late stage of the war, with everything cut to the bone, the LNER still supplied, on a daily basis, its drivers and firemen with a soft, white cotton 'sweat rag' and, in addition, for wiping the driver's hands, his oil feeder and any oil dribbles down the oil bottles, a large bundle of cotton waste, which was then used for wiping down the boiler black plate, leaving it clean and shiny.

Having been joined by my mate, Freddy Durdon, I checked over those parts of the engine which concerned me, the fire and firebox, then making sure the smokebox door was screwed up tight, the side water tanks were full to capacity, and the ash pan clean. With those tasks completed, it was time to move off the shed. Poor worn out 4514. As we left the shed, everything which could knock, knocked. Whilst the big ends rattled the shaft, her axle boxes jolted the frames, and her side rod bushes tinkled as they played around her crankpins. As for her valve gear, it sounded like the inside of a mad blacksmith's shop!

Leaving the shed line at Botanic Gardens for the first time required some instruction. Gone was Springhead's simple three warning pops on the whistle. Now, with the signal box controlling access to Paragon Station some distance away, and with several different routes, each requiring its own train formation, it was essential the signalman knew, in strict order, which engine was leaving the shed, and all importantly, what its destination was. At that moment, I had not only to juggle with a bewildering array of push-button route indicators, but I had to know which route and destination we were to take. What howls of despair, what gnashing of teeth, what confusion, what fury would ensue if, in the half-light of a dawning day, in my ignorance I inadvertently pressed the wrong indicator, and we landed up with our dainty tank engine all ready to go, but coupled to a heavy main line train!

However, Freddy kept me right, explaining that our first trip was to the seaside town of Hornsea, and showing me which indicators to press. Leaving the loco yard, we wheezed and clanked our way along the engine line to join other waiting engines, our worn bushes tinkling and clinking as they revolved around the coupled crank pins. Waiting our turn, Freddy enquired what sort of fire I had put on. This was a normal fire for any medium-sized tank engine, flat and level, about nine inches deep with a slightly thicker back end, a fire designed to raise the maximum amount of steam. Freddy's enquiry therefore came as a bit of a surprise, for providing the fireman had everything under control, drivers, in the normal course of events, left them to get on with things undisturbed. "These ingins are a bit tricky," Freddy explained, and to examine the fire, swung open the firebox 'big door' on its hinges. "There's only one way to fire a Tanky," he continued. "For a start, fill the back end up level with the door, close it, leave the flapper wide open, and fill its aperture with coal. And as it burns through and the ingin needs firing, push that down and fill the door up agin."

Loading, or to be more precise, overloading, more than half a Tanky's short narrow box with a dense heap of largely unburnt coal, seemed a peculiar way of producing steam at the rate a speeding passenger locomotive required, and filled me with horror. Yet as Freddy piled in the coal, who was I, a first day fireman, to question someone, who in the past, had spent many years firing just this class of engine? Booking on, Freddy would have been made aware of the calibre of his fireman—"One hev them from Springhead", giving the unspoken implication I would know nothing about vacuum brakes, or the finer points of working passenger trains. As we backed on to our train and Freddy had corkscrewed himself into a position where he could both buffer up safely, and simultaneously apply the brake, he asked if I knew how to "Hang on?" With my experience as a lad porter behind me, I was able to reassure him on that score at least.

After coupling up, at this still mild and balmy time of the year, screw coupling and vacuum pipes only without the need for steam heater pipes, I stood on the footplate gripped with excitement, awaiting "Right Away!" and the thrill of working a train over an unknown railway, and through an equally unknown part of the great big world I lived in. But dominating all else, was the sheer exhilaration of firing a flying passenger locomotive!

It was Freddy, on the platform side who took the guards "Right Away." Peering back into the semi-darkness of the station's interior, he heard way back and over the sound of other train movements, a faint indistinct whistle, and caught the flicker of the guard's green flag. Wanting a clean uninterrupted start, and feeling for any indication of a slip, Freddy gently pulled open the Tanky's parallel regulator. By now I was relieved to see the firehole aperture ablaze with burning coal, an indication, I hoped, that the mountainous back end, which I viewed with increasing unease and suspicion, was now well and truly alight.

After the first exhausts I closed the 'taps' (cylinder cocks) and began to regulate the sight feed lubricator, an instrument of considerable efficiency, and for the convenience of the crew, mounted in the cab. Earlier, on shed, I had drained it of its steam and water, and filled it with 'black oil'. Now with a bit of careful fine tuning, it would, via the main steam pipe, lubricate the valves and pistons for the rest of the day. With 4514 well into its stride through Paragon's maze of lines, and pulling fiercely on its fire, Freddy indicated I should push the blazing coal in the firehole doors forward, to roll down the back end where it would replenish the front of firebox, and as part of the same firing process, I should recharge the flapper plate with fresh coal.

At the throat of the long and complicated station yard, the running lines, under the control of the busy 100-plus lever West Parade signal cabin, diverged in three directions: those on the left swinging away in a southerly direction to form the main western route out of Hull; the central lines heading due north became the Bridlington, Scarborough, and at Beverley, the now closed Market Weighton-York lines; whilst 4514, going grandly, swung to the right, picking up the Victoria Dock branch on its route through Hull, and dashing non-stop through Botanic and Stepney Stations, to our first stop, some three and a half miles from Paragon, Wilmington Station, which for workmen's purposes served Hull's main industrial area.

But on the footplate, even at this early stage, all was not well. Distracted at first by the unfolding panorama, which included a spirited dash around the perimeter of Botanic Gardens locomotive shed, I became aware the 4514 wasn't responding to my firing as it should. To my dismay the pressure gauge informed me, even before putting on the injector, and despite the strong pull of the exhausts (which had whipped the fire into a white heat), pressure was falling at an alarming rate. My first reaction was to lay the blame on the massive back end, and by implication, on the shoulders of Freddy, who had built it. Was he, I wondered, in some act of lunacy, 'having me on'? It was an unworthy thought, and one I dismissed at once.

Helpless, expecting to be stuck for steam at any time, and as such to become the laughing stock of the shed, I could only stare in disbelief at the pressure gauge and falling boiler levels. A sudden though occurred to me, and I quickly checked the Tanky's one and only damper, to see if it had fallen shut, only to find it wide open. With shoulders slumped in despair, and hands hanging down, at a loss to know what to do next, this wasn't the way I had dreamt things would go, and in an instant all my hope and aspirations had turned to dust and ashes. If this was firing a passenger train, then clearly, I wasn't up to it, and unable to see a future at Botanic, I began to think of having to give up my promotion, and return to Springhead where engines, running at slower speeds, behaved themselves.

Freddy, with one eye on the road, the other on myself and the falling gauges, came to my rescue. "Don't worry," he reassured me. "These ingins are all the same. They'll run all day on 120 lbs of steam, just keep firing as I've said, and you'll be all right." With hope restored and fears banished, I relaxed and was able to look around, and for the remainder of the trip, enjoy the sights and sounds around me.

During this trip, I began to experience another peculiarity of these unusual engines. With steam on, at speeds of about 35 mph and above, and as it increased, they began to progressively develop, under the thrust of their pistons, a pronounced and increasing bounce at the front end, above the bogie carriage, which in extreme cases became so violent it left me wondering whether or not the bogie wheels were lifting off the rails. However, engine crews seemed happy enough with this condition, often observing the engine was now 'doing evens' (keeping time).

Hornsea, when we arrived, proved an attractive terminal station, boasting three platforms, its own turntable, and several strategically positioned water columns. But despite its pretty face and compact layout, like all terminal stations, for the sake of safe and efficient working, the signals, movements, and working arrangement had to be learned.

Returning to Paragon, we carried out a well-practised drill. Each platform had its own water column, positioned near the 'dead end', just short of a crossover which allowed us, after taking water, to use the crossover to reach the opposite platform's empty road, and in preparation for our next trip, run round our train, which I now discovered was a short ten mile local to Beverley. I was particularly looking forward to this, not only would I revisit my old 'stomping ground' at Cottingham Station, but by unexpectedly turning up as a fireman on a locomotive, be able to preen a little, to show off a bit in front of my former workmates and confirm I had risen somewhat in the world. I knew the stretch of track from Cottingham South Junction to Cottingham from my lamping days as a lad porter, and also from the time I had to search the line up to Cottingham South cabin and back for a reported body which turned out to be an old, discarded overcoat.

Arriving at Cottingham I was delighted to be welcomed by the staff as a long-lost friend. The stationmaster, Mr Beckett, to whom I owed everything, acknowledged me with a glance and nod of his head. Looking back along the train, with platform duties completed, excitement overcame my natural caution, and reverting to some degree to my portering days, I anticipated the guard's "Right Away", and gave Freddy the 'tip' early, causing the guard to hurriedly board the departing train. We swept past Cottingham North cabin, where Steve Barley, the signalman, and an old friend, who liked to observe each passing train, was standing at an open window, where he twigged me and gave me the thumbs up. A mile beyond Cottingham North cabin, with the engine in its stride, and its front end bouncing on the rails, a gated accommodation crossing connecting two sections of Tomato West's land bisected the railway. This was also the site of Cottingham North's Up distant signal, where as a lad porter I often exchanged its lamps and polished its yellow and green aspects. It was also located in close proximity to the centre of Tomato West's business, and knowing most of his staff, it was usual for me when lamping to exchange a few pleasantries with them, weather permitting.

This morning, puffed up with pride and importance, I wanted to show myself dashing past at speed, and so approaching the crossing I moved over and stood behind Freddy, who in true Great Northern style, though he had no other option, was standing observing our progress through the front weather glass. In excited anticipation I scanned Tomato West's extensive packing sheds and greenhouses for anyone I could wave to, hoping that if they recognised me they might wave back, in the approbation my new position deserved. As my eyes swept over and around this yard, I became aware of an unusual figure, a smartly dressed man of professional appearance, sitting facing the railway on the top rail of the crossing gate, reading a newspaper. As my eyes swept past in that first fleeting glance, something struck me as a little odd: here was someone a long way out from the village, and completely out of place with his surroundings. Now nearly on the crossing, and intrigued by the solitary figure on the gate, my eyes swung round for a closer look, when to my astonishment, the man flung down his paper, leapt off the gate, and hurled himself over the crossing, in front of the train. In that split second my first reaction was one of disbelief, followed by the thought that this well-dressed man must be Tomato West himself, and that something urgent and immediate on the other side of the line had caught his attention. Watching him flying over the crossing, my next impression was, he was cutting things mighty fine.

In the meantime Freddy, standing close behind the screw reverser, and looking through his weather glass, had spotted something out of the corner of his eye—a fleeting blur, the merest flash of brown in front of his engine, yet nothing enough to cause him alarm. In an even voice, he asked, "What was that?"

Above the noise of the engine, I replied, "It was someone running across in front of us."

Freddy, surprised, shouted back, "Did you say somebody?" and to my affirmative reply, he shouted back, "Did he get across?" Fear for the man's safety was now growing, and back at my own side I looked back, anxiously searching the crossing and field beyond, for signs of the man, who I fully expected would be across, and giving me a reassuring wave. Freddy, now as confused and unsure as I was, had automatically left his regulator open and, under steam, 4514 raced on!

Asked again, I shook my head: "No, there's no sign of him, I don't think he got across." By now, several hundred yards beyond the crossing, Freddy asked again, "Are you sure he didn't get across?"

"Yes," I replied, "I'm certain."

"It looks as if he's a goner then, and there's nothing we can do about it," observed Freddy. "The best thing for us is to say we know nothing about it. It doesn't matter who asks, police or anyone. Tell them we neither saw nor heard anything." Hesitantly I agreed with him that, in the circumstances, it seemed to me the most sensible course of action. After all, we were by now well past the spot where the incident had happened, and to stop the train would have taken another half a mile. Even if we could have gone back, there would be nothing we could do, for when a fast-moving locomotive hits a person there is but one outcome.

Arriving at Beverley we stopped under the station's Andrews roof, where I climbed down from the driver's side on to the four-foot, before 'lowsing off' and running around the train. Curiosity (had we really hit someone?), together with a strong sense of duty, overcame any repugnance over what I expected to discover. What met my horrified gaze was enough to confirm my worst fears: below the running plate and side tank, from the leading bogie wheels, to the trailing radials, the whole set of wheels at that side was splattered with blood and human remains. And to emphasise that dreadful sight, tattered, blood-soaked clothing hung from the right front guard rail, brake hangers, brake rigging and springs.

Shocked by the extent of the carnage, I pulled myself together and uncoupled the engine from its train, and back on the engine informed Freddy of what I had discovered, adding, "I think I ought to report what I have found to the stationmaster." Leaving the engine, I met the station foreman hurrying towards me. Fortunately, things began to unfold in a way which favoured the story I had reluctantly agreed upon.

"Did you know you've killed someone between here and Cottingham?" he asked. This question gave me the opportunity to state the facts, whilst being just a little bit economical with the truth.

Adopting the same fake sincerity which is the hallmark of many a politician, I looked him straight in the eye and stated: "Yes, I've just found the engine bloodstained, and was coming to report it."

By the time we had run round our train and shunted across to the Up platform opposite, two of the best of Beverley's constabulary had arrived, post-haste, on bicycles. With notebooks poised at the ready, they began to question us both at length. No, we swore we didn't know we'd hit anybody until we arrived at Beverley and found the engine bloodstained (which was true—we didn't actually *know* until that moment). With that came the killer question: "If that's the case, how do know it's human and not animal?"

In reply, I had the unassailable answer, one which cemented our story hard and fast. "Because," I affirmed, "there's clothing caught up on the engine." Both peered down over the platform edge and, having seen enough to confirm our story, they snapped their notebooks shut and departed.

Unlike our first call at Cottingham, our second was a more sombre affair, with an air of gloom hanging over the station. The victim had already been identified, and his truncated and mangled body, guarded by a solitary policeman (none other than my old adversary and foe, PC Gray), lay covered by two of Tomato West's waggon sheets. It was not, however, Tomato West himself, but another man who'd been a popular and well-respected member of the village community. What possessed him to suddenly fling down his newspaper and tear across the tracks in front of a speeding locomotive will never be known. Absent now the cheerful greetings of the Cottingham Station staff, as we steamed past, my eyes averted and lips sealed, the only response from the station foreman, a raised arm indicating platform duties were completed and offering us the 'Right Away'.

Approaching Paragon, the first thing to meet our eye was a spare engine and crew waiting in the opposite platform to relieve us of our duties, whilst down at the end where we'd buffer up, two railway policemen prepared to question us once again. In spite of their persistence we stuck firmly to our story, and finally satisfied, they allowed us to be signalled to the shed where, as we each made out our reports, 4514 was sluiced down by the boiler washout gang, using high pressure washout hoses, which nonetheless, unfortunately, failed to reach the more inaccessible parts of the engine, as the malodorous cloying smell of decomposition hung around the engine for the next few weeks.

For a newly 'fligged', 'wet behind the ears', unsure and uncertain fireman, my first shift had proved an emotional roller coaster. One minute elated at unexpectedly finding myself in Tanky Link, and to cap it all, with my own engine, the next, all hope gone, as I tried in vain to make an unwilling engine steam; my cheerful welcome by old friends, the Cottingham platform staff, which raised my spirits to new heights; only for them to be dashed a few minutes later, when in disbelief I watched someone racing, full pelt, to throw himself headlong beneath our speeding train. Hanging heavily around my shoulders were the 'terminological inexactitudes' given to probing policemen. And adding to the burden I carried came the profound fear that, at some time in the future, I would have to maintain that economy of truth in the more formal setting of a coroner's court.

Leaving the shed, Freddy intensified the bother and upset which gripped me, when on parting, he confused me further by saying "See you at the inquest; and remember, we only knew about this accident when we got to Beverley." See me at the inquest, what's that about? He's my regular driver, isn't he, and I should be seeing him tomorrow, so what's all this talk about only seeing me at the inquest?

Booking on early the next morning and wondering what was in store for me during the coming day, I followed a driver booking on, who was greeted by the timekeeper with a "Morning Fred", followed by, "This is your new fireman." The driver turned to see what sort of fireman he had been landed with, and then what had puzzled me long into the night immediately became clear: here was the real Freddy Durdon, who had, for whatever reason, taken the previous day off. Yesterday's driver, as I later found out, had been sent from Dairycoates to cover for Freddy, and in the circumstances must have cursed his misfortune to high heaven! His name remains unknown to me to this day. As for the inquest I feared, fortunately I was never called to attend—a massive relief, as you can imagine!

Chapter 10
The Art of Administering Cough Drops

During the months I worked with Freddy (the 'real' Freddy!), we became good friends. Freddy, like most of Botanic's middle ranking drivers, Tanky and Push and Pull drivers, was happy to share the driving with me once I'd learned the different roads. And under his excellent tuition I proved proficient at working a locomotive under many different conditions, and more importantly, being able to brake a train smoothly and safely, whatever the gradients or weather.

To me, then an 18-year-old youth, nothing in the world could offer greater delight than the thrill of being in control of a speeding train, particularly when working one of the morning or evening fast trains over the Hornsea or Withernsea branch lines. In either direction, these express trains had to make a madcap dash through Hull, and with whistle screaming, pass over two of the city's main arterial roads, where, at that time, Hull being a city of cyclists, long lines of lesser mortals had to wait our passing, with patience as, with front end bouncing violently, we thundered past. Elated by an especially exhilarating dash, my chest swollen with pride and importance, Freddy came up with a blinder: "Any more driving like that, Blackie, and you'll need your jacket buttons sewed on with elastic!"

With time, and my growing experience of Botanic's Tanky engines, I began to recognise that 4514 differed from others of its class. Contrary to the others, with short chimneys, which, incidentally, gave them a dogged aggressive appearance, 4514's tall, shapely, 3 feet 3 inch chimney seemed to give it an air of graceful grandeur. It was also, at least as far as Botanic's stud was concerned, the only one with its jet, or as it's now more commonly known, its blower (although here, some might maintain its action on the fire was to suck, rather than blow, but one mustn't be too pedantic) was to be found on the driver's side, where I have always felt the jet should be, firmly under the driver's control.

Unlike the others, whose boilers were pressed to only 165 psi, 4514's boiler was set at a more respectable 175 psi, this working pressure being confirmed by a stamped copper disk on the boiler's back plate, below the water gauges. But for me, the engine's crowning glory was its magnificent pressure gauge. Unexpectedly for a company which built its locomotives to the highest standards of workmanship and finish, its boiler pressure gauges, from the lowliest shunting engine, to the famous Great Northern Atlantics, were usually poor insignificant things, only about 4 inches in diameter, devoid of any artistic merit, and tucked away, almost out of sight, as if afraid to show themselves. On the other hand, 4514's large and impressive pressure gauge would have graced any engine to which it was fitted. The face, embellished with large, elaborate numerals, was marked from nought to two hundred. The 200 at the top of the gauge being, one might say, on the top half stroke. To draw the crew's attention, an ornate and stylishly formed 'needle' pointed to the pressure, whilst alongside the 175 psi mark, a vivid red flash underscored the boilers working pressure. And to confirm the gauge's origin, around the lower half, in bold copper plate it bore the inscription 'Great Northern Railway'. Where it came from and how it arrived on 4514 is anyone's guess.

As mentioned, speed, in any shape or form, always held a fascination for me. As a firemen in Tanky Link, I quickly became aware that as a class, the 'C12' were reluctant to maintain full working pressure when running between stations and, despite their useful 5 foot 8 inch coupled wheels, were by no means the fastest horses in Botanic's stable, crews being lucky if they could get 50 mph out of them, and then only downhill with a strong back wind. Rightly or wrongly, I put this sluggish performance down to the miserable 120/124 boiler pressure they ran about on. So with the arrogance of youth to enthuse me, and disregarding what all these engines had taught generations of footplate men, I decided to try and maintain full pressure at all times by experimenting with different forms of fire, together with as many settings of the flapper as its ratchet allowed. Incidentally and unusually, the 'C12' Class had only one damper opening, a front one, which together with a restricted air space, may account for the steaming problems.

First I tried the traditional and trusted method, a medium-sized back end, and beyond it, the majority of the grate area covered with a flat level fire, which I varied in depth as I altered the flapper as the fancy took me. No improvement. Next, throwing caution to the wind, I risked a thick fire under the brick arch. A back end in reverse as it were, with the remainder of the fire level—an experiment not to be repeated. After much trial and tribulation, for all my efforts, which probably amused a watching Freddy, the only slight improvement, hardly noticeable on the 'clock', was achieved by the arduous task of continually 'peppering and salting' a thin level fire with the flapper closed. I soon abandoned this, however, as dropping the flap after each firing caused the engine to consume prodigious amounts of coal, much of it thrown out in a volcano of black smoke and large white-hot cinders, as 4514's chimney worked on the fire. Reluctantly admitting defeat, I accepted what common sense should have told me in the first place, and resumed filling the back end and fire door with coal. Yet to be frank, I enjoyed every minute of my experimentation, and it taught me a lot.

Sometime in mid-June 1946 I booked on to find 4514 gone, and in her place that day, 4348, one of Botanic's two Ivatt 4-4-0 runabout tender engines—engines heartily disliked by all true NER men for their minimalistic cabs and lack of seating. And because they were too long for the turntables at Hornsea and Withernsea, some of our work required tender first running, something not to be recommended with this type of locomotive, especially in adverse weather conditions when overcoats had to be donned, and collars turned up. Enquiries then led to me being informed that 4514 had gone into Doncaster plant for a much needed heavy repair job. For the next five or six weeks, during which 4514 was systematically taken to bits, then just as systematically reassembled, I went through the whole pedigree of Botanic's disparate engine fleet.

Depending on the job, it might be one of the shed's NER Class 'R' 4-4-0 (later 'D20') of 1899/1910 vintage, still full of life, and with five or six on, still good for a spirited gallop. Or any one of the shed's large 4-6-2 passenger tank engines of Classes 'A8', 'A7', 'A5' and 'A4', all easy on the fireman, and fast into the bargain. A favourite, and easily remembered, were the dandy NER Class 'C' 0-6-0 tender engines, which with a squeeze, just fitted on the turntables at Hornsea and Withernsea, this obviating the need to run tender first. Game they might have been, but with diminutive 4 feet 2 inch coupled wheels, they found the express trains to and from Hornsea and Withernsea rather trying.

Five or six weeks after 4514 had disappeared into Doncaster plant, I booked on, anxious to get grips with whatever the shed might throw at me. The booking-on clerk that day had lost an arm in World War I. Whether this coloured his outlook on life I don't know (although he can hardly be blamed if it had), but I always found his manner surly and unpleasant, ever-ready, day or night, to book anyone for being a couple of minutes late. As I stepped forward he automatically glanced at the office clock and, satisfied I was on time he announced, to my delight, "Engine 4514."

Standing on the far side of the locomotive yard, by herself, 4514 looked magnificent, the freshly varnished paintwork gleaming in the bright afternoon sunlight. With eager steps, I hurried to tread the familiar footplate. Instinctively I glanced at the pressure gauge, not only to note the pressure, but to also reassure myself the engine had returned with its original gauge. Thanks be, it remained there in all its glory. In the meantime Freddy had arrived, and whilst he went around the already prepared and oiled engine, 'putting in trimming' and checking the engine oil, I built up the back end. For whilst I hoped and prayed Doncaster had, by some magic, improved the engine's steaming, I wasn't prepared to take any chances.

Indeed, with the reputation the class held, I knew she would remain a stoddy steamer. But now, in stark contrast to the previous groans, sighs and whistles at the chimney top from worn and leaking valves, and the dull heavy thud of played-out big end brasses reverberating throughout the frame, and the clank of worn out side-rod bushes, the new engine moved out of the locomotive yard, along the engine line and onto our train soundlessly and effortlessly, apart from a soft gentle, barely audible, whiff of exhaust steam, which hardly raised a flicker on the fire. Once coupled up, I returned to the cab to begin 'gassing up' for the serious work ahead.

Standing in the hot cab, with the jet hard on, I watched the pressure gauge needle creeping up to the red mark, happy to have the engine 'blowing off' as we left. Then I became part of the most improbable event in the whole of an extensive footplate career, an event, or to be precise, events, for it continued as long as I remained with the engine, so implausible, that by continuing the story I risk being branded a fantasist, or at best a deluded, confused and senile old man.

Waiting for the 'Right Away', I watched the pressure, under the influence of the jet creeping up to the boiler's 175 psi working pressure. The needle touched the red mark, where I expected the lowest 'set' of the two valves to lift. As the needle continued rising, to my surprise the safety valves remained tightly shut. First 180, then 185, at which point, feeling the pressure gauge was at fault, I rapped it sharply with my knuckles. The needle twitched and quivered a little, but continued rising. As it continued its wilful climb, I waggled the gauge steam pipe, but to no effect. At 190 and still rising, the guard's green flag signalled the end of this intriguing affair. As far as the run to Hornsea was concerned, whilst it was an uncommon pleasure to be on an engine running as smoothly and quietly as the proverbial sewing machine, and with everything steam-tight, she still refused to steam.

With time on my hands, after running round the train at Hornsea, and in blissful ignorance of what was about to begin, yet with unquestioning trust in the engine's safety valves, I vowed to now get to the bottom of what was bugging me. At what pressure I wondered, would the safety valves finally lift? Exhilarated by the belief that higher steam pressure equated with greater speed, here I had the boiler before me to prove it. I enthusiastically turned up the jet, and with the fire made up, watched unconcerned, as the gauge needle once again rose above the 175 psi mark, and with equal indifference to the strains the boiler was undoubtedly experiencing, watched the needle climb remorseless to 200, the final figure on the clock, when the needle came to rest against the gauge stop pin. Standing behind the boiler's creaking backplate, I waited for the engine to blow off. After a full five minutes with the needle hard against the stop, the engine let loose, with both valves opening. With a bang that shook the engine and a roar which split the heavens, both valves picked up the boiler water, sending a huge plume of hot spray drifting the length of the platform—fortunately in the opposite direction to those members of the public, whose sole intention at that time was finding a suitable compartment, rather than showing interest in what type of locomotive was gracing the front of the train.

Now thoroughly alarmed, as much by the loss of precious boiler water that now drenched the station as by the noise and ferocity at the safety valves, I thought to quieten things down by applying the injector and easing the jet. In the meantime, Freddy, who had been in conversation with the guard, arrived all hot and bothered to know why I had let the engine blow off, blasting the heavens and wasting half a boiler of water. My shamefaced excuse was that I had inadvertently overfilled the boiler. The upshot of all this mayhem being, I left Hornsea with only half a boiler of water, and a struggle all the way home, as with the help of Freddy, who by long shut offs to regain steam and water, helped me on the approach to stations.

But, to return to the extraordinary lapse on the part of Doncaster, for it was surely an error on their part, during the overhaul, that had resulted in faulty safety valves. Lacking all knowledge of the plant's internal practises, how this perilous and fraught-with-danger fault occurred, can only be a matter of conjecture. One explanation I can offer is the following: after testing the boiler to its maximum pressure, the plant's boiler inspector signed off the test, then for whatever reason left, with the intention of setting the valves to the correct pressure on his return. In his absence, did he succumb to a heart attack? Was he knocked down by an engine traversing the plant? Or run over by a bus? This is something we shall never know. But with the paperwork complete and the boiler certificate signed off, there would be no further reason to delay the engine's return to traffic. However, as part of this breach of practise, just as inexplicable was the lack of concern on the part of engine crews, who seemed oblivious to the dangerously high pressure the boiler carried. I put this down to an absolute trust, by them, in the integrity of the safety valves being set correctly. And as a further dimension must be added the easy manner in which crews routinely accepted engines each day, more often than not, clapped out for want of a bit of inexpensive maintenance. Maintenance such as: easily adjusted wedges to take up axle box knock, the root cause of much knock throughout the running gear; marine-type big ends keyed down as knock developed; and out of sync valves set up to give precise valve events. Simple jobs, which would have transformed the majority of run-down engines into much more efficient machines. Unfortunately by the end of the war, this dedication had become a thing of the past, and here's the rub: drivers, not expecting much in that respect, only booked the most trivial repairs, unless it was something effecting the integrity of the machine; normally, just something to put in the repair book and show the driver had his eye on things. Even though Botanic's passenger engines rarely if ever needed them, sanders to put in working order was a favourite, as were ejector cones to clean, even though the ejector was working perfectly. Also a regular entry, brakes to adjust, and on older engines given to that complaint, piston glands blowing, to tighten. War has many casualties, we are told; unfortunately proper maintenance was one of them.

 At this point, observations on the efficiency, or otherwise, of 'cough drops', might be in order. In the early days of locomotive development, and as locomotives became more powerful and speedy, enginemen (never more so than the hardy souls on the open footplates of John Gray's celebrated Hull & Selby Railway, high-pressure, inside cylinder 2-2-2 express engines), found that a combination of fast running, very hot high pressure steam, and the enclosed valves and cylinders in close proximity to the radiating heat of the smoke box, made it difficult to provide efficient lubrication to the 'front end' valves and pistons. To that end, before departure, with the engine resting in mid-gear, and in that position, all four cylinder ports open to direct contact with the blast pipe, the driver or fireman would drop a ball of fat or grease, whatever came to hand, down the blast pipe, with high hopes that, on melting, it would provide sufficient lubrication to the valves and pistons. When waggon grease became freely available, this became the preferred lubricant, claims then being that it not only lubricated the front end, but cleaned carbon deposits and imparted a polish to valves and pistons, earning for themselves the title of 'cough drops'. There may have been some truth in these claims, for the former NER fitted a grease lubricator to the steam chest cover on its saturated locomotives, and this device, together with cough drops, remained an article of faith among engine crews of the NER region as long as saturated locomotives continued in service.

Finally, a word of warning regarding the application of cough drops: despite the sight feed lubricator doing its work delivering oil to the valves and cylinders, to perfection, dropping a cough drop down the blast pipe of 4514, or any other saturated engine I might be working, became something of an obsession, as I searched any convenient sidings for the increasingly elusive 'grease waggon' – a waggon with its axle boxes filled with splendid yellow, soda soap grease which, when administered, added, in my mind, a further dimension to the engine's performance. However, with this exercise, care had to be observed. If administered near to departure time, the unmelted and still solid cough drops would be discharged from the chimney with the velocity of an cannonball, to the consternation of any assembled bystanders, and the dismay of the engine crew, who watched its soaring flight open mouthed wondering where and among whom it might fall.

In mid-summer 1946, I returned to my lodgings to find waiting a buff-coloured envelope addressed to me, and bearing in bold type the inscription *On His Majesty's Service*. Mystified, I opened it to find I was being ordered to attend a medical examination for future military service. What's all this about then? This was the first I had heard of compulsory military service being reintroduced, after it had been made blindingly obvious every man was needed to help rebuild Britain and much of the rest of the world, shattered and bankrupt by war. At the time, I put rumours of a call-up to some government nonsense.

At first shocked and dismayed, I later reassured myself with the comforting thought: historically, footplate work has always been classed as a reserved occupation, and its workforce exempt from military service. And there was one thing of no doubt, I was firmly on the footplate. I reported for the medical with about 30 other young men, boys really. The room, in a public building, was large, and apart from a folding table at the door, with a clerk taking our personal details, completely bare of any furniture. As for the medical, like the room itself, there was nothing private about it. Once inside, we were brusquely told to strip naked, and thereafter treated like cattle by doctors who appeared to find the business as distasteful to them as it was to us.

Standing with arms raised, stark naked, each man's general wellbeing and condition was noted, before being ordered to turn around and bend over, as his nether regions were examined. This, in my case, was followed by a somewhat economical examination of my lungs, after which I was discharged with a curt "Get dressed, you're passed A1." If he had found me coughing or wheezing from one of my still frequent chest infections, the doctor's prognosis would have been considerably downgraded, of that I can be certain. After leaving I dusted my hands of the place, and returning to my lodgings, dismissing it as a day ill spent.

Brough, 10 miles to the west of Hull, the former site of Petuaria, the Roman settlement and fort, and as such the custodian of its Ermine Street Humber crossing, became the scene of a spectacular and unusual derailment, in which I was unfortunately involved. Innocently, I hasten to add. In 1946, Brough, now greatly developed, was a small village located to the north of the four-road Hull to Staddlethorpe section of the railway, whilst to the south, occupying land between the railway and the Humber estuary, lay the extensive Blackburn Aircraft Company works (no relation!), and its adjoining airfield. To service its workforce the railway provided a frequent service between Hull and Brough.

From the start this particular shift was a little out of the ordinary. That day 4514 was stopped for a washout and boiler examination, and in its place one of Wilson Worsdell's NER Class 'W' 4-6-2 tank engines, a 'Willie', was substituted. Next, I found myself firing to an unfamiliar driver, again a Spare Link man from Dairycoates. By mid-morning, after trips elsewhere, we arrived at our destination, Brough, where after running round our train, we were shunted across the station and into a lay-by loop adjoining the Down slow line, to which it was connected at both ends by turnouts, each controlled by dollies. Once inside we were out of the way of the heavy traffic occupying both the fast and slow lines. To further set the scene, the right-hand drive Willie was now standing at the east end of the station, pointing engine-first for Hull with, importantly, the loop's controlling dolly on the driver's side. Approaching train time, our next move, under the direction of our dolly, and with all the slow line signals at danger, would be to draw our train out of the loop and onto the slow line, before propelling into the slow road platform.

After a period in the loop, during which we grabbed the chance to eat our 'bungy' sandwiches and read our morning paper until, with a distinct double thud, came the sound of points being operated and the dolly being turned. Leisurely the driver put his paper to one side, rose, and without checking the dolly, dropped the engine into full fore gear, and opened the regulator. In the meantime, I prepared for the short run back to Hull. Then came a resounding crash, followed by the engine bucking and heaving after running through a set of open catch points, and gamely making its way over open ground. With a howl of dismay my unfortunate driver shut the regulator, at which all hell let loose. Down the slow line, and 100 yards further back, travelling at a steady 30 mph under clear signals, came a heavy coal train. Its driver, his long day nearly over, his fireman on top of his job, and everything under control, was, I suspect, smoking his pipe, and for the last few miles taking things easy.

Up to this point, his view through Brough Station had been obstructed by two overbridges, both located at the western extremities of the station's four platforms; the outermost, a substantial road bridge, the inner a footbridge. On bursting out from under them, the first thing to register, no doubt to his horror and shocked disbelief, was the sight of a passenger train steaming out of the loop, and about to occupy the slow line. Fully aware that, in the short distance left to him, it was impossible to prevent a catastrophic collision, he snapped his regulator shut and pulled his steam brake on so as to lessen the impact as far as possible, and whilst reversing his engine and applying steam, called for his fireman to screw the hand brake hard on. Now helpless in the face of disaster, his only other course of action was to hang on to the whistle, and by a series of urgent pops, attempt to warn the errant crew, or anyone else involved, of the danger they were in.

As the Willie shuddered to a halt, an even more frightening sound froze the blood of its helpless crew: the sound of a train bearing down on us, its brakes screeching and whistle screaming. As it crashed past in a welter of smoke and dust from its protesting brake blocks, I had a fleeting vision of its crew, both staring at us accusingly. The coal train came to a halt 300 yards beyond where the Willie was stood, off the road, lopsided and helpless, its front bogie wheels buried in soft earth. The coal train driver, white-faced and clearly shaken, came hurrying back, stumbling and tripping over sleeper ends, points and other lineside obstructions. "What were you thinking about?" he demanded. "Have you both gone mad?"

In truth, there was no danger of collision. The trap points positioned to prevent any such conflicting movement did their job, throwing the Willie clear of the running line. But for the driver of the coal train, unfamiliar with most of the station layout, the sight of a train leaving the loop was enough. How then did this sorry state of affairs come about? First and foremost the driver of the Willie was manifestly at fault, having, for some inexplicable reason, failed to adhere to the most elementary of practices, a simple act to an engine driver of checking his signals before moving off. Such an action was normally as automatic and unthinking as placing one foot before the other when walking, but in my experience lapses were more common than the general public were aware of. What then of the unmistakeable sound of points being set, and the dolly being operated?

Arriving in the loop, the Willie, standing at the east end of the station, had its controlling dolly just ahead of its right front buffer beam. As to the reason for my not monitoring it, I was on the opposite side, the fireman's side, and with train time imminent, the road set, and the dolly giving us permission to leave the loop, the next move involved us drawing the train out of the loop, through the turnout, and on to the Down slow-running line; then propelling it 'facing road' back along the main line, and into the station's slow road platform, thereby taking up a position behind the station's starter signal. In this case it was a double aspect semaphore signal whose other purpose was to process through-trains to the section ahead, and in its single or double form, common to most stations, and as such it was a signal planted firmly in every driver's mind.

If the villain of the piece was the driver of the Willie, the position of the starter signal in this instance bore a heavy responsibility, for it stood opposite, and in near proximity to the loop line dolly. Tucked quietly out of the way, and engrossed in his morning paper, it was not, as he too readily assumed, the sound of the points being driven home, followed by the dolly being turned, which roused him, but the sound of the double aspect signal being pulled off for the passage of the coal train. Shaking himself free of the little world his mind had been occupying, he unthinkingly set his train in motion. The rest, as they say, is history. Although not quite… as a few years later, in a remarkable coincidence, I was involved in exactly the same sort of incident, in the same loop, but this time at the opposite western end, with results even more spectacular (as you'll discover later on).

This leaves me to reflect on some of the major unexplained railway accidents of the past. The strange behaviour of driver Robins on the London and Southwestern Railway express, which on 1 July 1906 derailed at high speed on the curves approaching and through Salisbury, killing 28 people including himself, two firemen and the guard. Or the equally bizarre accident in September of the same year, when driver Fleetwood, working a Great Northern semi-fast from Kings Cross to Edinburgh, failed to make his booked stop at Grantham and derailed on curves to the north of the station, with the loss of 14 lives (more about this later). Perhaps the terrible accident at Quintinshill in the Scottish Borders on 22 May 1915, resulting in the deaths of over 200 people (and which remains the worst rail disaster in British history) might be attributed to the same cause, or the much later Harrow disaster, when on the morning of 8 October 1952, the driver of an overnight Glasgow to London express ignored a series of red stop signals, with appalling results: 112 fatalities and 340 being injured.

To this sorry list might be added other equally mysterious accidents, plus the many times when prompt but concealed action by the fireman prevented similar accidents. Were the protagonists, all long-serving highly-skilled men, each steeped in railway practise, suffering from a then unknown, but now familiar illness, Alzheimer's disease?

Chapter 11
Pounding the Main Line

Post-war, before holidays abroad, with its sun and sense of adventure, came within the reach of many, the holiday months were July and August. As a result of these holidays, Botanic, short of footplate staff and literally scraping the bottom of the barrel, had the added burden of coping with many Sunday excursions to the popular seaside resorts of Scarborough, Bridlington, Hornsea and Withernsea, as well as some further afield. Excluding these two holiday months, Botanic in effect closed down on Sunday, and in these circumstances engine crews, apart from Spare Link men, had little cause to examine the duty roster, their shift patterns set within the Link they occupied. But come the two holiday months one had to be vigilant and keep a close eye on the Sunday roster, with its list of excursion workings, for woe betide anyone who missed his rostered turn of duty without adequate explanation, as they were not easily forgiven and the penalties were severe.

In mid-July, at the end of an early morning Saturday shift, whilst examining the Sunday roster, I discovered, with a feeling of trepidation, I was booked to work, not as I might expect, a Hornsea or Withernsea excursion (work I felt more in keeping with my abilities), but to Blackpool of all places—somewhere far distant, on the other side of the country, and far beyond my knowledge. Why me I wondered, and not one of the senior firemen, until I realised the senior firemen were all Passed Firemen, and as such would be rostered out on driving turns. With my experience limited to branch line stopping trains, I wondered if I could cope with high speed, non-stop running. But to comfort me I had Freddy Durdon's sage advice: "If you can fire (and by fire, he meant maintain steam and water) a small engine, especially a GN Tanky, you can fire anything." And to further cheer me, I recalled my main line trips over the H&BR systems when, as a cleaner, lacking both polish and finesse, I had successfully fired a variety of eight-coupled goods engines.

Over the next few hours my mind was occupied with what sort of engine might be allocated tomorrow. Perhaps any of the shed's Shire or Hunts? Or Botanic's solitary GN Atlantic? Possibly an NER Class 'S' 4-6-0 with its long narrow firebox to test my stamina and skill. Or a Dairycoates 'K3' 'Ragtimer', filling a gap, and dancing and jiving its way along, to the fascinating accompaniment of its lightweight, tinkling, nickel-chrome valve gear and rods. However, it was no good speculating, I would just have to wait until tomorrow and see.

I was immensely proud of my position and my uniform, and each week I started work with a clean set of blues, for which I paid my landlady an extra two shillings to wash and press. Nor was I the only one by any means who came to work with polished boots. So, on that splendidly summery Sunday morning, donning my clean blues and leaving nothing to chance, I stepped out early for what I thought a very pleasant 7 am start, my intention being to arrive on shed at about 6.30 am, and then alone go around whatever engine I'd been allocated, checking my side of things, and generally weighing it up. Booking on duty, the timekeeper ran his finger down the roster. "Ah, here it is," he exclaimed. "It's 2165, it's in the shed doorway, prepared and ready to go."

For a moment I was thunderstruck. Since I first watched in delight 2165 thundering through Cottingham Station, and afterwards, waiting each morning entranced by her beauty and speed, I had never once thought that one day, somewhere, somehow, I might have the privilege of riding the footplate of one of the most beautiful class of engines to ever grace a railway.

She stood just outside the shed, looking magnificent, having arrived overnight from Springhead, where Harry, the cleaner foreman, and his gangs of cleaners had done her proud, 'bulling' her up for the occasion, even burnishing the wheel splasher brasses and outside oil boxes, using a mixture of bath brick and paraffin. I climbed into the low-slung NER cab, where, standing between the driver's and fireman's footstools, the boiler back plate reared above my head. I looked around, and even if the ghosts of generations of enginemen seemed to permeate the cab, it was like meeting an old friend. There on the backplate, the Detroit lubricator, which had once gulped a mass of scalding hot cylinder oil down the back of my neck when I'd had the privilege of helping prepare her for her next turn of duty. And the NER door and flapper plate, through which at times I had been encouraged, as a cleaner, to help the fireman by making up his back end.

Upon entering the cab I stowed my black jacket and grub tin containing the still-rationed dry 'bungy' sandwiches within the fireman's box seat, and placed my screw-topped bottle of tea on the hot plate above the firehole door (for until the end of steam, all northern enginemen carried their day's supply of tea this way, and which, when placed on the plate, stewed away gently, becoming more appetising, or less so, depending on your taste). Then, after checking steam and water gauges I went over to the stores to draw my firing shovel, slecker pipe and hand brush, together with an engine crew's generous daily allocation of a new, white cotton sweat rag each, two 'washed' sweat rags for dirty work, and a large bundle of cotton waste. Then, leaving nothing to chance, on my return I began an examination of whatever I felt might affect the engine's steaming.

Dropping the NER-style firehole door I began a close examination of the firebox and its contents, paying particular attention to the condition of the fire and firebars by making sure the preparing fireman had cleaned both properly. I found them as I expected: clean, with the advantage of a clear, bright and level fire. Next I examined the tube plate for signs of incipient 'birdnesting', a condition which to a greater or lesser degree blocked the tubes, and which, if found, I was prepared to dislodge using the engine's straight dart. This was followed by an examination of the firebox brick arch. It was well used, its firebricks fused together, with the underside melted into stalactites by the intense heat, but I knew it was sound, and good for many more miles. Satisfied, I closed the firehole door and turned my attention to the smokebox. In the way of things, I found the fall plate in front of the smokebox swept clean of smokebox ash and dust, and on opening the smokebox door I found the smokebox clean, its tube plate, tubes, steam pipes and blast pipe joints steam tight. With everything in good order, I closed the door and screwed it tight. More as a formality, I went underneath to check the ashpan and dampers. Once again, the preparing crew had been thorough in their work, with the ash pan raked clean, and the dampers in good working order.

No longer afraid of asphyxiating myself, looking inside a smoke-filled smokebox I made up my fire. With a tender of Springhead's South Kirby hards, success or failure now lay in my hands, and using large knobs I carefully formed an impressive back end in the deep firebox, before firing round the remainder of the firebox with small coal. With the blower (EAR's preferred term for a jet) open only enough to prevent smoke and fumes coming back into the cab by way of the firehole door, and also to prevent the engine blowing off to the annoyance of the nearby stores, mess room and offices, I climbed over the tender to make sure its tender tank was full to capacity, and to check whether or not it carried a spare firing shovel. If being up a creek without a paddle is a misfortune, then the damage or loss of an only shovel on a steam locomotive can only be classed a disaster.

Before the driver arrived and I came under scrutiny I felt the need to familiarise myself with the fireman's injector, an early Metcalfe Type F exhaust injector and known sardonically as 'Metcalfe's Masterpiece'. Unlike later automatic exhaust injectors, which changed automatically when the regulator was opened or closed, Metcalfe's Masterpiece knocked off each time and had to be restarted, and as such, with its separate and complicated steam and water valves, could be a tricky bit of kit to operate. With its reputation going before it, and before I was out on the raging main line and things got hot, I was anxious to get the better of it, if only in its live steam mode.

Before we set off on our journey to Blackpool, however, let us pause a moment for another sort of illumination, that concerning the character of NER locomotives and the men behind their designs. Throughout its existence, the NER continued a long and proud tradition pioneering locomotive development, reaching back to the Stockton and Darlington Railway (S&DR), and its distinguished engineer, William Bouch, Locomotive Superintendent, and brother of Thomas Bouch, designer and architect of the ill-fated first Tay Bridge. William was the mechanical engineer responsible for the splendid, long-lived 0-6-0 tender goods engines which, day and night, thrashed their smokebox rivets loose on way up the fearsome grades of the S&DR, hauling iron ore, limestone and coal for the ever-hungry and expanding Cleveland iron mills. Resplendent in all the glory of its S&DR black and green colours and embellishments, one of these remarkable locomotives, number 1275, is fortunately preserved for all to see in the National Railway Museum in York.

To take greater advantage of the hard graft these engines were now putting in, and to further exploit the still searingly hot firebox gases being ejected, Bouch designed an effective feed water heater, which was coiled within the circumference of the chimney. However, unlike his very successful Class '1001', Bouch came a cropper when, far ahead of his time, he trialled not only piston valves, but piston valves of extreme diameter, allied to cylinders of advanced design with a 30 inches piston stroke, on his brand new 4-4-0 outside cylinder, bogie passenger engines. His forward thinking came to naught when his piston valves, lacking spring rings and despite the frequent 'cough drop' down the blast pipe, persisted in seizing up and wrecking the valve gear, or alternatively, quickly wearing out and blowing heavily, shooting coal consumption up alarmingly, and effectively prevented the engines ability to keep time. But from an engineman's point of view, his crowning glory was his provision of a larger, comfortable, and by the standards of the day, luxurious all-weather cab, which in the fullness of time came to be adopted first by the NER, and later by the LNER, thereby earning Bouch, in a roundabout way, the gratitude of generations of appreciative enginemen.

Edward Fletcher, a Northumbrian through and through, served his time helping to build George Stephenson's famous Rocket, and other early steam locomotives at the company's Gateshead works. In 1854, after the formation of the NER, Fletcher was appointed Locomotive Superintendent, and as such inherited a motley collection of widely differing locomotives from the 74 independent railways which now formed the mighty NER. In his long tenure of 28 years 'Daddy' Fletcher maintained the S&DR's reputation for locomotive experimentation and innovation, during that time being responsible for some outstanding locomotives. There are three types which deserve mention. Firstly, his impressive '708' Class 0-6-0 Standard Goods, which for many years remained the mainstay of the NER goods and mineral workings. Powerful and free steaming, they enjoyed the respect and admiration of the men who worked them, and spreading throughout the system, eventually reached a grand total of 324 machines. Even more impressive were his famous '901' Class 2-4-0 Express engines, with 7-0 foot coupled wheels, which dominated the main line, earning for themselves a reputation for fast free-running, aided no doubt by Fletcher's patent cylinder 'taps' (known as such because the early cylinder cocks had, on being opened or closed, a simple rotating tap-like action, this terminology remaining in the north-east until the end of steam). But back to the '901' Class: Fletcher's taps were designed to reduce or eliminate the effects of 'back pressure'. This is excess steam trapped in the cylinders at the end of each stroke, when the engine was working hard and fast, and which had a retarding effect on its running. For many years the '901' Class dominated the NER main lines, putting in astonishing mileages between the repairs, and averaging an impressive coal consumption of just over 28lbs per train mile (although admittedly the loads were light) over the 124¼ miles between Newcastle and Edinburgh. On the even more arduous Newcastle to York to Leeds route, however, coal consumption only rose by a meagre 1lb per train mile, to 29lbs per mile. The author well remembers old drivers who had fired the '901's', reminiscing, "Why them old injins could catch pigeons, an' they steamed all day on next to nowt." Finally, Fletcher's renowned 0-4-4 Bogie Tank Passenger (BTP) must not be forgotten. Of an excellent design, and solid build, with a little tweaking now and again they gave splendid service for 47 years, being taken into LNER ownership in 1922, and ending their days as well-regarded Push and Pull engines.

In January 1885, Edward Fletcher, after building the most efficient and forward-looking Locomotive Department in the country, announced his retirement, the vacant position being occupied by Alexander McDonnell, who for 18 years had been Locomotive Superintendent of the Great Southern and Western Railway of Ireland, and director of its famous Inchicore locomotive works. Despite McDonnell's sound engineering background and brilliant academic record, he quickly lost the respect of the footplate staff, when one of his first actions was the removal of the cherished Fletcher taps. Resentment may well have died down if his own express engines, engines designed to take over from the '901' Class, had lived up to their promise, for McDonnell's express engines had an attractive and graceful appearance.

However, to the dismay of the deeply conservative NER drivers, happy and content with Fletcher's pair of fixed leading wheels, which having plenty of side play in each outside axle box, jiggled about splendidly when taking curves or other inequalities in the track, Fletcher's 2-4-0 now became a 4-4-0. Gone were the polished brass safety valve covers, to be replaced by open safety valves. And whoa, what's all this about then? The familiar right-hand drive had changed to the left. With most station platforms, and the majority of signals to the left of the engine in the normal direction of travel, this might seem a logical arrangement, and one, finally adopted as standard by Edward Thompson and the LNER in the early 1940s. But to engine crews this adaption was not always as welcome as it might seem.

My first experience with left-hand drive locomotives were the two Class '01' 2-8-0's, Thompson rebuilds of Robinson's heavy goods engines, allocated to Springhead in early 1944. Like the NER enginemen of old, I too was never fully at ease on a left drive locomotive, the driving position never feeling quite right. As for firing, here I was all at sea, for no matter how I tried, I never got the hang of firing left handed. I often missed the firehole, and scattered coal around the footplate to the annoyance of whoever I might be firing to, for drivers liked clean and dust-free footboards. To emphasise their displeasure at my lack of skill, they would grind beneath their heels any fragments of coal that came their way. Being forced to fire right-handed on a left-drive but roomy footplate, this didn't much matter, but on an engine with restricted footplate space, say a Thompson 'L1', which to the onlooker offered a longer and more handsome cab, but which on closer inspection had three feet or more of boiler occupying much of its interior, then firing (with a necessarily foreshortened shovel) and scrunched up close against the driver, became a much more personal affair.

Adding to the men's frustrations, McDonnell express engines were soon found wanting. Despite their pleasing good looks and an air of power and speed, they suffered the double whammy of being under-boilered and heavy on coal. McDonnell, fed up with it all, departed after only a few months in office, leaving a growing void. For under new arrangements the Kings Cross to Aberdeen night train (and no UK train was more prestigious) was to run the Newcastle to Edinburgh section non-stop, a trying 124¼ mile gallop. Whilst on the crack NER trains, McDonnell's 4-4-0 were rather like a baby's backside, not to be relied on. And although Fletcher's '901' Class were stout engines, they were not really up to this non-stop running, thus, with time against them, the Locomotive Department needed a new engine, and quickly.

Fortunately, the NER carried a cadre of well-qualified mechanical engineers, who were called in from their respective divisional headquarters or locomotive works, and under the chairmanship of the General Manager, Henry Tennant, were tasked with a new fit-for-purpose express locomotive. The committee quickly thrashed out a new design, the result of which was a triumph of collective engineering. Among that distinguished group was one Wilson Worsdell, a name that looms large in the annals of NER locomotive development, and who as McDonnell's principle assistant was the one who in the past had to bear the brunt of the men's displeasure. Perhaps heeding Worsdell's warnings, the new engine signalled a return to Fletcher's well-tried features—except this was a more noble locomotive.

Built like a battleship, it had massive double frames, 7 feet 1 inch drivers, cylinders bores increased by one inch from 17 x 24 to 18 x 24, a larger boiler and an extended grate area. Adding to the men's approval, Fletcher's exhaust taps were reinstated, whilst McDonnell's unwelcome left-hand drive was consigned to the past, together with his unwanted bogies. Powerful and free steaming, the new engines were welcomed with open arms, after proving themselves the masters of 'The Aberdeen'. But what of the engine crews? Long experience leads me to nothing but admiration for those hardy souls, on open footplates, driving hard through the night in the depth of winter, across the bleak and rugged northern fells.

But we must move on. For, whilst the 'Tennants' proved an outstanding design, a design which earned the first, number 1463, a place in that hallowed hall of fame, the National Railway Museum, in York, they, being straightforward machines with no frills, did little to further the NER's compulsive quest for greater thermal efficiency, and for that we must look elsewhere.

Thomas William Worsdell, then aged just under 47, became the next to occupy the Locomotive Superintendent's chair. Of wide experience, he had gone to America as a young man where, after entering the service of the Pennsylvania Railroad, he rapidly became Master Mechanic, in charge of the prestigious Altoona Works. Returning eventually to England, he accepted the position of Works Manager, Crewe, where he assisted F. W. Webb, the London and North-Western Railway Locomotive Superintendent in his compounding[17] work, and where he became a devotee of both compounding, and Joy's valve gear. In 1881, after leaving Crewe, he accepted the position of Locomotive Superintendent of the Great Eastern Railway, where he introduced both compounding and Joy's valve gear to his two types of passenger locomotives. The first, a stylish 2-4-0, and the second, an even more handsome 4-4-0. Unfortunately both proved a disappointment, by all accounts suffering from poor steam distribution, and other ailments brought on by the complexities of compounding. In 1885 he accepted the position of Locomotive Superintendent at the NER mainly, it has been suggested, for his outstanding administrative abilities, rather than his engineering prowess. At the same time, his younger brother Wilson, aided by his gifted Chief Draughtsman, the Scotsman, Walter Smith, concentrated on locomotive design and development.

With marine compounding proving such a success, there was little wonder railway engineers began to see it as the way forward. However, his years at Crewe had made the elder Worsdell wise to the failings of the Webb compounds, which struggled against a defective and never-resolved front end layout, a layout

---

[17] A type of steam engine where steam is expanded in two or more stages, rather than being expended on each stroke.

which sometimes did peculiar things, often locking the engine up, and to the dismay of the crew, refusing to move either forwards or backwards. Or to further unsettle the unhappy men, setting off in the opposite direction to the one expected.

Well aware of the Webb compounds defects, one can reasonably imagine the two Worsdell brothers, over brandy and cigars, and in company with the alter ego of the team, the clever engineer Walter Smith, enjoying a few convivial evenings together, with slide rule and paper to hand, as they thrashed out the problems of fitting an efficient and balanced compounding system within the narrow confines of a locomotive framework. And this was achieved by improving a largely discredited two-cylinder compound arrangement, an arrangement whereby a single high pressure cylinder, at the end of each stroke, exhausted into a much larger low pressure cylinder, before its terminal discharge to atmosphere via blast pipe and chimney. To gain the improvement required, much thought and many hours of studied calculations, along with considerable ingenuity, was needed, including a profound rethink of normal draughting arrangements for a system with only two exhausts for each revolution of the driving wheels—a condition emphasised by a soft, woolly and much lighter final exhaust.

For it to be rated by the NER as a success, compounding required application to as wide a variety of locomotives as possible. From the company's hard driven, long distance express engines, to the less powerful secondary passenger locomotives, where frequent restarts from stations, and subsequent working up to speed each time, required skilful handling if an alarming drain on the boiler was to be avoided. Equal consideration had to be given to other types. The slogging main line goods engines handling heavy coal trains or mixed freight, often at express speeds. And designed for shorter work, a powerful and versatile 0-6-2 tank engine, equally at home on the fearsome grades of the former Cockermouth, Keswick and Penrith railway, where they earned their laurels hauling mineral trains from Darlington to Cockermouth over the wild and windswept Stainmoor summit, and on each return working, iron ore for the ever hungry Durham and North Yorkshire blast furnaces. Or else they were pottering along between stations on some routine stretch of railway for spells of shunting, on pick up duties.

By 1886, with the Industrial Revolution in full swing, and to meet a pressing demand for more powerful locomotives, the NER began a concentrated programme of new-build compound engines. Commencing with the Class 'C' 0-6-0 express goods, of which no fewer than 170 when built over the next four years, and of such outstanding design and workmanship that after more than 60 years of hard graft, I found them, although in their rebuilt simple form, a delight on local passenger trains. Then, with Stephenson's link motion gnashing away between the vermillion-coloured frames, the old girls could still whip up enough enthusiasm to run like the wind when asked.

With the Class 'C' came a return of the American, fully enclosed, side windowed all-weather cab, a cab which thereafter became the standard for all future NER and LNER tender engines. And what of the Americans? Let it be remembered, they knew a thing or two about working engines in extreme weather conditions. This capacious cab was identical to the one William Bouch had unsuccessfully tried to introduce in 1860 on his two innovative and futuristic, outside cylindered, piston valved Stockton and Darlington 4-4-0 express locomotives, the Broughton and the Lowther, when it was put about, rather disingenuously I've always thought, that the footplate staff preferred the rigorous and harsh realities of an open footplate, with nothing more than the boiler backplate for protection. After my own experience of running tender first in all weathers, it's a claim I found difficult to accept, and one reinforced by a saga recounted to me as a boy by an elderly lady, as I listened enthralled when she spoke of her great grandfather, a Doncaster driver, employed by the Great Northern, and who, one bitterly cold winter's night, drove his open footplate express engine from Doncaster to Kings Cross through repeated snow storms, before arriving, on time of course, suffering frost bite to his face and hands.

I am now more inclined to the view that the failure to provide protection was part fear of the driver falling asleep if made comfortable during their long and arduous 12 hour shifts, and in part (with little thought of the crews) a reluctance to spoil the outline of their splendid locomotives with anything as outlandish as a well-designed cab. This corporate attitude persisted well into the 20th century, as a survey of the cabs adopted by some of the major railways of the day clearly confirms, and where, on many locomotives, a simple extension to the cab roof would have proved a great blessing. Two examples of the many badly-designed cabs spring to mind: the minimalistic cabs favoured by the Stirling brothers, Patrick Stirling of the Great Northern, and Matthew Stirling, Locomotive Superintendent of the H&BR, whose shallow slab-sided cabs, although enhancing the general outline of their tender engines, offered neither much in the way of protection, or help when controlling the engine's movements. This was particularly true, as the 'Rule Book' warns, during the hours of darkness, in fog or falling snow, when the driver, on the lookout, with senses sharpened, yet hampered by the adverse conditions, and the unhelpful shape of the cab, and reaching for a regulator or brake handle tantalisingly positioned just out of reach, by some draughtsman who felt they looked attractively laid out on his drawing board, must have often been startled by the unexpected jolt of a sudden and unexpected 'buffering up'.

In 1890 T. W. Worsdell retired, full of honour, to be succeeded by his brother Wilson, likewise, once a pupil of the Altoona Works. Under his captaincy, and aided by two outstanding mechanical engineers, the department's Chief Draughtsman Walter M. Smith, and Worsdell's personal assistant, Vincent Raven, compounding began to lose favour, though mention should be made of Smith's later tour de force, that masterpiece of design, his two splendid 1909, four-cylinder compound Atlantics, which possibly being over engineered, were never repeated. With compounding losing favour, out went Joy's valve gear, and in came Stephenson's link motion. And here as a point of interest, to northern enginemen, valve gearing was always referred to as 'motions'. At the same time came in Smith's segmented piston valves, and because the East Coast route between London, Edinburgh and Aberdeen was, for passengers, becoming increasingly important, the need for faster more powerful express engines became an urgent requirement. To that end, Gateshead began the production of a new class of engines.

The first of these, number 1620 of the 'M' Class series, a 4-4-0 with 7 feet 1 inch coupled wheels, and 19 by 26 inch cylinders, was, like the remainder of its class, the most powerful express locomotive in Britain at that time, and proving, in traffic, to be flyers. Among the many outstanding runs attributed to the M's, the concluding night of the 'Race to the North' set a record for the 124¼ miles from Newcastle to Edinburgh, which years later, the best of the LNER Pacifics found difficult to equal. That night, 20 August 1895, with engine 1621 (which now rests in all its glory within the National Railway Museum, York), driver Robert Nicholson of Gateshead, aided and abetted by his fireman Tom Blades, another firebrand, ran the Aberdeen night sleeper the 124¼ miles in a whirlwind 113 minutes. That's an average speed – average mind you – of 66 mph, despite slowing for tight curves at Morpeth, Alnmouth and Berwick, followed by the 4¾ mile climb over Cockburnspath Bank, and on approach to Edinburgh that hot

August night, the slow negotiation of the Portobello curves. It is difficult to imagine what conditions were like on the footplate, as, at full throttle, with wheels pounding the open joints of the short rails then in use, over track not quite up to later standards, Tom Blades, feet firmly planted on the rocking footplate, fired quickly and deftly through the open flapper, whilst a stream of white hot cinders drawn from the very depth of the fire bounced off the roof of the train.

If the conditions on the footplate were extreme, spare a thought for the passengers, for whom that wild ride through the night must have been the stuff of nightmares, including those who, having paid a premium, and hoping therefore to take advantage of the sleeper's comfortable bunk beds, now lay awake in mortal fear, as the short length four and six wheel coaches tore through the night, flanges grinding against the rails, jerking and gyrating as if to jump the track at any moment.

For those detraining at Edinburgh, the stop for a change of engine crew must have come as a blessed relief. In the meantime, backing down on the train came one of Matthew Holmes' North British, four coupled bogie express engines with 7 foot driving wheels. If those travelling on to Dundee, or further to Aberdeen, were hoping for a more gentle, less frightening experience, they were in for a shock. Manning the engine, the Scottish driver and fireman, names unfortunately unknown, but men with backbone and fire in their bellies, were more than happy to take up the challenge, and on the 'Right Away' ran the switchback, sharply curved, 59½ miles to Dundee, including speed restrictions over the lengthy Tay Bridge, in an astonishing one hour (yes, over 59 mph, on average). And on the continuing 71½ miles to Aberdeen, over heavily graded and reoccurring lengths of single track, in a blistering 77 minutes (an average 55 mph).

As someone who spent years struggling with what was then a class of modern engines, built in 1947 and 1948, but which were, despite this, much given to running hot in bearings, side rod bushes, knuckle pin joints and big ends, I can appreciate how mechanically sound and efficient those small locomotives were, able to travel long distances without running hot and with boilers able to maintain boiler pressure under extreme conditions. All of which reminds me, with a sardonic twitch of the lips, one old driver's maxim: "Why, nowt's hot 'til it takes tha skin offen the back of your hand." An exaggeration, of course, but you get the idea.

In 1896, William Worsdell, delighted with the performance of the Class 'M' flyers, designed a larger and more powerful version, designated Class 'Q', with the same 7 foot 1 inch diameter coupled wheels and cylinders bored out to 19 x 26 inch. And at the same time, in obvious anticipation of further races, and on the same frames, he built two pure racing machines, the splendid Class 'Q1' 4-4-0's, with 7 foot 7.25 inch wheels, 20 x 26 inch cylinders and a longer firebox. In view of the out-and-out risks taken during the races, it was perhaps fortunate for all concerned that the Class 'Q1's' were never called upon to race to Edinburgh against the London and North-Western Railway's finest. Sadly perhaps, no attempt was ever made to determine the 'Q1's' top speed.

But the two Class 'Q1' engines whose beauty of line and refined proportions made them arguably the most elegant 4-4-0 to grace any railway anywhere, were merely the forerunners of an even more outstanding class of locomotives, the famous NER Class 'R' 4-4-0 (LNER 'D20'), locomotives with 6 feet 10 inch coupled wheels, 20 x 26 inch cylinders governed by 10 inch piston valves, and whose large boiler was pressed to an unusual 225 psi. Built to exacting standards throughout, they became a byword for reliability and hard work. The first, number 2011, entered traffic in August 1899, and double-manned with its own crews, and often with loads exceeding 300 tons behind its intermediate drawbar, ran six days a week from Newcastle to Edinburgh and back in the morning. On its return it would go on shed where the Dust Hole men cleaned the fire, cleared the smokebox of accumulated cinders, and the ash pan of ash, before making its way round to the coal stage for coal and water. Afterwards oiling the engine all round and turning it for the next crew and its return trip to Leeds later in the day: a monumental 2,700 miles a week. Even more remarkable, 2011 clocked up an astonishing 284,000 miles in just over two years, before its first visit to Darlington Works. And if that record wasn't enough to seal the Class 'R's' claim to fame, the remainder of the class were rattling up similar mileages.

Despite the triumphs of the Class 'R's', pressure was mounting for larger and more powerful locomotives right across the board. As a consequence, Gateshead's spacious drawing office was already preparing drawings for a splendid head-turning 4-6-0 passenger engine, with the classification 'S', and the honour of being the first British passenger engine of that wheel arrangement, although, with its smaller 6-foot 1-inch wheels, it would strictly speaking, be classed later as a mixed traffic engine. Unfortunately, the first three, Nos. 2001, 2002 and 2003, had to be built with foreshortened cabs to accommodate the existing turntables, which not only spoilt the engines' appearance making them look ungainly, but reduced the distance between the tender and the firebox to such an extent that with their 23 square feet of grate area, and long narrow firebox, these first three must have proved a very difficult and laborious engine to fire. But with 20 x 26 inch cylinders, 10 inch piston valves, 200 psi boiler pressure and an adhesion weight on the coupled wheels of 42½ tons, they, like the Class 'R' before them, proved impressive locomotives, as I was to find out working them in the mid-1940s and early 1950s. By then the 'R's' were still a useful secondary express engine, capable of fine work. Whilst the final run of the 'S' Class, the powerful 3-cylinder 'S3' line, whose 6 feet 1 inch coupled wheels gave them a handy turn of speed, were, even late in life, important enough for Edward Thompson to rebuild, with raised running plates and Walschaerts valve gear replacing the customary Stephenson's inside link motion.

With modern piston valves and streamlined front-end steam passages to improve steam flow, whatever may be laid at his door, Edward Thompson, true to his NER roots, and as such, ever mindful for the wellbeing of engine crews, fitted his locomotives with carefully arranged controls, rocker grates, drop-down ash pans, and self-cleaning smoke boxes. And to the envy of any driver or fireman seated in those 'foreign' (i.e., non-NER) engines, with their open draughty Spartan cabs (of which many remained until the end of steam) I might well add, luxurious bucket seats. I remember picking one such up at York. New out of Darlington Works and making her way south to Hull Dairycoates, resplendent in fresh paint and varnish, and smelling of newness and the work done on her, she was, as expected of an engine straight out of shops, tight throughout, and in that condition steamed effortlessly, riding like a first class carriage. She went like the wind on the express back to Hull.

In 1913, one of the 'S3' lineage, number 825, became the subject of extended trials with Stumpf Uniflow cylinders, this being a revival of an 1849 experiment, which failed mainly because of the inability at that early stage, of keeping the cylinders steam tight. Even in 1849, the cooling effect on live steam, using the same ports and passages as exhaust steam, with its subsequent loss of power, and increased fuel consumption, was well understood. By having separate admission ports, and separate exhaust ports, Uniflow cylinders were an attempt to overcome this problem. This was achieved using Walschaerts valve gear, with piston valves to control admission, cut off and notching up. Exhaust was via ports halfway along the cylinder being overridden by a piston. This gave a short, very direct communication with the blast pipe. Elderly drivers who had fired 825 spoke of her short sharp and very precise exhaust, her free running, and as one veteran put it, her ability to steam on: "Nowt but a few shovelfuls of coal." After some two years hard running, during which her coal consumption showed a distinct reduction against others of the class, she was, for whatever reasons (which must have been compelling), rejigged with ordinary cylinders.

In 1901, Wilson Worsdell, impressed with Ivatt's GN Atlantics, and even more by the Philadelphia and Reading Railroad's exemplary high flying 4-4-2, sailed to America with several of his staff, to observe and study the work of the Reading Railway Atlantics, now making a name for themselves in the world. On his return, fired up by what he'd seen, he set about designing his own 4-4-2 locomotive. The result, number 532, outshopped from Gateshead works in late 1903, being the forerunner of 30 two-cylinder Class 'V' Atlantics. Boasting a 5 feet 6 inch diameter boiler, with a working pressure of 200 psi, cylinder volume was increased from the NER standard for heavy engines of 20 by 26 inch, to 20 x 28 inch, and 6 feet 10 inch coupled wheels This imposing machine, the most powerful passenger engine yet seen in Britain, caused a stir on its release to traffic. Set to work on the demanding Newcastle-Edinburgh turns, she quickly proved to be the best.

Worsdell now had a stud of exceptional engines to his credit. He had his Class 'T' 0-8-0 heavy mineral engines (used mainly for moving coal), his Class 'S' 4-6-0 engines, and also his famous Class 'R' 4-4-0, notable for the outstanding work they did. And then there were his new and more powerful 'R1' series engines, with the same 5 foot 6 inch diameter boiler as the Atlantics, but with pressure upped to 225 psi on the clock, 10 inch piston valves to give free admission and exhaust, variable blast pipe, and to prevent slipping with the heavy East Coast trains, the extraordinary 42 tons resting on the coupled wheels, all of which made them exceptional.

Add to this, there were a variety of other worthwhile types, including the Class 'X' 4-8-0 heavy duty three-cylinder tank engines, through which he introduced to the NER three-cylinder simple propulsion. Wilson Worsdell can be said to have ushered in the NER's big engine policy, and in 1910, after a distinguished career marked by greatly increased loads and speeds, Worsdell, leaving behind as legacy a huge increase in the company's motive power, which was to serve it well into the future, and fêted by his peers, chose to retire. His position, now classed as the more familiar Chief Mechanical Officer, was taken by his long term friend and personal assistant, Vincent Lichfield Raven who, having spent the whole of his professional life serving the NER, was an engineer steeped in its history and traditions.

With the demand growing for even more powerful locomotives, Vincent Raven introduced the Class 'Z' Atlantics which, whilst closely following the outline and style of his predecessor's Atlantics, benefitted from three-cylinder propulsion and superheating. Although in its infancy, and sometimes uncertain in action, the most effective Schmidt-type superheating was chosen, giving a marked reduction in water and fuel consumption against the Class 'V' Atlantics.

Anyway, enough digression, for we still have a train bound for Blackpool awaiting us at Paragon Station, and the passengers are getting fractious. Yes, 32 years after number 2165 had first entered traffic in June 1914, and on that splendid summer's morning, I stood on her deep footplate with a profound sense of her history and exploits, and with the shades of those hardy men, who in all conditions, had driven her hard, resting heavily upon my shoulders. Satisfied I had the hang of Mr Metcalfe's injector and I wouldn't have to go cringingly cap in hand to the driver and ask for help with its bewildering array of water handles and steam valves, I began to clean and polish the boiler back plate and its fittings using a handful of oily cotton waste, for it was not only drivers who liked the footplate clean and tidy. Part way through, behind me, I heard the lap plate between engine and tender give a little as a weight came on it, and turning I faced the driver. A tall chap, hawk-faced, and of about 60 years of age, and rather slim after years of rationing. His dark eyes, fixed on me, now held the faraway look of someone who had spent his life, despite what weather may have thrown at him, searching the distance for those all-important, but often elusive signals. At that moment I dubbed him 'Hawkeye'. He was unknown to me, a stranger, perhaps from one of the opposite shifts, for at Botanic the twain hardly if ever met. Or perhaps from Dairycoates and none the worse for that, although that may be a matter of some dispute. In any case he had probably spent many years at Botanic, for he knew his way around the place.

Observing my youthful figure, whilst no doubt hoping for a more experienced workmate, he asked, "Are you the fireman?"

Somewhat awed by his presence, I replied, "Yes."

His next question inevitably being, "Have you ever fired one of these before?"

"No," I had to confess; was that a slight trembling on his lips, as he turned away, his worst fears confirmed? Taking a bottle of tea from the pocket of his black jacket he placed it on the tray above the firehole door, next to mine, and lifting the lid of his box seat he stowed away his 'grub tin', a round topped tin, shaped to take a sufficiency of sandwiches, and if Lady Luck smiled, an onion. Then slipping off his top jacket, he carefully folded it and placed it alongside.

Alluding to the engine's stores and equipment, and its general fitness to leave the shed, he asked, "Have we everything?"

"Yes," I reassured him, thinking of the spare firing shovel I had placed at the back of the tender, just in case I broke the shaft of my own, or so I had one to fall back on in the unlikely, but not unknown, event of mine being lost overboard.

"Alright for water?" he queried.

"Yes, a full tank," I replied. Taking his oil feeder, which as custom dictated I had filled and wiped clean, he went round the engine, checking its trimmings, and where necessary, topping up its oil cups and boxes with engine oil.

With Hawkeye busy elsewhere I took the opportunity to examine the fire, and found myself in a bit of a predicament. Twenty-one sixty-five stood alongside and in close proximity to a row of buildings comprising the booking on office, the drivers' and firemen's mess room, and the stores, and in those conditions, allowing the engine to blow off or make a reek, risked bringing a storm of wrath around my head from irate staff, and for those reasons I had unwisely neglected the fire. Now to my dismay, I found much of it burnt out and dead. Fortunately, Lady Luck was about to smile on me: I still had a large back end, which I was prepared to sacrifice, and which was well burnt though and red enough for me to spread around the grate without making a stew and upsetting everyone. Then with care, and little softly-softly firing, I was able to more or less retrieve my fire.

After checking the oil boxes and trimmings, Hawkeye returned to cast another critical eye over my youthful frame, which in his eyes spelt trouble, and a fraught and difficult trip ahead. "Are you fit?" he asked—a local way of asking if I had everything under control and ready to go. After firing on the H&BR main line with heavy trains and a variety of engines, including Robinson's 'O4's, Thompson rebuilds of the same engines, and a variety of 'khaki coloured' engines, the eight-coupled War Department engines. I felt I could make a decent hand of today's beauty. Rather, though, it was something quite insignificant that bugged me, as we moved off in reverse gear. It was something which was about to expose my youth and lack of experience, and perhaps what I feared most: the lash of Hawkeye's tongue, if he vented his frustrations. At the departure end of the loco yard, where it led out onto the station's engine line, was located, within a stout weatherproof box, a series of push button route indicators, which when pressed informed Paragon's signalmen, A) that an engine was about to leave the shed, and B), where and what its destination was. But here was the rub. I had no idea the whereabouts of Blackpool, or what our route should be. It was all vague and distant. And whilst I could discount the more familiar H&BR section, and the Hull to Scarborough line, I was at a loss to know our route. Was our path via Sheffield, Doncaster, Leeds or York, all marked as destinations in the indicator box, but nothing marked for the distant Blackpool. Meanwhile, with Hawkeye's age, austere manner and negative attitude hanging between us like a veil, I feared his reactions and the lash of his tongue at being burdened with a no-hoper, as I was forced to ask which indicator to press. In my anxiety I was perhaps misjudging him, for his reply was quite even tempered: "Leeds lad, push Leeds."

Trundling out of the locomotive yard, we joined others waiting to be directed on to their respective trains. This gave me time to strengthen my fire, whilst being careful not to make smoke, for to the left, the engine line was close to Victorian terrace housing, whose wifely inhabitants were always ready to complain if the washing they had laboured over became marked with engine soot, and to the right of the engine line, on the far side of the through running lines, reared the Western General Hospital, with its many open windows and spirited matrons and ward sisters eager to report any engine crews who allowed offending smoke to drift their way. For the careless fireman this meant receiving a dreaded Form One, a printed form which stated: "You have committed the undermentioned irregularity. Your explanation is required within 24 hours." If the explanation was unsatisfactory, a note to that effect was entered into the man's service history. Another, and more serious offence, was being late for work, but with only three minutes leeway allowed at Botanic, it was easy to slip up a little when booking on for an early morning shift. Having said that, I have every sympathy for a harassed shed foreman dashing around with his 'flapper down' seeking a replacement for a late or absent fireman or driver.

As a young railway employee, it was not unknown for me to occasionally get into scrapes, both on Cottingham Station and at Springhead. At neither did I ever hear a whisper of a Form One, leaving me to wonder if they even knew of their existence. But Botanic Gardens, despite its visions of a gentle horticultural way of life, was different, being rather free and easy with its Form Ones, as the following story indicates. Booking off duty one evening I was handed a Form

One. Because of safety concerns, a Form One was only handed out at the end of a shift (possibly to prevent upset and consternation when the soon-to-be-recipient of the form was still working). Surprised and mystified by this unexpected dampener on what until then had been a pleasant trouble-free day, and reading on, I was charged with causing distress to a female by discharging hot cinders from an engine whilst passing beneath Selby Street footbridge. I was a bit miffed by this, feeling my only part in this unfortunate affair was to throw coal into the firebox, whilst the driver was responsible for throwing it out! But that said, it begs the question, had this been to the detriment of the lady's underwear? Because service history remained undisclosed and secret to employees, and no one knew if and when an adverse entry had been recorded, it was the fear of receiving a Form One which had the ability to intimidate and keep in line the more junior members of the footplate staff.

But to return to the 'engine line' and the job in hand: with my fire knocked into shape, our turn came to leave and, under the guidance of subsidiary signals, take up the long diagonal 'gathering line', which stretched the width of the yard, giving access to Paragon's 14 platforms, its yards, stock sidings and large domestic coal depot. Arriving on our train Hawkeye let 2165 roll back gently onto the train's buffers, as excited passengers, glad to escape the war-ravaged city, with its streets of wrecked buildings and heaps of stinking rubble, crowded the platform. A little group of interested spectators had gathered to see what kind of locomotive was, for a few brief hours, about to whirl them away to a more attractive environment, namely the exotic delights of Blackpool, with the more knowledgeable gazing down between the engine's claret frames to examine its middle engine, the three sets of Stephenson valve gear and, on its driving shaft, fitted with the precision a Swiss watchmaker would have been proud of, the engine's middle big end and six eccentrics.

It was the fireman's duty to couple up, or as the local idiom would have it, to 'hang on'. Afterwards, walking back through the knot of onlookers carrying the tender lamp, prior to fitting express headlamps for the first time in my life, proved one of my proudest moments up to that point. Back on the footplate once more, I looked around. Through the open flapper the fire slumbered a dull red. In the two gauge glasses the boiler water bubbled near the top nut, whilst the pressure gauge showed a full head of steam. The boiler back plate and its fittings glowed brightly as the morning sun struck across the cab, and the footboards, swept clean earlier on, would remain that way for the rest of the trip. I had stuck my trusty shovel, its shaft polished by months of work, and ready for whatever was needed, firmly into the coal on the tender shovelling plate. Meanwhile Hawkeye, having blown off the train brakes, sat on his seat, relaxed and at ease with the world. Satisfied everything was in good order, I turned to look at the platform colour light. As I did, it flicked from red to green. This was it then, something I had longed for and dreamt about, but never expected. I was, I felt, now at one with the valiant souls who, in the past, had worked this splendid locomotive in hard and difficult circumstances.

Excitement welled up as I peered down the length of the train, eyes searching the shadows for that flash of green from the guard's flag. Faintly heard above the noise of the station, I caught the warning whistle, and in the shade cast by the station's canopy, I saw a flicker of green. Turning to the silent austere figure seated opposite, and hardly able to control the excitement in my voice, I gave the "Right away!" Hawkeye stirred, his dark gimlet eyes fixed firmly on his colour light, and spun his reverser out of mid-gear, down to its stop on full travel. And with the regulator within hand reach, and senses awake to any slip of the mighty coupled wheels, he opened the regulator. In a flash, steam flooded the engine's three steam chests, blowing past the valves and into the cylinders. 2165 stirred, shook herself a little, and began to move. As the first few exhausts took effect on the fire, they raised a swirling blizzard of loose white ash within the firebox. Picking up speed, we threaded our way through the station yard, before leaning into the curve at West Parade to follow the line along Selby Street and its infamous footbridge—yes, the one which had once earned me a totally unwarranted Form One. Hereabouts, with 2165 now working hard, its fire incandescent and wearing thin, was time for some serious firing.

My first shovelful went into the back left hand corner, producing an explosive eruption which flashed like the corona of a distant sun around the open flapper, whilst at the same time, producing a momentary darkening of the engine's clear exhaust. As I continued firing, the exhaust thickened, and with it, the open flapper plate became a mad inferno of flame, with a white-hot radiance at its centre. Legging it down the main line, I began to recognise that despite its size and impressive appearance, 2165, without its tender, was an engine that was no larger than those 'A7' and 'A8' 4-6-2 tank engines that I'd fired in the past. By now I'd got the better of Mr Metcalfe's exhaust injector which, purring contently, was working perfectly on my side of the cab. Heartened by this, and by the fact that despite her heavy train, 2165 was steaming freely, I settled down to enjoy the trip and all it had to offer.

I knew the road as far as Brough. Beyond, lost in a faint blue heat haze, the track lay straight and level for many miles, and as such was a notable galloping stretch since the days when John Gray's remarkable 2-2-2, high-pressure 'express engines' of 1840, romped along the Hull and Selby Railway. But to me that sunny morning, an unknown country lay ahead; my *Ultima Thule*, yet with a promise of rare delights and unknown surprises. Steaming along merrily Brough passed in a blur, the kettledrum rattle of points and crossings to mark its position, followed by a succession of stations, each one greeted by a shrieking, long drawn out whistle, warning tardy railwaymen or others crossing the line that we were approaching, and approaching at speed. Exhilarated by my first experience of main line express running, and for my heightened senses, all too soon Hawkeye was shutting off for Barlby Junction and the slow approach over the River Ouse swing bridge to Selby and the tight curves through the station, where just to the north I caught my first sight of the impressive Selby Abbey in all its honey-coloured magnificence.

Then, leaving Selby behind, Hawkeye put his left arm to work on the regulator as he lifted the train the six miles up Micklefield Bank. The next day, Monday, my regular mate Freddy asked me if I noticed Micklefield Bank? Truthfully, I could say "No." Perhaps at this point I was busy firing and using the slecker to prevent tender dust blowing about. From the top of the bank the line ran level, passing the huge Crossgates armaments factory, before descending the few miles into Leeds Central. Along here, especially at lower levels, I was in for an eye opener: the beautifully formed and aligned brickwork of the massive retaining walls of Richmond Hill cutting. Part tunnel and part cutting, this was before I learned the history of this unusual section of railway.

Excavated in 1834 by the Leeds and Selby Railway, it initially formed the disreputable Richmond Hill tunnel, whose notoriously dark and greasy interior proved such an obstacle to the orderly progress of trains facing the eastward climb out of Leeds, that eventually a kind of lobotomy was performed, when the worst sections were opened out, exposing the track to the kindly effects of drying sun and wind but leaving the graceful curved walls of the original tunnel for me to admire.

On arriving at Leeds we ran down the platform where, waiting at the water column and ready to help was our London, Midland and Scotland Railway

(LMS) pilotman[18]. Whilst I scrambled over the tender to take water, he swung the column round. Monitoring the flow I noticed one of those small inconsequential things which for some reason remain vivid throughout life. Unlike the footplate men I worked with, who traditionally carried their food to work in a 'grub tin' which fitted comfortably in a pocket of their outer black jackets, and in the other, a bottle of tea, the pilotman carried his 'bait' (a West Riding or 'Wessie' term for his bottle of tea and sandwiches) in a square ex-army gas mask holder slung over his shoulder. Ideal for the job, but at the time I thought a bit *infra dig*. After taking water, and back on the footplate, I found Hawkeye giving a good look at my fire. I was a bit put out by this, for unless he was in trouble, the driver left the fireman to get on with the job in his own way, and in my case I had provided Hawkeye with all the steam he required, plus a bit on account. However he quickly smoothed my ruffled feathers by announcing that he felt like doing a bit of firing, something that happened more frequently than the travelling public were aware of, when the man at the controls was the fireman, and the man wielding the shovel was the driver. In this case it was the pilotman driving, whilst Hawkeye gave a masterclass in the art of firing.

This was the one and only time I worked to Blackpool, and consequently I have little recollection of the route beyond Leeds, apart from heavy industrialised towns along the way, and the attractive country between. Arriving at Blackpool Central, to the cheers of excited trippers, we went on shed to prepare the engine for the return trip. After coaling, watering and turning, we moved to the ash pits, where I cleaned the fire and emptied the smokebox of its accumulated ash—hot work on a hot day—and Hawkeye oiled all around. During this time a steady stream of LMS enginemen came to view and pass comment on this unfamiliar, high stepping intruder, which having 'LNER' in bold lettering on its tender, seemed to compound its air of loftiness. With engine duties completed, the pilotman reversed into a quiet dead-end siding, for us to work our way through the coarse bread and 'bungy' sandwiches of the day. Board of Trade regulations at that time allowed engine crews a 20 minute food break between the third and fifth hour of each shift, but in practice food was often snatched 'on the hoof', as and when opportunity afforded. After completing engine duties we still had a couple of hours before 'train time', which I spent listening open mouthed as the two drivers swapped yarns. The pilotman, we learned, had been a Lancashire and

---

[18] A driver who specifically directs trains through stretches of track unknown to the train driver.

Yorkshire Railway man, a 'Lankyman' who, in his younger days, worked J. A. F. Aspinall's 4-4-2 High Flyer express engines through to Hull. Among his many reminiscences were the many hard run races with NER trains between Hull and Staddlethorpe Junction. All too soon for my youthful interest he was examining his pocket watch and declaring it was time to go. Back on our train, the return trip became a repeat of the morning run, except this time Hawkeye, perhaps feeling his age and aware of the work yet to come, left the firing to me. Under the expert hands of the pilotman, 2165 put in another magnificent performance. On full boiler pressure, heaving its heavy train up the more distinct grades with gay abandon and a roar from the chimney enough to wake the dead.

Finally, as we approached Leeds Central, the pilotman vacated the driving seat. "It's a clear run down to the water column from now on," he informed Hawkeye. "Just drop me off at this end of the platform. It will save me walking all the way back." After slowing to walking pace, the pilotman dropped off, and with a wave of his hand, and clutching his precious gas mask case, was gone. From here on, it would be tedious to recount the run from Leeds to Hull, but my first descent of Micklefield Bank deserves a mention. This section was always run at high speed, and this time was no exception. After breasting the summit at about 60 mph, the pace rose steadily as 'shut off', but unchecked, we ran down the six-mile gradient.

I found this an intoxicating experience which ended abruptly at the foot of the bank, where we hit the 'flat' square on South Milford crossing with a crash that seemed to threaten the stability of the engine, followed almost immediately by further heaves and lurches as we drove over the points and crossings of the two-directional Gascoigne Woods Junction, leaving me to fear for the engine's springs, and pondering how, under such everyday punishment, the crossing and junction were both maintained in safe working order.

We arrived back in Paragon late in the evening, when the station's colour lights showed bright against the deepening shadows. I was tired after a long day, but excited and feeling fulfilled and complete by the day's events, and cheered by having laid to rest the nagging doubts I had over my ability to produce the steam that a hardworking express locomotive surely required. Regretfully, as stated, this was the only time I worked to Blackpool, but an even greater disappointment, this proved to be the only time I had the privilege of working that pinnacle of Northern Eastern Railway's express locomotive design, a Raven Atlantic; a type constantly admired since years before, and one that had caught my attention when, in all its glory, it came thundering through Cottingham Station at full stretch. A few months after my Blackpool trip, 2165, now numbered 2971, under the LNER post-war numbering system, worked a train northwards to Darlington via York in, I am sure, as sprightly manner as ever, after which, somewhere behind Darlington Works, unseen by ordinary eyes, she regrettably met her end.

And here, with us back at Paragon Station, it might be of interest to examine the workings of what was then a complex and labyrinthine yard, with over 800 different movements to juggle with. Nor must we forget those periods of bad weather, when dense fog or equally impenetrable falling snow hampered a driver's ability to observe either his fixed signals or his shunter's hand signals. Let us, then, go back to a grey overcast winter's morning, many years before—to the morning of 14 February 1927, in fact, when, despite every safety device man's ingenuity could contrive, two passenger trains met in a head-on collision on the approaches to Paragon Station.

The details of this catastrophe, where 12 passengers were killed and 24 were seriously injured, have been reported many times before, but the incident's inclusion within the pages of this book is apposite due to one important visual reminder that is often omitted: the high boundary wall separating the Western General Hospital from the station yard. This wall is directly opposite the point of collision and, whilst only faintly visible, for the bricks were an excellent match, closer inspection shows that a large section of the wall has been rebuilt. Running in and out of the station as a fireman, I assumed this was a result of one of the air raids on the city, until a driver, who as a fireman had witnessed the collision and its aftermath, assured me this was the point where the rescuers and hospital staff had broken through the wall in a desperate attempt to transfer the injured into hospital as quickly as possible.

The precise location of the collision acquired something of an evil reputation, and I could see why, when in 1944, 20 years later, on the way into Hull by train, I passed the bodies of a signal fitter and his mate, killed when they stepped out of the way of one train and into the path of another. Sufficient to say, the inevitable consequences of the 1927 collision were a complete rejigging of the station's signalling, when the multitude of lever-drawn signals and calling-on boards were replaced by push button, electric colour lights, and points and crossings controlled by an electro-pneumatic system.

For reasons of safety and simplicity, all movements within Paragon Station and yard were now governed by two easily understood principles. The first applied to drivers shunting the station, its sidings and yards, and also light engine movements in either direction between the station and the loco shed, the watchwords being 'Sub to Sub' and 'Sub to obstruction'—i.e. move from subsidiary signal to subsidiary signal, or more importantly, from subsidiary signal to obstruction. An obstruction could be coaches left in platforms for any reason, or trains made up and awaiting and engine, or vehicles in stock sidings, the coal yard or one of the station's other yards.

For trains departing, including those working empty stock or Walton Street washing sheds, a different maxim applied, with colour-light to colour-light now being the 'truth and the way'. For those trains a green light at the end of the platform signalled the road was set through the yard to West Parade, a manually operated signal cabin, and the point where the main running lines diverged, 'A' line swinging south through the city before curving west to follow the River Humber as far as Staddlethorpe Junction, where its slow line swept south to Goole, Doncaster and Sheffield, whilst the fast line continued on to Selby and Leeds. Centrally, the Hull, Scarborough and York Railway, the 'B' line, headed due north, whilst the former Victoria Dock railway, the 'C' line, bore right to skirt Botanic Gardens locomotive shed, before winding its way through Hull to Wilmington Junction, where it separated into the Hornsea and Withernsea branch lines.

Incoming trains were likewise led on the basis of colour-light to colour-light, the final colour light normally showing a yellow cautionary aspect, indicating the receiving line was clear up to the red signal on the dead-end buffers. Occasionally, in place of a yellow, a Sub was showing, warning the driver that the platform he was about to enter was occupied, to a greater or lesser extent, and he must now proceed with all due caution from Sub to obstruction. Perhaps only Paragon could get away with a manoeuvre as fraught with danger as this. In its defence, and thanks to the vigilance and skill of engine crews, no accidents occurred during its many years in operation, and for all that I know, despite the station and its environs now only a shadow of its former self, this system might, in its depleted form, still be in operation.

Chapter 12
A Failed Experiment

In around 1946, more modern and more powerful locomotives, though mechanically not better machines, were arriving on the scene. Also, with heavier trains, the 4-4-2 wheel arrangement, lacking the adhesive grip of a six-coupled engine, were becoming redundant. It seems an unfortunate oversight that not one of these superb machines, resplendent in NER livery, their trailing splashers adorned with the NER coat of arms, all brass work highly polished (including the large oval brass number plates which had been such a feature of the cab sides), were saved for future generations to admire.

Around this time Tanky Link worked the last train of the day to Brough, home of the Blackburn Aircraft Company, where many of the nightshift detrained, and a place made famous throughout the war for the aeroplanes and cigarette lighters it produced (some claiming it produced more lighters than planes). This train returned to Paragon empty stock, a short non-stop run of about 10 miles, but one longer than the short hop between stations, and one taken easily as the driver nursed his out-of-breath engine home. True, a GN Tanky would run all day with a reduced pressure of around 120 psi on the clock, a pressure just sufficient to maintain 21 inches of vacuum throughout the train, but leaving little to play with. This was never good enough for me, however, and I strove mightily and with all the ingenuity I could muster, to maintain a high boiler pressure, still believing (quite erroneously of course) that higher steam pressure meant higher speed.

Meanwhile, booking on duty on Saturday afternoon, after a week which included working the last train to Brough, Freddy and I were advised because of weekend engineering work occupying much of Brough Station, that we would have to run forward to Staddlethorpe Junction and run round our train there. This would then entail a return, non-stop, empty stock run of about 20 miles, which, apart from the approach to Hull, is fortuitously on straight and level track. Nevertheless this was far in excess of the short four or five mile hops between stations which was about all the GN Tanky's, as a class, could manage with any degree of efficiency, before their chronic state of breathlessness overcame them. Despite everything I had experienced, I felt, given favourable conditions and a fine bit of timing, this could be a golden opportunity to urge an unresponsive old slug into something of a racer.

My stratagem was to simply run my boiler down on the approach to Staddlethorpe, and whilst running around the train and taking up position on the Down side, fill the boiler to its maximum. At the same time, with the jet fully open, I'd maintain as high a firebox temperature as possible, with a view to an all-round red-hot start, which I hoped, before the inevitable fatigue overcame her, to whip 4514 into a gallop—a gallop I felt she would maintain, even when gasping on reduced boiler pressure.

At Staddlethorpe we ran round our train before coming to a stand on the Down line, opposite the junction cabin. With the jet hard on, the injector working, and the boiler water now in the gauge glass top nut, everything now depended on how quickly we were given the road. Too much delay and I would have to shut the injector off before the boiler swamped. Already the steam pressure was somewhere off the gauge, and anxiously I gazed along 4514's creaking groaning boiler, where receding into the distance whilst I prayed they would turn green, a succession of red signals led on. With the whole of the engine in a very hot condition, shutting off the injector would, without any shadow of doubt, cause the old girl to react violently, lift her safety valves, and by so doing pick up her water and empty her boiler, resulting in the loss of my dream, an ignominious crawl home with frequent stops for a 'blow up' (to build up steam pressure), and harsh words from the normally placid Fred.

Deeply concerned at the way things were going, I was on the point of closing the jet and shutting the engine down, when in the distance, as mere pin pricks of light at the limit of my vision, I saw the first signals turn from red to green, followed by others in succession. In the dim light from the cabin I saw the signalman 'pull off' as our starter turned from red to green. Freddy gave a pop on the whistle as a thank you to the signalman, who raised his white rag in reply. "Take her easy," I warned, "she's full to the whistle." Cautiously, with only a little regulator, so 'she didn't get hold of her water', Freddy moved off. This was it, the launch of my experiment!

By the time water began to show in the water gauge, Freddy had 4514 in her normal running positions of regulator and reverser. With steam pressure still off the gauge, and streaming a plume of white hot cinders from her tall elegant chimney, my bonnie black beauty, her front end beginning to bounce, was into her stride. I had a critical 10 minutes or so of extremely high steam pressure in which to discover if for once she would break into a proper gallop, before falling boiler pressure and water required me to turn on the injector, an action I knew would quickly knock the steam pressure on which I was relying back to 120 psi or so. By Crabbly Creek crossing, 4514's front end was bouncing to such a degree that I began to wonder, though not for the first time, if there was enough play in the bogie guides for the axle boxes to move freely up and down, or was there a tendency for the axle boxes to seize and lift the bogie wheels clear of the rails?

On our right, the Humber flowed dark and menacing. Whitton Sands lightship with warning lights flashing, tugged and heaved in the strong current, and across the deep-flowing estuary, the blast furnaces of Frodingham West's steel works flamed vivid red against the night sky. Approaching Brough, Freddy hung onto the whistle, a warning to the engineering gangs working by the light of large Tilly lamps. Here water levels had fallen to half a glass, and with steam pressure beginning to show just below 200 on the 'clock' I had no other option but to put the injector on, an action I knew would quickly reduce the pressure I was relying on. However, we roared through Melton Halt, spitting fire and brimstone, and on through Ferriby Station. By the time we reached Hessle steam pressure was down to 130, but 4514 was maintaining her speed, and with little more than a mile to go, where on the rise to Bridge 5A, Freddy would be shutting off to negotiate the reverse curves at Hessle Road Junction, by which time my experiment would be over and done with.

Years later, as a Passed Fireman[19] working a driving turn, I experienced an unexpected and major shock hereabouts. Just a few hundred yards forward of Bridge 5A, in the Down direction, stood Hessle Road crossing's distant signal, followed, on the curving downgrade beyond the bridge, by the crossing's outer home signal. At the foot of the downgrade, Hessle Road crossing, the most notorious of Hull's level crossings, bisected the railways which carried many of the trains, both passenger and goods, entering or leaving the city, and as such

---

[19] A 'Passed Fireman' was the terminology for a fireman passed for driving e.g., when short of drivers.

was the cause of much delay to road users, and here, partially obscured by the looming bulk of the former H&BR high-level Neptune Street steel girder bridge, which formed its backdrop, stood a diminutive, rather obscure home signal, protecting a crossing always teeming with buses, lorries, cyclists and pedestrians. Behind the signal arm, as a sighting aid, was affixed a white sighting board, a board somewhat faded and discoloured by weather and the smoke and fumes from passing trains. It was the practice of drivers approaching Hull in the Down direction to shut off on the rise to Bridge 5A, thereby slowing the train for the falling curve leading to the infamous crossing, and just beyond it Hessle Road Junction. Approaching Bridge 5A on a day of blinding snowfall, driven on by a fierce south-westerly gale, I had already marked Hessle Road's distant signal in the off position, and lured on by my love of speed had delayed shutting off until I had cleared Bridge 5A. With snow driving past my side glass, I caught the crossings outer signal as expected in the off position. Running fast and leaning into the curve after being given a clear section, it was a mere formality to pick out the elusive home signal. Nevertheless, training and discipline ruled and I was on my mettle.

When it came into view, indistinct through the swirling snow, I saw with heart stopping suddenness that the signal was not, as expected, in the off position, but firmly on. In a flash I became engulfed in a sea of helplessness, horror and utter confusion. Helplessness, because I knew I was about to overrun the crossing by several hundred yards, and horror at the carnage I was about to inflict on those using the crossing. At the same time a riot of confusion and doubt swirled around me. Could I by some strange aberration, some quirk of the mind, have misread those two all-important signals, the distant and the outer home? With a cry of the damned, I threw on the train brakes, a feeble ineffective gesture, and hopelessly, applied the engine's steam brake.

Alerted by my cry of despair and unexpected application of the brakes, the fireman leapt across the cab. Standing behind my back I heard him whisper, "Oh my God." Impotent, stiff with fear and shock, and with nothing left to avert disaster, I could only await the inevitable. Then through the driving snow, to relief beyond understanding, I saw the gates closed to road traffic, giving me a clear uninterrupted run over the crossing. With brakes screaming the length of the train, I swung round the curve to come face to face with the home signal, when in an instant my fears fell away.

With a relief, which only a condemned criminal must have felt on being reprieved moments before execution, I gave a shout of exultation, "It's off, the signal's off." Now close up, I discovered that driving snow had obliterated both the signal arm and sighting board in a blanket of pristine white snow, but leaving untouched on the sighting board, as a dark shadow, the distinct shape and form of a semaphore arm set at danger. Arriving at Paragon, a few minutes later after my alarming brake application, I received some questioning looks from those passengers in the 'know'.

For all the trouble I had gone to on my epic empty stock dash from Staddlethorpe to Paragon, did 4514 break into the hoped for gallop? Not a bit of it, despite my best efforts, like the rest of her class her indifferent front end arrangements choked on its own steam, building excessive back pressure in the cylinders, and effectively preventing the engine from running free. And whilst she lifted and bounced her front end in splendid style, she cantered along at her usual steady gait, finally demonstrating to me it was impossible to make flyers out of this class of locomotive. Moving on with this narrative: about this time the LNER post-war renumbering scheme came into operation, and I well remember the confusion when booking on early one Monday morning: chaos reigned as drivers and firemen, having risen from warm and comfortable beds and in some cases reluctantly it must be said, were given unfamiliar numbers now attached to their engines. Echoing around the booking on hall were cries such as: "Come on Freddy, wake up, the number's 7371, not 4514."

Returning to my lodgings one damp and miserable November afternoon I met an old acquaintance from my days as cleaner at Springhead. We had been good friends, but having moved to Botanic Gardens we had lost touch. On that basis I was happy to stop and renew a friendship. His first words, spoken in shocked disbelief, were, "I've just received my calling up papers for the army!" This announcement came as a complete surprise.

Despite always taking a morning paper, this was the first I had heard of compulsory military service being reintroduced. It seemed very strange and unreal, as the war had ended more than 12 months previously, and servicemen were being demobilised as quickly as possible. At that time, Europe, indeed much of the world, lay in ruins, and in Hull itself shattered buildings and broken streets lay all around. Now in peacetime the world was trying to rebuild shattered infrastructure and revive bankrupt economies, and I'd heard from friends in the building trade that bricklayers and joiners were being encouraged to help rebuild

London. A well-kept secret from those difficult and hard-nosed post-war years, when rationing was its most acute, concerns mainly drivers, who, at the end of each shift, with their grub tins now empty, took the opportunity to fill them with bits of coal to supplement their meagre coal ration—an act of desperation by desperate men in desperate times.

In Britain, on the one hand, the government was demobilising service personnel, and on the other reintroducing conscription. So what was that all about? You tell me! It was a question that puzzled me then, and still does. Was it all a gigantic piece of social engineering by a very left-wing government, a government exemplified by Aneurin "Nye" Bevan's disreputable speech, when he asserted that Conservatives were "Lower than vermin." Anyway, all this call-up nonsense was no concern of mine, for I reasoned that my friend was still in the cleaner grade, open to this unexpected interference, whilst I was comforted by a long-established Act of Parliament which had exempted footplate men from military service on the grounds of essential service during both world wars. And being confirmed as a fireman months before, I was confident I was secure.

Of course, I felt for my friend in his predicament, knowing that his widowed mother relied on him greatly, and on saying goodbye I wished him well, and secure in my mind, I confidently walked the remaining short distance to my lodgings whilst praising God, and others, for the minor miracle of gaining, against the odds, my promotion to fireman and exemption from military service.

Entering my lodgings, I found the house empty, its interior cold, dark and musty. To save on the meagre ration of inferior coal, the fire remained unlit. Only when the cold began to bite would it be lit, to give a little warmth and comfort during evening hours. Glancing around I saw with mounting horror and disbelief, a buff coloured envelope on the table. Scarcely believing my eyes I picked it up. Addressed to me, across the top in bold print, it carried the ominous heading *On His Majesty's Service*. Thunderstruck (but recalling my medical examination some five months before), I didn't need to open it to know the bitter message it contained.

With trembling hands, I tore it open anyway. It informed me that I must report to Victoria Barracks, Beverley on Thursday, January 16th, 1947, for two years compulsory military service. At once, in a flash, all I had worked for, my pride in my work and its position, and my aspirations for the future, were gone. Apart from the shock, which left me in a fog of despair and disbelief, for I was a railwayman not a soldier, I was left with a problem. In effect homeless, what was

I to do with my few possessions—my footplate uniform and my civilian clothes—and just as importantly, where could I stay when on leave? In these circumstances I could hardly expect my landlady to keep a valuable room free for the next two years.

With a couple of weeks to my call-up, my first duty was to inform the shed. The next morning, with this in mind, I took my call-up notice to work, and handed it over to the booking-on clerk, who, faced with a new situation, examined it slowly before announcing he'd pass it on to the chief clerk, and return it when I booked off. After being granted leave of absence on the following Sunday I went to Cottingham, to the family home now occupied by my elder brother and his wife, to ask if I could store my effects with them, and also if I could stay during periods of leave. Childless, with three double bedrooms, thankfully, they readily agreed.

National Service was now imminent, but before its commencement I had one more adventure with Freddy and 7371. Early that morning my jangling alarm clock woke me to one of those raging snowstorms which in winter frequently pummelled the East Riding (or at least they did in those days). I battled through the driving snow, glad to reach the comfort and shelter of the shed and the cosy warmth of 7371's cab. Freddy and I were booked to work the first train of the day to Hornsea, all stops. On our departure from Paragon we found the colour aspects of the line's semaphore signals pretty much obscured by snow. With, as yet, no fogmen[20] at each distant signal to offer help, and acutely aware of the danger of overrunning any of the city's level crossings, we battled on. Once we had left the outskirts of Hull, with its dense buildings echoing our passage, we entered the flat, windswept, open Plain of Holderness, where in these conditions it was easy to lose one's sense of exact position. Even so, by a combination of dilatory timings, set for the equally dilatory Tankys which worked this train, plus the fact that Freddy, from long experience, could have worked this train blindfolded, we managed to keep time. Here as a matter of interest, it may be a surprise to many to know that drivers were never issued with a working timetable, each trip being worked on the driver's skill, judgement and experience.

---

[20] Railway workers tasked with laying detonators (fog signals) on railway tracks during foggy, snowy, or other low visibility weather conditions, to warn drivers of signals, speed restrictions or track works ahead

We reached the isolated Whitedale Station, so plastered with snow it was almost impossible to pick it out from the surrounding countryside. In these blizzard conditions there was no way of catching the guard's 'Right Away', and as things were, foolish of him the leave the guard's van. As we waited, some fiendish Abominable Snowman, a snow-covered apparition, appeared alongside the cab to startle us. This was in fact Whitedale's porter/signalman, who came to give us the 'Right Away', along with the welcome news the section ahead was clear, with signals pulled off into the next section and into the next station. With a warning whistle, Freddy opened the regulator. About 150 yards or so beyond the station the line entered a shallow cutting, 60 or 70 yards long, and no more than six or seven feet deep at the maximum. With 7371 having regained her breath, we were off to a good start, with both of us standing (no seats remember) looking through the front weather glasses into impenetrable darkness. Entering the shallow, hardly noticeable cutting, we became aware of a slowing of the engine's beat. Our first reaction was to glance at the vacuum gauge to see if the communication cord had been pulled. No, it stood at its full 21 inches of vacuum. Mystified as the engine continued to slow, things on the footplate became a bit of a jumble until, glancing over the side of the cab, the reason became clear: a wave of snow streamed over the buffer beam, beating against the smokebox door and flooding the running plates. During the night, wind-blown snow had filled the entirety of this shallow innocuous cutting. In a flash Freddy pulled the Ivatt horizontal regulator from its normal first valve running position, opening the fearsome 'big valve', and at the same time spinning the reverser down into full travel to gain maximum tractive effort. Barking like a hound out of hell, and sending up a plume of fire high into the air, her side valves groaning and squealing under extreme pressure, 7371 slowly forged ahead. In the meantime, realising the ash pan was scooping up snow and delivering it to the underside of the fire grate I shut the damper, fearing a violent and possibly fatal blow back. Then, acutely aware a slip would bring us to an abrupt standstill, leaving us snowbound and helpless, I quickly worked the sanders. Shuddering throughout her length, 7371 gamely held her feet. Blinded by the dark of early morning, and the swirl of snow around us, we hung on with gritted teeth, our only guide to progress or failure, the slow thunderous bark of our exhaust. Then, barely noticeable, the exhaust began to slowly quicken. By a miracle 7371 was hauling herself and her train out of the snowbound cutting and on to clean windswept rails. At that moment, my fervent cry was 'Thank God!' for the high boiler pressure our engine carried, for I am convinced to this day that any other of Botanic's Tankys, each with its miserable 120 psi of boiler pressure, would have stuck fast.

This was only a brief interlude in a trip fraught with difficulties from the start. Having freed ourselves from the cutting, I was faced with a fire now shot to pieces. As feared, I discovered my thin front end, apart from a few larger coals, more or less bare, blown out of the chimney by the tremendous exhaust the 'big valve' had generated. With steam pressure and water levels falling rapidly I had to act quickly, for to fire black unburnt coal over the bare bars was to invite disaster (i.e. such firing wouldn't make steam). Speed therefore was of the essence if I was to avoid the inconvenience and humiliation of a long and costly 'blow up'. Taking the engine's bent dart fire iron from its accustomed place atop the fireman's side water tank, and by now certain the ash pan was clear of snow, I opened the firebox door, and quickly pushed the remainder of the back end forward, covering the exposed bars with well-burnt coal, leaving a thin, level, but effective fire for me to work on at my leisure.

As a point of interest, now might be the appropriate time to examine the action of the double-ported regulator valve carried by the majority of Victorian designed locomotives, one eventually abandoned for more effective designs. The double ported regulator valve comprised first the small, or as it was known the first valve, followed in a vertical plane by a larger port, the big valve. Both were covered by a sliding flat valve and governed by the driver's regulator. Only twice have I seen the 'big valve' opened: that time at Whitedale Station, when 7371 groaned 'under its lash', and the second time was by someone who should have known better—a running foreman. On that occasion the effect on engine 7280, an NER Class 0-4-4 passenger tank engine of 1896 vintage was profound, with the engine notched up to near mid-gear and the regulator open full (or as former NER men would more descriptively put it, 'open full hole'), almost defies description. With full or very nearly full boiler pressure acting on the engine's two slide valves, the valve gear fought the excessive pressure in a crescendo of knocks and groans. So extreme was the strain, visions of bent valve spindles, burst expansion links, and in extremis, a general collapse of the whole valve gearing flashed across my mind, with the broken eccentric rods and other bits and pieces flailing around below the boiler. Adding to this cacophony of groaning slide valves and tortured valve gear, the cylinders and pistons, now deprived of a sufficiency of steam by a cutoff the engine was never designed to endure, complained bitterly by jerking the engine along in a most unseemly manner, whilst emitting from its chimney a series of woeful and discordant exhausts.

In view of the effects of opening a flat-valve engine 'full hole', and the well-grounded reluctance of drivers to do so, it has remained a mystery to me why the Victorian mechanical engineers continued to employ the two port regulator valve, rather than a single port, opening progressively at the driver's discretion. But there it is, perhaps I've missed something here. Be that as it may, in my experience, covering both goods and passenger work, on these old engines, the first valve, with a longer or shorter cut off as required, was sufficient to work the heaviest goods train, or the fastest express. In view of this experience I'm willing to bet my bottom dollar that the famous 1898 high speed race to Aberdeen was achieved using the first valve only, helped by each driver's expert manipulation of the cut off, of course.

As to the rest of our journey to Hornsea, well, despite the deep carpeting of snow that Mother Nature had bestowed upon us, we finally ploughed our way to our seaside destination and discharged the remaining passengers, before preparing for the run back to Hull. And what of the intriguingly named Whitedale, that snow-lashed isolated station set in a flat and featureless landscape, far from anything called a dale in the conventional sense? Perhaps in the distant past, with the line under construction and station's name yet to be agreed, a fiendish snowstorm howled in, as in 1946, filling the newly excavated cutting, the only one hereabouts, and thus endowing the nearby station with its unusual name.

Chapter 13
National Service

My final trip before call-up had proved a sombre affair, and that evening, arriving back on-shed for the last time I said goodbye to Freddy (as so often happened in footplate work, I never saw him again) and leaving my trusty shovel, its shaft and handle polished by hours of work, for another to wield, I rolled up my slecker pipe, itself in many ways a badge of office, and with hand brush attached, left them both in the stores. It was time to leave a way of life which fascinated me and leave my beloved 7371 for an unwelcome and uncertain future. It would be nearly three years before I returned to a much-changed railway. Now bear with me a little, for my army service, whilst throwing up some surprises, did, to a little extent, mirror my railway vocation. My enlisting date fell on January 16th, 1947. Despite its implications I enjoyed my walk from Cottingham to Beverley Barracks, the Home Depot of the East Yorkshire Regiment. The day was glorious, with a clear blue sky and, surprisingly for the time of year, a warm gentle breeze caressing my cheeks to help me on my way. With the instinct of a countryman, I cocked my eyes heavenwards, wondering if this beautiful day heralded a 'weather breeder'.

Despite my dismay and reservations, I stepped out determined to make the best of what I could not alter. Unfortunately, despite my good intentions, I made a bad start: entering the barracks, at this point just a hutted camp, I had to pass the guardhouse, a brick built two-storey affair with a balcony from which most of the camp could be kept under observation. On the balcony, flanked by two regimental police, stood the regimental Provost Sergeant, in immaculate uniform, highly polished boots, white belt and white gaiters (of course there was always a prisoner or two in the guardhouse to maintain his appearance). A wide red sash adorned his uniform, and on his head a red roofed 'cheese cutter', its peak flat on his nose. Finally, a highly polished East Yorks cap badge gilded this particular peacock. All very well if you like that sort of thing.

Something about my appearance seemed to amuse him, and pointing his swagger stick at me, he made some remark, a remark which brought a snigger to the faces of his two companions. Immediately my hackles rose, and all my pent up frustration and deep resentment burst out. From the moment I opened my mouth I knew I'd made a grievous mistake. Yet those three grinning faces spurred me on, and despite his uniform and rank, in my eyes this man was a bum. With deliberate emphasis on the first two words, I called out to him, "Hey mate, where do I want to be?"

In a flash, his attitude changed, and with a howl of rage heard a mile away, he flew down the steps. "Mate, is it?" he screamed, shoving his face incredibly close to mine. "I'll show you if it's Mate! Get yer bloody heels together and stand to attention. What's yer name?" he howled.

Still putting up a resistance of sorts, I merely replied, "Blackburn."

"Blackburn? Blackburn? Blackburn what?" he bellowed.

Admitting further resistance was useless, I replied, "Blackburn, Sergeant!"

Dropping his voice to a whisper, his face as close as paint on a barrack room door, he cautioned, "Watch your step, little boy. I'll remember your name, and if I want to, I'll make your life a misery."

Despite a somewhat unfortunate introduction to army life, I was impressed with the speed and efficiency the East Yorks were able to absorb what up to then was only the second intake (the 102 Group) of National Service recruits. But with my enlistment came a medical diagnosis which put the whole of my railway future in jeopardy. After being checked in I was given a thorough medical examination by the regiment's medical officer, during which I was handed a booklet, each page a blank except for a large circle of multi-coloured dots, and told to read off the number within each circle.

As page after page turned, I tried in vain to identify each number. With suspicions aroused, was this man having me on, or was this some kind of trick, a trick to detect how stupid or otherwise the conscript was? Then as the pages turned, and the dots became larger and more open, through the blur of colour, I began to work out the first shadowy outline of a number. Triumphantly I announced my discovery. The orderly taking the test then reported to the medical officer and delivered a verdict which poleaxed me: "This man is colour-blind," he announced.

Shocked beyond belief and unable to accept this outcome, after the many colour tests taken, the multitude of signals observed, not to mention the hues of everyday life flashed before my eyes. "This is impossible!" I protested. "I'm a railway fireman."

The orderly's reply brooked no argument. "You are colour-blind."

Hopelessness and despair gripped me like a vice. Was this then the end of something I loved with a passion, which dominated my life? Shaking myself free of such pessimism, I took stock of my position. On the grounds of colour blindness, could I wangle a discharge? A happy thought, but dismissed at once. If my brother, hampered by only one eye, had fought as an infantryman, I was convinced the army wouldn't let a little thing like colour-blindness stand in its way. With this thought came the alarming realisation, if I was discharged the railway would want to know on what grounds, thus bringing a sure and certain end to my dreams. Better, I thought, to knuckle down, keep quiet and hope for the best.

After being tested for tuberculosis and found clear, each conscript was 'jabbed up' with a needle, which having done the rounds that day, required some effort to insert into the arm of the quivering recruit. As each man was processed, the company clerk made out his Pay Book, a booklet carried in the left breast pocket of his battledress, ready to produce on demand and containing a record of his military service. But at this juncture, only date of enlistment, category of fitness, inoculations and, as a means of identification (alive or dead) age, height, colour of eyes, and any other distinguishing marks, were recorded. Adding to this ritual, each man was issued with two identity discs, stamped with his army number, and worn around the neck at all times—in the event of death, one to be buried with the body, the other to be retrieved and sent to the army records office.

From the medical centre we moved to the stores for fitting out. To some readers, what follows may seem a needless and tedious account of something long gone, and now of little consequence, but the burden to the long-suffering tax payer of equipping and maintaining the army of conscripts was crippling, extending for many years to come and resulting in even more severe rationing regime than the one in force during the war. Even more damaging to the nation, many conscripts were employed in the building trades, and as such would have been better employed by remaining in those cities destroyed and crying out for rebuilding. As far as I am aware, the political reasons for this mass conscription have never been properly explained. At the stores, each conscript was issued with clothing and equipment which, apart from a refurbished rifle, bayonet and steel helmet, were all brand-spanking new. The following list gives some indication of the cost of equipping a 1947 foot soldier, for what seemed to me, some dubious political experiment:

Issued: two pairs of black leather 'ammunition boots' (I have no idea why they were so called, unless in the days of muzzle loading cannon, with cannon balls expended, they were stuffed up the barrels and fired at the enemy—probably with great effectiveness). Each boot was nailed up with heel and toe plates, and the regulation 13 studs—something to be jumped upon if one was found missing during frequent boot inspections; four pairs of undyed, pure wool socks; two sets of underwear, vests and pants; a PT vest and shorts; two shirts, khaki; a total of four uniforms, comprising a 'best uniform' for walking out or special parades, a second best uniform for more mundane occasions, and two sets of working denims for everyday use; two pairs of ankle gaiters; an army great coat, with an ample collar (which no matter how savage the weather, we were forbidden to turn up); likewise, a pair of woollen gloves, worn only when off duty; and to complete his uniform, each man was issued with an army beret and East Yorks Regimental cap badge.

Our webbing equipment, known as Field Service Marching Order, or FSMO for short, included the soldier's broad canvas waist belt, to which was attached, via webbing, a large pack; a small pack containing, among a few personal items, two tin plates, knife fork and spoon; two field service mess tins, which in the absence of a drinking mug, often had to serve instead (as best they could). Attached by straps to the small pack, a rolled up waterproof groundsheet, which during periods of rain served as a cape; and arranged to fit across the chest, two ammunition pouches and gas mask container. Miscellaneous equipment included two excellent bath towels; a 'Housewife' containing needles, thread and darning wool; a shaving brush and razor; a pair of boot brushes, a brass polishing brush and brass 'Tidy', inserted behind whatever was being polished, to prevent polish marking the uniform below. And last but not least, the old kit bag, thrown up by a comrade to rest on top of the large pack, when on the move. Equipped thus, and entirely self-contained, each soldier could be moved instantly, anywhere.

Once kitted out, we paraded for inspection by the company sergeant major. At such inspections I found that CSM's normally spoke, as this one did, in a quite even voice. He moved along the ranks giving a bit of gentle advice here and a word of encouragement there: "Remember lad, stand to attention and call me Sir when I speak to you" and "Now my lad, stand a bit closer to the razor next time." To another: "Shoulders back, young man, you're no longer bending over a desk." One he told: "Tighten your belt, son, I fear you might slip through it and be lost."

Anyway, all went well until he came to Williams, who was a bit of a 'wide boy' and spiv. In those days, the normal male haircut was a short back and sides, and this was in keeping with army tradition. Williams was different, however, his hair long, black and luxurious, and combed straight back from his forehead, lying thick above his ears, and cut off sharply at the rear to rest in a thick bunch on his collar. This was an unnecessary import from America I believe. The sergeant major halted. "Haircut before first parade in the morning," he calmly ordered. Williams, jealous of his locks, chose to ignore him.

A few minutes after parade, waiting our turn for the cookhouse, we witnessed something which sent a chill of foreboding through each one of us. Marching with precision, an NCO shouting the step, and other NCOs urging them to greater effort, came our predecessors, the 101 intake. In his left hand each man carried his two tin plates, his arm forced up his back at a painful and unnatural angle, whilst in his right hand he carried his knife, fork and spoon, with eyes staring blankly ahead, and faces set in stone. To a fearful company of recruits, each knowing they too, would shortly be one of them, they marched more like automata than human beings. The cookhouse, where you got what you were given, gave us further insight into army life. We queued along a counter lined with large steel bowls, and even to this there was a drill which had to be followed. Here you held out your plate, holding it just below the rim of each bowl, whilst the cook, taking a ladle of, say, mashed potato, struck the handle sharply on the rim of the bowl, directing the ladle's contents. *Splat*! onto the plate. Occasionally, but also inevitably, some misdirected food would fly onto the well-trodden concrete floor, at which times the hapless recruit was told sharply: "Pick it up!"

I should mention that this culinary imposition was not as bad as that to which my brother Bernard was subjected when he was in the army. Sentenced to a period in the 'glasshouse' for striking an officer (what prompted the offence is now lost to history), he shared a barrack block with eight or so other offenders. At mealtimes they were indulged enough to receive the same fare as their fellow soldiers, but in their case it was put into in a large metal bowl, in which the main course, pudding, and milky tea were tipped in together, with each man having to fight with his spoon to receive his fair share of this disagreeable concoction. One of the punishments Bernard was subjected to involved him shovelling, at speed, a pile of gravel or some other such aggregate through a hole in a purpose-built wall, whilst being harangued by the guards. Once he'd completed this task, he was required to run round to the other side of the wall, and shovel it all back again. How many hours, days or weeks he was made to carry out this futile work is anybody's guess.

Getting back to my first day as a pressed man, that evening we spent sitting on our beds (the army didn't provide seats), adjusting and polishing our webbing equipment. Lights out was sharp at 10 pm and it was here Jimmy Gossop came into his own. Jimmy Gossop, a school friend and fine cornet player, was the regimental bugle player who later became the Bandmaster and Drum Major of the East Yorkshire Regiment. Each night his role was to give the regiment a virtuoso 'Lights Out'. Pure and clear, perfect in every note, each tripping off his tongue flinty sharp in the cold night air, it was a joy I looked forward to each night, and a pleasure which has remained with me.

At 6 am the billet door was flung open with a crash and the light switched on by the Orderly Sergeant. "Reveille!" he howled, "Reveille, get yer feet on the floor, and the last man up will be on a fizzer." During the night the weather had changed, and as he left, leaving the door wide open, a thin curtain of snow drifted in, the first gentle, indication of a long and brutal winter. After cookhouse, in light snow driven by a freshening wind, the company sergeant major came to see how we were shaping up. He walked round, passing Williams without comment. Completing his inspection, he called one of the NCOs and pointing his pacing stick at Williams, said, "Escort that man to the barbers!"

The parade shifted uneasily, afraid of what may come next, but the CSM turned and walked away. Twenty minutes later, as we heard Williams being marched back, we were brought to attention. What met our nervous gaze brought a gasp of disbelief. Deprived of his beret Williams arrived with shorn head, and as the flecks of blood on his bare pate showed, shaven with a heavy and unsympathetic hand. Further humiliation was heaped on his shoulders when he was made to sweep up his own hair. For the remainder of our time at Beverley, Williams, much reduced in style and swagger, was made to march around the camp scalped and bareheaded, a warning to the rest of us not to flout the army's diktats.

Another poor soul, even more unhappy than the rest of us, for none of us with our own lives to lead wanted to be where we were, was a certain King. King was probably suffering from autism or some similar affliction, a condition that, I believe, was unrecognised at that time. King had all sorts of problems, the two most manifest being his inability to march in step (resulting in him swaying wildly from side to side, therefore spreading dismay and confusion to those around him), and the disconcerting way his arms moved in unison with his legs. Despite their best efforts the NCOs were unable to break him of these decidedly unmilitary actions, so, finally admitting defeat, King was removed to the guardroom from where he emerged a few days later with a bruised and swollen face. Whether these injuries were self-inflicted, or were due to the regimental police 'roughing him up' (possibly to dissuade others from getting the ideas of trying a similar course of action) we had no way of telling. For the next few days, King was confined to barracks, spending his days sitting on the bare frame of his bed before being discharged.

By now we recognised we lived in a different world, in a kind of state within the state. A state with its own laws which differed wildly from those which had hitherto ruled our civilian lives; a state where even a lost boot stud, lost perhaps as we marched onto the parade ground, or a simple hook and eye incorrectly fastened, assumed a matter of grave importance. It was also effectively a prison, for no National Servicemen wished to be there. But it was a prison the army of 1947 could easily control without the need for high walls, barbed wire or prison bars, for in my three years of military service I never once heard of anyone going AWOL (Absent Without Leave) despite conditions at times being almost unbearable. Some might dismiss all this by saying we were weak and easily knocked into shape. My reply: we were as tough and hardy as the best of the present generation, having endured six years of 'total war'.

As day followed day, the weather increased in severity, blocking the parade ground with deep snow drifts and preventing parade ground drill. However, the East Yorks had an answer to that: some battle drill. Lined up along the edge of the parade ground in Battle Order, that is, small pack, ammunition pouches, gas mask, steel helmet, rifle and bayonet, we were told we were about to attack an enemy strongpoint in the shape of a hut, and when a whistle was blown, this would indicate we were coming under fire and to take cover by diving to the ground. In view of the depths of the snowdrifts, we were not too happy with this arrangement, feeling there was room for mischief, and sure enough, with a perverseness hard to believe, each time we reached the deepest drifts the enemy, without fail, always opened fire, forcing us to throw ourselves forward into the drifts, where the snow forced its way up the sleeves of our greatcoats, down our necks and under our helmets, at the same time blocking our rifle muzzles and jamming the bolt mechanisms. As pressed men we didn't think much of that as a game at all.

Except for isolated incidences, much of the six weeks' primary training passed in a blur, but other events remain deeply embedded in my memory. Twice a week, and dressed only in PT vests, shorts and boots, and regardless of the weather, we went on what was euphemistically called a 'PX march' (possibly standing for Physical Xercise, who knows!). Designed to take it out of us, it was a forced march at speed. The more mean-minded among us thought it training for one of the British Army's favourite manoeuvres when, with all equipment abandoned, and in the face of the enemy, they beat a hasty retreat. During one such march, as the weather took its toll, my dodgy chest began to complain, and coughing and wheezing like a broken winded horse, I fell out to make my own way back. Nearing the barracks I met a solitary figure, an old countryman, coated up under several layers against the cold, and carrying a bundle of hay on his shoulders. Visibly shocked, he exclaimed, "Good God, they haven't got you out dressed like that in this weather have they?" Well, yes they had.

Another memorable event occurred on a day spent on the open rifle range where, laid out on the snow and under a strict counting of our fired ammunition, we aimed at various targets. This coincided with a visit from a lady dental officer, who in the absence of drilling equipment, spent her time yanking out any teeth showing signs of decay. Blessed with sound teeth I was fortunate to escape her attention. As she fought to extract some deep rooted and decaying molar from the squirming victim, she offered a little light relief by saying, "If I'm hurting you, put your hand up." This innocent remark seemed to offer some amusement to the more coarse minded amongst us! But more to the point, as each treated man returned to the firing line and laid out on the snow in the open, with blooded mouth and aching jaw, they were to find that the recoil from their rifle sent a splatter of blood over the small of the butt, making the rifle difficult to handle, and further staining the already blood-flecked snow around. Not for nothing, methinks, were the East Yorkshire Regiment, the illustrious Duke of York's Own, nicknamed 'The Snappers'.

Reaching the end of our basic training, a number of the intake were ordered to 'Stand To' and prepare for an early morning posting to separate Corps Training camps. Three of us, one a joiner by trade, one a bricklayer (so much for rebuilding bomb-shattered towns) and myself, a railwayman, were being sent to a Royal Engineers camp outside the small town of Lockerbie in south-west Scotland (that quiet unassuming place which suffered so grievously when years later a Pan Am aircraft crashed on it after being destroyed by a bomb[21]. Early the next morning, after being roughly roused from sleep, we marched to the cookhouse through falling snow where, in addition to our breakfast, each man was issued with 'travelling rations'—two thick 'bully beef' (corned beef) sandwiches, which for convenience we carried in our ammunition pouches.

Around 5 am we moved off in single file with rifles reversed, each man holding the muzzle of the rifle in front, and guided by a Lance Corporal with a torch. By now the roads and streets were blocked by snow and abandoned vehicles, with only narrow winding routes through them to Beverley Station. In complete darkness, lashed by wind and snow, we slipped and slithered along under the weight of our equipment, until eventually a faint light marked our destination, whereupon our guide suddenly disappeared. One minute there, the next gone, and who can blame him! Beverley Station lays on a north-south axis, and that morning a cruel wind swept under its over-all roof and along its two platforms, but free of camp discipline we were able to pull on our warm woollen gloves and turn up the collars of our greatcoats whilst awaiting the first train of the day, a Push and Pull from Hull, and incidentally the same train which years before in those blissful days on Cottingham Station, I had sometimes begged a barrowful of coal for the porters' room fire from its helpful fireman.

Time passed and no arrival. Eventually I made enquiries, to be told Hull Paragon was snowbound, its multitude of points frozen solid under the snow and with no trains arriving from either the York or Scarborough directions, this confirmed, if confirmation was needed, that both these route were blocked by snow, and it was now a waiting game. The long morning wore on until about midday the crash and bang of the stations gates heralded the approach of a saviour. A saviour in the shape of a local three-coach train arriving from Hull, headed by a GN Tanky. Eagerly we piled into one of its warm, inviting, steam heated compartments, glad to be out of the biting wind. At Paragon we had to be

---

[21] Pan Am Flight 103, brought down on 21st December 1988.

careful. Military Police (Redcaps), ever ready to stop and publicly humiliate low-ranking privates, for their own amusement, prowled its extensive platforms and halls. Here we had to change to a Leeds train, and once again our little group of three had a long wait, and of the trip to Leeds I have little recollection beyond seeing the Humber, for the only time in my life, largely frozen over. Arriving we found the Leeds to Carlisle departure platform thronged with patiently waiting passengers. With my travelling instinct honed by years of railway work, I moved close to the platform edge, ready on the train's arrival to make a dive, equipment and all, for the nearest door and, I hoped, a favourable place within. When the train eventually rolled in, in the rush to board I took little notice of its locomotive but it was one about to give us a gallop, despite the snowbound conditions.

When the train stopped it was with a corridor end door opposite to where I was standing, and squeezing in I found the train already crowded, with passengers standing along the length of the train. The mass of boarding passengers pushed me along the short length of corridor, and the next coach or coaches were first class, with the vestibule door locked against intruders. Crushed against the locked door I found myself standing in the gangway, on the two overriding lap plates. I don't know who the engine crew were that night, London men perhaps, working through? Possibly Crewe men, but most likely a Leeds driver and fireman to work the penultimate section. Whoever they were, they proved to be a pair of fire-eaters, working their engine hard and tearing along the old Midland main line as if the devil was after them, and giving me, riding the wildly bouncing lap plates in a cold and draughty vestibule, a ride to remember. After standing on the madly thrashing lap plates between Leeds and Carlisle, I detrained with my two companions, to catch a train stopping at Lockerbie. We were out of our depth regarding our destination, and I sought the help of the train guard who generously agreed to keep us right.

Our train proved to be the last of the day, leaving us when we arrived stranded on a deserted station. Whilst it remained bitterly cold, it appeared the further west and north we travelled, the less snow had fallen, leaving a thin covering blowing about in the wind. Lockerbie Station platform proved an inhospitable bed for the night as the three of us huddled together on a platform bench, waiting for the morning shift to come on duty, when contact with the camp could be made. About 9 am a lorry arrived to collect us. Halleaths Camp, Lockerbie offered no visible grounds for optimism. Obviously occupying the grounds of a former country house, that now, lucky for them, formed the officers' mess, it consisted of decaying Nissen huts dispersed beneath clumps of trees, in groups of two or three, over a wide area. I know nothing of the camp's history beyond that it was built on what was obviously once a country estate, and as such had all the hallmarks of a camp built hastily just before or just after war was declared, and then abandoned after D-Day. Everywhere were signs of neglect and decay, with Nissen hut doors hanging on sagging hinges and window frames warped and open to the elements. Even the parade ground, hallowed in all regiments, was a crumbling mess, with grass growing through its broken surface (it was re-tarmacked whilst I was in residence). Together with my two companions we were housed in a rusty, mouldering, Nissen hut. Two unshaded low wattage bulbs illuminated its gloomy interior, and in the centre stood a small coke stove which, because of a national shortage of fuel, we were forbidden to use in any circumstances.

Beds were non-existent, and in their absence we were issued with a 'bed board' to sleep on, a paillasse, which we filled with straw, and a 'bed box' for our uniforms and personal effects. Three thin blankets were issued to each man, one to be wrapped around the paillasse, the other two to serve as not very effective coverings. We had no pillows and at first we used our rolled up greatcoats until we hit of the idea of using the half empty kit bag, and although the canvas was hard and unyielding it proved better than waking with a large brass button tormenting one's ear, and also meant our greatcoats could be used as a further blanket. The cold was so intense that to get any sleep we were forced to go to bed in our uniforms.

Front entrance to 'The Kennels', Halleaths Camp, Lockerbie, taken by the author in the 1970s, long after the camp had been decommissioned.

At Halleaths the duty sergeant and his bunch of ruffians each carried a pick axe handle as a badge of office. Reveille was called at 6 am when this group of ne'er-do-wells went round waking up the conscripts by shouting in a loud voice, and hammering on the outside of each Nissen hut with the pickaxe handle, before dragging it along the hut's corrugations, terrifying those inside before the door was flung wide open. The effect on the unfortunate sleepers by the wall where the blows first landed was enough to induce a heart attack in any but the most stout-hearted. After cold water ablutions (wash and shave) we stored our greatcoat and kit bag in our bed box, folded our blankets in the required formation and placed them in the centre of the bed board. By 7.15 am we were formed up and marched to the cookhouse.

Cold, unheated, its inside walls distempered long ago but now dirty and flaking, it was a building as dreary and uninviting as the rest of the camp, with four rows of bare rickety trestle boards serving as tables. At Beverley each man had been issued with a knife, fork and spoon which he retained for the rest of his service life, along with two tin plates and an enamel mug, which had to be handed in on posting. At Halleaths no such luxuries existed and we had to rely on our two awkward and cumbersome 'mess tins'. Whilst in no way blaming the cooks, who battled with limited and poor quality rations, and even less in the way of equipment, the food was, to put it mildly, awful, raising the cry: "We can't eat this."

After a couple of days, however, and by not examining too closely what had landed in our mess tins, we were glad to eat anything, including, if only we could, the mess tins themselves. As a kind of protest against the abominable food, we deliberately broke step and slugged our feet as we marched to the cookhouse, leaving the NCOs racing up and down the column trying to restore order. It was a futile gesture on our part and one which was to have consequences later. Once having eaten, we were allowed to make our own way back. But this was not without its own hazards.

Almost opposite the cookhouse we had to pass 'The Kennels', the former estate's purpose-built dog kennels—a series of brick-built structures around three sides of a stone flagged square. Completing its outline, the front was made secure by heavy ornamented railings, and ornamental iron gates. But in 1947 it was used

The rear of 'The Kennels'.

for a more baleful purposes, for those in detention, this was the regimental prison, where those in confinement were imprisoned within its narrow cells, unless, as they could be seen at times, marching under escort, to perform some degrading task. This place was somewhat dark and sinister, and we hurried past with eyes averted. Two regimental police stood outside the ornamental gate at mealtimes, and as was the nature of the beast, these two were ready to call you over and subject you to some verbal abuse, or if they felt that way, to detain you.

Now began six months of intense Royal Engineers training, when, day after day, in all weathers, we built Bailey bridges, until even in the dark it became second nature. Each day, as part of our training, we carried a 28-inch 30 foot rolled steel joist (RSJ) for about 50 yards on our shoulders, over broken, frozen and usually snow covered ground. Assembled shoulder to shoulder along its length, we slowly lifted this enormous weight under repeated commands from an NCO. Then, placing our feet with care, and with a slow and deliberate "Left, Right, Left" we moved the joist from one place to another. Even more difficult and tricky was the act of moving it off our shoulders and lowering it, without mishap, to the ground. Looking back now, it seems a miracle no grievous accident ever occurred.

Two events happened around this time, which serve to illustrate the severity of the 1947 winter, the first instance being what amounted to an act of gross stupidity. Situated close to Halleaths and the village of Lochmaben, with a ruined castle guarding its head, the pretty Castle Loch was used at that time by the Sappers to teach watermanship—without putting too fine a point on it, messing about in the water. One morning, with our small packs firmly strapped on our backs, we found ourselves lining its shore. Thick ice and frost covered the surface of the loch, and showing through the ice, barely visible, were several sunken bridging pontoons, with a sorry-looking and waterlogged rowing boat, each crushed by the ice. Trapped with them, but undamaged, were a number of inflatable rafts.

Clad only in our boots and everyday denims, we viewed the scene with mounting horror, praying that not even the army at its most unfeeling would send us into this frigid water. Unfortunately our prayers went unanswered. But first gun-cotton charges were laid on the ice, and in a spectacular explosion, shattered it around the wrecks. When things had settled down, our worst fears were confirmed when we were marched in, knee-deep. Gasping and reeling from the shock of the cold we were told: "You are all wet now, so no hanging back." The taller of us were ordered in even further with instructions to attach stout lines to the nearest pontoon. Even to our inexperienced eyes, hauling ashore a pontoon filled with several tons of water, and firmly grounded, seemed an impossible task, and so it proved.

Taking hold of the line, we were given the preparatory order: "Take up the slack." At that we laid our weight along the line and waited for the now familiar "All together", a slight pause to ready us, then the dominant order "Heave ho!" With one mighty heave, the line with 120 men on it snapped like a length of rotten thread, throwing us all either into the water or to the ground, and failing to move the pontoon a fraction. Repeated attempts by doubling the line proved just as futile, and eventually that idea was abandoned in favour of retrieving the inflatables. Between each event, to keep some life in our frozen feet and limbs, we were made to double round for a few minutes. Gasping and heaving for breath, it was something I found nearly as bad as paddling around in the ice-cold water.

Around midday, two army lorries arrived bringing that most welcome of army standbys, tea and bully beef sandwiches—a blessing which in their hour of need had sustained countless soldiers. I remember when the container lids were lifted how the tea steamed in the frosty air, but by the time it reached the lips, by way of a flat cold mess tin, it too was cold and had lost its appeal. In the afternoon we turned our attention back to retrieving the inflatables, but by now with cold and exhaustion affecting many of the men, the whole madcap scheme was abandoned. However, this was not the end of the matter. The next morning at reveille a cry of dismay went up when we tried on our boots. Still wet from the day before, overnight they had frozen solid. Like the NCOs at Beverley, those at Halleaths pushed us hard, but it must be remembered, these were veterans of World War II who, having fought a formidable enemy for so long, would have thought wet feet the least of their concerns.

Our second struggle with the elements came when we were called upon to aid the civil authorities, or to be more precise, the railway administration, and whilst this action could only be judged a failure, it had the merit of being a worthwhile objective. For several days a fierce blizzard swept the south-west of Scotland, piling snow on snow. As it abated we were each issued with a shovel and told to prepare for an early start the next day. No information as to what this was all about was forthcoming, but at around 3 am we were roused from sleep and marched off through the darkness, into the unknown: which turned out to be a railway line close to where bridge-building was practised. A place where, when a train had dashed past, I had often gazed at it lovingly, wishing I was on its warm and familiar footplate. This morning we found ourselves unexpectedly boarding a waiting train, and making ourselves comfortable, we quickly fell asleep. I awoke as the train ground to a halt, in a snow-covered landscape, miles from anywhere, but with clear blue skies and sparkling sun. We detrained on to a low embankment, and with two railway workers as guides, made our way along the track to where a rounded hill next to a deep cutting, now filled with wind driven snow, barred our way. Ominously in my eyes, the telegraph poles alongside the railway began to progressively get shorter, disappearing under a mountain of snow as they entered the cutting. We climbed the hill to where the telegraph poles barely showed above the snow, and once there we were informed that, somewhere below us, entombed, lay a train[22]. Our job, we were told, was simple: dig it out. This wasn't too bad a task we thought, it was a beautiful day, the sky cloudless and the sun warm, and we had the benefit of a flat calm to work in. So, piling our greatcoats on top of the telegraph poles, we set to work with a will, attacking the snow both from the rail level and from above. Unfortunately despite our enthusiasm, we soon ran into difficulties, as disposing of the snow we had dug out became a problem, severely hampering our efforts.

By mid-afternoon, having failed to make much progress, we became aware, far down the line, of a mighty and unnerving roar, at first faint and indistinct, but growing in volume until it became deafening. Then, coming into view, propelled by a locomotive, came a bogie flat waggon, on which was mounted some kind of infernal machine blasting out white hot flames, and crewed by RAF men. We had never seen or heard its like before, and could only think this was some kind of mighty flame thrower. At the time it never crossed our minds that, constrained to a railway line, it was unlikely to be of much use on a battlefield. To give it a free hand we moved away down the railway, and my last view was of it being inched forward and blasting snow in all directions. To this day I have no idea where in Scotland this, my first encounter with a jet engine, a technology that was about to change the world, took place.

---

[22] Throughout Britain the winter of 1946/47 saw large snowdrifts blocking roads and railways, disrupting coal supplies to factories, power stations and homes, and causing severe hardships in a country still recovering from the war. Food became scare as supplies were cut off, and in the countryside, vegetables were frozen into the ground, and herds of animals froze or starved to death.

Captain Van Reenan, as his shoulder flashes confirmed, was of the South African Army. Apart from being an expert on bombs, mines and booby traps, he was also very fierce, and as such used to put the wind up me mightily. He instructed us on how to deal with deadly devices, including the much feared German S (for shrapnel) anti-personnel mines, which when activated sprang some three feet out of the ground before exploding and sending a lethal swathe of ball bearings for 300 yards around. If this occurred, we were told that the only thing to do was lay flat on the ground and hope for the best. Our first lecture set the tone.

Captain Van Reenan came in. "Right," he said, "stop your coughing, sneezing and farting, and pay attention." As he droned on about Teller mines, the hard to detect Japanese clay mines and the rest, inevitably the cold and half rations we were on took effect, and heads began to droop. "Wake up, you fools!" he barked. "I'm trying to save your lives. If you can't stay awake sitting, I'll make you stand!"

Weeks later, we found him inspecting our rifles. Mine, issued at Beverley, was a much-used and worn wartime weapon, still showing traces of khaki paint in the more inaccessible parts of its bolt mechanism. Van Reenan tapped the rifle with his stick. "Rust," he pronounced.

Having been among guns most of my life and proud of my ability to maintain them in good order, I bridled a little. "Khaki paint, Sah," I replied.

"Rust," he countered.

Still determined, I made the point again, "Khaki paint! Sah!"

Tapping the rifle a little harder, his face beginning to set, he snarled, "Rust!"

Once more I tried, but I got no further than "Kha—"

"Yaaah!" he howled. "Don't you argue with me!" This outburst so frightened the man next in line that he dropped his rifle, upon which Van Reenan turned all his attention on him, venting the full fury of his spleen. Thankfully, he never took the matter of my 'rust' any further, having, I think, accepted my explanation.

In spring, as the weather improved, we loaded our bed boards, bedding and bed boxes onto lorries, and moved to a wet bridging camp, somewhere near Castle Douglas, on the River Dee. It was a small unoccupied camp of about four Nissen huts, with a Nissen hut cookhouse. Due to meltwater from the winter snows, the river was in full spate, and for a week, without lifebelts or any other safety equipment, we tried in vain to bridge it. We tried anchoring each pontoon with several anchors—I recall the team used anchors in 'kedge' (coupled together)—but the pontoons refused to stay in line, heaving and swaying in the floodwaters to an alarming degree. Finally giving up before a tragedy occurred, we returned to Halleaths. So ended my one and only attempt at bridging a river.

When marching to the cookhouse we still indulged in breaking step and sludging our feet. One Saturday morning, not long after our failed attempt at bridging the Dee, we were ordered to dress in our best uniforms, boots and gaiters and fall in with our rifles. Rumour spread we were about to have a company photograph taken. As usual on parade, I was ordered to take the 'Right Marker' position. Marching down to the parade ground, I spied the disquieting figure of drill sergeant Vickerman standing in the centre of the square, with his fierce black moustache and huge barrel chest, which we judged he stuffed with a pillow, until 'shirt sleeve order' proved us wrong. His voice, deep and resonant, rivalled a foghorn, and when drilling it extended to the far reaches of the camp. All this made him the very essence of those caricature Drill Sergeants depicted in wartime cartoons.

Nothing seemed quite right. What is Vickerman (who, incidentally, was alleged to be of German extraction) doing here, and suspiciously, why is there no sign of the photographer? Well, we were about to find out. As my left foot touched the parade ground, Vickerman's voice with perfect timing, boomed across, "Ah, Left Right Left, ah Left Right Left!" The column marched to the centre of the parade ground, halted, and left turned. As a prelude of things to come, Vickerman kept us standing to attention, our rifles at the slope.

In silence, he walked up and down the three ranks as tension among us mounted. At long last, he spoke, "I understand you are unable to march properly. You have difficulty in keeping step, and you seem unable to lift your feet off the ground. This morning I am about to correct those faults, and I warn you, if any man falls out, he'll be in The Kennels before he knows what's happened to him!"

For the next hour, our rifles at the slope and bouncing at each step on our bruised shoulders we doubled round the square, until things became so fraught our own NCOs began to encourage us, urging us to "Stick it, lads, show him you can take it." Finally, on the point of exhaustion, and punished enough, Vickerman called a halt, calling on those who hadn't had enough to take one step forward. Billeted in the same hut as me were two East End cockneys, who clung together whilst exhibiting an annoying air of superiority. Earlier I'd crossed swords with one of them and been invited outside for a bout of fisticuffs, which, with my height and long arms being an advantage, was something I readily agreed to, adding that I was game for anything, from tiddlywinks to manslaughter, upon which the matter was dropped.

Personally, I had had enough of this torment, but the two cockneys, full of bravado, stepped forward, and in view of the recent past I felt I too should step forward: if they could take more, I'd match them! Vickerman lined us up before the others. "Look at them," he urged. Now we're for it, I thought. "Just look at 'em!" Oh-oh, here it comes. "The only men with any guts! Fall out, you three," he ordered, "and take a rest."

Then he gave the remainder a few more gallops around the square. And here I wish to stress in the strongest terms that, despite the harsh discipline (and contrary to some modern television programmes showing 'squaddies' undergoing training), bad language, much less disgusting language, was never used, being beneath the dignity of the office that the NCOs held. In those days, the army didn't need to use obscenities to terrify us—in fact, resorting to such measures could be seen as a loss of control, and one thing that every officer unquestionably possessed was total, undisputed, control over us.

Twice a week, in the absence of any physical training instructors, we engaged in what was euphemistically known as 'Milling'. In this, men of roughly the same height and weight, dressed in PT kit and boxing gloves, stood outside a boxing ring. At the blast from a whistle they climbed in as fast as possible through the ropes, hoping thereby to catch their opponent off-guard and deliver the first and hopefully decisive blow. Usually, however, for a further two minutes, standing toe to toe, they knocked the living daylights out of each other—and then it was the turn of the next pair. For one such bout I was paired with a mixed-race opponent of African and English ancestry, whose father was none other than 'Larry' Gains, heavyweight champion of the British Empire. This did not fill me with optimism. In an effort to obtain some sort of parity, when putting on my gloves I got my mate to roll and bind them as tightly possible, giving them the consistency of wood, and I dived into the ring at the first blast of the whistle. Getting my retaliation in first I caught my opponent an upper cut as he was still getting through the ropes. Whereupon he sprouted 20 arms, and from then on all I remember is thinking to myself, "I'm on the floor again? How did I end up on the floor again?"

Even more brutal was the 'Blind Milling'. Eight men, all blindfolded, were lined up at each end of the ring, and on the blast of a whistle moved towards each other, arms flailing. When they met it became a bloodbath. In the ensuing melee men quickly became disorientated as blows rained from all directions, striking unprotected faces and heads, and most dangerously, the backs of necks. As men were felled, others tripped over them, only to continue pounding the body beneath. Lacking the presence of a medical officer or even a medical orderly to intervene if necessary, it now seems a miracle that, although we were all thoroughly roughed up, no one was seriously hurt. Welcome to National Service, army style, circa 1947. Quite what this taught us in terms of engineering, Royal or otherwise, I have no idea.

The bitter and prolonged winter of 1946/7 gave way to a scorching summer. At the end of June, an independent mobile column of about thirty men was formed to specifically overhaul a Bailey bridge and access road on the Balmoral estates. This was under the command of Captain Van Reenan, of all people, who's presence immediately spoilt any sense of the coming adventure, having always put the wind up me. Carrying full FSMO, including rifle, bayonet and steel helmet, were the natives in the northern part of the British Isles about to revolt, we wondered, or was it for the more mundane reason that Halleaths had nowhere to store our small arms? We travelled by train, first from Lockerbie to Glasgow, detraining at Glasgow Central, then marching through the streets to the city's Queen Street Station. The way was steep and lined with granite setts, and burdened by our equipment, our hobnailed boots quickly lost traction as we tried to hold our feet on the polished surface. Then something quite extraordinary moving happened. I have since spent many happy and rewarding holidays among the good folk of Scotland, always finding them willing to go out of their way to help, and that day was no exception. Seeing us in trouble, in an act of spontaneous kindness, the menfolk of Glasgow rushed to help, taking our rifles and kitbags, and with willing shoulders to steady us, helped us to the station. It was an act of goodwill, freely given, and one I shall never forget. At Queen Street we entrained for Aberdeen, where on arrival we marched to a regimental barracks, and there were welcomed, not as our warlike appearance suggested, by what some among us thought might be dissident Highlanders standing at bay, rifles and bayonets at the ready, but with open arms, a splendid evening meal and something we were unused to, a comfortable bed. The next morning, fortified by a good breakfast, we moved to catch a train for Ballater when, on arrival, we made ourselves at home in the empty but well equipped Royal Guards barracks, conveniently situated within the village. For the next six weeks, beneath the shadow of the mighty Lochnagar and Craigendarroch mountain, under the lightest of touches from Van Reenan, we worked on the Royal Estates.

Putting the skills we had learned into practice we first stripped down a Royal Engineer-erected Bailey bridge over the Linn of Dee River, now reduced by sun and drought to little more than a shallow stream, finding its way between large boulders. Once dismantled, we painted the bridge's steelwork, refurbished its decking, and to preserve it safe and sound, greased its securing pins, before rebuilding it in situ. Next we turned our attention to improving a dirt access road, which wound its way up the hills of which the Bailey bridge was part, by digging side drains along its length, then filling the bottom with large readily available stones, around which rainwater could percolate, before progressively filling the drains with small and smaller stones until it was level with the surface of the road. Where the road cut the hillside, we dug similarly constructed 'cats paw' drains to drain and stabilise the slopes. This was done day by day under a blazing sun, with a warning from Van Reenan reminding us that severe sunburn was classed as a self-inflicted wound, and as such a court martial offence.

Whilst not exactly eating from the fat of the land (and who, in 1947, was?), under Van Reenan's benign rule, our rations increased dramatically both in quality and quantity. And further, during our off duty periods, he (amazingly) arranged visits to places of interest, including one to Balmoral Castle where, despite none of the Royal Family being in residence, we were only allowed within the grounds. Interestingly, the house staff had spread out on the lawns the original deep blue tartan carpets, now threadbare in places, and were busily cutting them up to form a more presentable appearance. One highlight arranged by Van Reenan was a visit by an all-singing, all-dancing Scottish entertainment party, who giving their all, delighted us with an evening of song, pleasure and diversion. In view of his obvious concern for our wellbeing, I began to warm to Van Reenan. Years later I wondered who paid for the concert party? There could only be one answer: Van Reenan himself.

Chapter 14
Eighth Railway Training Regiment, Longmoor

On my return to Halleaths with 18 months of National Service remaining, I received some unexpected but exciting news: I was about to be posted to Longmoor in Hampshire—the HQ of all the military railways both in this country and abroad, and where I expected to be reunited with my beloved steam locomotives. That my colourful expectation never materialised is about to be explained. I have little recollection of the solitary journey I undertook, with its many changes of route from Lockerbie to Longmoor, except at Kings Cross tube station, were, lumbered with rifle and FSMO, I was squeezed, with pushes from behind, and pulls from the front, and good hearted quips from all round,

National Service, 1947 to late 1949. Quite what I found to laugh about I'm not sure!

into an overcrowded rush hour tube train, only to find my big pack preventing the train door from closing. At Waterloo Station I adopted my usual practice in these circumstances, of asking the train guard to keep me right for Liss, my disembarkation point for Longmoor and Longmoor Military Railway (LMR).

My first sighting of the LMR was a train standing in the military station, located side by side with its southern neighbour. A train made up of three coaches, headed by an ungainly Austerity 0-6-0 saddle tank, which at its appointed time waddled its way through woodland, consisting mainly of heather, bracken and furze, to Longmoor Downs, the camp's principle station. Detraining I found a large island-type platform, dominated by a brick-built signal box, and served each side by a through-running line, and obviously designed to facilitate the rapid deployment of a large number of men and equipment. Fronting the station, a public thoroughfare, the Liphook to Greatham Road, divided the station from the camp, where a substantial brick-built guard house formed part of the camp's main entrance. After reporting in I was marched by a very regimental Lance Corporal, full of wink and shout (which should have been a warning) to the HQ admin offices, from where, after being checked in, and given the once over, I was then marched to one of the 20 large modern brick-built, two storey barrack blocks, each spacious and airy, with large sash windows, each opened daily, precisely the same distance top and bottom. And what's this? Between each window a proper bed with, lo and behold, a steel cabinet in which to stow gear and hang clothes. After Halleaths with its rusty decaying Nissen huts dripping moisture, its unyielding bed boards and flatted straw paillasse, things were looking up. Allocated a bed I stowed my gear before being taken to the Quartermaster stores to draw blankets and the three 'bed biscuits' that formed a comfortable mattress.

It quickly became apparent that, whilst the railway staff, all regular soldiers, went about their rostered duties with much the same freedom as if employed on a civilian railway, for National Service men like me, Longmoor spelt strict discipline, a place where we experienced many spit and polish parades, including a full kit inspection each Wednesday and Saturday mornings, with each man standing by his bed, on which was laid, with meticulous precision and in set order, his bedding, his spare uniforms including his bulled up spare pair of boots, and even down to his lowly 'housewife', open to display its contents. Any infringement, however slight, brought the ire of the inspecting officer down on the poor man's head. For National Service men the camp's gymnasium, a large structure with spacious windows reaching down to near floor level, was the scene of a four weekly ritual, an 'FFI' parade: a Free From Infection examination, when each man, stripped naked in an unheated and often cold hall, was subjected to a close examination for head lice or other infestations, sore backside or festering feet, but above all, for 'the dreaded lurgy'—VD (a condition known among the more irreverent as 'Spotted Dick'). This was a court martial offence, punished by enforced treatment in the prison ward of a nearby military hospital, and for which Longmoor National Service men provided the guards. Locked in the ward on 24 hour turns, we had a grandstand view of the grisly treatment provided. Alongside the gym ran a footpath frequented by the wives of married officers, on their way to and from the NAAFI shop. I suppose the sight of 40 or 50 naked and fit young men gave them some relief from the boredom of isolated camp life. Well, I like to think someone enjoyed it.

Whatever the reason my being posted to Longmoor, it was, I was to find out, for anything but railway work—unless the time I spent digging out spent ballast and shovelling it into waggons, or loading condemned sleepers onto flat waggons, could be called railway work. Otherwise, like the rest of the National Service men, it was any one of the many mundane tasks around the camp. Each morning men were detailed off, for among other things, cookhouse duties such as peeling potatoes, preparing vegetables, and washing pots and pans etc. Along with others I spent about a week excavating some long-disused cess pits, the contents of which, having now become a fine tilth, were spread on the gardens surrounding the officers' mess. It was a task chiefly remembered for the profusion of large brilliantly coloured dragonflies flitting about the area. But many of the plum jobs were also filled by National Service men. Waiters and stewards in both the officers' and sergeants' messes, who were excused most formal parades, and as such were able to walk to work when the time of day, and the spirit, called them.

Rear entrance, No. 2 sergeants' mess, Longmoor, with the author on the left.

Mustered for work one morning, a call went up for a locomotive fireman. It says something about the disparate nature of Longmoor's National Service men that I was the only one to put his hand up. As an interesting fact, among the many National Service men at Longmoor I only met one other with a railway background. And whilst I did not know him personally, remarkably he hailed from a familiar location, the Alexandra Dock Junction signal cabin, whose 88 levers made it the largest cabin on the former H&BR, and one I got to know well from my time at Springhead.

As my hand shot up, so visions of a return to footplate work eddied and swirled around my head, only to be dashed in an instant when I was ordered to report to No. 2 Sergeant's Mess for cookhouse duties. Longmoor boasted two sergeant messes. No. 1, which I never entered, being the Sergeant & Warrant Officers' Club House, and No. 2, a much larger building serving as cookhouse and dining hall. Located some distance apart, both were built of rustic brick to an attractive neoclassical arts and craft design. No. 2 Sergeants' Mess, located in an isolated position, some distance away from the main camp, comprised a large, tiled, well equipped kitchen, with two coal fired ranges, and a central heating cum hot water boiler. Leading off, two useful walk-in pantries and a preparation room with sinks for washing kitchen utensils. But much the greater part of the building was formed by a spacious dining hall, with a later (wartime) attached, but no longer in use, framed addition. At the further end of the dining hall, a pair of heavy figured oak doors led to a surprise: an attractive, well-proportioned room with mullioned and leaded windows and dominated by a massive walk-in inglenook fireplace, supported by heavy oak beams. A room to be proud of, and used perhaps in its glory days for reunions or formal dinners. In all my time it lay empty and unused.

Reporting to No. 2 Sergeants' Mess I found I was elevated from humble sapper, and now classed as stoker, keeper of the cooking ranges and hot water boiler. The cruel disappointment I felt at being denied footplate work began to fade when I was told this was a permanent position, with unbelievably, its own private bunk accommodation normally reserved for none but senior NCOs. Adding to my growing wonderment, I discovered the staff left after the evening meal, leaving me in sole charge of the place. Surrounded by trees, isolated and quiet, it proved a soldier's paradise, an idyllic way of life spoilt (if that's the right word) only by being roused each morning at 5 am to light fires and whip the ovens up to scratch in time for the cooks coming on duty at 6 am. During the 20 months in that position I was only nabbed three times for parades, although each time was a drama fraught with anxiety and worth recounting.

The first came one very hot July morning, when Field Marshal Sir William Slim, of Burma fame, came to inspect the regiment. For this grand occasion everyone who could be spared was raked out of their hiding places and cubby holes, including myself. Dress was 'best battledress', medals (if any), boots, gaiters, rifle and bayonet. The fact that I was in a parade caught me on the hop. Fortunately as I only wore denim fatigues in the cookhouse, the rest of my uniform was in good order, and to bring my rifle up to parade condition only required a quick pull through and a dust down. Fishing my bayonet and scabbard from the bottom of my kit bag, I was dismayed to find the bayonet, long out of sight and out of mind, dirty, stained and flecked with rust. Annoyed at being nabbed for the parade I did something very silly. Instead of taking the few minutes required to clean and polish it, I threw it in disgust into the bottom of my kit bag.

The next morning, forming up with the rest of the HQ battalion, it began to dawn on me, by coming on this important parade improperly dressed, I was about to bring down on my head the wrath of both officers and NCOs. It didn't help matters when the CSM called on me to take position of Right Marker. What I recognised as a deep deep hole I was getting myself into, now in the exposed position of Right Marker, looked suspiciously like a grave, and I began to search for some way out. Before I could come up with a plan, we moved off under the direction of the HQ company sergeant major, and onto the main square. Once there the RSM took over command, forming the regiment up company by company in three lines across the square. Here, by the quirk of being the HQ company, I found myself as Right Marker to the rest of the entire regiment. Once settled down we were ordered to first stand at ease, then stand easy. I had come to the conclusion that the only way out of my predicament was to feign illness. Sweating profusely, part heat and part fear to achieve that end I began to sway backwards and forwards, something I found difficult to do in a convincing manner. Normally on parade the slightest flicker of an eyelid was enough to bring a swift response. Today perversely, no one took any notice.

Frustrated in my plan, I was about to turn to the nearest NCO and say I felt ill, when Slim, together with Longmoor's commanding officer and a retinue of others, stepped out of the imposing regimental HQ, overlooking the square. Too late, before I could act the RSM brought the regiment to attention, and with Slim and others in place, he saluted and handed the parade over to the commanding officer, who gave the order to "Present Arms!" From now on, under a succession of orders, things went from bad to worse. Next came the order "Regiment, Open Order—March!" followed by "Regiment, Fix Bayonets!" Praying I wouldn't be discovered, I went through the charade of pretending to fix my non-existent bayonet to my rifle. Brought to attention, now was the time of the greatest danger: an inspection by Slim and his coterie of officers and NCOs.

Fearfully, I watched Slim striding towards me. A short man, his legs could have done with being a bit longer, nevertheless he looked every inch a soldier, with his cap circled with a broad band of vivid red, its peak emblazoned with gold. His khaki jacket was set off by his highly polished Sam Browne belt, with medals glinting in the sun, and red tabs, and a profusion of gold tassels hanging from his right epaulette. To complete the picture he wore khaki-coloured riding breeches, brown riding boots and spurs. Yes, spurs! I tucked the muzzle of my rifle under my arm and into my armpit, hoping and praying he would fail to notice it lacked a bayonet.

After a brief glance, he along with others passed on without comment, and I knew I had got over the first hurdle. But this was by no means the end of the matter: worse was to come. Having inspected the lines of men from the front, Slim turned and inspected each man from the rear. I heard them approaching, then in a panic I realised what was glaringly obvious. I had no bayonet scabbard hanging from my belt. A moment's thought earlier, and I could have attached it, and no one would be the wiser. I cringed as Slim and his party arrived, fully expecting a tap on the shoulder, or a poke in the ribs from one or other of them, and a demand for my name. Each one, including our own company commander and his eagle-eyed sergeant major, passed without the dreaded dig in the ribs from a swagger stick.

By some strange affinity, some quirk of fortune, I had escaped this close inspection. But there was still a long way to go, and this was in fact only the start. And nagging me, the fear that our company sergeant major had noticed my default, but chosen not to say anything whilst on parade, but to leave it until back on home ground, where he had the opportunity of throwing the book at me with a string of charges. My next concern: the March Past, in 'Review Order', with bayonets fixed. Three times we swept past the reviewing stand, as we wheeled, the regiments bayonets, all except mine, glinting proudly in the sun. Surely at this critical point someone would note the offence? Perhaps by now the heat and indolence was taking effect among the senior officers, with minds fixed on cool drinks, and the lunch to follow.

Whatever, after the final march past, and after receiving permission from Slim, the commanding officer, a shadowy figure until now, dismissed the parade, leaving us to march off by our company commanders. Now was the crunch time! Would our company sergeant major, at his fiercest and most frightful, come down on me like a ton of bricks? Arriving back at the barracks I waited for the seemingly inevitable blow to fall. Instead, quietly, without fuss, we were dismissed, leaving me to ponder for the rest of my life, what sort of blessed guardian angel had sheltered me that day.

The second time I was prized out of my hidey-hole was to act as escort to someone up before the company commander. Usually this was for some minor offence—dirty boots for instance, or in my time, 14 days for a bent arrow or rusty quiver! But whatever the reason, by all accounts, being an escort was a dodgy business. The company commander's ire might just as well be turned on the escort, especially if he had had a difference of opinion with his wife the night before. Under the direction of a sergeant, with all the foot stomping which went with it, we marched into the CC's office.

Apparently, this unfortunate and misguided man had requested a transfer. "What's this all about?" demanded the CC.

The petitioner then went about things in entirely the wrong way. "Well Sir," he replied. "I'm sick of this place and want a transfer."

At that, the room exploded. "You're sick of this place?" howled the CC. "How dare you, you've insulted the camp, you've insulted me, and above all you've insulted the commanding officer. Now get out before I charge you with gross insubordination."

At that we scuttled out as fast as our stomping boots could carry us, glad that we too had escaped an earful. Two days later the unhappy sapper found himself posted to distant Kuala Lumpur(!), to spend the rest of his service sweating it out under a tropical sun.

Longmoor 1948, with the author on the left

For myself and the rest of Longmoor National Service men, my final parade proved a sombre affair. Drawn up on the main square we were told that, to counter the growing threat from Russia, our service was being extended by a

254

further six months, an announcement met with stunned dismay. To show our displeasure we marched off sludging and scraping our feet. Not that it made much difference as far as I was concerned, for shortly afterwards I was granted seven days leave, and told on my return I was being sent to the Great Western Railway (GWR) at Reading on a pre-release course. Cheered up no end and thrilled by this news, I went home.

However, whilst standing on the station platform at Liss I was taken by surprise. Running west, and flat out, came a train headed by, of all things, a GN Atlantic, leaving me wondering what on earth was a GN Atlantic doing on Southern metals? It was years before I discovered what lay behind this extraordinary event. As assistant to H.R. Ivatt, chief mechanical engineer to the Great Northern, D.E. Marsh had been closely involved in the design of the famous GN Atlantics. After his appointment as chief mechanical engineer to the London, Brighton and South Coast Railway, between 1905 to 1911, he knocked up a class of locomotives which closely resembled the GN Atlantics, and it was one of these clones, being driven with such obvious joie de vivre, that tore past me that Saturday afternoon.

At home I gathered my LNER blues and soft LNER cap together in readiness for my welcome return to footplate work. Then, back at Longmoor after my leave, I found I was being posted to an army camp somewhere on the outskirts of Reading, where on arrival I was told to report to Reading West, a former GWR loco shed, at 8 am the next day. Excited by what lay ahead I made a quick recce to discover its whereabouts. The following morning unusual things occurred in the life of the Reading army camp. I discarded my army uniform in favour of my blues, being careful to mount my Royal Engineers cap badge on my railway cap. If stopped and questioned I could legitimately say I was Royal Engineers and wearing an engineers' footplate uniform. Dressed thus, my appearance caused nothing but distress and confusion, first among the cooks when I turned up for breakfast, holding my plate out, then among the camp's officers and NCOs, especially the officers, who were thrown out of their stride when I saluted them with one of my best. The look on their faces spoke volumes. Was this some civilian taking the mickey out of them, and if so what was he doing on the army camp? Some returned the salute automatically, only to wonder why. Others merely glared. Infantile it may have been, but it tickled my fancy no end when it occurred, and at the same time frequently leaving the officers in need of a stiff whiskey as a sop to their agitation.

The next morning I reported to a typical locomotive shed, but one which held some surprises. My first impression of the loco yard was a number of what seemed to me as fairly archaic looking 4-4-0 passenger engines, remarkable in my eyes for still having outside frames with protruding cranks and side rods. And as if holding everything together, including bogie frames, an old-style smokebox wrapper plate with a multitude of prominent round-topped rivet heads. Adding to this air of vintage decrepitude, a foreshortened cab offered minimal protection during periods of inclement weather. But standing alone, one engine in particular caught my attention, the unmistakeable shape of a GC 'Puggy', a type I thought unique to the LNER, and for many years the mainstay of the Springhead's main line fleet. This was a mystery indeed, and I moved closer to investigate. Yes, despite a GWR style safety valve cover, and GWR writ large on its tender, this was without doubt a Robinson 2-8-0 heavy goods engine. How this embodiment of the LNER goods scene came to be a GWR engine I only found out later, in the fullness of time, as I learned the history of these remarkable engines.

To meet demand during World War I, the ROD (the Royal Engineers' Railway Operating Division) in France required a much more powerful locomotive than the motley collection at their disposal, the preferred option being the Robinson, of which a total of 518 were built. After the war, and no longer required, some were sold to overseas buyers, a few to the LMS, who didn't seem to care for them very much, and some to the GWR, with the majority going to the LNER, who snapped them up. In view of their distinguished service with the ROD, and the numbers involved, it seems unusual that, as far as I am aware, none ever returned to their spiritual home, Longmoor.

Standing out amongst the diverse selection of locomotives dotted around the loco yard (I never did know the name of the shed) were a couple of magnificent looking 'Kings', together with several equally good-looking 'Halls'. One unexpected intruder caught my attention, a Southern railway Lord Nelson Class, looking massive against its taper-boilered neighbours. Had it 'fallen down', I wondered, and been dragged into alien territory? But what a gasp of astonishment was caused by one Hall in particular: it carried a wholly unexpected name, Burton Agnes Hall—a local Elizabethan mansion nestling at the foot of the Yorkshire Wolds, in the heart of the bucolic East Riding. Reared in a narrow restricted environment I found it difficult to understand how this little-known but splendid house came to be celebrated on a GWR engine. Nevertheless my heart swelled with pride at the sight[23].

Reporting to the Shed Foremen, I was told to go to Reading West. Reading had two stations, Reading South of the Southern Railway, and Reading West, the GWR station, and once there join an autocar. Ah yes, an auto car, that must be one of the GWR streamlined petrol driven, single coaches, used upon branch lines, whose shape I had probably picked up from some pre-war cigarette card. I found such a vehicle tucked away in a short dead end bay, but empty with its doors firmly locked. Stymied I hung around for a while before returning to the shed, where the running foreman, a hatchet-faced character, demanded to know why I had returned? After some explaining it became clear that what the GWR called an autocar I knew as a Push and Pull train.

I remained with the autocar crew for the rest of the week, finding I had to adjust my firing techniques to a completely different way of doing things. For someone used only to hard, long-flame steam coal which, when the engine was working, filled the firebox with dense luminescent, multi-coloured flames, I was now firing soft friable Welsh steam coal, a coal with entirely different characteristics, being more like semi-formed anthracite in appearance and volatility. Even under forced draught, with the engine working, this coal produced little in the way of flame, and even less in the way of smoke. Nor, with the engine working and the firebox an incandescent white heat, did this Welsh coal react to fire irons in the same violent way as did hard steam coal, which if used in a last despairing effort, turned the fire bed into a clinging glutinous mess, killing the fire at once and spelling disaster for the unhappy fireman. In direct contrast, GWR firemen freely used a fire iron quite unknown to me, a poker, which as its name implies, they used to poke and prod the fire as and when they felt it necessary.

On the autocar I discovered I not only had to wield a shovel much larger than any found on the LNER, but had to form and maintain an entirely different kind of fire. Instead of the normal 'back end' with thin front end I was used to, I was instructed to shape a kind of hogs-back along the centre of the firebox, whilst keeping the edges thin, a fire which in all my experience would have quickly spelt death by a thousand puffs using the coal I was familiar with.

---

[23] No. 6998 is now preserved at Didcot Railway Centre.

Since the days of the broad gauge, the GWR, as I was discovering, ploughed its own individual and independent furrow, and never more so than in locomotive matters. One such difference, and very important to those using it continually, the design and mechanism of the firehole door. On the autocar I was faced with a different arrangement than any met before, with the firehole, when running, being covered by two heavy fireproof doors. When steaming, with a pull on the fire, the doors remained nearly closed, apart from a narrow gap, sufficient to allow an inflow of secondary air. To prevent cold air being drawn on to the tube plate during firing, a hinged baffle plate with attached chain was raised and lowered between each shovelful—heavy work when combined with GWR's outsized shovel, and often requiring the help of the driver.

After a week on the autocar learning the ropes, I was rostered to work 28 Class 2-8-0 heavy freight engines on return workings between Reading and Swindon, and with the engine's fireman helpfully working the firehole doors and baffle plates for me, I did the firing. The open and exposed footplate reminded me of early NER cabs before they became an enclosed structure in the 1850s, but it was a high summer, the weather kind, and in those conditions I didn't mind the unusual experience of, as it were, firing in the open air. And after nearly three years from the absence of the work I loved, I found it a deeply satisfying and fulfilling experience, adding to which, being goods work, it revived memories of the wonder and thrill I experienced during my first firing turns over the former H&BR main line.

After several weeks on heavy goods work I was privileged to spend the rest of my time at Reading on express duties, firing the ubiquitous Hall Class between Reading and London's Paddington Station. With its prominent sloping firebox, its sharply tapering boiler, and tall copper-capped chimney, I thought them a very handsome locomotive. Unfortunately, in many ways my initial encounter proved something of a disappointment. Used to LNER engines of whatever background, with low footplates where the bottom of the cab was in line with the bottom of the tender water tank, thereby ensuring a lofty spacious cab, I found myself climbing higher ever higher, until, with my head nearly touching the cab roof, and with a feeling of being hemmed in, I finally gained a flat and level footplate.

To prevent anyone dashing their brains out on the cab roof as they climbed in required a large section of the cab roof being cut away at the point of entry, a design fault from a long line of draughtsmen which left the crew to the mercy of the weather when the engine was at rest. It had more to do with how good it looked on the drawing board then any consideration for the well-being and comfort of those who spent most of their working lives in these conditions. Unfortunately it was a design that continued, via Stainer (by upbringing a GWR man) and the LMS, right through the standard engines of British Railways, which apart from the LNER Gresley pattern motion bars and cross heads, were of pure LMS design.

If, on looking around, I expected an upgrade from the austere 28 Class cabs, I was in for a disappointment. For such a sleek, modern looking locomotive, the cab and its fittings seemed curiously old fashioned and out of joint. From the heavy sliding fire doors and baffle plate of the firehole, to a regulator handle which, to operate smoothly, required a substantial counter weight. Affixed to the boiler back plate, an antiquated sight feed lubricator, its glasses usually gummed up with cylinder oil, did nothing to improve the look. Further proof of GWR eccentricities, the vacuum brake application handle had to be applied and released, not with the easy fore and aft movement of other ejectors, but in an unusual, wrist twisting across the body motion. It was a peculiar action, for which there didn't seem any sensible explanation. Then of course the other oddity, a vacuum pump driven by one of the engine's crossheads, for the GWR insistence on creating 25 inches of vacuum instead of the normal 21 inches, which didn't matter much unless a foreign engine was coupled onto GWR stock, in which case, each of the train's vacuum cylinder release valves had to be pulled by hand to prevent the brakes binding.

Glancing around the cab, I noticed a facility missing which at speed helped the crew maintain a sharp lookout, protecting the crews faces and eyes from hot smokebox cinders and the like: outside weather glasses; although on carefully looking round, it became plain the form and structure of the cab would have made them almost impossible to fit. But the need seemed unnecessary when viewed against something outside my experience and a real eye opener: the GWR fitted an Automatic Train Control (ATC), a system which gave a strong audible warning in the cab when approaching distant signals. If the distant signal was 'On' a siren sounded. And if this, for any reason was ignored, the train brakes automatically applied. With the distant signal in the 'Off' position a distinctive bell sounded, reassuring the driver the section ahead was clear.

For the first day or two on the Halls, I worked under close supervision of GWR firemen, who were at pains to warn me, in the limited boiler space available above the firebox, that I must maintain at least ¾ of a glass when working hard, or in no time I would discover the water level unexpectedly and dangerously low. Firing the Halls was the same as other GWR engines, although old habits die hard, and now and again I had to drop a couple of shovelfuls into each back corner. It was during this period on the Halls that I learned the true worth of the ATC, which engine crews relied on to the extent it was not unusual for a driver to calmly read the morning paper whilst running at high speed, something at first I found rather disconcerting (and hardly likely to have been prescribed in the GWR Rule Book). Equally memorable, and again something I found a little unsettling, if thrilling, was, during a week of dense fog with visibility down to zero, tearing along at undiminished speed, to arrive on time each day with the driver in complete confidence relying entirely on the ATC.

At that late period of 1949 an interesting experiment was underway on the GWR. Each morning, shortly after our arrival in Paddington, a train headed by a King drew up into the opposite platform. Nothing out of the ordinary in that, except this train was made up, unusually, by having the GWR dynamometer coach marshalled behind the tender, and a wooden shelter erected in the front of the smokebox, from which, draped along the boiler, ran telephone cables to the engine cab, and along the tender to the dynamometer car. In addition, and connected to the engine's main steam pipes, its steam chests and four cylinders, a variety of pipes and tubes. This was something new to me, and curious, I went over to the group of young engineers disembarking from within the shelter. They were friendly and enthusiastic, happy to explain what it was all about.

In conversation, they explained they were testing a high temperature superheater against GWR's all inclusive 'steam dryer'. As its name implied, it merely dried the boiler's saturated steam on its way to the cylinders. And with this experiment GWR's first mechanical lubricator and a different quality of superheated cylinder oils. All of this came as a surprise, and is an interesting bit of railway history, me thinking the advantages of superheating had been established many years before. But there again, perhaps the sharply tapered boilers, favoured at that time by the GWR, left insufficient room to fit a large superheater.

Chapter 15
Back to Civvy Street and Becoming a Passed Fireman

Returning to the camp one evening, after four or five weeks on the Halls, I was stopped at the guardroom by the duty sergeant. "Get your kit together," he ordered. "And tomorrow, report to Aldershot demob centre, you're overdue your discharge date." It was news I had waited three long years to hear.

With nowhere to go after my demob, and still under the age of consent (then 21), my brother and sister-in-law kindly offered me a home, and so I returned to where I had grown up, and where the presence of my father and mother still lingered. Anxious to resume work at the first opportunity, I reported to Botanic Gardens, where my sudden and unexpected appearance caused confusion and quite a bit of head scratching as seniority lists and charts were examined, and where, after some finger and thumb adding up, it was decided I was now in Push and Pull Link. "Start Monday for three days instruction on Pull and Push workings," I was told.

The author as a young man, after demobilisation.

At Botanic, as elsewhere in the north-east, Push and Pull trains were worked by the famous and indefatigable NER Class 'O', 0-4-4 tank engines (LNER Class 'G5') introduced by Wilson Worsdell in 1894, still hard at work and still completely reliable. They rode as smoothly as a first class carriage, steamed freely and, in the NER tradition, had cabs comfortably arranged and easy to work, and they were engines I loved. If they had a fault it was found in their slipper box crossheads which enclosed the single slide bars and which by their nature picked up any dust or dirt swirling about, quickly wearing down the white metal of the slipper boxes, which in turn affected the piston rod glands, causing them to blow heavily and continuously, and in doing so, enveloping the engine in clouds of steam, especially when departing stations, and continuing to blow heavily with steam on. Yet if the slipper blocks had been re-metaled as and when required, a fairly simple and inexpensive job, a serious and wasteful defect would have been prevented easily. But I regret to say, at Botanic, as at most other sheds, daily maintenance was then a thing of the past.

After my three days of instructions, and picking up where I had left off all those years before, I was rostered in my own right on an early Push & Pull shift. Booking on, I was told, "Your engine is 7280 [we omitted to use the 'BR6' added to all LNER engines], it's in one of the stalls on number one table, and your mate is George Ebbs." And thus began one of the most extraordinary and risky periods of my railway career.

In the darkness of early morning, and whilst looking around 7280's cab with the aid of a torch lamp reeking oily black smoke and soot, my attention was immediately and unfavourably drawn to the two Gresham and Craven combination injectors mounted on the back plate. They were of a type I was familiar with from other engines, but a novelty on the Class 0, the others of that class retaining their original NER injectors, being of an uncertain nature and at times difficult to start. Not a happy way to be on a speeding locomotive with a boiler rapidly declining. The combination injectors had a bad name among enginemen, but in my three years on 7280, they never failed to pick up instantly, and to thereafter sing contentedly until shut off.

George Ebbs was about 50 years old, from Hexham in Northumberland, with an accent so broad and irregular that few on the shed, including other Geordies could follow his manner of speech. Of medium height, slim and lithe, he shared with me a passion for speed, and in places where other drivers usually shut off, George, revelling in the sensation, would leave the regulator open. Another thing in his favour, he was happy to fire whilst I did the driving—a great thrill for a young man, especially on fast trains.

I found 7280 in poor mechanical condition, seriously out of beat, knocking like the inside of Gateshead's main blacksmith's shop, and leaking steam from every gland and joint. Yet, though in extremis, she steamed freely and ran like the wind. In some ways my early days on 7280 mirrored my early days of 4514, in so far as both engines were run down and neglected, and both, shortly after I joined them, left for heavy repairs—4514 to Doncaster Plant (it being a GN engine), and 7280 to either Gateshead or Darlington Works, when unbeknownst to me, she slipped away quietly. My first intimation she had gone was, when booking on duty, I was given 7311, a spare Push and Pull engine, which brings me to a deep and profound mystery, which due to a certain dullness of the brain, I had until recently failed to register. Now in my dotage it haunts me a little, that which should have been blindingly obvious, and which I failed to recognise, until in a sudden flash, it struck me, many years later when sat at my desk writing of 7280's abrupt departure for heavy repairs. In this I refer to the movement between shops, of those locomotives requiring workshop attention.

The mystery, for it is a mystery, is this: how did the city of Hull, with a huge fleet of locomotives to service its vast trade, and the many miles of docks, transfer its engines, on a daily basis, to and from the repair shops without it becoming apparent? To this tangle of engine movements must be added the *ad hoc* transfer of locomotives between Hull and other parts of the system. Tender engines, both passenger and freight, might unnoticed, double-head trains departing Hull, or, equally unnoticed, work trains forward by themselves. However, for smaller engines with limited water capacity, this was never an option, leaving only two alternatives. The first, to work them light under steam—but with long stretches between water columns, this was out of the question for the more diminutive engines. As an example the former H&BR Alexandra Dock loco shed can be illustrated. Remote from other railway activity, it seemed to exist in a world of its own, shunting the complex of docks with a substantial number of tiny 'bug-crushers'[24] aided by several of the diminutive NER Class 'K' 0-4-0's, useful when shunting warehouses, or digging out obscure dead ends, but little else. It was impossible for either to make their own way to the far distant repair works at Darlington and Gateshead. And to some extent this was true of other tank engines including Botanic Gardens' GN Tankys to Doncaster, and the ever faithful NER Class 'O', to Darlington.

This surely leaves only one other explanation: the smaller engines, unable to make the journey under steam, must, with connecting rods disconnected and stowed on either tank top, and with pistons secured centrally, have been attached

---

[24] A somewhat derisory term for a small engine.

to goods trains. Those to Doncaster plant going westwards out of Hull, and those to Darlington or Gateshead going north via Beverley, Market Weighton and the York line. But here's the rub: what irks me is why I never observed any of these 'dead engine' movements. Alas those in the 'know' and who might have enlightened me, have all long gone.

Seventy-two eighty was away for about three months. It seemed a long time when compared to 7371's six weeks, and in view of her condition I began to wonder if she had gone to be condemned and cut up. In the meantime I began to notice all was not well with George. Increasingly he was becoming emotional, lost and vague, his mind not always on the job, and at times breaking down. Asked what was the matter, his reply was he was having trouble at home. Concerned over his behaviour I began watching him like a hawk. In this I was not always successful. One day whilst propelling the train along the Hornsea branch, I had to shut the engine off and brake the train into a station. If this wasn't disturbing enough, worse was to follow.

Part of a morning shift was to Brough where, after the passengers had detrained, we shunted across from the Up slow to the Down slow, and from there into the accommodation loop where, years before, the NER Willie had derailed on catch points at its eastern end. Here we stood for about three-quarters of an hour as a succession of fast freights and express trains occupied the running lines. For several days I had dragged myself to work suffering a nasty chest infection, and standing in the loop a bitter wind blew through the cab making it unpleasant. In view of this, I decided to lie down in the comfort of the nearest compartment. Dozing, I was eventually roused when George began propelling the train out of the loop. As this was a normal everyday procedure, I sat up preparing to rejoin the engine when we stopped in the slow platform. Unlike the eastern end with its catch points, the western end had, as a safety measure, a short runoff leading into a dead end beyond the turnout points, its buffer stops located at the base of a steel column supporting one end of a long footbridge over the station. I roused myself and sat up. As I did so I was flung back into the seat, and accompanied by an almighty crash, the train lurching to a standstill. Horrified, I dropped the compartment window and looked out at a scene of utter devastation. Against the warning 'dolly', George had driven the train through the dead end, smashing through the buffers, and struck the steel bridge support, which promptly collapsed, bringing that end of the footbridge crashing down on the first coach, completing its utter wrecking. Thank God there were no pedestrians on the bridge at the time. In disbelief I realised I had become involved in a serious and unexplained accident; some might say, an inexplicable accident, and for the second time in the same loop!

Being absent from the engine, and feeling I might be judged equally responsible for the accident, I could see this might well spell the end of my career, for already rumour around the shed had it I was a 'Jonah', and as such to be avoided. People quoted my first trip, which ended in suicide, a time I collided with another engine on the ash pits, and now, for the second time, a cock-up in the same loop at Brough.

Leaving the wreckage of our two-coach train, its leading coach now reduced to matchwood under the collapsed footbridge, with the second reared-up, hump backed, its under-frame bowed, we returned to Botanic light engine. There, not for the first time or last time I was lucky. Booked off duty for the remainder of the shift, I left without being required to make a statement or write a report. But recognising my part in the accident and the precarious position I was in, and with visions of my career coming to an abrupt end, I cast around for a defence. That evening I went to the doctor who promptly signed me off as suffering from acute bronchitis. The stratagem seemed to work, for on my return the matter seemed to have been dropped, or perhaps wisely and generously, my absence from the footplate was something George chose not to divulge. Thereafter, once the footbridge was restored and resting on a stout brick built column, the loop became for evermore known as Ebbs' siding.

George no doubt received a dreaded Form One for this accident and must surely have received a penalty for his footbridge 'irregularity', but he still remained a driver, and not long after my return to work I became involved with him in a comedy of errors, which would have done credit to the Keystone Cops at their most zany, and further evidence of George's wandering mind. Preparing to leave the shed we discovered, most unusually, the engine's tanks required topping up. The nearest water column was just along the departure line, and was unusual in that it was hardly ever used, and what set it even more apart, its on/off water valve positions were in reverse to the remainder of the other shed columns.

With George on the running plate checking oil cups, I drew up at the water column. In these circumstances it was normal for the driver to put the long leather bag, or tube, through which the water flowed, into the engine tank, and to supervise the rest of the operation. George stood watching the tank fill, and when nearly full, shouted, "Steady." Automatically, I spun the water valve to the closed position, only to discover I was opening it further. Thoroughly confused, I spun it one way and then the other.

At this point George should have taken swift evasive action by hiding behind the smokebox door, but instead, ignoring his years of experience, he merely stepped back a couple of paces. As the tank filled and overflowed, the bag, pulsating along its length like some huge slimy grey-green monster of the deep, began to slither out of the tank. George still firmly held his ground, until with a whoosh it freed itself from the tank, and with its mouth flapping wildly, discharged a full pipe of icy water at George, hitting him fair and square in the face and almost sweeping him off his feet.

As was their wont, the water column arm now swung round to resume its normal position, and before I could shut it off had bored a hole in the soft surface about two feet deep by the side of the water column. George, dripping wet from top to toe, climbed down and advanced towards me in a manner most menacing. "What are you doing!" he roared. "Just look at me, I'm wet through from top to bottom!" At that moment, he sealed his fate by placing his foot into the water-filled borehole, pitching forward and falling headfirst into the seemingly bottomless pool left by the errant water column. Fortunately, this additional drenching seemed to cool his wrath, although to anyone observing our antics, it must have seemed as if two idiots had been let loose from a lunatic asylum!

After being away about three months, 7280 returned as quietly and unobtrusively as she had left. She seemed to have been away a long time when viewed against my only other benchmark, 4514, who earlier had six weeks in shop. Now she was back, and was well worth the wait. By more or less rebuilding her, Gateshead had done her proud, except for the ugly LMS type shed and number plate now disfiguring the expertly varnished smokebox door, and, as such, an anathema to LNER men, who preferred the number and shed allocation displayed proudly in bold ornate script on the buffer beam. Whilst at shops, under the British Railways renumbering scheme, a six had been added to all LNER engine numbers, making 7280 now 67280, a digit ignored by shed staff throughout the remaining years of steam.

At first, however, 7280 proved a disappointment. Comprehensively overhauled and refurbished, her big end brasses tight on the shaft, she was found stiff and unresponsive to an extent that it was difficult to keep time on inclined sections. This was aggravated by indifferent steaming, chiefly caused by the front end now being clean of carbon deposits in the exhaust passages and blast pipe, resulting in a soft and gentle exhaust which failed to lift the fire. As her motion loosened a little and a film of carbon coated her blast pipe, she resumed her ability to make steam and run freely.

Unlike engines rigged with balanced slide valves, the Class 'O' were encumbered with ordinary flat valves which, if provided with a reversing lever only, would have made them impossible to 'notch up' with steam on. In these conditions the only course open to a driver was to close the regulator, lift the jiggling valve gear, playing both on the lever and driver's shoulder, and with hope, drop the lever into the chosen slot—something not always achieved at the first go. When successful the regulator would be opened with a consequential snatch on the train, with its inevitable cause of alarm among the more gentle of the passengers. To watch a driver trying to notch up a lever-controlled NER Class 'P' 0-6-0 mixed traffic tender engine of 1896 vintage on a branch line express, was enough to bring on an attack of heartburn.

On the various runs 7280's valve gear began to attract my attention, in particular the position of the two adjustable weights, secured to the weight bar shaft by studs. What caught my attention was the position of the weights that, in keeping with the rest of the class, were located about half way along each arm. Their purpose, as I was aware, was to act as a counter to the weight of the valve gear, and I reasoned the length of the weight bar shaft arms would at the design stage have been carefully calculated to gain the maximum effect. If that was the case why were the weights not fixed to the outer extremities of the arms? It seemed that moving the weights was worth a try. One afternoon, after booking on early so as not to be disturbed by George or anyone else, I loosened the weights' retaining studs and slid the weights as far as I judged prudent, and with bated breath awaited the results. The result when out on the road was truly astonishing, transforming an ordinary run of the mill locomotive into a flyer. Not only that, using the lever only, the engine could be notched up easily against steam, using just one hand.

There are recorded instances of similar locomotives occasionally touching 80 mph, and with long experience of fast running I can confidently claim 7280 frequently exceeded that speed, and at such times, with wondering eyes, I would lean out of the cab to watch the side rods and coupled wheels rotating at what seemed impossible speeds. What was happening with the pistons hardly bears thinking about. Yet at these very high speeds, with 7280 consuming enormous amounts of steam, she continued to steam freely. This may have been in part because I always ran with both the front and back damper open. This was partly a reaction to my time on the GN Tankys, fitted with only a front damper, which because of a restricted airflow below the grate, failed miserably to maintain boiler pressure. But in addition, when at speed, they would blow from the ashpans the fine ash and grit which otherwise found its way into my lungs each time I raked the ash pan out. Nor fortunately did the blown-out grit seem to have any effect on the engine's working parts. Running an aged engine, much as Wilson Worsdell, chief mechanical engineer, of the NER had imagined 47 years before, fast, effortlessly, and gracefully even, was the stuff dreams were made of.

A Push and Pull worked the last train to Brough, returning empty stock. It was a short but fast run of 10½ miles, which 7280 accomplished as a matter of course in 12 minutes (an average of over 52 mph), start to stop, including the rather sedate passage through Hull and its environs. Even more exciting was the 08:28 morning business train from Hornsea to Hull, running on first class track on express headlights, and with 7280 in its restored condition, at record speeds (although with no speedometer I can't say what this would be). Among its distinguished commuters was Hull's then stipendiary magistrate, a Mr MacDonald, who despite his acerbic manner, was a keen observer of locomotive performance, and as such frequently came up to the engine for a chat, where I always felt he was scrutinising us both for any signs of criminal tendencies, which might land us up before him. He was once moved to exclaim, "Ah, the Schneider Trophy men!" Another time, on asking the age of the engine, he expressed amazement, and with his magisterial instincts to the fore, had to examine the engine's Darlington Works plate for confirmation.

On the Hornsea branch, Swine Station, of unfortunate name, was positioned some distance outside Hull's eastern boundary. Like many country stations its staggered platforms were bisected by a public road, thereby allowing easy access from the road to the station and its facilities. Over one Sunday, remedial work had been carried out on the crossing timbers, and perhaps packing work on the underlying track. Swine Station was on a slight falling grade, and 7280, running bunker first with steam on, was racing flat out. Both George and I were standing at our respective places looking through the bunker weather glasses whilst enjoying the sensation of speed and delighting in the smooth riding and quiet efficiency of 7280, when there was a heart wrenching crash which almost lifted us off our feet, as we hit the crossing, both feeling a sensation that the engine had lifted off the rails for several yards, before crashing down. Fortunately no harm appeared to have been done.

It was usual when arriving at Paragon for McDonald to raise his rolled up brolly in recognition of a good run. Not so this morning, he stopped at the engine. "That was a nasty bang at Swine?" he questioned. "What happened?" George made up some excuse, saying there must have been stones on the line or something. McDonald searched George's face for signs of a lie or deceit, then with a nod walked on as if to say, "Try pulling the other one, mate!"

A further well remembered trip also concerned the 08:28 Hornsea to Hull express. Overnight heavy snowfall had smothered the countryside in a deep blanket of snow, but by train time the clouds had drifted away into the North Sea, leaving a clear blue sky and light winds to cheer us on our way. With a depth of snow concealing the track and deadening all sound, riding the footplate proved an eerie experience, but as speed increased, something else began to occur. The train began to lift the snow in glistening swirling clouds which rose scintillating and flashing in the sun over and around the train, crusting the carriage windows and freezing the compartment doors fast against the frames. When we arrived at Hull we had the devil's own job of getting the passengers out.

But these short high-speed runs, exhilarating though they were, paled into insignificance when measured against a series of roller coaster gallops over the summer months, and which I christened the 'Foggathorpe Flyer', after a station on the Selby Market Weighton railway. Runs which, for performance and speed, would have done credit to larger and more modern locomotives.

At that time extensive work relaying the Selby Market Weighton railway began drawing plate-laying gangs from a wide area around Hull, and to return them each evening required a round trip of about 70 miles, for which the dependable free-steaming Class 'O's' were called upon, rather than the less sure Ivatt GN Tankys. Prior to this, the longest trip taken by Botanic Push and Pulls were the all-stops there-and-back to South Howden, over H&BR metals, a return trip of about 50 miles. However the Foggathorpe Flyer, with only one stop each way, at Market Weighton, to take water, was a different proposition altogether. And as if further proof was needed, it was working these Specials that 7280 demonstrated what an outstanding little locomotive she had become.

Leaving Hull propelling the train as empty stock, we ran at speed through Cottingham then Beverley, with a two-coach train, making light of the climb over the Yorkshire Wolds, and with steam on, racing on the falling grade to our first stop for water at Market Weighton. Replenished, there followed more high speed running, over the 15 miles of straight and level Market Weighton Selby track. Returning, now bunker first under express regulations, we again reeled off the miles to Market Weighton and a necessary stop there again for water, followed by the climb out of Market Weighton. Breasting the summit, George as keen as an Olympic runner, gave a Tally Ho! "Now, we'll see what she can do," he called out. Hereabouts drivers shut off to coast down to Beverley. However, aided by equally keen signalmen who, aware of our speed, were pulling off early, George with steely determination, left the regulator open.

Guided by furiously spinning bogie wheels below the bunker and cab, 7280 rode the long sweeping curve leading to Beverley North Junction, with silky smoothness, followed by a tearing rasping dash under the canopy roof of Beverley Station, followed by the final 10 miles of level track leading into Paragon, where we ran gently down to one of the water columns in preparation for our next trip. It was whilst taking water the ganger-in-charge of the relaying gangs approached. "You're mad!" he announced. "Both mad!" Since when, I've never quite made up my mind if this was a compliment or a reproach.

One thing these lengthy high-speed runs impressed on me: how effective were the primitive tail trimmings, then in general use, in maintaining the integrity of the oil film intact on bearings, bearings not only spinning at high rotational speeds, but under constant attack from the thrust of pistons and the relentless jar of rail joints. It speaks volumes for the efficacy of this simple device, the brainchild of some unknown but inventive mind, that even on the most run-down relics of the war, I never experienced a hot bearing.

Now, although I had to watch George like a hawk, I wasn't always able to monitor his every move, and he eventually, as it were, slipped the lead. He did this in a manner so bizarre it is difficult to believe, and one which must cause concern to even the most blasé of the travelling public, and which only by a whisker avoided a major collision. A collision, I might add, which would have surely ended with both George and I 'in the dock', charged with criminal negligence and possibly manslaughter. However, to better understand how this near disaster came about, a brief description of NER Push and Pull workings needs to be addressed.

Each Class 'O' Push and Pull engine had an arrangement whereby its main steam pipe to the cylinders was diverted to a chamber, fixed to the right-hand side of the smokebox, and containing an intermediate regulator valve. This valve was opened and closed by the action of a vacuum cylinder and piston, in much the same way as a vacuum brake worked. With the train about to be propelled, the driver left the engine cab and occupied a driving compartment which formed part of the carriage at the front of the train, which contained two vacuum-operated handles to control the train, the first, a straight vacuum brake application handle, the second governing the workings of the intermediate regulator. Communication between the driver, isolated in his little compartment at the front of the train, and the fireman on the footplate, was maintained by each having a vacuum gauge separate from the train brake gauge. As the driver either shut off or opened the intermediate regulator, this registered on a separate engine gauge, preparing the fireman to work the engine as the driver wished. Under this system, the driver, in theory, was able to operate the engine as if on the footplate.

In the minds of Push and Pull crews, however, this system held serious flaws. With the driver in his driving compartment some distance from the engine, isolated and out of earshot of its working, one problem was how to prevent it slipping violently when departing a station. But this paled into insignificance when viewed under a regulation stating: 'Before leaving the engine to take his place at the front of the train, the driver must open the engine regulator to its working position'. As can be imagined, this opened up the possibility for all kinds of mischief, even if in theory, this intermediate valve, now closed, was preventing steam from entering the cylinder and the train moving off.

Imagine us then arriving under Paragon's magnificent and ornate glass roof after running bunker first on a return trip from Hornsea. We had stopped at the water column and taken water, and now with the engine shut down and quiet, were waiting for our next trip—a run to Beverley and back. For a Push and Pull train, departure from Paragon was a well-practised routine. When passengers began entraining, George left the engine with the time-honoured phrase: "I'm going up to the front"—a clear and unambiguous statement, telling me he was leaving the engine to go to the front of the train, to enter the driving compartment in preparation for the propelling movement to Beverley.

Shortly before train time, and after the driver had left the engine and taken up his position in the driving compartment at the front of the train, it was normal practice for the station foreman to arrive. Walking from the front of the train to the rear, he would inspect the carriage door locks on his way, when arriving at the engine he would give the fireman the 'Right Away', who would respond by giving a warning pop on the whistle, before opening the regulator. This day was no different. After opening the sight feed lubricator located in the cab on the fireman's side, I opened the jet (blower) to ginger up the fire, and adjusted the flapper (the fire door's air deflector plate) and went on to blow the train brakes off.

With George as the driver, watching out for signals had become second nature to me, and bursting out from beneath Paragon's lofty and ornate roof, and gathering speed, I became aware the colour light starter signal located at the end of the platform was unexpectedly showing red. Anticipating George shutting off and braking, and whilst watching for the intermediate regulator's vacuum gauge to drop, I closed the regulator and lowered the reverser into full travel. With the distance between the train and the signal rapidly decreasing I found myself muttering, "Come on, George, time to begin braking."

At the last moment, and with no indication from either gauge, I flung on the vacuum brake. Shuddering to a halt and convinced George was seriously ill, or may have collapsed, I raced up to the front of the train, both to reassure myself we had not overrun the signal, and to come to George's assistance. Arriving at the driving compartment I peered through the side window, and as I did so something dreadful occurred. Sweeping across the path we were just about to take came an incoming passenger train. Shocked to the core by this near miss I looked for George, only to find his seat empty. Now certain George must have collapsed, I searched the cab floor without success.

Desperate to find him, I entered the luggage compartment, to find it also empty. Utterly confused, I returned and climbed down in front of the train and in desperation looked underneath. Still no sign of George, or his body there. I looked down the off-side of the train in the hope of seeing him, and then over the adjacent platforms. Nothing! George had vanished into thin air. Bewildered and lost I climbed back onto the platform and wandered about, not knowing what to do next. In this state I heard a shout, and turning saw George, arms waving madly, running down the platform towards me. "Have you got past the signal?" he shouted.

Part anger and part relief at seeing him flooded over me "No," I shouted, "and where the bloody hell have you been?" By now, the colour light had turned green. Without answering, George climbed into his cab. Lady Luck now smiled upon us: for some inexplicable reason, neither the signalman, whose cabin overlooked the platforms, other station staff, or members of the public seemed to have noticed anything amiss, and the incident passed without comment.

As a diversion from watching George, I received notice that my seniority was coming up, and I would be sent to York to sit the examination for promotion to Passed Fireman, a position giving me the authority to act as driver, if and when required. I was aware that the examination consisted of a morning spent both firing and driving a passenger train, and then an afternoon of questions on the Rule Book and on locomotive management. The Rule Book never being one of my favourite reads had left me rather shaky on its contents, and to remedy this defect I turned to an old friend, Steve Barley, signalman at Cottingham North and an authority on such matters.

One evening, before going up the next morning, Steve stopped me at the door as I was leaving and said, "Here's one for you, one I'd almost forgotten about: Does a locomotive ever carry a red headlamp during daylight hours?" This was a new one to me and threw me completely. Confessing my ignorance, Steve carefully explained, "Yes, it does, but only at those times when it's running facing road during fog or falling snow, or when passing through a tunnel." Armed with my new-found but somewhat arcane knowledge, I faced the following day with renewed confidence.

The next morning, in the company of another fireman also being tested, I travelled to York where, together with the examining locomotive inspector, we occupied the footplate of a splendid Harrogate-bound NER Class 'R' of 4-4-0 wheel arrangement, which I fired on the outward leg, and drove on the return. There are two things about this trip I mostly remember: the first, when I wound the 'owd lass' up, how she flew; and secondly, entering York Station, a station I was largely unfamiliar with, we were turned into a dead-end bay. Somewhere from the deepest recesses of my mind, I dragged up a memory of this short terminal bay we were about to enter, and receiving confirmation from the inspector, I carefully eased the train in, and with swelling pride, stopped a few yards short of the buffers.

In the afternoon, I felt Lady Luck had again deigned to smile on me when, in the course of my verbal examination I was, amazingly, asked Steve Barley's almost forgotten red headlamp rule, which I was able to answer without hesitation. What difference knowing it made I have no idea, but at the end of a gruelling afternoon I, along with the other fireman, were both informed, without congratulations or handshake, we had passed, and our respective sheds would be informed. It was my 23rd birthday.

A few weeks later, whilst preparing to depart with a mid-morning train for Brough, George, as always, announced he was going up to the front to the driving compartment. On receiving the 'Right Away' from Paragon's station foreman, I opened the engine regulator, and with the platform colour light showing green, and the bit between my teeth, I began notching up. Then, above the pounding beat of the accelerating locomotive something occurred at that juncture that I can only describe as a miracle. From a neighbouring platform came the piercing shriek of someone frantically whistling through his teeth. Alerted, I glanced across to see a figure gesticulating wildly and pointing to the platform I was leaving. Scarcely able to believe my senses, instinct nevertheless told me, however impossible it must be, George was again in a state of mental confusion, and had again escaped my attention and wandered away. Without hesitation I flung on the train brakes, and as it shuddered to a halt I looked back to see George, arms waving, running along the platform in what but for the Grace of God would have been a futile attempt to catch his train.

All those years ago, still my flesh creeps and blood curdles when I recall what might have been. Think on it. A train being propelled through Paragon Station yard, with its maze of converging lines, its shunting engines and its incoming and outgoing trains, with no one in control. Then, at multi-directional West Parade Junction, and still driverless, swinging south as it threaded its way through Hull whilst negotiating two notorious main road crossings, before turning westwards at Hessle Road Junction, where in full view of Dairycoates locomotive shed, 7280 would have tackled the short sharp climb to the bowstring girder bridge 5A over the Hull Central Line, before taking advantage of the following down grade, and at speed, passing on the left Dairycoates outward yard, and on the right the massive hump-controlled[25], inward goods yard. Blissfully unaware the train was driverless I would have continued firing and attending to the needs of the engine.

Passing Hessle East signal box, about a mile from Hessle Station, our first stop, would have found me preparing for George shutting off by opening the jet, to prevent a blowback at the firehole door, applying an injector to keep the engine quiet in the station, then with one hand on the regulator and the other on the reversing lever, and an eye on the intermediate regulator gauge ready to shut off. With that failing to materialise would come the dreadful realisation that I had

---

[25] A clever piece of engineering that uses gravity to sort rolling stock and build up trains, with a control tower diverting freight waggons to the correct lines.

been propelling a train along a busy stretch of railway with no-one in control. Assuming I'd got that far. In this case, however, the 'no-one in control' wasn't strictly true, as given George's state of mind I had been careful to observe all signals and was always prepared to act if they were adverse. But in the greater scheme of things, I'm afraid that would not have washed.

With the terrible realisation that I'd left George behind, and its dreadful implications crowding me, I would have taken over control of the train and guided it into Hessle Station. Fortunately that morning, by what can only be described as the Grace of God, some unknown person (surely another guardian angel, in human form) happened to be in the right place at the right time and, furthermore, had a skill, not always granted to everyone, of being able to whistle strongly through his teeth, together with the knowledge of what was going on and the gumption to act.

After George had regained his train, we completed the remainder of his day's work without further incidence. The feared demand to hand over the train to a new crew, following this near miss, never materialised, nor did a command to 'lowse off', leave the train and return to shed. At the conclusion of a shift fraught with angst, I expected to be called into the shedmaster's office for a grilling, but no one seemed aware of what had happened, and I booked off as usual. Despite the gravity of the situation, and contrary to everything one might expect, as far as I am concerned, nothing was ever made of it, either officially or as rumour and tittle-tattle around the shed. George, however, wasn't so fortunate. Booking on duty a couple of days later, I found another driver in his place. George, whilst remaining a driver had, to use football terminology, been relegated to a lower division, the Dust Hole.

Chapter 16
An Encounter with Some Crossing Gates

With poor George's demotion came an end to the fast exhilarating runs I liked so much. Bill Pickersgill, my new driver was a man of cautious habits, who, if speed rose above 40 mph, grew a bit wobbly. I gained the impression he would rather have spent his days at Alexandra Dock in a never ending series of shunting movements. But Botanic Gardens was much nearer his home in west Hull, and with only a bike for transport, this counted a lot. In keeping with his character, Bill, after each trip, would carefully examine the engine for signs of an overheating bearing. That he never found one did nothing to deter his dedication, which, if he had been at Alexandra Dock would, I am sure, have been extended to his 'bug-crusher' after each shunt.

He had an irritating habit of declaring he had never run an engine hot, and this didn't surprise me one bit, as he'd never gone fast enough, which led me to think that in his hands a squeaking wheelbarrow would be safe. It reminded me of the hoary headed old driver who, after taking a long satisfying drink of stewed tea from his bottle, was moved to declare, "It ain't 'ot till it takes the skin offer the back of yer 'and," bringing visions of a gulp, a curse, the distinct smell of burning flesh, and the sight of a patch of skin curling up at the edges as it stuck to the axle or bearing centre.

After all the mishaps with George, I was preparing to work the train over the former H&BR main line to North Cave, when a stranger in a blue serge suit and bowler hat stepped up onto the footplate. "Loco Inspector," he announced, and that was all. I didn't mind, I knew my job and I knew I was skilled at it. Under his eagle eye I worked the train forward, firing with my usual care, and maintaining as always, full boiler pressure. If by some mischance a little coal happened to fall from my shovel, I promptly swept it up using the hand brush for just that purpose, leaving the footplate as clean and dust free as my mother's kitchen. On the approach to each station: Springhead Halt, Willerby, Little Weighton, South Cave and finally North Cave, I stood by with my faithful combination injector hard at work and waiting and watching for the intermediate regulator gauge to fall when I closed the engine regulator with one hand, and with one deft movement of the other, lowered the reverser into full travel.

At North Cave, after the last of the passengers had detrained and the station staff had given me the 'tip', I gave a pop on the whistle and propelled the train over the station's crossover and behind its dolly. With the road made and the dolly turned I drew the train across from the Up line, through the crossover and into the station, where with a certain flourish and delicate touch of the brake, I brought it gently to a stand. Now for the first time after his curt introduction, the locomotive inspector spoke. Instead of patting me on the back and congratulating me on a job well done, and though I say it myself, carried out with some flair and panache, he spoke through grinding teeth.

"Touch that regulator or that brake again," he warned, "and you'll be looking for another job." Taken aback by this unexpected change of fortune, I protested, explaining this was the way I had been taught to work a Push and Pull unit, and at the same time pointing out that I was a Passed Firemen, and as such the great and glorious London & North-East Railway had granted me authority to drive any of its trains. A well-found argument, I thought, but one that didn't seem to work. "You heard!" was his answer.

It was only later I discovered it was the sole responsibility of the driver to open and close the engine regulator and operate the brake. But without going into tedious detail, this was an arrangement that, it was generally agreed, was fraught with difficulties and dangers, especially when darkness or bad weather intervened. It was obvious this examination was a direct result of George's misconduct. Needless to say Bill and I, together with the rest of the Push and Pull crews carried on with the tried and trusted system we were used to.

Despite a change of driver, I continued to cement my reputation as a Jonah, a plaything of the gods. On the evening of 31 January 1953, we left Paragon Station bound for Hornsea. The train, the 5.18 pm, a limited stop semi-fast was booked non-stop through the first two of the Hull's three stations, before stopping at Wilmington in the heart of the industrial district, to pick up those who grafted, and those who, by holding the grafter's noses to the grindstone, were whirled home, to their comfortable detached dwellings in the leafy suburbs of Hornsea in cushioned first-class splendour.

Our next stop, Sutton-on-Hull, a village not wanting in the necessities of life, and situated on the eastern extremity of the city, had its station located snugly in a cutting and as such well-placed for its industrious inhabitants, including the staff of a nearby hospital annexe. Though cold, the evening was fine and clear, but all day from the north a howling gale had hit the eastern seaboard counties, causing widespread damage, and a mighty sea surge along the coast, overwhelming many seaside towns and villages[26].

Departing Paragon, heading north out of the city, we were shielded at first by being directly head-on into the storm, but leaving Sutton-on-Hull with its sheltering cutting, overbridge and mature trees, things changed. The line, on a long sweeping curve, Swine curve, one of George's racing lengths, climbed gently to Swine, the next station. Along here, on open and exposed farmland, 7280, its train broadside onto the storm, and finding the going heavy, laboured, a torrent of fire streaming 'full hole' from her chimney. I had been forced by the gale to leave my accustomed position on the fireman's side, and seek shelter standing on the driver's footstool, close up against the engine's warming backplate, from where, on the approach to Swine Station, the 5:18 pm was booked to pass, and I began looking through the driver's front weather glass, diagonally across the curve for an early sight of Swine's signals. Swine, a typical branch line station had, in both directions, a minimum of signals: warning distant, home signals to protect its level crossing, and at each platform end, a starter signal giving, when lowered, engine crews the 'Right Away' into the next section. But in one respect Swine was different: three hundred yards beyond the Down starter, stood another, a very strange signal. Strange because in that isolated position it served no useful purpose, though at one time it may have controlled entrance to some long forgotten siding, of which no sign remained. Strange because, even on the darkest night, its aspect though lit, could only be observed at the very last moment, but strangest of all, for some unfathomable reason, its signal arm was fixed permanently in the off position, leading me to believe its sole purpose was to provide exercise for those station staff responsible for changing the lamps.

Fully expecting Swine's signals to be pulled off right through, my sighting would be a mere cautionary glance. Instead, peering through 7280's volcanic

---

[26] Known as the 1953 North Sea flood, it killed many people in the Netherlands, north-west Belgium, England and eastern Scotland, as sea defences were overwhelmed and extensive flooding ensued.

eruptions, I was met by a wall of impenetrable darkness. Realising Swine's signals must have been blown out, I prepared for Bill shutting off, and then creeping slowly forward to ascertain the true position of the signal arms. Instead, and rather alarmingly, Bill kept steaming on. Then, sweeping into view, and meaning only one thing, came a powerful green signal. Protected from the gale to a large extent by the station buildings, it could only be Swine's Down starter, and when pulled off, the last in the station's succession of signals, and as such a guarantee of a sure and certain passage into the next section. Reassured I began replenishing 7280's voracious firebox, when without warning I felt a distinct jolt. Alarmed, I looked up to observe both the regulator gauge and train brake gauge rapidly falling, and glancing out over the driver's side I was shocked to see white-painted wood and dark metal, twisting and grinding beneath 7280's wheels—we'd run clean through Swine's closed crossing gates! By something of a miracle, both the train's vulnerable brake equipment and the engine's equally exposed cylinder taps escaped damage as we overrode the wreckage.

Stopping in the station with a squeal of brakes my first concern was for Bill's safety, as he had little in the way of protection in his flimsy wooden driver's compartment at the front. Pressed against coaches that were swaying markedly in the storm, I fought my way along the train, hand over fist. The first coach had overrun the platform, and on reaching it I had to pass the starter signal, now defunct and useless, its paraffin lamp snuffed out, and barely visible in the darkness, its signal fixed firmly in the On position. Calling out to Bill, but fearing the worst, I climbed up into the driving compartment to find him shaken but unhurt. And as I did so, 300 yards ahead, malevolent and mocking, stood the station's peculiar outer signal, a will-o'-the-wisp, its lamp, whipped up by the wind, blazing a glorious and brilliant green for the first time ever.

But, and it was a big but, this accident raises some serious questions regarding the conduct of the signalman during that storm-wracked night. From his box situated close to the gates he had long uninterrupted views of his signals both ways, including sight of that dodgy outer signal. From his signals' back lights he must have been aware his advance signals had been blown out and were no longer effective. And whilst no one could expect him, in those conditions, to try and relight them, there were other steps he could take. One unusual aspect is why, after receiving 'On Line' from Sutton-on-Hull, and accepting it, did the signalman fail to open his gates and to pull off his signals right through, as he would do in the normal course of events? If for some reason his crossing gates had jammed, or in some way become obstructed, and in view of that sound and treacherous outer signal giving such a clear unambiguous green aspect, why did he fail in the simple duty of leaving his box displaying a red danger signal, and laying three warning detonators to alert the train crew? Don't ask me, I was only the fireman! And as before, incredibly, I was never required to make a statement or give an account of what happened. In this case I imagine that the signalman must have received a Form One.

In another incident involving Bill Pickersgill, we were returning from Beverley bunker-first with a late night train on a cold but clear night which made the colour aspects of the signals conspicuous for miles. Running at a steady 40 to 45 mph, with the flapper open, the fire's radiant heat provided welcome warmth to our backs and, in a blaze of gold, illuminated both the cab and its fittings. We both stood at ease, relaxed, each looking through our respective weather glasses. Far ahead on the long straight approaching Cottingham, was a succession of Up signals blazing bright and clear. Having been accepted, it was normal for passenger trains to be given the road, but this night, most unusually, Cottingham North's row of signals stood at red. Closing in on the distant, now showing an orange caution signal, and expecting Bill to shut off at any moment in preparation for stopping at the next signal, I moved from the cab window, opened the jet, and to prevent the engine blowing off, put my injector to work. Whilst thus engaged, and to give me an indication of its position, I tried to catch a glimpse of the distance back light, but this was lost in the engine's exhaust. Bill, as before, stood unmoved looking ahead. In the meantime, convinced by his attitude that the signals had been lowered whilst my back was turned, I leisurely resumed my place at the weather glass when, to my shocked disbelief, I discovered we were on top of the outer home signal still exhibiting red, whilst a mere 300 yards further along, and closing rapidly, Cottingham North's all important Inner Home, a signal protecting the busy Northgate crossing, also blazed fiercely red. With a cry of "Red, Bill, red!" I flung myself across the cab, and with a single sweep of my hand, threw the brake on full. Then, helpless as the distance between ourselves and the Inner Home rapidly decreased, I stood in mounting dread at the now unavoidable catastrophe unfolding before my eyes. Some 50 yards from the crossing, and still travelling at 20 mph, with no hope of stopping, in another astonishing stroke of luck the recalcitrant Inner Home swung from red to green. To our intense relief we swept safely past Cottingham North, to the astonishment of the signalman, who was left wondering how we had arrived so quickly from nowhere. But whilst we escaped by Divine Intervention, it seemed that in it were echoes of a more distant, more catastrophic past.

Specifically, the (previously mentioned) Grantham disaster of 19 September 1906, when the Great Northern 8.45 pm from Kings Cross to Edinburgh semi-fast overran its signals, failed to make its booked stop at Grantham, and at full speed, still under steam, passed through the station before derailing on curves beyond. Driver Fleetwood, a Top Link Doncaster driver, Talbot, his fireman, eleven passengers and a postal worker all perished in an accident which has remained one of railway's enduring mysteries. In the days that followed, many theories, most without justification, were produced. One claimed Fleetwood and his fireman had been seen fighting together on the footplate just before the accident, a claim so preposterous it was dismissed out of hand. Another, equally absurd, was that Fleetwood was hopelessly drunk at the time (but witnesses testified he was perfectly sober as he backed onto his train at the start of the journey).

One supposition, with some credibility, is that he had been taken ill suddenly, his fireman going to his aid. In these circumstances, experience tells me that the fireman would have taken control of the train before safely guiding it into the station. As for the charge of being drunk, or suffering a sudden and catastrophic collapse, surely these conditions would have been revealed in the post mortem. Most telling, and the greatest mystery of all, is the evidence given by signalman Day who, standing in his cabin, had followed the passing of the engine, and in the glare from its firebox had seen clearly, both men standing either side of the footplate, gazing through the weather glasses.

Much has been made of how skilled the fireman Talbot was, when by profession he was not a fireman as such, but a Doncaster premium apprentice, engaged that night in evaluating locomotive performance. As with all firemen, experienced or otherwise, working over unfamiliar routes, poor Talbot was dependent on the driver, even to the extent of not knowing which stations the train was booked to call at. So we have this young man, ignorant of his whereabouts, approaching just another of several stations passed at speed. Perhaps half blinded by a recent firing into a white hot firebox, and faced with a confusing array of unfamiliar signals, there's little surprise that he was content to leave things in the hands of a competent driver, seemingly in good health, and in full command of his senses and his locomotive. However, in the unfolding circumstances a more experienced fireman would have realised they were running against red signals and immediately have warned the driver. But that night blind fate decreed otherwise. With this simple decision to exchange one fireman with another, lay the genesis for the terrible events which followed. Whilst I can offer no explanation for Fleetwood and Bill Pickersgill's extraordinary behaviour, I can understand the events leading to the Grantham disaster, as I can well understand the reluctance of the GNR authorities to identify the true (i.e. novice) character of Fleetwood's fireman. And this brings us to the crux of the matter, which is, if Fleetwood's regular fireman, with his intimate knowledge of the road, its stations and signals, had been rostered with him that night, I am confident this dreadful accident would never have occurred.

In the light of my own experience, drivers overran signals rather more frequently than many, including the railway management, were aware of. By taking an ill-considered chance I once overran signals at Wilmington Junction, where the Hornsea and Withernsea lines diverged, and in full view of the signalman standing at his open window, who gave me a very pronounced thumbs down. I finally stopped opposite his box, half way across the junction, and with nothing worse than a few missed heartbeats, and muttered curses at my own stupidity. Things were patched up between us, to be heard of no more, although old MacDonald, at that time Hull's shrewd stipendiary magistrate, a passenger of the train, asked on arrival: "What happened at Wilmington then?" Unable to answer, I gave him a timid but cheeky grin, since when he probably marked me as some kind of subversive who needed to be closely watched.

Of course there were incidents which, by the very nature, it was impossible to keep under wraps. Such as the spare driver from Dairycoates who drove though catch points at Brough, derailing not only the engine, but the best part of his train. It was also at Brough, which seemed to have some malign influence over me, where George Ebbs demolished the footbridge. Under the circumstances we can forgive Bill Pickersgill for overrunning the signal at Swine and demolishing the crossing gates, but it's more difficult to forgive his extraordinary lapse when, like driver Fleetwood 70 years earlier, standing at his weather glass, he continued steaming against a series of bright unmistakeable danger signals. Whilst I can offer no explanation for this strange behaviour, I can understand why this Grantham accident, one of railways enduring mysteries, ended in such a tragic loss of life.

In the meantime, I wasn't done with Bill Pickersgill just yet, as you will see in a moment. But first, let us go back to a cold winter's morning before the age of the motor car, when those such as engine crews, with multiple pattern shifts, walked to work, if near enough, whereas for those like myself, living further afield, a bicycle was a necessary if a sometimes uncertain means of transport. Cycling to work through Cottingham that morning, in the early hours, I began to feel the dreaded thump of a puncture, as the wheel began to ride on its rim.

Fortunately, I was near a telephone box, and with an hour or more's brisk walk ahead, I telephoned the shed asking if they still wanted me to come in. "Yes," I was informed, "we'll find a job for you."

Pleased I was not going to lose a day's pay, I stepped out. Before I had gone far however, a motorcar, going in the same direction, overtook me—at that hour of the night a wholly unexpected occurrence. Having signalled it down, I found that inside were two men. "Can you give me a lift into Hull, please?" I asked.

"Yes, jump in," I was told.

One of them asked "Where are you going?"

"To work," I answered.

"Where's that?"

"To Botanic Gardens loco shed," I replied.

"Do you always walk to work?"

"No, my bike's punctured."

"Oh, where is it?"

"I've left it in a hedge bottom." By now I was becoming suspicious of these two and their persistent questioning and said, "I would be much obliged if you'd drop me off at Botanic level crossing, from where I can walk the short distance along a trod to the shed".

"No," one of them said, "we don't mind taking you to work."

"In that case," I replied, "if you turn first right past the crossing and drop me off at the entrance to Warmsley Street, it's only a short walk to the shed." Without replying, they drove me to the shed entrance and followed me in, standing behind me as they watched me book in.

Expressing surprise, the timekeeper said, "I didn't expect you so soon."

"No, these two gentlemen kindly gave me a lift in," I replied—yes, even to the extent of watching me book in! Plain-clothed police, of course, making sure I wasn't up to no good.

In similar circumstances, I once rode in standing on a trailer, drawn by a tractor going to an early fruit and vegetable market, which was memorable for how bitterly cold it was, standing on an open rully on a frosty morning.

To further cement my growing reputation as a 'Jonah', I became involved in one more accident. Leaving Paragon with an evening Push and Pull rush hour train crammed with commuters, we were side-swiped by an incoming train. Bill, as driver, had left the engine and gone up to the front of the train to occupy the driving compartment, and, with a green colour light and the station's 'Right Away', I set the train in motion. We had barely left the platform when, with an almighty bang, the train lurched to a halt, after the collision. More wrecked coaches!

Fortunately for all, there were, apart from shock, no casualties. I had to attend the subsequent inquiry and give evidence, but I never discovered its outcome. But before leaving Bill I discovered a very effective way of preventing that bane of a driver's life, wheel slip, a discovery which was to stand me in good stead in the future. At some time the Class 'O' had been fitted with the highly effective Mark 3, ¾ bore, gradable steam brake, which worked in conjunction with the vacuum brake, but could be operated independently with infinite variations. Leaving Paragon on a day of heavy overcast skies and greasy rails, 7280, traversing the jumble of points, crossings and turnouts which formed Paragon yard, was having difficulty 'finding her feet'.

Acting on an intuitive impulse, I applied a little steam to the engine's steam brake. The effect of the brake blocks gently rubbing the coupled wheels was instantaneous. Without retarding the engine in any way the slipping stopped immediately, even after I opened the regulator further. This was of course, only if the engine had been fitted with a steam brake, and the steam brake was of a type suitable for controlled application.

A new Link, the L1 Link, was formed using Edward Thompson's Class 'L1', a powerful (32,000 lbs tractive effort) tank engine, and as part of natural progression through the Links, I moved into it. I was never very impressed with any of the Edward Thompson engines I was familiar with, such as his 1940's rebuilds of Robinson's 'O4', eight-coupled freight engines, whose dull heavy thump and clank reverberated all around Springhead during my cleaning days. Likewise, his 'B1' and 'L1' passenger engines, both of which quickly developed pounding in the coupled boxes, and a severe knock throughout the valve and motion gear.

This was especially true of the 'L1' Class, earning them the derogatory nickname 'Cement Mixers'. Sometimes, when running at speed on a falling gradient, with the regulator closed, the big-end knock was so severe I began to fear for the integrity of the driving crank pins, half expecting them to shear off under the relentless pounding with the flailing connecting rods bursting through the side tanks. But set against these failing, which may in part be due to the post-war shortage of essential materials, must be Edward Thompson's deep commitment to the welfare of his engine crews—an understanding nurtured by his early years with the former NER, where roomy, weatherproof cabs with ergonomic layouts of cab features and fittings were the order of the day. In addition, he added comfortable padded bucket seats, and firebox rocker bars and self-cleaning smokeboxes to ease the toil of preparing engines for their next turn of duty, as well as electric lighting throughout, thus earning him (like the earlier William Bouch) the gratitude of his footplate staff.

Another driver of note I fired to, Harold Hines, remains to be described. As a resolute socialist, he refused on principle to make up lost time. Ten minutes, or whatever, late departure due to events outside his control (i.e., waiting for a connection), meant ten minutes late arrival. He was a good mate who never tried to impose his beliefs on me, although it did irk me a little when lost time could have been regained without much effort on our part, and we then had to suffer the disapproving glances from frustrated and angry passengers. It was all political, you see: "Make up lost time and them bosses [the sworn enemy] will use it as an excuse to cut running times."

His 'bible' I remember was *The Daily Herald*, which he read avidly, and whose extreme language and inflammatory articles were designed to provoke and excite its readers into paroxysms of fury over the capitalist society they were forced to endure. Sometimes, led on, his frustrations became too much, then with cries of anguish he would fling the offending newspaper into the firebox, where together with its extreme contents it was consumed in a flash.

One Monday morning, to illustrate his attitude to the cause, whilst awaiting the 'Right Away' signal from Doncaster Station, another driver arrived, heaved himself up into the cab, and announced he was learning the road. My mate welcomed him aboard where they engaged in friendly conversation. The driver, an elderly man of about 60 years had an unfamiliar accent and, intrigued, my mate remarked, "You don't seem to come from round here."

"No, I'm from Peterborough," he replied.

Astonished, my mate continued, "Peterborough, that's a long way away. What are you doing up here?" In all innocence, he was about to put his head in a noose—the poor newcomer informed us he was part of a new lodging turn being introduced between Peterborough and Hull. In a flash, my mate's attitude changed from one of friendly bonhomie to one of disgust.

This requires an explanation. Lodging turns were an anathema to Hull men who, before the war, had reached agreement that they would be exempt from any such working. With a snort, Harold turned his back on the blameless driver and announced: "We don't want your sort up here." For the remainder of the week, he refused to speak to him, even to the extent of failing to point out important parts of the railway infrastructure. This led to one of the most unpleasant periods of my entire footplate career. Nevertheless, it was a part, a very small part, of the life I loved.

However, there was an interlude, and a telling aside, which is worth repeating. On a very hot morning I had fired the 'L1' to Doncaster, and the interior of the locomotive's closed cab had become stiflingly hot. Now, on the return trip I was experiencing the same conditions, and once after firing round the box I turned to the Cambridge man and said, "I got a wet shirt coming up, and now I've got a wet shirt again."

He rubbed his hand over my blue jacket shoulders and made the following disclaimer: "Naw you ain't, not yet," making me wonder what the Cambridge fireman had to do to earn that dubious accolade 'a wet jacket equals a wet shirt'.

One of the L1 Link's morning shifts involved running a train engine first to Withernsea, where, because the turntable was unable to accommodate an 'L1', and for subsequent engine movements, it returned to Paragon running bunker first. On arrival and after taking water and leaving its train at the platform, the engine shunted across to Platform 9 and now facing engine first, worked an express to Doncaster. At Doncaster the drill was to 'lowse' off and run around the train, again reversing the engine's direction of travel. With the passengers safely entrained and now running bunker first the engine and train left Doncaster to pick up the East Coast Main Line for a gallop to Selby, the morning shift's final destination.

After uncoupling and leaving the train in the station, the engine, now engine first, ran the short distance into Selby loco, where the crew, after taking on coal and water, prepared it for the afternoon shift. With this complete, they both caught a train and 'rode the cushions' back to Hull. Likewise, the afternoon shift arrived 'on the cushions' to take over the engine and work through a train to Scarborough via the Selby to Market Weighton Railway, then over the 'Alps' (the Yorkshire Wolds) to Driffield. Then from Driffield to Scarborough, where, after running round its train with another change of direction, the engine again bunker first, and with all systems go, ran an express back to Hull.

Booking on at Botanic Gardens for the afternoon turn, I ran into the morning shift driver, who I expected had long since gone home, and expressing my surprise he answered by informing me a woman had committed suicide between Doncaster and Selby, and he had just finished making out a report. Remembering my own experience of a suicide, I expressed my sympathy, "That's all right, there was nothing we could do, she walked out in front of us and stood in the middle of the track, and as we were near Selby I reported it on arrival there."

Once on shed at Selby, my first task was to prepare my fire before checking the engine's tools, equipment and stores. And because night fell whilst running, I opened the dynamo generator steam valve and went round the front of the engine to switch on the express headlamps that we would be running under, and also to switch off any others showing. Satisfied all was in order at the front I went to check all the tail lamps were switched off. Rounding the bunker I was brought up short by the sickening sight of human body parts scattered thickly over the bunker back plate, including on the screw coupling and vacuum pipe, both of which I would have to handle when coupling or uncoupling. Leaving the shed with the engine in this condition was, of course, out of the question, and to make the engine presentable, hurried arrangements were made for us to go on the washout line, where the washout gang, using high pressure hoses, sluiced the engine down.

Why the morning crew failed to notice the state of the engine remains something of a mystery, perhaps explained in part by the working practices of the driver and fireman, who when stabling the engine, fastened it down and walked over to the station to catch the next train home. When preparing an engine, after first coaling and watering, the second shift driver, with oil feeder and two oil bottles (the larger, engine oil, the smaller, partly to differentiate in the dark, containing cylinder oil to top up the mechanical lubricator), would begin by oiling the engine. If right-handed, the driver would normally oil the left side of the engine first, finding it more convenient to use his left hand to unscrew the corks, and with better control of his feeder, use his right hand to oil the engine, working round, before finally finish his oiling at the opposite side of the cab, and without the need to go around the bunker. Meanwhile, the fireman, without leaving the cab at any stage, would carefully clean the fire before making up a new one, and on completion sweep the footboards and, using a swab of oily cotton waste, polish the boiler back plates and its fittings, and if required, clean and polish the cab side windows and weather glasses. Only then, with everything completed, its cab tidy and clean and its boiler full, would the driver find a quiet out of the way spot where, with its cylinder taps open, its reverser locked in mid-gear and its hand brake screwed hard on, he'd leave the engine. Following which, with a cough and a spit, he and his fireman would walk the short distance to the station to enjoy a well-earned rest, by travelling home 'on the cushions'. Consequently, there was a good chance this would remain unknown until the next crew (i.e. me and my driver) arrived.

Chapter 17
Stuck for Steam (Or, Not a Grand Day Out)

In the meantime, as a Passed Fireman, my tally of driver turns increased. One, however, has remained fixed and set in my mind, but for all the wrong reasons. One Saturday afternoon, Hull City Football Club (The Tigers) were playing an important game in Hull. With enthusiastic supporters expected from over a wide area, Botanic Gardens, having to provide motive power for the extra trains, had to pull out all the stops, to the extent of asking Dairycoates for help. To fill the gap I was rostered to work an empty stock train to South Howden, over the former H&BR under the banner of a 'Football Special', and on return working, calling at all stations except the last two, Willerby and Springhead Halt, both within easy travelling distance by other means to Hull City FC.

After being informed that my engine was arriving from Dairycoates I collected my fireman, a cleaner on one of his first firing turns. Together we walked out to West Parade Junction to await our engine stopping opposite the large and busy Parade signal cabin. I felt at ease both with the job and the inexperienced fireman, confident I could keep him right, and if necessary, do a bit of firing on his behalf. On arrival our engine proved to be a British Railways Standard 4 MT (MT for "Mixed Traffic"). Aware of the danger from frequent fast-moving trains, we carefully picked our way over the tangle of rails to relieve its Dairycoates crew, but to my astonishment, before we reached the engine they both quickly bailed out. Crews normally met on the footplate, and by exchanging a few words about the state of the engine, formally handed it over. There was something distinctly shifty and underhand in the way they scuttled past with only a brief "Everything's alright" from the driver.

Climbing into the cab, it was an automatic gesture to first glance at the steam and water gauges, when it became clear why these two malcontents had abandoned the engine in such haste. The steam pressure gauge stood at a miserable 150 psi, and even more alarming, the two water gauges showed less than half a glass. Problems were now beginning to crowd in on me. I had to back down into Paragon Station and couple up, and time was short. Also, ahead lay the brief but steep climb from the level to the H&BR 'high-level' section, followed almost immediately by the gruelling climb up the Wolds, with a cold engine already short of steam and water. Shouting up at the signalman I asked if they could give me a couple of minutes to 'gas the engine up' explaining it was as flat as a pancake. Being granted a little time I opened the alien LMS firehole doors. Apart from its LNER crossheads and slide bars, the whole engine was pure LMS design. Looking into the firebox I was dismayed to find a thin almost moribund fire, lacking any back end and in places with the bars showing through, and apparently composed of nothing but slack and to all intents and purposes on its last legs. It would take all my skill, and some good coal, to revive the fire enough to keep going. Taking the shovel and opening the tender door to find what it had in store, I discovered a tender of dust and fine slack, intermixed with odd pieces of small coal, and as such by far the worst tender I had set my eyes on before or since. Looking at it my heart sank: to call what it held as colliery yard sweepings was to honour it far beyond any virtue is possessed. At this point I should have sent my fireman over to the shed to report the engine was unfit for duties. However, I was a young Passed Fireman, without, at that time, the experience or authority for such extreme action. Yet, there was a glimmer of hope, for if I could resurrect a moribund fire and fill the boiler, I could, within reason, ignore the low steam pressure. My time on the GN Tankys had taught me, providing the vacuum ejector was still working effectively, engines ran freely on low steam pressures. In the circumstances I might just manage to scrape over the top at Little Weighton, before having to apply an injector with its powerful cooling effect on the boiler.

Unfortunately the signalman then called to say Paragon wanted to know where I was, hence it was time to go, and closing the firebox doors, so as not to disturb the fragile fire I had built up, I gently backed down through the station yard and coupled to my train. With the fire showing a bit of life and making steam, I was able to fill the boiler and raise steam pressure to about 170 psi on the gauge. Aware it was beyond my fireman's abilities to maintain steam and knowing that I would have to drive and fire for the whole of the trip, I set off. Lifting the train from the flat on to the high-level section of the H&BR, followed by the gruelling climb over the Wolds, firing became constant, producing a plume of black smoke, much of it unburnt coal dust which, thanks to the abysmal contents of the tender, was now drawn through the tubes without reaching the grate. Despite my exertions, and without using an injector, pressure fell steadily, until with a last supreme effort and with brakes beginning to go on, and barely an inch of water in the gauge glass, I crawled over the summit. However, I had succeeded. Before me lay the gaping entrance of Drewton tunnel, and with the regulator closed, both through and beyond, I had 10 or 12 miles of steam-free running. This interlude gave me time to rebuild my fire and replenish the depleted boiler, and with it came the knowledge that, whilst taking water at Howden, running around my train, and repositioning it in the Down platform, I could continue working on the fire. By now I had dug deep into whatever the tender held, and at Howden I told the fireman to shovel what was left forward. It was a position he was forced to maintain until entering the confines of Drewton's murky tunnel.

With a stout heart and full boiler, a full head of steam, a goodly complement of enthusiastic football supporters, and with the hope that my fireman might mine some decent coal from the confines of the tender, I struck out, taking advantage of the first few miles of level track to recover steam and water, and nursing the engine along using long shut offs on the approach to the stations. But from Newport, on a superbly engineered incline of a constant 1/150, began the eight mile section which in H&BR times proved such an obstacle to heavy Down trains that each had to be split at Sandholme, until the superb eight-coupled H&BR Tiny's came along, to relieve the situation.

Once on the grade, and feeling its effect, I began to struggle, and by North Cave I was down to less than half a boiler of water and 150 psi of steam. At the next station, South Cave, with my fire shot to pieces and low in water, I was forced to stick. Ahead lay the longest and most tortuous section of all: four miles of sinuous curves through Drewton Dale, with its two short tunnels, Weedly and Sugar Loaf, followed by the daunting 2,160 yard Drewton tunnel, its dark, sulphurous, smoke and steam-filled interior a trial at the best of times. To have any chance of clearing this section meant leaving South Cave with a full boiler, a full head of steam, and importantly, a fairly deep, well burnt through bed of fire—something not easy to achieve with the dusty low-grade rubbish in the tender. Ignoring the complaints of irate passengers coming up to the cab and demanding to know what was going on, and aware I was holding up following passenger trains and several coal trains, I worked for the next 40 minutes knocking the engine into some kind of shape.

Satisfied I could do no more I left South Cave, and with heavy exhaust already tearing holes in my carefully constructed fire, I began firing immediately. This was to little effect, only adding to the smoke disfiguring the otherwise tranquil landscape, as each shovel full of dust merely exploded in a flash at the firehole door. With steam and water falling at an alarming rate, it was apparent I would never make it through Drewton without another lengthy blow-up. Fifty yards from the tunnel entrance, the H&BR had erected, in case of emergency, signal D49, the only colour light on the system, and one in direct telephonic communication with the Little Weighton signalman. Also installed as a precaution against a coupling breaking in the tunnel and the rear portion running away to wreak havoc further down the line, a pair of trip points had been installed. With the engine dead on its feet I stopped at the signal. I had travelled a mere two miles since my last blow-up and at present could go no further. My first action was to make a full application of the brakes and to close the ejector steam valve, principally to prevent the train rolling back and derailing on the trap points beneath us as I worked, but also to preserve a little of my precious steam and water.

Contacting the signalman at Little Weighton, I explained the position and warned him of a further long delay, but would advise him when ready to move off. Facing my biggest challenge, things were now at a critical stage. The fire was so choked with residues of all kinds the only way for it to produce steam to the degree needed, was to clean it. But in the circumstances of time, and the rubbish in the tender, this was out of the question. Further adding to my anxiety, the tender was becoming depleted, and after working for several hours in the tender shovelling coal forward, my poor fireman was showing signs of exhaustion. Hanging over me was the concern of whether I could reach Little Weighton without sticking somewhere in the depths of Drewton, to the discomfort, alarm and despair of my unhappy passengers. Finally, with the boiler full to the whistle, the safety valves on the point of lifting, and the fire burnt through, I informed the signalman I was ready to go.

However, it was the same story repeated. Despite furious firing, and without applying an injector, steam fell whilst still in the tunnel, to the extent the vacuum ejector began to fail, and with growing concern I began to feel the brakes dragging. Then, with hope fading, through the dense clouds of steam and smoke, a faint lightening in the darkness began to show, then, before the brakes clamped on, I made a last desperate lunge which just succeeded in the engine's chimney, with its voluminous clouds of black stinking smoke, clearing the tunnel's entrance. However, half a mile short of Little Weighton station after another long blow-up, with the train and its trembling passengers stuck in utter darkness in the tunnel, I stuck yet again. This short section was level, and my concern was to raise enough steam to reach the station before everyone became pickled. The fire was now really at the end of its tether, but with steam raised I hoped to dig the train into the sanctuary of the station, from where, after another short blow-up, enough to keep the brakes off, and after regaining enough steam and water, I could more or less coast all the way into Paragon. My hopes were dashed, however, after only quarter of a mile, as short of steam I stuck outside the signal box. After raising enough steam to drag the train into the station I set about my fifth and final blow-up. If anyone doubts my ability to fire an engine, let me add, this was the only time I was ever 'stuck for steam'.

Reaching Paragon nearly three hours late, I must confess to an act of cowardice. Rather than face the wrath of the dispirited football fans, who had not only missed the match, but now found the return train waiting for them on the platform on the opposite side, I chose to dismount and hide on the blind side of the engine, from where I could hear not only their demands for my head, but for other parts of my body also! On returning to the shed it was rumoured that my novice fireman immediately handed in his notice, joined a travelling circus as an assistant to a drunken knife thrower, saying he found the erratically thrown knives less stressful than being on the footplate. Perhaps in keeping with the times, I was never asked to give an explanation for something which failed to dent the conceit of British Railways.

Two other events remain sharp and clear in my memory, both of which found me sailing rather close to the wind. To qualify for driving turns over those routes I was familiar with, I first had to sign for Paragon. Whilst I was familiar enough with the main running lines in and out of the station, and one or two other bits and pieces, the majority of that sprawling complex of yards and sidings remained a mystery, I never having been booked a shunting turn. As a consequence, in the hope that I would never be rostered on any of the shunting turns, I kept my fingers firmly crossed. It was all in vain. Inevitably, and to my dismay, the day came when I was rostered on the unpleasant 3.20 am Paragon shunt, a turn made more difficult for me by darkness and, in this case, thick fog.

From the moment I backed onto the first 'rake' of carriages (known as a rake because they were 'raked up'), the whole shift became a nightmare; a nightmare from which I feared I would never fully recover, and which should really have turned my hair white. After first coupling on, the shunter gave me his first set of instructions, which went something like this: "You've got eight on and you're going into seven. There's four coaches at the bottom. Leave four to make eight, then with four on go into two and leave them there for the first Withernsea. Then into stock sidings for the Yorkshire Pullman set and leave them in nine. From there into ten and clear it for the first Brough Push and Pull."

That was only the start! With each new set of instructions I nodded sagely as if I could follow the sequence of events and, more importantly, as if I knew how to carry each one out. Then, hampered by fog and darkness, unsure of what I was doing or where I was, I crept hesitantly from one obscured signal to another, never certain I had cleared the signals in my rear before setting back, and each time afraid I might cause an accident. By some miracle, my guardian angel kept watch over me, and I finished the shift without incident. Incidentally, I did learn to shunt the yard.

For many years after the war, a popular Saturday evening entertainment was a dance held at Withernsea, for which a special train was provided, and to which many of East Hull's young flocked. So as to not fall foul of strict Sunday entertainment laws, the dance ended at 11.55 pm, by which time many of the young men, fuelled by alcohol, had gained a reputation for some rowdy, but usually good-natured, behaviour, often wishing to climb aboard and drive the engine, and, whilst the train was in motion, for a bit of fun, frequently pulling the communication cord, bringing the train to a halt, a trick especially prevalent when arriving on the outskirts of Hull. This gave them the opportunity for a short cut home but extended the running time considerably.

One of the perks of the job was free entry to the dance, and whilst I never learned the art of dancing, I had no intention of missing an evening's free entertainment. Also, tell me this, what else is there to do on a Saturday evening in post-war Withernsea? To that end, by wearing a clean white shirt, clean blues, and a pair of polished leather shoes, I made myself look suitably presentable.

I had a trouble free run to Withernsea with an LMS style 4MT, and on arrival ran round the train and in preparation for our eventual departure, ran down to Withernsea's solitary and rather distant water column, and filled the tender tank. Whilst thus engaged I noticed the fireman's injector water valve leaking half a pipe of water. Jiggling the valve handle failed to cure the defect, and this was to have serious consequences later that night. Returning and coupling to the train, I settled the engine down for its long wait by screwing the hand brake hard on, fixing the reverser in mid-gear and opening the cylinder drain taps. At the same time I instructed my fireman, one 'Porky' Upton (so called for his rotund figure) to let the front of the fire die out, but build a substantial back end, ready to push down and spread before our departure. With our duties fulfilled, the dampers closed and the jet shut off, we both left to sample the enticing delights of the nearby dance hall.

Now Porky, unprepared for the dance floor, had come in stout working boots, and before long was making his mark on the dainty feet of whichever girl dared to dance with him. Inevitably his supply of girls soon dried up, and Porky came and sat beside me, complaining of his boots and the damage they were inflicting to partners and to his reputation. I cannot now remember whose idea it was, his or mine, but in next to no time he had expropriated my shoes, and though they were several sizes too large, was, not without some difficulty, but with gay abandon, happily steering them and a girl on his arm around the dance floor.

And so, lost in a world of music and jollification, the evening galloped on, until by 11pm my thoughts turned to preparing the engine for our return trip. With these thoughts came a memory of the leaking water valve and its drain on the tender tank. In particular, I was suddenly alive to the probable long delays inflicted by mischievous passengers on the way home—a common hazard. "Come on, Porky," I called. He was in possession of my own shoes, remember, and without them I was helpless, his boots being far too small for my Cottingham-size feet. Porky in the meantime, getting on famously with a bit of 'hot stuff' (who in turn seemed to fancy a 'bit of rough') chose to ignore me, until in the end I had to become quite insistent with him, threatening to punch him on the nose if he didn't come along, by which time it was approaching train departure time. Swapping footwear, we dashed to the engine to find it slumbering away with only a half a glass of water, and less than a 100 psi on the clock.

A quick check showed a significant loss from the tender tank, and with the probability of long delays looming, and a lack of water points between Withernsea and Hull, I decided to 'lowse off' and arrange a run down to the water column for a top-up. In the meantime Porky, having pushed the fire back end down and spread it around the grate was, by taking advantage of a tender-full of good quality hard steam coal, busy shaping up a sound and serviceable fire.

Back on the train I found the stationmaster in full uniform, as if to emphasise his authority, and demanding to know what the delay was about. I had a ready answer in the two delinquents wishing to climb aboard and drive the train, at the same time pointing out that neither he nor I knew when we might finally arrive back in Hull due to the likelihood of the previously-indicated interruptions to the journey, and in those circumstances every drop of water was precious. In any case I had decided to leave before the stationmaster made further enquiries. It was a bold, and on the face of it a mad and insane decision which, I'm somewhat ashamed to say, would put all the passengers at risk (such is the fool-hardiness of youth!). For, because of low steam pressure, when I blew the train brakes off, I could only raise three inches of vacuum against a working minimum of eighteen, leaving me with little or no braking power.

To work a train with less than 18 inches of vacuum was against the rules, and might seem just about as imprudent an action as was possible to undertake, and if discovered would surely cost me my job, if not a charge of serious criminal negligence. But as a young man made of stern stuff, I weighed things up with a cold, calculating and confident eye, in the sure knowledge that I knew each signal, gradient, curve and stop, and could adjust my speed accordingly whilst the vacuum pressure built up. And without further preamble, I left.

The return trip had only two booked stops. The first, Marfleet, a small urban station on the eastern extremity of the city of Hull, and then Southcoates Station serving the busy Holderness Road area of the city. Except on the most congested lines, even the most humble of freight trains could expect a clear run through, and I anticipated no less from the signalmen, giving Porky and me ample time to raise steam and water levels, and restore full braking power before our first booked stop. And if, as expected, we experienced any out-of-course stops, these would give Porky more breathing space to raise steam.

Praying the brakes had leaked off during our stay, I opened the regulator. My luck held, and with a clean bright fire to raise steam quickly, I left Withernsea behind. Before long the expected fun and games commenced, with some joker pulling the communication cord. This occurred several more times between Withernsea and Marfleet, to the accompaniment of raucous laughter and discordant singing, and though this was Sunday they were definitely not hymns! I made a perilous journey in the dark each time, to identify which tell-tale application disk was turned, followed by an equally perilous climb up the carriage to return the disc to its running position.

Between Marfleet and Southcoates Stations the railway skirted the eastern edge of the city. It was along this stretch that most of the communication cord applications occurred, when the East Hull worthies applied the brakes, giving them a golden opportunity for a short-cut home across the tracks. After a night of high drama, the curtain fell at Southcoates Station, and here a long delay took place whilst peering down the dimly lit platform for the 'Right Away'. Suddenly I became aware of a young lady (although I use the term 'lady' with some reservations) being escorted along the platform draped in a railway overcoat. It transpired later she had been discovered in a state of undress, many of her outer garments being thrown willy-nilly out of the carriage window as the train progressed. Whether this was the result of an enthusiastic game of strip poker, heavy petting, or simply a hot flush, remains a mystery. She seemed to take it in good part though, and her clothes were retrieved, so all's well that ends well. Finally we made it into Hull station, disgorging the remaining crowd of still-exuberant and giggling rowdies, who headed for the comfort of their own beds (well, hopefully), blissfully unaware that their mortal lives had just been imperilled by an inappropriate type of footwear!

One Sunday in 1953 I booked on with my regular mate to work a Troop Train Special to Hellifield on the Settle to Carlisle Railway. Our diagram showed us working express to Leeds, stopping there to take water and pick up a pilotman, before continuing on to Hellifield. There, time was allowed for us to complete engine duties and take a food break, before returning empty stock. Now, I have spoken somewhat of the character and nature of steam engine drivers as a group, and such drivers, like most of the human race, were creatures of habit. They drove much the same way each and every day. On the whole, conscientious men, they did what was required without imposing unnecessary hardship on themselves or their firemen. However, within that group lurked a substratum of other types. Among them were the 'Strong Arm Brigade', the 'Chimney Rappers'—men who liked to hear plenty of exhaust at the chimney top, and one driver by the name of Fred Dransfield, who rejoiced in the nickname 'Captain Blast', of whom it was said, all a fireman had to do was drop coal over the lip of the fire door and Captain Blast would spread it around the firebox. Among this collection were the 'Speed Merchants'—drivers who had the devil in them, and given half a chance would race their engines to the limit.

My then mate was a driver of that ilk, a short middle-aged man who favoured a 'Mainliner' flat cap rather than the regulation headgear. He loved a gallop, which actually suited me down to the ground. In my childhood Sir Henry Seagrove had been a world famous motor racer and speed champion, and in recognition of his dash and verve I secretly christened my mate 'Sir Henry'. We booked on to be allocated 1010, a 'B1'. Finding it rough riding and run down, Sir Henry had little incentive to whip it into a gallop. In any case, why be early and then stand waiting for the pilotman at Leeds, so Sir Henry ran strictly to time as far as Leeds. The pilotman stood at the water column as we arrived, and whilst I climbed upon the tender and put the water bag in he took control of the water valve. Back in the cab Sir Henry, as was normal, handed the engine over to the LMS pilotman. The only unusual thing I remember about this part of the trip was the astonished remark of the LMS pilotman as I commenced firing. Used to LMS fireholes with sliding doors, which when opened revealed the whole of the firehole to fire through, he stared in surprise as I began to fire through the much smaller aperture of a Doncaster type door. "Bloody 'ell," he remarked in a strong West Riding accent. "'Ow the bloody 'ell do you fire through that, it's nowt but a letter box?"

The following Sunday we booked on to work the same job, but this time in reverse order: empty Stock to Hellifield, and, after loading the soldiers (probably Territorial Army), express back home with a stop at Leeds for water and to say goodbye to the same pilotman as the week before. This time we found a Hunt, a poppet-valved racing machine, number 2754, waiting for us. A Darlington-built locomotive of traditional NER form, with a NER fire door hole, a type which I preferred. With a feather-light train of only four coaches we were up and away easily and going steady, until, passing through Hessle Station on the fast line, Sir Henry spied a 'fully fitted'[27] fish train making a run for it down the slow line. Alerted by the fast line signals being dropped, and in an attempt to outrun us, he began to produce an impressive amount of black smoke. Ahead lay 18 miles of straight and level track to race him on before the slow line curved away at Staddlethorpe Junction for Doncaster and all points further south.

This was too much for Sir Henry. He reached for the regulator and opened it further—he wasn't going to let some snotty-nosed, slack-arsed Dairycoates fish train driver get the better of him. Passing Brough 10 miles out we were going like the wind with 2754 dancing on the rails and beginning to roll and swing about, but now we had the fish train's guard's van within reach. Fish trains had

---

[27] Fitted throughout with vacuum brakes.

a maximum speed limit of 60 mph imposed, however in the heat of the race the fish driver was throwing caution to the wind in his effort to stay ahead. Little did he know he had Sir Henry on his tail, a man just as determined to overtake as the fish train driver was to stay ahead.

With 2754 heated up and raring to go, its rotary cam valves opening and closing with absolute precision, we were gaining on him fast. Would we be able to draw level before he had to shut off for the curve at Staddlethorpe Junction? That was the question! Running alongside and creeping up on his engine we could observe the effect the driver's somewhat cavalier attitude to the speed limit was having on his train, with each fish van oscillating violently. It seemed that when it came to speed, Sir Henry had as steely a rival as himself. It was a lost cause for our rival, however, for we had the faster engine, and as we drew level with his cab the fish train driver threw up his hands in mock surrender, whilst his fireman grinned in recognition of a hard run race. Running cab to cab, we knew why they had given us a good run: heading the fish train was a Thompson rebuild of an NER three-cylinder Raven Class 'S', large powerful and fast, and known inevitably as "Them new S's." We ran alongside for the last mile or so, then with a wave the driver shut off to curve away towards Doncaster and wherever was his final destination. He had given us a splendid run for our money, and we returned his salute.

On level track, one of the beauties of the Hunt class was their ability to run mile after mile with the regulator closed, due in no small part to its rotary valves, a gear which required negligible effort to operate, unlike normal valve gears which, after the driver had closed the regulator and dropped the engine into 'full travel', set up two unwelcome after-effects. Firstly, a pumping action from the cylinders drawing smokebox ash and other particles down the blast pipe, carbonising both it and the valves and pistons, and secondly having a strong retarding effect on the locomotive with its consequential strain on the valve gear, which in protest set up a myriad of knocks. On the other hand, the driver of a Hunt would, after shutting off, screw the engine into mid-gear, the effect of which was to lift all the valves away from their seats. In consequence, a perfect bypass action in the cylinders was realised, allowing the pistons to sweep back and forth unhindered and without putting strain on the reciprocating valve gear. Later in my footplate career I learned the value of bypass valves which achieved the same results, and as a consequence I have often wondered why they were not applied to British locomotives.

Sir Henry gave the Hunt a long shut off for the flat approach to Selby, negotiating Barlby Junction and the River Ouse swing bridge beyond with care and consideration, followed by a gentle traverse of curves through and beyond Selby Station. Beyond Selby, the six miles of the straight and perfectly aligned Micklefield Bank was tackled in a quiet and sedate manner as was the remaining 15 or so miles to Leeds. Arriving in Leeds we were welcomed as old friends by the same driver who had piloted us over the Leeds Hellifield section the week before.

Among enginemen it was normal practice for a pilotman to take the controls. This time Sir Henry had to instruct our friend in the peculiarities of an unfamiliar valve gear, and where to position the reverser when running shut off. He warned of the unexpected and unfamiliar impression Hunts gave when at speed on a falling or flat length of track with the regulator closed and the reverser lifted into mid-gear. As the steam exhausted from the cylinder, the engine, at first, gave a rather disconcerting impression of increasing in speed, a sensation enhanced by the complete absence of noise from the silently rotating valve gear.

Arriving at Hellifield, the same routine was observed as the previous week: lowse off in Hellifield Station, go on-shed to coal, water and turn the engine, then place it over the ash pit. Yorkshire Hard Steam coal was noted for its steam-raising qualities, but unfortunately it had a downside. Owing to its hard nature it was inclined to produce a rather large amount of ash and clinker, and whilst this had little effect when running, the rush of air between the firebars keeping them open, at the end of a trip as the fire cooled a transformation occurred. The ash fused and ran over the bars as clinker, forming an impenetrable barrier to the passage of air. The same effect occurred if a fireman was foolish enough to introduce a fire iron into a white hot fire, the results being catastrophic. In almost a flash the fire clinkered up, becoming dead and lifeless. The inevitable consequences of this mismanagement: an inability to maintain steam, and with it the certain failure of the locomotive.

With this in mind I carefully cleaned the fire of its dross and clinker, which on a hot afternoon was sweltering work. And then, as I had done the week before with 1010, put into 2754's belly a brand spanking new fire. Whilst I sweated over the fire a steady stream of Hellifield staff came to view, examine and scratch their heads over a locomotive with three-cylinders, three connecting rods but no apparent valve gear.

After the engine duties we had time to eat our 'bungy' sandwiches, relax a little whilst admiring the unfamiliar landscape, before returning to our waiting train, where the last of the soldiers, looking bronzed and fit after a week's camp, were entraining. We left on time, running under express headlamps under the control of our pilotman, with Leeds our one and only stop to take water and decant our friend. Approaching Leeds the pilotman slowed to a walking pace before handing the train over to Sir Henry with a request. "Drop me off at the platform's end, it'll spare me a long walk back." He left us with the rare compliment: "It's a grand engine you've got there, lads."

We climbed away from Leeds after taking water, through the impressive brick-lined Marsh Lane cutting, most of which had once been part of a 700 yard long Richmond Hill tunnel, driven through hard limestone rock in 1833 by the Leeds & Selby Railway Company. Unfortunately for the Leeds & Selby, its wet and greasy interior proved such a hindrance to eastbound trains, much of it had to be opened out, leaving its impressive brick lining as a reminder. With precise exhausts from our cam-driven valves echoing back from the former tunnel walls and my excellent automatic exhaust injector singing happily, such a friend to firemen, one needed only to open its steam valve and the injector automatically did the rest.

After five miles of collar work we gained the level at Cross Gates, after which came the descent of Micklefield Bank, a six mile stretch of 1 in 135 which Botanic men took advantage of, descending at a furious speed and hitting the flat crossing of the former York & North Midland Railway at the bottom with a crash—a frightening experience to a fireman unused to such goings on! It then required some heavy braking to negotiate the curves before and through Selby Station.

After a gentle passage negotiating the Selby Station curves, and again the equally strict observance of the speed limits imposed by the River Ouse swing bridge, Sir Henry came over to stand behind me on the footstool, ostensibly, as the line swung eastwards, to catch sight of Barlby Junction signals; signals which, in the normal course of events, I would relay to him with a twirl of my hand and a shouted "Right Away." But Sir Henry had other thoughts on his mind, that is, speed. Perhaps the earlier hair-raising gallop down Micklefield Bank had got his dander up.

Resting his hand on my shoulder, to better gauge my reaction he observed "A good injin this."

"Yes," I informed him, "it's a very good injin."

Then, using an old NER turn of phrase, he continued, "Fast enough to catch pidgins!"

"Yes, I should think so," I agreed, "fast enough to catch pigeons!"

"Right," he said as he reached for the regulator, "let's see what she'll do." As he reached for the regulator, I, knowing what was coming, reached for the firing shovel. (The astute reader will no doubt cock an eyebrow here, in recognition of the fact that the forthcoming escapade has already been hinted at in the prologue). With little regard for the speed restriction round Barlby Junction, beyond a warning to hold on, we tore around the curve at speed.

With a light train behind and 30 miles of splendid straight and level racing track for Sir Henry to exploit before us, it was more than enough to find out what our racing machine was capable of. Noted as free runners, the Hunts had another shot in their locker: with steam on, and all things being equal, the further they went the faster they ran. This was only governed by the punishment the crews were prepared to take, given that the engines themselves were built to run, and to run fast.

Blessed with a boiler which could provide Sir Henry with all the steam, and more, that he needed, he was prepared to ignore the histrionics the Hunt might deliver and test her to the limit. For the first and last time I was about to discover just how fast a Hunt could run—although I'd hints before. (One in particular is remembered: a Sunday evening express from York. Because of an original agreement with a pious landowner, no Sunday trains ran over the direct Beverley-Market Weighton route to York, instead taking a circular sweep by way of Selby and Church Fenton. Because of a late connection we left York 17 minutes late, and after a hair-raising run we arrived back in Paragon only three minutes late—a remarkable gain of 14 minutes!).

But back to the Hellifield to Hull wild ride. Now, 70 years on, it seems presumptuous of me to hazard a guess as to what speed we achieved on that splendid summer's evening between Selby and Hull. One hundred, one twelve, perhaps one hundred and fifteen miles per hour. With the Hunt being a right-hand drive, Sir Henry adopted the classical driver's position against the shocks and jars from an undulating and swinging cab. With his left hand within the easy reach of Gresley's pull regulator, his left foot rested comfortably on his footstool, whilst his right leg, bent at right angles, was supported by a flat steel plate, a continuation of the trailing wheel splasher and a mounting for his box seat, a handy store for his coat and 'grub tin'. To further arrange what might be a three-part suspension against the shocks of a speeding locomotive his right forearm lay lengthwise outside the cab on a convenient handrail, a little stroke of genius by some unknown NER draughtsman way back in time, which, if conditions on the footplate became too wild, was something one could grasp firmly to help further dampen the shocks.

With a fully opened regulator and the reverser well down, we accelerated away from Barlby, racing flat out for home. By five miles out we were running at an estimated 100 mph. Things on the running plate were becoming, shall I say, difficult, with the engine rolling and bouncing above its coupled axle boxes, and adding to the noise, in a cacophony of bangs and crashes, the lap plate between the engine and tender bouncing up and down. However, aided by my exhaust injector, I had no difficulty in maintaining steam pressure, although with the engine's wild swings I was finding it a test of skill to fire through the narrow NER fire door. Sometimes caught off balance, my shovel would describe a wide arc, then I had to call upon all my dexterity to avoid cutting into Sir Henry's exposed left leg and inflicting a nasty wound.

Ash from the ashpan and the blue asbestos lagging dislodged from the boiler swirled around the cab, and to add to the state of things, the right hand injector steam valve handle, dislodged by the vibrations flew off, to go skittering about the footplate from where I had to rescue it before it was lost overboard. After retrieving it I stowed it away for safe keeping in my box seat. The Hunts were fitted with steam chest pressure gauges, which I always found an interesting addition. Ours now began to show a distinct loss of pressure between the boiler and the steam chests. My first thought: jarring had partially closed the regulator, but a glance confirmed it was fully open. Puzzled, I wondered if the boiler pressure gauge was at fault, and to test it I fired a quick round of coal into the firebox, upon which the engine promptly blew off. Satisfied by the result I began to pay more attention to the steam chest pressure gauge which I noticed began to get the wobbles. As our speed rose the steam pressure in the steam chests began to fall until about 90 psi the gauge needle began to flicker.

Sir Henry noticed this, and to counter it, notched up a little, but without any real effect. As speed increased and steam chest pressure fell, another development occurred. The falling exhaust pressure affected the exhaust injector, which began to complain loudly. Its automatic change-over valve confused, it began rattling and banging in its body, allowing water to escape at the injector overflow pipe. I then had no other option but to turn the exhaust injector off and, after retrieving its steam valve handle from where I had placed it for safety reasons, turn and use the other, a live steam injector.

Hurtling along, trailing a fine haze of dust, Sir Henry, intent on squeezing every last bit of speed out of the engine despite conditions on the footplate, refused to close the regulator. At an estimated speed of 105 mph, steam pressure in the steam chests had fallen to 80 psi, with the pressure gauge beginning to oscillate. At around 110 to 115 mph the pressure gauge needle began to swing wildly, a clear indication the engine's internal steam pipes, its regulator valve and superheater, were no longer able to supply a full head of steam to the engine's three-cylinders, which were now gasping feebly for whatever the poppet valves could deliver. Number 2754, Mr Gresley's speed machine had, in effect, run itself short of breath, its flashing pistons draining steam faster than the regulator valve and superheater could deliver.

Arriving into Hull we criss-crossed the tangle of steel rails that made up Paragon Station's running lines, moving from D-line to C, to B, and finally to A-line, towards our destination at number two platform. A casual onlooker would, no doubt, think the engine looked in good shape, gliding in quietly, with just the wheel flanges protesting a little on the curves, the snifter valve flacking gently. No doubt the lowering sun was glinting on the burnished tyres and flanges of the leading pair of front bogie wheels, as they gently traversed beneath the engine, following their predetermined path. With approval such an observer might well note that the fireman had his side well under control, with the chimney clear of smoke, and as the engine passed they might observe, with some interest, the signs of high-speed running—the weather glasses coated with exhaust residue and oil, the soot-darkened faces of the crew, and, most telling of all, the marks on the main frame, scored by the coupled wheels as the engine had oscillated violently above its axle boxes. However, they would also hear the nearside injector singing healthily, and it would clear to them that the crew had everything well in hand.

After disembarking, our armed forces passengers came up to the cab and gave us a hearty cheer for what their commanding officer described as "An outstanding run!" If only they had known the conditions on the footplate they might have been less enthusiastic!

On the engine, Sir Henry 'ran down to the bottom' to wait for his train to be drawn by the pilot engine, allowing him to return to the shed. As the train glided to a stop Sir Henry made a full application of his vacuum brake, at the same time closing its small ejector steam valve, thus shutting off his vacuum ejector. The engine, when released, would now be worked back to the shed under the control of its steam brake.

At the same time, satisfied that I had both my fire and boiler where I wanted them, I shut off my injector, then eased the blower until it just prevented firebox fumes from venting back into the cab. Assured that all was in order, I stepped out onto the platform and rearranged the headlamps for light engine running back to the shed. Passing the cab, I asked my mate to "Nip 'em up", which Sir Henry obliged by screwing his engine into reverse gear, and with a whiff of steam to compress the buffers between engine and train, thus relieving the tension on the screw coupling and allowing me to 'lowse off'.

After uncoupling, I walked back to the cab and climbing on board, I glanced at the steam and water gauges. With three-quarters of a glass of water showing and nearly full steam pressure, I swung open the firehole door, the better to examine the condition of my fire. It was well run down; there would be no cause for the stabling fireman to grumble about too much or too little fire. Content with what I found, I closed the firehole door, and with the engine standing silent under the station canopy, I made myself comfortable to wait for the train to be 'drawn', releasing us for the shed. Heat still hung in the air and with it the distinctive smells of a large station, that heady combination of creosoted sleepers, steam engine fumes and hot oil. Over on the far side of the station a carriage examiner and his mate moved down the stabled trains, the ring of their hammers on the carriage tyres the only sound to disturb the tranquil calm of evening.

It was now time to relax, to ease the aches and strains of what had proved to be the fastest run I'd ever made, or, indeed, was ever likely to make on a steam locomotive, and where, thanks to a steam chest pressure gauge, I'd observed that peculiar effect at the locomotive's 'front end' when the cylinders appeared to be devouring steam at a faster rate than the boiler, at full working pressure, could supply them through the regulator valve and superheater. In effect, a locomotive running itself breathless.

Not all drivers, however, cared for the cut and thrust of passenger work, with its opportunities for a wild dash through the night, when the glare from the open flapper plate lit up their engine's streaming exhaust with all the colours of the rainbow. Many preferred the more sober life that a slow rumbling goods train offered. Some spent their entire working life, both as firemen and drivers, far from any hustle and bustle, on the mundane task of shunting their many miles of dock railway around the port of Hull. Not for everyone, when every second counted, the strains and tensions of running a train to time, especially when that curse of footplatemen, fog or falling snow, blocked out the semaphore signals and other familiar landmarks.

Captain Blast was a Selby driver who had transferred to Botanic Gardens. He liked to give anyone who might be watching the entirely false impression that he was always strong in the arm and heavy on the regulator. Once, when about to enter Drewton tunnel against the grade, he asked, "Is this a long tunnel?" Before I could reply, he opened the regulator further with the remark, "Yes? Well, I'll show you how to make it short!"

Captain Blast led a strange life. Having transferred from Selby loco to Botanic he still lived in Selby, and with shift work this meant on early turns he had to spend each night in the driver's lobby, trying in vain to snatch some sleep. On a late shift it was even worse. Then, having missed the last train, he had to spend the next 16 hours waiting for his next turn of duty. However, he never worked on a Sunday, and this gave him the opportunity after his last Saturday shift, to catch the next train to Selby, and spend the day with his family. And on this hangs a story.

All one week we had worked an early morning Push and Pull train. Now at the end of our Saturday morning shift we were about to put our train away just in time for Captain Blast to catch the next train home. Our destination was an empty stock siding located behind the engine line at the bottom of the station yard. Leaving the engine to go up front to the driving compartment, for the run to the siding, Captain Blast urged me to not hang about or he would miss his train. Given the 'Right Away', I opened up, rattling down Paragon's main gathering line. Then things began to go awry. From our approach, the stock siding was hidden from view by several engines waiting to move into the station. Unbeknownst to me, and for the only time in my experience, the sidings were occupied. Captain Blast, at the front, also expecting the sidings to be empty, was suddenly and unexpectedly confronted by a line of coaches. Collision was inevitable.

Flinging on the vacuum brake he hurriedly left the driving compartment for the greater safety of the adjoining luggage compartment. Caught unaware and almost thrown off my feet and against the boiler back plate by the collision, I looked out to find our two Push and Pull coaches raised up in an inverted 'A'. Once again I found myself hurrying to the front of a train wondering what I might find. Climbing up from ground level I looked around the driving compartment finding it empty.

In my search for Captain Blast, I moved to the luggage compartment. The luggage compartment contained two large fire extinguishers, and what met my eyes was a scene which would have been a credit to a Dad's Army sketch, with Captain Blast taking the part of Captain Mainwaring. In the collision the two fire extinguishers had broken away and now lay erupting in all directions. Searching for Captain Blast I found him crouched in one corner covered in a blanket of foam. Only his eyes, staring in helpless frustration, gave his position away. "Are you all right, Fred?" I asked.

"Get me out!" he yelped.

Trying to commiserate with him, I came up with one of my more inane, irritating and useless remarks: "Somehow, I don't think you'll catch your train today, Fred."

In terms of my railway career, I next moved from L1 Link into Spare Link, where I covered for any firemen, in both number one and number two Main Line Links, who was away on driving duties, or otherwise absent due to holidays, etc. But ominous clouds were gathering on the horizon as far as railways were concerned. There were line closures and rumours of further closures, and whilst this didn't directly affect Botanic Gardens, the Malton to Driffield Railway, which served isolated communities, was, in 1950, closed to passenger traffic, and talk was not just of withdrawing passenger services on the H&BR but of closing both the Hornsea and Withernsea branches, wiping out at a stroke both Tanky Link and Push and Pull Link. And looming over all was the recent introduction of single-manned diesel railcars, bringing a worrying downshift in both drivers and firemen. As an aura of doom and gloom enveloped Botanic Gardens I began to see myself landing at the bottom of the footplate heap and, if I did manage to escape redundancy, having to start all over again.

Then a ray of hope in an old and valued friend, Bill Etherington, appeared. Bill and I had sat together all our schooldays, but as often happens, our ways had parted when I left school at the age of 13 to become a farmer's boy, and Bill at 14, to pursue a career as a cabinet maker, and fulfil his lifelong passion for shaping fine wood. After serving his time as an apprentice, Bill too was called up for National Service, and as a soldier posted first to Palestine, where he found himself in the firing line between Jew and Arab, then to Kenya, and to a life which suited him so much he chose to be demobbed there. After knocking about a bit in Nairobi he had found employment with the East African Railways and Harbours (EAR&H, hereafter abbreviated to EAR), as a trainee Permanent Way Inspector. Despite having been recruited in Kenya and classed as a local, he was granted home leave, arriving in this country after an absence of six years. With our old familiar friendship resumed and much to talk about, especially when he drew a vivid picture of his life constructing the recently opened (but ultimately ill-fated) 132 mile Southern Province of Tanganyika (Tanzania) Groundnut Railway, a grandiose but abortive attempt by the 1945 Attlee government to grow groundnuts in Southern and Central Tanganyika on a massive scale. He spoke of building a railway in the tropical conditions of heat, whirling dust devils, safari ants, termites and poisonous snakes, along with all manner of other strange and fearsome beasts.

To disrupt the work, sudden typhoons, flooding and wash-aways abounded, and when he wasn't constructing bridges he was drilling solid rock to blast cuttings—work which earned him his Explosive Licence, and yet, despite all the difficulties, he was laying, on an average day, half a mile of solid well-built track. And in conversation he said something which has remained fresh and clear in my mind: "Along with my tent," he observed, "I always make sure my bench and tools come up to the railhead on a push trolley. And no matter what kind of day I may have had, if I can manage a couple of hours woodwork, I can put it all out of mind." Bill has now long gone, but I am the proud custodian of some of his exquisite African hardwood furniture.

In conversation between two old and trusting friends, I mentioned my concern for the future. "Why don't you join East African Railways?" he remarked. "They're always keen for British drivers, and if you want, I can give you the address of the Crown Agents, the recruiting agency."

Things were now looking bleak in the UK as far as promotion was concerned, and yet I was single, footloose, and fancy free, as they say, and encouraged by my friend's tales of exotic locations and manly exploits, and with nothing to lose, I applied for a position of driver with East African Railways. Events then moved swiftly, with an interview at the imposing Crown Agent's offices, 4 Millbank, London, where I was interviewed by a three-man team, as I learned later consisting of Gordon Gibson, the recently retired Chief Mechanical Engineer (CME) of EAR (and a former pupil of Sir Vincent Raven of NER fame, and the man chiefly responsible for the EAR post-war stud of magnificent locomotives), a Crown Agent representative, and a serving District Motive Power

Superintendent (DMPS) on home leave, who questioned me closely on engine management, and my attitude to working with the indigenous African population. This all seemed to go well, and I was next required to attend a Harley Street clinic for a medical examination. Shortly afterwards I received a letter confirming my appointment as Driver Grade V, on a salary of £15 per week, three times my Passed Fireman's pay on British Railways! What I didn't know then, but soon found out once my feet touched African soil, was that under the terms and conditions, I would have to put in three times the hours of work, and under the most arduous conditions! Also with the letter came the usual list of requirements, such as a valid passport (naturally), but also the need for certificates showing Smallpox and Yellow Fever vaccinations.

My last working day with British Railways chanced to be a cold foggy December evening, when I was rostered firing to a more senior Passed Fireman on a return Scarborough express. Whilst preparing to leave Scarborough he offered me the regulator. This was my last chance of a gallop, and in one of the Hunt Class with its precision rotary cam poppet valve gear to speed it along, thus I had the right sort of engine to indulge my fancy. With the regulator in my hands I drove the engine hard from Scarborough to Hull, an exhilarating ride, and what seemed a fitting end to a love affair with British locomotives which, as a boy, commenced with watching the procession of trains on the H&BR.

Chapter 18
Africa Ho!

Whilst air travel is now commonplace, in 1954 it was regarded as not only a great adventure, but with a certain amount of unease. I flew from the former London Airport, now called Heathrow, then an untidy jumble of ex-army prefabricated concrete huts with bare concrete floors. It was in keeping with Britain after a costly war, and under the thumb of an extreme left-wing government, where the only priority was imposing socialism on a tired and weary nation. I left with few regrets.

The aircraft I flew in, a large and handsome four-engined propeller driven Bristol Britannia[28], dwarfed the army hut which served as the departure area. To those unaccustomed with air travel, take off with a large piston-engined aircraft could prove a bit unnerving when, with engines screaming at full power, the aeroplane bucked and heaved against its brakes, before howling down the runway at full throttle. Another heart stopping moment came when, having gained some height, the pilot throttled back and altered the pitch of the propellers, causing the aircraft to fall away, before recovering, which made me think at the time that we were heading into the ground. In those early post-war years, the pilots were generally ex-RAF Bomber Command, quite used to that sort of thing, but also used to having a more inanimate payload.

We landed at Rome, our first stop, in driving rain and a shower of spray from the wheels. So much for sunny Italy I thought, when, with head bent against the rain and cold wind, I made my way with the other passengers to the airport

---

[28] A medium-to-long-range airliner produced to service Commonwealth routes, it was known as "The Whispering Giant" for its quiet exterior noise and smooth flying, although the passenger interior was less peaceful. It was, nevertheless, popular with passengers.

lounge. During the flight I had been allocated a window seat above the port side wing, and on our flight to Rome I had watched, with interest, dirty black oil, which looked as if it had never been changed in years, spreading from the outermost engine over the upper surface of the wing. None of the crew seemed concerned, and for the remainder of the flight that engine sang as lustily as did the others. Cairo, our next port of call had a different feel to it. It was hot and dusty, with a faint, unfamiliar and exotic smell about it, and my first taste of things to come. Lurching up into the sky again, we flew over endless desert to Khartoum in the Sudan, where, when gliding in, and following its course for several miles, I caught sight of the legendary Bahr al-Nil, or as we know it, the mighty River Nile; a river I was to become more familiar with in the years to come. Here I disembarked with a group of British administrators. Old hands, they had changed into tropical dress—white cotton shirts, white tailored shorts, white calf-length stockings, and to complement their appearance, polished brown leather shoes. They exuded an air of purpose, of knowing what they were about, of cradling a country safe and secure in their hands. That everything was to change in the next few years was not, I think, their fault. Leaving the aircraft for a refuelling break, I felt the full force of tropical heat, so intense that it left me wondering if, in the future, I would be able to stick that kind of roasting.

From Khartoum we flew on and further into the heart of Africa, our port engine still leaking oil, until I became aware of the clear limpid waters of Lake Victoria passing below, its shoreline fringed with vivid emerald-green vegetation, and coming into view, Entebbe Airport, Uganda. This was a cluster of white painted, red-tiled buildings, set in idyllic surroundings on the edge of a vast inland sea. Again a bevy of colonial types disembarked: district officers and the like, some with wives and children, to devote their lives to the fair and equitable governance of fractious tribes, often warring with each other over cattle and grazing lands. From Entebbe our route, taking a south-easterly direction, led to our final destination Eastleigh Airport, just to the east of Nairobi, once the HQ of RAF East Africa Command, but latterly used mainly by commercial airlines. I remember it as occupying a barren windswept plain of red murram earth where, at an altitude of 5,000 feet, the warm and pleasant climate reminded me of an English summer's day.

At Eastleigh I fell foul of a bristly Immigration Officer, a little martinet of a man sporting a fierce red moustache and little piggy eyes, which bored into me as he weighed my fate in the balance. "Passport," he snarled. "Where's yer passport?" He flicked through the blank pristine pages. "Who gave you permission to land in Kenya?" he demanded.

Taken aback by this strange question and his unpleasant manner, I stuttered that I was taking up a position with EAR. With ill grace he stamped my then pristine passport, allowing me, however reluctantly, to enter Kenya. But more was to come. "Where's yer luggage?" he barked. I placed what little I carried on the counter. From childhood I had used a shotgun, hunting rabbits and game birds, and in anticipation of some sport I had brought, dismantled and in a canvas 'leg of mutton' case, my Holland & Holland 12 bore. It was the time of the Mau-Mau rebellion, an event unknown to me, and as consequence things were a bit tight in that respect.

"Is that a gun?" he howled, his voice rising a further decibel or two, his little piggy eyes popping out. After my timid affirmation, he told me in no uncertain terms that my gun was confiscated. I think one way or another he had had a bad day. I offer this vignette to the reader, not merely as a simple distraction, but as a prelude to another interesting story, for many years later at another custom desk, our paths were to ignominiously cross again.

I and a man called John Millree, both newcomers to EAR, were driven the short distance from the airport into Nairobi, and my first encounter with Africa in the raw. Strolling along one of its main thoroughfares, and totally oblivious to anyone else, were three Masai tribesmen, each carrying one of the tribe's traditional broad bladed spears, and naked except for a blanket draped loosely over the shoulder, which blew open at each step. Welcome to Africa!

The Mechanical Department, aka the Locomotive Department, didn't altogether trust its new recruits with either its steam operated Westinghouse air brake, necessary on the Kenya Uganda section, where at Timboroa Summit the railway reaches an altitude of 9,136 feet, or with its splendid and immensely powerful Garratt locomotives[29]. As a consequence we spent three weeks in the railway training school at Nairobi learning EAR rules and regulations, and also, from the beautifully sectioned parts on display, the intricacies of the Westinghouse air brake. Many of the former NER engines (a Westinghouse railway) had that as the engine brake, and as such I was familiar with its actions, and what to do if the steam driven compressor stopped working. Our remedy was

---

[29] A type of steam locomotive that is articulated into three parts for easy negotiation of curves, with the boiler and firebox unit suspended between the two engine units, and invented by British engineer Herbert William Garratt.

to give it a hefty clout with a spanner on the steam chamber cap. EAR would have none of that, going out of their way to make it clear that such treatment would not be tolerated under any circumstances. We were taught instead to remove the reversing chamber cap (after shutting off the steam supply, of course) and apply a little cylinder oil to the main valve and reversing rod, before replacing the cap and restarting the pump. Whether, in an emergency, the painstaking EAR approach was more efficacious than a clout with a spanner, I cannot say. Likewise, time was spent under observation driving Garratt's to the first crossing on the steeply graded and tightly curved Nairobi Nakura main line, and in view of the long and heavy trains, an interesting experience.

After three weeks of instruction, and having decided we were unlikely to wreak too much havoc on their precious railway, John and I, were informed we were being posted to Tabora in Tanganyika. Word had it that Tabora, an 'up country' railway centre, where the vacuum brake still reigned supreme, was a punishment station, but I think this was more to do with its harsh and primitive living conditions than anything else. Having said this, as a one-time Arab centre and a base for Livingstone's explorations, Tabora had its appeal. Thus the day arrived for John and I to leave the fleshpots of Nairobi, and after managing to retrieve my shotgun, we boarded one of the railway's excellent Albion buses for the long journey south by road, crossing, somewhere in the dusty Masai steppes, an invisible border into Tanganyika, followed by our first halt, a stop for lunch at Handini, an attractive town in the shadow of Mount Kilimanjaro. During the First World War this had been the scene of a bitter ding-dong between advancing British soldiers and the resident German Shutztruppe, under the command of the formidable and wily General von Lettow-Vorbeck.

Finally, we arrived at Morogoro on the Central Line, hot, sweaty and covered in fine red murram dust: welcome to the 'Tanganyika sweat belt'! There we lodged in the European drivers' running room[30], a solid stone building of German origin, to await the arrival of the next Up[31] passenger train on its long 32-hour journey from Morogoro to Tabora, a train which was not due for the next couple

---

[30] Running rooms are where the drivers of single crewed locomotives would stay after completion of their run, before picking up their next duty, and as such were equipped with a dining room, beds, etc.

[31] 'Up' being the direction from Dar es Salaam to Kigoma. 'Down' being the opposite direction.

of days. During that stay we gleaned much useful information from the resting drivers regarding the railway.

Hauled from Dar es Salaam by a onetime Tanganyika Railways (TR) 4-8-2-2-8-4 Garratt engine, the train when it arrived consisted of old but very comfortable wooden-bodied TR stock, which in effect deadened the sound of the track. As a point of interest the train was marshalled as follows: immediately behind the engine were bogie goods waggons to make the train up to full load. Next, two first class bogies conjoined at either end to a dining car each with ten two-birth sleeping compartments, and access to the dining car via verandas and open gangways—what price health and safety? Then, three second-class composite corridor bogies and four-third class coaches, and then finally a postal van and guards brake van.

After the Garratt had gone on shed, it was replaced by a Morogoro-based 21 Class single crewed 4-8-2, for the arduous ten-hour overnight slog to Dodoma, a test of both the wood burning engine and its crew. After being made welcome by courteous and efficient Catering Department train staff—a peerless organisation which never failed to fill me with admiration—we were shown our sleeping compartment, each bunk pristine, with its crisp bed linen already made up. After settling in, we fell sound asleep to the sound of the 4-8-2 ripping the skies.

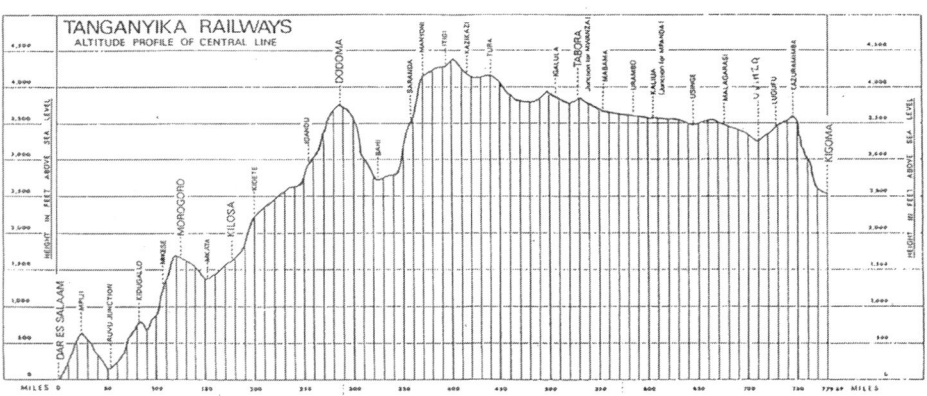

Gradient profile of the Central Line, from Dar es Salaam on the Indian Ocean, to Kigoma on the shores of Lake Tanganyika.

At 6 am the next morning, whilst passing through a dry and barren landscape, we were woken by the sound of a xylophone being played along the corridors, a gentle and relaxing way of rousing one from sleep. Already the catering staff were busy preparing the dining car for breakfast, and at 6:30 am we rolled into Dodoma, where, after a shunting engine had detached the goods waggons, a caboose double-manned wood fired 26 Class 2-8-2 Tabora engine, its Weir pump and preheater, a feature of TR locomotives, gently thwacking, backed onto the train. By 7 am, as the call for breakfast was being made, the 26 Class whistled up, and commenced its 13-hour trip to Tabora, which included, by way of Kigwe Bank, a descent into the Great Rift Valley, and following the run across it, the gruelling climb out via Saranda Bank, now with a banker engine[32] on the rear giving its all. This climb consisting of thirty-five miles of 1 in 50 elevation, to its summit, the high central plateau, and mile 380 on the railway. Here on the open main line, the banker, its piston rods now blue and cylinders smoking with effort, slipped its coupling and departed.

This area was tsetse fly country, which refers to a small brown but deadly creature, which in colour and form reminded me of the British cleg-fly. Feeding on the blood of animals and humans, they are vectors of microscopic trypanosome 'worms', which cause sleeping sickness and other diseases. To prevent them entering our compartment, for they were attracted to anything moving, we were advised to close the mosquito-proof window of our compartment. By 12:30 pm a splendid lunch was being served, with all those touches of gracious living which both railway hotels and dining cars were justifiably noted for. White linen table cloths, silver service and, as a distinctive feature gracing each table, a small cut glass vase holding a single red carnation with a dainty bouquet of maidenhead fern. Also peculiar to each dining car, a hen coop carried on the under frame, from whence, as required (well, there was no refrigerator), hens were snatched, necks wrung, and the unfortunate bird curried before you could say "Jack the Knife" or "Fanny's Your Aunt"!

By 8 pm, after a dinner, and after miles of interminable sun-baked bush, we arrived at Tabora. Like others along the line, the station was of a solid German-style construction. Messages had been passed between Nairobi and Tabora, and John Millree and I were expected. To greet us and take us under his wing was one of the British locomotive staff, who drove us to the Tabora Railway Hotel for the night. This was an imposing building, again of German construction, reputedly built for Kaiser Wilhem II as a hunting lodge. Because of the intervention of World War I and the 'advance' or invasion of German territory

---

[32] Locomotive stationed at the foot of steep gradients, and used to assist the train when climbing it. These were manned by African crews.

by British and Colonial Forces, it was never used for its original purpose. With Wilhelm's wonky arm this was perhaps just as well, as I doubt he was one of the best shots in the game!

Entrance was gained by wide sweeping stone steps leading to an extensive and open balustraded balcony and bar, set out with tables and comfortable colonial-style easy chairs. It was a pleasant meeting place and 'watering hole' for Tabora's European drivers. In keeping with colonial regulations, John and I had been granted a generous (for those days) allowance of £60, for the purchase of personal household effects. This included bedding, pots, pans, cutlery and crockery. Also included, what was a necessity for 'safari' men[33], a kikapu—a large, loosely woven native basket, used for the conveyance of food and bedding to and from the caboose (a railway vehicle with accommodation for the train crew, typically attached to the end of the train. They included bunk beds, showers and kitchen facilities). The next morning our guide and mentor drove us to one of Tabora's two 'dukas' (general stores, usually owned by Indians) to buy the necessary household items and food. This was a white building whose thick walls absorbed the heat, providing a welcome if temporary relief from the raging sun. From there we were driven to our furnished accommodation, one of several large spacious German-built houses located near the railway station, with high ceilings and wide verandas to provide shade and catch any passing breeze.

Having arrived at our accommodation, already the 'bush telegraph' had been at work, and a little knot of Africans had gathered, seeking the coveted position of 'house boy'[34] to a European driver—a plum job that involved keeping the house tidy and secure when the driver was away. For this service the houseboy was provided with excellent accommodation, electric light at the householder's expense (rather than the glimmering paraffin 'rush light' of an African hut), and a ready supply of food. I chose one dressed in a long white kanzu and red fez—a wily old African who seemed to have 'a bit more about him' than the others—whose name, Hamici-ben-Hamili, denoted Arab blood coursing through his veins. Over the next few years he rooked me no end. It was said, by those with

---

[33] Throughout, the word 'safari' is used in railway terms, meaning travelling with a train as part of work and spending a number of days (sometimes weeks, in the case of loco inspectors) away from home.

[34] Although the prefix 'boy' was always used, the incumbent of the post could be a male person of practically any age, and the suffix 'boy' was in no way seen as derogatory. In fact being a houseboy was a plum job.

ears to the ground and a fine command of the lesser-known verbs of the local Nyamwasi language, that he had been able to diddle me out of enough money to buy half of Tabora. Perhaps not the best choice I ever made!

With domestic arrangements completed, I reported to the shed for instructions. By 1945, Tanganyika Railways was exhausted by its efforts during the war, with a desperate shortage of spares and equipment, and suffering from a loss of experienced staff who, isolated and unable to return home, had worked on long after retirement age and now worn out had left, leaving the railway to manage as best it could. This was never more keenly felt than in the Mechanical Department, a division not only responsible for all locomotive matters, but as its name implies, for the vast majority of the railway's mechanical equipment.

In 1945, after the bloody partition of India, many of its railway staff, fearful for their lives, fled the country, and a good number made their way to Tanganyika, and were welcomed with open arms by the railway, to fill the gap left by the departing expatriates. At Tabora these included skilled machinists, fitters and drivers, including several of mixed European-Indian descent including the shedmaster, Willoughby Dalgains (now there's a name to conjure with!). Tabora was, and I trust still is, a busy railway junction, its trains, all with cabooses, running eastwards the 231 miles to Dodoma, the changeover point for Tabora engines, and westwards 261 miles to the township and port of Kigoma on Lake Tanganyika, with ship connections to the former Belgian Congo and south via lake steamer to Umpulungu in Northern Rhodesia, now Zambia. Also from Tabora was a 236 mile line of railway north to Mwanza on Lake Victoria, a port town with frequent sailings to Uganda and Kenya.

The shed advised me that I was booked the next day to learn the road[35] to Dodoma with two other British drivers, Bill Connell, previously of Polmadie shed, Glasgow, and Ron Kenyon, a former GWR man. Both were old hands, and knew their way around, having been recruited in 1945 by Tanganyika Railways. They lived just beyond my quarters, further along the tree shaded street. Ron was a bachelor, and Bill a married man with family. That day they were still out on safari, making their way home, and not expected back until mid-morning the next day. Time spent in the caboose was classed as time off duty. The crew arriving 'spare in', that is in the caboose, were deemed rested and ready for duty as soon as the engine could be made fit. It was a system that worked on the

---

[35] Learn the road: a railway phrase for committing a section of track to memory, including its gradients, curves, signals, timings, etc.

principle of 'first in, first out', and depending on how many repairs the engine required, giving crews little time at home. In our case we were rostered to work a Down Goods, leaving 16:00 the same afternoon. For this, the role of the engine crews reversed, Ron Kenyon having arrived home 'spare' (i.e. resting in the caboose) now worked out, whilst Bill Connell, having worked 'in', now went out 'spare' in the caboose. One trouble with this system was that it was often very difficult to sleep in the caboose due to the heat and the clattering of the train, and often the 'spare' was very far from rested when he arrived.

In spite of many hours on the footplate and having little time with his family, my friend Bill, on his way home, called in to make sure I was adequately prepared for the three-day safari, at the same time promising to pick me up at about 15:30 and see me installed in the caboose. At 15:30, followed by our houseboys carrying our kikapus, we walked the short distance to the station, with the train already marshalled. Here, I remarked that I must go to the shed to book on, whereupon Bill answered, "No, the guard keeps a tally of the hours we work."

"What about booking on when working out?" I asked.

"As long as you're seen at your engine and it leaves the shed on time, that's enough," Bill answered me. I rather welcomed this more relaxed attitude. Booking on, especially at Botanic Gardens, had always been a serious and formal ritual, with no give or take offered to young firemen if a minute our two late, whatever the time, and no matter how adverse the weather conditions.

Caboose furnishings were primitive to say the least. They were divided into three compartments: the first one for Asian crews, the centre for Europeans and the third for African guards and firemen. The European compartment had four bunk beds, two on either side, arranged one above the other. Between them, and affixed to the dividing wall at one end, was a small table with a cupboard below. As I was about to find out, this was an absolute glory hole for clumps of grossly fat and fleshy cockroaches who, with feelers waving, were not adverse to crawling over you when you were sleeping, or at least trying to. The other end of the compartment was formed by a lavatory cubicle, a sink with water filter above, and a Primus stove to boil water and make tea. With no refrigeration, and in the absence of anything else, food consisted of tins of corned beef, which in the searing heat of the caboose poured out of the tin in a kind of thick and not very pleasant soup. Later, as the territory's position improved, more kinds of tinned foodstuffs thankfully became available.

In the meantime, Ron Kenyon had been on shed for two hours preparing his engine and, now coupled to the train, was testing the brakes on the long line of vacuum-braked waggons. By now I was settled into one of the upper berths, my bed made up by my houseboy, and my kikapu, containing two tins of corned beef, small tins of *Carnation* milk (the only safe milk available to Europeans), plate, knife, fork and spoon, tea and sugar, and an enamel mug stowed beneath one of the lower bunk beds. I thanked Bill for his help and made my way to the engine, 2606, its tender further heightened by rails, piled high with hardwood acacia logs. As I approached the engine I noticed what became a familiar and interesting sight: African Pied Crows, circling in the steam as the safety valves lifted, and cawing with delight as they enjoyed the benefits of a free sauna.

Ron Kenyon, who I was about to meet for the first time, welcomed me on the footplate. A tall, rangy, bareheaded man, with a shock of red hair—hair which, among the Africans earned him the name 'Bwana Ekundu' (Mr Red). As I climbed aboard, heat from the boiler struck me in waves, forcing me to retreat to the rear of the cab where it was a little cooler. Purely as a means of identification, the railway issued uniforms only to guards and stationmasters. Such wood-fired locomotives required the combined effort of two firemen to feed the prodigious amounts of fuel consumed by a large firebox and which, in the absence of a brick arch, was maintained full to the crown sheet. Curiously, in my eyes, the crew wore everyday civilian clothes, the two firemen barefoot and stripped to the waist, their gleaming bodies slicked with sweat, stood waiting. Ron, bareheaded, but dressed in khaki cotton slacks, white shirt, as an added distinction sported a red neckerchief. This further cemented his African name, and was there to prevent perspiration from trickling down his face and chest.

With brake tests completed on the long train, the guard came up to record our names and keep a tally on our hours of work, at the same time giving Ron the load, which was 444 tons on 45 units. 2606 would certainly have to earn its corn over the 231 miles of undulating switchback grades to Dodoma. The 2-8-2 configuration of 26 Class, built in1947 by Bagnalls of Staffordshire, were a modernised version of the earlier 25 Class, which for 22 years, and over two million miles of service, had been thrashed along the Central Line. Building on the 25 Class, the 26 Class were favoured with a larger superheater, a MeLeSco multi-valve regulator, and an improved front end. Perhaps as an experiment for future designs, roller bearings had been fitted to both the pony and Bissell truck carrying wheels, but not, unfortunately, to the coupled wheels which retained plain white metal bearings, which despite being fed by a mechanical lubricator, caused endless trouble.

Train operations were controlled by the simple but effective Line Clear ticket system. The Line Clear issued by a stationmaster to the driver of a ready-to-depart train affirmed the line ahead was clear to the next station. With the engine's Weir pumps controlled by a simple steam valve from the cab, clacking softly, it delivered water to the boiler through a long pre-heater chamber, and, in its entirety, an apparatus so reliable and effective that I never once saw the 26 Class' two injectors used. Ron now stood ready, the Line Clear safely in his possession. To learn the road, drivers were given only three trips over each of Tabora's three main routes; however, this was insufficient for over 1,500 miles of railway, and for months after taking over driving duties I was completely lost (as you might imagine given the distance), relying on the two firemen to help keep me right regarding my whereabouts.

With a flag from the guard, and a whistle in reply, Ron opened the regulator and carefully picked up his heavy train. For me this was the beginning of a learning curve which saw many of my cherished beliefs concerning locomotive management thrown out of the window. And with that came a sense of shock at the parlous state of the Tabora shed, with its lack of stores and equipment and its effect on drivers and shed staff alike.

Underway, it immediately became apparent 2606 was in poor mechanical condition, not only knocking throughout its running gear, but riding dead and flat as if lacking springs, an effect which jarred and kicked the rear of the engine, banging and lifting the lap plate between engine and tender to the extent I was forced to retreat to the kinder and more steadily riding tender. Between Tabora and the first station, Igalula, I came to sample the unpleasant effects of burning wood as a locomotive fuel. Under steam the engine discharged a column of sparks and red-hot charcoal which, under differing conditions, either drifted as far back as the caboose, or fell in or around the cab, causing agitation amongst the crew as they sought to escape being burnt. On down grades, with the regulator closed, clouds of fine ash drifted along the boiler, filling the cab with a bitter acrid smog, burning the eyes and choking the lungs. Not very pleasurable, especially in the heat!

On reaching Igalula, 14 miles out, we stopped to await the Line Clear—a leisurely affair in those days. Here Ron got down and began to carefully examine the engine for hot spots developing. After only 14 miles, my reaction to this was: "Hello, we've got another Bill Pickersgill here!" It was, however, an incorrect and arrogant assumption on my part. Ron, with long experience, knew what he was doing, and quickly discovered one of those dubious white metal bearings already showing signs of overheating.

What followed astonished me, a jury-rigged fix I would never have thought of in a lifetime, but which in the future I ran on for thousands of miles: namely water, siphoned from the Wier pump pre-heater. To accomplish this Ron retrieved a length of armoured hose and attached it to a drain pipe leading from the Weir heater. Then, withdrawing the axle box flexible oil pipe, he inserted the opposite end of the hose into the axle box crown.

With the Weir pump never having found favour in the UK, it's likely that its actions require a little explanation here. With this system, exhaust steam from the cylinders is fed to a long box containing a number of heat transfer elements, through which cold feed water from the tender was pumped directly into the boiler. At this point the heat transfer from exhaust steam to feed water was so effective that the exhaust steam from the cylinders was discharged as hot water. For the next 92 hours, and 548 miles, both Ron and Bill ran this bearing on water only, before returning to Tabora, where a more detailed examination of the recalcitrant bearing would taking place. Anything which might overheat was pretty much guaranteed to do so at one time or another, so in this respect it was not unusual to observe a 26 Class arriving festooned with water pipes!

On any British railway, water intended for boiler consumption had to be reasonably pure and clean, but along the arid, dusty and wind-blown section between Tabora and Dodoma, with water at a premium, anything had to serve. At Nyahua, 39 miles out from Tabora, our first watering point, this 'clean water conviction' on my part, was radically adjusted. At several watering points along the line, water was drawn from a dam—an open reservoir relying on the rainy season for replenishment, but each now reduced to a pool of muddy water, among which swam or wriggled a multitude of strange unidentifiable creatures whose ultimate fate was delivery to a locomotive boiler. None of which, it has to be said, seemed to have any detrimental effect on the boiler's fabric or its ability to produce steam.

Tura station, 75 miles and five hours steaming from Tabora, was just such another watering point, delivering up the same quota of dirty water and lacustrine creatures as Nyahua. Here, whilst the fireman took water and Ron examined his engine, I decided I'd had enough of the footplate. Overcome by heat, noise and wood ash, my mouth as dry as the scorched wastes around and about, I left them to it. In any case night had long since fallen, leaving nothing to observe and mark beyond the headlamp's narrow beam. Back at the caboose Bill fixed up the Primus stove and made us both a mug of tea. This was an act of benevolence for which I was extremely grateful, but also one which gave me a taste of how a Primus stove could raise the temperature of the caboose from very hot to almost unbearable levels. Worn out, I fell asleep, to be woken the next morning to the sound of 2606 ripping the dawn with its exhaust. My first thought on waking was "My word, Bill's hammering the engine." Then, to my astonishment, I saw he was still laid in his bunk. With this came the numbing realisation that, after 16 hours of working under the most arduous conditions, Ron was still on the footplate working the train forward, and Bill accepted this as the ordinary course of events. Ominously, this scenario proved to be the template for my own future…!

During my time with Bill and Ron, the extent of the poverty which Tabora shed laboured under (for in the end everything comes down to money, or the lack of it) became more apparent. The only stores issued to engine crews was a ration of oil so meagre that the only way to get by was to ignore the engine's 16 axle boxes in favour of the more important big-end and side rod bushes. Nor were my spirits lifted when, with growing dismay, I observed, in the absence of oil feeders, engines being oiled using old baked bean tins. Even detonators and flags, essential to protect the train in the event of a breakdown or accident, were unknown to engine crews. Two additional items that were never kept in stock: tail and plug trimmings. In the UK, these were made by storemen during quiet periods. Unfortunately this service was unavailable on the Tanganyika section, and drivers had to make their own—a drudgery not made any more welcome by the fact that the shed had no copper wire to form them on. The answer then, was to go cap in hand to the district electrician, and beg for a length of suitable copper wire from him. Adding to my disquiet I discovered, to my alarm, the 26 Class, in the absence of modern piston gland packing, had to rely on asbestos packaging, of the kind George Stevenson and his contemporaries would have been familiar with, compelling drivers, often under difficult circumstances, such as during hours of darkness, or during a tropical thunderstorm, to set to and repack the failed gland, a task made more irksome by everything he touched or handled being exceedingly hot.

To repack the erring gland, all the driver had was a length of 3/4 inch square asbestos cord. This required him to unscrew the gland's retaining nuts and, not without difficulty, extract a hot and tight-fitting stuffing box, and with it dangling around, an equally hot piston rod, clean it of any remaining residue, and after repacking the gland using a block of wood carried for the purposes of preventing damage to the face of the stuffing box, tap it into position using a hammer. To be successful, this required some skill. After carefully measuring the circumference of the piston rod, and allowing for steam-tight diagonal joints, the length of asbestos packaging had to be cut, with the joints at 120 degrees to each other, to increase the glands ability to withstand steam pressure. With that completed all that remained was to replace the stuffing box cover and its retaining nuts and tighten them up. This was done whilst trying to avoid bare arms and wrists touching the hot piston rod. There was the further hazard of working under low, and very wide, running plates; plates so disproportionately wide I can only imagine their purpose was to shield the ordinary white metal bearings from the heat of the tropical sun.

Neither was I left jumping for joy when, in keeping with Tabora shed's poverty-stricken condition, I found drivers had to find, by way of purchase, their own engine tools. These tools included spanners to fit the engine's motion parts, and preferably of the ring kind, for this type could be hung on the engine's screw reverser lock, a gadget so unreliable on the 26 Class that to prevent the reverser spinning into full travel, it had to be held in position by some other means. A hammer was also required to test for loose nuts, slack taper pins, and occasionally for a suspected slack crosshead gudgeon pin, and equally indispensable when repacking piston glands. Equally important, a couple of heavy duty pin punches for withdrawing split pins, and for working in the dark, whatever the task, an electric torch, to be held in the hands of a fireman, was essential. Altogether this came to a not insignificant sum.

Putting aside this lack of one of the most basic items of locomotive equipment, brings me to another practice which stood everything I believed in on its head. From the earliest times, engine motions, that is the valve gear connecting rods, big ends, side rod bushes and knuckle pin joints, had been, and I suppose on active steam locomotives still are, oiled by way of a half-inch threaded hole drilled through each oil cap. To be certain each oil cap was fit for the work in hand, drivers had no other option but to fill them to overflowing—a time honoured but inevitably wasteful practice. After overflowing, each cap was sealed tight by firmly screwing in a cork. Using cork, we were given to understand, was the only reliable way of allowing a little air to filter through into the oil cavity to counteract a partial vacuum building up and preventing oil siphoning through, surely a fallacy, given that, for generations, the same material has been used very effectively to seal wine bottles.

In East Africa this long-held belief was cast aside in favour of just the opposite. There, each oil cap was sealed, once and for all, by filling it with white metal. At first this caused a sharp intake of breath from me, and the conviction that ignorant colonial railwaymen knew no better—a conviction I was forced to drop when the benefits of this custom became apparent. Drivers, when oiling, were compelled, using a ring spanner similar to ones I had been obliged to acquire, to unscrew each cap. Once fully open they were easily filled without any overflowing. It had one other important advantage, one well known to EAR locomotive inspectors, who being held responsible for all aspects of locomotive performance were very keen on that sort of thing, and this was that the engine's plug trimmings, now exposed to view, could be examined for signs of wear or neglect, in which case things were made uncomfortable for the offending driver.

By far the most ill-disposed of all the different types of locomotives it has been my lot to work with, the 26 Class suffered a number of serious defects, each worthy of attention. Perhaps they had been built on the cheap. If so it was an indication of British post-war austerity and the shortage of essential materials, but also of the parlous state that Tanganyika Railways had been left in after the war. What also cannot be ignored, are the further blows the railway was forced to endure when the newly elected Attlee government decided to press ahead with its inevitability ill-fated Tanganyika Groundnut Scheme (TGS)[36]. With insufficient motive power to move the expected tonnage, the near-bankrupt railway was obliged to put out to tender a contract to build twelve of an 'improved' version of the 25 Class, the infamous 26 Class, together with some 400 covered bogie waggons, which as far as waggons were concerned, at least set the railway up nicely when eventually the TGS collapsed.

Other burdens imposed by the TGS on the creaking railway, and one I referred to earlier in my conversations with Bill Etherington were the separate 132 mile Southern Province (Groundnut) Railway and deep water port of Mtwara

---

[36] Despite warnings that the environment and rainfall were unsuitable, after a tremendous effort and a cost of £36 million to the British taxpayer (equivalent to over £1 billion in 2020), the TGS was a calamitous failure and was finally abandoned in 1951.

(a costly undertaking to build and also operate), a 25 mile branch line from Msagali on the Central Line to Kongwa district, to serve a further groundnut experiment. In addition, in 1947, a short branch line about 9 miles in length built to connect the newly opened Williamson Diamond Mine with the Mwanza Line, was constructed. It was said of Williamson, a government geologist, employed at that time to find anything of use amid the empty wastes of Tanganyika, that upon termination of his employment at the end of the war, he immediately registered a claim on a parcel of land just north of Shinyanga, where, to few people's surprise, he quickly discovered, quite by chance you understand, a large and lucrative diamond field.

In the meantime, another important, as far as the railway was concerned, and expensive line had to be constructed. Large deposits of galena lead ore had been discovered in the isolated Mpanda district in the Western Province south of the Ugalla River. To retrieve the ore a branch line 130 miles in extent was built to connect Mpanda with Kaliawa, on the Tabora to Kigoma section of the Central Line. Built without telegraphic communication and as cheaply as possible, it was worked on the 'one engine in steam' principle, when, twice a week, a mixed train left the main line at Kaliwa, before clanking into the wilderness at a splendid 15 mph, to hopefully return (such was the condition of the track) fully laden, some time later, but not every time. Flying along the railway with Bill More-Gilbert, the Senior Game Ranger, as the pilot, the District Commissioner was horrified to spy the Mpanda engine, unknown to anyone, laid on its side. Immediately diverting from his destination the District Commissioner flew straight to Tabora to report the incident to the railway authorities. What caused this accident is unknown to me. Years later I was involved in retrieving two engines that had become marooned for weeks by flood water on the same line. The line's most imposing feature was a half mile causeway over the fast-flowing Ugalla River. Built of large boulders, it allowed the river to flow (relatively) unimpeded between them. There were, however, occasions when large dead and decomposing animals were caught up, and a fetid stench followed the train for miles.

This then was the background, in 1947, to the arrival of the first of twelve 26 Class at Tabora, where under harsh working conditions their many faults soon became evident. The primitive, by 1947 standards, rotating cylinder drain 'taps' were difficult to maintain steam-tight, requiring frequent grinding-in and rod adjustment. A more serious problem, thankfully common to the 26 Class only, but which in those times of 'make do and mend', stretched the shed to its limits, was that the coupled springs were all as soft as putty. The consequence, after a couple of thousand miles, was that engines were down on their box tops, with the boxes themselves taking a terrible pounding. This affected the white metal inserts, which soon became flattened and distorted, setting up lubrication problems on what I suspect were already inadequate bearings.

Whilst Dar es Salaam workshops seemed able to tackle pretty much any job, for some reason they were unable to master the simple art of tempering springs, these being returned little better than when they went away. I can't help thinking it was fortunate that, of all the locomotives and other rolling stock held by the railway, only the 26 Class gave trouble. In respect of springs, even this was enough to keep Tabora's drop pit gangs (responsible for dropping the wheels of engines to work on them) at full-stretch changing springs both night and day, and repairing and re-metaling worn or damaged axle boxes. The cost of sending flat springs back to the works for repair, on top of the unremitting toil of renovating and re-metaling axle boxes, proved a heavy drain on the shed's meagre finances and resources.

Another grave fault I might add, was that it was impossible to keep the coupled stay plates in position, and its bolts tight, resulting in the axle box wedges to which each was attached, falling by the same amount the stay plate dropped. Because of the limited space available for the coupled wheels and stay plate bolts, it required the engine being placed over a pit before the stay plate bolts could be tightened and the wedges adjusted. The inevitable result of this fault was heavy pounding between the axle boxes and horned cheeks when running with steam on.

Equally, and perhaps more damning in a modern locomotive (and one which bore heavily on drivers already beset with long hours, the fatigue this brought on, and all the other problems the 26 Class piled on their shoulders): the big-end and side rod bushes lacked elementary locking keys and keyways (slots with keys designed to prevent the bush turning in the eye of the rod and cutting off lubrication). Instead the 26 Class relied on a 3/4 inch diameter stud, machined to a tight fit to bear on the bush and rod. By their very nature the originals had long been lost, to be replaced, because of Tabora's poverty stricken condition, by any old bolt with the right thread. Ill-fitting and invariably protruding an inch or more from the rod, they were easily lost, despite being checked at every opportunity. Once lost the bush turned, cutting off its oil supply and running hot, with the driver having to rig up a water pipe to splash water over the offending bush to keep it both cool and lubricated.

Back on the shed it became the responsibility of the fitting gang to drop the rod, and by operating a screw press, remove the damaged bush. Then two members of the gang, using a long strip of emery cloth and a length of suitable cord wrapped around the crank pin, would, by see-sawing away, manually polish out the discolouration or scoring on the crank pin. The same was true of hot bearings, except the affected wheels and boxes had to be dropped in their entirety and moved clear of the engine before polishing could begin. Tabora had a small group of highly skilled Indian machinists who usually worked quietly and largely unnoticed in the machine shop, profiling worn tyres and forming new engine parts, until one emerged, micrometre in hand, to measure up (with a care and precision I always admired) a newly polished crank pin or bearing, before turning up a new bush.

Chapter 19
Feeling My Way

In the meantime, under the supervision of those two stalwarts, Ron and Bill, I continued to learn the road—sort of—between Tabora and Dodoma. This included negotiating the spectacular 2,000 foot deep Great Rift Valley, by way of the 25 mile, 1 in 50 gradient, Saranda Bank, blasted out of the hard unyielding granite outcrops, and in many places still showing the drill holes and blast marks left by its German builders. On the rift's opposing side was the similar and equally trying 22 mile Kigwe Bank. In between, along the floor of this massive fault, lay the dead Bahi Flats: thirty-four miles of straight-level track, which during the heat of the day became lost in a shimmering heat haze, distorting the eyesight of engine crews. During the rainy season the Flats flooded, becoming a sea of clear shallow water, the home of a little terrapin, an attractive kind of turtle, which, at the sound of an approaching train, leapt in droves for the safety of the water. It was also home to countless bullfrogs, whose strident croaks, rising above the sound of the engine, echoed throughout each warm and sultry night.

26 Class passing through rock formations on the approach to Mwanza.

As a potted history of railways in East Africa, the Usambara Railway was the first to be built by the Germans in their East Africa colony, and ran from the port of Tanga (with construction commencing in 1893) northwest to Moshi, near Mount Kilimanjaro, the track reaching there (kilometre 351) in 1911. This railway was followed by the Mittellandbahn, the Central Line, with construction commencing in 1905 at the port (and then capital) of Dar es Salaam[39], following an old caravan route west towards Tabora. The town of Morogoro (at kilometre 200), was reached in 1907, with Kilosa on the shores of Lake Tanganyika (kilometre 1252) reached on the 2nd February 1914—the eve of World War I. The war then brought an end to German railway building in East Africa.

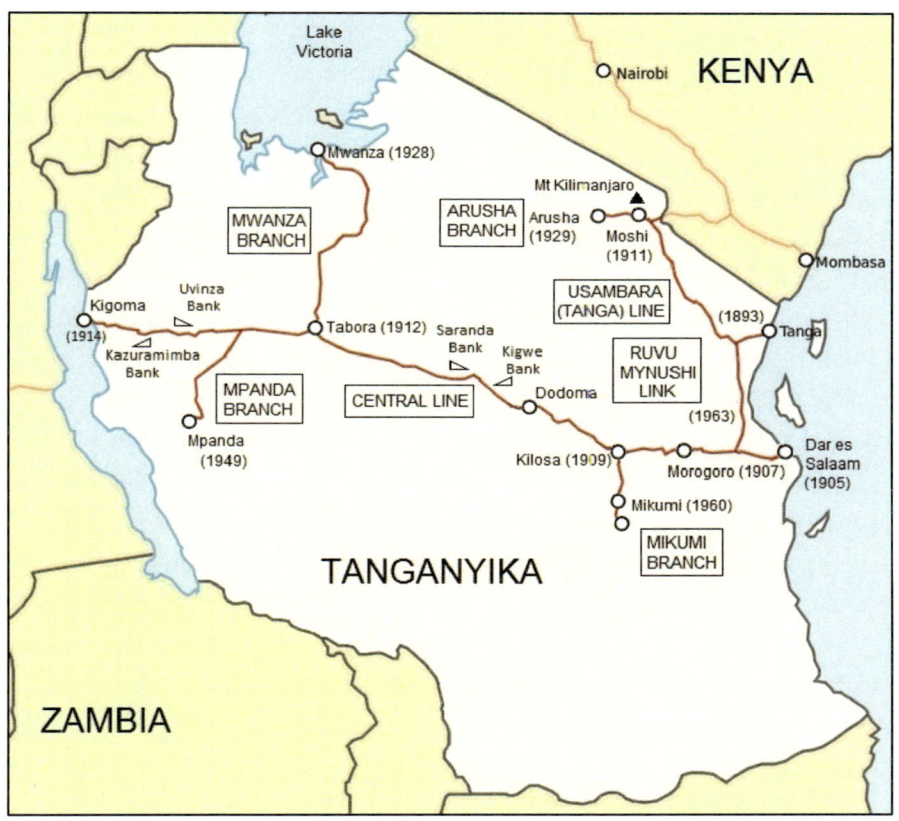

Map of Tanganyika, showing main and branch lines and the years they were completed.

Following the Armistice of 1918, administration of the territory of Tanganyika was granted to the United Kingdom under a League of Nations mandate, with Tanganyika Railways and Port Services being established to operate the railways. During the time of this mandate three branch lines were added to the Central Line.

The most important one, the Tabora-Mwanza line, ran north 379 km (235 miles from Tabora to Mwanza on the south bank of Lake Victoria) and was completed in 1928. The second, a shorter branch from Kilosa south to Mikumi, was built between 1958 and 1963, and the third, established in 1931, ran from Manyoni to Kiniyangiri, but was shut down by 1948. Meanwhile, in 1930, the Usambara Railway was extended another 86 km further west to Arusha. Then, between 1949 and 1950 another branch line, the Mpanda Line, was added to the Central Line, heading south from Kaliua to Mpanda.

Who the Germans employed to help build their railways is not clear. Perhaps it was African workers, although the British, when building railways in Africa, preferred to employ Indian labourers, who were no-doubt easily recruited and shipped in. Whether they found Indians better suited to the work, or more experienced in railway-building, or were just better able to communicate with them, I don't know. There are stories of African workers being employed in early railways construction, but disappearing into the bush once they'd been paid, only to be seen again when their money ran out. Whether these stories are true, or apocryphal, is not clear. Old photographs, dated around 1910, do, however, seem to show African workers during the German construction of the line.

After my three trips between Tabora and Dodoma, I was next booked on the Mwanza line, with two Eurasian drivers, chiefly remembered for them adorning their engine, a 26 Class, with brass trinkets, and the disparaging way they regarded their fellow compatriots, the full blooded Indians. They spoke in a kind of Victorian English, warning me about those "Bally Indians" who were "absolute rotters." Having to repeatedly listen to this refrain brought to mind the thought: "Well, you ought to know, both your mothers were Indian!" They went to great lengths to assure me of their parent's high status, having fathers who were British Commanding Officers of Indian regiments and mothers who were Indian princesses. Uncharitably disposed towards their snobbishness, I wondered if their fathers had really just been ordinary British soldiers and their mothers, perish the thought, simply girls from the local 'knocking shop' just around the corner!

The Mwanza line had a chequered history, forming a story in itself. Conceived by the Germans to connect the then Belgian Congo railways, north of Lake Victoria, they achieved about 60 miles of construction before the colony of

Deutsch-Ostafrika (German East Africa) was invaded by the Imperial and Belgian forces during World War I. This line remained largely forgotten until commercial pressure from the booming but isolated lake port of Mwanza forced a rethink by Tanganyika Railways. Work to complete the line as far as Mwanza was started in 1926, and by following the German survey, whose plans had been discovered in Tabora, was completed in 1928. The 60 miles of German construction had been built to their usual high standards, with solid stone built stations, bridges and culverts and the track laid on deep granite ballast. However, the British construction was, due to financial problems, built on the cheap using light 38 lbs per linear yard second-hand rail, laid without ballast on the bare earth, resulting over the years in much additional expenditure to both track and engines. That's not to say all was cheap and nasty. At Mwanza the terminal station was architecturally very pleasing, and to serve the township and the lake steamers extensive wharfage and port facilities were constructed.

Further rock formations on the approach to Mwanza.

Somewhere towards the end of German construction the railway left the dense tsetse fly infested bush surrounding Tabora, and from thereon to Mwanza entered open savannah grassland. As with the Central Line, the German surveyors had been at pains to avoid cuttings, which were death traps for wild animals, and in the case of a herd of larger animals e.g. elephants and the like, equally disastrous for the trains. Following the lie of the land from the footplate the rails stretched out seemingly as light and unsubstantial as lengths of wire. Unsupported by ballast, most, if not all, of the rails were hog-backed and suffered from 'pumping sleepers', which in the dry season puffed out clouds of red murram dust, and in the rainy season splashed out water in sufficient quantities to frequently undermine the track.

Working over the Mwanza line with its light rail and narrow railheads created other problems. Because of the reduced area in contact with the rails this exaggerated the tendency to slip. However, more seriously, it wore a narrow groove or channel around the rims of the coupled wheels. This didn't much matter until the engine had to work over the main line with heavier rails and broader railheads, leaving the coupled wheels with little contact between them and the rails. The Anglo Indian drivers overcame this problem by an arrangement with the shed to stick only to the Mwanza line and never venture any further. The 26 Class wasn't helped by being fitted with Lambert Wet Sanders, a sanding apparatus which failed in all respects to deliver sand. On this line there was little of note apart from where it passed through some spectacular kopjes (formed when the softer volcanic rock and ash has eroded to expose the underlying layer of ancient granite) on the approach to Mwanza South, and at Shinyanga, where a four-span straight girder bridge on granite piers had been erected over the Manonga River, and was the scene of a near-disaster involving Bill Connell, as explained below.

In the initial absence of a Rule Book (I received mine four years into my EAR career) we ran trains on word of mouth and our own experience. However, we were familiar with Warning Orders (WO), a form issued by stationmasters warning drivers of any hazard they may encounter in the section ahead. A frequent example was a plate layers' push trolley working somewhere in the section, and common sense dictated that, when his view was restricted, the driver would sound the whistle as a warning of a train's approach. However, some of the issues that prompted a Warning Order were long-standing, and with these a perilous flaw had been allowed into the system, for, after a few weeks, engine crews were judged to be familiar with the hazard, and the Warning Order was discontinued—a practice fraught with danger, misunderstanding and all sorts of mischief.

Such an example is as follows: Bill Connell had left Tabora for six months of well-earned home leave, and in the meantime a flash flood generated by an intense thunderstorm had undermined the two central piers of Manonga Bridge on the outskirts of Shinyanga, on the Mwanza line, causing them and the railway they supported to subside by several inches. Immediately a 3 mph speed restriction was imposed and a Warning Order issued, informing drivers of the condition of the bridge and the speed restriction imposed. After a few weeks, and here's the rub, the Warning Orders were discontinued as per regulation. A few weeks later Bill returned from leave, and before his feet had hardly touched the ground, he was booked to work 3 Up passenger, the Night Mail to Mwanza. Leaving Tabora at 19:40 hours and arriving at Shinyanga at 03:00 hours, the crew changing station. Unaware of any special speed restrictions (no Warning Orders), Bill was running through the hot African night at full line speed. Only one thing saved him and the train's many sleeping passengers: the position of Manonga Bridge. Just a few yards beyond the bridge, Shinyanga Station opened out, with its own speed restriction (though they were often exceeded) of 5 mph over its facing points. Bill had 'shut off' to enter the station and braked for the facing points; nevertheless, he struck the bridge at some speed. His first intimation of disaster came when, to his horror (he maintained it would remain with him for the rest of his life), the engine, rolling wildly, sank several inches, almost throwing him off his feet. Instinct and long experience of Africa in its many and extreme moods warned him it would be a disaster to stop on the bridge, which he felt was on the point of collapse. Instead, with heart in mouth, he opened the regulator a little, and with extreme caution, slowly drew the Mail clear of falling in the river below.

For weeks the rainy season had slowly gathered strength, with the Kaskani, the monsoon wind, blowing ever more strongly, and bringing with it towering banks of black rain clouds, against which snowy egrets, the traditional African 'rain birds', a forerunner of impending rain, flashed vivid white as they wheeled and soared against the overcast sky. With the egrets came a marked increase in humidity, when by some miracle of nature, and weeks before any rain fell, saw the ground carpeted with fresh grass and a host of wild flowers, with the bush springing from a dead and lifeless waste into a sea of lush and verdant green.

On one occasion I was rostered to work out with 31 Up Mwanza Goods, departing Tabora at 03:50 hours. The night was hot and humid with lightening continuously flickering behind dense rainclouds, and the train, made up of a full load, some 458 tons, was heavy enough to try the engine on some of the grades ahead. Leaving Tabora, the line, on a grade of 1 in 95, curved sharply as it climbed to a bare and desolate granite ridge, where, on reaching the summit, it swung to the west on the level for a few hundred yards, before falling for a couple of miles, then again on the level curving to assume its northerly direction. After this start, when both firemen had their work cut out, the line ran on a series of more easy grades as far as Shinyanga, the train crew changing station and water point.

After an hour of continuous steaming I became aware of a strong and rising side-wind beating against the side of the engine. This, with lightening, grew rapidly in strength picking up clouds of dust, loose grass and dried twigs, to batter the engine and drive me from my usual position. As the wind and lightening grew in intensity, it brought a welcome and long overdue fragrance, the sweet smell of rain falling on parched earth. Standing at the reverser and looking through the weather glass I saw the first raindrops, driven almost horizontally by the wind, flash through the headlamp beam. Taken aback by their unusual size, tangent and velocity I leant forward. I had become used to tropical rainstorms, but I was unprepared for what was about to follow. After the first few raindrops came an absolute deluge which swept across the footplate, this time driving me from my position, despite the engine's generous cab and long extended roof, to the fireman's side, from where, by being a little more sheltered from wind and flying debris, and leaving the engine to find its own way through the storm, I was better able to navigate the many hazards the railway was throwing at me. With light from the cab (it was tradition to run with the cab lights on) I could see the railway's side drains filling and in places the track was submerged under flowing water. Leaving the ballasted sections, track conditions became more uncertain, with long sections under water, the sleepers pumping and the track throughout feeling soft and spongy. Attacked on all sides by sheet lightening, horrendous thunder, torrential rain and dodgy track, and with little or no visibility forward, I was compelled to drive by instinct. Then something outside my experience occurred: torrential rain began penetrating the boiler cladding, producing masses of steam which obscured what little view I still had. Now blind, I crouched on the bouncing lap plate, and by using the lee side of the cab as shelter was able to keep an eye on trackside conditions and maintain my bearings. For months after, as Permanent Way gangs struggled to knock the line and its sinking and tilting sleepers into shape, it proved a nightmare for drivers. It was a miracle, and down to the skill of the drivers, that no derailments occurred.

Mwanza's 4 Down Passenger, comprising an auxiliary water tank bogie (WTB) holding 5,000 gallons, restaurant car, two first class sleepers, two second class bogies, three third class bogies, a post office bogie, a caboose and a bogie guards van, left Mwanza on its 912-mile journey to Dar es Salaam at 17:00 sharp. On this particular evening I was 'working out' and leaving the first station, Fela, with the line curving away on a rising gradient before it entered a shallow cutting near the summit. The train was heavy, confining the speed to a steady 10 mph. Entering the cutting, my view restricted by the boiler, I was alerted by an anxious shout from the senior of the two firemen: "Piga brake upesi, Bwana!" (Apply the brakes quickly, Sir!)

Without hesitation, I made a full application of the vacuum brake. In the centre of the cutting, his head close to the rail, lay an elderly African man. Willing the train to stop before it struck the inert body, I watched the closing gap with growing apprehension. With the brakes grinding hard on, the train had almost stopped, when the 'cowcatcher', striking the victim in the head, pushed him to one side. Jumping down, not knowing if the casualty was drunk, dead or injured, I examined him carefully. He was alive but deeply unconscious, with a nasty head wound from the engine's cowcatcher, and obviously needed urgent medical attention. Fortunately, for him, help was not far away. I knew that half a mile from Fela Station was a Catholic Mission with medical facilities. Aided by my fireman I lifted the casualty and laid him within the entrance to the first coach. Then against all the rules, I cautiously propelled the Mail Train back down the grade and into Fela Station. From here the victim was quickly transferred to the Mission. Out of this affair I was fortunate—the guard, probably as I was, lacking a rule book and just as ignorant of the more obscure rules, failed to report the matter. But then out in the wilds of Africa, away from prying eyes, drivers, hoping they might get away with it, frequently had to ignore a few rules and work on their own initiative.

Kasuli, on the Mwanza line, was a typical bush station, consisting of a station office and living quarters for the stationmaster. Its purpose, apart from being the first watering point after leaving Tabora, was to control trains over its adjoining sections and to act as a crossing place when necessary. However, in this respect it was out of the ordinary. Some distance from the station and the scattering of native huts which had grown up around it, stood a police post. This was manned by several African policemen under the command of an African sergeant. In 1956 it became the scene of a terrible massacre. Late one night, under some pretext or other, one of the constables lured the sergeant outside and, with a single blow to the head from a machete, killed him. Taking the keys for the armoury from the sergeant's body, the constable armed himself with a rifle and ammunition and systematically murdered the other constables, before disappearing into the bush. For a week or more a massive search was mounted with distressing reports coming in that the constable was shooting anyone, men, women and children, unfortunate enough to cross his path.

As can be imagined, all this had an effect on the railway and its operations. Whilst goods trains continued running, all passenger trains were cancelled, leaving myself and other engine crews passing through the area, or taking water at Kasuli, feeling particularly exposed to the maniac and his rifle. Eventually, hunger and thirst drove the errant constable to seek shelter. Approaching an isolated African hut he asked for food, but the 'bush telegraph' had been busy, and the occupants, an elderly couple, were well aware of the danger they were in. Nevertheless they offered him food and a place to sleep. Under cover of catching and preparing a chicken, the old man, risking his life and that of his wife, hurried to his nearest neighbour asking him to contact one of the police patrols combing the area. Later the same day armed officers arrived and, after making sure the old couple were out of harm's way, set up an ambush and called on the policeman to surrender. When he refused they raked the hut with rifle fire, killing the occupant and, to our relief, bringing to an end his murderous spree.

Despite these events, working over the Mwanza line was little different to those other lines radiating from Tabora, and in what might be termed a tale of two water columns, two recollections, each of them ordinary enough, have, by some quirk, remained locked fast in my memory. Let us return again to that place of ill repute, Kasuli Station, 75 miles out and the first water stop from Tabora. Before the introduction of the 30 Class with massive tenders, each train left Tabora with a water tank bogie attached to the tender, and whatever its quality and wherever available, both tender and water tank were as a matter of necessity filled to capacity. However, unlike most watering points, Ikasule water was plentiful and pure, to such an extent that it was one of only two places I dare fill my water bag with water straight from the column. To stir the senses and delight, around this column had grown a huge bed of canna lilies, fed by the overflow from the column, throwing a welcome and exotic mix of deep crimson red and brilliant golden yellows to glorify the station, even in the most barren months of the year.

Situated mid-section on the treeless veld, miles from anywhere, was the second of the two water columns, and its purpose was to provide for the next waterless 80 miles between Kasule and Shinyanga. Hereabouts the population were few and widely scattered, each hut isolated from its neighbour by the need for grazing land, and surrounded by prickly euphorbia hedge, whose thorns and milky acidic juice defended the domestic animals corralled within each night. In the absence of wood, its inhabitants relied on dried animal dung for fuel. Mile 90 water column was located where the railway swept around the base of a prominent hill, and it was here, taking her time from the position of the sun, an elderly African woman met the trains on the bare windswept hillside, and would barter a few small hard-boiled native eggs for kuni, the sweet-smelling acacia wood used as locomotive fuel. Perhaps she lived alone and as such was no longer able to look after the livestock, which would have provided her with the source of kindling she needed. With agreement reached, she would bind her kuni with a rough rawhide thong, securing it around her forehead, which after a lifetime, had left a deep and permanent imprint. Aided by her staff she left after thanking us with a soft and gentle "Santi sana" (thank you very much) and as I watched her toil up the steep and rugged pathway home, me thought, old age is not for wimps (a conviction which I can now verify, from direct experience!).

However, all this was in the future. In the meantime I had, for want of a more precise expression, to 'look over' the Tabora-Kigoma section, and in the three trips allowed, try and get a grip and make sense of it. Taking both directions into account this amounted to 502 miles of railway, with a 'ruling grade' of 1 in 50, including two nasty gradients, Uvinza Bank in the Up direction, a bank made more difficult by the final two miles consisting of a series of tight curves which had a tendency to heave the engine over, causing it to lose traction and slip. If that wasn't a headache enough, the whole of the train's wheels were strung around several curves, caused the flanges to bind against the rails, imposing further retarding friction. To slip to a standstill here was to court disaster, for if 60 minutes were lost during the whole run (which could easily happen during the process of sanding the rails, setting back, and hand-sanding the rails ahead of the train) it would be classed as a failure, requiring a please explain in the form of a detailed written train delay report.

Tabora European drivers celebrating Christmas 1956 at the Tabora Railway Hotel. From top left: Bill Connell, John Millray, Jon Luis; from bottom left: Dennis Cregan, the author, and Ron Kenyon.

In the Down direction, after leaving Kigoma came the laborious 27 mile '1 in 50' slog up Kazuramimba Bank, interrupted by a water stop at Kandaga, a closed station, but one which gave the drivers the opportunity to take water and examine the engine. In both directions several hefty grades intervened, such as the 79 minutes of '1 in 92' rising grade between Uvinza and Malagarasi in the Down direction, which saw the engine working to its limit. Midway in this section the climb was interrupted by a short falling grade leading down to a single span steel girder bridge straddling an intermittent water course, and I used to take advantage of this short respite by whipping the engine as fast as I could to build up some momentum for the climb ahead. It was in this section that I regularly played a game with a pair of small brown falcons. At the brow of this down grade trains were often met by the two small birds, flying from behind at high speed, and then diving down with rapidly beating wings, both would pass the cab within touching distance. Then, suddenly, at rail level, they would swerve across the cowcatcher to pick up any insects leaping or flying out of the way of the locomotive, before repeating the manoeuvre several times in an amazing show of speed and dexterity. It was always a pleasure to renew their acquaintance, and though I always tried to outpace them I always failed.

This time my mentors were Sikh drivers, workmanlike, hardy and efficient. On wood burning locomotives they had a problem, though: hot embers discharged by the engine had the unfortunate effect of lodging in their turbans, and alerted by the pungent smell of burning head gear they were forced to temporarily forego their religious beliefs and whip the turban off and douse it under the tender water tap before clapping it back into place. They did, however, then get the added benefit of their heads being cooled by the evaporating water.

In future years two sections of this line were to prove a challenge, which in my youthful enthusiasm I was more than willing to take on. The first, Usinge Swamp, is a five mile stretch of (usually dry) black cotton soil which the railway crossed on a seven foot unballasted embankment. However, after flooding, the water rose to a nine foot deep lake, extending south to what seemed like infinity, and immersing the track under more than two feet of water, resulting in traffic being disrupted for several months. The swamp was remarkable for an unusual type of palm tree which grew there, and the enormous ant hills which dotted the surface and which ecologists assured us were several thousand years old. The second concerned the Malagarasi swamp. Spreading to the size of Yorkshire and extending north for 200 miles, and as such becoming almost another arm of Lake Victoria. It was drained by the Malagarasi River, flowing south into Lake Tanganyika, and in the dry season this river was nothing more than a placid stream, flowing smoothly and darkly. It was said, however, to be the home of voracious monster crocodiles, although in the many times I crossed it I saw nothing on or beneath its smooth surface to affright me.

The river became a different matter in the rainy season where it became a 20-foot deep flood sweeping south. The railway crossed the swamp at its narrowest point on a substantial embankment, breached at intervals by a series of single-span girder bridges resting on dressed granite abutments. This allowed flood water to pass through, before the line crossed the Malagarasi River itself on an imposing girder bridge of overhead construction. Whilst not a great engineering feat in itself, nevertheless I found much to admire in its granite piers and Herr Krupp's[37] latticed steel crossbars, girders and transoms. Regarding these two swamps, Malagarasi and Usinge, and the work I was called on to perform regarding them, and conditions I had to endure, all that lay a long time in the future and the reader must bear with me a while before a detailed account is provided.

After what amounted to little more than a cursory inspection of more than 1,500 miles of varied railway I was paired with a driver by the name of Dennis Cregan on engine 2612, a partnership that proved long and fruitful. Dennis, a

---

[37] Of the steel-making dynasty fame. The particular member of the family in charge of the business at the time the steel was produced for German East African Railways would likely to be Gustav Krupp, born 1870, died 1950.

genial southern Irishman, had form. Not, I hasten to add, of a criminal nature, but form nevertheless. Born and raised in the 'bogs', his words not mine, the youngest of a large family, from an early age he was destined for the priesthood, or the 'Monk House', as he called it (as in "When I was in the Monk House…!"), where he was taught the Swahili language, and afterward shipped off to Tanganyika as a missionary priest, until one day it came to an abrupt end. According to Dennis (and who is to doubt the word of a priest?), one sunny morning the Bishop, no less, was riding his bicycle along a dusty rural pathway when he inadvertently chanced upon Dennis, not only in dalliance with a local maiden, but in full *flagrante delicto*. The upshot of this encounter was traumatic (probably for all of them) and Dennis did a runner to eventually land up in Dar es Salaam, living rough and sleeping on the beach—probably one of the few priests to be defrocked for being defrocked! From the Dar es Salaam beach he was rescued by one of the Mechanical Workshop supervisors who put him to work painting locomotives after heavy repairs, and within a few months he transferred to footplate work, becoming first a fireman, then in due course a driver. As such, possibly the only Roman Catholic priest who became a professional engine driver! My only thoughts are that, if his tutors had taught him less about Swahili, and more about morals, he may have fared better as a priest; but on the flip side, he was a very good engine driver.

A few weeks after pairing with Dennis, on returning to Tabora from safari I found big changes afoot—and changes not for the better. Out went the current DMPS to be replaced by one Frank Kent. Out also, Willoughby Dalgains, Eurasian shedmaster, together with the locomotive inspector (whose name I can no longer recall), to be replaced by Snellings as loco inspector, and Wright as shedmaster (Wright by name but not by nature!). These senior officers, who I came to call the 'Unholy Trinity', arrived blowing off steam and determined to shake things up, and this regime change signalled a time of bullying and intimidation, resulting in an unhappy period in the life of the Tabora shed.

Gone also was Ron Kenyon, a long-time and experienced driver, shipped off to Dar es Salaam for no apparent reason, though it may have been ill will in the Kremlin. Six months later Ron sadly died in mysterious and unexplained circumstances. He was booked to work the Sunday 12:30 Up Mail, drank a single bottle of beer with a little group of other drivers, but left after refusing another drink, saying he had to work the Mail Train. Failing to turn up for work, a call boy was sent to his accommodation, an upstairs flat, where to the boy's dismay he found Ron at the bottom of the outside stairs, dead with a broken neck. The day before he had caught his houseboy pilfering and had sacked him on the spot. Word went round that the houseboy may have laid in wait and pushed him over the rather low stone balcony; there didn't seem to be any proof, however, and I never heard that any arrest had been made. Also gone without trace were the two Eurasian drivers that I had learned the road to Mwanza with: here today, gone tomorrow, one might say. Dismissed out of hand, never to be seen again, John Millree (who joined EAR at the same time as me) although he was, admittedly showing a distinct liking for the bottle. And for those of us left there began a period of oppression, especially for the shed's British drivers who refused to acquiesce to the system of 'brandy repairs'[38]. Anything that could be thrown at us, was, including being blamed for the manifest shortcomings of the 26 Class, with multiple long reports being demanded with menaces, in the little time granted between safaris, all adding to the sense of being wronged.

Here it may be appropriate to say what my terms and conditions of employment were. As mentioned earlier, I was paid £15 per week, and for this, drivers were required to work 208 hours a month (52 hours a week). Every 12 months we were given two weeks' paid 'local leave', and every three years we were granted six months paid 'home leave'. Included in this package was my EAR accommodation.

Since my arrival at Tabora I had, however, begun to learn the downside of working for EAR, which if brought into the open at my interview, may well have changed my mind about signing up. With British Rail I'd worked a forty-four hour week, with overtime pay for Sundays and public holidays. I now found out the 208 hours a month was at a standard rate, with no extra rate for night work, Sundays or other holidays. On opening my first payslip, having been required to work a good many long stints, I was cheered no end to find that after 208 hours work my pay was all at the overtime rate—until it was pointed out to me that this was only an extra shilling to every pound of flat rate earned. Little wonder therefore we were kept at work as intensely as possible. I had accepted the lack of equipment at engine stores, and the primitive conditions a caboose offered, but I now learned, under the new regime, of something I had never heard of before: the use of "Pay Fines".

---

[38] Where, as the name suggests, a bottle (or some other little incentive) was quietly slipped on to the shedmaster's desk by those willing to buy his goodwill, securing improved maintenance and a speedier return of their engine.

Directed mainly at the white drivers, or so it seemed, up to fourteen days without pay could be imposed, without appeal, and largely on the advice of the loco inspector, who was responsible for all footplate staff. True or false, a story went the rounds which perfectly illustrated the indifferent attitude senior officers had to the problems experienced on a daily basis by drivers. It was reputed that a Nairobi driver, when rounding a curve with visibility restricted, had crashed into a recent and unreported wash-away. Ignoring the trauma he suffered he was then arbitrarily charged with 'Failing to keep a proper lookout', without being able to give his side of the story, and without right of appeal, and was fined fourteen days of pay—in other words he was forced to work for a fortnight without pay. A similar sanction was imposed on a Tabora driver whose engine failed, after an ill-fitting clack box cover lifted off, taking the clack valve and the contents of the boiler with it. Any failure reflected deeply on the shed concerned, its shedmaster, shed inspector, and its DMPS, whose combined ire was then directed at the hapless driver.

Because of Frank Kent's attitude to the white footplate staff, and his quick and ruthless disposal of those he wished to be rid of, I dubbed him 'Fearless Frank'. In this he was aided to some extent by a form of dismissal when a person was declared 'temperamentally unsuitable'—a charge which could cover a multitude of sins, or none at all, and one to which there was no answer. This vindictiveness, not only on the part of Fearless Frank, also extended to the shedmaster and loco inspector, began to tell on me, and was emphasised by a further incident.

Late one Sunday night I was called to the shed and told to trim a 26 Class after mileage repairs, and now awaiting a test run in the morning. It was, however, a set up: whilst the shed's stores carried trimming wool, as reported earlier, they lacked the copper wire with which to form new trimmings, the old plug trimmings having been cut in half when the big end and side rod bushes had been pressed out and new ones fitted. Unable to trim the engine, and recognising I'd been set up, I awaited my fate. This was not long in coming: the imposition of a three-day pay fine. Three days working long hours under the most difficult and trying conditions without pay.

One particular failure was adjudged so grave it ran to six pages of the Motive Power Manual (a catalogue of misery if ever there was one) issued by the Kremlin. But to condense its six pages into more brief and understandable proportions, its gist was this: any locomotive arriving at its destination sixty or more minutes late due to lost time was deemed to be a failure. This charge was not easily avoided given that each trip took three days and the timings were calculated based on an engine in perfect working order. With an unreliable 26 Class, however, there were just two ways the failure could be avoided. The first, by making up lost time (yes, by speeding) to somewhere below the critical sixty minutes (a strategy not without danger, but one encouraged by the unjust penalties, as any competent administrator would see); the second, as practised at Tabora, but kept hidden from the authorities, by asking the guard to book the train's arrival time to something below the sixty minutes. And whilst the driver still had to account for the time lost, having just two minutes, or even one minute, in lieu, allowed him to escape the dreaded failure charge and its hefty pay fine.

In respect to the pay fines, much to my vexation, on one occasion I was harshly penalised for running a big end hot, despite it being no fault of mine. In this case the engine was in poor condition, and at each stop I'd gone round with a spanner tightening ill-fitting bush securing bolts. My first warning came on a long uphill pull when the right-hand big end developed an ominous 'thwack'. By the time I was able to examine it the bush, having lost its badly fitted bolt, had turned, cutting off its oil supply and running hot to the extent it was beginning to disintegrate, bringing with it the very real danger of knocking out a cylinder cover. For the remaining two hundred miles of my trip much of my time was spent nursing a poorly engine home. Did I lose sixty minutes. No, I did not (well, not according to the guard's journal!)—just a mere fifty-eight minutes. Nevertheless, without the opportunity to present my side of the story, and without leave of appeal, I was docked four days hard-won pay.

Also at this time the shed used a cunning and devious ploy, whose only purpose, as far as I could see, was to keep the white drivers under the thumb, which, in relation to myself, worked thus: wait for when I came on shed in the early hours, after working a twelve to sixteen hour shift, then give me an hour or so to have a bath, something to eat, and fall into bed more or less exhausted (but not forgetting to tuck my mosquito net in firmly all round, of course, for Tabora's malarial mosquitoes were large, with many producing an anaphylactic effect). I would then drift off in the sure knowledge that the shed staff would take several hours to knock 2612 back into shape, before I would be called back on duty. However, after an hour or so of sleep, the tactic was to send for me, saying I was required at the shed… "immediately!" Rubbing sleep from eyes, still red-rimmed and sore from kuni exhaust dust, and fearing a serious accident had occurred, I would rush to the shed, stumbling and tripping over points and crossings, whilst dodging shunting engines in what was an extensive, and at that time unlit, station yard. Imagine then my bewilderment, which quickly turned to fury when, handed a train delay report going back weeks, for an insignificant few minutes lost in some section of which I had no recollection (and of so little consequence I was unaware it had occurred), and which was in all probability 'cooked up' in the shedmaster's office the day before. I in no way blamed the hapless shedman who handed over the demand for an explanation. This I knew came from a higher authority. And this made all the more nonsensical by the fact that goods trains, at that time, worked from station to station on a "pick up" basis, attaching and detaching waggons if and when required. With this arrangement, a few minutes here and there along the way was as nothing. Neither did it interfere with train crossings, as they were arranged by stationmasters to suit the work in progress.

At the time I was quite happy to work long hours, to forego basic equipment and lack of stores, and put up with primitive working conditions and the wayward and unreliable 26 Class, for I was doing the work that I loved. But I was no longer prepared to bow to the vindictive attitude of the Unholy Trinity. In fact I was prepared for a fight. Dennis Cregan had a droll Irishism for them, a sentiment I suspect long directed at the English. "Bastards!" he declared. "All three, bastards! They should be shot with a ball of their own shit!"

Not that Dennis seemed anti-British. He once remarked: "I have lived under that good old Union Jack flag for many years and it's always looked after me."

So, in the circumstances, and whatever the consequences, I decided to have it out with Fearless Frank. The DMPS's office was located some distance from the shed and, lucky for him, beneath the cooling shade of a splendid mango tree. On arrival I knocked on his door. Probably thinking it was one or other of the district's more senior officers, the district engineer or the district traffic superintendent, he called, "Come in." Seated behind his desk and very much the senior officer, he looked surprised to see me enter. "Yes?" he demanded. "What do you want?"

I was fed up at being at the receiving end of continual and petty harassment, and I was up for a fight by way of telling him what I thought of him, his shedmaster and his loco inspector—which I did in no uncertain terms. Outraged, he told me to get out, and when I refused he threatened me with instant dismissal, making the point I would have to repay the £60 allowance I had been granted. That didn't worry me. I was single, with enough money to cover personal effects and to see me home if I wished. Besides, there were other African railways not too far distant. Rhodesian Railways, Beira Railways, Nyasaland Railways, and the transcontinental Lobita Bay Railway, all of which would be glad to take on an experienced driver. By now I'd had enough of what I increasingly viewed as little more than a Keystone Cops kind of railway, and as I left I threw down an ultimatum: "Suspend me, and I'll bring my resignation and throw it in your face."

At this, Frank, perhaps thinking the Kremlin might want to know why he'd got rid of so many of his, by grade, senior drivers, calmed down, and in a more amicable manner asked "What do you want then?" We discussed the pay fine and how I'd been led into a trap. Our conversation ended with me pointing out that the cause of so many 26 Class bushes running hot was the surprising lack of a key-way and key in the side rod and big end bushes.

Wood-burning 2612 climbing Kigwe Bank, on the Rift Valley's eastern escarpment.

After crossing swords with the DMPS I left to resume my duties and await developments. Happily, the expected pay fine failed to materialise. Perhaps the Kremlin authorities were showing concern at the number and severity of the punishments being meted out, although a notice came round to the effect that anyone wishing to contact the DMPS had to do it through the shedmaster. And in that I wished them well! But even more importantly, my 'frank discussion' with Frank had the result that, as each 26 Class locomotive went into shops for heavy repairs, it returned fitted out with key-ways. Whilst things had settled down, it was still prudent to keep out of the way of both the loco inspector and Shedmaster Wright, in particular the latter, an unpleasant domineering type who tried to make life difficult for the white drivers. Quite openly he continued a tradition of 'brandy repairs', which favoured the Asian drivers. In fact, you only had to listen to the sound the engines of subscribers to this system made, when coming out of the shed, to know that they were better maintained than the engines of non-participant drivers. One day Wright asked me to come over to his office and deliberately kept me awaiting his pleasure in the middle of a tropical downpour (which at least was nice and warm). When a Sikh driver arrived, having just returned from India from a long leave period, and knocked, unlike me he was greeted with a broad smile and a "Ah, come in, Singh, what can I do for you?"

"Sahib," he replied, "please can I have my engine back?" (and here it's worth saying that each driver preferred his own engine, knowing its characteristics and its maintenance history).

"That's a nice watch on your wrist," the shedmaster observed, holding out his hand. The Sikh slipped it off and handed it over. "Is it gold?" he asked.

"Yes, it is," the Sikh confirmed.

The shedmaster laid it on his desk, saying, "Yes, you can have your engine back." And as I looked on, that was that. The driver left happy, having got his own engine back, leaving the shedmaster equally happy. Sometime later, however, the shedmaster was dismissed, much to the European driver's delight, for a serious misdemeanour involving empty petrol tankers.

To understand his felony, a brief description of the characteristics of railway petrol tankers is required. After a tanker had been decanted, a gallon or two of petrol always remained swilling about in the 'empty' vessel, before finally filling the empty decanting valve. On arrival at Dar es Salaam, the oil companies became concerned at finding these valves frequently empty, and consequently contacted the railway police. Incidentally, it was teasingly said of railway policemen that, if a woman ran to them saying she had just been molested, they would automatically ask "What's the waggon number?" Putting that slur to their good name aside, the police quickly identified the culprit by simply asking the owner of Tabora's only petrol pumps if any of his car-owning customers had stopped purchasing petrol in the last few months. When the answer was a definitive "Yes, the shedmaster", his fate was sealed.

The police escorted him to the DMPS's office, who brought his career to an abrupt end by informing him "You are dismissed with the loss of all privileges." This was an extreme penalty, leaving the dismissed person, from that moment, to fend entirely for himself and, if a family man, having a heavy bearing on his loved ones.

Apart from wages earned and any personal effects, everything else, including accommodation, furniture, local and home leave entitlements, and most important of all, your pension, was deemed a privilege. Consequently, 'loss of all privileges' meant that these things immediately became null and void, leaving the offender homeless and sometimes destitute, in the middle of Africa. From there, by whatever means he could contrive, he (and his family) must make their way to Dar es Salaam, and as a DBS (Destitute British Subject), cast himself on the mercy of the colonial administration, who had to find a friendly homeward-bound ship's captain who was willing to let those involved work their passage home. In colonial times, any DBS was considered beyond the pale, and to prevent a repeat of the situation, they had their passports automatically confiscated on arrival in the UK.

The most disturbing of these actions, which showed East African Railways at its most heartless and vindictive, involved a Tabora driver, his wife and three small children. The driver, a highland man from the Kyle of Lochalsh Railway, in the north of Scotland, had been at Tabora, his first posting, for only a few months. He spoke in a soft Scots burr, prefacing his conversation with a quiet "Surely, surely." As a result, he was nicknamed (what else!) "Surely Surely." On the face of it, his downfall seemed to have been the result of a carefully engineered management plot. At least something must have occurred very much out of the ordinary, about which I have no knowledge. All I know is "Surely Surely" was informed he was demoted to working engineering trains.

Engineering trains were always worked by African drivers, being the next step up the promotion ladder from that of shunting driver. Also, for the very good reason that Africans were better able to 'live off the land', having contacts amongst the rural population, and better able to cope with the harsh conditions during those weeks out in the bush. As far as I'm aware, "Surely Surely" was the only European, or indeed Indian, to have that sanction threatened, and for these reasons he refused. Immediately he was suspended, without pay, for refusing duty.

2612 tackling the same bank, with a Down train, under the charge of Dennis Cregan.

The suspension continued for one month, then two, during which Surely Surely

347

supported his wife and children by writing out cheques, in the mistaken belief, it seems, that whilst he still had cheques in his cheque book, he still had money in the bank. Inevitably, his cheques began to bounce.

Taken to court for the non-payment of debt, Surely Surely was sentenced to three months in prison, followed by deportation. I was unaware of any of this, until arriving home one afternoon I was met by his distraught wife begging for help after being told she and her young children were being deported the next morning, and had to travel, not by passenger train, but in the guard's van of a goods train—a thirty-six hour journey to Dar es Salaam in the tropical heat, without food, water or toilet facilities. It reminded me, if not resuting in the same outcome, of Jews being herded into goods trains by the Nazis. I cast around for some way to help without it becoming too obvious.

My first thought was to seek help of the local church of England vicar, the Reverend Backhouse, an elderly and genial Australian, who for those interested in genealogy was the offspring of parents who had emigrated to that country from Beverley in East Yorkshire, and who carried a name still common in that ancient borough. Likewise, when I was visiting a friend in central Kenya, I was introduced to a lady in her ninety-fifth year, who had an interesting story to tell. She had been born in the village of Leconfield, just north of Beverley, her parents being of farming stock, having farmed Leconfield Grange before migrating to the wild uninhabited Kenya White Highlands.

This was before the coming of the railway and meant an eight-month trek via four-wheeled cart drawn by six oxen, over what was then trackless country. I asked her if she ever missed Leconfield. "No," she replied, "I'd been too young to remember." All she could recall was the grinding poverty of her African childhood. the life of hard graft and toil her parents had experienced, and how she was brought up living off ugali, an African cornmeal gruel. This poverty lasted until the 1939-45 war brought a demand for increased food production, and with it a better standard of living.

But, back to the problem at hand. I dropped the idea of approaching gentle old Backhouse, thinking it would carry more weight if Surely Surely's wife and children went up to the hospital to put their case to the hospital doctors, who I felt certain would have put a stop to what was, by any standards, gross mistreatment of innocent victims, and at least allow them to travel in a civilised manner on the next Down passenger train. I don't know whether they went to the hospital or not, as I was back on duty within the next few hours, and when I returned the family had left, and so in the circumstances I lost track of them. I often wondered what became of them though.

Anyway, getting back to my pairing with Dennis and 'learning the road'. For the first few months, every trip proved a leap in the dark. Lacking guidance in the shape of a rule book or timetable, and unable to converse with my native firemen (or Dennis, who was of course off duty in the caboose), I was faced with a bewildering succession of unknown and isolated stations, each bearing an unfamiliar Swahili name, a name which had to be remembered when accepting a 'Line Clear'. Adding to my anxiety was my responsibility to keep the locomotive (a machine hardly fit for purpose) up and running under the most trying of conditions, a problem compounded by the lack of equipment and stores. However, stopping every 25 miles, or so, in mid-section, to take on a tender full of kuni wood did give drivers an opportunity to examine the engine and carry out a few repairs. The concessions to provide kuni were often held by Asian's, with Africans employed to gather it and stack it on raised platforms by the side of the track, where upon stopping two attendants could easily load it into the tender. Before the 30 Class came into operation, goods trains ran on a pick-up basis, dropping off and picking up waggons when and where required, and this together with stationmasters' somewhat tardy approach to issuing Line Clear tickets gave drivers a further opportunity to carry out inspections and repairs.

As I became more and more 'bush-hardened', in other words largely immune to heat, lack of food and water, I began to be affected by a manifestation common to caboose crews, the inability to sleep during off-duty periods. This was due, in part, to extreme daytime temperatures within the caboose, partly because of the ever-changing patterns of work which drained the body of its ability to adjust and also, when on the move, due to the incessant drum from the caboose wheels reverberating through ones pillow. Although in all fairness I must mention the superb riding qualities of the EAR cabooses, which were able to absorb to a high degree the irregularities in unballasted track such as the Mwanza and Mpanda lines.

On the footplate, staring fixedly along the beam of a headlamp for hours on end, whilst fighting an overpowering urge to sleep, produced some strange effects. Eyes became heavy and dull, reluctant to follow any movement of the head. Checking steam and water gauges required real effort to slowly drag fixed eyes from the headlamp beam, and slowly adjust them to a different focal length.

The same effect applied when the head swung around again, leaving the eyes still fixed on the gauges.

At night illusions began to take effect as exhaustion developed into confusion. One night after 12 hours gazing along the headlamp beam, I picked out a cluster of grey granite boulders in the distance, alongside and almost fouling the track. This threw me into even more disorder. For many miles along this section of railway there were no exposed rocks, and fighting exhaustion I tried in my confusion to make sense of what I could plainly see illuminated at the very limit of my headlamp. Or was it just a figment of a hallucinating mind? Then panic set in, had I fallen asleep, passed through a station (each a 'blockpost'[39]) and was now travelling, without authority, through another (boulder-dotted) section? Any Line Clear irregularity was followed by immediate suspension without pay, and in extreme circumstances, with no if's or but's, instant dismissal. I tried to pull my jumbled wits together and sort out what to do for the best. The surrounding countryside, veiled in darkness, offered no hint or comfort as to my whereabouts, and which at any time now could be the scene of a catastrophic head-on collision. Then, as I prepared to shut off and brake the train to a standstill, the cluster of grey granite rocks began to disperse and move away from the lineside. Of course, what my weary and overstretched brain had taken for rocks was, in truth, a herd of elephants which, with trunks raised, ears flapping and tails swinging, had the instinct to head off for the safety of thick bush, rather than take on the might of a 600 ton train running at speed.

Home for a few hours and yearning the company of others I made my way to the Railway Hotel. The night was dark and overcast with the threat of rain, and on arriving I found only the postmaster and his wife, together with the then British hotel manager and his wife, seated around a circular drinks table on the wide open-fronted balcony, who invited me to join them. After some pleasant chit-chat, and as the night wore on, the hotel manager's wife suggested, as a diversion, that we set up an Ouija board. This was something outside my experience and, whilst sceptical, I was anxious to observe the outcome. With the alphabet marked out in chalk around the table, and using a beer mat to spell out its replies to questions, we were each instructed to place a fingertip lightly on the beer mat and see if we could make it 'talk'.

---

[39] Whereby, for safety reasons, the line is divided up into a series of sections or "blocks", with only one train being allowed occupy a block at a time.

Slowly but deliberately, the pointer moved about the board, spelling out answers to the various questions we asked it. As it did so I watched closely for any underhand manoeuvring, but failed to spot how any one person could control its movements. After a little while, the postmaster, sitting next to me, declared, "I'll fettle it—I'll ask it something that no other person on this earth knows! My mother died when I was little, but she used a special name for me which not even my wife's aware of. I'll try it with that." Having addressed the board with the question, the beer mat slowly and methodically spelt out a name (one I can no longer recall it), after which the postmaster rose, his face deathly pale, pushed his chair back, and in a state of agitation stated, "I want no more to do with that. I'll never try that again."

Surprised by the reaction of the postmaster, his question had nevertheless revived in me the memory of an old friend, Lionel Cowper, who years before had emigrated to South Africa, and so, undeterred, I asked, "What's the name of my old friend who went to South Africa?" By now it was apparent that the power of the Ouija board was becoming exhausted, its pointer growing slow and hesitant, and finally it conked altogether. But and make of this what you will, not before it spelt out the word "L-I-O-N."

And so, to return to more sober railway matters. By the time the 30 Class arrived, all EAR locomotives had been converted to oil firing, and as such only required a single fireman, who as a job lot were not above snatching a crafty forty-winks as and when the opportunity arose. Whilst descending Kazuramimba Bank, and for all the reasons given earlier, I momentarily dozed off, and I could not have picked a worse place, the approach to Kandaga station, a closed station and watering point. This approach was marked by the railway circling around the base of a large and prominent hill and ending with a tight reverse curve leading into the straight and level station. Before the advent of the 30 Class with their massive tenders, each and every train stopped at Kandaga to take water, and for those working in the Down direction, against the grade, moving off proved a nightmare. From its position at the water column, the engine's pony wheels were already on the first tight curve with its daunting 1 in 50 incline, a combination which acted to prevent the coupled wheels obtaining a grip, so here I was happy to bring into play the steam brake to prevent slipping and gain the required traction. This particular time, whilst descending the bank, and just before the reverse curve, exhaustion gently and quietly closed my eyes. My first intimation of danger was being nearly flung out of my seat, as the 30 Class, with its long coupled wheelbase, hit the reverse curve at some speed. How the engine and its following train held the rails has remained a source of amazement to me. The shock, however, was so traumatic that sleep fled, and I remained utterly wide awake for the rest of the trip.

Likewise Mohan Singh, a veteran Indian driver, and his fireman, both overcome by the lack of sleep, succumbed on the same descent. Their saga mercifully developed, not into a disaster, but something of a comedy, which is best explained by first describing the layout of the 30 Class vacuum brake arrangements. On this class the ejector body, a powerful Gresham and Craven super-solid jet, was mounted on the outside of the cab, and for the very commendable reason of keeping the cab as cool as possible; as were all three of the engines injectors, two on the firemen's side and one on the driver's. The vacuum brake application valve and handle, laid on a flat plane, were arranged within the cab on a vertical three-inch steel vacuum pipe, within comfortable reach of the driver's left hand. In its running position the application handle was seated at a 6:30 position, and an application of the brake was made by moving the handle through 90 degrees.

As the train descended Kazuramimba Bank in the early hours, the guard became aware it was, for no apparent reason, slowing to a halt. He waited for 10 minutes, but nothing happened. Twenty minutes passed with the train standing on the grade, silent and unmoving. Finally, after 30 minutes, the guard, now deeply concerned, left the safety of the guards van, which in view of the risk from wild animals required stern resolve, and set off in the darkness to walk along a train which at any moment might move off, leaving him stranded on a narrow single track miles from anywhere, at the mercy of any wild and dangerous beast on the lookout for an easy meal. Reaching the engine, he called up for the crew, but received no reply. Now mystified, and feeling that he had some kind of *Marie Celeste* on his hands, he climbed aboard, where to his astonishment he found both Mohan Singh and his fireman sound asleep. What had occurred became immediately apparent. As Mohan Singh braked continuously during the descent, sleep, the close companion of exhaustion, had stealthily, silently and insidiously, closed his eyes. Fortunately, as he slumped in his seat, so his extended left hand slowly made a full application of the brake. I say fortunately, for the train had stopped at the commencement of a half-mile stretch of straight track, and with no intervening curve to jar Mohan Singh into wakefulness, the train would have quickly run out of control on the descending 1 in 50 grade, to derail on the first curve, with results which can only be imagined.

Tabora running shed was one of the largest and most important on the whole system, providing motive power for the four lines radiating from its centre. And now, perhaps a summary of the types of locomotive available might interest the reader. The most venerable, the 22 Class, was a non-superheated flat valve 4-8-0 tender engine, built by the Vulcan Foundry in 1918 for the former Uganda railway, and was the first 8-coupled engine put into operation by that railway. With a tractive effort of some 20,000 lbs they were nominally a little more powerful than the famous GN Atlantics. After many years of unblemished service, and overtaken by the need for more powerful locomotives, they were relegated to Tanganyika, where they were used for shunting at Tabora, Mwanza and Kigoma, as well as on the districts' engineering trains under the directions of the Engineering Department, where they roamed often far from home for a fortnight at a time, before returning to the shed for a wash and brush up. The 22 Class also worked the monthly Pay Train which, whilst distributing its largesse, made its slow and stately progress through the district, calling at all stations and Permanent Way camps. As a matter of interest, most of the Pay Train was made up of early German 4-wheeled passenger stock. The axle boxes, still retaining DOAE (Deutsch OstAfrikanische Eisenbahn—German East African Railways) markings. Although sun-bleached and weather-worn, they proved an interesting insight into early German coaching stock, with features such as the large sun blinds on the windows.

Another splendid product of the Vulcan Foundry, were four 25 Class locomotives still in service, 2501, 2504, 2506 and 2511. Each was a superheated piston valved 2-8-2 tender engine, brought into service between 1925/26. They were utterly dependable and free-steaming, even during the rainy season when the kuni wood fuel was wet, thereby reducing an engine's ability to make steam. This propensity, a much valued quality, was enhanced by the Weir feed water heater, fitted to each engine, a system which supplied a steady flow of hot water to the boiler by means of exhaust steam fed into a long pre-heater box containing heating elements mounted on the left running plate, alongside the smoke box. Worked by a steam-driven Weir pump the system was at its most efficient when the engine was being worked hard, and the exhaust steam discharging at high temperature. As an aide to efficient working, the 25 Class were the first in a line of Tanganyika Railway locomotives fitted with large capacity bypass valves to the steam chests. When coasting, the cylinders of a locomotive tend to act as pumps, drawing in smokebox gases and particles of unburnt fuel, hence bypass valves were fitted to eliminate this tendency. In addition, they reduced wear and tear on big ends and side rod bushes and gave a much easier and freer motion to the freewheeling locomotive. As a class, engine crews greatly preferred them to their more modern but problematic 26 Class.

I was once called upon to work a Kigoma train with 2506, and despite having nearly two million miles under her wheels, she responded to virtually all the calls I made of her. On rising gradients, in an attempt to maintain 30 Class timings, I thrashed the smoke box rivets loose, but this was asking too much of her, and I had to make up lost time by racing her along more favourable sections. In this, finding the mainline German track superb, I frequently took a chance, even though on the diminutive EAR one metre gauge, exceeding the set speed limits was considered a heinous crime, with a reduction in salary for the first offence, and dismissal for any further infringement. However, it was with a sense of satisfaction that I was able to bring the train in on time.

Here and now, I confess to a flaw in my character, one which has driven me all my life: the need for speed—a curse which always ruled the hand which controlled the regulator! Providentially, on this occasion the traffic Department failed to examine the guard's journal in any detail, or the speeding offence would have been laid bare. Consequently, I escaped a speeding charge, as I continued to do for the remainder of my driving career.

The next locomotives in line, 17 American built 2-8-2 Austerity engines. Purchased after the war by Tanganyikan Railways to fill an urgent need for more power, they proved as tough and reliable as a blacksmith's anvil, and as such were held in high regard by both shed staff and engine crews. Erected on stout bar frames, with high running plates that gave drivers an easy and uninterrupted view of the internal parts of the engine, axle-boxes and stay-plates. A design feature later adopted, to the delight of engine crews, on the 30 Class. These were locomotives which could and were thrashed to the limit of their capabilities all day and every day, without any components working loose. Unlike British locomotives of the time, the cylinders and steam chests were cast in one piece, to form a rigid immoveable cross section to which the bar frames were attached. On a railway with severe grades and tortuous curves, the 27 Class' sanding arrangements came as a godsend. In keeping with American practice, and after all they know a thing or two about climbing steep grades, each engine carried a large sandbox mounted on the crown of the boiler. Leading from it, four gravity-fed sand pipes delivered sand, two to leading pair of coupled wheels and two to the main drivers, and operated from within the cab by the fireman working a handle back and forth. New to British-trained drivers, the engine bearings ran on a hard grease, pumped into the axle-boxes under high pressure, a system which in my experience never failed, even under the most trying of conditions.

As an example, two of this class were stabled at Manyoni, a station a few miles below the summit of the Rift Valley, where for ten years, under the care and direction of an Indian fitter-in-charge, they carried out the arduous task, on a round the clock basis, of banking trains up the arduous 1 in 50 Saranda Bank. Arriving at the crest of the bank, after working flat out for two hours, each in turn offered a sight few if any in Britain had ever experienced: resting under the harsh African sun whilst being uncoupled, and providing indisputable evidence of the work done, the whole of the engine's front-end, its cylinders steam chests and piston rods, now an attractive shade of blue, were wreathed in smoke.

Banking Saranda was an interesting operation, and both it and the geography of this section are worthy of examination. Clawing its way out of the Great Rift Valley for thirty-five miles on an incline of 1 in 50, the Saranda Bank section remains a lasting tribute to the tenacity and skill of the German surveyors who quartered the ground, and against appalling odds, charted a way up its steep and rugged slopes. Equally it is a tribute to the same determination and expertise of the engineers and builders who followed on behind.

Commencing at Makatapora, a station hard up against the Rifts western scarp, the line climbed, on a series of curves, the first fifteen miles to Saranda, a station and watering point, and where clear pure spring water was greatly appreciated by thirsty engine crews (and their engines). From Saranda, and still on a succession of curves, the line took on a different hue, entering a land of massive rocks, the home of poisonous snakes and their like. Mid-way, the heavy grind was relieved by a sharp half mile descent to a two-span steel girder bridge over a dry barren wadi; a bridge which suffered a great deal of ill treatment, when both crews whipped their engines into a gallop for the climb ahead, hitting the bridge's level deck with a wallop. Manyoni, the next station on Saranda Bank was a fuel and watering point with a small shed, and home to the two banking engines. It gave drivers time, whilst the engines were being fuelled and watered, to examine the engines, especially the unreliable 26 Class.

Quiet and peaceful against the station's northern edge lay a small German cemetery. Reading the gravestones, one discovered a mother and two children buried together. A little further along, but apart, a young man's tombstone showing a different surname. And somewhat oddly, still further apart, lay the husband of the family. All had died on the same day. Not, as one might expect, the result of some tragic accident, but a tragic personal drama, as related to me by local Africans, whose parents' had witnessed the outcome of a dreadful and poignant turn of events.

According to the story, the husband who is now buried in the separate grave, returning from a period of maintenance work at the railhead, discovered his wife was having an affair with the young man who now lies betwixt the family. Driven to despair and taking his hunting rifle, in a fit of blind rage he shot his wife and two children, before turning the hunting rifle on the young man, then himself. There they lie, in a secluded corner of Manyoni station, the little cemetery which, as with other German graves dotted the length of the Central Railway, was maintained clean and tidy by the British railway administration.

With engine duties completed, the train left for the final seven-mile climb to the summit which, at 4-5000 feet above sea level, was the highest point on the Central Railway. There, in mid-section, on the open main line, the banking engine left the train and returned tender-first to Manyoni. On call for the next Up train, a banker engine ran the 25 miles from Manyoni to Makatapora, tender first, where, after being turned into the loop, it ran to the end of the loop to await the arrival of the next train. After crossing the rift, it was practice for the train driver, unsure of the length of his train, to run up to the 'fouling mark' at the far end of the station. Common to all Tanganyika railway stations, this mark formed a rudimentary but effective signal, being nothing more than a steel sleeper, painted white and laid between converging lines, beyond which a collision would occur. With the train at a standstill, the banking engine, under the direction of the stationmaster, left the loop and was coupled to the rear of the train. Isolated from the action by the length of his train, its driver was kept abreast of things by the diminution (on his gauge) of the trains continuous brake, and after coupling on had been completed, by the return of vacuum on the gauge (which was, because of the altitude involved, some three inches lower than standard British practice). Saying this I am not forgetting the GWR engine vacuum pump, which as I remember, whacked the vacuum up to a whopping twenty-three inches.

After overseeing the banker's movements, the stationmaster returned to the station office to arrange with Saranda, the next station, the train's safe passage through the section. When this had been confirmed, the stationmaster filled in a Line Clear form to hand to the train driver. As a guarantee of safety (and his life might depend on it) the driver would examine it carefully, making sure it was correctly made out, for the station ahead. Defacement or loss of this flimsy ticket was a serious Line Clear offence, open to grave consequences. To make sure it was carried safely, drivers normally tucked it into a convenient pocket. With everything completed the driver, after a glance at the main gauges, water, steam and vacuum, on his engine, and finding everything ready, whistled up the banker and on its reply opened his regulator.

Banking from the rear continued a venerable Tanganyika Railways custom and had much to commend it. Attaching and detaching the bankers was accomplished quickly and easily with minimal delay to the train, and more importantly, when one engine was on a curve and inclined to slip, the other was usually on a straight and still plugging away. Towards the end of 1956 orders came from 'The Kremlin' (East African Railways HQ in Nairobi, so called not only for its red stone construction, but more so for the tone of its edicts) that with immediate effect, Saranda banking engines must couple to the front of the train and lead.

From a slipping point of view, this was no bad thing. With a 27 Class leading round each curve, the effect of its sand on the rails was transmitted to the second engine. The downside was, the banker engine from now on had to run a further fifteen miles to Itigi before it could detach and run round the train, all in all adding thirty miles to each banker's mileage. To prevent this wasteful time-consuming practice, a new station, Aghondi, with run-around facilities, was built at the lines highest point. This operated for a few years, during which a scattering of native huts grew up around it, until, with devastating effect, plague struck. As a precaution against the disease spreading, the station was closed, the stationmaster evacuated, its points clamped shut, and through running, with strict instructions to run through at maximum line speed, substituted. The huts, harbourers of rats, the alleged spreaders of disease, were burnt to the ground.

The quarantine remained in force for several years, during which the Kremlin issued further banking instructions: now the train engine (i.e. the main locomotive hauling the train) and its crew had to take up the leading position, with the banking engine slotted between it and the rolling stock. To accommodate the extra shunting required, both Makatapora, and in the absence of Aghondi, Itigi the next station, had to be rejigged at considerable expense. What the purpose was of this change in instructions, involving a great deal of expense, I have no idea.

But let us return to the train standing at Makatapora. Within a short distance of leaving the station, the line began to rise, but in this instance, was straight for the first 200 yards, before the first of many curves tried the skill of both drivers. To gain traction both engines departed on wide-open regulators and full travel, a state of affairs which would continue for the next thirty-two miles. With kuni-wood engines, under these conditions both sets of firemen had to work non-stop, the 'second fireman' passing kuni logs to the 'first fireman', feeding them into the firebox. Along the length of Saranda, as with the other banks, Kazuramimba, Uvinza, Kigwe and all along the long thirty-five mile 1 in 95 pull between Uvinza and Malagarasi, the lineside was strewn with lumps of charcoal ejected by hardworking engines, providing a welcome source of fuel to the Permanent Way gang camps[40] dotted along the route, at least until this welcome bounty was swept away by a deluge each rainy season. Here it's perhaps as well to remind readers that it is not the severity of the grade, but rather what the locomotive has to lift against it which is the ruling factor. And in Tanganyika, on those inclines, trains were made up to the limit of the engine's power.

Arriving at Saranda after a fifteen mile climb, with a banker coupled to the rear, each engine had to take water. Two water columns had been provided by the original builders which, the length of trains having increased fourfold since those early days, could no longer be carried out within the station limits, allowing (after the train driver had received the Line Clear for the next section, Saranda to Manyoni) the train to draw forward, for the banker's tender to be topped up, leaving the leading engine and part of its train standing on the grade. To the viewer this glaringly emphasised the difference between the level station and the incline. Unlike Kandaga on the Kigoma-Kazuramimba section, when after taking water the engine stood both on a curve and the incline, and where, if there was any hope of starting the train, the lines had to be hand sanded, at Saranda the line ran straight for a short distance, enabling both train engine and banker to get a purchase. Again both had to be worked flat-out on the ten mile climb to the next fuel and watering point, Manyoni. This twenty minute stop gave the train driver

---

[40] A permanent abode used by the men employed to maintain the railway.

time to check his capricious 26 Class and prepare it for the remaining 10 mile climb to the summit. On a 26 Class, this kind of treatment sometimes affected the cylinder and steam chest castings, which sometimes worked loose on the frames. Securing them required very careful and precise work by the shed staff. If memory serves me correctly, each cylinder casting was secured by thirty-eight 1½ inch bolts. On repair, all bar one at each corner were withdrawn and the loose casting accurately positioned, and each bolt hole lapped to a bright finish. Then each hole was individually 'miked' (i.e. measured with a micrometre) and a new and slightly oversized straight bolt was turned up to fit each bolt hole. This was then driven in cold by shed staff using sledgehammers. This, by any standards was slow, heavy work, lasting over many hours.

In 1949 a Down 'mixed train', in the charge of an African driver, entered Manyoni station. It consisted mainly of goods vehicles but also two third class passenger coaches marshalled immediately behind the tender. After detaching the two coaches the engine commenced shunting operations. On completion, with the two coaches attached, at 18 inches of vacuum on his gauge and the Line Clear in his possession, the driver left for the direction of Saranda. As speed increased the driver began applying the train brake. To his horror, however, he received no response, and hence made a full application, but speed continued to rise. In desperation he reversed the engine and called for the fireman to screw the handbrake hard on, whilst using the steam brake in a last effort to control the train. The result was inevitable. On a curve the train left the rails, causing a scene of utter devastation, with coaches piled up in a heap, resulting in the deaths of many of the passengers. Examination of the wreckage discovered a fateful error: when coupling the two coaches to the train, after shunting had ceased, whoever was responsible had failed to connect the vacuum to the main train, leaving only the two passenger coaches with active brakes. As a consequence, where the line began to fall, a 'Stop Board' was erected with a dire warning that all drivers must, by stopping, test the train's brakes, an injunction I carried out faithfully until the introduction of the 30 Class and through running. And thereby hangs a tale to be explained later, when I got into trouble for ostensibly calling a guard a fool.

In 1956, Tabora received its first oil burning locomotive, bringing with it a system that went on to transform the lives of engine drivers and firemen. Gone the dirt, dust and sheer hard work other fuels brought, replaced by an absence of smoke, both at the chimney top and in the cab, with the cab remained remarkably clean at all times. It fell to my lot to work the first oil burner, a 27 Class from Dodoma forward to Tabora, and in doing so I made a complete mess of things by failing in mid-section and receiving a black mark, though thankfully not a pay fine.

For reasons I no longer remember, my co-driver Dennis Cregan was absent on this trip. In his place I had Gulum Nabi, a large rotund Indian driver on the verge of retirement, whose engine was on its way to the railway workshops in Dar es Salaam for heavy repairs. Both of us thought that it would be an ordinary, straightforward trip, working a Down train to Dodoma, and returning with an Up train. We arrived at Dodoma station during the night and left our shop-bound engine on-shed for servicing and a new crew. It was then that we learned our engine for the Up train was an oil burner, which stood half in half out of the shed doorway, blowing steam, its blower hard on. It no longer had a fire grate or an ash pan, only an air scoop from which, to our consternation, fire flashed and roared.

Our instructor was waiting, and after telling us to always beware of the airscoop and its violent and turbulent flames, we mounted the footplate for instructions on how to manipulate the oil burner equipment. At this Gulum Nabi's rolls of fat began to tremble. "No, Sahib," he wailed, beads of sweat on his forehead and his skin growing pale. "It glows all orange and greatly dangerous for me!"

More certain in my ability to cope than I should have been, and always ready to jump when others more sensible would have refused, I agreed to work the train back to Tabora by myself (i.e just me and my fireman, without a changeover with driver Gulum), a 260 mile 16 hour trip. During this time Gulum cowered in the caboose. In all this noise and confusion I failed to notice the engine was blowing off very lightly, something not always easy to see due to the hot night-time temperatures. This was, as I was about to find out, to have serious consequences on the way back.

All went well to start with—the oil firing was simple, requiring only two adjustments to the apparatus, the first to a steam jet which blew oil through the burner into the firebox, the other, a small ratcheted hand lever which precisely controlled the flow of the thick crude oil to the burner. Incidentally, this oil, when it's supposed beneficial effects became more widely known, was used by tribesmen to treat leg ulcers, open wounds, and for all I know, any other complaint. Upon request, "Nataka mafuta, bwana" I would open the fuel tank drain valve alittle and fill the small proffered gourd, or in some cases a rusty bully beef tin, with the thick black oil, the recipient thanking me profusely. Continuing on my way back, part way through the longest stretch without water, 60 miles of dry barren bush, disaster struck, as without warning the fireman's injector 'kicked off'[41].

By now, aware of a dicky safety valve and the effect it was having on the boiler, I tried my injector. When it failed to start, fearing the worst I stopped the train, and climbed over the tender to investigate. Opening the tank lid and finding it empty, my worst fears were confirmed. It was some time about mid-day, and with the sun at its zenith was very hot. As a little aside, I found myself surrounded by African honeybees, not attacking, for none stung me, but seeking moisture. In an effort to save precious boiler water my first instinct was to shut the engine down and take stock of my position. I was ten or twelve miles from the next station and its water supply. I could stay put and wait for a search party, but that would mean long delays to other trains. Or I could 'louse off' and make a dash for it. Choosing the latter, and with three-quarters of a glass of water and a heart full of hope, I flashed up the fire and set off.

Alas and alack, just four or five miles short of deliverance, boiler water was just visible bobbing about in the bottom nut. To proceed further risked dropping the lead plugs, misconduct which I knew would bring the harshest penalties down upon my shoulders.

Finally admitting defeat, I stopped and shut the engine down and handed the Line Clear ticket to my fireman, instructing him to take it to the next station and hand it to the stationmaster. At first he was a bit reluctant to walk unarmed through country teeming with wild animals, though in reality the railway was often used by the native population as a convenient pathway through the bush. In one respect I was fortunate, as the fireman arrived at the station around the same time as a Down train, whereupon arrangements were quickly made for that train's locomotive, with my fireman acting as conductor, to enter the section. This was set up by the stationmaster taking possession of my Line Clear, and issuing his own, together with a Warning Order detailing the situation. Cautiously, feeling it's way along, and sounding it's whistle continuously, the relief engine crept towards the failed engine and train. I waited impatiently until eventually I heard the sound of a distant whistle, and in the absence of warning

---

[41] Meaning it stopped working because there was no water left in the tender—a very dangerous situation to be in!

detonators or a red flag ('For Want of a Nail …!') I walked out the last few hundred yards to direct my rescuers.

After being hauled into the station, the first thing was to replenish the tender with water. I then witnessed something which, until then, would never have been believed mechanically possible. By now boiler water was out of sight, but more important to this narrative, the boiler pressure gauge had for some time registered nil. With a lot of residual heat remaining in the firebox my concerns for the safety of the lead plugs were growing. Despite the excellence of the American injectors that were fitted to the 27 class, I was a little put out to discover my fireman engaged in a futile attempt to start his injector. I can offer no explanation, if indeed there was one, for what followed. To my utter disbelief he told me the injector was working, and when I checked and found it was not only working, but to my astonishment, was working strongly and cleanly without wastage from its overflow pipe. With the relief engine recovering my abandoned train, and the lead plugs now safe and secure, my thoughts turned to the risky business of trying to fire up the oil burner now that there was no steam and after the firebox had been cooling for hours, and, if successful, thereafter, raising steam and working my train to Tabora, and the wrathful gala awaiting my arrival. With half an inch in the glass to play with, I decided to give it a try. After telling the fireman to shut the injector, my main concern now was whether there was still sufficient heat in the firebox flash wall to ignite the oil, and in this was the danger: would the oil instead just vaporise, filling the firebox, the tubes and the smokebox with explosive gases, causing an explosion which, without a shadow of doubt, would mark the end of my career with East African Railways and quite possibly the end of myself.

After telling my fireman to leave the engine and stand well clear, I opened the heavy cast steel firehold door, a cover designed to protect the engine crew in the event of a blowback, and examined the flashwall below me. This revealed that heat still remained in the firebox, with the flashwall glowing cherry red— sufficient, I judged, to fire up the burner oil. I secured the firehole cover, then with hair prickling the back of my neck, gingerly opened the burner to oil. For a second or two nothing happened, and I began to get the wind up. I was about to close the oil valve when, with a bang and a flash, the concussion almost strong enough to blow the smokebox door off its hinges and damage the air scoop, the fire ignited. Thankful and relieved, I adjusted the oil flow to the burner until I had a clear smokeless fire filling the box and raising steam quickly. With a good head of steam the injector went off leaving me to work forwards to Tabora and finally arrive in Tabora at 05:30, very dehydrated after working thirty-six hours non-stop, without food or water. At that early hour there was no irate officers to greet me, and I left the shed as a bright new dawn tinted the skies. Unexpectedly, and to my relief, nothing much was made of what earlier would have been classed as a gross dereliction of duty, the expected pay fine failed to be imposed, and whilst I had to write out a full report I made the most of the difficulties encountered, whilst glossing over with a broad brush my own failings.

Reflecting on the thankfully muted response to my cock-up, I came to the conclusion the DMPS and his fellow cronies, the shedmaster and loco inspector, had been warned by the Kremlin: "Enough is enough!" There has been too many dismissals, too many pay fines, too many transfers of drivers who, being cursed with a fickle 26 Class, found themselves more sinned against than sinning. From now on we found ourselves benefitting from a more reasonable regime, although it paid to keep out of the way of both shedmaster, with a glint of avarice in his eyes, and the loco inspector, who spent much of his time on safari, riding the footplate, trying to find fault with driver performance. By now the reader will have gathered that each trip threw up its own peculiar set of circumstances (or 'challenges and opportunities', as they'd call it nowadays). This was emphasised by the heartfelt prayer to departing drivers: "Have a good trip!"

One such occasion was on a Down trip from Kigoma. My then co-driver, Dennis Cregan, had worked the train as far as Malagarasi, a fuel and water point and crew changeover station, where it was practice for driver to examine the engine all round, before being relieved. Malagarasi station was notorious for its vicious, biting safari ants, which took advantage from the run-off from the down water column, forcing drivers, to the amusement of the watching Swahili fireman, to continually stamp their feet as they attended to the engine. These large black ants, about an inch long, struck fear into both animals and humans, and their powerful jaws, locked even in death, were traditionally used by the natives to close open wounds.

As I was taking over as driver, the stationmaster arrived with the Line Clear, and informed us that we were to pick up a dead body at the next station, Nguruka, and convey it to Urambo where a post-mortem had to be carried out at the small bush hospital there. Apparently the deceased had arrived at the station in a distressed condition, begging for water, which the stationmaster had supplied him with. However, to the stationmaster's consternation the poor unfortunate fellow, after drinking deeply, dropped down dead at his feet, hence the need for a post-mortem.

Expecting a delay whilst the body was being loaded, Dennis said, "When you get to Nguruka, come back to the caboose and I'll have a cup of tea ready for you." It was a warm, balmy evening, about an hour before sunset, when we arrived, and sitting in the caboose with its windows wide open to catch whatever little breeze might have remained, we observed a small group of Kanzu-clad men about two hundred yards away carrying the corpse along a path to the station.

Already, the sickening smell of a body, in an advanced state of decomposition, began to fill our nostrils. Hurriedly, we closed the caboose windows and waited as the silent cortege shuffled past with its grim cargo, pervading everything around, as they made their way to a small four-wheeled covered goods van. For a train hauled by a 26 Class locomotive, the running time between Usingi and Urambo, a distance of fifty-seven miles, was two hours fifty-seven minutes, and as I ran into Urambo station the day had long given way to night, a warm, velvety, soft African night. The gentle breeze which earlier had brought the first disturbing whiff of death and decay had fallen away, and all was now calm and still. In keeping with the rest of the central railway stations, Urambo was unlit, and it together with a scattering of native huts around its perimeter lay in profound and total darkness.

Guided by my headlamp, I drew into the station, stopping just short of the fouling mark[42]. Not wishing to become mixed up with the carrying party as they went about their gruesome task I remained on the engine until I judged the coast was clear and the body was on its way to the tiny bush hospital, and the attendance of its resident Asian doctor. As I walked back to the caboose the clinging stench of a decomposing body became more apparent. I hesitated in my stride, wondering if the body had been left in my path and I was about to trip over it, or worse, step on it. At that moment I unexpectedly cannonned into one of the carrying party, whose flowing Kanzu robe stank of death and putrifaction. Repelled, I recoiled, only to collide with first one, then another, of that malodorous group. Disentorientated and in a flap I blundered amongst them, until finally, and with immense relief, and whilst gasping for a breath of clean pure air, I broke free and made my way to the caboose. Entering, Dennis wrinkled his

---

[42] A white-painted sleeper laid between the loop line and the main line, used to avoid collision between two trains on adjacent tracks.

nose and moved away from me. "You stink!" he observed. "Where have you been, you stink of rotting flesh!"

"I know," I replied morosely. And as I drank a mug of tea, as welcome as any before of since, I recounted my experience, Returning to the engine, I sensibly used the off-side of the train as a barrier between myself and any more unpleaseantness. For the remainder of the trip, some sixty-six miles, and four hours thirty-two minutes running time, I stood on an exposed part of the footplate where the wind generated by the passage of the engine helped dissipate some of the offensive smell, but which continued to pervade my clothes and nostrils.

Chapter 20
A New Class of Engine

Christmas day was the one day in the year when an effort was made to grant the European drivers a day off. Which is not to say the full twenty-four hours. As midnight fell one might still be ploughing on, many, many miles from home. And after midnight, Boxing Day, each driver had to be ready to go on duty again. But this short but welcome break gave the Tabora-based white drivers the opportunity to meet in the evening on the pleasant open balcony of the Railway Hotel, and to reminisce, pass the time of day (or night), grumble a little perhaps, and have a quiet drink together. One such driver was John Luis. His parents were of South African Boer stock, from somewhere up Eldoret way in the Kenya White Highlands. For whatever reason, John had chosen footplate work over farming, and had been transferred from the Kenya Uganda railway to replace one of Tabora's white drivers who had left in mysterious circumstances. John had spent the whole of his footplate career climbing the fearsome grades of the Eldoret section, but for some reason found it difficult to breast the final mile and a half of Uvinza Bank, with its series of reverse curves. Perhaps John was more used to the sixteen coupled wheels of a Garratt than the eight of a dodgy 26 Class. Whatever the reason, it meant at times that John had to adopt the 'yo-yo' system. After slipping to a standstill on the curves, and failing to restart, this approach meant falling back to a straight length of track, and trying again and again, up and down like a yo-yo, until success was achieved.

Sometime in mid-1956 Dennis and I caught our first sight of the locomotives which would transform not only the working of the Central Railway, but the quality of our work lives, the splendid 30 Class. We had heard via the bush telegraph that a new, larger and more powerful series of engine was on the cards, and in Dodoma station yard we discovered our first. Dennis and I had worked a Down train to Dodoma the administrative centre of the vast central province and the then changeover station for both Up and Down engines and crews. Dennis had worked 'In', arriving late in the evening, and after leaving 2612 on the shed for attention, made his way across the wide expanse of the unlit goods yard. In so doing he discovered, looming out of the darkness, the outline of a dead but very large and imposing locomotive. A flash from his torch revealed it a product of the North British Locomotive Company, Glasgow, and its number, 3003. A quick examination showed its side rods and connecting rods uncoupled, and as such stowed securely on its running plates, and both pistons held mid-cylinder with wooden blocks between the slidebars—a clear indication that we would be hauling it dead to Tobora for fitting up there. Excited by his discovery, Dennis called me, and together we went to examine this latest addition to the Tobora locomotive fleet. Seeing it looming against a clear, star-spangled sky, my first impression was one of size, it seeming to dwarf the engines we had become accustomed to. By the light from our torches we were impressed with its 2-8-4 wheel arrangement, and even more impressed with its all-singing, all-dancing, roller-bearing axle boxes throughout, including those on its massive 12-wheel tender, carried on two individual 6-wheeled American-style cast steel bogies, riding, unusually, on shock absorbers rather than the usual leaf springs. In water capacity, this was a tender designed to eliminate once and for all the problem of unreliable water supplies along the Central Line. We noted with approval the American-style running plates, with enough headroom to stand beneath, giving a clear view of the engine's cast steel bar frames, and exposing to our examination the return of an early idea, compensating beams between each of the coupled axle boxes. We examined with interest the massive hollow-cast Delta bogie, below the cab, giving the promise of a smooth and easy ride for both engine and crew. Climbing onto the footplate and looking around, we discovered a cab palatial in its fittings and layout, offering large bucket seats with ample legroom, and even padded armrests. Louvred side windows with outside weather glasses, and setting it all off, a polished tongue and groove African hardwood finish to the inside of the cab's extensive roof, giving the cab an air of opulence that even Edward Thompson would have found difficult to match.

As a new feature we found interesting the Australian-designed SCOA-P type[43] coupled wheels, with spokes of hollow 'U' form rather than the conventional oval shape. This design was intended to provide a light but stronger

---

[43] The spokes being hollow with a U-shaped cross-section, making them considerably lighter than a conventional spoked wheel.

wheel centre. In practice they were not (if you'll forgive the pun) all they were cracked up to be, developing fractures in the spokes close to the rim of the wheel, and hinting at some deflection of the rim itself. Repairs were not easy to effect, with the crack having to be 'V'd out and the ensuing gap refilled with weld by allowing the spoke and its welds to cool between each quick pass. Even with extreme care a click often indicated the weld had failed, with the whole laborious 'V'ing out process having to be repeated. Another problem was broken coupled wheel spring hangers.

However, after these initial teething troubles had been sorted out, the 30 Class ran between 200,000 and 250,000 miles entirely trouble free, not even developing a knock in the big end and side rod bushes, and running on a minimum of lubricating oil for many thousands of miles, without any signs of overheating. This is in contrast to the unhappy 26 Class which, after shaking themselves to bits each trip, required a full page of repairs to put them in any kind of running order.

In keeping with oil burning engines, the 30 Class eliminated the need for the dirty, time-consuming and arduous work of firing, smokebox and ash pan cleaning, and bringing with it the added advantage of escaping the expense of maintaining brick arches and replacing worn or defective firebars. From a crew's point of view, oil firing provided a clean smoke-free environment, whilst relieving the fireman of the sometimes back breaking work of hand firing, and giving him at the same time the ability to maintain full boiler pressure under all circumstances without blowing off and wasting steam.

After a few weeks in traffic, however, a potentially more serious defect was discovered in the first two engines, 3001 and 3002. In this case it was not a design fault, as with the SCOA-P coupled wheels, but a defect of manufacture. During routine boiler inspections, depressions were found on the firebox inner steel plates that were sufficiently deep to compromise the safety of the firebox, causing alarm bells to ring all the way to the Crown Agents in London, and to the locomotive manufacturers North British Locomotive Works in Glasgow. Both of them sent engineers on the first outward bound flight, to investigate. The affected engines were stopped and the boilers blown down. The findings of the investigating engineers sadly offered no credit to that famous Glasgow institute, The North British. They found dirt of one sort or another had been rolled into the plates during manufacture (an event so unusual I wonder if it had been a deliberate act of sabotage by some disgruntled employee). It left a thin skin of steel disguising the defect, and this skin was melted and blown away by the first blast of the engine's oil burner. This led to the replacement of the firebox plates of these two engines, a big job, but once done they maintained trouble-free steaming for many thousands of miles.

Now make of this what you will, but back in 1947, when the 26 Class began to arrive, Bill Connell and his co-driver Ron Kenyon, and Dennis Cregan and his co-driver (his name now lost to me), were by grade the most senior drivers at Tabora. However, despite their seniority, Bill and Ron had to await the arrival of 2606 before being allocated a 26 Class. Dennis Cregan and his mate then had to await 2612, the last of the series to arrive. The same occurred with 3003, the engine we'd hauled dead from Dodoma. The first two 3001 and 3002 had been allocated to Morogoro shed, where they were being used to trial experimental running of the 403 miles between Morogoro and Tabora. Bill and his most recent co-driver, an ex-Rhodesian Railways driver of Welsh and GWR antecedance, had to wait, co-incidentally perhaps, for 3006 to come along. Whilst Dennis and I, co-incidentally or otherwise, had to await the arrival of 3012. John Luis and Jim Parker, the latter a former Rhodesian Railways driver, had to wait much longer, finally being assigned 3020. In the meantime, every other 30 Class had been allocated to Asian drivers.

My first sight of a 30 Class in action was at Itulu, the first station in the Down direction from Tabora, where I'd been turned into the station loop, to await the arrival of an Up train. In advance of me, the line ran straight on a rising grade before being lost in the heat haze and whirling, dancing, dust devils of the dreaded Methundu Wa Kali, the 'Land of Heat', an area, apart from one exception, without surface water and extending in from the Malagarasi River in the west to Dodoma in the east, 365 miles of stifling heat, dust and tetse fly. Although, as I was to discover later, this extended a further 110 miles beyond Dodoma to where the railway met the Makndoa River at Kilosa. How slaves, under the lash of Arab slave traders, survived the Land of Heat is something quite beyond me. The only exception to all this was Nyahua swamp, 47 miles in the Down direction from Tabora—a five and a half mile stretch of clear running water, and as such not really a swamp in the accepted sense, its crystal clear water, five or six feet deep, fed by meltwater from distant Mount Kilimanjaro. These waters ran gently south before being lost to heat and evaporation somewhere in the wastes of Central Tanganyika. The railway crossed this section by means of an embankment and a succession of single-span steel girder bridges, each resting on finely dressed granite piers.

I used to welcome Nyahua swamp, not only for its limpid waters, but also for its waterlilies. Stretching as far as the eye could see, and beyond, it was the home, during daylight hours, of a species of leaf hopping bird which, ignoring passing trains, stepped daintily from one lily leaf to another. The home

Brian Duffell with 3002.

also of iridescent dragonflies and flittering, fluttering butterflies. And for those sharp eyed enough, sinister and deadly green mamba snakes, swimming among or resting coiled up on a convenient lily leaf. Throughout the hours of darkness, in contrast, the swamp became illuminated by countless winking and blinking fireflies. Leaving Nyahua swamp in the Down direction, the line curved away to the right on a rising embankment. Within its somewhat tight radius, and sheltered by the embankment and overlooking the open waterway, lay an area of level ground dominated by an ancient kapok tree, its green triangular trunk and spreading canopy offering shade and rest. Although no evidence of it existed, this idyllic place must surely have been where those German surveyors and engineers who were engaged in building the railway pitched their camp. Opening the regulator further to climb out of the swamp, my minds eye could see them after a day's work, sitting at ease on folding canvas chairs, at hand bottled beer cooled by the clear flowing water of the swamp, which still had a hint of its birthplace, the snow and ice of Mount Kilimanjaro. Facing west with its wide, uninterrupted views, in the hour before darkness fell, the air heavy with the faint, indefinable scent of waterlilies, and with the sun's declining rays gilding the heavens, it must have been a balm to the weary.

As I waited at Itulu for the crossing, out of the Methundu, with it's dancing, swirling dust devils, like a mirage, came an Up train, headed by Locomotive 3002, now on the final 23 miles of its journey to Tabora, where it would be turned on a newly-laid triangle, the shed's 60 foot turntable being too short for the 30 Class. Thereafter, being watered and serviced, before making its way the 403 miles back to Morogoro. Unlike the knocking, rattling 26 Class, 3002 rolled into Ituli silently. At its controls an unknown European driver. As he drifted past me we exchanged salutations and for me, that was that. But after stopping, to my surprise the driver left his engine, and running back mounted 2612's footplate, where with a cockney accent he introduced himself with a "Watcha' mate, I'm Brian Duffell." It was the start of a long and happy friendship which continued until his death many years later.

An interesting account of the arrival, erection and testing of the first of that Rolls Royce of steam locomotives, the 30 Class was published in the February 1956 edition of the EAR magazine, and is as follows:

The first of two of the new 30 Class locomotives arrived at Dar es Salaam on the SS Govenor, on the 23rd of June 1955. Despite delays in getting these ashore, the first out, number 3001 was in the erecting shop on the 4th July 1955, in readyness for erection. It is interesting to note here, that although erection drawings were unavailable at this particular stage, this locomotive was completely erected by the 14th July 1955 (i.e. 10 days after the arrival of the pieces in the shop, and just a month after its arrival in the port).

These 147 ton locomotives arrive in parts, consisting of three main units of frame, boiler and tender, whilst all the rest of the parts are in packing cases (including boiler mountings). Their rapid erection, testing and handing over to Traffic is therefore quite a considerable feat, and one which earns congratulations for the staff concerned, more particularly when it is remembered that no drawings were immediately available on the arrival of the first two locomotives.

Owing to the high axle load of 13 tons, the locomotivs are prohibited from working over certain parts of the Dar es Salaam Morogoro section, and local trials could only be run on the short section from Dar es Salaam to Pugu. By 24th July, number 3001 had completed preliminary tests and was enroute from Dar es Salaam to Morogoro as a dead engine to be ready for running in trials on the Morogoro-Dodoma section, before the first caboose run to Tabora.

The trial runs were completed satisfactorily and the test caboose run was accordingly scheduled for one Up goods on 3rd August. The load to be hauled consisted of through traffic from Dar es Salaam to Tabora and Kigoma, and amounted to 32 units of 530 tons.

The overall journey time for the 403 miles from Morogoro to Tabora was 19 hours 42 minutes, giving an average speed of 20.4 mph, during which time the locomotive was stationary for only 84 minutes, a very favourable reflection on the traffic organisation of crossings. During the run a rigid observance of all speed restrictions was made easy for the driver by keeping a constant watch on his speedometer, but in spite of this a steady gain over most section running times was made. The main impression gained on the footplate were the superior standard of comfort provided for the crew, and the convenient layout of the cab fittings, and the extremely smooth riding qualities provided by the four-wheeled trailing truck, the roller bearings and the two six-wheeled bogies on the tender.

The return trip was started after a turn round of 4 hours 15 minutes, running in the timings of 8 Down and was equally successful, although not quite so fast, being completed in 23 hours, thus giving a complete round trip time of 46 hours. The overall consumption figures were: water 39.7 gallons per mile; fuel oil 4.02 gallons per mile, or 7.66 gallons per thousand gross-ton miles.

The result of these tests indicate that the locomotives can run in regular service between Morogoro and Tabora, taking water at only two intermediate stations and oil at only one. This will give much greater operating flexibility.

During the periods 31st August and 1st September, and the 5th and 6th September, trial run were made with 30 Class engines on the Tabora-Kigoma and Tabora-Dodoma sections, respectively.

On all these trials the engine was driven by the Tabora District Locomotive Inspector Mr Snellings. He was instructed to drive the train as near to the speed limit as possible, but of course not to exceed it. With sustained running at approximately the limit of 45 kph it soon became apparent that very considerable improvements were being made on section running times and that with capable handling of the engine and efficient exchanging of Line Clear tickets, goods trains could be operated on this line very much faster than hither to. When Malagarasi, the first station with a reliable all year round water supply, was reached, there was still 2 feet 3 inches of water in the tank and by a rough calculation, this amounted to 3000 gallons of water, it was decided on the spot to proceed to Uvinza the next water point. At this station the water remaining in *the tank amounted to approximaely 1800 gallons and it was again decided to proceed to the next watering point Kandaga. On reaching this station there was still roughtly 800 gallons and so the train proceeded to Kigoma. The total run, therefore, of 251 miles had been done without taking water at any intermediate point. Certainly an acheivement of driving, but one which proved conclusively these locomotivs can operate regularly between Tabora and Malagarasi without taking water in between.*

The total time for the run, including an 8 minute stop at Uvinza was 9 hours 52 minutes. The fuel consumption totalled 730 gallons or 2.91 gallons a mile. The water consumption was roughly 30 gallons a mile. Up to February 1956 20 of these locomotives had been erected and placed in traffic whilst 2 are under erection and the components of a further 4 are on the water. They have already proved themselves by having revolutuonised traffic operations on the Central Line.

After this official report concerning the erection and two test runs of the 30 Class, the comparison of the 26 and 30 Class is made of the leading dimensions of the two classes of locomotive, as follows:

Attribute	26 Class	30 Class
Wheel arrangement	2-8-2	2-8-4
Lenth of wheelbase	25 feet 6 inch	63 feet 8 inch
Boiler pressure	180 psi	200 psi
Total heating surface: Firebox, tubes and superheater	1731 sq ft	2272 sq ft
Cylinders	2: 16 x 24 inch	2: 18 x 26 inch
Tractive effort at 90% boiler pressure	23651	29835
Water capacity—tender	4166 gallons	7000 gallons
Oil fuel capacity	1350 gallons	1950 gallons

With the arrival of 3012 (named '*Makonde*') imminent, Dennis and I were sent to learn (observe would be a more accurate description), in three trips, the 176 miles from Dodoma to Morogoro. This section had always been operated by single crews, and lacking a caboose we made our base in Dodoma's European running room, working from there to the European running room at Morogoro. From Dodoma the line threaded its way through Wagogo country, a land of the peculiar 'upside down' bayobab trees, sparse bush and distinctive Wagogo tribesmen, distinguished by their unusual red clay hair decoration which resembled the shape and form of a Roman soldiers' helmet. Some carried at their waist a short Roman-style sword, and as dress they wore a knee length Roman-style tunic, making me to ponder the question, did Roman soldiers make their way here in the far distant past? The Wagogo women, likewise, wore a kind of miniskirt, a shuka, made from merikani, a blue cloth, originally from the mills of Massachusetts (the Swahili name derived from the word "American", its place of origin). Should they wish to urinate, this was was easily accomplished by the simple practice of opening their legs. Speaking of their lack of modesty, where a train entered a station, the moving piston rod frequently drew the attention of the younger women who, giggling, nudging and pointing, made rude gestures at the engine and its crew.

In the Up direction the main feature of this section was the 26 miles of mainly 1 in 100 between the stations of Kilosa and Kidete. To keep time along this stretch an average speed of about 22 miles per hour had to be maintained. With 620 tons behind the tender draw bar, this required the engine being worked to its limits. In this respect two features of the 30 Class and its attribute of being oil-fired stand out. Firstly, despite the sustained thrashing, oil firing (when set up correctly) produced, with capacity to spare, a clear smoke-free exhaust, and the steam required to produce the constant boiler pressure of only a couple of pounds below boiler working pressure was easily maintained. An added advantage, so quick was the response to the drivers actions, the engine never wasted steam by blowing off. The second which, after my years of British practice came as a real eye-opener, was how little cylinder oil was fed into the cylinders to lubricate them. In 25, 26 and 27 Classes, the favoured means of lubrication was by a Detroit sight feed lubricator, when, as an interested observer, I was able to watch how slow and infrequent each drop was fed into the valves and pistons by the engine crew. As an example, the 30 Class's mechanical lubricators were set to a miniscule one pint every one hundred miles, half a pint of cylinder oil for each steam chest and cylinder. Yet under the most extreme conditions this was enough to maintain (without the pistons groaning) sufficient lubrication. An important trade off to this was a total lack of carbon in the cylinders, steam ports and blast pipe.

A further feature of this section of railway was twenty-nine miles of low-lying black cotton soil and stagnant blackwater pools, between Kimamba and

Kilosa, which Henry Morton Stanley, the Victorian explorer dubbed 'The dreaded Mkata Swamp'. However, over the years the Kilosa-Kimamba section of this malodorous swamp had been drained and turned over to huge Greek-owned sisal estates, stretching on to a range of distant blue-grey hills. The remaining 29-mile Kimamba-Mkata-Masimbu section, however, remained a quaking bog, the abode and refuge of all kinds of creepy-crawly creatures, poisonous snakes, and who knows what else in and around its fetid pools. A hundred yards beyond Kimamba station, haunt of the Greek community, the Planters Hotel reared its 1930's-style art deco façade.

Tormented by thirst, I once stopped at Kimamba station and, whilst waiting for the Line Clear, went over to sample an ice-cold *Coca-Cola*—a drink not entirely to my taste, but at that time the only soft drink available on the market. Standing at the bar, drinking deeply, I noticed on display a bottle of South African wine, its name 'Gratitude' drew my attention, leading me to ponder what story of trial and tribulation, toil and tears, and final success, lay behind the bottle's rather prosaic label.

Over time, I had developed an admiration for the quality of the German-built Permanent Way, laid on heavy cast steel sleepers, resting on two feet or more of indestructible granite ballast, meticulously maintained. Each rail carried the name and date of manufacture, mostly by Krupps of Essen, but a few here and there by the German Union Steelworks. Instead of being stamped in, the name and date formed part of the rail casting itself, giving the impression that each rail had been expensively cast, rather than the cheaper option of being rolled. These rails were very hard, it being easier and cheaper to replace the tyres of locomotives and rolling stock than to replace worn rails out in the middle of nowhere. Such was the quality of this splendid track, it was an open invitation for me to consider line speed limits as advisory, and on those trips unhindered by loco inspectors, let the engine romp away.

Because of my physical appearance—I was tall, slim with a longish neck—I was known among the ordinary Africans as Bwana Twiga (Mr Giraffe), but among African fireman I developed a more ominous title. To them I was Bwana Ndege (Bwana Bird), and this wasn't because of my sweet singing voice! When it came to their part several refused to act as my fireman. Why this never reached the ears of the loco inspector or the shedmaster remains a mystery. But one stout hearted soul, with the intriguing name of January Pace Mbili (January Twice

Quickly) stepped forward, exclaiming, "If I die, the bwana dies with me"—a sentiment I had no intention of allowing to happen!

January had an amusing habit. Every so often he would ask, "Sa ngapi bwana?" What time is it? After looking at my watch and telling him in my halting Swahili, he would then look at the sun. I was never quite sure if he was checking the sun to see if my watch was correct, or vice versa. January will remain with me a long time, my faithful companion of the footplate, on which we both liked to fly.

With the advent of the 30 Class, things began looking up in the Stores Department. In place of baked bean tins, each engine was issued with a jealously guarded oil feeder and a generous supply of engine oil and cylinder oil. Drivers were still responsible for making their own trimmings and maintaining them in good order, and for drivers long frustrated by having to beg bits of spare copper wire from the district electrician, copper wire was now available in quantity. Each 30 Class required sixty-six tail trimmings and eighteen plug trimmings, and making them was something I took pride in, forming the wire round a short length of ½ inch diameter copper pipe. It was caboose work, when sleep was denied.

By now, indoctrinated with the need to be careful with oil, I made trimmings to suit the job they were intended for. As an example, I made two-strand trimmings for lightly stressed parts such as the valve spindle slides and the pony pivot, the Delta truck pivot and the two six-wheeled tender bogie pivots. For axle box faces and the compensating beam fulcrums with which these engines were fitted four-strand trimmings were sufficient to take the continuous up and down movement created by variations in the track. Taking the full thrust of the pistons, the side bars received six-strand trimmings, as did both piston rods.

Built like a battleship, the 30 Class proved a superb, trouble-free locomotive. Fitted with manganese steel roller bearing axle boxes throughout, with large, generous faces, massive horn cheeks, set up to a tight sliding fit to the axle boxes, and to equally large and firmly secured stay plates, eliminating knock throughout the engine. Indeed, when the 30 Class were called to shops after about 200,000 miles of running and three years of hard work, they seemed on the face of it to require very little attention, beyond reprofiling the tyres. But as a matter of sound engineering, each engine had to be returned to traffic 'as per drawings'.

Over the years a great deal has been written condemning the use of a jimmy, the fireman's friend, a bladed device with a view to improving steaming, and secured centrally across the top of a blast pipe to split and sharpen the exhaust. It is said that it's use was frowned upon because of increased coal consumption and its tendency to throw fire. East African Railways, which included the former Tanganyika Railways, took a different view. To reduce cylinder back pressure when working hard, a large diameter blast pipe was adopted, bringing all the steaming problems of soft exhaust. So to counteract this, each blast pipe was fitted with a more scientific form of jimmy called Goodfellow tips. Four v-shaped bars of about 1 inch long by ¾ deep were set flush within the top of the blast pipe, and extending to about one-third of the blast pipe's diameter, leaving a central solid jet of exhaust, and spreading the remaining exhaust steam into eight distinct jets. After some 200,000 miles and millions of exhausts, even these hardened tips showed distinct wear.

During the last few trips on my first tour of duty I developed some form of dysentery. I struggled on, however, but became progressively weaker, until in the early hours of one morning I fell asleep on the down grade approaching Munisagara, a station between Dodoma and Morogoro, an event which, for several reasons, should have been my undoing. That morning, however, for the first and only time, I was mercifully turned into the station's loop, and in doing so it woke me up and prevented me from passing through the station and entering the next section without authority—a Line Clear irregularity on such a scale as to warrant dismissal.

As the term 'loop' indicates, this was a curved piece of track and I had entered it far in excess of the permitted speed. However, if Lady Luck had smiled on me so far, I was doubly fortunate. Aided to a large extent by the quality (in terms of design, material used and construction) of the German track, 3012, a 147 ton locomotive with a long rigid wheelbase, miraculously held the rails, thereby preventing the train ending up in a jumbled heap spread around the station grounds. Rudely awakened after being nearly thrown out of my seat, and shaken and appalled by what had occurred, I still had time to apply the brake and stop the train within the station limits. Convinced some of the train was derailed on the crossover I went back and examined each vehicle carefully, finding, thanks to the splendid design of the track, that all was safe and well.

Engine 3012, Tabora.

Admitting, finally, that I was no longer fit for work, I reported sick on my return to Tabora (about 32 hours after my Munisagara incident) and attended the European hospital. The doctor, shocked at my emaciated condition (he said I looked like a concentration camp victim), ordered me to bed. The German-built European hospital (overshadowed further along the road by a more modern and comprehensively equipped African and Asian hospital), had been built in the shape of a hollow square. One side formed the female ward, the opposite formed the male ward, with both conjoined at the top by a pharmacy, the hospital stores and living quarters for the British nurses. Rather suspiciously, I was placed in a small room at the end, but separate from the main ward. It contained a single bed with a crucifix on the wall above it. I felt ill, but not, I thought (or hoped!), that ill.

After a couple of days of rest and food I was moved to the men's ward, when as the only inhabitant I reigned in solitary splendour (at that time the European inhabitants of Tabora must have been a healthy lot). I now came to an arrangement with the matron, a no-nonsense Scottish lass who agreed that, provided I return to the hospital by 9 pm of an evening, I could go down to the Railway Hotel and, if lucky, meet one or other of the British drivers. The Germans, with a grand scheme in mind, had laid out Tabora on a widely-spaced grid system, the development of which, apart from a few public buildings dotted about (the post office, the hospital and the municipal offices, etc.), had ceased with the advent of the First World War, leaving large tracts of open ground and country. The European hospital was about a mile from the Railway Hotel with nothing in between. One evening, making my way back to the hospital along the unlit road I became rooted to the spot when suddenly a large and ferocious animal, teeth bared, fur flying, came out of the scrub and hurled itself at me. Thinking my last few moments had arrived, the thought flashed through my mind as to what a poor sort of meal would I make in my present condition. With one last bound the creature flung itself at me. Only then did I discover, with a relief that can only be imagined, that what I thought was a large and ferocious lion was in fact a large and friendly Alsation. One which seemed as happy to find me as I was relieved to discover it was a harmless dog, looking for a friend and some companionship. It walked with me up to the hospital ward, it's tail wagging as it fussed around its new found friend. Never was I more glad to see a dog. Unfortunately I had to sever the ties between us and close the wards mosquito door to prevent it following me in.

Late one particular night my sleep was broken by loud and anguished cries from ouside the ward, along with some complaining, "Leave me alone, you're hurting me!" The mosquito door swung open and an elderly man in obvious pain was carried in accompanied by his daughter who put him to bed, where he spent a disturbed night. There was now two of us occupying the ward, and the next morning I went over to have a chat with the old boy and see if I could help in any way. In conversation I discovered he lived with his daughter, who was in charge of a small bush hospital at Shinyanga, halfway between Tabora and Mwanza, and the changeover point for engine crews. It was inhabited by a scattering of Europeans, which included the district doctor, the district agricultural officer, and that's about all.

"Pop", as I came to call him, in deference to his age, had become concerned about a tree whose branches were in danger of breaking a hospital window, and deciding to do something about it, climbed the tree and promptly fell, breaking his hip. With only limited facilities, his daughter loaded him into a Landrover, and after a harrowing 123 miles of deeply rutted and badly corrugated murram road, delivered him straight to the better equipped African hospital. There the staff aligned his hip and fixed him up with a plaster cast. Later that afternoon, his daughter, covered in red murram dust, arrived to see how he was getting on, and bringing with her, to comfort him, several bottles of beer and, two bottles of whisky, Pop's favourite tipple. And I must say how grand they looked, lined up on his bedside locker.

In conversation, I learned he had been an engine driver on the former London, Brighton & South Coast Railway, which led to some interesting conversations between us. Suffering continuous pain from his hip, he complained bitterly about the cast being too tight. Unfortunately his complaints were ignored, with the result that his condition, both mental and physical, began to deteriorate. One day, in desperation, he began emptying the contents of his water jug over his plaster cast and over his bed, whilst trying to unpick the plaster with his dinner knife. Eventually, after closer inspection, the plaster was cut through and in response sprang open by several inches, thus relieving the intense pain he had suffered. By then it was too late, however, as Pop sank slowly into moments of mumbled incoherence.

The day came when he lay still and quiet, seemingly close to death. Having been in hospital for about a week I was now (January 1957) only a few days from the end of my first three-year tour of duty and an early flight home had been arranged for the next day, with instructions to report to the Liverpool School of Tropical Medicine for further treatment. That final evening there seemed little I could do to help poor old Pop, and I decided as usual to go down to the Railway Hotel. Before leaving I went over and asked Pop if he would like a drink of whisky. Slowly opening one eye, which fixed me with a helpless stare, he croaked a faint and feeble "Yes." Propping him up with pillows, I sat beside him dribbling whisky into his mouth from a spouted feeding cup, until his head slipped to one side. By then I'd put a fair old wallop of whisky into him (probably not treatment that the doctors would prescribe) and shaking my head I left with the thought, "At least old Pop will die happy tonight."

Honouring my agreement with the matron, I left the hotel in good time and returned to the hospital, fearing an empty bed or, more offputting, a sheet-covered body to keep me company overnight. Unsure of what I might find I approached the ward heart in mouth. The ward's night light shone dimly through the mosquito door's mesh screen. Carefully and cautiously I opened it. In a land replete with surprises I was never more taken aback than when I found Pop sitting up in bed smoking his pipe. I am unable to speak of whisky and its recuperative properties, but here was Pop, not only lucid for the first time in days, but apparently a new man, who to my amazement greeted me with a "Wocha, mate! Have you had a good night?" This seemed to me not just a recovery, but a ressurection!

I don't know what happened to Pop thereafter, as the next day I left Tabora for the flight home and my appointment at Liverpool. There I was escorted to a ward full of cheerful colonial types suffering from a variety of tropical nasties which included malaria, bilharzia, beriberi, foot rot and double vision. After giving me a cheer and an invitation to join the club I was put to bed, where for the next few days I underwent various tests, until one morning a doctor arrived at my bedside. "Ah, Blackburn," he remarked, "we've found out what's wrong with you." I shuddered a little, wondering what they had in store for me. "Fourteen days of Mepacrine [an old anti-malarial drug] should fix you." And in this he proved correct.

Engine 3012 after taking water, Kigoma.

After home leave, on my next tour of duty I returned to Tabora and engine 3012. At that time the overnight passanger train from Kigoma left on unrevised 26 Class timings, and over the 37 miles between Kigoma and Kazuramimba the more powerful 30 Class made up about 30 minutes on the 26 Class timings, arriving at Kazuramimba just as dinner was being served.

With 30 minutes in hand before departure time this gave me the opportunity to shut the engine down and make my way to the dining car and there, in oppulent surroundings (and in my perfectly acceptable work clothes), sit down to a proper meal. This happy state of affairs continued until someone in the Tabora Traffic Department noticed the difference between the two Class of engines, when thereafter, by a reduction in running time and an addition of loaded bogie waggons, the train was made up to exploit the full capabilities of the 30 Class.

3012 standing on the back road at Kigoma

381

Europeans generally were few and far between on the Kigoma part of the Down passenger train and, typically, on any one such evening only five sat down to dinner, a family of three, and in this instance a solitary male and me. After dinner, whilst tea was being served, the solitary male came over and asked if he could join me, explaining that he had overheard me in conversation with the Goanese steward, and recognised the voice of a fellow Yorkshireman. It emerged that he was a Nairobi entrepreneur returning from a business trip to what was then the Belgium Congo.

"Where are you from?" he enquired.

It was a question common among expatriates meeting for the first time, and thinking he had probably never heard of Cottingham, I replied with my stock answer: "I come from Hull."

His face lit up, and he sprang a surprise: "That's interesting," he remarked, "I come from Cottingham. On the western fringe of Hull." Cottingham was more of a town than a village, and because of its size, we had never met. For the remainder of our time together, we reminisced, recalling some of Cottingham's worthies, and some of its other less well-known characters. This was neither the first or the last of such encounters during my time in Africa.

For many years, Cottingham had been the residential home of Hull University students. Strolling along its main street when on home leave, I was met by a young Indian student who in passing gave me a long hard look. He stopped and asked, "Are you Mr Blackburn?"

I stared back in astonishment, thinking, *Who on earth is this, and where had he come from?* I answered, "Yes, I am Mr Blackburn." My confusion ended when, in reply to a question, he said he came from that dry and dusty township in the middle of nowhere, Tabora. I asked what he was studying.

"Law," he answered. "Law and Economics." Ah, I might have known—those well-established staples of Asian vocational education!

Dry and dusty Tabora, yet it had had its compensations (although lack of water was not one of them). Over the years both the railway and the civil administration had tried to find water without success. During the dry season water became so scarce throughout the township water trains had to be run on a daily basis. This involved a single-manned, tender first, overnight run of 160 miles from Tabora to Malagarasi, where each of the train's 5,000-gallon water tank bogies were filled from the stations water columns with water drawn from Malagarasi swamp, before returning engine first in time for the start of a new day. Here the water was decanted and pumped into Tabora's water supply, where it was quickly used up, leaving the town without water for the next 24 hours.

My first such trip caught me out. The night filled with the cloying scent of frangipani and the honeyed perfume of Indian cork trees felt warm and velvety as I walked to work clad only in a pair of shorts and a thin aertex shirt and battered old trilby. Who would dress otherwise on a night like this? One-hundred and forty-six miles of exposed tender first running quickly transformed a balmy night into eight hours of freezing cold and chattering teeth, and with it came a solid determination not to be caught out like that again.

Returning to home leave, and unusual encounters, my elder brother, Bernard, who you'll recall played the organ, was friendly with Peter Goodman, then resident organist at Hull's stunning Holy Trinity church, and keeper and organist of Hull's City Hall organ. Peter was preparing to give a recital and asked my brother if he'd turn the music pages for him. I was invited along during one of his practice sessions, my brother saying, "Peter has a bit of a surprise for you."

Now, I like a bit of organ music, providing it doesn't go off the scale and become alarming, and so I readily agreed. After the practice Peter said (and here's the surprise): "Of course, you'll know my brother?"

I raked about in the deeper recesses of my mind (somebody Goodman, somebody Goodman…?) and regretfully had to answer, "Er, no, I don't think so," to which Peter replied, "Oh I think you do. My brother's the Tabora tax officer"—a surprise indeed, as I then immediately recognised him as the man who took a good chunk of my pay off me each month!

But to continue along the same lines (if you'll forgive the pun), arriving at Dodoma with the Down passenger train I sometimes observed a European shepherding a group of blind African children from the train, and into a battered old bus, before driving off in a cloud of dust. He drew my attention because of a pronounced rye neck (torticollis), and his command of the Swahili language. I found out he was a Englishman, who together with his wife, had been sent to Tanganyika by the Church Army, to minister to and educate blind African children. During this time he not only built a school and its living accommodation from scratch, but had translated the bible into Swahili braille. An amazing feat of perseverance and endurance if ever there was one. Then, many years later, after retiring from EAR I set up home in a quiet East Yorkshire village where, after a few years a new vicar, the Reverend Gordon Johnson, and his wife Margaret, were inducted. By their selfless devotion to their parishioners they both earned the love and respect of all who knew them. You may say "What's that got to do with the story in hand?" Well, Gordon, a gentle and holy man, had a wry neck and a scholarly command of the Swahili language. Yes, incredibly, it was the very same person. God bless him!

In 1957, whilst on home leave, a surge suddenly seemed to have occurred in the world's economic fortunes, when to the delight of many, of both sexes, Dior's 'new look' burst upon the scene, and people began to throw off the drab austerity which had blighted their lives for so many years. This was never more apparent than when, despite official disapproval by the council, homeowners began painting their front doors in a variety of bright colours. This new-found prosperity even found its way to Tanganyika when, for the first time, lighting was installed in railway goods yards. And with this wealth came a dramatic increase in traffic, much of it railed to Kigoma for onward transmission to the Belgium Congo by lake steamer. This, to our wondering eyes included the unaccustomed sight of lines of shiny new motorcars heading that way on flat waggons. This unexpected influx of money gave engine crews cause for rejoicing, resulting in the issuing to drivers of top-quality oil feeders, the end of cut-to-the-bone oil rationing and, for making trimmings, copper wire on demand.

To accommodate this enormous increase in traffic, and to further exploit the outstanding capabilities of the 30 Class, it was decided, without any consideration for engine crews, to extend the working range of the Tabora-Morogoro run by including the Tabora-Kigoma section, adding to an already arduous 800 miles, and making it an eye-watering total of 1,308 miles for the round trip. This was achieved by first working the 250 miles from Tabora (mile 529) to Kigoma (mile 780) where the engine was left on-shed for the staff, who in preparation for its Down run of 654 miles, turned it, before taking on fuel and water. The Down run involved 53 station stops to exchange Line Clear tickets, and include taking on water and fuel at both Malagarasi (mile 675, water only) and Kaliua (mile 605, the junction for the Mpanda Line), where in preparation for the next stage, a run with no intermediate fuel points, from Kaliua to Manyoni (mile 370), a distance of 298 miles, water was always taken at Tabora (mile 525), to cover the same long, waterless run.

On reaching Manyoni, with water running low, I used to take a chance by only taking on fuel oil, preferring to run a further 10 miles with steam shut off, down the bank to Saranda (mile 360), to take, for my boiler's sake, a tenderfull of that sweet, untainted, pure spring water. Once, I must confess, my injector kicked off on the descent, but with a full boiler and the engine shut off, there was no cause for concern. The next and final fuel and water stop, Msagali (mile 243), gave a final run of 170 miles to Morogoro (mile 126), where on arrival the engine was left on-shed, and prepared for its immediate return journey.

As mentioned earlier, following a serious accident on Saranda Bank due to the failure to connect the locomotive's vacuum to the main train following shunting operations, a stop board was in place where the line began to fall between Manyoni and Saranda, warning that all drivers must come to a standstill, thereby testing their train's brakes. However, with the introduction of the 30 Class and through running, the train was no longer parted, shunted and reconnected, and with the driver being aware of the efficacy of the braking system from the down gradients he'd already encountered, there was no longer, in my mind, any valid reason to stop here. I was quite surprised then, on one occasion, when, having pulled up at Saranda, the guard came up to me and said I'd failed to stop at the sign. Making light of the situation, I replied in a jocular manner with the saying that "Rules are made for fools." However, it seems he thought I was calling him a fool, and taking it as a personal insult he submitted an accident telegraph detailing my failure to stop. Later, when questioned about this by the shedmaster I told him, not entirely truthfully, that I had slowed right down, whilst admitted that I didn't actually stop, following which I thankfully heard nothing more about it.

The author on the footplate of 3012

Whilst 'spare' in the caboose was classed as time off, for European drivers, vainly searching for sleep whilst crossing the unforgiving Mathundu Makali (Land of Heat), with its swirling dust devils, in these conditions rest time in a caboose could offer no substitute for time off in a large and airy house, cooled and shaded by majestic mwembe (mango) trees. To this end Dennis and I agreed to extend the distance between the traditional changeover points in the hope of giving crews travelling 'spare' sufficient time to discover the sleep which so often eluded them.

3012, dusty but unbowed, after its first 1,308 mile round trip.

On the first leg, the 250 mile Tabora-Kigoma section, we decided, whilst still taking water there, to ignore the time-honoured Malagarasi changeover, and work both ways as single crews, in a running time of 11 hours 30 minutes. Added to this, a preparation time of 2 hours at both Tabora and Kigoma, giving a shift time of 13 hours 30 minutes in both directions.

The relieving crew, taking over at Tabora, ran the 230 miles to Dodoma in a straight 12 hours, before being relieved there by the 'spare' crew for the final 164-mile, 7-hour run to Morogoro, which apart from one or two minutes at each station, exchanging Line Clear tickets, and 15 minutes at each water/fuel station, gave a time of 40 hours continuous running in the Down direction. Arriving at Morogoro normally on the dot, the engine was left on the shed for the shed staff to fuel, water and turn, and for the 'spare in' crew to oil it all round for the return trip, within 2 hours, such was how snappily the railway was organised. 3012, along with the other, would be back on its train for the 400 mile return trip, when for convenience we reverted to exchanging crews at Masagali and at Manyoni, each round trip taking just under five days to complete. It might be expected, after each trip, for crews to be granted a reasonable amount of time off, but

Tabora didn't work that way, the crew 'spare in' having in theory been fully rested were back within a few hours preparing the engine for its next marathon. Although it may seem extreme to modern sentiments, there were occasions when, due to a shortage of motive power at Tabora, an engine and its crew were turned around and sent off on another 1,308-mile round trip—a tribute not only to the efficiency of the 30 Class, but to the hardy men who manned them.

It may be of interest to more closely examine the 2-8-4 metre-gauge tender engine, capable of feats of haulage and sustained steaming such as those already outlined. 74 feet 7¼ inches over couplers, and too long for the existing

Side view of 3012, taken at the same time as the previous photo, and after hard running.

60 foot turntables, turning triangles had to be laid at both Tabora and Morogoro. Kigoma already had a triangle. Fitted throughout with British Timpkin tapered roller bearings, which completely eliminated hot boxes, the 30 Class weighed in at 147 tons in working order, each pair of four-foot diameter coupled wheels carried an axle load of a little over 13 tons, making available a weight of 51 tons 15 cwt on the driving wheels. The boiler, pressed to 200 lb/sq. inch, measured 14 feet 4 inches between the tube plates, and tapered from an outside diameter of 5 feet 5 inches at the firebox to 5 feet 3 inches at the smoke box, with the slab-sided Belpaire firebox adding a further 38 sq. feet internally. Interestingly, the firebox foundation ring rested on phosphor bronze expansion guides, atop the main frames, giving the boiler a visible expansion of about 1½ inches from cold.

Without going into the finer details of the boiler, the total heating area, including the 28-element superheater, came out at a very effective 2,290 sq. feet, delivering superheated steam to two 18 by 26 inch cylinders, which provided a calculated thrust of 29,350 pounds at 80% of boiler pressure. But thanks to oil firing with its precise control, pressure was continuously held at 198 psi, 2 pounds below full working pressure, adding a further 18% to the engine's nominal tractive effort. To overcome the enduring water shortage along the Central Railway, the massive tender, carried on two 6-wheeled cast steel bogies, held 7,000 gallons of water and 1,900 gallons of fuel oil, giving a working range of over 200 miles.

At this time Dennis and I had been rostered to work the Sunday passenger train, otherwise known by its old-time Tanganyika Railways designation, the Mail Train, or to give it its EAR designation, Two-Down Mail. For in truth it, like the other passenger trains, carried under lock and key the mail destined for several townships which had sprung up along the length of the Central Railway. This train ran from Tabora to Kigoma on Lake Tanganyika, back through Tabora, through Dodoma, and on to Morogoro, then finally back to Tabora, taking five days in all. Dennis worked the first leg of the 1,308 mile round trip, the Tabora-Kigoma section, leaving the engine on-shed for the staff to turn and service. With this three-hour break before train time it was a habit of mine to go on-shed early and, after oiling the engine all round, carefully clean its main frames, its wheels and valve gear by using the blowdown. Then, once it was looking all spic and span, I'd return it to the station for the overnight run.

View from the footplate when crossing the Malagarasi River bridge

A typical Kigoma to Tabora run, a distance of 251 miles, might be as follows: my fireman and I board 3012 and bring her in to Kigoma station, resplendent in the EAR's maroon livery and yellow detailing, and ready to set off at 18:00, just as the sun is beginning to set over Lake Tanganyika. Dennis and his fireman are safely ensconced in caboose, of course. On the footplate, satisfied that all is in order, the engine gently ticking over, we wait for the 'Right Away' and, precisely on the hour, with a wave of the guard's flag and an acknowledging blast of the whistle, I open the regulator, 3012's slow and deep exhaust beats increasing in pace and softening as we gain speed. I notch up the reverser as we leave the buildings and the main street of Kigoma behind, the sky gradually turning from blue, to dark blue, through hues of green, gold and orange, before reddening as the darkness of night approaches, the sun going down behind the hills overlooking Kigoma bay, nature's kaleidoscopic display played out to the beat of the engine.

A short pause at Luiche, one of the 16 stops on this section, and then on past the large banana plantation there, with the stars beginning to perforate the vast heavens, growing in number and intensity, until, looking up, we're steaming under the vaulted roof of a celestial cathedral of starlight (no light pollution here), the rhythmic beating of the engine and the swaying joint-clatter of train the only acknowledgement that we're earth-bound rather than flying through the firmament. On we steam through the warm night with its miles of twisting empty, night-curtained bush, eyes straining as the lance of the headlamp beam pierces the night, looking for any potential obstruction or defect in the track, my fireman keeping a steady eye on water, fuel, and boiler pressure, the engine eating up the empty miles. On past Kandaga (no need to stop here for water with the large-tendered 30 Class), and then the start of Kazuramimba Bank, and the challenge of the long 37 mile, 1 in 50 haul up it. I notch down, open the regulator almost to full, steam pressure 198 psi, locomotive working to the maximum, pistons and valve gear straining with the Herculean effort—no banker engine here to assist—the sharp exhaust barks reverberating off the surrounding escarpment slopes like rolling thunder.

Tenaciously, 3012 claws its way up the gradient, 331 tons behind the drawbar on a 2% grade, until slowly the gradient begins to flatten out and I ease off the regulator and adjust the cutoff, applying the brakes as we glide slowly into tiny Kazuramimba station at the summit.

We then commence the easy run on down to Lugufu and on through Uvinza, making fine adjustments to the position of the regulator and cutoff to maintain a steady speed over the changing gradients. The sluggish opaque waters of the Malagarasi River reflect in the pale moonlight as we rattle over the steel girder bridge, and then glide in to Malagarasi station where we stop briefly for water and fuel, and where passengers, mainly Africans, embark or disembark, despite the hour. Then on past Nguruka and through the flat expanse of Usinge Swamp, the giant termite mounds just visible above the dense night-shrouded vegetation, followed by a stop at Kaliua.

Tiredness now beginning to creep up on my fireman and me, as we approach Urambo, but we take heart as the stars slowly begin to fade and the first streaks of dawn steal onto the horizon, meaning we've not far to go now. The sky gradually lightening as darkness gives way to reds and oranges—empyrean skies framed by deep velvet blue with the dawn-fresh white clouds silhouetted in gold. The countryside now beginning to take shape as the night retreats, steaming through dry bush country of orange-red murram soil, picked out with the greenery of hardy trees and bushes, speed 30 mph. And as the sun tips the horizon its shafts glance down the length of the boiler, reflecting off its still-burnished surface, a heat-haze dancing above the chimney, its exhaust strong and smoke-free.

On past Mabama and into the outskirts of Tabora, past the large 'go-downs' of the Grain Storage Department (each acting as an insurance policy against the ever-present threat of famine should Mother Nature turn malevolent and decide to withhold the life-giving rains), on past the sidings full of goods waggons, with the distant rails dancing in the shimmering heat as slowly we pull into Tabora station.

On arrival at Tabora at 07:35, Dennis, with his kikapu basket, would relieve me to work on to Dodoma through the heat and burden of the day, as I dozed in the caboose. I would then take over again for the final 164 miles to Morogoro, which included the usual take-over pleasantries, and as expected with

 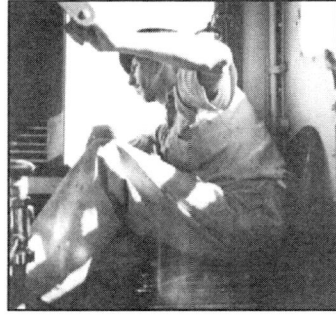

The author at the regulator.

the 30 Class, that Rolls Royce of locomotives, a brief "Yes, everything's alright"—for these engines could easily run the distance between heavy repairs. In respect of the 30 Class, the term 'heavy repairs' was a misnomer if ever there was one, for as they made their way to the shops in Dar es Salaam they seemed good enough for another 200,000 miles or so.

Unlike the dreadful 26 Class, whose repairs filled a whole page of the repair book after each trip, the only faults I recall were an occasional fractured spoke or spokes in the leading pair of coupled wheels, and in the early days, a tendency for the leading coupled spring hangers to snap, leading me to think that these leading coupled wheels were being overstretched. With still many miles to go, it came as something of a shock when I first discovered both leading coupled springs pointed skyward at an acute angle. But I consoled myself with the thought that the engine had continued in that condition for hours without harm and without any tendency to derail. And so, with no means of effecting any repairs, I had no other option but to carry on and hope for the best.

3012 crossing the Malagarasi bridge in the daytime.

Over many years on the 30 Class, the need to book repairs remained at an absolute minimum. Of these, three, all out of the way, I shall report later, but two, both connected, occurred in unusual circumstances. I rolled into one of the more distant stations as dawn was breaking over the bush, and to wake myself and stretch my legs I climbed down and walked around the engine, finding as I did so, the left eccentric rod covered in blood and animal hair, a sure sign we'd struck and killed some creature during the night. Looking more closely I discovered the collision had to some slight degree bent the eccentric rod, which I reported on my arrival at Tabora, where the rod was quickly dismantled, straightened and reassembled in time for the next trip. It was on this trip that I discovered another design fault, one peculiar to the 30 Class.

Working through to Kigoma on the next trip I again discovered damage to the same rod, when I stopped at Malagarasi to take on fuel and water. Instinctively looking around the engine, I discovered the repaired rod's fork-end a deep and attractive blue—a sure sign it had run hot somewhere on the seven-hour run between Tabora and Malagarasi. Although it was now cooled and swinging freely on its pin, further examination revealed its brasses had melted and deep scoring had occurred both to the pin and to the foot of the expansion link to which it was attached. On my return to Tabora, and my report, the shed's first instinct was to blame me for lack of lubrication, a charge I strongly denied. Fortunately, further and more detailed examination discovered the true reason. At the design stage of the 30 Class, some amateur draughtsman in the employ of the North British Locomotive Company had, whilst working on the form, shape and dimensions of the eccentric rod connecting pin, drawn it parallel throughout, without a shoulder to prevent its retaining nut being overtightened. In refitting the rod an unknown, but overenthusiastic member of Tabora's fitting staff had continued tightening the nut until it had firmly clamped the eccentric rod's fork ends against the expansion link foot. The rest, as they say, is history, but no amount of lubrication would have prevented the assembly from running hot once the engine was underway.

In all respects the trouble-free 30 Class proved a massive leap forward, for both engine crews and shed staff alike. When oiling or carrying out other duties drivers no longer had to scramble about under the low 25 and 26 Class running plates. Based on very old, at least a hundred years, American practice, the 30 Class had high running plates, at least 6 feet above rail level, and fitted with electric lights, giving drivers freedom to oil and examine the engine under very favourable conditions. Of inestimable value to drivers, forced in the past to repack blown-out piston glands every 200 miles or so, were the spring-controlled metallic packing rings which imparted a mirror-like finish to the piston rods, came as a blessing beyond belief. Equally important in maintaining steam-tight cylinders, the primitive rotating cylinder taps (drain cocks), which under the harsh conditions prevailing required constant attention to keep steam tight, were now replaced by simple mushroom valves, each working in a sleeve. Cylinder steam pressure held each valve tight against its face. But when running with the regulator closed the opposite occurred, with each sweep of the piston lifting the valves, drawing in air, which, in conjunction with large-capacity cylinder bypass valves, was then distributed around the cylinders and steam chests, bringing an added advantage to the wellbeing of the front end, namely the prevention of hot smokebox gases (or in the case of coal and wood-fired locomotives, hot gases combined with fine ash, grit and dust) being drawn down the blast pipe, where, mixing with cylinder oil, it formed a hard unyielding carbon deposit on valves and pistons.

The cab, spacious and airy, and with an extended roof, was by any standards luxurious. Fitted with outside sight glasses it had, as protection for the crew, sliding, unglazed louvred windows of polished African hardwood, and its cushioned armrests and padded seats offered a high degree of comfort (although being of no help to drivers fighting to stay awake). The cab roof, lined internally with an attractive, polished tongue and groove hardwood, leant a pleasing finish to the interior of the cab. Suspended from the roof by brackets hung two whistle pulls, the first giving a deep sonorous chime which, when drivers acknowledged a guard's departing All Clear signal, echoed melodiously across townships along the line. The other offered a more delicate and refined whistle. Asian drivers often fastened the two pulls together to give a more distinctive and oriental sound.

Because oil firing eliminated the dirt, dust and smoke connected with solid fuel, the cab fittings remained in pristine condition, its footboards whitened in the first place but the use of caustic soda and kept white thereafter by detergent and the use of the engine's slecker pipe. To compliment this finery the day shift polished the copper pipe and brass works to such a high degree they were only touched thereafter using a clean rag. On the fireman's side his two automatic Gresham and Craven injectors, the bodies mounted outside, in front of the cab, to keep its interior as cool as possible, with each actuated by a single pull rod. On the same side, two levers, the first operating the cylinder drain valves, and the second, in the absence of an ashpan, controlling the air scoop damper, the primary source of air to the firebox. Mounted in comfortable reach of the fireman, the American designed Caltech oil fuel manifold combined the jet (blower), steam valve, and, with its own pressure gauge, a separate steam valve supplying steam to the burner, together with a steam valve providing steam to a steam jacket surrounding the crude oil supply pipe from the tender to the burner (a bit of 'kit' never required in Tanganyika's balmy airs). And mounted as an integral part of the oil manifold, a short hand held ratcheted lever governing the supply of oil to the burner.

To produce perfect, smoke-free combustion within the firebox required something of a juggling act between the demands of the driver, the amount of fuel oil delivered to the burner, and the correct pressure of steam blown through the burner to throw the crude oil against a flash wall located across the rear of the firebox below the fire door aperture. Too much oil produced thick black smoke which quickly sooted up the tubes, affecting steam production, whereas too much steam on the burner resulted in white smoke, both bringing displeasure to any watching Mechanical Officer. It was a matter of pride that, notwithstanding how hard the engine was being worked, a boiler pressure of 198 psi, 2 psi below working pressure, above which the engine would blow off, could be maintained, with a perfectly clear exhaust, indefinitely.

The driver's position included a single automatic injector, together with a powerful Gresham and Craven super-solid jet vacuum ejector, the body of each being located outside the cab, and an easy-to-use screw reverser. Also, readily to hand, the driver's vacuum brake application handle with its vacuum gauge, and coupled to it, an automatic and graduable steam brake. Tucked away, so that it wouldn't be accidentally knocked open, was a lever for one of the engine's two manually operated blowdown valves. Finally, on the left, the two-handled pull-out regulator, operating a Superheater Company MeLeSco multi-valve regulator located within the smokebox. This arrangement of superheater and smokebox regulator, giving a short passage between the regulator and the cylinders, had the advantage over the steam dome regulator valve, insofar as the superheater elements always remained steam-filled and no longer required the fitting of a snifter valve (valves designed to draw air through the superheater elements to prevent them being burnt out by hot smokebox gases when running with the regulator closed). But as far as drivers were concerned it had other advantages, as anyone who may have observed an LNER Pacific restarting its heavy train whilst standing on the curves within York Station, for example, would realise. Any slip, and they were frequent and explosive, continued until all the steam had been exhausted from the engine's steam pipe and superheater. The same delay, with its effect on the train, occurred when the regulator was opened for another try. With a MeLeSco smokebox regulator, reaction when opening or closing its multivalve regulator was instantaneous—a reaction much appreciated by drivers on the more difficult sections of Tanganyika's Central Railway.

The main steam manifold lay crosswise, atop the flat-topped Belpaire firebox, and for the purpose, once again, of keeping the cab's interior as cool as possible, was, as with other steam fittings, located outside the cab, but with its row of highly polished brass handles protruding within the cab. Laid traverse across the boiler's backplate, and convenient from either side, the two-handled regulator occupied a prominent position; and just below it, from where it could easily be read by both the driver and the fireman, stood the boiler pressure gauge. Between the two-gauge glasses were a polished (but rarely used by me) automatic blowdown valve. I preferred to use the manually operated blowdown valves located just above the firebox foundation ring. Apart from the electric generator steam valve under the control of the driver, and its array of switches above the driver's head, all that remains of the cab fittings was a heavy cast steel firehole door, so designed to protect the crew in the event of a flashback and containing a peephole through which to examine the fire and burner when out on the road.

Arriving on shed to prepare 3012 I normally found it with its fire shut down and about 100 pounds showing on the pressure gauge, indicating that the engine had been slumbering, unlit for several hours, and as such a great deal of its boiler sediment would have settled around the firebox foundation ring, giving me the opportunity to clear most of it by fractionally cracking open both manually operated blowdown valves. This discharged a diminutive flow of thick white sludge from both valves, until such time as the outflow became clear water. Whether, in the long run, it proved beneficial to the boiler is a matter of conjecture.

At this time, I found another use for the blowdown. After leaving 2612 I retained one of its armoured hosepipes, with a view that it may come in handy one day. Its brass connecting nut fitted the threads of the 30 Class's blowdown drainpipes, giving me the idea that I could use it to clean the engine's main frames, its wheels and running gear, at such times as became convenient. My first attempt almost ended in disaster. Fully aware what steam and water could do at 200 psi boiler pressure (the bore of the pipe I intended to use was about the same as a square inch) I approached it with some caution, and after fastening the pipe to one of the blowdown cocks and holding the nozzle firmly in both hands, I instructed the fireman in my unpolished Swahili to "Sikia" (listen carefully) and to "Fungua ya blowdown polepole polepole, nakidogo sana" (to open the blowdown very slowly, and only very little).

To make sure he exactly understood my instructions, and the dangers involved, I called up to him, "Wewe najua? (Do you understand?)"

In reply, I received a confident "Deo bwana, meme najua" (Yes bwana, I understand).

Satisfied, I called out "Tiari fungua!" (I'm ready, open the valve!). At that, all hell broke loose, as with a howl and a scream, the pipe tore itself out of my hands, spraying steam and boiling water in all directions, hitting me on the back and knocking me to the ground with a blow that felt like scalding steam. Leaping to my feet, convinced I'd been badly scalded, I skipped and danced my way out of the torrent of boiling water, whilst shouting to the fireman to close the blowdown valve. By some miracle, which I still find hard to understand, I discovered I'd escaped the boiling water unhurt, which if it had hit me fair and square, would have flayed my flesh down to my bones, adding another grave to Tabora's European cemetery. My narrow escape taught me, henceforth, to manipulate the blowdown myself, and not rely on someone else, by laying the pipe out flat along the track before climbing into the cab and very gently opening the blowdown valve.

But to return, briefly, to the cab fittings, and one in particular that has a bearing on this narrative: it comprised a steel tray fixed above the firehole door. A tray seemingly common to all steam locomotives, and used by engine crews for a variety of purposes, and thereby hangs a tale—an incident involving my co-driver Dennis Cregan, who had a close brush with death. This incident, as recorded by Dennis, is enough to chill the blood of all but the most stout-hearted, and which, for the benefit of readers, I will shortly transcribe, in all its heroic but blood-curdling details, from the original text. First, however, we must go back to the events leading up to this tale of derring-do.

Whenever Dennis relieved me at one or other of the changeover points, he brought with him his kikapu, containing his wants for the day, such as an ample supply of the local *Crown Bird* cigarettes, a large, brown and thoroughly disreputable enamel teapot, veteran of a thousand such safaris, one enamel mug, a small tin of evaporated milk, a packet of the locally grown and excellent Simba chai (Lion tea), and a small container of sugar. After making a brew from one of the engine's injectors, Dennis would place the teapot on the aforementioned tray, and as and when required, draw from it throughout the day.

On this particular occasion, when relieving Dennis at Dodoma, our changeover point, he remarked he'd had someone riding on the footplate for a couple of hours who had identified himself as an author, by which time, Dennis went on, the man was "all in" with the heat, but he nevertheless was interested in the way things were done and enjoyed the ride. It was a passing remark as we changed duties, and on my part drew little attention, and as such was quickly forgotten. Months later, however, during which Dennis had left on home leave, never to return to Tabora, for on the expiry of his leave he had been posted to Mombasa a thousand miles away, in which circumstances we never met again.

I was looking around the Indian duka I traded with, when by good fortune—good fortune because, in Tabora reading material was even more scarce than rain—I picked up a magazine dated August 1961, and entitled 'Wide World'. An adventure magazine for men, it sounded promising, and among its contributors was a young zoologist called David Attenborough. Just the thing, I thought, to while away a few hours in the caboose, and picking out those articles that might interest me, to my astonishment I found myself looking at a photograph of Dennis Cregan, fag in hand, beret on head, leaning against the imposing front of 3012. Turning to the beginning of the article, headed 'Killer on the Footplate', I read the harrowing story of Dennis's life and death struggle with an enraged lion, which, for the benefit and edification of readers, I now append in full:

Killer on the Footplate

Facing a savage, wounded lion in a swaying railway-engine cab, their only weapons were a shovel—and a teapot...
By JULIAN NEALE

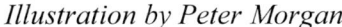

Illustration by Peter Morgan

Two thin bands of steel, a path through the bush country of Central Tanganyika. They are the tracks of the old Tanganyika Railway, linking the trim coastal city of Dar es Salaam with the twin termini of Kigoma and Mwanza, both busy harbour towns, although they are almost 800 miles from the sea.

Mwanza stands on the crocodile-infested shores of Lake Victoria, greatest of all African lakes, big enough to drown a kingdom. Kigoma lies on the banks of Lake Tanganyika, only a few miles from the spot where Stanley met Livingstone.

Those bands of steel that curve down towards the Indian Ocean are more than just railway lines. They are the nerves, veins and arteries of a dynamic African country approaching nationhood.

Huge tracts of Tanganyika are still without roads, air transport cannot fill the gap. It is the chugging goods and passenger trains that keep the economy of the country ticking over.

Take away the railway and Tanganyika might degenerate into the chaotic latter-day barbarism not far removed from conditions in the nearby Congo. Take away the top expatriate railwaymen and Tanganyika, now moving peacefully and smoothly towards independence might find its goal far harder to attain.

On one of those days, when the searing sun feels as though it could cook your brain, I stood in the swaying cab of a Tanganyika railway engine. Engine driver Dennis Cregan ran a thumb across his forehead and flicked the sweat expertly in the direction of the boiler where it spat and sizzled. "Hot enough?" he asked, with a grin.

"Well, I warned you we had no refrigeration facilities here for overheated journalists."

However, wild horses could not have dragged me back to my compartment, even though I stood sweating between the waves of heat beating outwards from the boiler, and the hot tongues of sunlight licking the back of my neck.

I had met Dennis at a wayside station a few miles back. To break the monotony of a long dry journey, I had wandered along the dusty, low platform as far as the engine.

He was standing in a minute patch of shade, smoking—a short, stocky man with an Irish brogue, a friendly grin and a beret perched at a jaunty angle on his head.

"It'll be a change for you to see the countryside from up here," he told me.

A change was what I needed. There is a dreary sameness to the interior of Tanganyika in the dry season, once the first novelty has worn off.

"I'm warning you, there won't be much excitement," Dennis apologised.

The train jerked out of the station, gathered speed, and rolled across the great emptiness of Tanganyika. As the sun's sizzling heat grew stronger, making man grow more irritable, Dennis reached for an ancient, battered teapot.

"Have some tea," he said. "It's drinking plenty of the stuff as keeps you cool."

He poured a thick, beery-looking brew into a chipped enamel cup and offered it to me. He then poured another mug for himself. "This is my lucky teapot and I wouldn't stir without it," he said.

Dennis Cregan has lived in Africa well over 10 years. He came to Tanganyika from his native Limerick, in Ireland, and was now driving Tanganyika's crack train—the one that shuttles the tourists, Asian shopkeepers, government officials and African marketswomen up and down the line between the scattered settlements.

Trackside Tombs

"Do you think we will see much game?" I asked.

Dennis shrugged. "Maybe. This is the dry season and animals keep close to the water holes. We don't reckon on seeing much game until the rains break in December. Of course, you might see the odd animal, generally in the evening, or early in the morning.

"How about a lion?"

Dennis shot me a quick glance. "Heaven forbid," he said, and pressed his lips into a tight line.

I looked at him in surprise. "What's the objection to seeing a lion? I reckon I'd get a terrible kick if I saw one at close range."

Dennis shook his head. "Some people might, but not me. That's another story, and not a very pretty one either."

He made no attempt to explain and pointedly changed the subject. "At out next stop, I'll show you something passengers don't usually see," he said. "When the train rolls along comfortably like this, you forget that someone had to put these lines here in the first place."

The train grated to a halt at a small station called Manyoni. It was typical of the tiny settlements in the Tanganyika interior.

Hordes of Africans—many of them vendors—clustered around the coaches. One wondered where they had all sprung from, when the country we had passed through seemed so sparsely inhabited.

Dennis dismissed the platform vendors with a wave of his hand.

"You can see these anywhere," he declared. "Come with me."

He led the way along a dusty path striking into the bush. A few yards ahead was an open place, and a few lonely graves, marked by grey-white headstones.

"This is what those steel rails mean," Dennis said. "They mean men's lives. These fellows here came out to Tanganyika, back in the days when Germany ran the place, to push this railway through to the lake.

"Man on the Line!"

"They were not heroes, just young fellows like you. I suppose they came for the adventure and the high pay. Who knows—maybe one of them came because he had a wild dream of building up a wild country. But they never went home again—the adventurer, or the greedy one, or the dreamer."

I walked over to the nearest grave, standing on a bare, sandy patch of ground a few yards away. Fading Gothic script identified the man as Heinrich Gastmeyer, of Lubeck. He had died in 1911, at the age of 23.

If he had not come to Africa, Heinrich Gastmeyer might still have been alive today. He had toiled under the imperial eagle of the Kaiser's Germany in an age of empires. He had died—perhaps of fever, or snake bite, perhaps killed by a lion—in this far-away, heathenish land.

Now this crumbling stone with the faded writing was his monument.

It was evening now. The east had turned slate grey as the sun set behind us, and soon we were enveloped by the velvety, caressing African night. The engine's searchlight cast its eye along the line, demolishing a great segment of the night.

"Watch the edges of the beam," Dennis said. "If there's any beasts out there, the reflection will show in their eyes. Like burning coals, they are, in the night."

He leant out and squinted ahead.

Suddenly, he let out a great yell, and leapt to the controls. Steel grated against steel and sparks flew, as the long train shuddered to a halt.

I leant out of my side of the cab and spotted a dark bundle across the tracks a few yards in front of us.

Dennis heaved himself out of the cab and with a curt "Follow me", walked quickly up the tracks.

Our shoes crunched against the gravel at the side of the line. The dark bundle resolved into an uneven shape, and then into a vaguely familiar form.

"It's a man!" I gasped, running forward.

Dennis leant over the still figure, and sniffed.

"Is he dead?" I asked.

He shook his head. "Dead drunk. Tight as a tick. He's been drinking some fearful bush brew laced with whisky, by the smell of it."

The two of us lifted the drunken African clear of the railway. He was surprisingly heavy.

"I suppose he'll wake up in the morning," Dennis grunted, as we laid him up against a rock a few yards away.

"What a stupid place to go walking when drunk!" I said.

"Nobody said he went walking."

"What do you mean?"

Dennis Cregan, the railwayman from faraway Limerick, who owns a lion-killing teapot

"I've heard some strange stories up and down the line," Dennis said with a wry grin. "If I'd not seen him, and the train had killed him, it wouldn't be the first time East African Railways have done the deed for murdering some bush African.

"Oh, I'm not saying this one was placed here deliberately, but it has happened before. It's easy to get one of these jonnies drunk and then carry him over to the line, dump him on the tracks, and wait for the next train to do your dirty work."

The train moved off again into the night.

"I always say, if it isn't the wild beasts, it's the Africans," Dennis said. "Sometimes I wonder which is the bigger headache for us poor drivers."

I smiled. "I should think most people would rather carry a dead buck on their conscience than a dead man."

Dennis lapsed into an uneasy silence. Thorny bushes and stunted trees hurried past, half-recognised in the dark.

"But it wasn't my fault," Dennis burst out suddenly. "And if it was, I paid for it in sheer terror."

"It sounds as if it must have been a pretty horrible experience—whatever it was," I said gently.

"It was horrible all right. I confess every time I go past the Bahi Bridge, I still feel my heart in my throat. The bridge isn't far from here, just a way down the line.

"I always knew that, when I passed by the bridge, I'd see some buck, or a few giraffes, or maybe a kudu. You can't miss a kudu: they're as big as cows, and about as stupid too.

"Those were the days when I was still driving goods trains with their little 26-ton locos. That's a lot smaller than this 80-ton giant we're in now. One afternoon, as I came near the bridge, I felt something was wrong. Nothing specific, you understand, but the nearer I came to the bridge, the more uneasy I felt."

Ominous Absence

"Have you ever walked into a house, and sensed something is amiss, even though ever stick of furniture, every ornament, is in the right place? That's the way I felt that afternoon. It worried and puzzled me as I took the train across the bridge, slow like. I'm not what you'd call a fanciful man, and I don't imagine things as a rule. Then, just before I reached the other side of the bridge, I realised what was the matter.

"I hadn't seen a solitary animal, not as much as a single buck, and this in an area crawling with game, like fleas on a dog. From outside, I could feel a silence pressing inwards on me. It seemed to me that, if I stopped the train, I would find that even the insects had ceased their humming and rustling.

"At that moment, I had a funny impulse to stop the train right there to see if I was right. I kept on going, of course, and it was probably just as well, because at that moment I spotted him, standing next to a bush, not 10 feet from the line. I gasped, and so did my fireman. Out there was a lion, and what a lion! In all my years here, I have never seen a finer specimen. He was standing there with his head thrust forward, as proud and disdainful as an emperor, and as still as a stuffed creature in a museum.

"I just stared at him open-mouthed. The lion is a funny creature. He doesn't usually hang around near railway lines, like a buck. But this one stood there fierce and strong, watching me go by in my engine cab, staring right at me.

"I'll swear that, as I went past, he winked at me, as though to say, 'Sure enough, Dennis Cregan, you and I are going to become better acquainted one of these fine days!' All I know is that I wanted to get out of that spot as fast as my engine would take me. As for my fireman, I'll swear he turned so pale you would have taken him for an albino.

"A few hours later, we were in Morogoro, which was the end of the line as far as I was concerned. Next day, I was on my way up the line again. Before I pulled out, I had a queer feeling of anticipation, like I knew this was a big day for all of us—the lion included.

"When I left Morogoro, late that afternoon, I could see a storm was building up, with great billowing clouds. By the time I was near the Bahi Bridge, it was dark, and the sky was growling with thunder."

Vision by Lightning

"Maybe it was just the thunder, and the electric feeling of approaching rain, but I felt myself beginning to sweat, and the hair at the back of my neck was prickling. All at once, I knew I had to come here at this moment, because something was destined to happen—something beyond my power to stop.

"I tried to take a firm grip on myself. One part of my mind told me I was acting childish—but the other, stronger part took possession of me, until I felt I was not so much a human being as a character in a film, forced to act according to the script.

"I suppose I was a few hundred yards from the bridge, when there was an unholy jagged flash of lightening, a roar of thunder, and the rain came down like some huge waterfall. I froze. In that lightening flash, I'd seen something that clung to my vision even after it was dark again. That lion was there again, as I knew he would be. Only this time he was standing right on the railway tracks facing the train, with his head thrust forward as though he expected us to stop at his command. Now he was caught in the searchlight, and we were getting closer every second.

"You ask any game expert, and he'll tell you that in 99 cases out of a 100, a beast on the tracks will run from an approaching train. Besides, it was pouring with rain, and lions are like your domestic cats—they'll slink away under cover as soon as they feel water on their skin. But this lion was different. He stood there, terrible in the storm, snarling defiance at us to do our worst.

"At least that's what it seemed at the time, because things were happening so quickly now that there wasn't time to work everything out logically. I remember thinking 'he'll surely leap off the tracks before we reach him.' And then, too late, I realised that he couldn't leap off, even if he'd wanted to. In those final seconds, I saw why the lion was roaring at us, instead of sheltering in the bush where he belonged.

"One of his paws was caught in the points, and he was trapped—forced to stand there whilst 26 tons of steel came at him, spitting fire and black smoke, and with a great single eye to blind him as we came in for the kill.

"In that moment, before the impact, I cursed myself for being a fanciful fool, and dreaming wild dreams when I might have stopped the train; but even that would have made no difference. We were unarmed. How could an engine driver and an African fireman have freed a huge, snarling lion from the railway line in the middle of the Tanganyika bush, with nothing to use as a weapon?

"He was 10 yards away now—five yards—then we hit him. There was a thump, and a howl, a thud behind me and then another howl—only this time it was my fireman, crying like a baby."

"He's Dead!"

"'Bwana,' he screamed. 'Bwana. Simba…' And then he howled again like a banshee. I twisted around to see what was wrong. I saw alright—but I wish I hadn't, because I have had to relive that moment a thousand times since then. When I turned around, I looked into the face of that lion, not 10 feet behind me. 'The devil,' I thought, 'it's a dream for sure, and when I wake up in a few minutes, I'll be safe in bed back in Morogoro.' But it was no dream. And just to remind me, my fireman let out another yell like an engine whistle.

"To this day, I don't know how it happened exactly. Perhaps when we hit that lion, we were going faster than I realised. Perhaps I'd picked up speed unconsciously, what with the tension and excitement. Maybe—well, who knows—maybe the beast made a frantic effort, and leapt free a split second before we reached him, so that we caught him on the spring. But whatever the cause, the force had thrown his body clear over the locomotive, and into the coal tender.

"There he was now, with his leg horribly gashed and looking as dead as mutton. But I knew, somehow, he wasn't dead—and again this awful, dull fear was upon me—the feeling that somehow I was watching the climax of a show over which I had no control.

"We were across the bridge by now, and chugging up the gradient on the other side. I knew it was going to be now or never. 'Come help me push him off,' I told my fireman. 'We can do it if we work together. He won't hurt you. He's dead—finished. Come on now.'

"But my fireman just rolled his eyes at me, dumb-like, and moaned—the kind of noise kids make when they play at being ghosts. 'Come and help me, curse you!' I shouted.

"It made no difference. That boy was mesmerised with the sheer horror of it all. I don't think he could have moved if the devil himself had appeared in front of him. I climbed up on to the tender in the blinding rain and made a movement towards the poor beast. I knew already I couldn't budge the animal myself. It must have weighed the best part of half a ton, and no man on earth could have done it without help."

Bared Fangs

"But there was no need for me to try. At that moment, the lion opened one eye and looked right at me. It was an eye full of pain, and fright, and sheer animal hate. Suddenly, the rain beating down seemed to be scalding me. I slithered backwards off the coal into the cab, quivering life a leaf.

"The lion lifted his great maned head a fraction of an inch and rolled back his lips to show his fangs. There was fight left in him, you could see that, though he must have been half dead with pain, and what was left of his life was oozing away through the gashes in his body. He snarled—a little inward sound like a pig grunting—and his front paw jabbed out at us. The movement dislodged a piece of coal, and for a moment I thought he might start a little avalanche and sweep himself clear overboard. But no such luck.

"There was another flash of lightning and a great clap of

thunder. It seemed to frighten the beast, because he twisted his head in the other direction and snarled again. Then he leant over and tried to lick one of his wounds. The lion gave a great roar of pain, and those eyes were full of hate again.

"I felt as though the last moments of my life were slipping away. Either he would bleed to death, or I would die. It was as simple as that. And then I saw it, just a foot or two from my fireman. 'The shovel!' I shouted. 'The shovel! Hit him with the shovel.'

"The boy made no move, so I threw myself over to grab it. It was no act of bravery, I can assure you—just the thought that a shovel could be used as a weapon, even though it might be a poor one to fight off a jungle killer.

"But I never got to that shovel, because my fireman got there first. Seeing me move broke the spell and he came back to life again.

"Maybe it was that last desperation man, the animal, feels when he is in a corner and death looks him in the face. Maybe it was some dim tribal memory of the days when his kinfolk used to hunt with spears to prove their manhood. Maybe it was just the fearful sight of that wounded beast poised to make its last spring.

"All I know is that my African fireman scooped up the iron shovel and hurled himself at the snarling creature. There was a horrible sound as the animal clawed at the metal, and for one moment I thought we were both goners. But the boy came up again with the shovel held in front of him, half a shield and half a spear.

"The lion shot his claws out again, and the shovel went spinning to the floor. The fireman gave a howl of terror, and I groped blindly for something—anything—to use as a weapon.

"My hand connected with my old teapot, the one I always carry, and before I realised what I was doing I had hurled it at the beast. It hit him on his side—not enough to hurt him, of course, but it gave the fireman a free moment to recover the shovel. I heard a thwack as the shovel connected, and then the rattle of falling coal."

Mascot of the Loco

"The blow had caught the lion off-balance; the swaying of the tender did the rest. I turned around just in time to see him slipping away, down the little mountain of coal, and over the edge. His eyes were glazed.

"I think he was dead before he hit the ground. I hope so. While it lasted it was a matter of our lives of his—but I wouldn't have wished any extra suffering on him."

Dennis Cregan paused and surveyed the track curving away in the beam of our searchlight. I could almost feel the wild memories receding in his mind.

"Have a cup of tea?" he said, reaching out automatically for his battered old teapot. "Yes, this is the same one. Now you know why I'd never stir out of the depot without this hanging in my cab. It's not every engine driver who has a lion-killing teapot as a travelling companion…"

From: The **Wide World** Magazine—August 1961, pages 80-85 and 115.

Despite exhaustive research, the contact details of the copyright holder could not be ascertained.

It was all guff, of course. A figment of Dennis's vivid imagination and his Irish blarney, for who on earth would lay points on a bridge in the middle of a section, and miles from anywhere? Besides, there's another reason that I know the story to be hokum: for when I relieved Dennis, all those months ago at that hot and dusty Dodoma changeover point, and he mentioned having had an author on the footplate, he finished by saying "…and I haven't half spun him a yarn!"

Chapter 21
A Non-Fictional Encounter with a Lion

And yet for all the whimsy of Dennis' story, a few years later I had an encounter with a lion eerily similar, and equally fraught with danger (and, incidentally, one which is true). At that time, I had for a fireman a locally born European, Alistair Christie. Having been raised by an ayah (an African children's nurse), like many such European children it might truthfully be said that Swahili was his first language. Together we were working a 114 Down Goods (the number 114 assigned for traffic purposes), departing Kigoma at 23:30.

This incident occurred at Luiche, the first station out of Kigoma, on the edge of a large banana plantation, and where it was usual for the guardsvan to be loaded with a large consignment of bananas. With a wait and a long night ahead, I told Alistair to shut the engine down, and with only the gentle hum from the electric generator, I settled down for a doze.

Not long after, Alistair roused me with a warning: "There's a lion walking down the line towards us," he reported. Looking through my weatherglass, I could see at the extremity of the headlamp beam an animal walking between the rails and heading in our direction. Some old Tanganyika veterans once told me lion's eyes, at night, glared red, and this creature's eyes showed a prominent green.

"No, Alistair," I sniffed, being a bit put out at being woken, "it's an old fisi (an old hyena)." And thus, having a wealth of non-experience and having delivered my considered opinion, I settled down once again.

With a "No, it's a lion", Alistair once again roused me. Rather sleepily and reluctantly, I gazed down the beam of the headlamp to be quickly jolted awake. Walking towards us, not 100 yards ahead, down the centre of the track, came a fully grown male lion with, I have no doubt, an empty belly. I sat watching it, expecting it to slope off into the bush at any moment and disappear. Instead, it stepped rather daintily over the nearside line and along the depth of the granite ballast which followed the line of the railway. Unperturbed by the size of the engine and its gentle hum, the lion loped alongside the engine, its lithe toned body lit fully by the inspection lights beneath the engine's running plates.

By now, I was increasingly concerned, not only for the little group of men loading bananas in the dark at the rear of the train, but also for Alistair and myself. One sniff of human flesh and a hungry lion, following its nose, would be up on the footplate in a flash. What to do? My first thought as it passed was to let it have the full force of the blowdown—a force sufficient to kill it instantly. But what if the blowdown was set too high and missed it altogether? Or worse, merely caught it a glancing blow when the jet of steam and boiling water might only serve to send the lion into a paroxysm of rage and fury. I withdrew my hand which was reaching for the blowdown lever, and peeping over the side of the cab, watched the lion disappear in the darkness alongside the train.

Then, filling me with anxiety and concern, was how to warn those at the back of the train? Was the lion looking for an easy kill? I thought if I moved the train forwards a little, it might alert them; but also, it might injure someone. Then I hit upon an idea I thought more telling—why not sound the whistle in a number of short, sharp and urgent blasts. Reaching up for the big whistle, with its deep melodious chime, I gave a series of quick blasts mingling with longer chimes.

Man, I felt, could do no more, and I resumed my wait. Shortly thereafter, the stationmaster arrived on the station side of the train, asking why I was whistling. After explaining that a lion was on the loose, somewhere on the opposite side of the train, he let out a wail of fear and despair and hurriedly departed. He did, however, return later bearing the Line Clear for the section ahead, but now escorted by the loading crew banging drums and tins and carrying burning torches.

A few months later, my fireman Alistair had a narrow escape from lions—one which, for a quirk of timing, would surely have cost him his life. We arrived at midday at Tura station's Down signal, which was unusually in the 'on' position. The signal was unusual for another reason, it being the only semaphore signal along this section of the Central Railway. The reason for this solitary signal, set far out in the bush, can only be a matter of conjecture, but it is reasonable to assume that on the former German Mittellandbahn, each station would be equipped with a semaphore signal. It is well documented as a matter of history that during the First World War that the Feldkompanien of the

Schutztruppe, the German defence force, retreated along the railway destroying as much equipment as possible, including sabotaging locomotives, blowing bridges and culverts, and destroying rolling stock. But for whatever reasons, perhaps hard-pressed by enemy forces, this solitary signal, though now of little use in the scheme of things, managed to survive.

I drew up to the signal, stopped and blew my whistle, and waited for the stationmaster to lower it. An amendment to the EAR General Rules, 1953, stated: 'Should a train be detained at a home signal, or stopboard, for more than 15 minutes, a driver must send his fireman to remind the stationmaster the train is waiting at the signal or stopboard. In addition, a driver must sound his whistle in accordance with rule 231, immediately his train comes to a stand'. I'd whistled up, and was on the point of sending Alistair to the station, when I became aware of a female lion standing quietly within the shelter of the bush. After observing the open stretch of railway, she stepped out, followed by a male lion and two cubs—just in time to catch Alistair if he had made his way to the station. His life hung by a few seconds one way or the other, an incident so close I never let on to him.

On a number of occasions, the shades of Jonah, the unfortunate, seemed to have followed me from Botanic Gardens to the wastes of Tanganyika. Whilst climbing Kazuramimba Bank on a left-hand curve, with my view obstructed by the boiler, I came upon a little group of three men standing on the embankment, who I immediately took to be track workers. What alerted me was that all three were bent forward, looking intently at the line, to the extent that I felt that something must be amiss. This was not the best place to stop, and because the three were well back and made no indication of any imminent danger, I left the regulator open, but acting on impulse crossed over to the fireman's side to look out. As I did so, there came a mighty crash and the engine bucked and heaved. Convinced the engine must have derailed, and to the accompaniment of more grinding and crashes, I hastened to shut the regulator and apply the brakes.

Dashing back to the fireman's side, I looked down to discover the extent of the derailment. What met my eyes filled me with horror. Beneath the rear tender wheels, in a tangled heap, lay the broken remains of a platelayer's trolley. Whilst this was serious enough, what made my blood run cold was that I could see within the wreckage lumps of torn and bloody flesh and shattered bone. Shocked that I had killed, however inadvertently, some of a platelaying gang, I jumped down to examine the carnage.

The wreckage lay in a pitiful heap, and steeling myself, I approached it with some trepidation. Peering down into the bloodied mass of twisted steel and broken boards I saw… fur and antlers! Instead of mangled human beings, it was the remains of a large antelope. After heaving a massive sigh of relief, I, together with the trolley crew, set about clearing the wreckage, and when completed I examined the engine for damage. There was none, apart from a few scratches to the wheel paintwork. I dropped back to a straight stretch of track, with the delicate task of getting the heavy train on the move again.

What the final outcome was, I do not know. I made out an accident report and thereafter heard no more. But it was clear that the trolley was occupying the line without the permission of the stationmaster controlling that section. If so, he would have issued me with a Warning Order, alerting me to a trolley on the line. One can only assume the dead antelope had been discovered by the platelaying gang, probably hit by ourselves on the way up, overnight, and not wishing to lose an unaccustomed but welcome source of protein to lions and vultures they, without permission, had launched a trolley to retrieve the prize and bring it in.

Caught unawares and heavily loaded, the linesmen would have had no time to unload the trolley and lift it out of the way. On the other hand, it may have got a bit out of control on the 1 in 50 down grade, which raises a moot point: did I run into the trolley or did the trolley run in to me? What remains a mystery was why the trolley crew made no attempt to warn me of the imminent collision. It may have been the African's fatalistic attitude to such events. It was "Shauri Mungu" (the will of God), and that's all there was to it.

Unbelievably, the same Shauri Mungu occurred again the very next trip, with the same Down train, at nearly the same spot, when I almost cleaned up another trolley. I had just cleared a deep curved cutting and reached a length of straight track when unexpectedly (I had received no Warning Order), not a hundred yards ahead I perceived a trolley gang frantically throwing assorted tools and equipment off a push trolley. This time, however, they had time to lift the trolley off the track, allowing me to sweep by with a disapproving shake of my head.

The macabre spirit of Jonah continued to haunt me. One night I struck a body on the line. Was it already dead? The police who had the unpleasant task of retrieving the mangled remains seemed to think so. Sometime later, I found myself summoned to give evidence at a trial of three Africans, two men and a woman, accused of murder.

On another and more dramatic occasion, whilst working the overnight Mail from Tabora to Kigoma, I became involved in a serious chain of events at Urambo station. The Mail, a prestige train, was expected to run to precise times, and my first intimation that something was amiss was when the Line Clear failed to arrive. After waiting for several minutes, I left the engine to make enquiries, to be told by the stationmaster that one of the passengers, a European child, was seriously ill. I was directed to the compartment, a coupe, occupied by a Belgian family travelling via Kigoma to the Congo on one of the lake steamers, and there I found a distraught mother and father with a boy of about eight lapsing in and out of consciousness. He had found a packet of antimalarial tablets and, thinking they were sweets, had taken an overdose.

It was obvious that without medical attention, the boy would die, but what to do? The nearest hospital, at Tabora, was 56 miles back down the line. In view of the child's condition, it seemed to me the only course of action was to uncouple the engine, load the family onto the footplate, and make a fast run back to Tabora. On the face of it, it seemed a hopeless proposition. Tabora was two hours nine minutes running time from Urambo, and if I took a few risks with the speed, I could only shave a few minutes off here and there. But it seemed my only course of action, and informing the stationmaster of my intentions, I asked him to arrange a path by sending an urgent telegraph to all stations, warning them to give me a clear run.

Whilst I was making arrangements to uncouple and run round the train, I remembered a small Indian duka located some 200 yards from the station. At one time Urambo had been one of the main centres for the then British government's naïve groundnut scheme, a scatter-brained plan to grow millions of tons of groundnuts in some of the most desolate and arid parts of Tanganyika. Leaving behind a scattering of hardy expatriate tobacco farmers, after the scheme's failure, an enterprising Indian had set up shop there to serve their needs. I knew he owned a car, and though the road through to Tabora was the usual dirt road he could, if willing, cut my best time by half.

It was now about 23:00 and pitch dark as I groped my unsteady way along the unfamiliar road between the station and the duka which, as expected at that late time of night, I found bolted and barred and in total darkness. Shuffling around its thick whitewashed adobe walls I found the entrance door, and hoping my English accent might allay the duka-wallah's natural fears I hammered on the door shouting "I come seeking help!" Rudely woken, here I give him full credit, for without hesitation, he agreed to rush the family to the hospital. By the time I'd returned to the coupe, he had arrived at the station. On my part, all that remained for me to do was to help the family to the car and wish them well. Except for one thing: on my return to Tabora, in the little time between trips, I had to sit down and write a long and detailed train-delay report. As for the little Belgian boy, the centre of this drama, I'm happy to say that as far as I am aware he made a full recovery.

And so it went on, one thing after another, with the presence of Jonah ever near. Twice a year, to accommodate European children returning to boarding school, and the teachers, always women, escorting them, a further first class coach was added to the Mail Train. At 01:30 I arrived at Kidete station, on the final leg of the Morogoro run. The engine wheels had hardly stopped turning when one of the teachers came running up. "Oh Mr Blackburn," she wailed (I've no idea how she knew my name), "there's been a terrible accident! One of the boys has fallen out of the train somewhere along the line."

On hearing this, I feared the worst. This section, on a falling gradient of 1 in 100, was straight more or less throughout its length, and relying on Mr Krupp's splendid track I'd fairly zipped along. There was really only one course of action for me to take—uncouple the engine, and after being given the Line Clear for that particular section, return and search along the line to find a badly injured child, or more likely, recover a body. Then, as I was making arrangements with the stationmaster, all of which took time, to everyone's intense relief and delight the little boy came marching stoutly into the station. It transpired that, half asleep, and wanting to visit the lavatory, he'd taken the wrong turning, opened the wrong door, and stepped out into thin air.

Picking himself up, by some miracle uninjured (he must have been made of India rubber), he watched the train rapidly disappearing into the night. But, nothing daunted, though he admitted he was afraid of meeting one of Tanganyika's more carnivorous animals, he set off after the train. The end result: another long and lengthy train-delay report.

By now the former triumvirate, the Unholy Trinity, had long been dispersed: Wright, the corrupt and unpleasant shedmaster, dismissed on the spot with loss of all privileges; Snellings the locomotive inspector, promoted to become Principal of the Locomotive Training School, Nairobi; and Fearless Frank Kent, my former adversary, on his way up by way of Works Manager Dar es Salaam. Happily, this meant things were running more smoothly, with them being replaced by more understanding officers and a more amiable DMPS, as follows: Ralph Frazer, ex-LNER, as shedmaster, J.E. Fuller, mechanical engineer, as DMPS, and a locomotive inspector whose name now escapes me. It was just as well for me and my service record that these new officers had a more understanding attitude, the reason being that one night I committed the cardinal sin of setting off without the Line Clear authorisation, an error compounded by confusion, lack of sleep, general exhaustion, and a mix-up between the stationmaster and myself, and by some strange quirk of fate, occurring once again at Kidete station.

Arriving in the early hours my fireman, an African (now that Alistair Cristy had been posted to Nairobi to take up driving duties), had some bearing on events. The stationmaster turned me into the loop line to await the arrival of an Up train. Switching off my headlamp, so as not to blind the incoming driver, I settled down for a few minutes' peace and quiet, before being roused by the sound of the approaching train. In the time available between its arrival and departure I decided to top up a few of 3012's more prominent and easy-to-get-at oil boxes.

Returning from the engine's blind side, following the departure of the Up train, I was just in time to catch the stationmaster walking away from the engine and back to his office, having to all intents and purposes delivered the Line Clear. However, to make certain, I called out to him, "Line Clear ready?"

His answer, "Yes", came clear and definite, and not wishing to delay the train, I could see the guard's 'Ready' signal, and confident the Line Clear had been delivered I climbed into the cab and, after whistling up, opened the regulator. Then, expecting it to be in his possession, I turned to the fireman and asked, "Line Clear, wapi?" (Where's the Line Clear?)

The reply was devastating: "Hakuna hapi (It's not here)," he answered. I was already moving out of the loop line at that point, and I at once snapped the regulator shut and made a full application of the brake. It was too late, the points were still laid for the Up train entering the station, and on departing the loop, with a crash I split the points wide open.

I was clearly at fault, but there may have been a subtle clash of language at work here. The stationmaster was African, and though proficient in English, his interpretation of the word "Ready" may have been different to mine, and so what follows is pure supposition. Can it be that, after obtaining permission to proceed from the station in advance, but before setting the points for me to leave the loop, the stationmaster had already made out the Line Clear ticket, leaving it on his desk, and as he saw it, now ready? Thereafter confusion reigned. We shall never know why, on a pitch dark night, the stationmaster left his office and walked, for no apparent reason, and for some distance, to the engine. This was the nub of the whole sorry affair—a possible explanation and one not unknown: perhaps overnight the stationmaster had indulged a little too freely in pombe, the native beer, and decided to go 'walkabout'?

Here I should state that the penalties for Line Clear irregularities, as laid down in the East African Railways Motive Power Manual of 1962 were as follows:

A. For the first offence—Reduction in Salary;
B. For the second offence—Reduction in Grade for a specified period;
C. For the third offence—Dismissal.

Back at Tabora I was met by the Duty Shedman, an Indian who, with rolling eyes, informed me that I was required in the shedmaster's office "at once!" Entering I found both the shedmaster and the DMPS waiting. "What's all this about then?" the DMPS demanded. I covered myself to some extent by saying there had been a right mix up, implying that it was not altogether my fault. "Go on," I was told. Knowing much depended on my explanation (my future career, for instance), I glossed over the minor details whilst making sure I emphasised the more favourable elements. I left the office hoping my explanation might wash—and it seemed to have worked, when to my astonishment the penalties, which I have appended above, were quietly dropped.

As an aside, the fireman involved with me in this incident came from Dodoma, and on one occasion, on being granted a week's leave, he purchased return tickets from Tabora to Dodoma for himself and his wife. Starting work the following Monday morning, as we got underway he appeared to be ill, hardly able to hold his head up and lolling about in his seat. Concerned, I asked him if he was unwell. "Hapana bwana," he replied. "Nimechoka (No, I'm tired)."

That seemed a bit odd, given he'd just had a week's leave, so I spluttered, "What do you mean? How can you be choka when you've just had a week's leave?" Then the whole unhappy story came out.

Arriving at Dodoma, and for some reason I was never able to establish, both tickets were taken off him by the ticket collector—perhaps by mistake, or possibly for some nefarious purpose of his own. Either the unfortunate fireman's protestations fell on deaf ears, or he simply didn't question the decision, but immediately both he and his wife turned around, and began walking the 250 miles back along the railway, including crossing the lion-occupied Bahi Bridge. It took them a full week, arriving back in Tabora on the Monday morning, just in time for him to begin work. Whilst I felt for my fireman's plight, my sympathies lay chiefly with his wife—for tradition had it that she would be the one carrying the burden of their belongings on her head. And in that respect I still have nightmarish visions of her walking the first 70 miles, then toiling up Saranda Bank in the heat of the day with a large and heavy bundle, and with another 180 miles to go. If my fireman was tired, I hate to think what condition she was in when they eventually reached Tabora!

As for old Fuller, the DMPS, years later, having returned to the UK, our paths briefly crossed. After a chance encounter I had been asked to help the fledgling North Yorkshire Moors Railway, in the course of which I'd taken the railways newly acquired 0-8-0, the former North-Eastern Railways T2, on a test run on the gradients between Grossmont and Goathland. I found the fireman, who to spare his blushes remains nameless, a little out of his depth, and we arrived at Goathland with the engine rather out of breath. As I stopped at the station, out of the shadows stepped my old boss. With many years of railway experience he immediately recognised that we were a bit short of steam. We shook hands and with a wink and a smile he revived old memories: "What's this, Blackburn? Short of steam! You're dismissed! Dismissed with loss of all privileges!"

However, back to the Central Railway, and its capacity to surprise and at times discomfort. One hot and sticky morning, whilst working an Up goods, I arrived at Tura, a station 84 miles and five stops from Tabora. Stopping at the fouling mark I awaited the Line Clear. Looking back down the train I became aware of some unusual activity at the far end of the station, but in the circumstances took little notice.

Eventually, the stationmaster arrived bringing, not the expected Line Clear, but an unwelcome demand. "There's a body which has to be conveyed to Tabora," he informed me, "and as there's nowhere else on the train, we're bringing it here to be carried in the engine cab."

In short order, I told him, "No, you're not. Put it in the guard's van. I'm not having it in my cab."

He answered, "But there's no room in the guard's van, it's full of parcels and merchandise." I was aware that if a body had to be moved to Tabora, instead of being buried locally and quickly, some sort of mischief was afoot.

Remembering my earlier encounter with a decaying body at Urambo, in the Kigoma section, I asked, "Does it smell? Is it decomposing?"

"No," replied the stationmaster.

Thinking about the dilemma I faced, I came up with a solution. "Bring the body up, and place it on the flat plate across the front and below the smokebox. We'll get it to Tabora that way." Shortly thereafter, a little group of men arrived carrying the body, as was usual, on a native bed—a rough frame held together by strips of rawhide, and supported on four crudely shaped legs. The body, wrapped in banana leaves, secured by lengths of string-like fibres, was lifted off the bed, and under my supervision, laid lengthways across the flat plate forming part of the locomotive below the smokebox door.

Before reaching Tabora, I had a further four stops: Malongwi, Nyahua, Igalula and Itulu. At each station I went to the front of 3012 to make sure the body was still safe and secure, and at each of them, the sight of a dead body laid across the front of the engine aroused little if any interest, as, with a shrug of the shoulder, for the dead are dead, and it is "Shauri Mungu" (the will of God). If I'd arrived into Paragon Station in the Hull with a dead body on the front of the engine, I think it would have been a different matter, but in Africa the populace were a tad more philosophical about such things. On reaching Tabora, I was met by African police officers who, thankfully, took charge of the body.

After Dennis left on home leave, his place was taken by an Indian driver, Ujagar Singh, whilst about the same time, Brian Duffel, who became a lifelong friend, and about whom I have more to say later, was transferred from Morogoro to Tabora. I had a lot of time for Ujagar because not only was he a first class engineman, but his down-to-earth ways struck a chord with me. I well remember in our early days, he was approached by Wright, the unsavoury shedmaster, who ignoring my presence said to Ujagar, "It's Christmas, Singh"—the inference being clearly understood, and one the majority of Ujagar's compatriots would have acted upon, but not Ujagar.

Throwing away any chance of grade promotion under Wright, he replied, "Yes, Mr Wright, it is Christmas, but it's your Christmas, not mine."

Against all the canons and virtues of his religious beliefs, Ujagar smoked cigarettes, and not only any old gasper, but an extremely strong cigarette made from a brand of black Rhodesian tobacco, which for its lung-tearing effects had earned them the nickname of 'kali', the Swahili for 'sharp' or 'keen'. Ujagar's father was the Tabora stationmaster, an eminent position, and when convenient he would come along to see his son off.

If Ujagar and I were in the caboose together, and I saw his father approaching, I would warn him, "Look out, Ujagar, your father's coming!" For although Ujagar was in his mid-30s, married with children, he still feared his father's tongue. At that Ujagar would throw away his kali, and adopting an air or innocence, greet his father. Whilst I, to disguise the smell of Ujagar's illicit cigarette, would puff away on my own *Crown Bird* smokes.

Unusually, for one of his religion, he was happy to take off his turban in my presence and comb out his beard and hair, sometimes saying "Bloody turban, it puts years on me!" We only once ran into a spot of bother, which occurred whilst working an Up goods train-cum-water-train, a train supplying Permanent Way railway gang camps along the railway between Tabora and Kigoma. I had worked out as far as Malagarasi, our changeover station, where I replenished the tender and water tanker bogie (WTB) marshalled next to the engine, during which time Ujagar came up to relieve me.

After crossing Malagarasi swamp the line swung northward, clearing a range of low, sun-bleached and barren hills, before resuming its westward alignment. On breasting the summit, Ujagar would have wound his engine up into a shorter cutoff and eased up on the regulator, as he followed a three-mile length of straight and level track, which he was covering at a steady 30 mph.

Taking my ease in the caboose, I was alerted by a sudden and vicious jolt, followed by an immediate application of the brakes. For some unexplained reason the WTB had jumped the rails. As soon as the train came to a halt I left the caboose and went up not only to offer help, but to take over. This statement is no way a reflection on Ujagar's ability to cope, but rather to carry out an instruction which declared: 'In the event of an accident the senior person on the scene must take charge'. Being several grades higher than Ujagar, this clearly applied to me. Also, if things went wrong thereafter, there was someone to blame.

I was aware that the next following train was the Mail Train, and importantly, was in direct connection with the lake steamer Liemba, on its twice-monthly passage south to Mpulungu on the southern extremity of Lake Tanganyika. To give the Mail Train and its passengers an uninterrupted run, my first consideration was to clear the line as soon as possible, which at this point ran on an embankment 15 to 20 feet high. To that end I decided to roll the WTB down the embankment after draining it of water—a course of action that would eventually require the steam crane and its accompanying breakdown train and crew to travel the 697 miles from Dar es Salaam before the WTB could be retrieved. Because of the cost, something the senior engineers in Dar es Salaam might not altogether agree with.

About half a mile from the point of derailment, alongside the railway, in an isolated windswept position stood another of those Permanent Way camps, and whilst the WTB was being drained I sent one of the firemen to raise the alarm and bring as much help as possible. In the meantime, with the WTB drained and empty, it was drawn forwards a few yards, before being uncoupled from the engine, ready for the back breaking toil of winching it to the edge of the embankment, before tipping it over and letting it roll clear of the railway. This proved much easier than I at first thought, the ululating gang men, armed with crowbars and led by a singer with a strong, clear bass voice, slowly worked the WTB to the edge of the embankment and with the ululations rising to a crescendo, and with a final heave, sent it crashing down in a cloud of dust.

With no apparent reason for the derailment, the Engineering Department having said Mr Krupp's track was in perfect condition, which was true, suspicion of speeding fell on the driver, Ujagar. Consequently, I was called in to the shedmaster's office and questioned, first about my decision to tip the WTB down the embankment, and secondly about Ujagar's alleged speeding. I was able to convince Ralph Frazer, the then shedmaster, there had been no speeding, and in Ujagar he had a careful and reliable driver and a first class engineman. And on Ujagar's behalf, even though it was stretching the truth a little, I made the point that between the climb out of Malagarasi swamp and the derailment, there was insufficient length of level track to whip up excessive speed.

By now, although it still reared its head at times, the railways rigid, monolithic order had given way to a more benign rule. To the relief of drivers the demand for long and detailed reports, often about trivia, had been dropped, and enquiries into minor offences and incidents, apropos Ujagar Singh's derailment, were conducted at district level. This may have been, although still far off, the inevitability of the coming independence, a process which signalled the end of recruiting British drivers, and the advancement of Africans to driver status, many of them illiterate, and unable to write reports in Swahili, never mind in English.

With the 30 Class proving masters of their work, and mechanically sound in all respects, I began, against all regulations, to tweak 3012 with a few of my own gimmicks. Forming part of the casting, the four oil reservoirs to the valve spindle guides, whilst fully effective, detracted from the appearance of that part of the engine. Contracting one of the Erecting Shop machinists, he turned out, from solid brass bar, four handsome screw-capped oil cups which fitted the existing threads and in doing so enhanced the appearance of an already striking engine no end.

From somewhere I acquired an old-fashioned cylinder ball lubricator which I attached to the steam brake by unscrewing its top nut. It was a superfluous addition, but it added a little more to the footplate's well-polished fittings. Filled with cylinder oil, its delivery controlled by a fine-needle valve and adjusting wheel, it ensured instant action of the brake. After a while a further idea crossed my mind. There was always a plentiful supply of powdered graphite to be had. It was used to dry-lubricate the slides of points and crossings or anywhere else subject to the effects of dust and dirt on oil. Thinking about its lubricating properties I came up with the idea of mixing graphite and cylinder oil, and using it in the ball lubricator. The effect was so positive, I reasoned what's good for the goose is good for the gander, and set about ways of introducing my mixture into the engine's valves and pistons.

Having given up the idea of pouring it down the blast pipes, I turned to plugs in the steam or valve chests. Each steam chest had two plugs. A glance at the position of the connecting rods and big ends told me which steam port would be open to admission, and it was quick and easy for me to unscrew a plug, and just before departure time, with the cylinder drain valves shut, go round and administer a dose of my special 'emollient' to each steam chest.

The railway complex at Tabora stood on a level plateau from which the main line fell away in both the Up and Down directions. After receiving the proceed signal, the first gentle breath of steam spread the graphited emulsion throughout the steam chests and cylinders. In a short distance of leaving the goods yard, steam had to be shut off for the down grades when for the next three or four miles the engine ran steam-free, spreading the graphite all around the cylinders, steam chests and valves. Did it work? Yes, it did, splendidly! With further thought I toyed with the idea of mixing graphite with the oil in the mechanical lubricator, thereby ensuring a continuous supply of graphite to the valves and pistons throughout the journey. But I gave up on that idea, as I saw a danger from the graphite blocking the lubricator pumps and check valves, thereby depriving the valves and pistons of lubrication, and consequently causing considerable damage to the engine's front end—something I felt that neither Ralph Frazer nor the DMPS would approve of!

During the long hot hours in the caboose, when the monotonous drumming of its wheels on endless rail joints and the occasional attention of a tsetse fly failed to lull me to sleep, I cooked up a new idea. On my return to Tabora I visited its only hardware store, a small but well-stocked Indian-owned duka, from where I purchased two oil feeders, later, cutting their spouts down to make a tight fit within 3012's cylinder drainpipes. After filling each with my special tonic, and with the cylinder drain valves shut, just before departure from Tabora I inserted the oil cans into the pipes which drained each cylinder, the intention being to infuse each cylinder and piston rod with graphite. After leaving Tabora, and within a short distance, steam had to be shut off, as mentioned above. Running without steam, each stroke of the piston lifted the drain valves off their faces, drawing a little more of the preparation, which then, by way of four large-capacity bypass valves, was distributed around the piston valves and cylinders. Arriving at the first station some 20 miles from Tabora, it required only a few moments to retrieve the now empty oil can feeders. I don't know in the long run how much this treatment reduced wear on valve rings, valve liners, piston rings, cylinder bores and piston rods, but traces of graphite were still visible on the piston rods at Morogoro, after 400 miles and 20 hours of steaming.

In the meantime, moves were afoot. Brian Duffel and family had been transferred from Morogoro to Tabora, an event which has some bearing on this narrative. Ujagar Singh went on home leave to India, and on his return was posted to Dar es Salaam, working Garratt engines over the heavy grades between there and Morogoro. I lost my fireman, Alistair Christie, who had been posted to Nairobi to commence driving duties, and on his departure I shook his hand and wished him well in the future.

With Ujagar going on home leave, I not only lost a friend and companion, but I also said goodbye to a period when I ate well in the caboose, this being due to the fact that before each trip, Ujagar's wife prepared a tiffin (tin) of chicken curry, rice and chapattis. Arriving at Morogoro, I always felt it was my turn to replenish the larder for the return trip. Morogoro's main street was always resplendent in beds of roses, each carefully tended by two expatriate ladies, notable for their homemade straw hats. Morogoro also boasted a Greek-owned butcher's shop, from which I purchased stewing beef and kidneys. Taking advantage of the cool, well-watered slopes of the Uluguru Mountains, below which it nestled, Morogoro offered a plentiful supply of fresh vegetables, of which I purchased potatoes, onions, tomatoes, cauliflower and juicy red and green peppers, allowing Ujagar to prepare a splendid and mouth-watering curry, sufficient in bounty to last us both all the way home.

Eating the curry together, Ujagar would sometimes ask "Is it hot?", my usual reply being "No, it's just right," when, with a lifetime of curry experience, and just the right emphasis, he would answer "Ah, it is!" Whenever he relieved me on the engine, he never failed to remind me, in his gentle way, to "Take good rest!"

Ujagar's place was taken, not by John Luis, the Kenya-born white driver, but by John Stuart, an African of the Chagga tribe, from the foothills of Mount Kilimanjaro. Being Mission-educated, he spoke perfect English. On his upgrading to main line work, I was taken to one side by the shedmaster and in confidence told to look after him, as he was expected to, and indeed did, become the first African locomotive inspector.

For some reason, now lost in the mists of time, I began toying with the notion of experimentally changing 3012's plug trimmings in the big end and side rod bushes, with pins of some sort. Not something the 'higher-ups' would have condoned at all, of course! But I thought, my idea a good one, and so I proceeded. From one of the erecting shop mistris[44], an Indian overseer, I acquired a sufficiency of 4½ inch split pins, to carry out what might well prove a complete disaster. A disaster because I feared if too tight a fit, the pins would cut off the supply of oil to the crank pins, and if too slack, quickly empty the oil reservoirs, again denuding the bearings of oil. On that basis I moved with caution, choosing what I considered were the least stressed of all the crank pins, the trailing pair on the driver's side, which I could keep an eye on when in motion and perhaps 'sniff out' if it began to overheat.

A problem occurred when, instead of being a tight but sliding fit, the pins had to be hammered home with some force. I then examined them carefully, finding the two flat faces of the pins tight together, and with the pin itself tight

---

[44] Mistri being an Indian term for a master-craftsman, foreman or supervisor of manual workers.

in its housing there seemed no way it could deliver an adequate supply of oil to the bearing. But instinct indicated otherwise, and despite doubts I decided to give it a try. About 10 miles into the first section I stopped the train, climbed down, and examined the bearing. Finding no sign of it overheating I continued on to the first station, where I again examined the bearing, feeling round it carefully with my fingertips. Finding it cool, and encouraged by the experiment, over a period I slowly extended the use of split pins to all side rod and big end brasses. It never failed to astonish me how little oil was required to keep them cool, whatever the strain imposed upon them.

The Welsh loco inspector had also left by now. Unusually for one of his ilk, he'd always treated us drivers with consideration and respect, and was perfectly happy to join us for a drink and a chat on the veranda of the Railway Hotel. In his place, and full of his own importance came one Barber—a reject, I suspect, from Nairobi—who seemed determined to make his mark. If memory serves me right he didn't last long. I was perhaps unfortunate, for on his first look around the district he decided to couple his coach to the train I was working. The loco inspector's coach and its occupant, usually carried as an 'overload', was never a welcome addition to one's train. Mounted within the lounge part of the coach, an automatic speed recorder traced, on a wax roll, for later examination, the time and speed of the train for every inch of the way.

We met for the first time when, just before departure for Kigoma, he mounted the footplate. I nodded to him and said, "How do?", a greeting he chose to ignore. From then on, the remainder of the trip descended into something of a farce. Leaving Kigoma, with the engine still cold, Barber noticed a faint, almost imperceptible, wisp of steam from the right-hand valve spindle gland, and decided to make something of it, until I pointed out it was on the exhaust side, and as such of little or no importance. And in any case, as the front end heated up, it would take up and seal. My dismissal of his criticism seemed to upset him, and had later consequences. More to my way of thinking, 3012 had developed a barely audible tap in what I identified as the left leading coupled axle box. A little tap so indistinct that it only became evident when working flat out.

Approaching the climb through the sun-parched hills of Kazuramimba Bank, Barber found his voice: "Thrash it!" he yelped. "Thrash it! It doesn't feel anything, it's made of steel!"

Whilst loco inspectors wielded a great deal of authority, I'd now been on the go for a long time, which in itself brought a certain amount of say-so. "Calm down," I told him. "Everything's under control." With a gradient of 1 in 50, a full load of 488 tons, plus an inspection coach adding a further 16 tons, a hefty 504 tons, 3012 had to be worked close to its maximum to keep time. To lighten the mood a little, I asked Barber if he could identify the elusive knock, but he turned away without replying.

At Kazuramimba station, Barber left in a huff, to rejoin his coach, where he remained out of sight for the next 6 hours, by which time I'd reached Kaliwa, the junction for the Mpanda branch. There he detached his coach to await the next Mpanda train, before carrying out an inspection of the locomotive water and fuel installations at Mpanda. As he surfaced, he handed me a sealed envelope, with instructions to hand it to the shedmaster on my arrival at Tabora. And that was the last I saw of him for some time.

Arriving on-shed, I handed the envelope to Ralph Frazer, asking him if Barber had mentioned a knock in the left leading coupled box, to which he replied "No." Ralph opened the envelope and began to read. "Do you know what's in it?" he asked.

I answered, "No, it was sealed when I received it."

Ralph smiled. "He wants me to charge you with negligence and inattention to steam and water."

It was a charge too ridiculous for words, and I responded by saying, "The man's an idiot!" before making a further observation: "What does he think the fireman's paid for, to sit there like an ornament?" Ralph laughed, screwed the message and envelope into a ball, and threw them into the wastepaper basket.

As an interesting footnote to the axle box saga, I consulted my East African Railways Motive Power Manual for the axle box tolerances on the 30 Class, to find that they were a microscopic 15-thousanth of an inch. A figure so astonishing I checked to see if this was a misprint, but failed to find any amendment.

My encounter with Barber brings me to Brian Duffel, who you will remember had been transferred to Tabora. Brian had a wonderful gift of being able to conjure up amusing limericks to suit whatever occasion. Recounting Barber's charge of inattention to steam and water, Brian instantly came up with this concise beauty: "Do your job," he intoned. "Do your job as you should oughta, keep your eye on gauges, steam and water!"

As a follow-on, I recount a whimsical event involving Brian, his family and me; an event which throws light on an aspect of life in the former mandated territory of Tanganyika. About this time I was due for home leave, but in those days, before being allowed to re-enter the UK, I had to be in possession of valid inoculation certificates. My smallpox vaccination was about time-expired and had to be renewed, something I mentioned to Brian, who likewise was reaching the end of his present tour of duty. On those grounds it was decided that Brian, his wife, his two small children, and I, would be vaccinated together as a group. Under the hot sun the walk from the railway quarters to the hospital was long and tedious, but happily, midway into Tabora itself, was located a dispensary, presided over by an old-time African dresser who would cheerfully carry out any procedure asked of him. Approaching the dispensary, Brian's two little girls began to voice growing concerns, so to calm their fears, and show them there was nothing to be afraid of I elected to be vaccinated first, and bravely offered up my exposed arm to the dresser, who carefully sterilised his scratch knife. Then, before he vaccinated me, he just as carefully wiped the blade between his thumb and forefinger.

An accident at Tabora, as a result of an Indian driver entering the station yard at excessive speed. It was his first trip, and thereafter he was transferred to the Carriage and Waggon Department.

Not at all impressed, Brian made his excuses and left, with the intention of going on to the hospital with his wife and family, to be vaccinated under more hygienic conditions, whilst I left and returned home. Later, Brian popped round, and with his cockney humour to the fore, explained how things had gone from bad to worse. Arriving at the hospital dispensary he was met by another old dresser, a doppelganger of the first who, after sterilising his blade, began to vaccinate Brian. After sawing away at his arm without much success, the dresser decided his knife was blunt and required sharpening. Bending down he honed it on the dispensary doorstep, over which, I might add, many bare and callouses feet had passed. Satisfied that he had an edge the dresser tried it with his thumb, before vaccinating the family.

For once Brian was too lost for words to invent an appropriate ditty, but he did go on to wonder, gloomily, which one among us would, within the next few days, have the most pronounced and swollen arm from blood poisoning; a prediction which thankfully failed to meet his prognosis, as none of us developed anything more dreadful than a scab and an itch. Years later, whilst reminiscing, and in reference to me, he came up with another of his witticisms, largely lost, unfortunately, to the sands of time, but ending with a prophetic line: "…too many *Coca Cokes* and *Crown Bird* smokes, and now he's in the hospitali." (Swahili for hospital, of course.)

Chapter 22
Funny Business at the Shed

Only once did I cross swords with Ralph Frazer. It happened at a time when a series of unexplained and suspicious circumstances occurred at the shed. The first concerned a British driver, Bob Mackensie, recently transferred from Kenya, where, unlike Tanganyika, with its vacuum brake, the Westinghouse air brake reigned supreme—a difference that may have had some bearing on what followed. On Bob's first trip, and shortly after leaving Mabama, the first station on the 251-mile Tabora—Kigoma section, he suffered a complete engine failure.

Allow me to elucidate: from Tabora the line runs for its 24 miles on easy grades to Mabama. Although being nothing more than a block post and crossing station, Mabama had two distinguishing features. Firstly, it was the scene of a bitter and bloody battle during the First World War between advancing Belgian forces and the German Schutstruppe, intent on delaying the Belgians entering Tabora until most of its essential infrastructure had been destroyed and the German population evacuated down the line to Dodoma. Used as a blocking position and strong point, the station and its buildings were totally destroyed during the battle, thereafter, being rebuilt by the Belgians in a much more utilitarian style than that adopted by the Germans. The second remarkable feature was an extensive but much decayed Belgian war cemetery, facing the railway and located about 200 yards beyond the station limits. It was (and I presume still is) dominated by three large and imposing marble war memorials dedicated to the fallen.

On leaving Mabama the first two miles involve a pretty stiff gradient, meaning hard work for the engine of 63 Up Goods with its full load of 510 tons on 30 units. As Bob lifted the train up the grade, he noticed the needle of the engine's vacuum gauge gradually begin to fall, despite the boiler pressure gauge registering 198 psi. This fall continued despite Bob's efforts to overcome the deficiency by opening his large ejector steam valve. Finally, just short of the summit, its brakes hard on, the train ground to a halt.

Convinced the train had developed a pronounced leak somewhere in the braking system, Bob set about examining each vehicle, including the engine, with the intention of rectifying the problem, if possible. Unable to discover the fault, Bob had to send his fireman back to Mabama station to declare—for no obvious reason—his train a failure.

Back at Tabora, this set the cat among the pigeons, and because of the trouble and delay in recovering a failed train (which reflected deeply not only on the driver, but on the shed, the shedmaster, the locomotive inspector, and ultimately the DMPS), things there began to 'hum'. After being recovered back to Tabora a detailed examination of the train found its brakes in perfect working order and suspicion fell on the engine.

During testing of the locomotive's vacuum ejectors it was noticed that the boiler pressure gauge still stood at 198 psi, despite the fire having been shut down for several hours, during which time some fall of pressure would be expected. A faulty boiler pressure gauge was an unheard-of occurrence, and highly suspicious when only a few hours before the boiler had been examined by the shed's boilersmith, who must have found the gauge in perfect working order. Nevertheless, the gauge was removed and taken to the shedmaster's office to be stripped down and examined, whereupon it was found to have been tampered with, to the extent of having its pointer jammed at 198 psi, leaving both the driver and fireman believing that full boiler pressure was being maintained on the climb out of Mabama. The defective gauge had little effect on the easy alignments between Tabora and Mabama, but on the climb out of Mabama, with the locomotive at full stretch, a failure became inevitable.

But there was a sequel to this. Also, about this time I was rostered to work the 40 Down Goods leaving Tabora at 03:45. As I walked over to the shed 3012 was, as expected, standing silent in the warm tropical night, its fire shut down. Climbing aboard I opened the generator steam valve prior to switching on the engine's electric lights. A quick look around showed a full boiler and nearly 200 psi on the pressure gauge. Satisfied all was in order I went around the engine putting in trimmings and filling the oil cups. On my return I told my fireman to fire up, and turning to the oil manifold the fireman reported, "Blower kabisa! (The blower's broken!)" I examined the valve, finding the valve wheel and spindle broken off close to the gland in what appeared to be either an act of gross mistreatment, or deliberate sabotage.

Without a spare valve this was deemed a 'shed failure', which put the responsibility into the hands of the engine shed staff. However, my mind then began to turn to the many times I had, in perfect safety, run down grades with the damper closed, the fire shut down and the blower closed, something that could only be performed with an oil burning locomotive, even if this was against the rules. Why do such a thing? Well, simply because of the quiet that resulted. A favourite stretch of mine in which to do this, especially at night, was the 27-mile run down Kazuramimba Bank: winding through silent hills, with only the gentle hum of the generator and the soft click of the Delta truck on the rail joints to mark our passage, but with all the blaze of heaven to wonder at.

Despite the British administration of the railway coming to an end, if only slowly, the ethos of railway service still ran deep, and a failure on-shed, with its staff and extensive equipment, reflecting on the shedmaster and his ability to run the shed in an efficient manner. I weighed up the pros and cons of the situation, my mind following the topographical details of the 1,300-mile round trip, with the Central Railway's many and varied gradients and station stops, and I came to the conclusion that, with intelligent use of the damper and fire, the trip could be accomplished without a blower, and without damage to the boiler in any way. But before leaving the shed, and to cover myself, I made a succinct entry in 3012's repair book stating that I had discovered the defective blower before leaving the shed at 03:20 hours, and had it countersigned by the shed man.

I worked the first stage of the Morogoro trip, the 250-mile Tabora-Kigoma section, without a hitch, my African fireman, used to my ways, responding immediately to my calls for him to 'funga damper' ('close the damper'), 'funga moto' ('close the fire') and 'funga blower' ('close the blower'). On shed at Kigoma I was relieved by John Stuart, my African co-driver, who expressed concern at the lack of a blower. I explained in detail the art (for it could be called an art) of working a heavy train without that essential piece of equipment, emphasising the need to first close the damper before shutting off steam as a precaution against admitting cold air into the firebox and damaging the boiler. John was an intelligent man, and was quick to cotton on, but to make sure he understood the drill, I rode with him as far as the first station, reminding him that damage to the boiler would result in both of us seeking further employment! As expected, the trip passed without incident, with John and engine 3012 arriving back at Tabora after five days of continuous steaming with the boiler in perfect condition, its tubes steamtight and watertight. Thankfully this flagrant and deliberate flouting of the rules governing engine management, which carried a heavy penalty, seemed to have escaped the authority's attention altogether. Times had changed since the days of Fearless Frank Kent, the DMPS, Snellings the locomotive inspector, and renegade Shedmaster Wright. And nothing was made of the fact that I had ignored a 'Kremlin diktat', i.e., 1) oil burning engines must not be driven when the fire is not burning, and 2) failure to comply will lead to severe disciplinary action being taken against the person or persons involved.

Following these two incidents, a third event, just as unusual or suspicious (take your pick) occurred, when I was rostered to work a Saturday night Sunday morning goods, leaving Tabora at 00:30 hours. Climbing into 3012's cab I followed my usual routine of first switching on the cab lights and looking around, whereupon I found the pressure gauge showing only 90 psi. With the intention of raising steam, I further opened the firing valve a little more, before oiling all round. Returning, I was surprised to find the gauge still showing 90, rather than the expected 150-160 psi. Puzzled by this I rapped the face of the gauge sharply, but without response. Immediately I took hold of the gauge pressure pipe and to my dismay found it disconnected, together with the gauge's inside mechanism loose, whereby I found, with a bit of judicious juggling, that I could fix the pointer anywhere on the gauge. This gauge had been working perfectly whilst on safari a few hours earlier, and was now the second highly suspicious case of a pressure gauge becoming defective whilst on shed.

This time there were too many imponderables to go off lacking a vital piece of equipment, and with Bob Mackenzie's failure in mind, I reported it to the shed man, who was the equivalent of a running foreman on British railways, and asked him to arrange for a gauge to be taken off another engine to replace the defective one. Also, I informed him that, to save time, I was about to leave the shed and couple onto my train.

After half an hour, a fitter arrived and started to replace the defective gauge, and at about the same time Ralph Frazer, the shedmaster arrived, and climbed up into the cab. Shedmasters were on 24-hour call-out, and late on a Saturday night, perhaps with other things on his mind, including the looming engine failure, Ralph was in a bad temper. "What's going on?" he brusquely demanded.

"My pressure gauge has been tampered with," I replied. The impact of this seemed to have escaped him, for he came up with an astonishing reply for someone of his experience.

Looking at his watch, and with a threat in his voice, he demanded, "Can't you go without it?"

"No!" I informed him.

Ralph, becoming more and more agitated and ill-tempered, said I was being disruptive, upon which I told him to calm down. After some chitchat between us, in which I felt I held the moral high ground, Ralph suddenly came up with a threat: "I'll put you on a shunting engine for this," he warned.

It was ridiculous and I became sarcastic: "Well, that's alright, Ralph," I replied, "don't you know all steam locomotives are much the same? Anyway," I continued, "if you're going to put me shunting the goods yard, make it the day shift, as I like my nights in bed."

By now, the fitter had changed the gauge and was busy opening the manifold steam valve that had isolated it. Even at this late stage of European administration, the weight of a failure hung heavily on Ralph's shoulders. Ralph looked at his watch again. "We're a failure!" he wailed, as a vision of a black mark swept his eyes.

I now played my trump card. Patting him on the shoulder, and with a wink, I told him, "Don't worry, Ralph... I'm still waiting for the Line Clear." And so ended my one run-in with Ralph Frazer.

Who it was that had tampered with vital bits of equipment, and why, remains a mystery.

Having now spent a good many years in East Africa, I had become familiar with the way members of one tribe treated members of another. This was at its most obvious when women folk of one tribe came asking for water from the engine crew of a different tribe, and were often flatly refused. The following story concerns the jolly and amicable John Stewart, at the time my co-driver.

Early one morning, John had taken over from me for the final leg to Morogoro, where on arrival at the shed, I relieved him by asking, "Is everything all right?" meaning is the engine all right?

"Oh yes," he answered, "but I'm in trouble." It emerged that the Kilosa stationmaster had sent an accident telegram in which he accused John of entering the station at excessive speed, a charge which could well be true. Approaching Kilosa in the Down direction, the line runs level for about a mile, previous to which the line fell for 26 miles on a grade of 1 in 100, keeping John busy for an hour or more as he controlled the speed of the train.

I knew this section well, and approaching Kilosa during the last hours of darkness I was aware one had to fight sleep every inch of the way, thus I thought it probable that John, somewhere along this final stretch had fallen asleep, only to be wrenched wide awake as he rattled over Kilosa's facing points. I commiserated with him, but he assured me he had made things right. This puzzled me, for I failed to see how you could get around an accident telegram, but as always, I was anxious to hear of ways to get out of trouble, and at this my ears pricked up.

Kilosa was one of the two or three stations along the line with a semaphore signal, the others, I presume, having been demolished by German engineers as the German Army retreated down the line. "Yes," continued John, "I went back to the guard and asked him to book the train as standing at the signal for two minutes." With the two minutes recorded in the guard's journal, there was no way the charge could be made to stick. This was a new trick, one that impressed me, and one I vowed to remember.

John was a Chagga from northern Tanganyika, and apart from the Swahili language, the *lingua franca* of East Africa, he had little in common with other tribes along the Central Line. John continued by saying, "I'll get that stationmaster!" (What tribe he was from, I've no idea.) Now, the possibility of pinning something on a stationmaster was almost non-existent, and hoping it might be of use to me sometime in the future, I listened carefully to what he had to say. However, what followed next turned my blood ice cold.

To understand what John was intending, a brief description of the line in the Up direction from Kilosa is required. For the first two miles, the line ran in a series of curves winding through elephant grass eight or ten feet tall, effectively deadening the sound of an approaching train, which was especially dangerous to men working on the line or riding a push trolley. In these circumstances the Kilosa stationmaster issued a Warning Order to the drivers of Up trains, an order which was read, acknowledged and signed for, and such drivers thereafter entering the section continually sounding the deep chime whistle. With tribal instincts to the fore, John's intention, as he explained to me, was to pretend to sign for the Warning Order, but to do so with a false signature, take the document, pass through the section without sounding his whistle, and if possible run down some hapless Permanent Way men. If such an accident did occur, he would then lay the blame squarely on the stationmaster by saying he had not issued a Warning Order, and must have falsely signed it to look like he had. Of course nothing did happen, and the stationmaster continued his long tenure at Kilosa. Cowardly it may have been, or perhaps prudent, but from then on I never signed a Warning Order using my own signature.

In the Down direction, this section of the railway between Gulwe station and Kilosa follows the Mukondokwa Valley and the course of the Mukondokwa River. Normally a clear and gentle watercourse, about four feet deep and 20 feet wide. But during the rainy season this frequently became a raging torrent of muddy water, spreading far and wide, and carrying all kinds of debris. Under these conditions a 50 mile stretch of railway came under attack, in effect becoming an overflow channel for the river, scouring out the earth beneath the track and sweeping away the ballast in places, leaving the track suspended in thin air.

There is a long history to this phenomenon. In the archives are World War I photographs showing a British troop train in this section, gingerly creeping along over lengths of temporary sleeper trestles spanning washaways. Tanganyika railway history records washaways in 1924, between Gulwe and Kidete, disrupting traffic for nearly three weeks. In 1926, the Gombo Lake, near Kidete, across which the railway ran on an embankment, rose above the level of the rails, closing the line for 14 days, with extensive flooding occurring with catastrophic consequences. At the same time the line between Gulwe and Munisagara stations was breached in six different places. On 5 January 1926, a bridge between Godegode and Kidete collapsed under the pressure of water, and once again the level of Lake Gombo rose, submerging the railway and eventually causing that stretch to be abandoned in favour of a new higher alignment, much of it having to be blasted, at great expense, through solid granite.

Not far from Kidete station, just below the present alignment, between the railway and the river, and on a stretch of bare level ground, lie the remains of a German troop train, with steel under-frames, wheels and couplings torn away and scattered about. This, sadly, is the result of a high speed derailment which killed many of the Askaris[45] being rushed to the defence of Morogoro against the British. On 6 January 1926, a further washaway occurred between Munisagara and Kidete, but by 13 January (a day of ill omen), it was considered safe to send

---

[45] Local native soldiers who served in the armies of the European colonial powers.

an engine across Lake Gombo to test the track. Unfortunately part of the embankment had been undermined, with the engine capsizing. As far as I am aware it is still laid in its watery grave beneath the still waters of Lake Gombo. Between Godegode and Kidete a temporary bridge replaced one washed away, but this also fell victim to flood water, with normal service suspended until 24 February. During this period the line further east was beset with floods, with ten separate washaways, and miles of ballast swept away. On 5 March, between Munisagara and Kilosa, an overnight cloudburst caused two more washaways and the wrecking of an engineering train which fell into one of the breaches. Then, on 1 April 1926 Lake Gombo rose again, preventing all train movements until 8 April, and it was not until 23 April, nearly four months after the railway had first succumbed to washaways, that a normal service was resumed.

In 1936 flooding occurred along the length of the Mukondokwa Valley (also sometimes known as Mkondoa valley), when, thanks to its new alignment, the railway escaped. But on 26 December 1955, after several days of torrential rain, flood water struck again, with the line between Kikombo and Igandu inundated to the extent that only the tops of telegraph poles marked the line of the railway. By the 29th, the flood waters had largely receded, and by immense effort the damage was made good. Then luck changed, however, with heavy and continuous rain the River Kinyasungwe, normally a dry river bed, altered course and struck the railway hard between Godegode and Kidete, scouring away more than 200 feet of embankment, again leaving the rails suspended in mid-air. However, by a stroke of good luck and the sharp eyes of one of the engineers, it was found possible to build a 900 feet diversion on slightly higher ground, which became the Permanent Way, and thanks to superhuman effort by African labourers was accomplished in a mere 36 hours.

Fortunately I experienced washaways only twice along this section. This was post-1956 when the 30 Class with its large tender had made through running between Tabora and Morogoro possible. In 1958 mother Africa again turned capricious, when the River Kinyasungwe again flooded, attacking the railway and undercutting a mile long section between Godegode and Kidete and stopping traffic for the next four days. With the line patched up, trains were allowed over the affected and still unsteady section at 5 mph. This was reduced to 3 mph where the line elevated at the point new ballast was being laid.

In 1959 a cloudburst above the hills of the Mukondokwa Valley sent a wall of water sweeping down the sandy bed of a deep dry wadi, undermining the substantial granite piers supporting a steel girder bridge and leaving them leaning at outlandish angles. I was the first train to pass over the destroyed bridge. But for the next 48 hours I was stopped from further movement at Gulwe, a bush station surrounded by a few Wagogo huts set among massive Upside Down trees (Boab trees[46]) whilst a temporary bridge, supported on steel sleepers was erected, the approaches dug out and the line slewed into position.

During the 48 hours of waiting I ran out of food and water, but fortunately Gulwe, despite its isolation, had a duka. Well, a duka of sorts—a miserable disreputable affair, whose Somali owner scraped a precarious living selling lengths of cloth and the odd machete to the local tribe. But the duka had a paraffin fridge containing ice cold *Coca-Cola*, which in the circumstances, and as a teetotaller at that time, I found extremely palatable. Amazingly, you could be in the most out-of-the-way fly-blown place in the middle of nowhere, but if it happened to have a little duka, nine times out of ten you could buy *Coca-Cola*. Here, I was able also able to purchase several tins of Tanganyika Packers bully beef, a product I normally avoided at all costs! Tanganyika Packers would accept any poor animal that was still just about alive, the end result bearing no resemblance to other brands of bully beef, being as dry and tough as the native animals it was derived from, and in appearance and colour, not dissimilar to chewed up cardboard.

After a cooling drink, taken out of one of the Somali shopkeeper's not very sanitary glasses, I loaded my purchases into my kikapu and made my way back to the caboose through a grove of giant boab trees. Eventually I was allowed to proceed, stopping at Kidete to be warned of the temporary bridge and 3 mph speed limit imposed on it. It was still daylight as we approached the scene of the wash away, and about 300 yards short of it I was stopped by a hand signalman who required me to fill in a book giving the number of my train and the time of my arrival, each confirmed by my signature.

Very cautiously I approached the temporary bridge, to find to my dismay its level several feet below the level of the main line, leaving me to suppose the steel sleeper'ed cribs had been built up to their maximum allowed height. Of equal concern, the steep grades leading onto the temporary bridge had been laid with curves of acute radius, leaving me to ponder if a 30 Class with a fixed coupled wheelbase of 13 feet 3 inches could negotiate such curves. It required very

---

[46] A species of what are commonly called baobabs, of the genus *Adansonia*.

careful driving as I inched down under light steam, the coupled wheel flanges protesting a little on the curves. Whilst carefully watching my progress I looked down to see the large cast steel Delta truck, that carries the weight of the firebox, protruding beyond the straight lines of the engine, showing just how tight the radius was. Alive to every movement that 3012 made, I crept very very carefully onto the cribbed bridge. With 150 tons bearing down on them for the first time the cribs shifted uneasily, groaned and settled down, providing a moment of heart stopping fear and causing my fireman to comment 'Nimeogopa, bwana' (I am frightened, Sir). From my position, and ready to apply the brakes at a moment's notice, I could observe the train descending the steep incline and snaking around the tight curves, the vehicles swaying about alarmingly on the bare unconsolidated earth. The climb out of the gap was equally fraught, a repeat of the descent, but now I had to use a lot more steam to lift the heavy train. Back once more on to the main line, to my relief and that of my fireman, I stopped the train and looked back to make sure it was all in order before exchanging signals with the guard and opening the regulator.

In the bad old days, any extraneous comments written in the hand signalman's book would have brought severe disciplinary action. But times had changed, and Brian Duffell (the jolly cockney, you'll remember), after noting his time of arrival and his train number, penned one of his witty jingles for the amusement of other drivers. It gives a picture, exaggerated of course, of negotiating a washaway by a temporary rickety bridge—a picture which I hope the reader will find as entertaining as it has always been to me, and which I append below:

> *If across this bridge I dash,*
> *Then I know my tea I'll splash,*
> *And make the sparkling footboards dirty,*
> *Then the DME[47] will get quite shirty.*

I only once worked a trip with Brian, and one which almost ended in disaster. We had worked a Down train to Morogoro, and on our way back to Tabora with 49 Up goods, I had taken over from Brian for the middle leg, which included the long climb up Saranda Bank. In Tanganyika Railway days, trains up Saranda

---

[47] DME: the District Mechanical Engineer

were always banked from the rear. From an operating point of view this was ideal, for if one of the engines was on the curve and liable to slip, the chances were the other was on a straight and better able to 'hold its feet'. Then, under new EAR regulations, the banker had to bank from the front, and after a few years this was again changed, as previously mentioned, with the banker now inside, with the train's engine and crew leading.

On this occasion it was nearly midnight, and with both engines working flat out I had almost reached the top of the bank. Within a few minutes I would reach Manyoni, the next change-over station, and I expected Brian to already be stirring in the caboose. The banker had slipped a little on one or two of the sharper curves, but with the steam brake rubbing its coupled wheels I was holding 3012 steady. I had just entered such a curve and was on my mettle, ready for the banker slipping, but confident I could hold my own, when from behind, with an explosive roar from its exhaust, the banker slipped. This was followed by a tremendous jolt as 3012, still holding its feet, took the full weight of both banker engine and train, snapping the coupling, a heavy steel forging, like a carrot, and sending 3012, now relieved of the train, flying forward under full steam, until, as a reaction to the parted vacuum pipe, the brakes automatically rammed full on, bringing both engines and the train to a shuddering stop.

Confused, I sat for a moment unsure of what had occurred, but looking back I could see 3012 had parted from the train. In East Africa the vacuum brake had a reputation for leaking off quickly, and my first reaction to this was to promptly move along the train's 30 units screwing on their hand brakes, to prevent it running away down the 2% grade, with consequences too awful to contemplate.

Gathering myself together I hurried down the train intent on screwing handbrakes on as tight as I could, but about half way along I heard the sigh of a releasing vacuum brake and felt a faint tremor in the waggons. Fully aware that once the train began to move nothing could stop it, a wave of fear and indecision swept over me. What ought I do for the best? Should I leave off applying the handbrakes and run down the train to warn Brian and others to jump for it? Or in a desperate attempt to save the train, continue applying handbrakes? It was a fine judgement either way, but I chose to stick with the train. Then ahead of me as I moved along I heard the whisper and clunk of brakes releasing, and to my horror and disbelief, came across Brian releasing the vacuum brakes. These were the brakes I was relying on to hold the train as I worked down it putting on the handbrakes!

At my shouted warning Brian stopped, and together we screwed on the remaining handbrakes. Brian, it transpired, in preparing to take over, had been alerted by the banker engine slipping and the train coming to a shuddering halt. Unaware of the events up ahead, Brian assumed that binding brakes (a not uncommon occurrence in that dry and dusty part of Africa) had brought the train to a standstill. Hoping to assist, Brian, started releasing brakes. If I had taken just a little longer in deciding what to do, Brian would, on that windswept ridge high above the Rift Valley, have sent the train, including the banker engine, its coupled wheels locked by the steam brake, sliding helplessly backwards. It was only by a whisker, and the Grace of God, that the train on that dark moonless night was saved from running away to certain destruction.

After securing the train, two options remained open to me. The first, to dismantle the broken coupling and replace it with one taken from the rear of the guards van—a long and difficult job at the best of times, but more so in the dark with only limited tools. The other option, the use of an emergency coupling, in the shape of a thick wire hoop which in the event of a broken coupling could be fitted over the central draw gear. This had been introduced a few months earlier, after a spate of broken couplings in Kenya, caused by mishandling of the recently introduced and powerful diesel locomotives. Each engine had been issued with this emergency coupling, but to me it didn't seem strong enough, even on the level, to pull a full 30 Class load, never mind on a 1 in 50 rising grade.

Now with the train made safe, Brian offered to help with the recoupling, a delicate operation in the circumstances, for a too-vigorous nudge whilst backing on could still send the train speeding off. With recoupling successfully accomplished and full brake power restored throughout the train, it was time to test the rather dubious emergency coupling. However, first as a precaution against another disastrous slip from the banker, the rails around the curve were hand sanded.

To test the coupling I gave 3012 a whiff of steam. The coupling tightened on the central buffing gear, then without complaint held firm and tight. Now was the time to unscrew the handbrakes, and whilst I held the train against the grade, Brian on his way back to the caboose released the brakes on each vehicle. After pre-arranged signals with Brian I whistled up for the banker's attention, and still fearing for the coupling, I opened the regulator. Silly me! Of course the wire hawser held. It had been designed to take far greater loads than any exerted by one 30 Class on Saranda Bank.

Having earlier drawn a picture of the problematic flood-prone stretch from Gulwe, through the Mukondokwa Valley to Kilosa, there remained hereabouts one further section giving trouble. From Kilosa to Mkata the railway crossed what Morton Stanley, the intrepid Victorian explorer, rightly called the dreaded Mkata Swamp. a 29 mile stretch of boggy quaking black cotton soil. From Kilosa to Kimamba, the intermediate station along the swamp, a distance of 12 miles, the swamp had been drained and given over to extensive sisal estates stretching away into the far distance, and this was the site of the Planters Hotel, wherein wealthy Greek estate owners sat drinking their lives away. But in the remaining stretch between Kimamba and Mkata the land was covered by rank swamp vegetation, growing 10 feet tall, and pressing hard against the railway. The formation had always stood up well to the lighter and less powerful 21 and 25 Class locomotives, but under the pounding of the heavy 30 Class it began to deteriorate quickly. Speed was first reduced to 20 mph, then 10 mph, finally to 5 mph. At these low speeds, especially in the early hours with no passing breeze, heat from the boiler rolling back became so savage footplate crew had to seek refuge on the tender, where in a state of stupor I, for one, had to fight an overpowering urge for sleep.

However, worse was to come. For several months, the water supply to Morogoro locomotive shed had failed, something that may have happened in the past, for halfway between Kimamba and Mkata, hidden by thick fetid vegetation, stood a solitary fixed water column, from which, in the circumstances, we had orders to stop and take water. This was not easy, and never more so at night with a heavy train and a large 25 foot long 12-wheel tender. This was especially so if working in the Down direction, with the water column now sited on the driver's blind side, and hauling a variety of vehicles marshalled in a variety of ways, with greater or lesser wear in brake blocks, trunnions and running gear, meaning that no two trains reacted to brake application in quite the same way. Consequently, it was a supreme test of driving skill to stop at this column first go.

In the dead of night, even worse might follow. Whilst the fireman scrambled over the tender to a place of safety, the driver, to reach the column's water valve, had to climb down and force his way through a dense tangle of 10 foot high reeds and vegetation, hoping all the time that a scorpion or similar unwelcome visitor, on being dislodged, wouldn't fall down the front or back of his open shirt. If that wasn't bad enough, here also were snakes, which if inadvertently trodden on could result in the driver's permanent discomfiture, or worse. Equally, there was always the chance of stumbling upon a hungry carnivorous beast lying in wait. Speaking for myself, it was always with a profound sense of relief that I regained the safety of the footplate unmolested and in one piece. Here I must remark that, among the tsetse flies, mosquitoes and other insects sent to try us, were a species of brown 'stink' beetle—a flying insect that, in the mistaken belief that locomotives were some kind of big red animal, would launch themselves in that direction, with the result they frequently landed down the front of an open-necked shirt or became entangled in one's hair or beard. From this location they emitted a stench so vile and disgusting it used to leave me heaving, to the widespread amusement of the African firemen.

I was now nearing the end of my third three-year tour of duty, and although unaware, the end of my eight-year love affair with 3012, the twelfth of a Class of 26 quite extraordinary locomotives, 24 of which were allocated to Tabora. After returning from home leave, I found myself posted to Nairobi, with its luxurious hotels, smart shops, cinemas and night clubs. But before home leave, one of my last Tabora trips had an unusual twist to it, which occurred between Usinge and Kombe stations whilst working a goods train from Kigoma.

Along this section the line, though undulating a little, ran straight for several miles. Along here, in close proximity to the railway, the German builders of the Central Railway, justifiably proud of their achievements, had erected an impressive monolith marking the one thousandth kilometre from Dar es Salaam. Along this stretch, in the distance, and totally unexpected in an area of dense uninhabited bush, I marked a solitary figure walking beside the track in the same direction of travel as mine.

Mystified, I assumed it to be an African on some walkabout or other, though where they were going, so many miles from anywhere, was quite beyond me. Imagine then my astonishment, when approaching nearer, I realised this was a European with a backpack, striding out under a blazing midday sun. A gaunt European dressed in ragged shirt and shorts, but with a stout pair of leather boots to help him on his way. Stopping my train, but unsure of his nationality I greeted him with a "Jambo" (hello), the common form of Swahili courtesy.

"Jambo," he replied, at least we were on some common ground, it seemed.

"Unaenda wapi? (Where are you going?)" I asked.

"Urambo," he replied.

Urambo was a good 40 miles further on—two days hard walking in fierce heat through uninhabited country. Welcoming him aboard, I invited him to

"Come up", and throwing up his backpack, he climbed into the cab, when I discovered he was not only of German nationality, but also a White Father[48], a Roman Catholic priest, returning to his Mission after four months in the bush doing whatever White Fathers did. He spoke educated English, if anything, rather better than mine! Lean and bony, I had nothing to offer him but a ride home, a drink of cool water from my water bag hanging over the side of the cab and some company.

In Nairobi, after the customary three-day trip between Nairobi and Nakuru and back, which included familiarising myself to the whims of a new and unfamiliar type of locomotive, the Diesel-Electric 90 Class, my first solo trip proved a bit of a sweat. This was because I found myself with two 90 Class diesels coupled together working in tandem, giving a combined tractive effort of 100,000 lbs on a train of 1,400 tons with 60 units and, for the first 50 miles, on a rising grade of 1 in 66. Unlike Tanganyika, each station in this section was equipped with semaphore signals, and on the climb to the summit my main concern was being stopped at one of the signals, and thereafter my ability to restart such a heavy train on a stretch of line I was still largely unfamiliar with and with locomotives I was equally unfamiliar with. Also lurking at the back of my mind was the fear of breaking a coupling, bringing with it all sorts of problems, including the wrath of the Nairobi mechanical establishment.

With exhausts roaring and both locomotives opened out to full power I climbed the grade at a steady 12 mph. An annoying feature of the diesel locomotives was the foot pedal that the driver had to depress every few minutes, otherwise the train's brakes would be automatically activated—a type of 'dead man's handle'. I say annoying, but don't dispute that it was a good idea, given the unquestionable danger of drivers falling asleep due to the long and unsociable hours. All went well through Kibera, the first station, but at Kikuya, a station approached on a series of embanked curves, things began to look decidedly tricky.

From some distance away, across the winding track I could see the station's signal in the stop position—the very worst place to restart a train held tight by snaking around a series of reverse curves. In an attempt to warn the stationmaster of my imminent approach and hoping he would lower the signal I blew a series

---

[48] A member of the Society of Missionaries of Africa, a Roman Catholic order founded in Algiers in 1868.

of loud blasts on the diesel's horns, an action replicated, as was every other action, on the second locomotive.

Alas and alack, the signal remained in the 'on' position forcing me to stop, and in my uncertain condition, this was an unhappy position to be in. However, experience gave me an edge. For the last 100 yards I had opened the sanders, which again was replicated on the second locomotive, and after coming to a stand I let the locomotives and train roll slowly back before stopping over the now well-sanded section of track, giving me the added advantage of opening the sanders once again after being given the 'Go Ahead'. When the signal was lowered I began to release the train brakes and apply power. This was the test, would the two locomotives pick up a train with its combined total of 264 wheel flanges binding against several tight curves, or would they slip with possible dire consequences?

With gritted teething and sweating brow, and whilst taking my cue from the air brake gauge, I applied power sufficient to hold the train against the grade. Then adding more power and more sand, I began to slowly lift the train from the standing position. Unlike a steam locomotive, the diesels gave no indication of an imminent slip, and because of this, moving off under these conditions remained a matter of guess work. To my relief and the help of my sanding strategy, both locomotives moved off cleanly without the dreaded slip.

Returning to a well-worn theme: one afternoon waiting in Nairobi yard for the Line Clear tablet (in this respect the Kenya Uganda section was ahead of the Tanganyika Central Railway, which still relied on the archaic paper Line Clear tickets), I was approached by a European, who called up to me, "Hello, remember me?"

Glancing down on the face of a stranger, I shook my head. "Sorry," I answered, feeling I ought to apologise, "I don't seem to know you."

"Well, you should!" he replied. "I used to give you your pay packet every Friday at Botanic Gardens."

Hey ho, let's be honest, I admit freely and openly I was more interested in the contents of my pay packet than in the somewhat shadowy indistinct figure handing it to me through the booking office window. They say it's a small world, and it seems that nowhere can this universal truth be better demonstrated than in the domain of colonial railwaymen!

Chapter 23
Locomotive Inspector, Tabora

Walking to work in Nairobi early one afternoon (it must have been in 1962) a car drew up alongside me, its driver none other than the senior locomotive inspector, and as such the man responsible for all the other locomotive inspectors and, by definition, responsible for all the footplate staff throughout EAR. After a cordial greeting, he asked me: "Do you fancy the job of loco inspector Tabora?"

I hesitated. Nairobi, its climate kind and agreeable, offered in abundance those necessities, and then some, that Tabora lacked. Further, I was aware that the Tabora Locomotive Inspector carried a heavy burden, being directly responsible to the DMPS for the safe and efficient workings of all parts of his far-flung empire. This included examinations of locomotives on the road, riding on footplates and giving instructions to both firemen and drivers on the most efficient and economical way of working locomotives and being responsible also for the smooth and effective workings of Tabora's two sub-sheds, one at Kigoma and one at Mwanza. This also included a twice-yearly check on all tools and plant, a wearying exercise if ever there was one.

In addition, on a regular basis, it involved checking oil levels, records and the general good order of the district's five widely dispersed oil fuel installations, based at Shinyanga, Mwanza, Mpanda (at the far end of a rickety branch line), Malagarasi and Kigoma. Also, at Kigoma, under the control of the locomotive inspector, three running rooms and their staff, one for each of the separate races, African, Indian and whites, which had to be inspected and checked over on every visit.

This was a type of work I didn't much fancy, and so I hesitated. Then common sense kicked in. All around the world the British Empire was being dismantled with unseemly haste, and with little regard for the welfare of the indigenous people and their future. I could see in the not too distant future my career with EAR coming to an end. Better, I thought, to retire on the pension of a Grade II inspector than a Grade V driver. With that in mind, I nodded my agreement.

With this agreed, I went off on safari, and on my return was told to transfer to Tabora as quickly as possible and relieve 'Legs' Baldwin (how he acquired his nickname remains a mystery), who was in turn, required in Nairobi to take over the position of senior locomotive inspector from its present incumbent, who was due to retire at any time. I decided that my quickest means of travel was to load my car with my personal effects and travel by road from Nairobi to Kisumu in Uganda, a township and port on the shores of Lake Victoria, and from there take the road to Mwanza, which required the use of a ferry to cross Musoma Gulf, a broad inlet and as such part of Lake Victoria.

I made good time to Kisumu, arriving travel-stained but in time for lunch. I found a hotel where, not to overly offend its regular and more sartorially dressed diners, I chose a quiet corner table. Whilst there, however, I heard disquieting rumours regarding the road between Kisumu and Mwanza. Apparently, for I knew nothing about it, unprecedented rains had for months swept the Western Provinces of East Africa, and the roads were far from good, and so to fully ascertain the situation I called in at the local police station to make enquiries. Perhaps the British officer in charge somehow took a dislike to my face, or maybe my grimy appearance offended him, for he summarily dismissed me with a bland assurance the road was open.

Replete with lunch, full of fight, my heavily laden Volkswagen Beetle car, its petrol tank filled to capacity, and with replenished water bag conveniently hanging from a side mirror, I struck out for distant Mwanza. Leaving Kisumu's smooth tarmacadamed streets I quickly discovered the Mwanza road resembled more the mud of a World War I battlefield than anything else. In first gear, slithering and sliding about from one deep rut to another, I crept forward. However, the Beetle's four cylinder air-cooled engine continued to roar lustily and confidently.

After about four hours of fighting the mud I arrived at a watercourse which ran over the road on a concrete ford. Normally a dry wadi, it now ran in full flood, its murram-red waters pouring over the ford before plunging over the edge in a series of waterfalls to a pool fifty or sixty feet below. I didn't like the look of things and stopped and went forward on foot to investigate. Wading across I found the water about 18 inches deep and tugging strongly at my legs. However,

I took the view that with the weight of myself and its cargo, the Beetle would 'hold its feet', and with it in first gear I inched across. Safely over, but hours behind schedule and with night approaching, other concerns began to grow. Under such conditions it would be impossible to continue after dark, hence it was imperative I found a firm stretch of road on which to spend the night. If I didn't manage this I might wake to find the car sunken into the mud, and not be able to get it out.

Near despair turned to jubilation when, on this isolated and abandoned road, I espied through the gloom a group of mission buildings, and turning off the road onto firm ground I made for its main part, to be welcomed by a group of White Fathers expressing amazement at my appearance. "Where have you come from?" they wanted to know.

"From Kisumu," I replied.

They threw up their hands. "But how did you get over the ford?" they enquired.

My answer was simply, "Well, I drove across." Then the whole grisly story came out. A couple of days before, and running short of provisions, one of the Fathers volunteered to try and reach Kisumu. Failing to return, a search party went out only to discover his wrecked car containing his drowned body submerged in the lower pool. Later I was invited to share their meagre meal—a slice of mission-produced cheese and a glass of boiled and filtered water, which was nevertheless most welcome, and as such gratefully received. Afterwards I was told the Musoma ferry was out of action, its landing stages submerged by rising lake levels, effectively cutting the road between Kisumu and Mwanza. In the morning there would be nothing for it but to return on the many mud-choked miles to Kisumu (where I felt like having it out with the snotty police officer), and there book a passage to Mwanza on a lake steamer. That night I was shown to a narrow cell with a small bed. Was this the unfortunate brother's, I wondered. There I spent a comfortable night.

Leaving early next morning without meeting anyone, I left a hundred Tanganyika shilling (£5) note on my freshly made bed for my meal and accommodation. If this seems to the reader like scant remuneration for my hospitable night's stay, I should mention that it was a third of my then weekly salary of £15. Retracing my route I found the ford still in full flow, treating it this time with rather more respect. Arriving in Kisumu I found I was in luck—a lake steamer bound for Mwanza was leaving the next day. A steamer tramping the lake and picking up cargo when and wherever it could, it had accommodation for four or five first-class passengers and I was more than happy to book a passage and see my car slung aboard by crane and stowed safely on deck.

Arriving at Mwanza, a typical East African earth road ran 250 miles to Tabora, and depending on its surface corrugations and any washaways that may have occurred, was a five or six hour drive. Messages had flown between Nairobi and Tabora and on arrival I found my accommodation had been arranged at a fine, old, solidly built, spacious German villa. Originally the residence of the German works manager, it had, as its name Snake Villa implied, something of a reputation. But more of that later.

In May 1962, reporting to the DMPS (a new boss) I was ordered to leave by the next train and make my way to the flooded Usinge Swamp, a five mile stretch of low lying terrain spanned by the railway on an eight foot high but unballasted embankment, now under still rising water. This stretch of railway was being kept open to goods trains (the passenger services had been suspended on safety grounds), and it was the inspector's duty to drive each train the 19 miles from Usinge Station on the edge of the swamp to Nzabuka, the station on the other side. Usinge Swamp was just dry black cotton soil, even in the rainy season, and encompassed a vast area, dotted about with huge ant hills said to be over 1,000 years old and containing enormous colonies of ants.

Promotion to locomotive inspector meant that I was provided with my own inspection coach, consisting of a lounge, with a desk and chair, and on the wall were a vacuum gauge and a speedometer, along with speed recording equipment, allowing me to monitor the speed of the train. It also contained a small kitchen, a bedroom, and a bathroom, including a small bath (filled using a bucket of scalding hot water from the locomotive injector, obtained from the fireman). All very comfortable and well-appointed, although on the move it was a jolting and weaving contraption.

On arrival at Usinge Swamp, however, I was rather dismayed to be told that, because of the need to remarshal trains at each of these stations, there was no room for an inspection coach, and my accommodation was therefore a tent, a camp bed, a Primus stove and a water filter. Apart from lack of creature comforts it seemed scant protection against a lion, or lions, sniffing around. In a place destitute of food, rations were sent up on a weekly basis, with a few tins of Tanganyika Packers grisly corned beef supplemented by tinned peas and baked beans, together with tea, sugar and tins of evaporated milk. One week, after some 'cock-up on the catering front', my rations failed to arrive, leaving me no other option but to report that I was 'forced to live on grass'. An exaggeration of course, but all I had were the wild banana's growing nearby. Small green, dry and bitter, it was an experience that put me off bananas for a very long time!

Meeting 'Legs' at Usinge Station we discussed operating methods, and then, adopting a grave face, Legs began to dramatize the dangerous condition the unballasted section of track over the swamp was now in. Taking in every word, I nodded my understanding, but my thoughts ran in a somewhat different direction. I reasoned that it would be very much a feather in Legs' cap if, on arrival in Nairobi, he could say he had kept the line open, but Eric Blackburn, faint of heart, had closed it. Waving him a cheery goodbye I vowed to take a feel of the track and form my own opinion. Trains were only allowed over the swamp during daylight hours, and each morning before the arrival of the first train, it was my duty to examine the submerged track.

For this I was provided with a plate layers push trolley and a gang of men to propel it along. Each morning at 6 am, as dawn was flushing the eastern skies, I set off, the trolley men running barefoot along the top of the rails. It was really a useless exercise, the embankment and track being hidden by a foot or more of muddy water churned up by the passage of trains, and the light push trolley was unable to give me any true feeling of the condition below the water level.

Since being placed in service the 2-8-4 30 Class had dominated the Central Railway between Morogoro and Kigoma, but at 150 tons dead-weight they were much too heavy for this delicate and unstable section of flooded track. Instead, light axle load 27 Class locomotives, coupled in pairs, now worked 30 Class loads over the Tabora-Kigoma section.

Arriving at Usinge in the Up direction, or at Nzabuka in the Down direction, the engines were remarshalled, and to spread the direct load on the unstable and waterlogged embankment, the leading engine was uncoupled, run round the train and attached to the rear. For safety reasons it would no longer take an active part in steaming across the flat swamp, for if it was pushing from behind and the line collapsed beneath the lead engine, it would push that engine and its load into the swamp. In the meantime, the now leading engine picked up three bogie flat waggons, each loaded to capacity with boulders, and each weighing in at 50 tons. These were propelled ahead of the train to both test the track and act as a safety measure in the event of an embankment collapse.

My first trip over the submerged embankment went better than expected. At a steady 5 mph the unballasted track seemed pretty firm; however, as the weeks turned into months and the flood waters continued to rise, the sleepers with the track they carried sank into the water-saturated surface of the embankment, making each trip something of a nightmare, with the engine rolling and dipping, making me wonder sometimes if it would recover from its tilt, or finish up on its side in the swamp. Looking back at the train was equally disturbing, its vehicles swaying from side to side in an alarming manner, all this forcing me to reduce speed to 3 mph. Even so I was acutely aware that the port and township of Kigoma depended on the railway for its myriad supplies, and I was determined to keep the railway open as long as possible.

Unfortunately, other problems began to develop. One such was occasioned by the fact that the rising water had begun to submerge the train's axle boxes, so that once both locomotives had lifted the train up the gradient out of the swamp, I had to open each axle box to examine it for water contamination, adding considerably to the time taken in the section. Remarkably, and a tribute to the design of the axle boxes, I never discovered any ingress of water. To carry out the examination I usually stopped opposite the line-side grave of a German construction engineer. In keeping with Christian tradition, its stone cross faced east overlooking the swamp, its occupant awaiting the day of resurrection.

But as time moved forward, an even more dangerous condition began to develop, one so serious I would be forced to close the line until such time as the floods began to recede. The issue here was that the water had now almost reached level with the firebox air scoop. If water was drawn up into the firebox in any quantity it would cause its collapse, resulting in a massive explosion. When shut, the air scoop damper, general speaking, fitted closely, and I thought long and hard about running the engines over the swamp with dampers closed. Unfortunately I had no guarantee that over time these would remain sufficiently watertight, and it was just too much of a gamble. To get a better view of the proximity of the water to the air scoop, at one time I hired a native dugout canoe, and paddled this alongside the train, whilst my old mate Ujagar operated the engine. Closely monitoring a situation that looked increasingly bleak, I began to prepare myself for closing the line. Then, as frequently happens in these parts of Africa, without warning the skies cleared, the rain clouds disappeared, and the sun, in all its glory, came out to work its magic. Day by day each 12 hours of sunshine produced, by evaporation, a half inch drop in water level, marked by a succession of water marks on each of the steel railway telegraph poles. Within a month railheads began to show, and after a further 18 days the embankment with its sunken sleepers could be examined by the Engineering Department and work commence on strengthening and stabilising the more affected parts. With the track knocked into better shape John Stuart, the first African locomotive inspector came out to relieve me six or more weeks after I'd arrived. In August 1962 I was pleased to receive a Letter of Commendation from the DMPS, Tabora, thanking me for my efforts in keeping the line open.

Crossing the flooded section of railway demonstrated in no uncertain manner the power of steam locomotion, especially at low speeds on level track. As stated, each train was drawn by two light axle load 27 Class locomotives. Both were made up to a full load of 297 tons for the 1-in-50 Tabora-Kigoma section's rising grades, making, altogether, a train of 594 tons. But, as indicated earlier, to cross the swamp must be added three loaded flat bogie waggons, being propelled ahead of the train, and each weighing in at 50 tons, thus adding a further 150 tons. Also the weight of the leading engine, now marshalled at the rear of the train and under instruction to take no further part in crossing the swamp, thereby adding a further 93 tons, making the train a massive 877 tons, for a locomotive with a tractive effort of 19,950 lbs. And yet, despite this colossal weight, all it took was a whiff of steam to draw the train across.

Returning to Tabora I occupied Snake Villa, one of four houses, but with the other three being unoccupied. It lay at the end of a quiet and peaceful dirt road shaded by splendid mango trees, and within easy walking distance of the isolated German-built locomotive works. It had a certain air of importance about it and it was easy to imagine the former German works manager waving goodbye each morning to his wife and striding off to his office, his walking cane, almost a badge of office, flashing in the dappled sunshine.

Behind the house the land rose steeply among a jumble of large granite boulders, the home of a variety of snakes—hence its name and dubious reputation. To the front, beyond the road, the house overlooked a wide and shallow grassed fold in the ground, upon which antelope grazed. As reported, the works manager occupied this house, which like the majority of German buildings, had a cool mosquito-proof veranda running its width. By all accounts he was an excellent shot, and from this veranda it was his wont to shoot an antelope for the pot, as and when required. As testimony to the truth of this story,

I discovered an unobtrusive aperture set within the mosquito screen, just the right height for a shot.

I had no sooner occupied the house and hired a houseboy-cum-cook, than I was sent out to retrieve two 27 Class engines marooned by flood water for several days on the Mpanda Line. The water was too deep to send a relieving engine and so I was given a gang of men. Working waist deep in water, we first split the tenders from the locomotives, and after draining them of water pushed them out by hand. The first part went according to plan, but then trying to push a 50 ton locomotive with only a handful of men proved too much. The track hereabouts, although level, had undulations, and with only a few men able to find purchase it was an impossible task. Tabora then sent up what I can only describe as a homemade Heath Robinson contraption, with a large flywheel and powered by a petrol engine. Despite an ear splitting roar from its open exhaust and a madly spinning flywheel, it too, together with my gang, failed to budge either locomotive.

Things seemed to have arrived at an impasse when I had an idea. The recovery had been hampered by how few men, half a dozen perhaps, I could muster around the engine—four pushing behind the cab and drag box, and one on each cylinder. Between them the gang had several pangas (machetes), a universal tool for either cutting back vegetation, defence, or murder—take your pick! I sent them off to cut some stout poles, and with one laid behind the cab across the lap plate and the other inserted through the bar frames behind the smokebox saddle, I was able to utilise every man.

With the contraption's engine roaring at full pelt, under the command "Moja, mbili, tatu, kuinuka!" (One, two, three, heave!) and with much ululating, shouts of jubilation, and deep-throated chanting (I always loved to hear Africans working to song), the first of the locomotives began to move. Alas my idea came to nought. In a somewhat deeper undulation the engine stuck fast again. With all hope gone it seemed there was nothing else for it but to return to Tabora and await such time as the water fell and an engine could get through. Then chugging through the flood water came a EAR motor trolley, sent by Tabora shed. Shackled together, it and the Heath Robinson contraption, along with all the gang pushing, succeeded in recovering both locomotives.

In late 1957, I took local leave to climb that wonder of East Africa, Mount Kilimanjaro, and was joined on this venture by the Tabora District Traffic Superintendent, who was born in Ceylon. Our base for the expedition was the fine old Marangu Hotel, a former German settler's homestead located on the lower slopes of Kilimanjaro. From the hotel, Kibo, the highest of Kilimanjaro's two peaks, rising to nearly 20,000 feet, was plainly visible, separated by a long 13 mile saddle from older Mawenzi, at just over 5,100 feet, with its craggy rocks and shear faces. Having spent the night in one of the hotel's separate guest lodges our group set off the next day carrying our daypacks, through the rainforest covering the lower slopes, with its damp moss-covered trees, masses of ferns, and vocal but elusive monkeys. Gradually this thinned and at about 9,000 feet we came out on open moorland stretching upwards to around 13,000 feet, and covered with heather, pretty mountain flowers, and with brightly-coloured little birds hopping and flitting about, including a type of hummingbird, jet black but with an iridescent green breast, a malachite sunbird. Six of us were on the climb, including two women, and a young German man, a visitor to Tanganyika. Accompanying us were an African guide, along with African porters who carried up our bedding, foodstuff and suchlike, thus completing our little group.

There were three climbing huts on the route up, and as the sun was setting on the first day we stopped at the first one, above the clouds, and looking over the rainforest towards the South Pari Mountains. These huts were primitive affairs, just small wooden structures with tin roofs and plank beds inside. The following day, looking up at the mountain towering before us we could see the bright snow-capped top of Kibo standing out in the sun, and not long after reaching the moorland we met a party coming down, led by a European guide. He stopped briefly and said to us, the tenor of his voice his emphasising the gravity of what he had to relate.

"The conditions up there," he said, "are terrible. And I ought to know because I'm a guide in the Swiss Alps," which rather brought things home to us. Nevertheless, we hadn't come all this way to give up before feeling snow under our boots, so we pressed on. Besides, this was probably the only opportunity any of us would have of climbing this iconic mountain. Having passed the sites of old fumaroles and lava flows, at about 10,000 feet cloud started rolling in over the moorland. Above this moorland it started to get very cold, an enormous contrast to the climate I'd become used to in Dar es Salaam, and by now the air was beginning to get very thin, making us puff and gasp with the effort of climbing.

Above the moorland was nothing but rock, classed as Alpine desert (a strange concept to grasp, on the equator), although the sun was still warm, and occasionally we'd take a break and shelter from the wind amongst the rocks. Having made it to the long saddle we walked along it towards Kibo, but trudging quite slowly given that we were all feeling the effects of altitude. The last hut before the summit, Kibo Hut, was at just over 15,500 feet. Above that, at around 16,500 feet arctic conditions prevailed (an even stranger concept to grasp), and as I stood outside the hut at sunset, the landscape in darkness, the snows of Kibo peak shone out radiantly, the sun still on them, and below to its left, hanging in the sky, the full moon also shining brightly.

Early the next morning, we set off for the summit and initially made good progress, but conditions soon began to deteriorate, and the last 4,000 feet were in a tremendous snowstorm which, despite our thick coats, hats and gloves chilled us to the bone. By now we were pretty fatigued, and at one point we all just lay down on the ice and snow, breathless and exhausted, as the snowstorm assailed us. One of the African guides, I remember, was quietly singing a Christian hymn, and I began to think that if we don't do something, and move, we were all going to freeze to death, so struggling to my feet I urged the others on. After a tough slog through blinding snow, enveloped in a world of whiteness, we made it to the summit. We should have arrived just as dawn was breaking, but because of the snowstorm, which had then passed, it was quite daylight when we got to the top. In those days Kibo's crater was a vast ice field with large glaciers, but I understand that, incredibly, the majority of this snow and ice has now sadly gone, leaving bare rock and just a small tract of dirty ice, a pale shadow of its former pristine frozen glory.

Having conquered the summit we slowly made our way down and by the time we got to the moorlands we had a spring in our step, passing mountain streams that provided a cool refreshing drink, through the moorland, where giant lobelia grew about 10 feet tall in places. It was the custom of the African guides, if the summit had been successfully reached, to make a little garland for each climber, using flowers from the moorland, which we gladly accepted. Finally, we make it back down through the rainforest to the welcome simple pleasures of the Marangu Hotel: a bath, a decent meal, and comfy beds in which to dream that most improbable of dreams: of a mountain harbouring snow and ice on equator, of Kilimanjaro, the White Mountain.

Back 'on shed' after my week's leave, Ralph Frazer had long since departed elsewhere, his place taken by Bill Gorman, late of Nyasaland Railways and a former Dar es Salaam Mechanical Inspector. Bill had rather a short fuse, but we got on well together, although years before, when I was a driver I'd had a bit of a run in with him. As Mechanical Inspector he had been sent up to set the valves on a particularly recalcitrant 26 Class. Watching him at work, he became aware of my presence and straightening up, he demanded, "What do *you* want?"

Always eager to increase my knowledge of steam locomotives, I replied, "I'm interested in what you're doing."

"Bugger off!" I was told.

A few months after my appointment as locomotive inspector, I saw Bill cross swords with Frank Kent. By now Frank had risen through the ranks to become assistant chief mechanical engineer, and as such had arrived unannounced one Saturday morning at Tabora. I was in conversation with Bill when he appeared out of nowhere, and gathering both of us up with him he began an inspection of the shed. All went well until we arrived at the machine shop. Levelled up and supported by screw jacks in the erecting shop, with wheels dropped, a 26 Class was having its tyres re-profiled.

With eyes as keen as the Jodrell Bank telescope, and attuned to locomotive defects, Frank Kent immediately picked up on excessive tyre wear. Calling for a tyre gauge he measured the degradation on both tyres and flanges, and finding them worn beyond established limits, he rounded on Bill, who gave as much as he received. I moved away, reluctant to eavesdrop on the ding-dong between them. Eventually, Bill stomped off, and Frank Kent, of southern stock, and perhaps remembering his run-in with me years before, asked, "Is Gorman a Yorkshireman?"

Around 1960, I took another week of local leave and booked a cruise on Lake Tanganyika on the MV Liemba, the former Tanganyika Railways passenger and cargo ferry which plied between Kigoma in Tanganyika to Mpulungu in the former North Rhodesia (now Zambia)[49]. This was a week-long cruise and part of a well-known holiday trip, involving numerous stops to pick up and set down passengers and goods, with small boats coming out to do the ferrying. Often these would be simple dugout canoes, but sometimes more advanced African sailing boats of a Arab design made an appearance, and occasionally a motor boat. On one of the stops nuns, in their dazzlingly white attire, including their white cowls, disembarked to return to one of the nunneries along the coast. Often, as the ship appeared, the locals would come to the lakeside and wave at the

---

[49] And, as of 2023, the Liemba still plies the same route, so I understand, continuing to give good service over 100 years since she was built.

people on deck, and on a few occasions I, along with my fellow holiday passengers disembarked to have look around some of the lakeside villages, with their picturesque, thatched huts. Many villages on the lakeshores relied on the Liemba for supplies.

The MV Liemba had an interesting history. She was built by the Germans in 1913 and named the Graf von Goertzen, and brought up to Kigoma in pieces, where she was re-erected. Then, during the First World War, as the Belgians advanced on Kigoma, she was scuttled by her captain, with a British Royal Navy salvage team raising her in 1924, where she was returned to service in 1927 as the Liemba. As of 2023, over a hundred years after her initial construction, she is, to my knowledge, still plying the lake.

Whilst back on safari, in August 1962, I received an urgent message to return to Tabora at once, and in the absence of the sick Bill Gorman, to take up the position of shedmaster. As a locomotive inspector, this was out of my 'line of promotion', but with my experience of the perverse 26 Class and with a tried and trusted staff from the Indian chief clerk to the skilled machinists and fitting staff, it was a post which held few concerns. As I saw it, the shedmaster's main problem was the wayward 26 Class. With the railway's financial position improving, cast iron packing rings had been fitted to the piston glands in replacement of the original asbestos fittings, which eliminating the need for the drivers to repack them at frequent intervals, although continuing to replace weak and spongy coupled springs remained a drain on the shed.

If my years on the 26 Class had taught me anything it had made me aware that many of the ills they suffered stemmed from the coupled stay plates working loose and bringing with them fallen wedges. When this happened they produced a tremendous box knock, reverberating throughout the engine, setting the engine crew's teeth on edge and affecting the integrity of the main bearings, connecting rod big ends and side rod bushes, to say nothing of many of the engine's other bits and pieces. What I intended was a simple mechanical solution, but one strictly against regulations, as laid down in the Motive Power Manual, which stated, "No alteration may be made to any locomotive without the chief mechanical engineer's permission."

If memory serves me right the shed undertook interim repairs to the 26 Class every 5,000 miles—a low mileage for a modern engine. This included machining new axle box face and side liners, and afterwards securing stay plates and setting up wedges. At this time, the 26 Class were the mainstay of the Mwanza line, its unballasted track, with light hog-backed rails and sunken rail joints guaranteed to give any coupled boxes a hammering. With interim repairs completed and unbeknown to the boss I gave orders that, after its first trip, a trip sufficient to bed in the new liners, the refurbished locomotive was to have its plain standard stay plate and wedge securing nuts changed to deep, specially machined and castellated replacement nuts. With the stay plate replacement nuts tightened to the maximum and the wedges adjusted accordingly, I ordered holes to be drilled through each retaining bolt at this point and split pins to be inserted to keep the nuts tight and prevent the stay plates falling, bringing with them the axle box wedges. The effect was immediate. In the repair books repairs fell away from the usual 20 or more to just a few, caused mainly by wear and tear from the track, making the 26 Class an altogether more dependable and economical engine. Of course I never received recognition for this, as I never let on about this invisible fix, given that it was against regulations to make alterations without the agreement of the Kremlin.

Whilst continuing to act as shedmaster two incidents occurred which I managed to bring to successful conclusions, and which I feel rather proud of. Each morning after going through the repair books the chief clerk brought me a pile of store requisition forms to check and sign. Sitting at my desk I was alerted by a dreadful knock from a Down train entering the station, its left big end thrashing about wildly to the disturbance of everyone around. Arriving on shed I went to examine the defective big end to find for the only time in my career that the big end bush had disintegrated and gone, leaving the eye of the connecting rod distorted. How the cylinder cover had not been knocked out remains a mystery—perhaps the Americans built them tough?

When I questioned the African driver over what had happened to cause a complete failure of the big end brass, he could or would only answer it was "Shauri Mungu". It seemed that God had left me with a problem, a connecting rod fit only for the scrap heap, and possibly with it a locomotive, for we had no spare rods and the cost of some British firm forging one and sending it out was prohibitively expensive, not to mention the time it would take.

However, I was blessed with a first rate Indian blacksmith, and together with one of the machinists we discussed whether the rod could be saved. The machinist examined the distorted eye and went into discussion with the blacksmith. Sucking at their cheeks and looking suitably grave they informed me it was difficult but could be done. At this point I informed the DMPS, now a man named Jackson, based at Tabora, who came out and, after examining the damaged rod shook his head exclaiming, "No, it's beyond repair."

"At least let me give it a try," I entreated. After a bit of persuasion he agreed, with the proviso that he examine the rod after completion and before a big end bush was machined and fitted. The blacksmith had a forge and anvil in one corner of the shed, and for the next couple of days the shed rang with the sound of the blacksmith's hammer. Announcing it was ready I informed the boss. I don't know who was the most astonished at the result, him or I. It looked perfect in every way. Using a micrometre, the boss carefully measured around the eye before congratulating the blacksmith and machinist on the quality of their work. Incidentally, as will be described later, this was only a temporary reprieve not only for this locomotive but for the whole class.

The next problem I faced concerned a 27 Class which had been involved in a shed collision, resulting in its mainframes being bent downwards, just forward of the smoke box, a deliberately designed weak point to protect the remainder of the main frames. With the running plate below the smoke box removed for close examination of the frames I sent for the boss. It was then I received a lesson from the boss on how not to use a delicate piece of equipment. It was a lesson I have never forgotten.

To mark out the radius of the bends I sent for a straight edge and a piece of chalk, only to find I was unable to get a true reading because of a build-up of dirt and old paint along the top of each frame. Taking the straight edge and using the end as a scraper I scraped away only to be halted by the irate voice of the boss who demanded to know what I was doing? "I'm cleaning the top of the frames to get a level," I replied simply.

"That's a straight edge you're using, not a scraper!" he bellowed. He had a good point, and suitably chastised I sent for a scraper. After examining the frames, the boss announced it was a job for Dar es Salaam workshops. I disagreed, explaining Tabora had straightened bent frames before.

This was achieved by building, from fireclay, a beehive-shaped furnace around the bent part of each frame, open at the top so more fuel could be fed in[50], and each connected at the bottom to oxygen cylinders to supply and control an

---

[50] This fuel was a sort of 'petcoke' (petroleum coke), derived from locomotives where the burners were misaligned, causing a build-up of a carbon-like deposit on the flash wall. This was found to burn at a very high temperature when air was blasted at it, and hence was ideal for smithy work.

air supply. After each furnace had been formed the fireclay was allowed to harden, and then each furnace ignited using an oxyacetylene torch and fed with fuel as required. With the engine standing on level track two hydraulic jacks were positioned on the forward frames to extend an upward force when they had reached a critical temperature. Levelling was achieved in the vertical plane using a plumb line down the face of the front buffer beam and in the horizontal plane using a spirit level on the same beam. With the frames judged straight and true the furnaces were left to die out and then broken up, and when the metal was cool it allowed the blacksmith to hammer a fine finish on the straightened parts.

During my time as shedmaster, I bought myself a new car. My old second-hand 1952 Beetle had roughed it over the years and was showing the effects of Tanganyika's dirt roads. I was by myself, single, and on a good salary, and so I indulged myself by buying a low-slung two-seater Volkswagen Karmann Ghia, and as such by far the smartest car in Tabora.

The author proudly showing off his prized Karmann Ghia.

After seven or eight months, I was relieved by John Pinkney, returning from home leave. It was his line of promotion and I returned to my locomotive inspector duties. In December, however, I received a letter of thanks from the chief mechanical engineer stating that I had "performed the duties of shedmaster in a surprisingly efficient manner"—a somewhat backhanded compliment, but one I was happy to accept, along with a post-dated duty allowance to compensate for "helping the administration to the detriment of his own pocket"; i.e., foregoing my usual loco inspector travelling allowance.

Then, in December 1961, Tanganyika was granted independence[51]. It was something we had seen coming for some years, its message promoted among the native population by visiting agitators such as Hugh and Dingle Foot, brothers of Michael Foot, the radical British politician, and both, in my eyes, 'useful idiots' for a government wishing to be rid of an empire and its responsibilities as

---

[51] Tanganyika became independent on 9th December 1961, with Julius Nyerere becoming its first Prime Minister, whilst retaining the British monarch as Queen of Tanganyika.

quickly as possible. Such types were happy to abandon the ordinary African to whatever fate awaited him or her.

At first, independence had little effect on our working lives, apart from the first day when the police went round the Indian owned dukas destroying bottles of South African wine and Rhodesian tobacco and cigarettes. One poor unfortunate to be caught up in this frenzy of destruction was the Goan manager of the Railway Hotel. Not only did he see his stock of South African wine destroyed, but out of habit he had unthinkingly raised the Union Jack on the hotel flagpole that morning. The police arrived and whilst he was roughed up and threatened with prison the flag was torn down, stamped on and set on fire.

One day, at about this time, my boss came up with an idea which, although it gave me more work, I thought had much to commend it. During one of our scheduled Sunday morning meetings, where I'd apprise him of the state of the network, he handed me a large sheet of graph paper with instructions to take readings of oil fuel and water consumption each time I rode on an engine, and from the top left of the paper lay them out in series of descending graphs, with each small square representing a mile of travel. Along the bottom edge I recorded the stations at which readings had been taken and on the left, as a separate column, I had to record the date and engine number. This was like holding my nose to the grindstone on every safari, but it could be read in an instant and showed if engines were being competently run or mismanaged. It also came in handy when one driver failed by running short of water. Working back along the graph from the point of failure it became obvious that he had, in error, departed Tabora several thousand gallons short of a full tank.

Around this time poor Bill was having increasing trouble with his legs, and was having to use a stick to get around. The last time I saw him he was making his slow and painful way on two sticks. I didn't ask him what the trouble was, as he would no-doubt have told me to "Bugger off!"

Also during this time I was aware that engine 3013, the next one up in the series from my engine, was lying on her side in Malagarasi swamp. Two years before, during extreme weather conditions, the embankment over the swamp, undercut by flood water, had collapsed under the locomotive's weight. Perhaps her number was unlucky. As I understand it, the driver and fireman escaped uninjured, and thankfully there were no passengers, it being a goods train. Now, however, the engine, along with its tender, lay 20 feet down the side of the embankment, having plunged into the swamp slightly smokebox down. At the time, Fearless Frank Kent, now Assistant CME East Africa Railways, had made it his business to fly to Tabora and had gone from there by train to examine the accident site, afterwards declaring it would take three months, and all the resources that Tabora shed could muster, to recover it. And so 3013 lay there, a forlorn sight, covered almost entirely by flood waters each rainy season, and by sun-baked mud each dry season, when its dirty black bulk was visible to all who steamed past it—a sorry testament not only to Tabora's inability to recover it, but to East African Railways as a whole. For the present, we're going to have to leave poor 3013 there, slowly rusting in the swamp, but fear not patient reader, for we will revisit her soon!

Around this time John Pinkney was courting a nursing sister from the hospital, and having decided to marry they invited my then boss (I am minded not to state his name for reasons of prudence), his wife, myself and one or two other guests, to the wedding, which was conducted by the old Australian vicar, the Reverend Backhouse. The reception was held in the Railway Hotel, Tabora, with the Railway Catering Department living up to its reputation for excellence, putting on a splendid spread. The happy couple were flying out of Tabora on their honeymoon, and it was decided to drive with them the few miles to the aerodrome, a grass strip with a reception hut and scales to weigh passengers' luggage, and wave them off. Gathered outside the hotel the boss's wife, a very attractive woman in her early forties, dropped a bombshell. "I'm going to ride with Mr Blackburn in his lovely motorcar," she announced!

Instead of wearing a light cotton dress, as was normally demanded by the hot tropical sun, she had, in view of the occasion, chosen to wear a smartly tailored 'home leave' suit, with a tight matching skirt, sheer nylon stockings, and high heels. Squeezing into the low and somewhat cramped passenger seat was a manoeuvre she executed with commendable dexterity, considering the shortness of her skirt, but once settled in, she was quite content to show off her long legs whilst I drove through Tabora and out onto the dirt road leading to the airport. European women were few and far between, and despite the fact that I was 32 or 33 years of age I was unused to female company. Having said that, it in no way prevented me from appreciating the aesthetics of a shapely ankle.

As I drove along, my brain exhorting my eyes to remain firmly fixed on the dirt road with its corrugations and potholes, she chattered away to me happily, glad, I suspect, of my company, given that it was a lonely life for the majority of white women. At some point, however, my peripheral vision registered a 'sweet disorder in her dress'—a fold, a small wrinkle in the knee of one of the stockings of her outstretched legs. Would it be a gallant act, I wondered, to offer to smooth out the unwanted blemish? It would be an offer welcomed if made, I fancied. But hang on a minute! She was someone else's wife, and not only someone's, but the boss's no less, and that had implications for my future; and so my morals (as well as my judiciousness) won out, and my hands remained firmly on the steering wheel.

Among the guests we were the first to arrive at the airport, with the boss in his Morris 1000 chugging along some way behind us, no doubt through the clouds of dust I'd raised. As the boss's car finally appeared, his wife edged out of the car, straightened her skirt, and walked past me to rejoin her husband. As she did so, she gave me a coy look and whispered, "You missed your chance!" The boss, on approach, gave me a long hard look, to such an extent that (despite my innocence of deed) I felt it advisable to make myself scarce and clear off on an inspection safari as soon as possible!

Chapter 24
Rescuing 3013

Not long afterwards the boss reached the end of his current tour and departed with his wife. His place was taken by Frank Kirton, one of a band of what we called 'retreads'—retired mechanical engineers with overseas railway experience and hired on individual three-year tours. On account of a somewhat prominent backside, he quickly earned the nickname 'Bwana Bata' (Mr Duck). He, my new boss, was a former Doncaster Plant-cum-Nigerian Railways engineer, and as fellow Yorkshiremen we understood each other, and to some extent he relied on me to help him keep right in the way we did things in that part of the world.

That didn't work every time, though. I was in my office a few months later when he called me in to inform me, "I want you to get 3013 out of the swamp."

For a few moments, I hesitated—it wasn't my job for a start—but with many of our expatriate staff leaving there was no one else to retrieve 3013 from its watery resting place and (if feasible) return it to traffic. Also, it pained me to see a fine locomotive abandoned and looking increasingly likely to be left to slowly sink into the mud. Was it even possible to get it out though? The words "Three months, and all the resources that Tabora shed could muster…" ran through my mind.

However, steaming past 3013 on numerous occasions, I'd thought long and hard on potential ways to recover it, and felt I had a feasible plan. Confident, and up for the challenge, I nodded. "Give me a couple of days to arrange things, and I'll then see what I can do." Arranging things included getting together a gang of reliable men along with four bogie flat waggons loaded with boulders in order to build a suitable platform on which to re-rail 3013. In addition, I asked for the assistance of the Carriage and Waggon Department supervisor (a man we affectionately knew as 'Spunky' Pennell—bearing that moniker because he was fit and full of vim and vigour, apparently a former weightlifter), who was in charge of Tabora's breakdown train, and responsible for its upkeep, stores and equipment—a necessary requirement for the task ahead.

With a gang of about 20 men drawn from both the Locomotive and the Carriage and Waggon Departments, and with my inspection coach attached to the rear of the breakdown train as accommodation for Mr Pennell and myself, we set off for Malagarasi, a station on the edge of the swamp. We were fortunate in one respect: instead of having to stable the breakdown train (which included accommodation for the 20 or so men) on the normal single loop line, where our sleep would be disturbed when it was shunted for crossing trains, the isolated Malagarasi station had a further line leading to, of all things, a 60-foot turntable!

One might ask what's a turntable doing in a bush station a long way from anywhere? The answer lies in that interesting part of Tanganyika's history connected to World War I and its aftermath;

3013 (side rods removed) and tender in Malagarasi swamp.

Tanganyika, the former Deutsche Ost Afrika, was invaded by joint British and Belgian forces, the British coming down from Kenya and the Belgians by way of the Belgian Congo. Overwhelmed, the Germans retreated into the interior, with the Belgian forces halting on reaching Tabora and declaring the ground they had won, extending from Lake Tanganyika to Tabora, as Belgian territory, and which included Kigoma and the railway to Tabora. At the end of the war, under pressure from the United Nations, the Belgians agreed to pull back to Malagarasi and use the Malagarasi River and swamp as a new frontier. To avoid tender-first running in both directions (i.e. on the west to east stretch for the Belgians, and east to west stretch for the British), the turntable was erected at Malagarasi. This continued for a few years until the League of Nations stepped in, decreeing the whole of the former German colony be administered by the British under mandated conditions, which was one of the reasons it remained largely undeveloped, the other being that, whilst its vast coal and iron ore reserves were known about, these were far from the existing railways. For Britain, impoverished and bankrupt after World War I, the cost of building new railways on such an extensive scale was beyond its abilities.

Beginning to extract the tender.

But back to the job in hand, rescuing 3013. My intention was to lay rails from the embankment down to the level of the swamp, but with no sure foundations we would have to build a stout platform using the boulders we had brought. Then, by using six hydraulic jacks, each of 20 tons capacity, jack the engine upright and onto the rails laid on the platform. It would then be a matter of hauling it up the slope and on to the main line. In theory it seemed a fairly simple operation, but in practice I knew there would be many and varied problems along the way.

Our day began at around 6 am when we breakfasted on 'Breakdown' rations, *Tanganyika Packers* corned beef along with the local and excellent *Simba Chia* (Lion Tea), with evaporated milk and sugar. By about 6:30 am, with the workforce gathered and ready for work, we walked the half mile or so along the embankment to the accident site. It was a pleasant walk, the air fresh and cool before a harsh and relentless sun cooked up dust devils, sending them dancing and swirling over the length and breadth of that ghastly sun-baked swamp.

The first days were spent building the platform, and from there a way up to the main line. The tender, which would have to be recovered first, was laid on its side at an awkward and crooked angle to the engine, and would have to be cut free at its intermediate coupling. It still contained a significant amount of water and fuel oil, and whilst the water could be drained off using the drain valve, there was no means of pumping out the fuel oil, so it would have to remain as something of a fire hazard. However, before I could tackle the tender, my first job was to remove, as an encumbrance, the left engine, comprising the piston valves, the piston, its connecting and coupling rods and valve gear. With these stowed safely in one of the vans and despatched to Dar es Salaam workshop, I could turn my attention to recovering the tender.

By a careful positioning of the jacks I was able to slowly jack the tender upright until, with infinite care, and without inflicting any damage to it, it touched down onto the platform's rails. The next move was the delicate task of hauling it out. This required co-operation with the Malagarasi stationmaster, to close the station and that section of railway to traffic during this operation. Malagarasi Permanent Way staff then had to split the main line and connect it with the temporary track laid down the platform. I was unsure if this temporary and not very stable track leading down to the swamp would bear the weight of a locomotive in full working order (i.e. the breakdown locomotive), but was delighted to discover a suitable length of steel cable within the depths of one of the stores vans of the breakdown train. It was long enough to shackle one end to 3013's large tender and the other to the breakdown engine, standing safe and secure on the main line.

3013 with connecting rods, side rods and pistons removed.

Slowly and cautiously the tender was hauled out and up onto the main line where I checked all of its 12 axle boxes, finding, to my surprise, that they were watertight and still full of roller bearing oil. Before moving off to Malagarasi station I oiled the axle box slides to make sure they were free to move up and down within the guides, and by way of its oil cups I poured a quantity of oil down into the bogie swivels. Confident the tender would run without derailing I accompanied it to Malagarasi station where, after a close examination, I declared it fit to run, it was stabled to await forward transmission to Dar es Salaam workshops for a complete overhaul and the continuation of its illustrious career.

It had only taken three days' work to recover the tender, and whilst this surprised me, I was aware the engine would prove far more difficult. It lay on its right side, down at the front to some extent, and at an angle fouling the embankment. Like its crew who had escaped uninjured, it was quite undamaged, to the extent that its louvred cab windows and glass on the side it was resting on remained intact. From this I assumed that 3013, cushioned by the soft crumbling embankment, had slid slowly to rest in the swamp's turbulent flood waters. It lay not only nose down but more than half-way over, and I knew before I started to jack it onto its 'feet' that I would first have to level it up and then line it up with the tracks that I'd already laid. For this I used ordinary screw jacks, and for the recovery men this was exhausting work under a blazing sun. However, encouraged by a lead singer, they chanted their inspiring work songs, and pressed on with the arduous but worthwhile task, until after 12 hours of gruelling work I surveyed 3013 and declared her to be laid level and true.

The author directing operations.

In preparation for jacking the engine over, the next half day was spent bringing hydraulic jacks and further balks of timber down to the site. Unmarked except for its several immersions, I didn't want to inflict damage on 3013 by the careless positioning of the powerful hydraulic jacks, and I intended to use the balks to act as cushions.

After levelling the engine, it still lay somewhat towards and into the embankment, and in its present position I gauged I would have to dig into the foot of the embankment a little; in total a section of about three feet deep by four feet in length.

I was about to make a start on this when John Cruden, the district engineer, arrived. In his soft Scottish burr, he asked me what my next move was. In all innocence, I replied that I was about to give myself some rerailing room by digging a small section of the embankment away. At once the friendly attitude disappeared, to be replaced by one of stern disapproval. "Interfere with that embankment in any way," I was told, "and you'll be in serious trouble."

Well, after all I was a footplate man and not a civil engineer, but I immediately understood his concerns. However, this left me with an almighty problem. I would now have to think of some way of slewing 100 tons of locomotive away from the embankment before I could jack it over. To achieve this I decided to exchange the plain screw jacks that the engine was resting on, for traversing jacks, and slowly, inch by inch, swing the engine away from the embankment. After 10 or 15 minutes traversing, 3013 suddenly gave a shudder, and with a crack, and to my horror, one of the traversing jacks flew out, narrowly missing some of the workforce. Plainly that idea had failed, leaving me at my wits' end.

At a loss of what to do, I studied the engine and its position on the jacks. It lay on its side, flat and level throughout, about two feet above the platform we had laid. I debated with myself whether it was feasible to erect a kind of pivot for the engine to swing on, but dismissed this idea, chiefly because I lacked a square of thick metal plate to act as a pivoting point. In its place I thought of using Herr Krupp's heavy cast steel sleepers, but had nightmare visions of them slipping, with the whole project ending in deadly disaster. Faced with an impasse, and almost in despair, I had another look around the engine, trying to reason another way of slewing it.

Suddenly, in a moment of enlightenment, I realised the answer had been staring me in the face all along. Why not, I reasoned, erect a wooden crib beneath the engine to line up with a pair of its coupled wheels and use the lower of these wheels to form a pivot. The more I examined the pros and cons the more I became convinced this was the only way out of my predicament. To allow the coupled wheels to pivot freely I would need to dismantle the surviving connecting rod, the side rods and the valve gear on the underside. For this, I needed a greater height to work in, for this was the most dangerous and difficult part of the operation.

I commenced by raising the engine a further two feet, and to make it safe and secure, laid it on four wooden cribs erected at each corner. Knowing I would require assistance for this dangerous operation, working beneath the engine, I called for volunteers. Never lacking in courage, the African workforce responded to a man, raising their fists and calling, "All is in God's hands; we are your men, Bwana, ready and willing."

Choosing three of the strongest and most able, we crawled under the engine, dragging between us a quantity of tools to loosen off the pins and nuts and to secure the rods during dismantling. This included four hydraulic jacks to carefully lower the heavy and cumbersome parts to the ground. Working upwards all the time, showered in dust and dirt, we fought to release pins and nuts rusted in by long immersion in Malagarasi's flood waters. Finally, after each separate part of the running gear had been safely lowered to the ground it was drawn out using ropes.

The commencement of jacking operations.

With this task completed, I turned my attention to building a stout wooden crib, one strong enough to bear the full weight of the engine. On a rough reckoning I calculated the main driving wheels would provide the best point of balance between the heavy 'front end' and the equally heavy slab-sided Belpaire firebox. This proved to be the case when, a short time later, 3013 was lowered to rest on this central crib and on to its lower main driving wheel as a swivel point. This was met with shouts of jubilation from the workforce, and the engine settled, balanced delicately on its lower driving wheel, and with the screw jacks and cribs out of the way, it was time to put my plan to the test.

Gathering the workforce together I warned them to swivel the engine "Polepole" (slowly) and "Kidogo kidogo" (bit by bit). To my profound relief it proved a complete success. With the workforce pushing, the engine swung freely on the driving wheel pivot point, lining up parallel with the embankment in the precise position I wanted. Here I digress a little, for whilst working around 3013 I noticed its wheels stamped with my old engine number, 3012, a clear indication Dar es Salaam workshop swapped sets of wheels to suit their circumstances.

With the engine in position for lifting, and to make it safe and stable for the removal of the now redundant and obstructive swivelling crib, I laid it on four temporary wooden cribs. Once in place it was time to bring on the big guns, in the shape of the hydraulic jacks. So as to prevent an accident, each jack had to be positioned with very great care, and never more so as the engine assumed a more vertical position and the angle of thrust and inclination increased. I was anxious also not to inflict damage on a largely unmarked locomotive by the careless positioning of jacks.

Hauling 3013 up the temporary track incline.

To this end, I chose a jacking point below the heavy double frame cast steel Delta truck, and after removing the steam dome cover I used the steam dome as a jacking position. I did toy with the idea of using the chimney, but they often seemed rather fragile and one of the first things to go in the event of an accident.

Instead, I used the multi-valve regulator cover on the smoke box, which to some extent I came to regret, as I had assumed the cover to be of cast steel, but in the event found it was of plate, and whilst it withstood the forces applied to it, the jack left a distinct impression on its otherwise flat end—a permanent reminder of the adventure 3013 had experienced.

To position another jack, I used the expansion link bracket—a large steel casting firmly bolted to the main frames and extending the width of the engine, a casting which carried the two expansion links plus much of the weight of both valve gears. Finally, I also found a place for a jack on the pony carriage truck.

I couldn't be everywhere at once, so I warned the workforce to stop jacking the moment they saw any adverse movement in any of the jacks, and immediately call me. As the engine became more and more upright and the angle of attack more acute, each jack required a 'blocking' wooden crib to both raise its height and resist its thrust—a delicate and time consuming, but necessary, operation.

Once initiated the jacking went very well. The men working the jacks had experience of them around the shed and at the slightest sign of danger a shout of "Simama!" (Stop!) would go up and the jack or jacks would be repositioned. As the engine assumed a near vertical position I expected that the weight of its cylinders, undercarriage and wheels would bring it crashing over and down on to the temporary rails. It came as a complete surprise, therefore, to find we had to continue jacking all the way, until the wheels finally rested on the rails.

3013 being examined, having been drawn up on to the main line.

Once upright poor old 3013 looked in a sorry state, with her smokebox filled with sand and other rubbish, as was her once pristine cab. Inside the firebox the firebricks and flash wall had collapsed and lay in a jumbled heap. Outside things looked even worse, with the underside encrusted with sand and black cotton soil and dead rushes. In this condition I felt that the axle boxes, by an accumulation of rust and foreign matter, might well be seized in the axle box guides, bringing with it the danger of a derailment when it was moved. I therefore arranged for the axles boxes and coupled compensating beam trunnions to be cleaned, and to penetrate and free the moving surfaces I had them flooded with thinned engine oil. Whilst this was taking effect I examined the engine's 14 roller bearing axle boxes, but again found each untainted by water and containing the correct level of oil.

Up to this point the recovery had taken 16 days of continuous work, and each evening, before darkness fell, Spunky Pennell and I stripped to the buff, with each standing beneath one of Malagarasi's water columns to sluice away the day's dust, dirt and sweat. That this was water straight out of the Malagarasi River (no-doubt teeming with water-borne parasites) didn't seem to matter at the time.

On the Malagarasi turnable

469

Spunky Pennel after a hard day's work (this time, at the scene of a suspected act of sabotage on the Mwanza line).

With 3013 standing on the stone platform, I left it overnight for the penetrating oil to work its magic, and in the morning made arrangements to haul it out of the swamp. To prevent the weight of the breakdown engine spreading the temporary track, I attached the steel cable to 3013's drag box, and doubled it by passing it through the intermediate coupling slot, before laying it out full length. My next move, after again arranging for the Malagarasi section to be closed and its main line slewed and connected to the temporary track, was to divide the breakdown train and propel the divided part down the slope to where I could shackle the cable to its leading van.

The African crew of the breakdown engine, standing on the main line, were experienced men, but having remained apart from the recovery site I reminded them of the dangers, and to draw out 3013 "Polepole". Under my direction, they carefully tightened the cable, and with everything secure began the slow pull up the steep incline out of the swamp and on to the main line where it

The author, after an equally hard day's work, at the same Mwanza line location.

was received with shouts of jubilation, and decorated in the African way with palm fronds. After a further application of engine oil to the guides and a careful examination of the axle boxes and their freedom to move up and down easily within the guides, the engine was drawn the half mile or so into Malagarasi station. With 3013's only coupling attached to the front buffer beam the engine was facing the wrong way round, and the problem of securing it to the rear of the breakdown train in this condition, and running it the 157 miles to Tabora for turning, was one fraught with danger and uncertainties.

Here again the long-disused Malagarasi turntable proved a blessing. Using balks of timber as buffing gear, 3013 was nudged onto the table, balanced and turned, then stabled up whilst the breakdown train returned to the site to recover its equipment and to tidy up. After this 3013 was coupled to the rear of the breakdown train to begin the first stage of its long journey to Dar es Salaam. Here it was cleaned, overhauled, painted up and returned to traffic looking as good as the day it was first erected. (Not that I got any thanks for its recovery, of course!)

Following 3013's extraction from the swamp I was due some local leave (this must have been about 1960), so I booked a two-week trip on Lake Albert and on up the Victoria Nile to see the Murchison Falls. I began by boarding the lake steamer the *SS Robert Coryndon*, a very attractive ship and, like all the passenger vessels operated by EAR, was very well appointed.

Built in England in 1929, all her parts were numbered and she was then taken apart and transported in kit form to Lake Albert, where she was reassembled. I can't honestly remember much about her interior, but according to Winston Churchill she was "The best library afloat", whilst Earnest Hemmingway called her "Magnificence on water"[52]. It was a very agreeable journey, watching the lakeside scenery slip past, seeing lake steamers plying their trade, and native canoes being vigorously paddled along, their occupants going at some speed, but to who knows where.

The *Robert Coryndon* took passengers as far as Nimuli, and then, because the Nile became too shallow, passengers transferred on to the paddle steamer *Grant*[53] (irreverently known to its passengers as 'The Grunt'). It, too, was very well appointed, with excellent accommodation on the upper deck. Being a stern paddle wheeler it propelled barges lashed to its bows, as it made its way along, passing Nile trading vessels that visited the little ports or jetties along the way, and which were used to load cotton and other goods.

---

[52] Sadly, she ran aground in 1962, around the time of Ugandan independence and was left to rust, being broken up for scrap between 2009 and 2012.

[53] Built in Paisley, Scotland, in 1912. Ultimate fate unknown, but certainly no longer extant.

Often, as night descended, beautiful sunsets would appear over the river, with just the sound of the steam engine puffing away as it drove the big paddle wheel, the water gently lapping against the ship as it made its slow but stately progress upriver. Part of the trip was spent going over into Sudan, with a visit to the 'Traveller's Tree', under which various famous explorers (Giovanni Miani, Sir Samuel White Baker and Emin Pasha) had rested in the early years of African exploration.

One of my fellow passengers was Bob Foster, our boilersmith, who had a number of pipes he used to smoke, one of which was a fancy long-necked one made out of a gourd, with a meerschaum centre. I recall that one of the lady passengers, an attractive young woman, picked it up, unlit, and jokingly pretended to smoke it to the amusement of the other passengers; however, she must have accidentally inhaled some of its dormant but malodorous contents, for she very quickly put it down, whilst making a half-theatrical choking performance which plainly declared, "Oh my word!"

From the Grunt, we were transferred to two smaller launches, as the paddle steamer could go no further, and passed what may have been the District Commissioner's safari launch, used for inspecting his wide and watery domain, which was riding at anchor. On the riverbanks were elephants, water buffalo, hyena, hippopotamus, and crocodile, as well as numerous birds. As we got closer to the falls, we exited the launches due to the turbulence of the water, and walked the last mile or two. The Murchison Falls see the whole of the River Nile forced through a narrow gap in the rocks just over 20 feet wide, with an overall fall of about 200 feet. The roar of this water can be heard from miles around and grew in intensity as we made it up to the top of the falls. Here a narrow iron girder footbridge had been thrown across the top, which visitors stood on to look down on the boiling, churning water directly beneath—an amazing spectacle.

Some historians believe that a party of Roman legionaries dispatched by Nero reached the Murchison Falls in 61 AD, although what evidence there is for this, if any, is unclear. If true it would be an incredible achievement; and who knows, may help to explain the distinctive 'Romanesque' attire of the Wagogo tribespeople, although they do live another 500 miles further south, so perhaps not. As we made our way back from the falls I noticed a European standing on a large rock near the base, fishing, probably for Nile perch that had been concussed by the falls, and wondered if this was the District Commissioner himself.

Following my leave, I returned to normal duties, firstly travelling to Mwanza to inspect the Locomotive Department's facilities there and report on them. The locomotive heading the train was one of the American built 27 Class. After checking the condition of the engine and in particular its trimmings, I rode on its footplate. Several of this Class had been built (perhaps for colder climes) without cladding to the boiler back plate. This engine was one of that number, and whilst observing the actions of its crew, I noticed a fine hairline crack in the boiler back plate extending about an inch from one of the stay bolt heads and marked by a microscopic, almost indistinguishable, seepage of limescale. This was just about as serious as it could get, and aware of the immense steam pressure surrounding the crack I resisted the temptation to give it a tap with my inspection hammer.

My concern grew as I examined the fracture more closely and I decided to forego my Mwanza inspection, and keeping a close eye on the backplate, ride with the engine on its return trip, and as a matter of urgency report my findings to John Pinkney, the shedmaster. On receiving this information John immediately stopped the engine and had it blown down for a boiler examination. This, it turned out, marked the beginning of the end for the 27 Class, and although some continued for a few more years it was found the boilers had, broadly speaking, reached the end of their life after about 20-odd years. In conversation with my boss I was told a new boiler would cost £10,000—an enormous sum in those days, and one unjustified by the general condition of the Class. And so after years of sterling service, one by one they arrived at the scrap line behind Dar es Salaam workshops.

Chapter 25
Keeping Mwanza Going

My next brush with destiny occurred when I was ordered to Mwanza on 'special duties'. An odd term I thought, more in keeping with the British Army than a railway directive, and which if I had remained a soldier may have meant being drafted into a firing squad or sent to quell some rebellion, which I suppose in one way or the other it was. For a reason or reasons I've never established, in February 1960 the 30 or so African staff at Mwanza had gone on strike, leaving only the Indian stationmaster and the Indian fitter-in-charge of Mwanza South locomotive shed remaining. On arriving at Mwanza and looking round I could see, to use an old NER footplate expression, that 'I had all my water on', with work stopped, goods piling up, both yards blocked by a jumble of both loaded and empty waggons, and the township without a railway connection to the outside world. At the same time traders were crying out for vehicles to be positioned for either loading or unloading, and those loaded to be marshalled on to Down trains.

Although at that time a large deep water port was being constructed at Mwanza South, Mwanza railway installations, that is Mwanza Station and Mwanza Port, were divided by a half mile branch line. Mwanza Port was visited by lake steamers and fitted out with quays, cranes and storage sheds, and Mwanza station, with its long loading and unloading platform and marshalling sidings, was the place where Up trains were sorted and Down trains formed.

I must confess that shunting has never been my strong point, my experience being confined to a few infrequent shunting turns whilst a cleaner at Springhead, when to be quite frank I had no idea what was going on. In addition, I'd made the odd carriage movements at Hull Paragon where I was equally lost. Yet even to my untrained eyes, both Mwanza Port and Mwanza station looked in a mess, each blocked by a mass of both empty and loaded waggons.

The shunters had their own unique way of doing things, pushing long trains of waggons, both loaded and empty, back and forth around the two yards, and after forming them into trains, splitting them up as and when required – a long and time consuming way of working. Being without help of any kind, I had neither the time nor freedom of choice to continue the practice, and to give me room to work I came to the conclusion I would first have to clear both yards of the clutter of unused vehicles by storing them in little-used sidings. This included that 'holiest of holies', the judge/governor's siding, an idyllic grassed and level amphitheatre surrounded by a natural circle of huge granite boulders. Here, when on safari, with personal staff and guarded by a detachment of police, a high court judge, or the governor general, if on a visit, would spend his leisure hours.

Having decided on a plan of action, and after obtaining a 'Line Clear' from the Mwanza stationmaster for my return with an engine, I walked the mile or so to the locomotive shed, where I hoped the fitter-in-charge had maintained one of Mwanza's two 27 Class (used for shunting in that faraway station) in steam. After checking the engine over I drove it back to Mwanza where, snatching a little sleep when or wherever I could, weeks of working around the clock awaited me.

My first priority was to sort things out and get traffic moving. All up trains had been halted at Tabora until the situation at Mwanza improved. With space at a premium I began the task of cleaning up both Mwanza Station and Mwanza Port by parking empty and for the time being unwanted vehicles in any empty space I could find, and digging out loaded waggons and forming them into the next Down train. After 20 hours of non-stop toil I advised Tabora that I was ready to receive Up trains and despatch Down trains.

Both before and during shunting movements, of which there were hundreds during any 24 hour period, I had to operate all the points myself. This was wearying work. When propelling vehicles I had to gauge over some distance, stopping just short of each pair of points, not always easy during daylight hours and much more difficult during the hours of darkness. This was equally true when drawing vehicles out of sidings and slotting them in elsewhere. Then I had to clear the points before I could turn them back. With that accomplished and after securing the engine from running away, which would add nothing to improve my reputation, I had to climb down and walk back to the points before turning them back to the original position.

To save my legs, I had two options: either stop just clear of the points, which were hidden during the hours of darkness and by the length of the train when propelling, and bringing with it the danger of still fouling the points, then having to walk back and start all over again; or, draw the train well clear of them, which might mean turning more points, then waste time and effort walking the extra distance. You may ask, why didn't I negotiate with the striking workers, as sorting out their grievances might have taken less effort than running Mwanza's railway facilities single-handedly. However, industrial relations wasn't my job, and I had been given no remit to negotiate with them, and hence I continued to shunt waggons and form trains.

Coupling up was, however, the most frustrating job of all, at times almost driving me to drink. The slightest misjudgement would nudge vehicles away, leaving me to walk back to the engine and try again and again until I succeeded. The Up Mail Train, unlike goods trains, each with its varied waggons for different locations around the station and port, was in comparison a quick and easy train to rejig into the Down Mail Train. Twenty minutes before its arrival the stationmaster, as per regulations, would warn shunting operations to stop, and the shunting engine moved clear of the running lines and parked up until such time as required. On arriving at Mwanza, the Mail Train, under the supervision of the stationmaster, would be directed into one of the station's two platform lines, from where, after the passengers had detrained, it would be remarshalled for its return. First the guards van was uncoupled, drawn out and placed at the bottom of the adjacent empty platform, followed by the caboose, then to fully form the train, the coaching stock would be added. When completed this allowed the engine to move out before proceeding to Mwanza South for refuelling and attention.

After about a month of working on my own, often for about 20 hours per day, doing the job of the 30 or so striking African staff, but during which I had been able to re-establish a regular train service, one of the African shunter drivers thankfully returned, giving me the opportunity to leave the footplate and direct the shunting operations. However, in the meantime two things had occurred. My right arm, always being in contact with the cab's window frame, became increasing raw from the wrist to the elbow, to the extent I had to purchase bandages and lint and for relief bind it up against the constant rubbing and pressure it received. The second was a more painful, and in the circumstances, a very unwelcome incident.

This occurred due to the fact that I was having trouble with the engine's steam brake cylinder, which on a 27 Class locomotive was located centrally between the frames and midway between the smokebox saddle and expansion links bracket. Whilst waiting for an incoming train I decided to investigate, and armed with a large and heavy spanner I leant over with my ribs resting on one of the engine's radius rods, whilst I fitted the spanner to an equally large and reluctant nut. Then, unthinkingly, and exerting all my strength, I gave a great heave, with the result that much of the force was transferred to my ribcage, causing excruciating pain. Incapacitated for a few minutes I gathered myself together, and convinced I needed medical help, informed the stationmaster before going to the local hospital. There I was seen by its the resident doctor. I forget her name, which is a pity, for years later in Dar es Salaam, at Ocean Road Hospital, she delivered my first born, a fine healthy boy.

Anyway, getting back to my ribs—in the absence of X-rays, she examined me carefully, before declaring (and I remember her words clearly for the genuine concern they held): "You poor man, you've broken two ribs." She then strapped me up before warning me to rest for the next few days. I thanked her and, on my way back bought a couple of packs of *Aspro*, a then very effective form of pain relief. Although frequently in pain for the next few days, I found that with repeated doses of *Aspro*, I was able to continue with what the railway expected of me.

During the time that I had the shunter driver as an aid, a serious accident occurred which went on to develop into something of a Fred Karno[54] circus act. I had taken to shunting Mwanza Port by digging out, at first light, loaded waggons for transfer to Mwanza station, and replacing them with waggons either for unloading or loading. Depending on the arrival of an Up freight or a ship's departure time, I occasionally had to return with waggons requiring urgent shipment. On this occasion I had to return, across lunchtime, with three or four bogie waggons, and it being a straightforward movement I left it to the shunter driver, whilst I grabbed a bite to eat.

My accommodation was an empty one-room structure, without furnishings of any kind, although I had found a wooden box to sit on. It was then that my dining arrangements (meals consisting almost entirely of bully beef) were suddenly interrupted when the shunter driver burst in saying there was a

---

[54] Frederick John Westcott (1866-1941), credited with popularising the custard-pie-in-the-face gag, and considered by some to be the man who originated slapstick comedy.

derailment. I asked him, "Wapi?" (Where?), and his reply could not have pointed to a worse place, and the accident could not have come at a worse time. Immediately after leaving the station limits, the Port Line crossed the only road linking Mwanza town with the European Quarter. It was whilst crossing this road that the engine had derailed, completely blocking the thoroughfare used by Mwanza's European commuters, whose rumbling bellies, it being lunchtime, required immediate sustenance.

Concerned by the seriousness of the situation I dropped everything and hurried to the scene of the accident, where I found the engine with all its 12 wheels derailed, but surprisingly neither its tender nor its waggons. Of equal concern to me was the long line of cars building up, whose occupants were anxious to get home. In view of all this I came to the conclusion that my only course of action was to reverse the engine, and whilst praying this didn't cause further havoc, try and propel the engine and waggons back into the station and just clear of the road. Climbing into the cab I prepared the move. From then on things became farcical. In his panic the shunter driver had left the injector on, and by now the boiler was full to its steam dome and just about at bursting point—something, in the urgency of the moment, that I failed to notice. Winding the engine into back gear I prepared to move, and with the intention of testing things slowly and gently, I laid my hand on the regulator handle. At that all hell let loose, the regulator, to my dismay, springing fully open. In an instant the engine picked up water, flooding all its internal steam pipes and both its steam chests and cylinders with water at full 175 psi boiler pressure. And with that, as I tried in vain to close the regulator, she gave a massive lurch, and with a horrible groan from her cylinders, set off backwards, bouncing and lurching over each unforgiving steel sleepers whilst spouting a dense column of water from her chimney and every gland and joint. Out of my control and afraid of a pile-up within the station yard, bringing with it not only the decimation of waggons, but much of the valuable cargo they contained, I turned in desperation to the engine's reverser, quickly screwing it into mid-gear. After about 25 yards of groaning and spitting water all over the place, this brought her antics to an end, just within the station and clear of the road.

Climbing down, expecting to see bent piston rods, cylinder covers knocked out, and even more extensive derailments, I was met by a beaming Englishman with outstretched hand. "Congratulations!" he enthused. "I've never seen anything like it in my life before. If I hadn't seen it with my own eyes I would never have believed it, I just don't know how you did it!"

Mystified, I glanced at the engine and did a double-take: miraculously, she had re-railed herself. Despite it being a situation I had no control over, I puffed up my chest with imitation pride and, putting on an air of nonchalance gave him a wink, casually remarking: "Ah well, it's all part of the job, don'tcha know!" As a celebration of this unexpectedly good outcome, I treated myself to a packet of *Crown Bird* smokes, and, to lubricate my dry throat, a couple of bottles of ice-cold and refreshingly fizzy *Coca-Cola*.

Getting back to the derailment, it proved a mystery from beginning to end. After a cursory examination of the cylinder covers and the piston rods, which I found undamaged (the Americans made them tough), I turned to the track which hereabouts was straight and level and inspected it for defects or an obstruction, finding it in perfect order. In any case the engine would have been passing over the crossing at a sedate walking pace making a derailment highly unlikely. At a loss I turned my attention to the engine and in particular its pony arrangements. Perhaps through neglect, I thought, the pony pivot had seized—a most unlikely event, but something which had to be explored. However, I found it well lubricated and in perfect working order. Scratching my head whilst making short work of a packet of *Crown Bird* smokes, I next examined the pony axle box guides, finding every indication the boxes were free to move up and down. To make sure I had the shunter driver run each pony wheel individually over a spanner whilst I confirmed they were able to move vertically without hindrance.

And so that was that. Well, not quite, for by regulation the District Permanent Way Inspector had to examine the track after a derailment. Also the engine wheels (which looked all right to me) needed to be gauged and the flanges and tyres examined for wear or misalignment, which, whilst waiting for the Mechanical Inspector to arrive from Dar es Salaam, would stop the engine for several days. In view of the delay to traffic and other manifest complications at that time, I elected to overlook the rules, say nothing, and carry on as usual. I disclose this 60-ish years later in the hope that my confession will in no way affect my modest overseas pension and my only hope of escaping the penury of the workhouse!

Chapter 26
Upheaval and Mutiny

About this time (and here I am a little uncertain whether the following event occurred before my Mwanza stint or after) I was called to accompany a 'Special' empty stock train to Kigoma, and arrange transport to Dar es Salaam for about 300 Belgian refugees, men, women and children, including a group of nuns fleeing across the dangerous and frequently storm-tossed water of Lake Tanganyika by whatever means they could, as the former Belgian Congo descended into anarchy, rape, murder and civil war[55]. Arriving about midday, I found them in a pitiful state, all huddled together in the port area, traumatised, dirty, without food or shelter. In their fear and exhaustion they seemed to view me with distrust and suspicion, as if I were some official intent on sending them back.

At this point I was approached by a tall middle-aged Belgian man with torn clothing who limped towards me bearing all the signs of a prolonged and savage beating. He said to me (in broken English) "They fighted me all night," from which I interpreted he had been assaulted throughout the night. My thought at the time was that, despite the state he was in, he'd been fortunate to get away with nothing worse. He begged help for his fellow refugees, and I was able to assure him he and the others were now safe, and I was there to arrange transport to Dar es Salaam as quickly as I could. As always, Kigoma lay quiet and peaceful, slumbering in the heat of the midday sun, its few European inhabitants

---

[55] Known as the Congo Crisis, this was a 5-year period of political upheaval and conflict that began almost immediately after the Congo became independent from Belgium in 1960. Something of a proxy conflict during the Cold War, the USA and USSR supported opposing factions, resulting in mutiny, massacre, and an estimated 100,000 lives lost.

widely dispersed and unaware of the suffering on the other side of lake, or even nearer to home, down at the docks. I later learned that many of the women I'd seen, including nuns, had been molested.

With the train remarshalled and the engine turned and prepared I led a sorry procession from the docks to the station where they entrained, if not in comfort, at least safe and sound. At Tabora, and no longer taking part, I left the train and went straight to the boss to report. Later I heard that many of Tabora's African Asians and European residents, warned of the refugees plight, had arrived at the station with food and drink and offers of help—a heart-warming display of humanity in a time of need.

My next assignment was to accompany a train of Indian infantrymen bound for the Congo on peacekeeping duties. So few were they, for the enormity of the task ahead. Their CO, a splendid looking Sikh, his khaki turban set off by a red plume, was enjoying the luxury of travelling in the former Tanganyika Railways Senior Officer's inspection coach, a bogie vehicle heavy with polished African hardwoods and redolent of late 1920's art deco. Arriving at Kigwe in the evening the CO sent his orderly, asking if I would like to join him for a drink. I found him seated at a large mahogany table within the coach's spacious lounge, a bottle of whiskey, and two cut glass whiskey tots at the ready. In perfect English he offered me a 'sundowner'. Being more or less teetotal at the time I declined as graciously as I could. Instead, he offered me a long drink of lime juice and soda water. This was something new to me and quite delectable, and furthermore I vowed, in future, to carry a supply when on safari. As we parted I shook hands with him and thanked him for his hospitality, and because I thought he needed it, wished him well.

The second battalion, the Tanganyika Defence Force, a militia still under the command of British officers and NCOs had barracks just outside Tabora, with many of its personnel, both British and African, former members of the proud King's African Rifles (KAR). I had two close friends stationed there, Major Jack Leeson and his wife Mary. Jack was a bluff experienced soldier, a veteran of World War II and later the Kings African Rifles. He was a shooting companion of mine, and a first class shot, who swung at passing game birds (and seldom missed) with graceful ease. We shot duck and spur-winged geese on the flooded Wemberi plains 70 miles north of Tabora, way off the Mwanza road, and also large red-legged partridge and guinea fowl in the bush around Tabora, having several adventures and narrow escapes together.

Once, whilst travelling to the Wemberi we stopped off to track a flock of guinea fowl gathered at the roadside, who all scuttled off at our approach. Parking by the side of the little used Mwanza road I made a point of standing square on to the bush and carefully took my bearings. Satisfied I knew what I was doing Jack and I set off to follow the guinea birds through an expanse of flat featureless bush marked only by small and infrequent acacia bushes and the dreaded ngoja kidogo or 'wait a bit' thorn, a dense bush growing four of five feet at its maximum and bristling with a mass of curved needle-sharp thorns, which penetrated the flesh and held you fast. To inadvertently brush against one and instinctively pull away as its curved thorns struck home was to pull most of the bush against your trembling body, with distressing consequences.

After about a mile, during which the guinea fowl trotted ahead, just out of gunshot all the time, we gave up. I turned around a full 180° and said, "That's where we want to be."

"No," Jack replied, pointing in quite a different direction. "I think it's that way." Convinced I was right, I disagreed, with Jack then giving up and saying, "You've been out here a lot longer than I have, we'll go your way." We trudged back through the scrub, our guns and other accoutrements becoming heavier at every step. After about a mile we stopped. Before us lay nothing but a sea of endless sun-blasted bush, before fading away into a blue grey heat haze.

We carried on for a further half mile when I stopped. "We are lost, Jack, I just don't know where we are or what direction to take."

Jack's military instincts came to the fore. "Let's think about it for a minute. We know the Mwanza road runs north to south, we went into the bush facing west, with the sun in our faces. If we walk with the sun behind us, we should eventually hit the road."

We set off again, our hopes raised, but after another mile without sign of the road my fears began to grow. Then, to our intense relief, we stumbled across a red scar in the bush, the Mwanza dirt road. Halleluiah! However, our ordeal was by no means over, as our eyes searched in vain for the car, was it north or south of where we stood? Tired as we were, there was nothing for it but to walk along the road in opposite directions until one of us found the car. It was Jack's car, and in common with VW Beetles of the time had only one key, and that was safely in Jack's pocket. If I found the car it meant retracing my steps until such time as I met Jack, then both of us walking back to where the car had been left. Holding my shotgun by the muzzle, I laid it over my shoulder, open but loaded (for one never knew what we one might come across in the bush) and set off, leg weary, along a deserted and heat filled road. Mile after mile was tramped without success until I heard the sound of a car approaching from behind. Turning I saw one of the ubiquitous VW Beetles, the only car able to withstand the rigours of Tanzania's dirt roads without the doors falling off, tearing towards me trailing a cloud of dust. Whoever it might be they would prove a saviour. In the event it turned out to be a sweat-drenched dust-plastered but beaming Jack whose first words were, "That's the last time I go into the bush without a compass," to which I could only say a silent "Amen!"

One day, after a fruitless shooting expedition around the western edge of Tabora and our arrival back at Jack's married quarters, an attractive colonial style bungalow, he suggested it might pay to have a walk through the bush around the camp's perimeter. Straight away we picked up a narrow path hemmed in by tall elephant grass. In the lead, and striding out, I began to open my cartridge bag and select a couple of cartridges for my empty gun when, horror struck, I found I was about to step on a puff adder—a highly venomous snake with the unnerving ability to not only strike forward with lightning speed, but equally adept at striking backwards. In shock I rammed on all my brakes, stopping just short of the snake's striking range. Now Jack, as I have mentioned before, was bluff], and as befits a man of his rank, a little portly in build, carrying the air of a prosperous farmer, as well he might for he came from a farming background. Never to be found wanting, Jack was striding out too, and keeping pace and close behind me. As I stopped without warning, Jack, unsighted, collided with me, his rather ample belly pushing me towards the snake which was in an aggressive mood. Unable to jump over it I gave a cry, half fear and half despair, and leapt to one side, just missing the snake's backward curving swing. Jack shocked by my near escape, his gun as empty as mine, was unable to despatch the creature, which disappeared into the long grass. Dispirited by all this we abandoned our quest and returned to the safety of the barracks as quickly as our legs would take us.

Occasionally, an instructor sergeant joined us on our forays. He had a little black dog, a bitch of indeterminate parentage and undisciplined nature, called Bonnie. I used to view it with some disfavour, for it persisted yapping loudly whilst running ahead, disturbing the sport. The three of us were doing a sweep in the vicinity of the newly constructed Queen Elizabeth dam, a large reservoir which, it was hoped, would bring to an end to Tabora's chronic water shortage.

Out of the blue we were alerted by a howl from Bonnie, who we then saw laid on her back, her legs in the air, and overshadowed by a large black spitting cobra, its hood outstretched and jaws agape, from which one bite would prove fatal.

Knowing the dog was in mortal danger I instinctively raised my gun, and leaning forward a little, took a long raking shot at the snake's rearing head. In doing so I had raised the muzzle slightly, praying the bottom spread of shot would miss the dog, but its wide spread might find its mark. At my shot the snake dropped, and the three of us, guns at the ready and moving cautiously, found it was indeed dead. Was it the result of some fine shooting or a bit of luck? Only shooting men can judge! Finding the snake dead, we turned our attention to Bonnie who lay on the ground whimpering and clawing at her eyes, having been struck by a stream of venom from the snake's fangs.

There was only one chance of saving the dog's eyesight—flush her eyes quickly, but with what? None of us carried water[56] and the dam lay a mile or more away behind some low hills, and time was of the essence. The only answer lay in urine, that last resort. I asked Jack, "Can you wee?"

Not such a silly question when heat and sweat had left each of us short in that department. "I'll try," Jack answered manfully.

"Right. I'll hold one eye open at a time and you let fly." With what little Jack produced splashing over my hands, the colour of fine brandy, this purged the venom, and there were still two of us to perform. Happily, this unorthodox eyewash saved her eyesight, and after a few days of swelling and discomfort, her eyes recovered. Not so fortunate was poor Mr Giles, a large golden retriever labrador, whose size and heavy build indicated a somewhat dubious father. But for all that, he was always affectionate, ready to snuggle up for a pat or stroke and a kind word. He had been left with Jack after its owner, a fellow officer, had been recalled to the UK, and because he was steady and biddable he became a firm favourite on our shoots together.

One day we decided to take an old back road, a sand track really, perhaps last used when the Germans retreated from Tabora. It was a track we were familiar with as it had offered us some fine sport in the past. Half way along a shallow grass valley, dotted with odd clumps of trees and dense thorn bushes, ran off into the far distance. Here we stopped, and with our shotguns at the ready, moved along the valley floor, Mr Giles accompanying Jack. We reached the first

---

[56] Unlike today, when it seems that people can't even step out their suburban houses without a single-use plastic bottle of water!

clump, and as Jack went round one side I went around the other. Part way round I heard a shot, followed by Jack's agitated voice calling for Mr Giles. Expecting trouble of some kind I dashed around, finding Jack, along with Mr Giles, his tail wagging and looking pleased with himself, standing together. In answer to my concerns Jack said he had disturbed a large snake which had reared above him in such close proximity he had neither the time or space to mount his gun and aim it properly, instead firing it on instinct from the hip. The snake promptly dropped and slithered away unharmed. In the meantime, hearing the shot, Mr Giles had rushed in, with Jack now saying, "I think Mr Giles met the snake and has been bitten."

I examined Mr Giles carefully, paying particular attention to his head, muzzle and chest, but finding no sign of blood or other evidence of a snake bite we continued on our way. After a couple of hundred yards, Jack stopped. "Where's Mr Giles?" he asked. At once dreaded certainty struck home.

With a cry of dismay, I said, "Quick, he's been bitten, we must go back and find him." We discovered him stretched out, his golden coat blending with the sun-blasted grass. The poison was already at work, his body shaking with outbreaks of tremors. Unable to lift his head, he rolled his eyes towards us with a look which said he knew his end was near.

We carried him back to my car with the intention of racing back to Tabora and the district veterinary officer. It was at the time I still had my old VW Beetle, a car that was able to stick to Tanzania dirt roads no matter how driven, and whilst I drove like a madman, Jack tried to keep Mr Giles conscious and alive. By now he was in a dreadful condition, his tongue hanging out and his body wracked by convulsions.

Still ten miles or more from Tabora, Jack said, "We've lost him, he's gone." We drew up at the veterinary offices and at our request the vet looked at Mr Giles.

"He's been dead about 15 minutes," he announced, then with a thoughtful gesture, "Would you like me to look after him?" I drove Jack back to his bungalow and went in with him.

The first thing Mary asked was "Where's Mr Giles?" It was a sombre little group which sat down. Jack offered me a whisky which I accepted, not for the drink, but as we raised our glasses it was to the passing of a gentle and faithful friend.

During my to-ing and fro-ing between home and the barracks, I began to notice a sullen attitude developing in the Tanzanian Defence Force soldiers. Meeting the occasional army lorry I now had to swerve out their way as they purposely took up most of the road or drove deliberately at me. Instead of a smart salute, a legacy from the famous King's African Rifles, at the barrack gates I was now left waiting, until with a show of indifference, someone reluctantly opened the barrack gates. Taking as an example the Congo soldiers still running amok, I asked Jack, who by this time was preparing to depart for home and retirement, "When's this lot of yours going to mutiny?"

"Don't worry, we're keeping our eye on them," Jack replied. "We have the keys to the armoury and everything's under control."

Thank heavens for that, I thought, reassured.

Unlike my usual Saturday morning visits to the shed, where I might, ironically, be examining footplate staff for sight and colour vision (the blind leading the sighted, if you believe the army medical orderly's diagnosis), or checking engines for signs of wear or neglect, Saturday, 25 January 1963, found me with John Pinkney, the shedmaster, interviewing a small group of hopeful Africans, wishing to fill vacancies in the footplate staff[57]. At about 8.30 am, and part way through the interview, we were interrupted by a burst of rifle fire from somewhere behind the shed, followed instantly by the shed staff and all our interviewees streaming out and racing away in all directions.

The shedmaster's offices had large windows on two sides, one overlooking the locomotive yard, the other the locomotive shed. Taken aback by the gunfire and unaware of what was going on, we were both surprised when three armed soldiers walked out of the shed and made their way towards us. Lulled into a sense of security by Jack's reassurances, and thinking the soldiers must be on some kind of military exercise, I said I would have a word with them. It was a grave misjudgement on my part, and one that nearly cost me my life. Two of the soldiers carried rifles and bayonets, the other a Bren gun. As I approached them I saw with some apprehension they were in a state of extreme agitation. Before I could ask a question they began pointing their guns and in a mixture of English and Swahili began hurling abuse at me. Rooted to the spot by the violence of their outbursts, and recalling the situation in the Congo, I was about to make a retreat when, at point blank range, one of the soldiers fired his rifle at me. The

---

[57] Other sources say that the events I'm about to recount took place on the 20th January, but I maintain that they happened on Saturday the 25th.

bullet fortunately missed, but the blast of his discharge, hitting me fair and square in the face and shoulders, sent me reeling backwards deafened and unsure whether I had been hit or not. His next bullet fired at my feet sprayed me with sand and pebbles sending me from a head-in-arms crouched position to one bolt upright. This was followed by another deafening shot that passed my head which again sent me staggering about. Expecting to be shot at any moment I experienced a strange out-of-body experience, a dispassionate feeling of indifference to it all. With my eardrums bursting I stood up straight and faced my tormentors, who I realised were shouting and waving at me to go in to the office, where I found John Pinkney, having witnessed what he expected to be cold blooded murder, standing with his back to the office wall, a look of horror and distress on his face.

As I joined him two of the soldiers, both in a state of high excitement, appeared at the open windows. One with a rifle fired into the confined space, the bullet ricocheting off the concrete floor and fortunately, for us, flying out of the open door. The other, the Bren gunner, poked his weapon though the opposite open window, when in a detached way I thought if he pulls the trigger there's going to be one hell of a mess in here. They then hassled us out and at gun point marched us across the station yard with the threat that we would both be shot in front of the station buildings. At this point they tried to make me raise my hands, but I felt strongly about this, and refused to lift my hands in feeble surrender. In response the soldier behind me kept jabbing me in the backside with the bayonet attached to his rifle which, fortunately for me, being blunt, had little effect. As I carefully made my way over sets of lines, it somehow seemed important not to trip over points and locking bars, and therefore make a fool of myself. Perhaps I thought that they would have more contempt for an idiot sprawled on the floor, and it would take less justification to kill such a man?

We were both marched through the station entrance hall, which opened out into a large square, and there my courage began to fail. Perhaps until this point I had deep down, believed the soldiers were merely playing a game, a bit of cat and mouse to put the frighteners on us. At bayonet point we were prodded through the entrance hall into brilliant sunshine and a square filled with a mob of jeering mutinous soldiers, one of whom rushed at me with a bayonet, intending, I suppose, to run me through. He was prevented by the timely intervention of a corporal, who went unrecognised except for his stripes, but who may have saved my life. At this, things became confused. Above the howling and yelling I could hear shouted and confusing directions, either 'Nenda nyumbani!' (Go home) or 'Nenda boma', boma being the former German fort overlooking Tabora and used in World War I to hold British prisoners of war. Walking away from the mutinous soldiers I expected to be shot in the back, and in anticipation I lowered my head and hunched my shoulders and waited for oblivion.

As we made our way along the road, the shouting and the tumult mercifully became more distant, at which point John said he was going to the European hospital to see if his wife, a nursing sister, was safe. Feeling helpless, I agreed to go along with him. On our way we were met by a Land Rover driven by Bill Moor-Gilbert, the game ranger, who shortly after sadly lost his life when the aeroplane he was piloting crashed on take-off.

Stopping, he enquired, "What's going on?" and in answer to the information we gave said, "Jump in, I've got half a dozen rifles in the Boma." Seeing the danger and futility of such action, and unaware of the nature and extent of the mutiny, my repressed fears welled up.

"Bugger you and your rifles, Bill!" I burst out. "What can three of us do in the Boma? They'll soon winkle us out, and if we kill one of them, the rest will murder every white person they can lay their hands on."

Convinced by my argument, Bill volunteered to drive us to the hospital, where we found John's wife safe and well, but deeply concerned by the distant rifle fire and for the safety of her husband. The hospital contained two patients, a young very ill White Father, brought in suffering from Blackwater Fever picked up on some Mission through the bush, and the wife of the battalion's British adjutant. She had given birth the day before by caesarean section, and now fed by a drip, also lay helpless. At first, she refused to believe the soldiers had mutinied. "Our boys would never mutiny, only this morning, a little group came to see me and the baby," she confirmed.

I sometimes wonder if this was a ploy by the soon-to-be mutineers to allay suspicions. She asked if her husband was all right, but with the fate of the British officers and NCOs unknown, we reluctantly told her we didn't know.

Gunfire, sometimes heavy, increased our anxiety, and for some reason not now apparent to me we decided to evacuate the patients from, what on account of its quiet position and its facilities, was as far as the two patients and ourselves were concerned, probably one of the safest places to be at that time. Unfortunately the hospital staff had fled at the first sound of gunfire, leaving only

John Pinkney's wife ministering to the sick. It was under these circumstances, together with the stress of events, we decided to move the two patients. It might have been more logical to move them to the larger and better equipped African hospital just down the road, but in our confused and panicky state this was something we overlooked. Instead, with herd instinct as a strong compelling force, we decided to move the patients to be among their own in the European railway quarters.

Guided by John's wife, we laid the Father, mumbling incoherently in his delirium, onto a stretcher and carried him to the Land Rover, where we slid him in the back before returning for the adjutant's wife and baby. Whilst she was being stretchered out by John and Bill, I helped by carrying her drip. The Land Rover, shaded by splendid mango trees, was parked on the road outside the hospital. The Germans, with the intention of developing Tabora into a garden city, had laid out its streets in a spacious checkerboard pattern, and facing the hospital lay an extensive stretch of open country. As we manoeuvred the second stretcher into the rear of the Land Rover we noticed, with mounting alarm, a group of armed soldiers running towards us across the open space. Still holding the drip, I hurriedly squeezed in the back of the Land Rover, whilst Bill, John and his wife, with an equal sense of urgency, filled the front. But alas, as Bill, with the intention of making a quick getaway, struck up the engine, a warning shot was fired, and realising we were too late, Bill just as quickly turned the engine off.

Whooping and pointing their rifles the mutineers surrounded us, demanding to know who we were and what were we doing? In faultless Swahili, Bill explained what we were about. After more argy-bargy and rifle-waving, they agreed to let us go. Sitting in the rear of the vehicle as we departed, with a clear view of the gesticulating rabble, I was once again horrified to see two of them raise their rifles and take aim. I suppose by now I should have got used to this sort of thing. It was the third time in so many hours I'd expected to be shot full of holes, but despite being allowed to leave I still found it a deeply disturbing experience. Fearing we might run into less accommodating soldiers we drove slowly and carefully through a Tabora now eerily devoid of life. Arriving at John's house without further incident we offloaded our two patients, the Father, still mumbling, and the adjutant's wife weeping for the unknown fate of her husband. After making them as comfortable as we could I went over to the house of 'Bwana Bata', Frank Kirton, my boss, to discuss the situation, where I discovered that our HQ in Dar es Salaam, by using the railway's secure telephone lines, had already been in contact to pass information on. By some obscure means, never divulged, they seemed to know more about what was going on in and around Tabora than we did ourselves. They informed us the British officers and NCOs were unhurt, but held under armed guard at the airport, awaiting the arrival of an RAF transport aircraft to evacuate both them and Tabora's tiny band of European women and children. However, with this information came a chilling warning. Leaving our posts and flying out would be deemed as breaking our contract and terminating our employment with East African Railways. After what we had already gone through, and with the threat of more violence and discord hanging over us, and with the very real threat we might not be as fortunate next time, this was much to ask. For John Pinkney, newly married, this was especially true, but also true for myself. We both had long service, and by leaving, had much to lose, and though we felt our lives were at risk, after some deliberation we chose to stay.

As I was about to leave the boss and pass on the good news concerning the fate of British soldiers, and to assure the adjutant's wife her husband had escaped unharmed, suddenly, from somewhere in the direction of Tabora shed, came a dull deep thud. We had heard no gunfire for some time and at once the same thought flashed through both our minds, something which in the stress and strain of the moment we had overlooked: the engines on the shed had been left unattended. Still in steam, abandoned, and with fires lit, and now short of water, had a firebox crown sheet collapsed and its boiler exploded? And if so how many more boilers were at risk. Despite my misadventures earlier in the day, and as foolish and as rash as ever (will I never learn?), I volunteered to investigate. First I returned to John Pinkney's and the little group sheltering there, and gave them the latest information.

After some discussion it was agreed that, whilst I made my way to the shed on foot, Bill would convey the patients to the aerodrome for evacuation. With extreme caution, I made it to the shed, stopping frequently to look for soldiers on the rampage, but nothing disturbed the deserted streets. The air was hot, breathless, heavy and oppressive, unable even to stir the flowers and leaves of the jacaranda and flame trees lining the roads. Even the odd 'shenzi' (native) dog that you usually saw had gone to ground, and the profusion of tropical birds that were always flitting around were now absent. It was quiet and eerie.

With every stop fraught with peril I took a long circuitous route so as to avoid the station, which I felt the mutineers might still be occupying, and arriving at the shed's main entrance gate, unsurprisingly I found it wide open, the gatekeeper having fled at the first sign of trouble. It was through this gate the three soldiers, intent on mischief had arrived. What further dismayed me was that my pride and joy, my elegant two-seater VW Karmann Ghia, was gone. This rather bald account requires some explanation: whenever I visited the shed in my capacity as locomotive inspector or shedmaster I left my car just within the main gates, where under the watchful eye of the gatekeeper it remained safe enough for me to leave it unlocked and with the keys in the ignition. Crime wasn't usually an issue in Tanganyika anyway, and the theft of an automobile was unheard of. However, the gatekeeper's hasty departure at the first gunshot left my car wide open and ready for theft.

As I cautiously approached, the whole area seemed abandoned. Slowly and carefully I made my way through the shed's interior with the intention of checking over any engine which might be in steam. Suddenly from behind one of the dead engines stabled within the shed the figure of an African stepped out. Silhouetted against the bright sunlight I feared this was yet another soldier I had stumbled upon. Unsure of what fate awaited me, a wave of cold sweat swept over me, then the reassuring voice of my African assistant calmed me. "It's me, John Stuart, go away and hide!" I asked him if everything was alright. "Yes," he assured me, "I'm looking after the engines, now go away, it's too dangerous to stay."

I instructed him to shut all the engines down except for one which could be used to light the others up when things returned to normal. Convinced the engines were in safe hands, I thanked him, and made my way back, avoiding any danger spots, and on arrival reported to the boss. I informed him John Stuart, at no small risk to himself, was looking after the engines, that there had been no boiler explosions (I never did find out what the deep thud was) and I had ordered him to shut all the engines down except for one to be kept in steam. With evening approaching and everywhere quiet I decided, after a wearying day, to spend the night in my own quarters near to the station.

We then entered a strange and uneasy period. Dar es Salaam HQ informed us that the soldiers had returned to barracks, and under some form of internal discipline, seemed prepared to remain there. From 11 am all Tabora-bound trains, that were then halted at out stations would be allowed to return, but no further train movements were to take place until the situation became clearer. For a week Tabora remained a ghost town, deserted but heavy with menace and foreboding. As each engine returned to shed it was serviced, its tender filled and refuelled with furnace oil, before being shut down and stabled. Also, at some point that week my car was recovered and was, thankfully, undamaged.

The following Saturday morning after the initial unrest, Dar es Salaam secretly warned us via the railway's secure telephone line that an RAF Regiment would be flying in about midday to secure the airfield for the later arrival of Royal Marines, and ordered Bwana Bata, John Pinkney, and me to be there to liaise with them. By the time we were ready to move off things were already hotting up again in Tabora. Word had gone round that Dar es Salaam's Colito Barracks, the HQ of the Tanzania Defence Force, had been attacked by Royal Marines, who had inflicted a number of casualties, before the remainder laid down their arms. Hearing this and expecting savage reprisals, our staff, who had dribbled back during the week, now melted away again, leaving us again feeling exposed and vulnerable.

Arriving at the airfield without further trouble we were alarmed to discover a detachment of the shadowy armed and native-led riot police. Unsure of the reception we might receive we nervously took up a position at the end of the landing strip. As we did so the riot police, without speaking, moved in behind us, giving us the distinct impression we were about to be held hostage to prevent a British landing. Around midday we heard the sound of heavy aircraft approaching. Meanwhile, the riot police, standing relaxed and chatting amongst themselves, seemed unconcerned, and we then began to form the impression that, rather than holding us hostage, they were to protect us against mutineering soldiers. Here the plot thickens: were wheels within wheels at work?

With secrecy paramount, we had been led to believe that in Tabora only the three of us were aware of the impending landing. Yet here were the riot police, ready and waiting. Surely the explanation was that, somewhere, someone in the 'know', certain of where the riot police's loyalties lay, had been in communication with them and arranged for them to guard us. Who that person could be was a mystery. The other possibility, which didn't bear thinking about, was that someone had let slip word of the RAF's imminent arrival, and a much less well-disposed 'welcoming committee' had been despatched by the mutineers.

From the direction of Dar es Salaam, and pretty much on time, the sound of approaching aircraft grew louder. Now we would find out whose side the shadowy riot police were really on—was the knowledge or instincts of that 'mystery someone' correct, or were we about to be used as pawns in a deadly stand-off? The aircraft came in low, about 300 feet, and instead of landing made several passes over the airfield, which did nothing to allay our anxiety. In an attempt to discover the mood of the riot police I glanced back at them. Instead of showing signs of tension they stood relaxed, more interested in the aircraft flying overhead than anything else. After several passes the aircraft came diving in at speed, one making directly for the airport's solitary office, the other towards our anxious group. Both landed heavily in a cloud of dust, to the extent that one damaged its landing gear and was unable to take off at the end of the operation. However, getting in fast once the decision had been made had obviously been the main priority. The other, its propellers whirring at full throttle, hurled towards us and with a screech of brakes stopped short and swung round with its rear facing us.

Now occurred the most dangerous part of the operation, an incident which could easily have led to bloodshed. As the first RAF men dashed down the ramp, rifles at the ready and fingers on the triggers, one, in his haste, slipped and fell. Several of these following tripped over him in their haste and also fell. It sounds comical, but it wasn't. My feelings were if one of those RAF men, in falling down, had accidentally fired his rifle, the remainder, on instincts of self-preservation, would have opened up on anything which moved and that would have been ourselves and the riot police. Fortunately strict discipline prevailed and in the spasm of fear my next impression of those confused few moments were of the RAF Commanding Officer walking imperturbably down the ramp whilst pulling on a pair of pristine white cotton gloves. Radiating a self-assured dignity and composure, here was authority personified. With an immense feeling of relief I could have kissed him!

Shortly after that three RAF fighter jets came screaming in and 'buzzed' the barracks, attacking not with rockets or cannon fire but with the thrust of their engines, a display of power. Sweeping in low at high speed, each pilot flew his aircraft into a vertical climb over the barracks, assaulting it with a roar which split the heavens. Later, after the RAF Regiment had taken control of the airfield, we discovered why they had been so hesitant in making a landing. Flying over they noticed three Europeans standing together with armed and uniformed

Africans behind them, and using binoculars had spent time assessing the situation. After deciding there was nothing to be gained and much to lose by delaying further, they came in hard and fast.

At about 4 pm, and still on the airfield with the RAF Regiment, we heard the throb of heavier aircraft approaching, then sweeping into view came two large troop carriers. It came as no little surprise the way they both lined up for the single landing strip, almost as if both pilots had experience of flying into Tabora and knew exactly where they were. The landing strip was on the short side for such large aircraft, but in a cloud of dust, with brakes hard on, and engines howling in reverse thrust, the pilots were able to avoid over-running the strip and ending up in the bush. Experience from my time as a soldier told me that during any troop movements each soldier carried his equipment and belongings on his shoulders in the shape of a Field Service Marching Order webbing and packs, or if going into action, the much-reduced Battle Order pack. Imagine my astonishment, then, when each Royal Marine disembarked carrying a large brown suitcase, as if arriving on a safari holiday! It still takes some comprehending.

Once landed, and to our incredulity and dismay, word went around that the first thing these dapper chaps intended to do was get a good night's rest, having already been in action that morning, and needing to recover from a rather arduous plane journey. What we found out later therefore came as something of a surprise: in the pitch dark, at 1 am that morning, they arrived at the gates of Tabora barracks silently and in full Battle Order. The mutineers, still maintaining a modicum of discipline, had ensured the guardroom was kept manned, whereupon its occupants found themselves staring down the muzzles of no-nonsense Marines, who gave them very clear orders not to raise any alarm. Then quickly, so as not to disturb those inside, each barrack block was surrounded. At 6 am a Marine bugler sounded reveille, whereupon, on rising, the mutineers found themselves held under armed guard without a shot being fired. Perhaps, then, the suitcase performance on the runway was merely a ploy to lull the mutineers into a false sense of security?

The next day we were asked to identify the main mutineers. We found the battalion drawn up on the barracks main square, under the command of Marines at attention and in open order formation. Each mutineer was shorn of rank, and dripping sweat and shaking with fear, as if expecting to be shot out of hand. Accompanied by a Marine, I went along each line of soldiers. If I had recognised the corporal who had intervened outside Tabora railway station, I would have stopped and explained that this man, at no little risk to himself saved my life. But apart from the distinction of a corporal's stripes, his face in the general confusion had failed to register. This was just as true for the others, and I was unable to point an accusing finger at anyone.

Whilst all this was going on, Julius Nyerere[58], the former anti-colonial activist and now socialist president who liked nothing better than to declare: "The British left us nothing but wild animals" had, in a panic, fled from the State House (the former Tanganyika Governor's residence). His policies against the whites, and in particular the British, didn't, in his hour of need, prevent him from seeking the aid of those he frequently condemned. Whilst it was all kept quiet, it was said he had sought refuge first in the British High Commission, before being smuggled aboard a British freighter which had promptly raised anchor and sailed beyond the three mile limit where it 'hove to' until the maligned British had restored law and order on his behalf.

In direct contradiction to Nyerere's assertions that the indigenous residents of East Africa had been left with nothing but open bush and wild animals (whereas in reality they had been left a much-developed country), it may be of interest to some readers to know the extent of British projects, both before and after independence, and which ran into many millions of pounds in order to support Tanganyika/Tanzania's frail and fragile economy. In terms of exports the country produced mainly sisal—not, I imagine, much of a money spinner— about enough to keep the Greek plantation owners in brandy at the Planters' Hotel at Kimamba on the Central Railway. One such project was the 50-mile Mukondokwa Valley Railway branch line, built with the intention of opening up this fertile valley to agriculture and sugar production. The magnum opus of the line, which crosses the Tendiga swamp and skirts the Mkegumba Mountains, was a bridge over the Mkondoa River at Kilosa, which consists of three spans, two of 95 feet and one of 120 feet, with two piers and two abutments. To find bed rock, pile driving of up to 90 feet deep required months of toil. The end result, painted silver, offered a striking spectacle, although it alone must have cost the British taxpayer a pretty penny.

---

[58] Julius Kambarage Nyerere governed Tanganyika as prime minister from 1961 to 1962, and then as president from 1962 to 1964, after which he led its successor state, Tanzania, as president from 1964 to 1985.

Similarly, the German-built Tabora-Mwanza line was in the process of being ballasted throughout, and laid with heavy, long, welded rails. This was achieved in the first place by converting the long disused German locomotive works at Tabora into an arc welding plant, and welding rails into quarter mile lengths. After welding each rail joint was carefully examined for integrity and its surface ground true before being drawn out on rollers onto bogie flat waggons. It was something of a sight to watch the lengths of rail snaking around curves heading out of Tabora. Arriving on site the rails were affixed to already laid and prepared steel sleepers, then thermite welded into half-mile lengths with a ten foot joint to take up expansion and contraction. All this required a degree of close cooperation between the Engineering Department laying the rails and Tabora locomotive shed, which had to provide locomotives and engine crews at different times and often at short notice. Again, I'm not convinced that the revenue made by the line would ever have paid for such extensive engineering works, and assume it can only have been possible due to the injection of large amounts of capital by the British government.

At Mwanza, a brand new anchorage, the Mwanza South New Port, six million cubic feet of landfill extending 400 feet into the lake, with an 860 feet frontage, held in place by innumerable 44-foot steel pilings topped by a stone bund. If the British government thought the above-mentioned post-independence largesse would sweeten Nyerere's attitude to them, they were in for a shock. Before long the British High Commission had been banished, and British-owned farms confiscated and the owners deported, to the extent that it was said among the surviving expatriates "I see another British farmer has been exported!"

And finally, two further examples of British munificence, both at Dar es Salaam: a brand new international airport, and an equally new university, both hacked out of the unforgiving bush, and at great expense.

Getting back to Tabora in 1964, if I thought I had done with mutinous soldiers, I was in for an unpleasant surprise. Bwana Bata, the boss, sent for me one day explaining that a train was leaving the next morning for Mpanda and he wanted me to travel with it and check Mpanda's oil fuel equipment and remaining fuel level. Later the same day I made arrangements for my inspection coach to be attached to the Mpanda train, and about 7 am the next morning my house boy, carrying a kikapu on his head containing my bedding and such tins of food as I would require on my safari. On his return an hour later, after cleaning and dusting the coach and making up the bed, I set off to walk the half-mile or so to the station. For a short period at this time of year, around August, the first few hours of daylight remained refreshingly cool and pleasant, with a gentle breeze dispersing the heavy cloying scent of the frangipani trees lining my route. Tabora, now having recovered from its fright and fears, had resumed an air of normality, with many and varied birds flying about and darting between the trees, and with them the return of the odd native shenzi dog. Making my way to the station light of foot, I exchanged greetings and pleasantries with the local Africans, many of them old acquaintances. At the station I strode into the entrance hall, and then in dismay stopped short.

Drawn up under the levelled rifles of the Marines, the mutineers were being herded onto the Mpanda train, where, as I discovered later, they were to be disbanded and abandoned, without food or water, in the dry and barren wastes of the Mpanda region, to make their own way back to their home villages and families. Being the only European on the train, the engine crew being African, the 16-hour trip between Tabora and Mpanda became a nightmare. At each stop on its 207 mile journey mutineers gathered round my coach, jeering, issuing threats and spitting on the ground. Fearing for my life I locked the coach doors, but these gave me little confidence in their ability to withstand an assault from mutineers awaiting their humiliation and seemingly bent on revenge. On this isolated railway it would be easy to dispose of my body by throwing it into the bush to be devoured by wild animals, or dropping it into the broad and swift-flowing Ugalla River, with its numerous hungry crocodiles. Well, that's how it seemed to me at the time.

Sun-baked Mpanda consisted of nothing but the mine and the railway station, and for that reason, on arrival, and feeling apprehensive and alone, I remained locked in my coach until the mutineers had dispersed and things had settled down, and I felt safe to make a survey of the oil fuel depot and its installation, before returning to Tabora.

Chapter 27
Life at Dar es Salaam

A few weeks after my latest 'mutineer misadventure', I left on my second home leave, and there I renewed acquaintance with the woman who became the love of my life. To make it somewhat clearer, this rather bold statement perhaps requires some further explanation. A few years before the war, in 1936/7, housing developments began to spread west of Cottingham, and with it came my future wife's parents with their only child, an 18-month-old daughter. At that time, I would have been six or seven years old, and whilst our two families, being close neighbours, became friendly, like most young boys, I had no interest in girls, least of all this little girl growing up next door, quietly playing with her teddy bear and dolls. Just before the war, our neighbours moved into Cottingham to take up the tenancy of an off-licence, whereafter our two families lost contact with each other.

Fast forward to the winter of 1957, and back in Cottingham for six months home leave, I often found it convenient to purchase my cigarettes from the nearby off-licence, where in the absence of one or other of the parents, I was sometimes served by a comely young lady called Shirley, none other than the little girl with the teddy bear and dolls. On my return to Tanganyika, I once again immersed myself in work for the next three years. On my next home leave, in 1960, I returned once more to buying my *Capstan Full Strength* cigarettes (the nearest equivalent to the *Crown Bird* smokes I was used to, and no doubt an equal destroyer of lungs) from the off-licence where I was occasionally served by the very attractive Shirley, who seemed happy to share my company and my tales of Africa.

By now I was in my thirties and on the way to becoming a confirmed bachelor. The shadow of my mother's bitter rejection hung heavily on me, as did the memory of the two lady teachers who had scarred my childhood. Miss

Thomas, the school music teacher, whose entrance filled the classroom with fear, and Miss Brown, general teacher, with her Marcel-waved flaming red hair and a temper to match ('Ginger Brown' we called her), leaving me hesitant to establish a relationship with any member of the fairer sex.

When I returned to Tabora for my next three-year tour of duty my thoughts increasing turned to the attractive woman in the Cottingham off-licence. In this my feelings were in no way diminished by Indian friends and acquaintances, who reminded me of my failure to marry and have children. "Mr Blackburn, sahib," they would gently chide, "why you not married, you must have children to look after you in old age?"

"Yes, yes, I know," I would answer, "all in good time."

I had always been a heavy smoker but this had increased over the years until it had become a serious addiction which now irked me no end, a habit not helped by years of dust and fume-laden footplate work, further shrinking my lungs, which I now feared resembled the size, colour and consistency of two dried prunes. At the time I was smoking about 100 *Crown Bird* cigarettes (small but potent gaspers) a day. So on the basis that smoking was doing me far more harm than good, I decided to put an end to it. I found this easier than I had previously thought possible (I would take a couple of puffs on the cigarette, and then throw it away, gradually increasing the interval between cigarettes, until I stopped craving them altogether).

In the meantime, I had been posted to hot and steamy Dar es Salaam, to take over the administration of the Locomotive Training School there. With more and more European staff leaving, I was frequently called on for other duties, which included a six month stint as senior locomotive inspector on the Central Railway, and in the absence of the shedmaster, on home leave, six months as acting shedmaster. Fortunately, during a hectic three years when other duties piled up, I had a capable assistant to look after the training school during my periods of absence.

On my next home leave, in summer 1964, whilst flying out from Nairobi International Airport, to my surprise and consternation I met the irascible little red-headed piggy-eyed customs official again. "Blackburn? Blackburn?" he exclaimed, staring hard at me and then my passport photograph. I was, however, reassured by the fact that he must have seen thousands of people since our less-than-pleasant encounter of several years ago at Eastleigh Airport.

Also, I was dressed differently and, now with a tanned and 'bush-hardened' appearance, no doubt looked a lot different from that pale, callow youth of years gone by, so putting on an air of nonchalance I awaited his pleasure. After a short pause, and to my utter amazement, he suddenly demanded, "Where's ya gun...?" Flabbergasted, I stutteringly told him I'd sold it to a gentleman in Tanganyika several years ago, whereupon he stamped my passport, slapped it back in my hand, and I was contemptuously dismissed.

Back in Cottingham, I found Shirley still single and unattached, and we began to go out together. At the time she was working for the University of Hull as a secretary in the student accommodation department. As our love blossomed, I plucked up the courage to propose, and to my delight she agreed to marry me.

Shirley and Eric, after their marriage at Huntington Chhurch, York, January 2nd 1965.

She only revealed later that she remembered me from when she was little, and thought I was "a big lout of a boy", which was probably a fair assessment of me at that time.

Taking advantage of two weeks' local leave I flew home for four days, and on 2 January 1965, on a day of hard frost but with a beautiful clear blue sky, we were married before a large gathering of friends and well-wishers in the ancient Parish Church of Huntington, in York[59]. This had proved an enormous step for Shirley. Her father had sadly died a few months before, and her mother was elderly and in the process of giving up the off-licence. To complicate matters, she and Shirley were in the process of buying a new-build house in Cottingham. My new wife, adjusting to married life, now faced the daunting prospect of leaving all behind, including her beloved mother, and living in a not-altogether-stable tropical country.

---

[59] As I write this I am proud to say we have now been happily married for 58 years, and she hasn't murdered me yet!

Husband and wife descending a very icy path.

Having flown in to hot and humid Dar es Salaam, as a way to help Shirley adjust to conditions in Africa I'd arranged for part of our honeymoon to be spent at the Maranga Hotel, with its equitable climate and an open view of Kilimanjaro's mighty snow-covered peak. Whilst there we explored the rainforest paths, the flora and fauna, with Shirley delighting in paddling in one of the clear, but very cold, mountain streams. From there we went to the nearby Ngurdoto Crater, surrounded by rainforest and famous for its wildlife, with herds of buffalo, several species of monkeys, birds, dikdiks, elephant and giraffe. Following this we travelled via Nairobi, to Jinja in Uganda, to view the country and stay at the Lake Victoria Hotel, Entebbe, overlooking Lake Victoria, and from there to meet my old friend Bill Etherington, the Permanent Way Inspector, and his wife and children..

On honeymoon, with the rapids below Owen falls in the background.

After our honeymoon, to get back to Dar es Salaam, we then drove the almost 1,000 miles from Jinja back home in one go, setting off at around 8 am (stopping only for petrol), and arriving in Dar es Salaam at 8 or 9 am the next day – a long and tiring journey mostly over dirt roads[60]. This was marred by one heart-stopping experience. After about 14 hours driving, in the darkness of night, somewhere south of Nairobi on the endless Massai Steppes, I remember accidentally straying off the main road and on to a narrow back road. Confident it would bring me to somewhere more recognisable I continued, only to be stopped by a small group of Africans carrying machetes. At that late hour and in those unusual circumstances I sensed danger and left the engine running and my hand on the gear lever. They asked, politely enough, for a lift, but I explained that the car was a two-seater with no further space, and at the first opportunity, with heart in mouth, I accelerated away, only to be stopped a few miles further along by a roadblock manned by armed police who explained they were on the lookout for a gang of robbers who had committed murder most foul. I told them of our encounter and after thanking me they moved us on. This confirmed my suspicious feeling that I had been fortunate, to the extent that if any of them had been able to drive, the outcome for Shirley and me would have been very different indeed. Fortunately, both these conversations were in Swahili, leaving Shirley in blissful ignorance of what was going on. It was only some years later, after we had permanently left Africa, that I felt able to reveal the danger we had been in.

Shirley and Eric with Mrs Etherington and family.

---

[60] Editor's note: Modern maps show the shortest route is 869 miles (without any unplanned diversions!), and on average takes 23 hours 57 mins, so an extraordinary achievement and feat of endurance in 1965.

Shirley in the grounds of the Marangu Hotel.

Photograph of the author, taken on his honeymoon.

Our bungalow in Dar es Salaam was set in its own grounds, and consisted of lounge, dining room, a relatively large kitchen, bathroom and two bedrooms. At the time I was generally working the very equitable hours of 7 am to 4 pm at the Locomotive Training School, with occasional safaris in my own inspection coach, on some of which Shirley accompanied me. When in 'Dar', after a hot day at work, we'd often meet up with friends and go down to the beach with its white-sand beaches, and go swimming in the warm waters of the Indian Ocean. Another favourite destination was the Seamen's Mission, with its well-kept pool, also good for getting some relief from the heat and humidity. Then, in mid-1965, to our delight, we found that Shirley was expecting our first child.

Shirley, on the beach at Oyster Bay.

But returning to the subject of work, the trialling of locomotives after heavy repairs was the responsibility of the senior locomotive inspecting officer, Dar es Salaam. This was carried out by attaching the test engine to a convenient goods train and working it for 12 miles to the first station Pugu. The initial four miles was level track, followed by eight miles of a 1 in 45 gradient. It was my practice to run with only a breath of steam on the level stretch. Firstly, this was to run the engine in a little and put a polish on its moving parts, for everything was stiff and tight, and secondly, to relieve the train engine of what was, in effect, an overload. On the 1 in 45 winding through the Pugu Hills I would lay into the test engine 'full hole', to prove under the most trying of conditions its ability to steam freely and to expose any mechanical shortcomings. In this there was never cause for concern, for in Chris Collard, the erecting shop foreman, the workshops were blessed with a foreman of exceptional ability who let nothing escape his eagle eye, and in so doing turned out locomotives immaculate both in appearance and mechanical condition.

This, however, leads me to recount an unseemly clash I witnessed between two senior railway officers. Already attached to a train was one of Tabora's 26 Class locomotives, 2607, that I was about to take on a test run. At this time Frank Kirton (Bwana Bata, the 'retread') was in charge of Dar es Salaam workshops, and in that capacity was rarely seen. I was therefore unprepared for his unexpected appearance, and received a bit of a jolt when I saw he was accompanied by none other than the assistant CME, 'Fearless Frank Kent' whom I expected to be 500 miles away within the Kremlin's hallowed walls, and whose presence usually spelt trouble.

Shirley at home at 15 Kurasini, Dar es Salaam.

Readers will remember that Frank was the DMPS at Tabora at the time when the shed struggled to keep the 26 Class on the road, and as such was fully aware of them returning from each trip little better than wrecks (that is except for those allocated to certain Asian drivers which, under the then shedmaster, were maintained to a much higher degree—a source of irritation to those drivers who were not willing to participate in the 'brandy repairs' arrangement). Despite this painful experience, on his elevation to Works Manager Dar es Salaam, frugality became the watchword. One of his crafty arrangements was to send an engine back after heavy repairs with its tyres nearly down, or even down to scrap size. As a result, *his* works balance sheet may have found favour in Nairobi and helped him with accelerated promotion, but it did nothing to help the other struggling sheds along the Central Railway, now burdened with the task of dropping the wheels after a few thousand miles and the expense of railing them to workshops in exchange for sets with new re-tyred wheels.

26 Class awaiting test after heavy repairs, and fitted with Giesle chimney and blast pipe, as well as Metcalfe-Oerlikon automatic type FV-4 air brake.

The test engine, now fitted with a Geisl ejector and blast pipe, stood resplendent in the harsh sunlight. Its Weir pump supplying water to the boiler clacked away gently, its side rods, connecting rods and valve gear gleaming, and its lined-out maroon paintwork a picture of perfection. About to board, I was drawn into the conversation when, before they examined the engine, they asked me a few questions. 2607 stood proudly on a brand new set of tyres, and immediately these drew the attention of Frank Kent. Rounding on Bwana Bata he demanded an explanation. Of Yorkshire stock, an accredited mechanical engineer some 10 to 15 years senior in age to Frank, a product of both the Doncaster Plant and Nigerian Railways, Bwana Bata didn't take kindly to being spoken to like an errant schoolboy and he sharply told Frank to mind his own business and not to interfere in something of which he was no longer a part. A bit of a ding doing then took place as they argued the toss, and I used the opportunity to slope off and complete my inspection of the engine's trimmings. However, it showed a strange quirk of nature on Frank's part when, long after things had changed, he was still so strongly against the fitting of new tyres to engines leaving workshops.

My stint as shedmaster Dar es Salaam, which in the absence of anyone else meant that I was still required to take trial engines on test runs, made an interesting comparison with the larger and more diverse Tabora locomotive shed I was more familiar with. Without stations at Kigoma and Mwanza, and long distance caboose-working over four separate routes (Tabora-Kigoma, Tabora-Mwanza, Tabora-Mpanda and Tabora-Morogoro), the Tabora shed maintained a stud of 57 locomotives. These comprised twenty-two 30 Class 2-8-4 tender engines, twelve 26 Class 2-8-2 tender engines, seventeen 27 Class 2-8-2 tender engines, two elderly knock about 25 Class 2-8-2 tender engines and two 11 Class 2-6-2 side tank shunting engines. This was in comparison to Dar es Salaam's more modest nineteen locomotives, which consisted of two unfamiliar 82 Class flame-proofed (for going in the oil and petrol sidings) 0-6-0 diesel shunters for work in the port's extensive oil and petrol depot, and two powerful 12 Class 2-6-2 tank engines for shunting elsewhere. Also retained for odd job work were two elderly (they entered service in 1928) Vulcan Foundry 21 Class 4-8-2 tender engines. These were used to haul miscellaneous trains such as engineering trains and the monthly Pay Train, which slowly and laboriously called at every station and plate layers gang camp between Dar es Salaam and Morogoro. The cream of the shed were the thirteen 4-8-2 and 2-8-4 Garratt engines, used for working the arduous 126 mile 1 in 45 grade Dar es Salaam-Morogoro section. This required a gruelling ten hour stint for the Garratt's single crew, who on arrival rested in Morogoro's rest rooms before returning with a Down train.

Whilst I was occupying the shedmaster's chair many of the mainly, but not wholly, Asian shed staff began to arrive at my office requesting an hour off. When asked for the reason I was somewhat surprised to be told it was to visit the British High Commission. This was the time when the British government was benevolently granting British citizenship to the many millions of its former and current colonial inhabitants. Taking advantage of this offer most, if not all, the Asian community of Dar es Salaam descended on the British High Commission requesting British passports, which without question were freely given, with no background checks of any sort.

At the time the British High Commission occupied the top floor of the Standard Bank building in Dar es Salaam, which before independence was known as the Standard Bank of South Africa, a name they had to drop on Independence Day, or woe betide! Situated on the waterfront, and one of the largest buildings in the city, it was strategically positioned overlooking the harbour, giving the Commission a clear view of all that went on there, which after independence (with the sudden increase of foreign vessels transporting who-knows-what) was no-doubt enough to keep communication between it and London sparking away full-time.

Under Julian Nyerere, the red-hot socialist president, whose rule eventually brought Tanzania to the brink of penury, both Russia and China became interested in Tanzania as an open door to the interior of Africa, with Russian cruise ships beginning to arrive. The passengers, middle-rank peasant-faced commissar officials and their wives, each perspiring freely in ill-fitting clothes, the womenfolk with heads wrapped in Russian-style headscarves, standing out distinctly from the rest of the European population.

Attracting close attention and much more sinister were the Chinese freighters, calling on an increasing scale, and each notable for the secrecy surrounding its activities. Anchored beyond the reef awaiting a berth, each ship had its superstructure shrouded in canvas, effectively preventing anyone, including British officials watching from the top floor of the Standard Bank, observing what was going on shipboard. Unlike other ships, a blaze of lights during the hours of darkness, the Chinese ships maintained a complete and utter blackout, except for essential masthead navigation lights.

Once berthed, and before unloading commenced, the crew, who appeared to be naval personnel, cleared the docks of all staff, then transferred the cargo onto covered bogie waggons. If the Chinese thought that, once sealed in railway waggons, their cargo was safe from prying eyes, they were mistaken. Each waggon was labelled with its destination and its contents—mainly small arms and ammunition, and I became aware of this traffic when travelling on official duties by goods train. Most of this was destined for Kigoma and then onward distribution to freedom fighters, or terrorist groups—take your pick—in other parts of the Continent. If the train carried a detachment of soldiers I knew it carried arms and ammunition. I then made it my business to walk down the train at a convenient halt, ostensibly reading the labels. This seemed to upset the soldiers, who, whilst recognising me as some sort of railway official, followed me around unsure of how to treat me. I used to greet them jovially enough but, aware I was baiting them a little, they maintained a sullen silence, apart from an occasional muttered and derogatory remark thrown my way. In some quarters at least, it seemed that the once happy and harmonious relationship between Tanzanian Africans and Europeans had become a thing of the past.

But to return to the Dar es Salaam branch of the Standard Bank. One morning whilst visiting on business, and within the space of a few minutes, I had two remarkable encounters. Beside the bank ran a narrow side street, and taking advantage of one of its shady trees, I parked my car beneath it and made my way towards the bank's entrance. Part way along I was stopped by an Englishman who enquired if I could direct him to a decent hotel. Approaching I had already noted his appearance which didn't quite fit the Dar es Salaam scene of shorts and loose cotton shirts. Dressed in 'up country' attire of well-cut bush jacket and slacks he wore a bush hat and carried a backpack and, unusually, on his feet, wore a pair of brown officer-style leather boots. I looked at him hard. Short and stocky he had the air of a military man, the air of a hard bitten infantry officer or sergeant major. This was at the time the former Belgian Congo had descended into rape, pillage and murder and the time when European mercenaries were trying to bring order out of chaos, and he made me wonder. My suspicions became confirmed when he remarked he had left the Congo and was making his way to South Africa. I advised him against trying to make it overland, warning him the 2,000 miles swarmed with armed dissidents, and suggested he go by ship, even if he had to work his passage. Wishing him well I shook his hand and left with the cheering thought that here was a man well able to look after himself.

A little further on, I passed two young white men, unusually both dirty and unkempt. Because one in particular was very blond I assumed, perhaps a little unfairly, they were crew members off a German ship. When I returned they were both in the same place and as I prepared to pass one stepped forward and, dispelling my allusions of ethnicity, spoke to me in perfect English, and to my astonishment asking, "Are you Eric Blackburn?"

Taken aback, I answered, "Yes."

"Don't you know me?" he enquired. Mystified, I looked him over closely and wondering how this ragged creature knew my name, shook my head. "I'm Mike," he announced.

Still in the dark, I again shook my head. "I'm sorry," I replied, "I'm afraid I don't recognise you at all."

His response left me both astonished and for a few moments speechless. "Remember me, I'm Michael, Michael Guravitch."

Now, his answer requires an explanation. I had a distant and tenuous connection to the family of this ragged unshaven young man, through my eldest brother's wife, whose sister had married Maximillian Guravitch, a Jew. They had two children, a boy and a girl, and the last time I had seen Michael was when he was six or seven years old, and in stark contrast to the present appearance, a picture, as always, of motherly love and attention.

Recovering from this revelation, I asked if he'd been looking for me. "No," he replied, "I didn't know which part of Africa you lived in, and it was just luck we bumped into you."

I asked, "What are you doing here and why in this state?"

Michael explained they had been travelling, and arrived in Aden, which with all its unrest seemed a strange place to visit[61]. After a few days and short of money they decided to head for Southern Rhodesia, at that time a state like South Africa (an anathema to the Tanzanian government) and once there help Ian Smith in his struggle for independence[62]. "If you had no money, how did you get from Aden to Dar es Salaam?" I asked.

"By Arab dhow," Mike answered, which sent a shudder through my frame and left me wondering why the Arab captain had resisted the temptation to cut their throats, seize the few belongings they had, and tip them overboard somewhere in the Indian Ocean.

I had to warn Michael to lower his voice and be careful what he said, for nearby loitered two Africans who might be plain-clothed policemen, and I for one didn't fancy a few days in the Central Police Station followed by deportation.

---

[61] A British Crown colony from 1937 to 1963, Aden consisted of the port of Aden and its immediate surroundings (now Yemen). Anti-colonial sentiments led to the Aden Emergency, commencing in October 1963, followed by outright hostilities against the British, with repeated guerrilla attacks resulted in the British leaving Aden at the end of November 1967.

[62] Ian Douglas Smith served as Prime Minister of Rhodesia (now Zimbabwe) from 1964 to 1979, and unilaterally declared independence from the United Kingdom in November 1965, following a prolonged dispute over British demands for black majority rule.

I advised then against trying to reach Rhodesia and suggested I took them home for a bath and square meal.

Safe in the privacy of our own home, Shirley and I managed to convince them, penniless as they were, that they had reached the end of the line, and the only sensible course of action was to put themselves into the care of the Canadian High Commission, acting now on behalf of the closed-down British High Commission. Once clean and tidy, and after a good meal, I drove them to the High Commission. That was the last anyone ever heard of Mike and his companion. I sincerely hope I'm wrong, but I can only assume they refused repatriation and, making for Rhodesia overland, had fallen foul of one of the guerrilla bands roaming the bush, being summarily executed and thus leaving their bleached bones somewhere in Africa. But there is a twist to this tragic story. Years later I discovered they had a good reason for not wanting to be returned to the UK. Far from being innocent travellers, they were in fact deserters from the British armed forces stationed in Aden.

Around this time, a new continuous brake was being introduced on the Central Railway—the automatic FV4 Metcalfe-Oerlikon air brake, and as such alien to drivers familiar with their tried and trusted Gresham and Craven vacuum brake. The new brake was a bit tricky both in its operation and its effect on the train. Unlike the vacuum brake which on a downgrade could be applied and released frequently without loss of brake power, the Oerlikon brake, despite two large powerful air compressors, could become denuded of air, with obvious consequences if mishandled on long descending grades. I therefore spent a lot of time travelling between Dar es Salaam and Tabora instructing drivers on its safe and proper workings, and the care and maintenance of the air compressors.

Shirley loved to accompany me on these and other safaris, delighting in the endless African skies, the vast open spaces and the teeming wildlife, with the stations, and the life around them, intriguing her, especially the larger ones. Morogoro, with the Uluguru Mountains forming a magnificent backdrop, was particularly striking. Sometimes we visited a duka in Dodoma which sold a raw, rough, yet eminently drinkable red wine produced by the local White Father Mission (which also made a not-easy-to-come-by but equally fragrant and desirable 'White Father Cheroot', that I occasionally indulged in during my smoking days). On our visits, Shirley and I made a point of walking into town, and to help us on our way, purchase a couple of bottles of this splendid red nectar (having now forsaken my teetotal stance, its demise coming in the form of shandy, in which the proportion of beer slowly increased as time went by). Dodoma, arid and windswept in the dry season, was awash with scorpions both black and white, when an infrequent rainstorm swept the area, leaving its inhabitants to gingerly pick their way amongst them.

After steaming through heavy rain once, when I was still a driver, I stopped at Zuzu, the station before Dodoma, to find the side drains blocked by heaps of drowned scorpions. Sweeping all before it this was the first rain to fall in seven years, and whilst waiting for the Line Clear to arrive, and amazed at the vast number of these dead scorpions, I asked my fireman where all these malign creatures came from, for normally they were notable by their absence. "Ah," he replied sententiously, "they live in secret places!" Yes, I thought to myself, they probably do!

Shirley, outside 15 Kurasini, Dar es Salaam.

Of course there were plenty of other 'creepy crawlies' in East Africa (such things were generally captured by the word 'dudu' in Swahili). One of the most impressive types of creature were the large millipedes, about a six inches long, and known as 'Tanganyika Trains', their legs moving rhythmically as they effortlessly traversed rocks and other obstacles. If threatened they'd curl into a tight spiral, as millipedes do, but they also secreted an irritating liquid, making them one of the few invertebrates that safari ants weren't able to take as prey. As mentioned, safari ants themselves were something to be avoided at all costs. At times they'd form marching columns composed of literally millions of ants, which would fiercely defend themselves against anything that attacked them or unintentionally blundered into their path, with their bite being extremely painful. There were large centipedes too, which could give a very nasty nip. One night when I was asleep a dudu of some sort (thankfully a small one) decided to make its home in my ear, and after 'fettling' it with ear drops I spent several weeks picking bits of body and legs out of my ear with a matchstick.

Accompanied by Shirley I once spent a fortnight on safari at Manyoni, the water and fuel point on the edge of the Great Rift Valley, and home to two 30 Class banker engines, and from there instructed Down drivers how to negotiate the long and tortuous Saranda Bank in safety, using the new and unfamiliar air brake. Lacking a provision store, this introduced Shirley to living entirely on corned beef. Occasionally when sitting down to a meal I thought I detected a tiny flicker of distaste on Shirley's normally placid features, a little Déjà Vu, as she surveyed a plate of Fray Bentos' finest! With a refrigerator as part of the inspection coach equipment we could at least sit down to solid meals, rather than pouring it out of the tin!

Shirley, with faithful old Bess, outside the inspection coach at Manyoni station. A banker engine is in the background.

Between trains, in the cool of the evening, we explored the station and its vicinity, including the little German cemetery where we examined the graves, each with its headstone and surrounding kerb stones, and each with its own tragic tale to tell. A cemetery under British administration was kept tidy and well cared for, but was now becoming neglected and overgrown. Also, the earthworks of the abandoned 120 mile northern aligned Manyoni-Mkalama branch line, closed after failing to sufficiently exploit a well-watered area south of Lake Eyasi, and proving thereafter a crippling drain on Tanganyika Railways' limited resources.

Whilst I was busy with the Oerlikon air brake, the 50-mile branch line extending south on the Central Railway was nearing completion. First it skirted the Tendiga swamp, then the Mkegumba Mountains, in the broad and fertile Kilombera Valley, bringing with it with the hope this would not only become the breadbasket of Tanzania, but eventually provide a link at Broken Hill with the then Rhodesian Railways and the remainder of the railways south of the equator. At Broken Hill a change of gauge from the East African Railway gauge of 1 metre to the Rhodesian 3-foot 6-inch gauge was required. This was, however, already catered for with East African rolling stock tyres positioned for both. With an easy ruling grade of 1 in 100, and ready for opening to traffic, I was tasked with establishing running times and providing charts and graphs on locomotive fuel and water consumption over the new line.

When not on safari Shirley and I attended Sunday evensong at Dar es Salaam's Mission to Seamen which, because of its straightforward no-nonsense Book of Common Prayer service, suited my Congregational upbringing. Standing in spacious grounds the Mission included a well-used open air swimming pool (about which I will have some more to say later). The building contained living quarters, a reading room, and leading off from the chapel, a drinks bar. Receiving seafarers from all parts of the Christian world, the worship not only offered an interesting take on some aspects of life for expatriates in a tropical environment.

During prayers American sailors were inclined to make us fidget and open our eyes a little when at the end of each prayer our quiet contemplation was interrupted by arm waving and shouts of "Hallelujah! Praise the Lord!" The pastor, a Welshman, kept his finger firmly on the pulse of the port and the arriving ships, by visiting those which might welcome him aboard, and in doing so reminding the crew there is a place of welcome open at all times for friendship, prayer and worship. Occasionally a German captain with some of his officers and crew would attend, then in fellowship and led by our accomplished musician on the harmonium, the hymns would be of German origin. Unlike the British, who during prayers remained seated with heads bowed, the Germans rose and stood reverentially. Once in a while, the pastor would announce the arrival of a Welsh-crewed ship, then lifting our voice in praise we sang traditional and well-loved Welsh hymns.

At the start of each service, the Mission's cat, in solemn procession, followed the pastor down the aisle to take its place by his side. Cats in Africa being prey to all manner of creatures, it led a charmed life, and I can go as far as to say this was the only cat I ever saw in this part of the world. I sat on the outside of a row of chairs, and to add further interest to the service a native shenzi dog always came and sat beside me. If our singing pleased it enough he would join in by howling whilst I tried to hush it. Sadly, one Sunday evening, missing from its accustomed place, word quickly spread that he had fallen down into the hold of a ship he was investigating, and had been killed. At the end of every service the congregation, perspiring freely due to the heat and also from its enthusiastic singing, found itself disadvantaged by the pastor, who, processing out first, led the charge to the bar and its ice cold beers.

To return to the Mission swimming pool as promised, in 1966 a visiting German sea captain, about fifty years of age and strongly built, vowed he would swim the pool in full uniform if West Germany lost to England in the July 1966 World Cup Final, which of course they did. The next time he docked in Dar es Salaam he arrived at the Mission looking splendid, in full white tropical uniform, and smoking a large and expensive cigar, with the announcement he was about to honour the debt. Climbing to the top of the diving frame he walked the length of the diving board, and balancing on the very end tested its flexibility. Satisfied, he set his white and gold-braided cap at a more jaunty angle, and to the chant of "One, Two, Three!" from the onlookers, in a cloud of cigar smoke, he launched himself into the water, before disappearing from view, to emerge minus his cap but with his bent and waterlogged cigar still clenched between his teeth. Swimming back on the return length he picked up his half submerged cap, and ignoring its full contents, replaced it on his head. Completing his swim he climbed out of the pool, shook himself to rid some of the water, and with water still spurting out of his shoes, trouser bottoms and the pockets of his uniform, acknowledged the approving cheers of the spectators.

'Big Jock Smith', a large braw Scotsman, and chief boiler inspector for the Central Railway, shared an office with me in Dar es Salaam. He was past the retirement age of 55 but had agreed to stay on and help out due to the exodus of experienced personnel. On the departure of the last governor of Tanganyika, Sir Richard Turnbull, Jack had somehow acquired his official car, a magnificent Armstrong Siddeley saloon, its tapered bonnet seeming to go on forever, whilst its polished hardwood dashboard boasted a bewildering display of knobs, switches, levers, dials and gauges. Whilst driving from home to the office one morning, Jack began complaining of the heat, which for someone who had spent most of his life in the tropics seemed a little unusual.

As time went on his lamentations increased, until arriving at work covered in sweat and staggering about, he began to say he didn't think he could stand the heat much longer. Although we all perspired in the heat and humidity, this was more serious, and fearing heat stroke or something similar, steps had to be taken to discover the cause of his obvious discomfort. Eventually the source was tracked down. Confused by the array of instruments on his dashboard we found Jock had inadvertently switched on the heater, with the inevitable result that by the time he reached work, the inside of his Armstrong Siddeley was hot enough to roast a turkey!

My wife Shirley was now heavily pregnant, and so on a Sunday, to escape the draining humidity for a few hours, and providing I was not on safari, we would motor to Morogoro, a round trip of 250 miles over a dust-laden dirt road with corrugations on which care had to be taken over the more treacherous sections. I remember one particular tragedy when the wife of an Indian doctor, an attractive young woman with blue eyes of either Afghan or Pathan (Pashtun) genealogy, lost control of her car and was killed whilst travelling between Morogoro and Dar es Salaam. After lunch at Morogoro's Greek-owned hotel we used to drive up into the nearby Uluguru Mountains to enjoy, briefly, the waft of cool scent-laden breezes and its mossy glades, where Shirley could dangle her feet in one of its many cold, clear mountain streams, before returning to Dar es Salaam in time for evensong.

On 10 May 1966, our first child, Richard Thomas, was born at the Ocean Road Hospital, an old German-built hospital, but none the worse for that, which faced the Indian Ocean. Here he was delivered by the same lady who, you'll remember, had strapped my broken ribs years before at Mwanza. At that time we had an old black labrador bitch by the name of Bess, which we had been landed with when her owner had left the service and returned home, and she became very protective of baby Richard. Our quarters had a deep open veranda to its front, and during the day this was the coolest part of the house, and to take advantage of this we used to lay Richard in his cot on its tiled floor.

Faithful old Bess, ever watchful, would lay beside the cot and carefully interpose herself between the cot and the big bad outside world. She was equally mindful for Shirley when we went for a swim at one of Dar es Salaam's several beaches. Then she would swim around Shirley and try to nudge her out of the water and back onto the beach. A very intelligent dog, somewhere in her canine mind she knew where danger lurked, and did her best to protect the vulnerable from it. Good old Bess, she only had one fault: her nose often led her to a rotting fish somewhere along the beach, then she took an obvious delight in rubbing her nose in it and rolling in it. Even after enticing her back into the sea for a wash down for the ride home, and a proper bath, the journey was anything but a pleasant experience!

By now, the Chinese were beginning to take more than a little interest in the newly independent state of Tanzania. They already had a vast embassy surrounded by high walls topped by coils of barbed wire, the embassy roof bristling with radio and electronic equipment, and its staff noticeable for driving to and from the ruling TANU (Tanganyika African National Union) party headquarters in expensive Mercedes saloons. On one occasion a group of Chinese mechanical engineers arrived to make a survey of the railway workshops, where they bombarded Kit Collard, the erecting shop foreman, with questions regarding the minutiae of workshop production and practice so remote that they left Kit Collard lost for an answer. In conversation later, Kit disclosed that much of what they asked. had, for practical reasons, never been explored in general practice by EAR engineers. For example, as a guide to workshop proficiency they wanted to know the kilowatts of electricity per hour used to re-tyre wheels of a locomotive. Examining a 60 Class Garratt undergoing heavy repairs they came up with another beauty: what, they asked, was the amount of deflection in the connecting rods of a 60 Class running at the maximum permitted speed on level track?

HQ staff, Mechanical Department Dar es Salaam. Centre bottom row, DME Mr Domanic. Top left, Erecting Shop Foreman Chris Collard. Middle row, third from left, the author.

Around this time a new boss, as District Mechanical Engineer (DME), arrived, again a 'retread', but this time in a more exotic mould—a former Argentinian Railways engineer of Anglo-Argentinian stock with the surname Domanic. Aged about 60 years old, he was of medium height and still slim and athletic, and in manner and appearance very much the gentleman. Understandably lacking knowledge of the Central Railway, he relied on my experience for the everyday workings, part of which was a new requirement for me to phone the Morogoro and Tabora shedmasters at 9 am sharp for an account of their dispositions, and report back to him. This got me into trouble with the Tabora DMPS, who rang me in rage when he discovered I was reporting things he preferred to remain unknown. This was a man I didn't care much for, and I shut him up by pointing out I was acting on the orders of not only my boss, but also his boss. Much of the telephone conversations were for urgent store requisitions to be sent up, and I spent a lot of time at the main stores, a large complex on the edge of town, arranging these articles.

When Richard was about six months old Shirley received an airmail letter, the only means of communication open to us at that time, saying her mother was in the last stages of leukaemia. Although I rented a post office mailbox, this letter unfortunately arrived over a weekend, and on the Monday coincided with the touchdown of the Chinese Premier Zhou Enlai, on a two-day state visit. This came with the warning that anyone seen at an upper window would be shot. Under this edict, travelling to and from work could be dodgy, very dodgy, and having had enough of looking down barrels of rifles waving about in front of my nose, I decided my allegiance to EAR could be put on hold for a couple of days.

Shirley and her mother wrote to each other once a week, and knowing how much she treasured her mother's letters, on the Wednesday morning, after returning to work and on my way home, I called in at the post office. Whilst being of no great age, Shirley's mother's hand writing had deteriorated very quickly, which caused me some concern, but she always wrote saying she was fit and well. On opening the post box I discovered a solitary letter addressed to Shirley in an unfamiliar hand, with 'Urgent!' scrawled across its heading. It carried devastating news: Shirley's mother was in the final stages of life. Without hesitation Shirley chose to return home as quickly as possible, so after some frantic efforts I managed to secure a place for them on the next plane home, withdraw enough funds to pay for the tickets and ensure Shirley had enough money to see her over the foreseeable future, and arrange for Richard to be vaccinated. Thus within the space of four hours both were on a de Havilland Comet airliner on their way home.

I mention this because whilst they were away I had two close encounters with death. The first brush occurred on my way home after finishing work for the day. For about a mile my route led me along an old, little used, German-built road, lined either side with mango trees, forming a dense canopy. Half way along I found the road blocked by a litter of sticks and stones, and whilst slowing down to clear my way through I noticed on my left a motor scooter (a 'Pigi-Pigi') laid on its side between two of the trees, having all the appearance of a serious accident. I stopped the car, and walking around its front went to investigate, I had almost reached the Pigi-Pigi when with a fearful buzz I was attacked by a swarm of very angry African bees—bees noted for their ability to kill. Followed by the swarm I raced for the shelter of the car, and once inside began brushing the bees off my body. Dressed lightly in shorts and open-necked shirt the bees were all over me, in my hair, all over my face and neck, inside my shirt and crawling and stinging my naked legs. This was serious and I frantically swept them off before realising this was having no effect on the numbers filling the car. Then I remembered I had been driving with the windows open, so leaving off killing bees (which was probably making their compatriots more aggressive anyway) I closed all four windows before returning to the task of disposing of as many as I could and as quickly as possible. After making an impression on them I drove the half mile to a neighbour's house to seek help. He, together with his wife, spent the next hour extracting stings, and lacking salve, balm or other soothing embrocation, they wiped my affected parts (which was most of me) with all that was available: water, cooled by ice, from the fridge.

The same evening I had been invited to a 'sundowner' for a retiring Asian member of staff, so despite the painful bee stings, and because I didn't want to cause offence by staying away, I decided to attend. As befitted formal occasions, such as Sunday evensong, etc., I dressed in light slacks, white shirt and tie, and at about 7 pm drove round to my host who met me with cries of dismay. "Oh Mr Blackburn, whatever has happened?"

"Beeez," I mumbled through swollen lips and half-closed eyes. "Wran into a zwarm ov beeez an got stug." Concerned about my condition, he asked if I had been to the hospital.

"Doe. Ad all wight," I replied. Apart from multiple swellings, the bee stings seemed to have had little real effect on me, other than to make my face look like that of the Elephant Man.

Now, although we knew how deadly African bees could be (the death toll even among the much lower non-African population bore witness to this), none of us had heard of anaphylactic shock and its ability to kill, sometimes after only a single bee or wasp sting. At that time, our thinking was that death occurred after the poison of multiple bee stings brought about organ failure, and I didn't feel that way at all, and so in reply to my host's concerns I thanked him and replied I didn't feel as if I needed hospital treatment. However, after an hour I began to develop a headache and a feeling of intense weariness and a shortness of breath. Making my apologies I left with the intention of following a long-held custom of mine of going to bed early when feeling ill, in the firm belief I would wake up next morning feeling much better. It never occurred to me that I might fall asleep to never to wake up again. So, tucking my mosquito net in all round, I fell asleep, to wake next morning feeling groggy and ill enough to report in sick for the next two days. The wonder of it is, what little effect the hundreds of African bee stings had on me, and in retrospect how fortunate I was to escape with my life.

Later on I came to believe the incident had been caused by local Africans throwing up sticks and stones into the mango canopy, hoping to harvest a bounty of large ripe and luscious mango fruits, and inadvertently dislodging a bees' nest, and then fled for their lives. As for the owner of the Pigi-Pigi, he must have run into the same swarm, and after abandoning his machine had also fled for his life.

My second narrow escape whilst Shirley and Richard were away, and which was entirely my own fault, proved to be even more serious, and occurred after I had accidentally taken an overdose of anti-malaria tablets. Our quarters consisted of a modern detached bungalow with a Bangalore tiled roof, standing in its own grounds. As accommodation it had only one fault, its false roof was occupied by swallows and fruit bats, with the result that the place reeked of bird droppings and, even worse, the pungent stench of bat urine. It was something quite common in Africa, and whilst there was nothing I could do about the swallows and bats who came and went as they pleased, in anticipation of Shirley and Richard's return I decided to make the place a little sweeter by entering the roof space and shovelling out the accumulated droppings.

On my next free weekend, I climbed up into the roof space and, by removing sections of the easily refitted roof tiles, began shovelling out a thick layer of debris, which consisted not only of droppings but the dried and desiccated remains of birds and bats, and the maggots feeding off them. In the roof space the heat and humidity was intense, like nothing I had experienced before, and in the confined space my shovelling raised clouds of malodorous dust. And here's the rub, beyond knowing Dettol was superior to iodine for treating cuts and abrasions, and my mother's potent ipecacuanha cough medicine was most effective when treating chest infections, my medical knowledge was nil. So with sweat pouring out of me and no thought for my health I shovelled away whilst breathing in clouds of choking dust. It took me the best part of two days to complete the task, which to be frank made little, if any, reduction in the overall smell.

The following morning, I went to work feeling unwell. By this time, Big Jock Smith, the senior boiler inspector, had been replaced by a South African, Jeff Dyson. I must have looked even worse than I felt, for straight away Jeff asked if I was all right. After admitting that I felt a bit rough, Jeff assumed that it was malaria, and asked if I had any 'dawa'—the Swahili term for any kind of medicine. It has to be said that we were all a bit offhand when it came to taking anti-malarial tablets, and having run out some time before I answered, "No."

"Jump in the car," Jeff offered, "and I'll take you down to the chemist." It was generally recognised that after a couple of years on one anti-malarial drug it was advantageous to change to another. Jeff told me a new and highly effective *Nivaquine* had come on the market. "Yes, that'll do me," I replied. Dar es Salaam had only one chemist, and whether the Asian proprietor was a qualified chemist or just a purveyor of pharmaceutical goods I'm not sure, but he stocked, and I acquired, a packet of *Nivaquine*, and that's when my troubles began.

Back at the office, I read the instructions, which said take one tablet a week as a prophylactic against malaria, and that was all right. Feeling ill I may have misread what followed, which, although it seemed plain enough at the time, should have sent alarm bells ringing. In effect it advised (or so I thought) that anyone actually suffering from malaria should take four tablets, a usual full month's supply, in one go. But worse was to follow when it advised taking a pill every two hours until the fever had subsided. With my brain fogged, I began popping pills at the recommended rate of a pill every two hours. By about 3 pm, with the room swimming, my breathing very shallow and my heart rate slowing down, I knew I needed help. At the time I was by myself, Jeff being in the workshops examining boilers, and so I decided to drive to the hospital.

Our office, which was part of the old German Railway HQ, was located above a large room occupied by African clerks and typists, under the control of an Indian chief clerk. Now desperately ill, I left the office staggering and swerving through the pool of astonished onlookers like a drunken sailor on his first day ashore. Reaching my car, I had a struggle to open its door which left me exhausted, and whilst trying to climb in I collapsed. Laid half in and half out of the car and barely conscious, yet feeling strangely peaceful and comfortable, I was ready to drift off into a gentle all-enveloping sleep. However, before I did so forever, an alert African gatekeeper discovered me and raised the alarm.

In a collapsed semi-conscious state, I was bundled into the splendid and recently opened Queen Elizabeth Hospital, where I clearly remember the English matron saying, as they carried me in, "He's still got a pulse." After being examined and asked what I had taken, I was laid on a bed in a single room, where a series of African 'dressers' watched over me night and day, to see whether I lived or died. With the drug absorbed, I could well understand there was little else they could do for me.

For two weeks I lay in a state of exhaustion and vertigo, which left me clutching the sides of the bed as the room swung wildly from side to side—a most unpleasant sensation which I can only describe as feeling as if my brain was loose and rolling about in my skull. After a fortnight, and still very weak, the vertigo had subsided to the extent I could sit upright in a chair, but I still found going for my ablutions like charting a course through a storm-lashed sea. Finally, after four weeks of hospitalisation, I was discharged fit enough to resume my duties, although the after effects of the overdose, a weakness and a slowness to react remained with me for a long-time.

Shirley arrived in the UK only a couple of days before her mother died. After winding up her mother's affairs Shirley and Richard returned, and I met them at Dar es Salaam airport as they flew in on another handsome Comet airliner. The introduction of the Comet jet airliner almost halved the flight time between London and Dar es Salaam, but of course the early versions of this aeroplane (which I flew on several times) did have a tendency to fall out the sky, their catastrophic mid-air break ups caused by metal fatigue. Thankfully, though, by the mid-1950s the design flaws of this new type of aircraft had been rectified (although not before the USA aircraft manufacturers caught up with and surpassed the British). Because the lavatories on the Comet were situated just behind the engines, when you opened the lavatory door and stepped inside you received the full howl of the wing-mounted engines. This proved a traumatic experience for Richard when requiring a nappy change, and later, when we were back living in Britain, he used to be frightened to death when he heard a jet plane approaching, and would run screaming into the house.

Chapter 28
Goodbye, Mr Krupp

Around the time of Shirley's return, changing circumstances impacting on Tabora shed were afoot. Because of continuing civil war in the Congo, traffic to and from Kigoma had dwindled away to a trickle, reducing that section to the status of a branch line, whilst in comparison, traffic through Mwanza from Uganda and western Kenya had increased dramatically, forcing EAR to upgrade the Mwanza line by ballasting it throughout, and relaying it with heavier, long, welded rails.

With the upgrade of the Mwanza line nearing completion, urgent action was required because 13 out of the 17 locomotives of the 27 Class were stopped, due to boiler degradation, and were under sentence of death! This left the four remaining locomotives working, with reduced boiler pressure, as shunting engines at Mwanza and Kigoma, resigning the struggling 26 Class to bear the burden of the Mwanza's lines increased traffic. With only a little relaying and tidying up work at Mwanza station and the two docks (Mwanza South and Mwanza North) outstanding, I was sent in to prepare that line for the heavier and more powerful 30 Class.

The one and only combined fuel and water point on this line was located at Shinyanga, 123 miles from Tabora, and the precise midway point. It was notable also for its constant supply of clean sweet water from the nearby mountain-fed river, and as such was positioned well within the range of a 30 Class with a tender capacity of 7,000 gallons of water and 1,900 gallons of fuel oil. At a pinch, this Class could run the whole 246 miles without taking water or oil fuel. As an example, during my driving days, in order to gain the benefit of a tender full of pure spring water taken at Saranda, I used to run the 269 miles on one tender of water (although admittedly it was cutting it a bit fine). And so, with no concerns with the 30 Class as regards water and fuel oil, I was able to concentrate on establishing faster running times between stations.

After one such trip, I renewed my acquaintance with the Pinkneys, spending an evening with them at the splendid Tabora Railway Hotel 'watering hole', where frequent clientele included Prince Bernhard of the Netherlands who, piloting his own plane, flew in on big game safaris. Another was General Franco's daughter, who liked a bit of game hunting and wasn't above joining the hoi polloi at the bar. Also, several times a year, one or other High Court judge arrived to dispense justice in that part of the country, and they always sat by themselves at a corner table, indifferent to the rest of us, and guarded by a native policeman.

Another visitor was a large and imposing Australian with a fearsome black beard and moustache, who I can only describe as a roving government dentist. He disembarked from the train carrying his gear in a large brown suitcase whose horrors included a grindingly slow foot-pedalled drill, which he set up in the hospital. Then there was the odd traveller passing through, and a sprinkling of European and American trophy hunters.

The rainy season was approaching at this time, with huge banks of menacing black clouds boiling up and towering high into the sky, whilst in the gaps between the sun burst through with its usual malevolent intensity.

Two Down Mail Train on the Rift Valley escarpment as evening falls.

Leaving the hotel, I walked the half-mile to the station where my coach was stabled. The night was hot and humid with lightning continuously flickering behind the clouds, silent and ominous. Reaching my coach, I was more fortunate than the Pinkneys, who I later learned had returned home to a scene of devastation and filth. The culprits here were large black aggressive safari ants who, sensing rain, had invaded and passed beneath the doors and through the house, driving the Pinkney's two Alsatian dogs into a frenzy of fear. In an attempt to escape, they had flung themselves at the windows, torn down the curtains, clawed at doors, smashed precious ornaments and, most unpleasant of all, in utter panic defecated over the beds.

But to return to railway matters—at this time, Tabora was still feeling the loss of most of its 27 Class, leaving it short of motive power, and whose duties had of necessity been taken over by the 26 Class. To fill the gap, an old but still reliable 52 Class Garratt (it had entered service in 1931) was sent from Nairobi to Tabora via the recently opened Link Line from the Central Line. 'Legs' Baldwin accompanied it with its train as far as Ruvo Station, the Link Line connection with the Central Railway, and some 49 miles from Dar es Salaam where, taking over, I attached my coach to the rear of the train to spend the next 48 hours monitoring the engine over the 600-odd miles to Tabora.

For the next fortnight, using Tabora as a base, I conducted a series of tests with the Garratt over the Mwanza line, which included fixing running times and fuel, and in particular water consumption, which was always a cause for concern. The water supply to Shinyanga was ample and of good quality, but north of Shinyanga on the arid grasslands, locomotives were, for the next 100 miles, served by only two water points, one of which was brackish, which as the day wore on became more and more salty, and as such was to be eschewed if priming on the heavy grades was to be avoided. To overcome this it was practice to attach a water tank bogie to the tender of each engine, and whilst at a push the 52 Class could have managed without, the margin was too narrow for everyday operations, and as a safety measure I recommended the use of a water tank bogie with the Garratt. Finally, satisfied, I handed my report conclusions and graphs to the DMPS Tabora, and instead of returning home on my jolting and weaving inspection coach, I chose the luxury of the Down Mail Train, which meant a prepared meal and smooth running in a comfortable bed for the night.

At this point in my career, I'm sorry to say I was turning somewhat jumpy, being affected by any sudden or sharp noise with what would now be diagnosed as a form of post-traumatic stress, brought about, I think, by what I had seen of the traumatised Congo refugees and the events during the army mutiny, but triggered now by matters nearer to home. Not far away a camp under control of elements of the Chinese Army had been set up for one of Tanzania's semi-military youth organisations, and from which, unexpectedly and at odd intervals, a fusillade of rifle fire would burst out, bringing with it each time a shock which left me a bag of nerves, and with the harrowing thought that this might be armed men once again running amok, and I had nowhere to hide my wife and baby.

After several months of this torment, I applied for a transfer to Kenya, a more stable country, I felt, even if this meant running the gauntlet of the irascible little red-headed piggy-eyed customs official (just the man for the job!) who I was convinced, upon me handing my passport to him, would turn it over and ask, "Is this for your 12 bore?" Unfortunately, my request was turned down (for reasons unknown), and regretfully, for I considered more at home in East Africa than in my homeland, I felt I had no option but to tender my resignation to EAR. For the next six months life had to go on, and this included my only trip over the 117 mile rail link, connecting the Central Railway with the Tanga (Usambara) Railway via Mnyusi to Moshi and its union with the Kenya and Uganda system, a trip which unfortunately developed into a nightmare.

The train left Dar es Salaam in the early hours, headed by a French-built Franco-Belge 4-8-2-2-8-4 Garratt, under the charge of an African crew. The engine was in good condition except for a pronounced blow from its front right hand piston gland. This, to say the least, was quite unusual, being the only time throughout my career when modern segmented cast iron piston rod packing had failed in service. It was also unusual for another reason: having arrived on shed defective and blowing, it should, as a matter of course, been taken down and repacked. Why this wasn't done remains a mystery.

From my coach, I could hear throughout the remainder of the night the piston gland growing steadily worse, and with scoring to the piston rod from the disintegrating cast iron packing very much in mind, I decided to investigate at first light. By some miracle, I found the piston rod unmarked, and with fingers crossed I elected, whilst examining the piston rod at every station, to carry on and if necessary take down the gland and clean it of broken packing. With this kind of gland it involved a long difficult and wrist burning operation, causing delay to the train and a sharp demand from the Operating Department for the reason. Mystified by the packing's failure, I examined the crosshead to see if its slide had suffered excessive side wear, therefore throwing the piston rod out of true at each front admission, but finding no fault there, I could only conclude it was one of those rare and unexplained 'failure of material' occurrences.

At one station, after being turned into a loop for a passing Down train, and whilst examining the Garratt's piston rod, I was shown the future of the former happy and peaceful Protectorate. As the opposing train passed through I saw it was made up of two passenger coaches plus a number of flat bogie waggons. It was what the flats carried which caught my attention and my breath: each flat waggon carried field guns, and the passenger coaches were crammed with soldiers, who I took to be either Russian or some other Warsaw Pact nationals. Or they could have been Chinese, for the Chinese were becoming far more dominant and conspicuous in Tanzania's affairs. After landing unobtrusively at the quiet harbour of Tanga, rather than the bustling port of Dar es Salaam where many interested eyes would have marked their arrival, they were now on their way to, well, who knows where?

Arriving at Moshi, the railhead of the Tanga line, I met the shedmaster, a Mr Singh, an old acquaintance of mine from Tabora days, and a Sikh 'pretty boy'— for, there, as fitter-in-charge of a shift, he was remarkable for never dirtying his hands, and for his always pristine attire, which included a variety of turbans, each of a delicate pastel hue and each drawn up to a splendid peak. But above all he was known for his ability to dodge doing repairs. Whatever the repair, he could give 50 good reasons for it to be left to carry on.

Entering his office, I was greeted like a long-lost friend. "Ah, Mr Blackburn, welcome, can I offer you a cup of tea?" Recognising this as part of his 'softening up' process, but not wishing to appear unfriendly (an unfortunate failing of mine in these circumstances), I agreed, although I had to stomach the weak and intensely sweet tea I was about to receive.

"Chia!" the shedmaster shouted with an imperious wave of his hand, and within a few minutes one of his minions appeared with a tray carrying two glasses, which with the sun striking through each one, did nothing to improve the appearance of the concoction they contained. Disguising my aversion, I sipped away, whilst telling Singh of the blowing gland and its need for repacking.

The return trip was booked for a 20:00 departure, and seated in my coach, I heard the Garratt coming off shed, its piston gland blowing to such an extent that every fourth exhaust was barely audible. My first reaction was: the bugger's got away with it again! Now I may be wrong, and perhaps Moshi shed didn't, after all, carry a stock of 60 Class piston rod packing material. But this is doubtful, as 60 Class locomotives worked from Tanga through to Moshi, as they did from Nairobi to Moshi, and on that basis I am certain Moshi locomotive shed held at least some suitable packing.

So to this day, I remain convinced that the rotter had (speaking in modern parlance) 'shafted me'. There was little if anything I could do about it except ride in my coach whilst listening to the distant but distinct blow from Mr Singh's pistons gland. About 22:00, as the coach waggled about on its four wheels with a motion more akin to a small boat caught in some turbulent cross-current, I wedged myself in its bunk and fell asleep, only to be jerked awake by the Garratt slipping to a standstill. For some time, I lay listening to the driver trying to restart his train, and when I was convinced it was safe for me to leave the coach without being left stranded in the middle of hostile bush, I dressed, and in the depth of an inky-black night went up to the engine.

It had long been a boast of mine that I could, by using the steam brake with a light and delicate touch, give its coupled wheels something more to bite on, preventing the engine slipping. Alas and alack, with a 60 Class I found myself thwarted. The steam brake as a component part was directly controlled by the air brake, and as such unable to act independently. So if I was to restart the train and counter the engine's tendency to slip, I would have to call on all my ingenuity and skill.

For the best part of an hour, at my command, and whilst blasted by red hot steam from the open piston gland, I struggled to restart the train. I used all the sand in the sandboxes, not by the way of the Lambert sanders, they were as hopeless as ever, but by the engine crew scooping the sand out of the boxes with their bare hands and spreading it along the tops of the rails. As a substitute I could have used the normally sandy topsoil on either side of the railway, but hereabout it was red murram earth, lashed by countless rains and baked hard by the sun. Unfamiliar with any of the railway, and in the darkness unable to judge the severity of the grade we were on, I juggled the train back and forth trying to find a grip. It seemed unusually reluctant to move either forward or backwards, and I came to the conclusion that there would be nothing else for it but to spilt the train and take the front half to the next station and then return for the remainder.

Fretting over how much water I had remaining, I asked the driver how far the next water point was? "Mbali sana," he replied (very far), his long drawn out syllables expressing a long way, though that could mean almost anything. Leaving the engine, I carefully made my way along the train to about half way, then fumbling about in the pitch dark, and anxious not to leave several fingers in the coupling hook, I detached the front half. Even this brought its concerns. Lacking detonators or even a red lamp to protect the remainder of the train, in the circumstances this was an action fraught with danger, something requiring the utmost vigilance if a collision was to be averted on my return with the engine to pick up the remaining part of the train. In the meantime I had other concerns.

A quick look at the Garratt's two water tanks confirmed we were running dangerously short of water, and with the driver's warning of "Mbali sana" very much to the forefront of my thinking, I was aware of an imminent failure with all the disruption and misery that would bring. I knew I was cutting things rather on the lean side.

After a six-mile climb with the forepart of the train, the driver warned me that we were approaching a station, and to my relief adding, "Maji hapa bwana (Water here, Sir)." It was none too soon, as we shunted the first half of the train out of the way the injector kicked off. But we had arrived in the nick of time, safe and secure, with a still full boiler to play with. After filling the Garratt's two water tanks to capacity, I returned for the rest of the train, and although I had marked the distance in my mind's eye, in the dark, on a falling gradient, with exhaustion dragging at my eyes, there was plenty of room for error. But with the engine crew helping by keeping a sharp lookout, this was achieved without mishap.

Exhausted (I was still suffering the aftermaths of my *Nivaquine* overdose), drenched in sweat from hot steam blowing back from the defective piston gland, and tormented by thirst, I took the opportunity to leave the rest to the engine crew, and whilst cursing the black-hearted villain whose dereliction of duty had led to all this upset, return to my coach and snatch some sleep.

The first blush of dawn was streaking the sky as I walked back to the coach. Part way along the train, and outlined against a spreading golden hue, I noticed, now just visible, two covered goods bogies (CGB's) out of line with the rest of the train. With a jolt of dismay I knew in an instant that both waggons had derailed, and this was the reason that the Garratt, loaded to its limit, had slipped to a standstill on the grade, and thereafter obstinately refused to budge. After the first wave of dismay came a profound sense of relief. I had discovered the derailment before the Garratt, now relieved of most of its load, had moved off, dragging the derailed waggons with it and tearing up miles of track and damaging the waggons beyond repair.

My first instinct was to prevent this happening, and I snapped apart the two nearest brake pipes, rendering the rest of the train immobile and preventing a further blot on my reputation. With the train now locked and unable to move, I went up to the engine to arrange for the driver and fireman to shut the engine down. Recovering the two screw traversing jacks which each engine carried in case of derailment (and used to lift the locomotive and move it sideways before lowering it back onto the track), I lugged them, for they were heavy, to the scene of the derailment where we could start the long and wearying task of rerailing the two waggons. Whilst making arrangements the driver volunteered information which lifted my spirits no end: he informed me of a Permanent Way gang camp about a mile ahead. What a blessing for a distracted soul, a gang camp with 20 or more strong able-bodied men whose routine included the use of jacks and other lifting equipment. Heaving a sigh of relief I sent the fireman to seek help with the request that the camp sent a runner to the next station to inform the stationmaster that this was the reason for the non-arrival of the remaining section of the train.

Within the hour a push trolley arrived loaded with lifting jacks, crow bars, thick balks of timber and enough men to almost bodily lift each waggon back on the rails. After about two hours of hard graft both waggons had been re-railed and with the train ready to go I examined the two waggons for fitness to run.

3012 after heavy repairs and alterations.

After bumping from sleeper to sleeper I expected the axle box brasses to have been dislodged and broken, and my examination confirmed this. Under these conditions I knew the axle boxes would quickly run hot, but there was nothing else for it, so whilst watching from the coach and ready to apply the brakes at the first sign of irregular running we set off at reduced speed, with each bearing squealing in protest at its displaced brasses, and the axle boxes began to stream smoke as the bearings ran hot, boiling the oil they contained, and setting fire to the oiling pads. Happily we arrived at the next station without further trouble piling up. Having detached the two defective waggons—these were now someone else's headache—and after remarshalling the train, and my work concluded I went back to the coach for a well-earned rest.

The sun was now well up and the coach, its flanges grinding noisily against the rails, was hot and sticky inside. Although tired, the sleep I craved eluded me. My days with EAR were now coming to an end, and with it, sadly, my railway career. Restless and ill at ease I lay and reviewed my years on the footplate, and it seemed to me that this, my last safari, had much in common with my first day at Botanic Gardens many years before. Both had been fraught one way or another, and both were to be remembered for all the wrong reasons.

Back at headquarters I made out my reports, putting as much gloss on them as I could, and continued with my day to day duties, until called by the workshop to trial an engine after heavy repairs. I was delighted to find it was my old engine 3012 standing in the works entrance, but in a much-altered condition. In place of its attractive 'windjabber' style chimney it now had a Giesl chimney and multiple blast pipes, which I approved of for its ability to clear exhausts in sharp clear beats. In any case I thought the wedge-shaped forward-facing chimney added a note of distinction to the engine. Less pleasing to the eye and the result of being fitted with the Metcalfe-Oerlikon air brake during its stay in the works, were two large and powerful air compressors that had been attached to the side of the smokebox and two ungainly air reservoirs that had been mounted on the topside of the left-hand running plate, all of which were completely at odds with the engine's former simple and uncluttered appearance. But despite 'it's made of steel and doesn't feel anything' as I walked towards it, it was like meeting an old and well-loved friend.

Even so, at this late stage in my career it would never do to conk out on a trial run, and I began a preliminary but careful examination of the engine by checking both air pumps to see if the topside lubricators had been filled and at the same time opening the smokebox door and examining the inside of the smokebox for any defects. Reassured I went to the cab to test the air compressors and check out the air pressure in the engine's brake system. Once I had opened the steam valve both compressors ran smoothly and I watched the air pressure rising on the gauge until it stopped at a little over the 70 psi regulation pressure, which I adjusted by manipulating the regulating knob on the driver's brake valve. With air pressure held at 70 psi I shut the compressors off and turned to the boiler water gauges, testing each one individually by blowing them through and at the same time asking the firemen to try the injectors and test that the air scoop damper was in good working order. I then examined the firebox where I found everything was steamtight and the oil burners correctly aligned.

As far as cab fittings were concerned, I had one further test before checking the remainder of the engine. In my earlier days I had discovered that on many British locomotives the reverser didn't always show the true position of the die-blocks in the expansion links, giving a false reading on the reverser's scale. In practice this didn't much matter because when 'notching up' the locomotive was operated by sound and feel rather than by the reverser's position. However, since becoming locomotive inspector, this had developed into something of a fad of mine, especially in the case of engines coming out of shops, though I must confess, I had never found fault. I did once, however, have a bit of a head scratch with a test Garratt. On this occasion Chris Collard was on local leave and in no way to blame, but on its first move under steam it 'lay down' on me and refused to budge. I tried it in reverse with the same result, and it wasn't until I examined the position of the die blocks that I discovered it had been set up to move in opposite directions at once. However, to satisfy my need I placed 3012's reverser in mid-gear and went and examined the position of its die block. As expected I found both lined up perfectly midway in the links. Better to check though, and be safe rather than sorry!

Since my arrival in Tabora and my daily tussle with the cranky unpredictable 26 Class, or should that be the predictably cranky 26 Class, I found it useful to carry a hammer, which I used for testing the tightness of nuts or anything else that might be working loose. Not a big heavy hammer you understand, but one just heavy enough to give a sharp rap, and through sensitive fingertips give a clear indication of any slackness developing in nuts, bolts, taper pins, and side rods discs, which on the 26 Class were prone to work loose, as were even cross-head cotter pins. Now as I examined 3012's lubrication points and tapped around, I took the opportunity to pump a little oil into the side rod and big end bushes using the plug trimmings. With my inspection complete I drove 3012 around to the waiting train. Although everything was tight as a drum 3012 ran smoothly and silently, her Giesl exhaust 'soft as the breath of ev'n'[63]. On test I would find out if she lived up to her previous good name and was able to maintain both steam and water under the most extreme of conditions.

I backed onto the train I was about to head and coupled onto the train engine, a 60 Class Garratt, explaining to its driver, a Sikh, my intentions. For the first

---

[63] Hymn, 'Our blest Redeemer', Harriet Auber, 1829: "And his that gentle voice we hear, Soft as the breath of ev'n, That checks each fault, that calms each fear, And speaks of heav'n."

few miles the track ran straight and level before climbing through the Pugu Hills to Pugu Station on a rising grade of 1 in 48 for the next 12 miles. At Pugu station I would detach and run back light engine to the workshops for a final check all round. With Carriage and Waggon Department staff in attendance, I made several full and complete applications of the brake, mainly to test the efficiency of the air compressors in recharging the brake system, and also to test the new FV4 driver's automatic air brake valve and its ability to maintain the regulation 70 psi. Satisfied on both scores I sat back in the driver's seat and awaited the Line Clear. On receipt, and ready to go, I whistled up for a flash of the guard's green flag, and with an answering whistle from the train engine I opened the regulator.

Whilst it couldn't be said of 3012's new valve and piston rings, which still needed working in, I was aware its cylinders and steam chest liners would be polished to a mirror finish, and to bed the rings in and spread a little cylinder oil around the front end before the real test began, I ran the level stretch at line speed but with only a whiff of steam. The real test of 3012's mechanics, and the ability of Herr Giesl's ejector to clear steam and maintain both water levels and steam pressure under the most trying conditions, would come in the climb ahead, when I prepared to thrash 3012 to the limits of its capabilities. Running on a comfortable 20% cutoff under light steam I reached where the line rose visibly, and when I hit the grade I opened the regulator to full. Immediately the exhaust rose from a soft purr to a staccato roar, and as the train left the level and began to feel its drag I slowly wound the reverser down to half a turn from full foregear. With the exhaust rising to a crescendo the fireman, intent on maintaining steam pressure and water levels, further opened his ratcheted firing lever. Under perfect combustion the firebox became incandescent, each and every part of its construction standing out in sharp white relief.

Even under these extreme conditions, and owing much to the skill of the American Caltech engineers and North British design teams, 3012, despite two injectors being used on occasion, steamed freely with a clear smokeless exhaust. Out of interest I went over to check out how much fuel oil was still available to the burners and was pleased to discover the fireman's control lever had still a few notches left on its ratchet before it was fully open.

As the 1 in 48 grade took its toll and speed on the 12 mile climb fell away, the roar of 3012's chimney became a series of distinct and individual beats, each one explosively sharp and precise. With the 60 Class Garratt meanwhile thumping away behind, speed through the rolling Pugu Hills was held at a steady 15 mph, a gain of 3 mph on a Garratt's normal velocity. After an hour's climb we arrived at Pugu station where I uncoupled from the train and ran around into the loop to await 'permission to proceed', and whilst there I took the opportunity to check the big-end and side rod bushes for signs of overheating. With arrangement for my return completed I left tender first, drifting down the grade at a steady 20 mph with the regulator closed. Back on the workshop line I began a detailed examination of 3012 including the engine's multiple valve MeLeSco regulator, its superheater elements and the blast pipe joint and ring. Looking impeccable in lined-out maroon and finished with several coats of *'Best Copol Varnish'*, I readily signed 3012 off as 'fit for traffic' and reluctantly said farewell to her.

The following Sunday, as a family, we went down to the harbour to welcome into port the SS Rhodesia Castle[64], then on her way down to South Africa. On her return we would board her for our voyage home, thus ending my career as a railwayman, for by union decree I was not allowed to rejoin British Railways in a footplate capacity. In the meantime, apart from my continuing duties, I had much to arrange. This included settling my income tax affairs, without which I would be unable to leave the country and arranging for Shirley and I to be 'jabbed up' against bringing into the United Kingdom those plagues and fevers endemic to Tanzania.

Also, another time-consuming and expensive task, the sorting out of personal effects, the disposal of those we didn't want or couldn't keep, and the boxing up of those we did by one of the port's shipping companies, prior to loading onto the Rhodesia Castle on its return to Dar es Salaam. Poor faithful old Bess was rehomed with her third adopted family. All these leaving preparations were done with a heavy heart. I'd originally set out on my 'African odyssey' in search of more assured employment, and perhaps some adventure, but I found more than this, and quickly grew to love the country and its people. I'd also considered that, in a small way, I was helping to make Tanganyika a more prosperous, more secure and better place to live for all its inhabitants.

A few days after 3012's engine test, the boss, who occupied a large and airy top floor office, rang down for me to attend at once. He informed me a head-on collision had occurred on Saranda Bank, and as a former Argentinian Railways

---

[64] Built 1951 for the Union-Castle Line, with a gross registered tonnage of 17,041. Scrapped in 1967.

engineer he was unfamiliar with EAR drill in the event of a major accident. As the senior loco inspector, I suggested his presence there would be welcome, as would any advice he could offer. The best way to get there quickly and efficiently was to hire a light aircraft and fly, at the railway's expense, to Dodoma, and then take a motor trolley the remaining 70 miles to the scene of the accident. In the meantime I would arrange for the senior officers' bogie inspection coach (BIC) to be attached to the next Up train with instructions that it be detached at Dodoma where the excellent Railway Hotel, with all its facilities, was within easy walking distance of the station.

A couple of days later, Domanic returned, and without discussing the cause of the accident, which would remain sub-judice until an enquiry took place, we exchanged views on the fate of the 30 Class engine which, leading the train, had felt the full impact of the collision both to its front and rear, destroying its large 12-wheeled tender and leaving the engine a near write-off. The boss felt the engine could be repaired, and by using one of the now defunct 27 Class tenders, of which a couple still awaited the cutter's torch, it could usefully spend the rest of its life banking trains up Saranda Bank.

This proposal sent alarm bells ringing. I remembered how 3012's forged steel coupling hook had snapped like a carrot when a banker engine slipped, and in my mind's eye I could see the rather light wartime-built 27 Class tenders being torn in half as two 30 Class engines, with a combined tractive effort of 60,000 lbs, and over 500 tons of train behind, fought to get a grip on any one of Saranda's many curves. I explained my concerns and wondered if a tender could be strengthened, and if not (and here's the rub: for EAR didn't like to change things once they became established practice), go back to Tanganyika Railways' approach, when the banker was coupled to the rear, the advantage being that the tender was then in no way involved. Secondly, of great importance, I pointed out, when one engine was on a curve and inclined to slip there was every chance the other was on a straight, holding its feet and flat out still plugging away. Another option I suggested, and one we discussed at length, was returning the banker engine to the head of the train, thereby reducing the forces resting upon a 27 Class tender by half.

During my last few working days the locomotive most damaged in the Saranda collision had been returned to the workshops for assessment and possible repair. Out of curiosity, and armed with a camera, I went to investigate, and found it minus its tender, side-lined on a length of empty track behind the works. From a distance I could see its smokebox door and surrounding plates had been stoved-in towards the bottom right-hand side, the side which had taken the brunt of the impact, and which gave a clear indication that the collision had occurred on a right-hand curve, leaving those involved little time to react. As I got nearer to the engine I became confused by the pattern of its damage which bore no resemblance to what I had expected.

Locomotive at Dar es Salaam workshops after the Seranda accident.

Looking at the locomotive side-on I could see that the cowcatcher, projecting forward just above rail level, and which one would have expected to have taken the full force of the collision, remained untouched, whilst the coupling with its buffing gear had been destroyed, but leaving the steel buffer beam to which it was attached relatively undamaged apart from a slight deflection of its right outer edge. Even more baffling to an observer was the path of the opposing locomotive, which must have ridden up and over the buffer beam, tearing off the right-hand climbing stanchion and leaving it laid on the foreplate, and by some miracle missing the two Great Western Railway (GWR) style stay rods helping to support the smokebox, and thereafter tearing a hole in the smokebox door. Equally puzzling, the right-hand running plate had been bent backwards some distance without in any way affecting the engine's right-side cylinder and steam chest or its two prominent bypass valves, and, perhaps most astonishing of all, avoiding on that side the two long cylinder drain pipes. Finally, the headlamp, bent backwards and now perched incongruously above the wreckage, remained, by some quirk of fortune, with its glass still intact, a testament to the freakish nature of the accident.

I then moved along the left hand side of the engine to see if the compressors had been damaged and found the smoke box and cylinder at that side covered in a fine white powder, residue from the boiler at the moment of impact, and a clear indication the regulator was still open and had carried the water surge over into the cylinders, and proof also that the engine crew had been caught unawares, and without time to close the double-handed pull-out regulator. Edging along on the lookout for further damage I came to the cab and looking up for the cast brass engine number I saw with a mixture of dismay and disbelief the number: 3012.

A short two weeks before I had taken her out fresh from the works, on test, delighting in her condition and performance. My old engine, which I had cherished and which had served me well morning, noon and night, over many years, now a wreck. Yes, it was made of steel and didn't feel anything, but of the 26 locomotives of its Class, why my Old Faithful,

Damage to the smokebox door, showing the extraordinary nature of the accident.

leaving me to wonder if, even at this late stage of my career, the shades of the malign and malevolent Jonah still hung around my shoulders. I never found out what became of 3012. On the surface the damage was negligible, but did it run deeper, fracturing many of the boiler stay bolts and boiler to such an extent that it made the engine uneconomical to repair? I never discovered 3012's ultimate fate[65], for on the following Saturday (6 October 1966) we boarded the Rhodesia

---

[65] A search of the internet (in 2023) does not reveal the fate of 3012, although Wikipedia does record that her stablemate, 3020, is preserved at the Nairobi Railway Museum. Given this, the only conclusion is that 3012 was, at some point, scrapped. But steel, of

Castle, in port embarking and disembarking passengers, whilst loading Congolese copper.

The next morning, I woke early, disturbed by the sound of the ship's engines being turned over, and after dressing went on deck. Apart from the engine room staff and a glow from the bridge, where the ship's officers were preparing to sail, the ship was still asleep. Alone on an empty deck, I stood looking over the still calm waters of Dar es Salaam harbour, towards the town and its familiar landmarks. Behind me, the first light of dawn was suffusing the sky with a wealth of colour. The air was breathless with heat and humidity, and in the half-light, the harbour stretched out before me, its surface grey and motionless.

After 12 years in Africa, I bade her farewell, turned away and went to rejoin my family. After breakfast, we went on deck, and already the Rhodesia Castle was on the deep ocean, out of sight of land and heading north for Cape Gardafui, Aden, the Red Sea and beyond.

Eric Blackburn,
April 2024

---

course, is a valuable and reusable commodity, so who knows, perhaps there's a bit of 3012 in the metal of the lamp you're reading this book by, or in the metal parts of the glasses perched on your nose, or in the pen I used to write this book. It's an intriguing and somewhat comforting thought!

The author in 2024, aged 96.

Epilogue

On the six-week voyage home, Eric, Shirley and baby Richard passed through the Suez Canal, visited Cairo with its museum, its antiquities and the pyramids, explored Pompeii during a stop at Naples, and called at Gibraltar for a day or so, before passing through the straits bearing that name and braving rough seas in the Bay of Biscay, finally arriving in London in November 1966.

It is amazing that someone who came from such humble beginnings, and with the most rudimentary of schooling, managed to go so far in life (geographically and vocationally), and achieve so much. Largely self-educated, Eric is capable of quoting from memory innumerable tracts of poems and hymns, and excerpts from erudite literature, quite justifiably declaring, "I've always had a good memory"—a claim which I'm sure you'll agree with, having read the above work.

Eric was very forward-thinking in terms capturing his African adventures, taking a cine camera with him on a number of his train journeys and on leave trips, as well as capturing scenes of family life—there's even some cine footage of Shirley riding a camel, captured on that final voyage home. Despite some deterioration in the film before it was digitised, the clips nevertheless make fascinating viewing!

Once Eric and family had arrived home, he took a job with a firm of auctioneers and estate agents in Driffield in East Yorkshire, and the family lived in a modern, if modest, bungalow in the little village of Wetwang, atop the Yorkshire Wolds, with views over the rolling countryside. In 1967, their second son, James, was born (a delightful baby!). Then, in 1968, Eric and Shirley bought a coal merchant's business (well, what else could they do, given their surname?), and the family moved to a more spacious house in a little village at the foot of the Yorkshire Wolds.

The next 25 years were a hard slog for both of them—Eric carrying literally thousands of tons of coal in that time, working in all weathers ('stinking' hot and choking on coal dust in summer; cold and wet in winter—in the days when we had proper winters!), a relentless battle to supply customers, often working late into the evening to get the lorries loaded for the next day. During these times, Shirley would drive the little grey 'Fergie' tractor, loading coal into the hopper for Eric to bag up, after which they'd 'do the books' on a night, only to find that the incomings barely balanced the outgoings.

After leaving school, I was privileged to work for Eric and Shirley for about four years (during which time it seems they managed to make a bit of profit—I can't recall what they paid me!), prior to their well-earned retirement in 1993. Amongst my many memories of my time 'coaling', I have a vivid recollection of helping push the big, heavily-laden, Commer lorry through virgin four-foot snowdrifts, up to the isolated village of Huggate on the top of the Yorkshire Wolds, and having got there, a lady customer looking at us with astonishment and just a hint of suspicion, declaring: "You can't be 'ere, we're cut off!"

Eric's chronicling of his life story has been a labour of love. At least, it started off that way 10 years ago, before it turned into something of the Labours of Hercules, especially when he accidentally threw away a good portion of his hand-written manuscript. Twice! However, I consider that it's a book he can be proud of. His rationale for putting it into print has been that he's had "an interesting life!"—a sentiment I hope you agree with. During its 10-year gestation, he's always maintained that it was a book about steam engines. Clearly though, it's much more than this—it's also a social history, as well as a personal narrative, and a window on a time gone by.

Eric is now very old (95 at the time of writing this), and like a hard-worked and archaic locomotive, his side rods (legs) and his pistons (lungs) are, understandably, worn-out. Nevertheless, he and Shirley continue to live in the house at the foot of the Wolds, and they are both are very happy there.

James Eric Blackburn,
May 2024